E-Government Development and Diffusion:
Inhibitors and Facilitators of Digital Democracy

Ganesh P. Sahu
Motilal Nehru National Institute of Technology, India

Yogesh K. Dwivedi
Swansea University, UK

Vishanth Weerakkody
Brunel University, UK

Information Science REFERENCE

INFORMATION SCIENCE REFERENCE
Hershey · New York

Director of Editorial Content:	Kristin Klinger
Senior Managing Editor:	Jamie Snavely
Managing Editor:	Jeff Ash
Assistant Managing Editor:	Carole Coulson
Typesetter:	Carole Coulson
Cover Design:	Lisa Tosheff
Printed at:	Yurchak Printing Inc.

Published in the United States of America by
Information Science Reference (an imprint of IGI Global)
701 E. Chocolate Avenue,
Hershey PA 17033
Tel: 717-533-8845
Fax: 717-533-8661
E-mail: cust@igi-global.com
Web site: http://www.igi-global.com/reference

and in the United Kingdom by
Information Science Reference (an imprint of IGI Global)
3 Henrietta Street
Covent Garden
London WC2E 8LU
Tel: 44 20 7240 0856
Fax: 44 20 7379 0609
Web site: http://www.eurospanbookstore.com

Library of Congress Cataloging-in-Publication Data

E-government development and diffusion : inhibitors and facilitators of digital democracy / Ganesh P. Sahu, Yogesh K. Dwivedi and Vishanth Weerakkody, Editors.

p. cm.

Includes bibliographical references and index.

Summary: "This book provides a comprehensive, integrative, and global assessment of the e-government evolution in terms of real-life success and failure cases"--Provided by publisher. ISBN 978-1-60566-713-3 (hardcover) -- ISBN 978-1-60566-714-0 (ebook) 1. Internet in public administration. 2. Information technology--Government policy. 3. Internet in public administration--India. 4. Information technology--Government policy--India. I. Sahu, Ganesh P. II. Dwivedi, Yogesh Kumar. III. Weerakkody, Vishanth. JF1525.A8E198 2010

352.3'802854678--dc22

2009001031

British Cataloguing in Publication Data
A Cataloguing in Publication record for this book is available from the British Library.

All work contributed to this book is new, previously-unpublished material. The views expressed in this book are those of the authors, but not necessarily of the publisher.

Dedication

To my wife Seema and daughter Geet...

G.P. Sahu

To my sisters: Asha, Sandhya and Santosh...

Yogesh K. Dwivedi

To the memory of my late father...

Vishanth Weerakkody

Editorial Advisory Board

List of Reviewers

Table of Contents

Detailed Table of Contents

In this chapter, authors present a framework of managerial considerations for the development of e-government portals. The framework builds upon available literature in the field of e-government and public administration. It consists of eight key front-office and back-office considerations that contribute to successful development of an e-government portal. It provides an excellent platform for future research on e-government portals. The framework can also be extended to managers as a useful tool for ascertaining the effectiveness of their government portal development.

This chapter attempts to address e-government interoperability issues and presents a framework for aligned development. The chapter begins by arguing the view that mobilization of electronic information across government organizations has the potential of modernizing and transforming information exchanges. The

This chapter outlines how, by leveraging the power of grid computing India is moving towards an e-governance grid. Towards this objective, existing computing networks such as NICNET with all its SAN Data Centres connected with each other and also the other state owned Data Centres and SWANs (State Wide Area Networks) are required to be connected with each other to ultimately form the e-governance grid of India (e-GGI). The chapter narrates how, once this is achieved, the web services which offer citizens services will be effectively supported by the powerful resources of this e-GGI, ensuring nonstop, fast and efficient delivery, with all the due backup, mirroring and recovery features in place. The authors argue that consequently Web Services Repositories can be successfully operationalised at the District, State and National levels on the e-governance grid of India, thereby delivering citizen services across the country. An architectural framework for citizen services delivery is also proposed based on e-GGI.

This chapter presents a case on one of the e-government initiative in India. ICTs are increasingly being recognized by the people across the globe as essential tools of development–tools that can empower them, enhance skills and increase productivity. Technology, science and other aspects of affluence have widened the gulf between rich and poor. On the other hand, they have also brought the world closer, in terms of connectivity. This has resulted in stupendous growth in terms of information exchange, business, education, agriculture, infotainment, inventions and better contact between places and people. The concept that the authors present within this chapter represents this very dream of brining villages, towns and cities closer, in more ways than tying them by technology. This chapter mainly reviews the conceptual frame work of e-halli in an Indian context.

This chapter aims to examine e-government activities in the Sultanate of Oman and to identify factors that are currently impeding e-government development and implementation. While issues such as lack of legal frameworks, strategy, project plans, usability issues and information quality are identified in the published literature as impeding e-government progress in Oman, this chapter suggests that factors such as web accessibility and integration of various government agencies also pose a major challenge for e-government implementation in Oman.

Foreword

E-GOVERNANCE: TAKING A STEP FORWARD

Information and communication technology (ICT) in public administration has been an issue since the earliest applications of ICT. Although these early applications may be unique and have contributed to some change, all too often adoption and diffusion was difficult. Only in the last decade, we have seen that ICT can have an enormous impact on the entire governance system. Governance has to do with reinventing relationships between the various parts of society. It is also about putting the citizen at the centre, stimulating economic developments and bridging the digital divide. It involves looking beyond what we are doing now and shaping society. Given its relevance and potential to contribute to a better society, it is with great pleasure that I write a foreword of a book that addresses such an important topic.

Taking e-governance a step forward requires sharing experiences and creating new knowledge. Given its complexity and scale, the actual adoption and diffusion of e-governance is a daunting task, some of which needs to be managed carefully to reduce manage risk and deal with the complexity involved, while other elements need to be realized as soon as possible, preferably yesterday. A typically complex task involves the creation of horizontal and vertical interoperability at all levels of government, which requires the creation of an interoperable infrastructure. Although by now the digital divide should already have been bridged, we are still removing the barriers to a free and effective interaction. The chapters in this book clearly demonstrate that, although bridging the social divide and realizing democracy in an online world is no easy task, it can be achieved if we keep on trying and learn from past experiences.

To develop effective e-governance, we need to overcome tremendous technological, managerial, institutional and political challenges. The need for e-governance is clear. It should be realized as soon as humanly possible, which is why the adoption and diffusions of e-governance is an increasingly important issue that is high on the political agenda. This book contains a variety of case studies and useful insights, and provides a rich set of relevant examples. The inhibitors and facilitators of adoption and diffusion, and of the digital divide and democracy, are discussed with regard to various areas of e-governance and by various authors, providing support to elected officials and public servants as well as consultants and service providers in their attempts to take the next step and realize e-governance. We need to be aware that, despite this valuable support, it will still be an arduous process. However, once the barriers will be overcome, the results will be worthwhile.

I hope you will enjoy reading this book, as I did, use the knowledge it provides in your everyday practice and let it inspire you to generate new knowledge,

Marijn Janssen
Faculty of Technology, Governance and Management
Delft University of Technology
The Netherlands

Marijn Janssen *is an associate professor within the Information and Communication Technology section and director of the interdisciplinary SEPAM Master programme of the Faculty of Technology, Policy and Management at Delft University of Technology. He has been a consultant for the Ministry of Justice and received a PhD in information systems (2001). He serves on several editorial boards and is involved in the organization of a number of conferences. His research is published in a large number of conference proceedings, book chapters, and international journals. More information: www.tbm.tudelft.nl/marijnj.*

Preface

Governments of many countries in both the developed and developing world are in the process of using new ICT opportunities offered particularly by the Internet for providing integrated delivery of services to citizens. Currently, services concerning payment of bills, information about government services, applications forms, identity and other record authentication and entries into governmental records are delivered on e-government platforms. However, they still need to address services requiring cross-referencing, discretion, evaluation and judgment. To deal with the delivery of such complex services, user's acceptance of e-government systems is one of the major issues facing governments. Since the inception of the concept in the late 1990's many developed as well as developing countries have faced problems in implementing e-government. In particular, the diffusion of new digital services have been slow in many cases as the users have shown a reluctance to adopt the new web based systems due to several behavioural and system security related issues (Sahu and Gupta, 2007[1]). Successful e-government also requires cultural and attitudinal change of the society as a whole. It will be quite naïve to consider that without existence of a strong culture of participatory governance both within the government and among the citizens, or the lack of a legal framework for freedom of information, implementation of e-government would suddenly make the system of governance open and, transparent or encourage the citizens to participate in governance (Shetty, 2003[2]). Therefore, greater accessibility and higher usage leading to e-government success would greatly depend on these factors.

E-government implementation is generally aimed to get rid of many problems of existing democratic structures in public services such as delay in processes, uncertainty, lack of transparency, and corruption to a great extent. However, existing literature suggest that failure rate of e-government project implementation is also very high. This means that there are likely to be various types of inhibitors and facilitators of digital democracy and electronic government implementation. In order to encourage and facilitate e-government implementation, it is important to document real-life cases of success and failure from various parts of the globe; this will provide a significant contribution to e-government knowledge and benefit e-government researchers, students and practitioners. The overall mission of this book is to present a comprehensive knowledge on e-government related issues (such as success and failure) for identifying inhibitors and facilitators of digital democracy. To achieve the overall mission, the book fulfils the following objectives:

- To presents different types of frameworks for guiding egovernment development and implementation;
- To highlight the inhibitors and facilitators of e-government implementation;
- To explore the effect of e-governance on rural development and digital divide;
- To describe useful technologies and cases on implementation of online services;
- To explore the extent of published literature on the issues related with e-government; and

- To present the views of practitioners involved in the development and implementation of electronic government.

In line with these objectives the book contains five sections to provide, address, and explore five areas related with electronic government and associated issues. Two core focuses (i.e. inhibitors and facilitators) of the book are explicitly and implicitly grounded within chapters included in all five sections. The 16 chapters which are included within this book have been organised into the following five sections: *Frameworks for E-Government Development and Implementation* (3 Chapters); *E-Governance, Digital Divide and Rural Development* (4 Chapters); *E-Governance and Online Services* (4 Chapters); *E-Government Research* (1 Chapter) and *E-Government Practice* (4 Chapters). All 16 chapters included in the various sections are briefly described below.

Bharat Maheshwari, Vinod Kumar, Uma Kumar, and Vedmani Sharan in **Chapter I** present a framework for e-government portal development. Electronic government (e-government) portals are considered one of the most popular conduits for offering government services online. Successful e-government portal development projects have been lauded in several academic and practitioner papers. These projects have concentrated on integrating government agencies by working to break the traditional silo-based view of the government and providing seamless integrated online services to citizens. However, the rate of adoption for e-government portals by citizens has been much lower than expected. A major reason identified in the literature for this is a lack of understanding of managerial considerations that affect portal development and subsequent adoption. In this chapter, authors present a framework of managerial considerations for the development of e-government portals. The framework builds upon available literature in the field of e-government and public administration. It consists of eight key front-office and back-office considerations that contribute to successful development of an e-government portal. It provides an excellent platform for future research on e-government portals. The framework can also be extended to managers as a useful tool for ascertaining the effectiveness of their government portal development.

Chapter II authored by Petter Gottschalk attempts to address e-government interoperability issues and presents a frameworks for aligned development. The chapter begins by arguing the view that mobilization of electronic information across government organizations has the potential of modernizing and transforming information exchanges. The current information exchanges are, however, often inefficient and error-prone, causing interoperability problems for electronic government. Then, based on a literature review, this chapter presents some of the many frameworks for aligned development to improve e-government interoperability.

Md. Mahfuz Ashraf, Jo Hanisch, and Paul Swatman presented an explorative study of dynamic influences on ICT-led developmental impact at community level in **Chapter III**. Authors begin this chapter with views and arguments that while there is hope that ICT interventions will lead to socio-economic development in developing countries, there is a dearth of research concerning ICT-led impact studies aiming to identify either potential or actual development at the community (individual/family/group) level in rural areas. This chapter then presents an exploratory and interpretive study that investigates the human development perspective at the centre of the research. Authors present data gathered from a village in rural Bangladesh where an ICT intervention; namely Gonokendra (multi-purpose community access centre), has been incepted. From a thematic analysis of the data, issues such as access to technology/information; skills building; income opportunity; health/legal awareness; and gender implications, have emerged. This chapter concludes that development at the community level is a dynamic process emerging from the complex social interaction of actors' (for eg individual, family/group and society) interests. This chapter uncovers that the interactions are further influenced by other dominant forces, including social constraints over individuals or family interests and decision making.

In **Chapter IV**, Marc Holzer and Aroon Manoharan examined the association of the global digital divide with societal divide. The chapter is based on a study of global municipal web portals conducted through a collaboration between the E-Governance Institute at Rutgers-Newark, USA and the Global e-Policy e-Government Institute at Sungkyunkwan University in Seoul, South Korea. The joint study ranked municipalities worldwide based on their scores in five e-governance categories of security and privacy, usability, content, services and citizen participation. Crucial trends in the development of the municipal web portal indicate a growing digital divide between cities belonging to the OECD and non-OECD nations. This chapter attempts to understand the correlates of this divide, by exploring the association of this digital divide to other divides - social, political, economic and literacy divides among nations, particularly those between OECD and non-OECD nations.

Chapter V, coauthored by Charru Malhotra, V.M. Chariar, and L.K. Das, attempts to explore the role of community knowledge systems for making information and communication technologies more meaningful for governance in rural areas. In this chapter the authors acknowledge the positive role played by ICT enabled e-government as means of attaining good governance, but question the sustainability of majority of rural ICT interventions in the light of disparaging results in developing countries. The study of literature attributes this negligible success rate to several factors including neglect of traditional indigenous knowledge in the projects designed for rural masses. Authors of this study propose that by defining a proper framework and by use of proper methodologies, community knowledge systems (CKS) of a rural region, when incorporated in an e-governance initiative can assist various actors and processes of governance to attain good governance. Projects based on the proposed CKS based G2C2G framework are assumed to be more sustainable and effective for ushering development in the rural areas. Implementation of such projects would however require synergetic efforts between the government functionaries, aid agencies, non-profit organizations and the rural citizens. The prime hypothesis is that the assimilation, improvisation and dissemination of the traditional community knowledge systems using ICT initiatives for rural governance, would help to liberate local ingenuity to catalyse sustainable rural development

Chapter VI, coauthored by Sandeep Kaur and N. Mathiyalagan, examines the impact of e-government implementation on poverty reduction in rural India. Authors share the views that ICTs in general and e-governance in particular offer tremendous opportunities for improving demand-driven transparent and accountable service delivery targeting the underprivileged. The objective of this chapter is to examine the effects of e-government implementation in the context of widespread poverty in India through an extensive secondary data analysis on selected pro-poor initiatives in reducing poverty and improving rural livelihoods. Analysis also includes various contexts in which these ICT based interventions operate. Specific recommendations are made to involve the socially excluded groups in the design, implementation and access to e-government services. The chapter draws conclusions that governments should design appropriate public policies in implementing socially inclusive e-government strategies in the emerging information society.

Subhajit Choudhury and Sudhir Kumar in **Chapter VII** introduce ICT and its importance with respect to digital divide. Digital divides is the connotation of three terms global divide, social divide, democratic divide. Further, it discusses the role of United Nations and United Nation's Millennium Development Goals for bridging digital divide amongst the under developed and developing nations. It also relates e-democracy with citizen empowerment. Some projects related to e-governance in developing society in India, Nepal and Bangladesh are discussed. The chapter also suggests that Library and Information Centres have been given utmost priority in these countries to maintain the e-governance projects so that these projects can be better maintained with proper information and become more citizen-centric.

Siddhartha Ghosh then describes application of natural language processing (NLP) techniques in e-governance in **Chapter VIII**. The author argues that effective and efficient e-governments deploy ICT systems to deliver services through multiple channels that are accessible, fast, secure, reliable, seamless, and coherent. The chapter outlines that in order to implement better government-to-government (G2G), government-to-business (G2B), government-to-enterprise (G2E) and government-to-citizen (G2C) services, a good governance should not only utilize ICT, but it also has to be serious about implementing natural language processing (NLP) Techniques to reach up to the masses and make e-governance successful. This chapter shows the need of applying NLP technologies in the field of e-governance and also tries to focus on the issues, which can be resolved very easily with the help of these modern technologies. It also shows the advantages of applying NLP in e-governance.

Chapter IX authored by Anand Agrawal empirically assesses e-governance online-service quality (EGOSQ). A primary goal of e-governance is providing online-services to citizens over the internet (web portals) to facilitate government to citizen (G2C) and citizen to government (C2G) interactions and transactions. This chapter provides a perspective on the users' perceptions of the attributes which determine e-governance online-service quality. The research based approach is used to first develop the discussion on the needs of quality "e-governance online services" (EGOS) and then a research study is used to demonstrate development of measurement instrumentation to measure online service quality from the users' perspective. The author suggests that the presented method and the instrument can be adopted in any country/state with minor contextual modifications.

Chapter X authored by Sundresan Perumal presents a model to understand e-governance better and at the same time to help avoid possible problems during the period of transition from traditional government to e-government. Towards introducing the new model, the authors also identify a few unique cases of e-government. As the heat of the business to consumer e-commerce (B2C) sector grows, public services are entering the frame whereby government-to-business (G2B) and government to citizen (G2C) services are becoming popular at local, regional, national, or even supranational level, albeit at a comparatively slower rate. Further, the concept of the traditional government model is a more conservative entity, slower to change into new initiatives, than operators in the commercial field.

Shafi Al-Shafi and Vishanth Weerakkody in **Chapter XI** examines the adoption of free wireless internet parks (iPark) by Qatari citizens as means of accessing electronic services from public parks. The Qatari government has launched free wireless internet parks concept under their national electronic government (e-government) initiative with a view of providing free internet access for all citizens while enjoying the outdoors. By offering free wireless internet access, the Qatari government hopes to increase accessibility of e-government services and encourage their citizens to actively participate in the global information society with a view of bridging the digital divide. The adoption and diffusion of iPark services will depend on user acceptance and availability of wireless technology. This chapter examines an extended technology acceptance model (TAM) that proposes individual differences and technology complexity to determine perceived usefulness and perceived ease of the iPark initiative by using a survey based study. The chapter provides a discussion on the key findings, research implications, limitations, and future directions for the iPark initiative in Qatar.

Yogesh K. Dwivedi is attempted to provide readers an exhaustive list of references focused upon electronic government related issues in **Chapter XII**. The chapter also presents information on a series of variables which were extracted after conducting a Bibliometric analysis of 1037 articles on various aspects of electronic government research, published in 19 peer reviewed journals between 1986 and 2008. Author believe that results of this research may have implications for authors/researchers, journal and book editors, reviewers and universities.

C.S.R. Prabhu presents electronic government development and initiatives in India from the practitioner's eyes in **Chapter XIII** which is briefly described here. The National E-Governance Plan (NeGP) proposes citizen service delivery up to the village level through various channels including village kiosks. The citizen services to be delivered are going to be web services (as against the present simply web enabled services) based on the service oriented architecture paradigm. These Web services expect adequate networking and computing resources for effective and efficient service delivery. Grid computing is the new computing paradigm. According to Gartner, computing (scientific, business and e-governance based) will be completely transformed in this decade by using grid enabled web services to integrate across the Internet to share not only information and application but also computing power. The latest grid computing standard open Grid services architecture (OGSA) integrates the power of the grid with that of the web services–both stateless and stateful, based on service oriented architecture (SOA). This chapter outlines how, by leveraging the power of grid computing India is moving towards an e-governance grid. Towards this objective, existing computing networks such as NICNET with all its SAN data centres connected with each other and also the other state owned Data Centres and state wide area networks (SWANs) are required to be connected with each other to ultimately form the e-governance grid of India (e-GGI). The chapter narrates how, once this is achieved, the web services which offer citizens services will be effectively supported by the powerful resources of this e-GGI, ensuring nonstop, fast and efficient delivery, with all the due backup, mirroring and recovery features in place. The authors argue that consequently Web services repositories can be successfully operationalised at the district, state and national levels on the e-governance grid of India, thereby delivering citizen services across the country. An architectural framework for citizen services delivery is also proposed based on e-GGI.

Swamy Tribhuvananda H.V. and Gopakumar K. presents a case on one of the e-government initiative in India in **Chapter XIV**. ICTs are increasingly being recognized by the people across the globe as essential tools of development–tools that can empower them, enhance skills and increase productivity. Technology, science and other aspects of affluence have widened the gulf between rich and poor. On the other hand, they have also brought the world closer, in terms of connectivity. This has resulted in stupendous growth in terms of information exchange, business, education, agriculture, infotainment, inventions and better contact between places and people. The concept that the authors present within this chapter represents this very dream of brining villages, towns and cities closer, in more ways than tying them by technology. This chapter mainly reviews the conceptual frame work of e-halli in an Indian context.

In the pen-ultimate chapter, **Chapter XV**, Moaman Al-Busaidy and Vishanth Weerakkody aims to examine e-government activities in the Sultanate of Oman and to identify factors that are currently impeding e-government development and implementation. While issues such as lack of legal frameworks, strategy, project plans, usability issues and information quality are identified in the published literature as impeding e-government progress in Oman, this chapter suggests that factors such as Web accessibility and integration of various government agencies also pose a major challenge for e-government implementation in Oman.

Finally, **Chapter XVI** examines the 'publicness' of the telecentres in the framework of public sphere as defined by Habermas. The paper uses telecentres as representative of 'technology mediated public space' created by ICTs and Internet and examines two approaches to the Telecentre movement, analysing whether Telecentres can meet the requirements of the rational-critical discussions and if and what factors influence the extension of the public sphere. The chapter concludes that while the telecentres create opportunities to improve communication and reconnect citizens to the State, offering greater access to information and support for group based discussion, they are likely to support only incremental modifications to the democratic system because the current use of information communication technologies (ICTs) concentrates primarily on information provision, and not linkages that improve the quality of democratic discourse.

Considering the richness and depth of the content illustrated by the brief description presented above, we firmly believe that this book will be an excellent resource for readers/audiences who wish to learn more on how to encourage the successful development and adoption of electronic government and its exploitations for improving various democratic processes particularly in the context of rural development and empowerment. The chapters included in this book are also useful for readers who are interested in learning about how various research approaches and methods fit with different theories. The target audience for the Handbook includes policy makers, academics/researchers and students.

We sincerely hope that this book will provide a positive contribution to the area of information systems in general and electronic government specifically. In order to make further research progress and improvement in the understanding of this area, we would like to welcome feedback and comments about this book from readers. Comments and constructive suggestions can be sent to the Editors of IGI Global at the address provided at the beginning of the book.

Sincerely,

Ganesh P. Sahu
Yogesh K. Dwivedi
Vishanth Weerakkody

December 2008

ENDNOTES

1. Sahu, G. P. and Gupta, M. P. (2007), Users' Acceptance of E-Government: A study of Indian Central Excise, *International Journal of E-Government Research*, 3(3), pp 1- 23
2. Shetty, K.A.V. (2003), Why most e-Government projects fail. Business Line, *Internet Edition*, November 15,2003, Retrieved May 10, 2005 from http://www.blonnet.com /2003/11/ 15/stories/2003111500050800

Acknowledgment

A number of people have extended their help in the development of the ideas presented in this handbook. We take this opportunity to convey our regards and thanks to those who have helped and supported us at various stages in completion of this work.

This handbook would not have been possible without the cooperation and assistance of the authors, reviewers, our colleagues and the staff at IGI Global publishing. The editors would like to thank the people at IGI Global, namely: Kristin M. Klinger for handling the handbook proposal, Jan Travers for managing the contract, Heather A. Probst and Tyler Heath for managing this project especially for answering queries and keeping project on schedule. A special word of thanks also goes to reviewers for their useful and constructive comments that have been incorporated in the final versions of the chapters. We are highly grateful to Dr. Marijn Janssen for providing the foreword.

Last but not least, we bestow our unbounded gratitude and deepest sense of respect to our families whose blessing, concerted efforts, constant encouragement and wholehearted co-operation enabled us to reach this milestone.

Ganesh P. Sahu
Yogesh K. Dwivedi
Vishanth Weerakkody

Section I
Frameworks for E-Government Development and Implementation

Chapter I
A Framework for E-Government Portal Development

Bharat Maheshwari
University of Windsor, Canada

Vinod Kumar
Carleton University, Canada

Uma Kumar
Carleton University, Canada

Vedmani Sharan
Carleton University, Canada

ABSTRACT

Electronic government (E-government) portals are considered one of the most popular conduits for offering government services online. Successful e-government portal development projects have been lauded in several academic and practitioner papers. These projects have concentrated on integrating government agencies by working to break the traditional silo-based view of the government and providing seamless integrated online services to citizens. However, the rate of adoption for e-government portals by citizens has been much lower than expected. A major reason identified in the literature for this is a lack of understanding of managerial considerations that affect portal development and subsequent adoption. In this chapter, we present a framework of managerial considerations for the development of e-government portals. The framework builds upon available literature in the field of e-government and public administration. It consists of eight key front-office and back-office considerations that contribute to successful development of an e-government portal. It provides an excellent platform for future research on e-government portals. The framework can also be extended to managers as a useful tool for ascertaining the effectiveness of their government portal development.

INTRODUCTION

Governments in both developed and developing countries continue to make massive financial and political commitments towards change initiatives that are enabled by advanced information and communication technologies (ICTs) (Fountain, 2001). Broadly, these initiatives that lead to the adoption and use of advanced ICTs in public administration by government organizations at all jurisdictional levels are grouped under the umbrella term "electronic government" (e-government) (OECD, 2003). The significant increase in the availability and use of government information and services online is a testament to the importance of e-government. However, several analyst reports point out that the return on e-government investments is very low or negative in many jurisdictions because these projects often fail to improve service quality (Accenture, 2005; Bhatnagar, 2002). Apparently, while the exponential surge in e-government initiatives promises widespread access, it also poses significant challenges for managers who are responsible for those initiatives in their respective jurisdictions. In this chapter, we focus on developing a framework of managerial considerations for the effective design and development of e-government portals.

Similar to majestic gateways of large buildings, in a literal sense, portals are anchor Websites. E-government portals provide a single jurisdictional window for offering services and information for all of a government's departments to the citizens/customers, government employees, and other stakeholders (Tatnall, 2005; Breen, 2000) and signify a move beyond information-only government Websites. E-government portals let governments reach out to the citizen/customer around the globe – inexpensively and around the clock as an integrated and single entity (Stauffacher, 2002; Heeks, 2001; McClure, 2000). A number of e-government portal development and implementation projects are being undertaken to improve the efficiency and effectiveness of government internal operations, communication with citizens, and online service delivery while cutting costs (Dittrich, Ekelin, Elovaara, & Hansson, 2003; Warkentin, Gefen, Pavlou, & Rose, 2002).

These initiatives require the managers in the public sector to consider issues of shared information resources and back-office integration (Weerakkody & Currie, 2003). However, the research on e-government development and implementation is meagre (Jaeger, 2003) and also quite diverse. A majority of the academic papers consider front-office and back-office attributes in isolation. Some academics consider measures such as navigability and aesthetics (Reichheld, Markey Jr, & Hopton, 2000; Chen & Stanney, 1999) and users' perspectives (Ghinea & Thomas, 1998). Others consider back-office integration (Ebrahim & Irani, 2005), content management (Dholakia & Rego, 1998), and branding and promotion (Kendrick, 1998). Considering this situation, this research is motivated by a need to develop a comprehensive framework of e-government portal development. This framework is an amalgamation of existing front-office frameworks and back-office frameworks. It consists of eight key e-government portal development attributes: segmentation, services, navigation, content management, implementation approach, governance, user adoption strategy, and IT architecture. The identification of key attributes was based on the review of e-government and portal development literature as well as our review of several e-government portals.

We contribute to the e-government literature by synthesizing the managerial considerations that affect e-government portal effectiveness. The proposed framework expands on the literature by incorporating both front-office and back-office considerations for the design and development of e-government portals and provides a platform for further research and practice. The next section provides a brief background and a discussion on the evolution of e-government portals. Section 3 discusses the conceptual framework proposed in this research. Section 4 provides a discussion of the key front-office design considerations and some of the associated best practices, and Section 5 discusses the key back-office attributes. Section 6 provides a brief conclusion and suggests avenues for further research.

LITERATURE REVIEW

E-government portals have been a subject of many studies in the last few years. The following section discusses various e-government topics in detail ranging from their evolution and their definition to an explanation of existing portal development frameworks.

E-Government

The notion of e-government is quite diverse; it assumes a narrow perspective when defined as use of IT by government agencies and assumes a wider perspective when defined as a catalyst for inducing administrative and policy reforms (Kraemer & King, 2006; Marche & McNiven, 2003). Chaffey (2007) defines e-government as the application of electronic-commerce (e-commerce) technologies to government and public services for citizens and businesses. Heeks (2006) sums it all by stating that it is similar to a socio-technical information system.

The OECD has defined e-government as:

...the use of information and communication technologies, and particularly the internet, as a tool to achieve better governance. (OECD, 2001, p. 1)

Elmagarmid and McIver have expressed the notion of e-government similarly and defined it as:

...the political conduct of government and enhancement of services to citizens and other stakeholders via the use of ICT. (Elmagarmid & McIver, 2001)

The Gartner Group, a well known IT consulting firm, has defined e-government as follows:

E-government is the transformation of public sector internal and external relationships through net-enabled operations, information technology, and communications to optimize government service delivery, constituency participation and governance. (Gartner Group, 2000)

Fang has put forward the notion of democratic institution and customer-focus to define e-government as:

a way for governments to use the most innovative information and communication technologies, particularly Web-based Internet applications, to provide citizens and businesses with more convenient access to government information and services, to improve the quality of the services and to provide greater opportunities to participate in democratic institutions and processes. (Fang, 2002, p. 1)

Peng has infused integration and governance to define e-government as follows:

...the governance state that utilizes the internet and other information technology to offer integrated public services. (Peng, 2002, p. 3)

However, Grant & Chau summed up all the above mentioned notions very well in their definition of e-government which is as follows:

A broad-based transformation initiative, enabled by leveraging the capabilities information and communication technology: (1) to develop and deliver high quality, seamless, and integrated public services; (2) to enable effective constituent

relationship management; and (3) to support the economic and social development goals of citizens, businesses, and civil society at local, state, national and international levels.
(Grant & Chau, 2005, p. 9)

Table 1 lists the major e-government initiative attributes found in the literature.

E-Government Portals

Portals have become the preferred Web interface for providing users with current, up-to-date information and services offered by organizations. A portal is a Web site that offers numerous services such as e-mail, search engines, news and local information (Davis & Benamati, 2003). There are two types of portals – horizontal and vertical. Horizontal portals define their market space to include all users of the Internet, and vertical portals are focused around a particular subject matter or market segment (Laudon & Traver, 2001). The level of Web portal functionality is a function of the amount of underlying system integration (Layne & Lee, 2001). Successful deployment of Web portals, content management, and collaboration technologies is essential to the organization's success. Driven to reap return on investment (ROI) from real time data access and advanced collaboration among employees and partners, more and more IT executives are hunting for the right enterprise portal.

The concept of e-government started with the advent of government Websites in the early 1990s. However, with the progress of information technology (IT), the increased legitimacy of the Internet as a transaction medium, and the development of adequate infrastructure and regulations, government Websites soon evolved into a channel for supporting a gamut of the front-office and back-office activities of the government and for providing services online. Individual ministries, realizing the potential of the Internet, began to develop innovative ways to transform their Websites into service-delivery channels. Unfortunately, not all government and departmental Websites evolved in the same way. For example, a few considered online service

Table 1. E-goverment attributes

Attributes	Description	Key Studies
Use of ICT	E-government is the use of information and communication technology so it is just an extension of the government	2, 4, 9, 11, 12
Information and Service Delivery	The initiatives should be able to disseminate all information and services to citizens	1, 2, 5, 6, 10, 11, 12
Transparency and Accountability	An e-government initiative should be transparent and accountable to internal as well as external stakeholders to infuse trustworthiness	1, 5
Organizational and Structural Transformation	E-government initiatives often require the organization to undergo transformation so the objectives of those initiatives can be met	7, 11
Integration	Integration of different government departments and agency websites to give the user a single point of access	3, 4, 8, 9
Effective Governance	An effective governance model for the initiatives is important so that all the above-mentioned attributes are efficiently and effectively managed	1, 2, 5, 6

[1] Drigas & Koukianakis (2004); [2] Elmagarmid & McIver (2001); [3] Gant & Gant (2002); [4] The Gartner Group (2000); [5] Macintosh, Robson, Smith, & Whyte (2003); [6] McNeal, Tolbert, Mossberger, & Dotterweich (2003); [7] OECD (2001); [8] Ojala (2002); [9] Peng (2002); [10] Saxena (2005); [11] The Cabinet Office (2000); and [12] West (2000)

delivery as a high potential opportunity and made it a strategic priority; others were satisfied with establishing a basic online presence. Most e-government projects evolved in departmental silos (separately in each department) and lacked integration, which led to chaotic development and widespread inconsistency in the online service delivery networks of most governments. A strong need for integrated, structured, and standardized e-government was widely observed and reported by several analysts and researchers (Grant & Chau, 2005; Accenture, 2004), which prompted broad initiatives to revamp not just individual initiatives but the entire e-government strategy. The ultimate goal – to eliminate redundancy in service delivery and provide a "single window" for accessing all government services – led to the development of e-government portals. An e-government portal is the complete integration of all online government services through a one-stop-shop portal (UN/ASPA, 2002). The ability of e-government portals to access content and applications directly from different databases of individual ministries presents an opportunity to ensure a consistent and seamless experience for the user.

Stages of E-Government Maturity

Integration is one of the most important criteria in e-government portal development research. It has been analyzed in various studies by examining e-government maturity models. The maturity stage of an e-government is an indicator of the degree of sophistication and integration with its users (Hiller & Belanger, 2001).

Several maturity models exist in the e-government literature; they range from two levels to five levels. As the information in Table 2 points out, the stages in various maturity models are not consistent with each other and even differ in terminology.

Vertical and horizontal integration is a very challenging yet important aspect of a successful e-government portal development project. It demands a proper project development and implementation roadmap to ensure success. Additionally, political participation is also necessary for the success of the project (Moon & Norris, 2005). However, an e-government portal requires both horizontal and vertical integration.

Table 2. E-government maturity models

Authors	Model Description	Maturity Stages
Reddick (2004)	two-stage maturity model	catalogue, transaction
Howard (2001)	three-level maturity model	publish, interact, transact
Layne & Lee (2001)	four-level maturity model	catalogue, transaction, vertical integration, and horizontal integration
Moon (2002)	five-level maturity model	information dissemination/catalogue, two-way communication, service and financial transaction, vertical and horizontal integration, political participation
UN/ASPA (2002)	five-level maturity model	emerging, enhanced, interactive, transactional, and fully integrated
Safari et al. (2004)	five-stage development model	close, preparation, develop, manage, and seamless
Siau & Long (2004)	five-level maturity model	Web presence, interaction, transaction, transformation, and e-democracy

Existing E-Government Development Frameworks

Several instances of e-government portal implementation have been lauded in academic papers as well as analyst reports. Kling (1978) has posited that a comprehensive information systems (IS) design framework should consist of technical as well as social and political aspects of technology adoption. However, literature on e-government portal development and implementation is fragmented, and available frameworks focus mainly on the technical aspects of portal design and development. For example, Zhang & von Dran (2001) argued that e-government portals are similar to e-commerce Websites in terms of benefits to users. They posited that Website attributes – such as ease of navigation, clear layout of information, up-to-date information, search tool, and accuracy of information – play important roles in providing benefits to users in terms of Website quality. Similarly, a survey carried out by World Market Research Council (WMRC) and Accenture identified indices for evaluating performance of government portals; it discovered that information availability, interface, e-commerce, application services, and accessibility are the most important indices for evaluating e-government portal performance (WMRC, 2001).

In another study, Fang (2002) has proposed ten attributes of an e-government portal. He posits that an e-government portal should be comprehensive, integrated, ubiquitous, transparent/easy to use, accessible, secure, private, re-engineered, interoperable, and it should have developed e-governance systems. However, e-government portal initiatives are expected to offer seamless, integrated information and service delivery; in these portals integration across departments, transparency and accountability (Drigas & Koukianakis, 2004; Macintosh et al., 2003), and effective governance and organization (McNeal et al., 2003) are equally important considerations. A careful investigation and analysis of the available frameworks reveal that they only consider the social and technical aspects of IS, i.e., front-office attributes of the e-government portals. However, none of them is concerned about the political aspects of IS that also contribute towards the adoption and use of the portals.

We carried out a search of the current literature on e-government portal development and implementation. A search for papers that exhibited: (1) studies on e-government development and implementation, (2) reviews on e-government, and (3) studies in public administration and public policy making in various databases was carried out. This search led to the identification of several articles on e-government portal development and implementation. 21 papers that demonstrated a comprehensive approach towards e-government portal development and implementation were used to build the proposed framework. Table 3 synthesizes an extensive and comprehensive review of these 21 papers on e-government development and implementation.

CONCEPTUAL FRAMEWORK

The conceptual framework proposed in this study seeks to build upon the previous frameworks and models by incorporating the political aspects of IS and also by including back-office attributes such as portal governance, leadership, and implementation approach. Our proposed framework (Figure 1) consists of eight key e-government portal development considerations that have been categorized into front-office and back-office attributes; these attributes consist of administrative, technical, and political issues concerned with e-government portals.

Front-Office Attributes

Front-office design and development attributes are those that are visible on the client side of a system. We have identified four key front-office

Table 3. E-Government literature review

Authors \ Key Factors	Front-Office Factors				Back-Office Factors			
	Service Delivery	Customer Orientation	Usability	Trustworthiness	Implementation Approach	Governance	IT Strategy	Information Strategy
Layne & Lee (2001)	✓				✓			✓
Gant & Gant (2002)	✓	✓		✓				
Moon (2002)	✓			✓	✓			
Warkentin et al. (2002)			✓	✓		✓		
Bretschneider, Gant, & Ahn (2003)	✓							
Goings, Young, & Hendry (2003)	✓							
Jaeger & Thompson (2003)		✓		✓	✓	✓	✓	✓
Janssen & Rotthier (2003)	✓	✓			✓	✓	✓	✓
Lee (2003)			✓			✓	✓	
Macintosh et al. (2003)	✓			✓		✓		✓
Martin & Byrne (2003)	✓	✓						
McNeal et al. (2003)	✓					✓		✓
Safari et al. (2004)	✓				✓			
Carter & Belanger (2005)		✓	✓	✓				
Ebrahim & Irani (2005)			✓			✓	✓	
Grönlund (2005)						✓	✓	✓
Norris & Moon (2005)	✓			✓	✓	✓		
Saxena (2005)	✓				✓	✓		
Kraemer & King (2006)			✓				✓	✓
Beynon-Davies (2007)	✓				✓	✓		
Furuli & Kongsrud (2007)				✓	✓	✓	✓	✓

Figure 1. E-government portal effectiveness framework

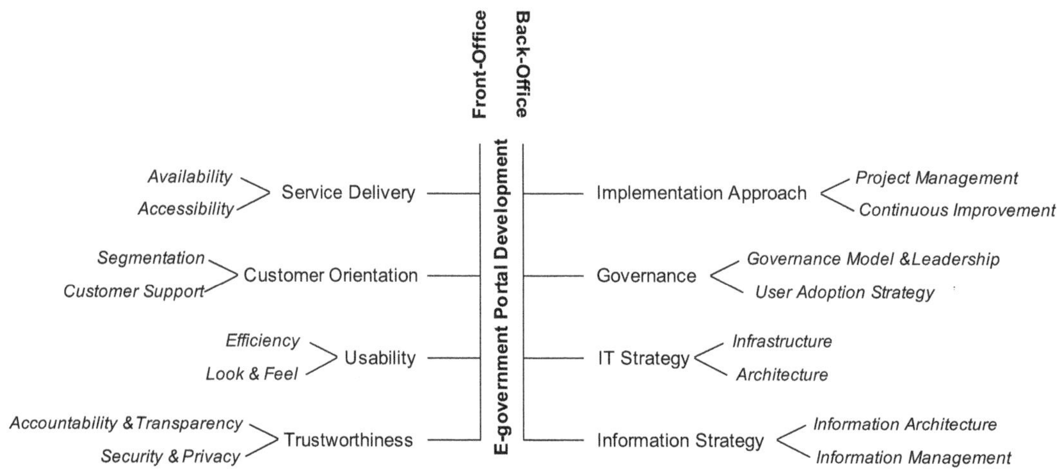

attributes as crucial inputs towards portal effectiveness: service delivery; customer orientation, usability, and trustworthiness.

Service Delivery

Service delivery refers to the process of offering government services through e-government portals. Services offered through an e-government portal are one of the key motivating factors for stakeholders to adopt and subsequently use the portal. The types and number of services offered through e-government portals depend, to a large extent, on the underlying system capabilities and integration of functional departments at the back office. However, adoption of a portal by citizen/customers is directly related to a) the availability and b) accessibility of various services offered on the e-government portal. This has prompted us to classify services as a front-office administrative attribute.

Availability

Availability refers to the types, levels, and number of services offered via an e-government portal. A vast number of services are already being offered via e-government portals in several jurisdictions (Bretschneider et al., 2003; Goings et al., 2003). Many studies (c.f. Safari et al., 2004; Fang, 2002; Peng, 2002; Moon, 2002; UN/ASPA, 2002) classify the types and number of services offered through e-government portals into five levels (Table 4). We argue that the availability of a threshold minimum number of services is important for the adoption of e-government portal by users, as stakeholders may not find the portal effective if important services are not available on the portal.

Accessibility

Accessibility refers to the ease of attaining information and services offered through an e-government portal (Criado & Ramilo, 2003). These services need to be accessible to all citizens/customers equally to ensure a wide reach and subsequent adoption of the portal. Disability and foreign language access are some of the attributes that ensure a wide reach and hence must be taken into consideration for an e-government portal development project (Criado & Ramilo, 2003; West, 2002).

Table 4. Levels of service availability

Levels of Services	Description	Types and Number of Services
Emerging	Gives a formal but limited website presence, mainly static information	Job search services; healthcare information; Social Security benefits
Enhanced	Provides numeric websites with more dynamic content and links to other websites	Ordering and downloading publications and forms
Interactive	Provides more sophisticated websites with government-citizen interaction	Filing complaints and online voter registration
Transactional	Enables secure and complete transactions, often using digital signature	User payments, online tax filing, online automobile registration renewal, and online procurement services
Integrated	Removes lines of demarcation between departments and provides seamless access to websites clustered around common needs	Online voting, and issuance of permits and licenses from different government agencies

- **Accessibility on multiple channels:** Accessibility of government services through multiple channels enables wider reach and increased adoption of an e-government portal by users (Accenture, 2005). Lately, other devices – such as digital TVs, personal digital assistants (PDAs), and mobile phones – are also being used to access the Internet. Thus, several governments are enhancing their portal technology to make their portals compatible for access through multiple devices.
- **Disability access:** Accessibility of services offered through an e-government portal to the disabled ensures the increased adoption of the portal by users of the portal. If an e-government portal is ill-equipped to provide information and services to people with any type of handicap, it fails in its attempt to reach out to as many people as possible (West, 2002). Hence, it should ideally have features such as Bobby-approved[1] (Accenture, 2005), that would provide access to the visually or hearing impaired (Criado & Ramilo, 2003; West, 2002). We found that governments in developed countries were particularly more attuned towards providing services for disability access.
- **Foreign language access:** Accessibility of services offered through an e-government portal in foreign languages warrants an even wider reach and increased adoption of the portal by users. Foreign language features on the portal allow access to individuals who do not speak the language and assist them with many accessibility features such as text translation of the information into a language of their choice (West, 2002).

Customer Orientation

Customer orientation is a key imperative for attracting more citizens/customers to an e-government portal and improving the service quality. Some governments, such as Canada and the United States, are changing the way they interact with citizens, businesses, and each other to ensure better information and service delivery (Accenture, 2005). We believe that better segmentation and improved customer support enable portal managers to increase the user adoption of the portal by making it more citizen/customer-centric.

Segmentation

Segmentation enables managers to target information and services towards specific customers

(Egan, 2004). It is an important attribute for ensuring increased user adoption of an e-government portal (Mohammad, Fisher, Jaworski, & Paddison, 2004). The following three ways of segmenting e-government portals (Criado & Ramilo, 2003) were used by some of the leading e-government jurisdictions we studied in this research:

- **By beneficiary:** This way of segmentation enables e-government portals to target citizens/customers by offering services for a particular group of customers who can find and use the services they need (City of Cape Town, 2003). E-government services are targeted towards four basic segments of stakeholders: Government to Citizen/customer, Government to Business, Government to Employee, and Government to Government; each segment uses these services for different reasons and can be further classified into sub-categories.
- **By department/agency:** This way of segmentation enables e-government portals to target citizens/customers by services offered by departments. Services provided by each department should also be listed and accessible through the portal. This is necessary to eliminate any confusion regarding the jurisdiction of departments over e-government service.
- **By life events:** This way of segmentation enables e-government portals to target customers/citizens by the stage of their life-cycle. Singapore's eCitizen Central Portal[2] is a successful example that displays government services according to stages in customers' lives (called "Life Journey" on the portal), beginning with registering a birth, through seeking employment or opening a business and retirement (Deloitte Research, 2000).

Customer Support

Adequate customer support is a key factor that enables citizens/customers to use the portal services fluently and, thus, aids the portal effectiveness by making it customer-friendly. E-governments portals that are equipped with customer support features are able to respond to citizens/customers better with respect to help and support requests. Customer support features put citizens/customers firmly at the center and help portal architects by organizing all the necessary information and services around use patterns and habits (Accenture, 2005).

- **Automated help and support:** Automated help and support features are installed in an e-government portal by default and are available to the citizens/customers automatically all the time. They act as guides for accessing information and services on the portal.
- **Human-intervened help and support:** Sometimes the automated customer support features are not able to guide or help the customers/citizens and human-intervened customer support is required. Human-intervened customer support can be provided online through integrated chat, email programs, or over the phone.

Usability

Usability refers to the degree of ease with which citizens/customers are able to use an e-government portal (Davis, 1989). Perceived ease of use and perceived usefulness determine the attitude toward the adoption of the portal, which, in turn, leads to intention to use the portal and the eventual acceptance of the portal (Moon, 2002; Bhattacherjee, 2001; Davis, 1989). Portal acceptance suffers if the citizens/customers do not perceive a system as easy to use and useful (Davis, 1989). We believe that the efficiency and layout of the portal are key considerations that enhance the usability of an e-government portal.

Efficiency

Efficiency of an e-government portal refers to the accuracy and completeness with which users can achieve specific goals (Nielsen & Levy, 1994). An e-government portal is termed efficient if customers/citizens/government employees feel that their output and job performance increases by using the portal. Several search and help features, error prevention and recovery, and other efficiency measures should be taken into consideration while designing an e-government portal.

- **Search and help features:** If the search feature on the e-government portal is easy to use, has the ability to provide relevant and accurate search results (information) to users, and has a lower response time, it amounts to higher efficiency (Kulviwat, Guo, & Engchanil, 2004).
- **Other efficiency mechanisms:** Several other efficiency enhancing mechanisms are discussed widely in the technical literature on portals. They include online interaction, faster download time, error prevention, faster recovery time, and session back-ups (Collier & Bienstock, 2006; Loiacono, Watson, & Goodhue, 2002; Yoo & Donthu, 2001).

Look and Feel

Symmetrical organization of the content, links, and navigational features, along with use of better aesthetics, improve the layout and design of an e-government portal. An e-government portal must be designed so that it is consistent enough to appeal to the citizen/customer. We believe that to achieve consistency, the portal should have the following features:

- **Aesthetics:** The aesthetics of the Website comprise graphics and layout, colors, multimedia, and other features that are critical to the success of an e-government portal (van der Merwe & Bekker, 2003). Consistency of the logo, Web page design, colors, and icons, however, have been found to be the most important factors that can improve site design and layout.
- **Navigation:** Navigation is defined as *"the process whereby people determine where they are, where everything else is, and how to get to particular objects or places"* (Mack, Ravin, & Byrd, 2001; Jul & Furnas, 1997). Navigation systems that are designed with user needs in mind can greatly enhance the usability of the portal. A well articulated navigation system for e-government portals should have proper menu systems, site maps, and moderated/non-moderated spaces for presentation of content (Jul & Furnas, 1997).

Trustworthiness

Trustworthiness is the perception of confidence in an e-government portal's reliability and integrity (Belanger, Hiller, & Smith, 2002). Lack of trust —specifically a user's belief in security, privacy, and dependability, especially under conditions of risk—can arise due to involvement of financial transactions and/or personal information. While citizens' reluctance to use e-government portals is a major challenge to their adoption (Kini & Choobineh, 1998), citizen trust is an important catalyst of e-government adoption (Warkentin et al., 2002). We have identified two ways to increase trustworthiness in e-government portals: (a) accountability and transparency, and (b) security and privacy.

Accountability and Transparency

Accountability is the relationship between an e-government portal and citizens/customers in which the portal is held to account for its performance by the citizens/customers (Kelly, 2003; Boyne, Gould-Williams, Law, & Walker, 2002). Accountability with respect to e-government portals is divided into internal and external accountability (Meijer, 2003). Internal accountability exists within the bureaucracy of the organization (Meijer, 2003) whereby the portal is accountable to the higher echelons of the organization for the information and services it offers (Griffin & Halpin, 2005). External accountability exceeds the boundaries of the organization where the portal is accountable to citizens/customers for the information and services it offers (Wisniewski & Stewart, 2004).

Transparency refers to the organization of information on the e-government portal that reveals the depth of access it allows the depths of knowledge about processes it is willing to reveal, and the level of attention to citizen response it provides (Demchak, Friis, & La Porte, 2000). The more transparent e-government portals allow citizens to monitor its performance (Reichard, 1998). Transparency in functioning can lead toward increased trustworthiness in e-government portals.

Security and Privacy

Security threat has been defined as a situation, condition, or incident with the potential to cause economic hardship to data or network resources in the form of destruction, non-protection, modification, and denial of services, fraud, mismanagement, and abuse (Kalakota & Whinston, 1996). Security can be defined as protection against these threats. Several studies have found that security is a potential indicator for consumers to take online purchasing decisions (Wolfinbarger & Gilly, 2003; Yoo & Donthu, 2001). Hence, security with regards to e-government portals can be conceived as transactional security, authentication, and functional risks. Secure e-government portals can lead to increased trustworthiness. For example, if citizens/customers are sure that the personal or financial information they enter in an e-government portal is secure and cannot be hacked or tampered, their confidence in the portal's reliability and integrity increases and trust is generated.

Privacy breaches can shatter public trust in e-government as e-government portals hold vast amount of personal information. Online privacy issues are major concerns for citizens/customers (Yoo & Donthu, 2001); they include spam, unauthorized tracking and data collection, and sharing of information with third parties. Citizens/customers are always concerned about privacy issues, especially disclosure and misuse of personal information (Ranganathan & Ganapathy, 2002). These issues influence citizens attitudes towards the portal and can impede the adoption of the portal. If the citizens/customers are sure that their personal and financial information are kept private and cannot be used without their authorization, their confidence in the portal's reliability and integrity increases and trust is generated.

Back-Office Attributes

The back-office design and development attributes of an e-government portal are those that are not visible on the client side of the system. These attributes include implementation approach, governance, IT architecture, and content strategy.

Implementation Approach

Implementation approach refers to the process through which an e-government portal is built and implemented. With a high number of services being offered and critical information provided, the task of implementing e-government becomes very challenging. Several issues—such as security of on-line transactions, consistency of applications, and integration of all the functional departments—must be taken care of before the implementation project is rolled out (Beynon-Davies & Williams, 2003). An e-government implementation project requires project management and continuous improvement for improving portal effectiveness.

Project Management

Project management is a key factor in ensuring that an e-government portal implementation project is carried out successfully; the implementation project requires careful planning, management, and development.

- **Project planning:** It includes the critical activities of informatics planning, including information audit and standardization; process mapping and design; authority strategy and modernization; informatics strategy; risk assessment; and cost–benefit analysis (Beynon-Davies & Williams, 2003). However, planning should also include considerations for key enablers of the internal value chain and supply chain of the e-government portal; for example, selection of partners for service delivery, selection of various channels for service delivery, and planning for the type of services the portal is going to offer.
- **Execution and change management:** This factor is concerned with the governance part of the e-government portal implementation process (Beynon-Davies & Williams, 2003). It includes electronic championing, electronic government organization, and the nature of any benchmarking exercise conducted or planned (Beynon-Davies & Williams, 2003). Management of the e-government portal implementation process is often vast and not managed within the internally available resources; this means that adoption of established protocols and standards are needed to minimize customization (Bhatnagar, 2002). In all, strong project management skills are needed to tackle the issues arising due to project execution and change management.

Continuous Improvement

There is an ongoing debate in the literature on whether to term an e-government portal initiative a project or an ongoing program. However, in practice we found that many e-government portal projects are never ending, as they become a way of doing business. Several governments are trying to enhance their IT capabilities for providing long-term value to their clients and stakeholders through e-government portals. Even when treated as projects, successfully implemented portals depend heavily on the continuous improvement process for greater effectiveness. Most of the desired potential business benefits are achieved through this ongoing process, where, along with some fine tuning of the technology, the organization modifies its work practices, skill-sets, business processes, and norms to develop a better fit, utility, and value (Bhatnagar, 2002).

Governance

Governance is a key factor that is required to provide a framework for decision rights and accountabilities to encourage desirable behaviour in the use of the portal (Weill, 2004). It includes the use of institutional structures of authority and collaboration for allocating resources and controlling activities of an e-government portal project. Governance can be categorized in two ways: a) governance model and leadership that is concerned with the authority or decision rights of e-government portals and b) user adoption strategy that is concerned with devising strategies to increase the adoption of e-government portals by users, such as branding and promotion.

Governance Model and Leadership

The objective of portal governance is to identify roles and relationships needed for policy setting, control, and monitoring the use of the e-government portal (Rau, 2004). Successful portals depend heavily on a sound governance model. Weill (2004) proposes five IT governance models that are listed below in Table 5. Most of the leading jurisdictions studied for this research used IT Duopoly governance models in line with recommendations made in the literature (Weill, 2004; Davenport, 1997).

The governance models require strong executive leadership that can guide the whole decision-making process with respect to the e-government portal project. Several papers suggest use of an IT governance council that assumes responsibility

Table 5. IT Decision/input rights (Source: Weill, 2004)

Governance Model	IT Decision/Input Rights
Business Monarchy	A group of or individual, business executives (i.e., CXOs). Includes committees comprised of senior business executives (may include CIO). Excludes IT executives acting independently.
IT Monarchy	Individuals or groups of IT executives
Feudal	Business unit leaders, key process owners, or their delegates
Federal	C level executives and at least one other business group (e.g., CXO and business leaders) – IT executives may be an additional participant. Equivalent to a country and its states working together.
IT Duopoly	IT executives and one other group (e.g., CXO and business leaders)
Anarchy	Each individual user

across all business functions for policy setting and control (budget approval, project authorization, and performance appraisal); performance management and reporting may be important for providing leadership for projects of such magnitudes (Rau, 2004).

User Adoption Strategy

The potential benefits of e-government portals—such as: improved service, greater efficiency, and potential cost savings—will not be realized if portal adoption by users is low (Malta e-Government White-Paper, 2001). Critical user adoption thresholds must be reached to make an e-government portal implementation worth the investment. Hence, different user adoption strategies—such as branding and promotion—need to be taken into consideration.

- **Branding:** Branding enables creation of a corporate identity for the e-government portal that is distinct from that of the functional departments providing the individual back-office services. The aim is to provide the image of government e-services as one homogeneous product (Mohammad et al., 2004). Branding increases the brand equity of the portal and ensures that citizens/consumers get emotionally and psychologically attached to the portal; hence, it is important in order to ensure high user adoption.
- **Promotion:** Promotion is the "voice" of the brand, and it is fundamental to brand equity (Mohammad et al., 2004). It is a very important tool for ensuring brand recognition, thus increasing the adoption of the portal by users. It includes all forms of communication such as TV ads, banners, interstitials, emails, coupons, and sponsorship deals that are designed to inform, remind, or persuade target customers.

IT Strategy

IT strategy refers to the underlying technological infrastructure and architecture of an e-government portal. The stability and scalability of the ITs are critical for successfully implementing an e-government portal. An e-government portal must be (Accenture, 2004; Breen, 2000):

- Able to cope with a variety of channels;
- Capable of providing access to all government back-end services from all delivery channels;
- Structured to accommodate different back-office requirements;
- Based on proven, widely available, and used technology;
- Scalable to accommodate growing and changing requirements with cheap incremental increases in size;

- Structured to integrate new delivery channels;
- Equipped to handle digital authorization; and
- Capable of handling unpredictable volumes of traffic.

Two requirements to successfully design and develop an e-government portal are: a solid IT infrastructure and a robust IT architecture.

IT Infrastructure

A sturdy IT infrastructure provides a reliable foundation for a successful IT strategy towards the development of an e-government portal (Ebrahim & Irani, 2005). The IT infrastructure includes computer and network hardware, such as servers and routers, and protocols, such as the intranets and extranets that are required for a robust IT architecture of the e-government portal (Smith, 2004). It involves a gamut of online and offline channels for unrestricted service delivery. It also includes the necessary IT standards and protocols in order to offer interoperability among various government departments and agencies (Ebrahim & Irani, 2005; Smith, 2004). Furthermore, IT infrastructure defines the success of online service delivery.

IT Architecture

The success of the IT strategy for developing e-government portals depends on the robustness of its IT architecture. Services offered through an e-government portal are developed in a very complex architectural and technological scenario (Arcieri, Melideo, Nardelli, & Talamo, 2002). A common IT architecture improves communication between different government departments and agencies by the means of system integration so that citizens/customers need not ask the same information or service separately from different government agencies (Tyndale, 2002), thereby removing confusion, ambiguity, and complexity. The IT architecture defines the ICT application and tools that should be used for information processing and knowledge sharing (Ebrahim & Irani, 2005); for example, this can be a selection of common applications and information systems – such as Web services, EAI, ERP, CRM, and data warehouses – that play a significant role in e-government operations. It enables the integration of front-office e-government layer applications with back-office activities to support the relationship and interaction of various segments such as G2E and G2G (Ebrahim & Irani, 2005).

Information Strategy

Information strategy is a key back-office attribute that decides what information is published and how it is published on an e-government portal. It is considered to be one of the most important design attributes of an e-government portal (Macintosh et al., 2003; McNeal et al., 2003). Implementing a cohesive information strategy requires effective information architecture and an information management system that enhances the government's administrative efficiency of publishing reliable and up-to-date information on the portal and, hence, improves the portal's effectiveness.

Information Architecture

The information published on a government portal has to be authentic, reliable, and up-to-date so that the users can take full advantage of the information and services (Bhatti, Bouch, & Kuchinsky, 2000; Lin & Lu, 2000). This calls for deployment of an organization-wide information architecture framework (Public Record Office, 2001). The information architecture framework defines low-level, organization-wide technical architecture as well as top-level, organization-wide policies for the information life cycle on the portal.

Information Management

Information management refers to the digital lifecycle of the content on an e-government portal. The digital information life cycle consists of six primary phases: create, update, publish, translate, archive, and retire. The first four phases deal with day-to-day information management in terms of creation, revision, publication, and translation of the information. The last two phases are special and are used when the information is no longer required to be on the portal. To ensure that all the information that is published on e-government portals can be accessed at a later period, they are added as separate records to a repository called archive. Unfortunately, most of the information on government Websites is hard-coded directly into HTML pages which make it very difficult and time-consuming to pull into a repository (Rusay, 2003).

CONCLUSION

In the recent past, research on e-government has received substantial attention. Yet it has not progressed in a coherent manner. For example, the definition of e-government still lacks clarity as the research is widely dispersed and fragmented. As Jaeger (2003) has pointed out, a proper research stream has yet to emerge in the field of e-government. Our review of the prior research on e-government reveals a wide diversity in topics and constructs, such as the dependent variable in various studies. Prominent research topics include e-government development, adoption, and evaluation, among others. Adoption, effectiveness, and efficiency of service delivery, and the governance and impact of e-government are some of the dependent variables used by various researchers in their quest to understand e-government. However, these topics have been researched in isolation. There is a need to round up these topics together to form a comprehensive framework of e-government. This, we believe, may help in increasing e-government adoption. Furthermore, our review of the literature suggests that prior research on e-government has put more emphasis on e-government adoption, governance, and its impacts. We argue that the successful development of an e-government portal may lead to an increase in adoption of e-government. Hence, studying e-government portal development assumes significant importance.

In conclusion, research on e-government portal development lags behind other topics in e-government research. This chapter identifies eight key factors of e-government portal development from the existing e-government literature and summarizes them. Subsequently, we propose a framework of managerial considerations for e-government portal development constituting the previously mentioned eight key factors. The key factors are categorized into front-office and back-office attributes. The framework highlights some of the prominent best practices associated with those key factors. E-government portal managers can make use of this framework as a tool to manage the design and development process of their portals. This research is still at an exploratory level – an empirical study is required to test the proposed framework. Additionally, issues of integration, interdependency, and public policy in public administration (e-government) are complex in nature and clearly warrant further probe. The study identifies several avenues for future research. The framework proposed in this study is based on an extensive review of the existing literature. There is a need to test this framework empirically, either through case studies or surveys. The literature identifies several complexities in the government that arise due to interrelationship among government agencies. These complexities span the goals of e-government to internal processes through governance to a final assessment of whether the goals were achieved or not. It will be worthwhile to learn how these complexities affect the portal development process. Third, e-government also initiates a lot of changes in the government, as it is transformational in nature. How these changes affect the development and implementation of the e-government portal is an important question if the success of the project is sought.

REFERENCES

Accenture. (2004). eGovernment leadership: High performance, maximum value. *The Government Executive Series, May 2004.*

Accenture. (2005). Leadership in customer service: New expectations, new experiences. *The Government Executive Series, April 2005.*

Arcieri, F., Melideo, G., Nardelli, E., & Talamo, M. (2002). Experiences and issues in the realization of e-government services. In *12th International Workshop on Research Issues in Data Engineering: Engineering e-Commerce/ e-Business Systems (RIDE.02).*

Belanger, F., Hiller, J., & Smith, W. (2002). Trustworthiness in electronic commerce: the role of privacy, security, and site attributes. *Journal of Strategic Information Systems, 11*, 245-270.

Beynon-Davies, P. (2007). Models for e-government. *Transforming Government: People, Process and Policy, 1*(1), 7-28.

Beynon-Davies, P., & Williams, M.D. (2003). Evaluating electronic local government in the UK. *Journal of Information Technology, 18*(2), 137-149.

Bhatnagar, S. (2002). Egovernment: Lessons from implementation in developing countries. *Regional Development Dialogue, 24*, 164-174.

Bhattacherjee, A. (2001). Understanding information systems continuance: An expectation-confirmation model. *MIS Quarterly, 25*(3), 351-370.

Bhatti, N., Bouch, A., & Kuchinsky, A. (2000). Integrating user-perceived quality into Web server design. *Computer Networks, 33*(1-6), 1-16.

Boyne, G., Gould-Williams, J., Law, J., & Walker, R. (2002). Plans, performance information and accountability: The case of best value. *Public Administration, 80*(4), 691-710.

Breen, J. (2000). At the dawn of e-Government: The citizen as customer. *Government Finance Review, 16*(5), 15-20.

Bretschneider, S., Gant, J., & Ahn, M. (2003). A general model of e-government service adoption: Empirical exploration. *Public Management Research Conference, Georgetown Public Policy Institute Washington, DC, October*, 9-11.

Cabinet Office. (2000). *Electronic government services for the 21st century.* London.

Carter, L., & Belanger, F. (2005). The utilization of e-government services: citizen trust, innovation and acceptance factors. *Information Systems Journal, 15*(1), 5-25.

Chaffey, D. (2007). *E-business and e-commerce management.* Upper Saddle River, NJ:Prentice-Hall, Inc.

Chen, J., & Stanney, K. (1999). A theoretical model of wayfinding in virtual environments: proposed strategies for navigational Aidiin. *MIT Press, 8*(6), 671-686.

City of Cape Town. (2003). *E-government services research project: Initial research to inform the design and development of e-government services.*

Collier, J.E., & Bienstock, C.C. (2006). Measuring service quality in e-retailing. *Journal of Service Research, 8*(3), 260.

Criado, J.I., & Ramilo, M.C. (2003). E-government in practice: An analysis of Website orientation to citizens in Spanish municipalities. *International Journal of Public Sector Management, 18*(3), 191-218.

Davenport, T. (1997). *Information ecology: Mastering the information and knowledge environment.* New York: Oxford University Press.

Davis, F.D. (1989). Perceived usefulness, perceived ease of use, and user acceptance of information technology. *MIS Quarterly, 13*(3), 319-340.

Davis, W.S., & Benamati, J. (2003). *E-commerce basics: Technology foundations and e-business applications*. Addison-Wesley.

Deloitte Research. (2000). *Through the portal: Enterprise transformation for e-government*. Deloitte and Touche.

Demchak, C.C., Friis, C., & La Porte, T.M. (2000). Webbing governance: National differences in constructing the public face. In G. Garson (Ed.), *Handbook of public information systems*. New York: Marcel Dekker Inc.

Dholakia, U., & Rego, L. (1998). What makes commercial Web pages popular? *European Journal of Marketing, 32*(7/8), 724-736.

Dittrich, Y., Ekelin, A., Elovaara, S., & Hansson, C. (2003). *Making e-government happen everyday co-development of services, citizenship and technology*, Hawaii.

Drigas, A., & Koukianakis, L. (2004). E-government application for supporting a network of distributed public administration units. *WSEAS Transactions on Computers, 6*.

Ebrahim, Z., & Irani, Z. (2005). E-government adoption: Architecture and barriers. *Business Process Management Journal, 11*(5), 589-611.

Egan, J. (2004). *Relationship marketing*. Harlow, UK: Prentice Hall.

Elmagarmid, A., & McIver, W. (2001). The ongoing march toward digital government. *IEEE Computer, 34*(2), 32-38.

Fang, Z. (2002). E-government in digital era: Concept, practice, and development. *International Journal of The Computer, The Internet and Management, 10*(2), 1-22.

Fountain, J.E. (2001). *Building the virtual state*. Washington, DC: Brookings Institution Press.

Furuli, K., & Kongsrud, S. (2007). Mypage and Borger.dk - A case study or two government service Web portals. *The Electronic Journal of e-Government, 5*(2), 165-176.

Gant, J., & Gant, D. (2002). Web portal functionality and state government e-service. In *Proceedings of the 35th Annual Hawaii International Conference on System Sciences, 2002. HICSS* (pp. 1627-1636).

Gartner Group. (2000). *Gartner's four phases of e-government model*. Retrieved from http://www.gartner.com.

Ghinea, G., & Thomas, J. (1998). *QoS impact on user perception and understanding of multimedia video clips*. pp. 49 - 54, Bristol, U.K.

Goings, D., Young, D., & Hendry, S. (2003). Critical factors in the delivery of e-government services: Perceptions of technology executives. *Communications of the International Information Management Association, 3*(3), 1-15.

Grant, G., & Chau, D. (2005). Developing a generic framework for e-government. *Journal of Global Information Management, 13*(1), 1-30.

Griffin, D., & Halpin, E. (2005). An exploratory evaluation of UK local e-government from an accountability perspective (pp13-28). *Electronic Journal of e-Government, 3*(1).

Grönlund, Å. (2005). What's in a field-exploring the e-goverment domain. *System Sciences, 2005. HICSS'05. Proceedings of the 38th Annual Hawaii International Conference on*, 125a-125a.

Heeks, R. (2001). Understanding e-governance for development. *I-Government Working Paper Series*, Institute for Development Policy and Management., *11*.

Heeks, R. (2006). *Implementing and managing e-government: An international text*. Sage.

Hiller, J., & Belanger, F. (2001). Privacy strategies for electronic government. In *E-Government 2001*. Oxford, UK: Rowman and Littlefield Publishers.

Howard, M. (2001). E-government across the globe: How will æeÆchange government? *Government Finance Review, 17*(4), 6-9.

Jaeger, P. (2003). The endless wire: E-government as global phenomenon. *Government Information Quarterly, 20*(4), 323-331.

Jaeger, P., & Thompson, K. (2003). E-government around the world: Lessons, challenges, and future directions. *Government Information Quarterly, 20*(4), 389-394. doi: Article.

Janssen, D., & Rotthier, S. (2003). How are they doing elsewhere? Trends and consolidations in e-government implementation. *Annual EGPA Conference, Oeiras.*

Jul, S., & Furnas, G. (1997). Navigation in electronic worlds. *CHI Æ97 Workshop ACM SIGCHI Bulletin, 29*(4), 44-49.

Kalakota, R., & Whinston, A. (1996). *Frontiers of electronic commerce.* Reading, MA: Addison-Wesley.

Kelly, J. (2003). The audit commission: Guiding, steering and regulating local government. *Public Administration, 81*(3), 459-476.

Kendrick, A. (1998). Promotional products vs price promotion in fostering customer loyalty: A report of two controlled field experiments. *Journal of Services Marketing, 12*(4), 312-326.

Kini, A., & Choobineh, J. (1998). Trust in electronic commerce: Definition and theoretical considerations. *In Hawaii: IEEE Computer Society.*

Kling, R. (1978). Value conflicts and social choice in electronic funds transfer developments. *Communications of the ACM, 21*(8), 642-657.

Kraemer, K., & King, J. L. (2006). Information technology and administrative reform: Will e-government be different? *International Journal of Electronic Government Research, 2*(1), 1-20.

Kulviwat, S., Guo, C., & Engchanil, N. (2004). Determinants of online information search: a critical review and assessment. *Internet Research: Electronic Networking Applications and Policy, 14*(3), 245-253.

Laudon, K.C., & Traver, C.G. (2001). *E-commerce: Business. technology, society.* Boston: Addison-Wesley Longman Publishing Co., Inc.

Layne, K., & Lee, J. (2001). Developing fully functional e-government: A four stage model. *Government Information Quarterly, 18*(1), 122-136.

Lee, J. (2003). A model for monitoring public sector Web site strategy. *Internet Research: Electronic networking application and policy, 13*(4), 259-266.

Lin, J., & Lu, H. (2000). Towards an understanding of the behavioural intention to use a Web site. *International journal of information management, 20*(3), 197-208.

Loiacono, E.T., Watson, R.T., & Goodhue, D.L. (2002). WebQual: A measure of Web site quality. *2002 Marketing Educators' Conference: Marketing Theory and Applications, 13*, 432-437.

Macintosh, A., Robson, E., Smith, E., & Whyte, A. (2003). Electronic democracy and young people. *Social Science Computer Review, 21*(1), 43-54.

Mack, R., Ravin, Y., & Byrd, R. (2001). Knowledge portals and the emerging digital knowledge workplace. *IBM System Journal, 21*, 54-80.

Malta e-Government White-Paper. (2001). *Vision and strategy for the attainment of e-government, Malta.*

Marche, S., & McNiven, J.D. (2003). E-government and e-governance: The future isn't what it used to be'. *Canadian Journal of Administrative Sciences, 20*(1), 74-86.

Martin, B., & Byrne, J. (2003). Implementing e-government: Widening the lens. *Electronic Journal of e-Government, 1*(1), 11-22.

McClure, D. (2000). *Electronic Government: Federal Initiatives Are Evolving Rapidly But They Face Significant Challenges*. Washington: US General Accounting Office.

McNeal, R., Tolbert, C., Mossberger, K., & Dotterweich, L. (2003). Innovating in digital government in the American states. *Social Science Quarterly*, *84*(1), 52-70.

Meijer, A.J. (2003). Transparent government: Parliamentary and legal accountability in an information age. *Information Polity*, *8*(1), 67-78.

van der Merwe, R., & Bekker, J. (2003). A framework and methodology for evaluating e-commerce Web sites. *Internet Research: electronic Networking Applications and Policy*, *13*(5), 330-341.

Mohammad, R., Fisher, R., Jaworski, B., & Paddison, G. (2004). *Internet marketing: Building advantage in a networked economy* (2nd ed., p. 743). McGraw Hill.

Moon, M.J. (2002). The evolution of e-government among municipalities: Rhetoric or reality? *Public Administration Review*, *62*(4), 424-433.

Moon, M.J., & Norris, D.F. (2005). Does managerial orientation matter? The adoption of reinventing government and e-government at the municipal level. *Information Systems Journal*, *15*(1), 43-60. doi: Article.

Nielsen, J., & Levy, J. (1994). Measuring usability: preference vs. performance. *Commun. ACM*, *37*(4), 66-75.

Norris, D., & Moon, M. (2005). Advancing e-government at the grassroots: Tortoise or hare? *Public Administration Review*, *65*(1), 64-75.

OECD. (2001). *The e-Government Project*. Retrieved July 7, 2005, from http://Webdomino1.oecd.org/COMNET/PUM/egovproWeb.nsf/viewHtml/index/$FILE/e_gov_project.htm.

OECD. (2003). *The e-government imperative: Main findings*. Retrieved from http://www.oecd.org/dataoecd/60/60/2502539.pdf.

Ojala, M. (2002). Forrester Research Hosts Portals Summit. *Information Today*, *19*(10), 1-2.

Peng, T. (2002). *From electronic government to online governanace: US versus Taiwan*. Macao Technology University, Macao.

Public Record Office. (2001). E-government policy framework for electronic records management. *Govt. of UK*. Retrieved August 8, 2007, from http://www.nationalarchives.gov.uk/documents/egov_framework.pdf

Ranganathan, C., & Ganapathy, S. (2002). Key dimensions of business-to-consumer Web sites. *Information & Management*, *39*(6), 457-465.

Rau, K. (2004). Effective Governance of IT: Design objectives, roles, and relationships. *Information Systems Management*, *21*(Fall 2004), 35-42.

Reddick, C.G. (2004). A two-stage model of e-government growth: Theories and empirical evidence for US cities. *Government Information Quarterly*, *21*(1), 51-64.

Reichard, C. (1998). The impact of performance management on transparency and accountability in the public sector. In A. Hondeghem (Ed.), *Ethics and accountability in a context of governance and new public management. Amsterdam etc* (pp. 123-137). The Netherlands: IOS Press.

Reichheld, F.F., Markey Jr, R.G., & Hopton, C. (2000). E-customer loyalty–applying the traditional rules of business for online success. *European Business Journal*, *12*(4), 173-9.

Rusay, C. (2003). *User-centered design for large government portals*. Retrieved from http://www.digital-Web.com/articles/user_centered_design_for_large_government_portals/

Safari, H., Haki, K., Mohammadian, A., Farazmand, E., Khoshsima, G., & Moslehi, A. (2004). eGovernment Maturity Model (eGMM). *ICEIS 2004: Software Agents and Internet Computing, 14*(17).

Saxena, K. (2005). Towards excellence in e-governanace. *International Journal of Public Sector Management, 18*(6), 498-513.

Siau, K., & Long, Y. (2004). Factors impacting e-government development. *International Conference on Information Systems 2004*, 221-234.

Smith, M.A. (2004). Portals: Toward an application framework for interoperability. *Communications of the ACM, 47*(10), 93-97.

Stauffacher, G. (2002). E-government as and instrument of public management reform. In *2nd E-Government Conference* (pp. 22-24). Kuwait Chamber of Commerce, Kuwait.

Tatnall, A. (2005). Portals, portals everywhere. In A. Tatnall (Ed.), *Web portals: The new gateways to Internet information and services*. Hershey, PA: IGI Global Publishing.

Tyndale, P. (2002). Will e-government succeed? In *2nd European Conference on E-Government* (pp. 429-438). St CatherineÆs College, Oxford.

UN/ASPA. (2002). *Benchmarking e-government: A global perspective*. Retrieved from http://www/unspan/org.egovernment/benchmarking%20Egov%202001.pdf

Warkentin, M., Gefen, D., Pavlou, P., & Rose, G. (2002). Encouraging citizen adoption of e-government by building trust. *Electronic Markets, 12*(3), 157-162.

Weerakkody, V., & Currie, W. (2003). *Integrating Business Process Reengineering with Information Systems Development: Issues & Implications*. In Lecture Notes in Computer Science. Springer.

Weill, P. (2004). Don't just lead Govern: How top-performing firms govern IT. *MIS Quarterly Executive, 3*(1), 1-17.

West, D. (2000). *Assessing e-government: The Internet, democracy, and service delivery by state and federal governments*. Retrieved from www.insidepolitics.org/egovtreport00.html

West, D. (2002). *Global e-government*, Policy Report of A. Alfred Taubman Center for Public Policy and American Institutions. Retrieved from http://www.insidepolitics.org/egovt02int.html

Wisniewski, M., & Stewart, D. (2004). Performance measurementfor stakeholders: The case of Scottish local authorities. *International Journal of Public Sector Management, 17*(3), 222-233.

WMRC. (2001). Global e-government survey. Retrieved from http://www.worldmarketsanalysis.com/pdf/e-govreport.pdf

Wolfinbarger, M., & Gilly, M.C. (2003). eTailQ: Dimensionalizing, measuring and predicting etail quality. *Journal of Retailing, 79*(3), 183-198.

Yoo, B., & Donthu, N. (2001). Developing a scale to measure the perceived quality of an Internet shopping site (SITEQUAL). *Quarterly Journal of Electronic Commerce, 2*(1), 31-45.

Zhang, P., & von Dran, G. (2001). User Expectations and Rankings of Quality Factors in Different Web Site Domains. *International Journal of Electronic Commerce, 6*(2), 9-33.

ENDNOTES

1. Bobby-Approved means that the site has been deemed disability-accessible by a non-profit group that rate Internet Web sites for such accessibility (http://www.cast.org/bobby/)
2. http://www.ecitizen.gov.sg

Chapter II
E-Government Interoperability:
Frameworks for Aligned Development

Petter Gottschalk
Norwegian School of Management, Norway

ABSTRACT

The mobilization of electronic information across government organizations has the potential of modernizing and transforming information exchanges. The current information exchanges are, however, often inefficient and error-prone, causing interoperability problems for electronic government. Based on a literature review, this chapter presents some of the many frameworks for aligned development to improve e-government interoperability.

INTRODUCTION

Alignment is the adjustment of an object such as a system, a procedure or a process in relation with other objects so that they work better together. For example, strategic alignment refers to business structure and information technology fit in relation to business strategy and external environment. When alignment is attained, then an organization improves its relative performance as compared to other organizations.

The concept of alignment was originally based on the fit in the context of organizational psychology and became an important concept in the management literature. The construct of alignment is difficult to develop, due to the ambiguity and complexity of management and organizational alignment. There have been a number of integrated conceptual frameworks in the recent decades attempting to understand and provide insights into the business-IT alignment complexity. Examples are Chan et al. (1997), Reich and Benbasat (2000), and Sabherwal and Chan (2001).

As illustrated in this chapter, there is no single framework for aligned interoperability development that will solve all interoperability problems. Rather, a combination of frameworks will be appropriate when trying to solve interoperability problems. Solutions to interoperability challenges are dependent on the situation, requiring a contingent approach to aligned development.

The purpose of this chapter is to illustrate the variety of frameworks available for e-government interoperability. Interoperability is referring to a property of diverse systems and organizations enabling them to work together (Cabinet Office, 2005a; Government CIO, 2007). Interoperability is the ability of government organizations to share information and integrate information and business processes by use of common standards (State Services Commission, 2007).

Interoperability is the ability of ICT systems to communicate, interpret and interchange data in a meaningful way (Archmann and Kudlacek, 2008). Interoperability is the ability of government organizations to share and integrate information by using common standards. Successful service innovation and multi-channel service delivery depend on strategies, policies and architectures that allow data, IT systems, business processes and delivery channels to operate, so that services can be properly integrated. If channels and back office processes are integrated, different channels can complement each other, improving the quality of both services and the delivery to government and citizens simultaneously. The ideal is to create an environment in which data, systems and processes are fully integrated and channels become interoperable instead of merely coexisting (UN, 2008).

1. CROSS-ORGANIZATIONAL BACK-OFFICE INTEGRATION

In electronic government, a distinction can be made between the front and back offices of public service delivery organizations. The interaction between citizens and civil servants occurs in the front office, while in the back office, the assessment of inquiries as well as the supporting registration activities take place. Back office activities normally require the exchange of information between the back offices of different agencies. However, back-office co-operation is found to be a serious problem (Bekkers, 2007).

Bekkers (2007) phrased the question: Given the political nature of back-office integration, should cross-organizational back-office integration be seen as a command and control challenge or a process of management challenge? He argues that comparative case study research has primarily shown that integration is the outcome of a process in which offices have been able to create a shared understanding about the necessity of integration and in which conflicting rationalities, with their own core values, internal logic and legitimacy, have to be weighed against each other. Integration is a goal-searching, incremental process, which should anticipate a changing political agenda in order to gain support.

Bekkers (2007) found that understanding is reached through the ongoing recognition of the interdependencies among back-offices, and as a result of a focus on the content of the problem and not on jurisdictions and costs. Trust and political and legal pressure are the lubricants that facilitate this process.

2. CROSS-ORGANIZATIONAL BUSINESS PROCESSES

Increasing interconnection of organizations is a global trend. Independent organizational units or entire organizations build temporary or permanent collaborations, which pool resources, capabilities, and information to achieve a common objective. New business models are emerging and existing procedures are redesigned, forming inter-organizational processes between several agencies (Greiner et al., 2007).

Inter-organizational processes are labeled cross-organizational business processes (CBP) by Greiner et al. (2007). The successful implementation of CBPs requires a clear understanding of the common processes across all involved stakeholders. It also needs a structured approach to interlink internal processes of en organization into a CBP.

3. ARCHITECTURAL OPTIONS

There are always alternatives when working on information systems generally and interoperability in particular. In a management perspective, it is always important to present alternatives. A nice example is Eckman et al. (2007), who present architectural options for health-care information exchange.

They found four major software architectures, or interoperability approaches, available to implement a health-care information exchange: data federation, data warehousing, information distribution (one-to-many, sometimes referred to as publish-subscriber), and one-to-one transactional messaging (Eckman et al., 2007):

- **Federated (decentralized) architecture.** In data federation, data is distributed among a number of independent repositories. Data may be stored in multiple locations, including, for example, at multiple health-care providers, each with a multiplicity of data repositories. The central infrastructure operated by the exchange accesses this data based on a central index. Information systems within an organization may have their own independent indexes. It is the responsibility of the central index in the operability stack to map to the appropriate data store.
- **Warehouse (centralized) architecture.** A data warehouse, a high-performance storage system including more than one repository for various data types, is maintained in the central infrastructure. For example, the entire history of all patients could be stored in the central repository, which would allow for the widest variety of uses for the data.
- **Information distribution (one-to-many) architecture.** In a one-to-many messaging architecture, each system shares information that is entered into the system and processes all information that it receives. The interoperability stack does not maintain a persistent store of the information, but is merely a clearing-house for information distribution. The transaction hub in the interoperability stack is defined as the component that ensures a reliable transmission infrastructure. Each published piece of data must be maintained in the transaction hub until it is delivered to all subscribers. The interoperability stack in the one-to-many architecture model operates much like an electronic mailing list server. Each enterprise within the exchange that has data entered into its systems publishes the relevant data outward to the interoperability stack. All other agencies participating in the exchange that have subscribed to data feeds receive the data from the transaction hub. The receiver of the data is then responsible for processing the information that it receives.
- **One-to-one transactional messaging architecture.** With the one-to-one architecture, each member of the exchange can communicate with other members. The interoperability stack for this pattern is the most lightweight and requires the least investment in platform components.

These alternatives do all have advantages and disadvantages. According to the contingent approach to management, situational factors for e-government will determine which architecture is better. Typically, there is a broad spectrum of stakeholders, each of whom plays a different role in deciding future interoperability architecture. When designing a real-world system, one should not consider the four alternatives as mutually exclusive. Rather, to satisfy all of the many stakeholders in a dynamic landscape of requirements, Eckman et al. (2007) argue that one should build into an interoperable infrastructure the ability to adapt to changing real-time requirements.

4. COLLABORATIVE NETWORKS

A framework for aligned development is the concept of a collaborative network suggested by Federowicz et al. (2007). A collaborative network represents the joint organizational entity, infrastructure, business processes, resources, and relationships, which support a shared effort to provide some collective benefit, whether it is a program, service, or a product. An inter-organizational system provides the connecting infrastructure (computing and networking hardware, application software, and databases) to support the exchange of information across organizational boundaries on a continuing basis.

Collaborative networks are created when agencies agree to share information on an ongoing basis. The collaborative network may be governed informally, or it may have formal governance mechanisms and an explicit organizational structure. Whether governed formally or informally, the collaborative network has its own strategy, governance structure, inter-organizational systems, and other systems, processes, and resources apart from the strategies, governance structures, systems, processes, and resources of each of the participating agencies (Fedorowicz et al., 2007).

5. ONE-STOP E-GOVERNMENT SERVICE PROVISION

Citizens and businesses face significant obstacles during their interaction with public administrations and governments, having to cope with bureaucracy, ambiguous procedures, functional disintegration, vague, and/or overlapping authority structures and information fragmentation. One-stop e-government represents an approach and a framework for solving such difficult problems, as described by Gouscos et al. (2007). One-stop e-government has emerged as a trend to offer electronically administrative service packages that meet the needs of citizens' life events and business transactions, with a promise to enhance service accessibility and alleviate service delivery delays and costs.

Gouscos et al. (2007) argue that traditionally, one-stop government developments have been based on approaches concerned with interoperability through standardization. Such frameworks call for some degree of technical "homogenization" of service provision schemes, based on communication and collaboration through common protocols and formats, as prerequisite to interoperability. However, one-stop government initiatives based on adoption of common standards and re-engineering of internal processes may face significant implementation risks due to a number of technical, organizational, regulatory, or political obstacles to standardization, especially in multi-national settings.

6. THE HONG KONG FRAMEWORK

In Hong Kong, the interoperability development framework supports the government's strategy of providing client-centric joined-up services by facilitating the interoperability of technical systems between government departments, as well as between government systems and systems used by the public, including citizens and businesses (Government CIO, 2007).

The interoperability framework defines a collection of specifications aimed at facilitating the interoperability of government systems and services. By bringing together the relevant specifications under an overall framework, IT management and developers can have a single point of reference when there is a need to identify the required interoperability specifications that should be followed for a specific project. By adopting these interoperability specifications, systems designers can ensure interoperability between systems while at the same time enjoy the flexibility to select different hardware, and systems and application software to implement solutions (Government CIO, 2007).

For existing systems, the framework says that conformance to certain specifications may not be readily achieved, given the diversity of current platforms and systems. Existing systems are required to consider conformance to the interoperability framework only when there is a new requirement for government to public integration, and only in respect of the modifications that specifically relate to external interfaces. Migration to the interoperability framework must be considered when a major functional change is being performed. In either case, connection or changes to existing systems are required to conform to the framework only when it is financially and functionally prudent to introduce compliance with the interoperability framework (Government CIO, 2007).

7. A THREE-LEVEL FRAMEWORK

In electronic government, the cooperation between agencies is specified in a changing environment. The aligned development includes a specification that is tailored towards information sharing and cross-organizational process enactment. Process enactment, however, relies on intra-organizational process specifications that have to comply with the infrastructure available in an organization for process and data management.

Therefore, Grefen et al. (2003) developed a three-level process and data specification framework:

- **Internal level.** The internal level is geared towards enactment of processes in the context of a specific organization, e.g. by means of workflow management systems. The internal level is a mapping of the conceptual level, where mapping is a combination of translation (specialization for a specific platform) and refinement. The internal process specification is used to have local parts of cross-organizational processes enacted by process support systems. Workflow management systems are a general infrastructure for the automated support of business process enactment. Often, these systems are separate entities in an information system infrastructure, and sometimes they are embedded in other systems.
- **Conceptual level.** The conceptual level is the centerpiece of process specification. It is independent from external use and internal implementation. It is used for conceptual reasoning about the process, e.g. for design and analysis purposes. The conceptual level is a combination of abstraction and aggregation of the internal level. The process exhibited by an organization to the outside world is usually less detailed than the implementation of the same process actually enacted by the organization. Consequently, several process aggregation levels exist. The mapping between these aggregation levels is dealt with by a process refinement hierarchy.
- **External level.** The external level is geared towards communicating process specification between different organizations. It can be considered a projection of the conceptual level, where projections uses hiding and

> translation operations. Interoperability of processes is the main focus of the external level. A process specification at the external level can be a high-level abstraction of a complex process that on the conceptual level is considerably refined into separate sub-processes. Still the process specifications at the external level should not be too general as they may turn the process of information exchange into a black box process, thereby not allowing the fine-grained cooperation that is required in dynamic relationships.

Grefen et al. (2003) argue that the three-level approach to business process specification provides a clear separation of concerns in business process design, thereby increasing quality, flexibility and reusability of process specifications in cross-organizational settings. This separation of concerns is becoming increasingly important, as the complexity of automated cross-organizational processes grows through the advent of digital government.

8. WEB-BASED INTER-ORGANIZATIONAL INITIATIVES

One of the most comprehensive institutional frameworks to study information technologies in government settings is the technology enactment theory, which explains the effects of organizational forms and institutional arrangements on the information technology used by government agencies. The technology enactment framework pays attention to the relationships among information technology, organizations, embeddedness, and institutions. Luna-Reyes et al. (2007) argue that institutional arrangements and organizational structures shape not only the enacted technology, but also other processes and results of government IT projects. They studied collaborative digital government in Mexico in terms of federal web-based inter-organizational information integration initiatives.

The national e-Mexico system is an "umbrella" initiative to develop government services and applications for the Mexican society. The mission of e-Mexico is to "be an agent for change in the country, integrating efforts from diverse public and private actors in the elimination of the digital divide and other socioeconomic differences among Mexicans, through a system with technical and social components to offer basic services on education, health, commercial interchange, and government services, being at the same time leader in Mexican technological development" (Luna-Reyes et al., 2007).

9. ELECTRONIC MARKETS

Markets have purely been the prerogative of business, not of government, which have relied upon bureaucracy as the way to administer society. The advent of e-government has created new opportunities to apply market mechanisms in government. Collaboration between agencies to solve complex issues, the citizen in focus, and public private partnerships are three examples to achieve better government using electronic markets.

The practice of markets has a long history. On a market, there is supply and demand. Electronic markets have supply and demand for information. Governments adopting electronic markets to inform citizens better as customers with a choice embark upon a line of development where information economics becomes relevant to the design of government triggered costs. Informed customers trade better than lesser informed which is why consumer policy and competition policy both support measures to ensure information quality and availability.

Embarking on digital government is more than applying information systems to government administration. It is to embark upon a trajectory of electronic markets according to the thesis of information value integration. Pedersen et al. (2006) claim that electronic markets represent a viable and fruitful conceptualization of the change from bureaucratic government to digital government, meaning government as a decision-making and allocating mechanism, wedded to periodic public elections of politicians constrained in the short run by constitutional institutions, yet having the potential power to change constitutional rules in the long run, legitimately authorized to govern and to appoint civil servants to enforce obligations and to service the needs of the public.

Electronic marketplace adoption by government is affected by several factors (Wang et al., 2006):

- **Performance expectancy.** An agency will be positive to electronic markets because of the economic and other benefits that electronic markets offer.
- **Effort expectancy.** An agency may adopt electronic markets if they are easy to use and implement.
- **Institutional influence.** Examples of such influences are trend followers, public request, and other influences.
- **Facilitating conditions.** Examples of such conditions include system compatibility, familiarity with business practices, and special funding for interoperability projects.

10. CONNECTED GOVERNANCE

Connected governance is a framework for alignment that ensures integrated information flows, new transactional capacities, as well as new mechanisms for feedback, consultation and more participative forms of democracy. Underlying the concept of connected governance is a systematic approach to collection, reuse and sharing of data and information. To achieve connected governance, the following steps are required (UN, 2008):

- Intra-government process re-engineering: efficient, responsive and tailored government to reflect citizen needs
- Inter-government process re-engineering: efficient, joined-up and borderless government:
  - o vertical cooperation/integration between levels
  - o horizontal cooperation/integration between agencies at same level
  - o multi-stakeholder cooperation (with private and third sectors)
- Re-engineer legacy technology, processes, skills and mindsets.

Underlying the concept of connected governance is a systematic approach to collection, reuse and sharing of data and information. The key platform on which connected government is built upon is the concept of interoperability, which, according to UN (2008), is the ability of government organizations to share and integrate information by using common standards. Strengthening connected governance concepts within e-government is an important step towards improving the coordination processes and systems within and across government agencies and organizations and changing the way that government operates. Improving the government agencies' capability to transfer and exchange information is critical and will require the improved interoperability between agencies' information systems. In the longer term it will require agencies to adopt and implement common information policies, standards and protocols.

Governments transform themselves into a connected entity that responds to the needs of its citizens by developing an integrated back office infrastructure. This is the most sophisticated level of online e-government initiatives and is characterized by (UN, 2008):

- Horizontal connections (among government agencies)

- Vertical connections (central and local government agencies)
- Infrastructure connections (interoperability issues)
- Connections between governments and citizens
- Connections among stakeholders (government, private sector, academic institutions, non-government organizations and civil society).

From the perspective of more horizontal but in reality networked governance solutions that are the essence of service transformation and effective security strategies, the two fundamental questions that remain stubbornly unanswered according to the UN (2008) are:

- How to motivate public managers to share data and, more generally, to work jointly for the public good
- How to understand and influence the range of barriers, from psychological and social to structural, political and technical, that mitigate across cross-agency initiatives

In order to better illustrate such tensions, the Swedish experience of public management and their recent quest for interoperability provides a useful case study as described by the UN (2008). Although one of the most prosperous and technologically sophisticated countries in the world, the Swedish government has faced critics both internally and externally pointing out that the traditional culture of decentralized agency autonomy does not lend itself easily to achieving government-wide capacities.

Swedish government, having studied several other European country experiences, concluded that many such models being developed elsewhere would not be workable in their context. The main reason is what they term as the contractual model of public sector management underpinned by a networked administration. According to the contractual model, an administrative unit decides for itself whether external services and functions are sufficiently attractive for the unit to use them or pay for this use. According to the networked administration, government is composed of independently managed units that rely on functions and resources provided by other such units or private companies, and form part of permanent and temporary cooperative structures.

11. MODELING METHODS FOR INTEROPERABILITY

A number of modeling methods and approaches exist for the purpose of aligned development. An example is the unified enterprise modeling language (UEML), which is an ongoing effort to develop an intermediate language for modeling enterprises and related domains, such as information systems. The aim is to support integrated use of enterprise and information systems models expressed using different languages (Opdahl & Berio, 2007).

The UEML construct template provides a standard, integrative format for representing modeling constructs. Entries of the construct template are derived from a UEML meta model. Template entries are filled in by gradually using concepts to build a UEML ontology that is rooted in central ontological concepts. This ontology grows incrementally as more modeling constructs are added, whether centrally by some UEML management organ or locally within an enterprise that uses UEML. As a consequence, when two modeling constructs, from the same or from different languages, have both been described using the UEML-template, the exact correspondences between them can be identified in terms of the common ontology. This paves the way for comparison, consistency checking, update reflection, view synchronization and model-to-model translation. Therefore, Opdahl and Berio (2007) define UEML as a web (or family) of languages that co-exist while at the same time relate precisely to each other.

In addition to UEML, there are a number of other modeling methods. Examples are activity diagrams, XML, and OWL. The idea is to improve interoperability through model-based generation of systems. For example, Touzi et al. (2007) demonstrated how a collaborative information system might be interoperable through model-based generation. In their approach, a collaborative process model focuses on process interaction, data interaction, and application interaction in a collaborative information system.

12. SERVICE-ORIENTED ARCHITECTURE

Another approach to alignment is service-oriented architecture (SOA), where the technology side is aligned to the business side by making the technology optional for systems. SOA is an architectural style that attempts to support business processes by being an independent infrastructure. It is an approach defining and provisioning the IT infrastructure that is supposed to allow different applications to exchange data and participate in business processes loosely coupled from the operating systems and programming languages underlying those applications (www.wikipedia.org).

Still in 2008, many government organizations seemed to have unrealistic expectations concerning benefits of SOA. While the idea and the concept of loosely coopled infrastructure and applications has great potential, experience so far in implementing this idea has for the most part been less successful.

With the increasing use of software applications for the conduct of business, the need to link software applications of co-operating organizations with minimal effort and in short timeframes is becoming ever more evident. This need for interoperability has stimulated not only SOA but also a similar approach labeled service-oriented computing (SOC). SOC is emerging as a promising paradigm for enabling the flexible interconnection of autonomously developed and operated applications within and across organizational boundaries (Dijkman & Dumas, 2004).

SOC is a distributed application integration paradigm in which the functionality of existing applications (the services that they provide) is described in a way that facilitates its use in the development of applications, which integrate this functionality. The resulting integrated applications can themselves be exposes as services, leading to networks of interacting services known as service compositions or composite services (Dijkman & Dumas, 2004).

SOC brings along a number of specific requirements over previous paradigms (such as object-oriented or component-oriented) that should be taken into account by service-oriented design (Dijkman & Dumas, 2004, p. 338):

- **Autonomy:** As services are expected to be developed by autonomous teams, service-oriented design is an inherently collaborative process involving multiple stakeholders from different organizational units. This raises the issue that certain organizational units may opt not to reveal the internal business logic of their services to others, making it difficult (yet indispensable) to ensure global consistency.
- **Coarse granularity:** Services are highly coarse-grained, at least more so than objects and components. Often, a service maps directly to a business object or activity (e.g. a purchase order or a flight booking service). It follows that the design of services (and in particular composite ones) is a complex activity. It involves reconciling disparate aspects such as the involved providers and consumers, their interfaces, interactions, and collaboration agreements, their internal business processes, data, and legacy applications.

- **Process awareness:** As services often correspond to business functionality exported by an organizational unit, they are likely to be part of long-running interactions driven by explicit process models. Hence, service-oriented design should take into account the business processes as part of which services operate and interact, and in particular, the integration (or retrofitting) of services into business processes. This effectively places service-oriented design at the crossroads between software and enterprise design.

At IBM, a top-down approach to service-oriented architecture was implemented. The IBM enterprise architecture is designed to ensure effective linkages between enterprise business and IT deliverables. It is a means to integrate business strategy, process, data, applications, and infrastructure. Enterprise architecture governance attempts to unify design approaches with a set of published principles, architecture criteria, standards, and guidelines (Walker, 2007).

CONCLUSION

A variety of frameworks and approaches exist to achieve interoperability in electronic government through aligned development. As governments evolve into more online and interoperable governmental processes and services, the traditional civil servant must develop as the organizer and manager of processes and services that increasingly propagate towards business, education, health and other domains critical to citizens. As a consequence, there is a need to train civil servants into their new roles.

Wilson et al., (2007) recommend training sessions on methodology to be organized as action learning and problem based learning. In addition, a range of support tools for service design exercises might be used as well. Case studies are also useful.

As shared services organizations become more popular as a service management and delivery option in government, properly defining and setting up the governance structure for aligned development continues to be a key success factor. A shared services organization is essentially a business unit or organizational entity within the public service that delivers specialized, value-added services across the entire domain.

REFERENCES

Archmann, S., & Kudlacek, I. (2008). Interoperability and the exchange of good practice cases. *European Journal of ePractice*, *2*(1), 3-12.

Bekkers, V. (2007). The governance of back-office integration. *Public Management Review*, *9*(3), 377-400.

Cabinet Office (2005a). *e-Government Interoperability Framework*. e-Government Unit, Cabinet Office, London, UK.

Cabinet Office (2005b). *Geographic Information: An Analysis of Interoperability and Information Sharing in the United Kingdom*. e-Government Unit, Cabinet Office, London, UK.

Chan, Y.E., Huff, S.L., Barclay, D.W., & Copeland, D.G. (1997). Business strategic orientation, information strategic orientation, and strategic alignment. *Information Systems Research*, *8*(2), 125-150.

Dijkman, R., & Dumas, M. (2007). Service-oriented design: A multi-viewpoint approach. *International Journal of Cooperative Information Systems*, *13*(4), 337-368.

Eckman, B.A., Bennett, C.A., Kaufman, J.H., & Tenner, J.W. (2007). Varieties of interoperability in the transformation of the health-care information infrastructure. *IBM Systems Journal*, *46*(1), 19-41.

Fedorowicz, J., Gogan, J.L., & Williams, C.B. (2007). A collaborative network for first responders: Lessons from the CapWIN case. *Government Information Quarterly, 24*, 785-807.

Government CIO (2007). *The HKSARG Interoperability Framework.* Office of the Government Chief Information Officer, The Government of the Hong Kong Special Administrative Region, www.ogcio.gov.hk.

Gouscos, D., Kalikakis, M., Legal, M., & Papadopoulou, S. (2007). A general model of performance and quality for one-stop e-government service offerings. *Government Information Quarterly, 24*, 860-885.

Grefen, P., Ludwig, H., & Angelov, S. (2003). A three-level framework for process and data management of complex e-services. *International Journal of Cooperative Information Systems, 12*(4), 487-531.

Greiner, U., Lippe, S., Kahl, T., Ziemann, J., & Jäkel, F.W. (2007). Designing and Implementing Cross-Organizational Business Processes - Description and Application of a Modeling Framework. In G. Doumeingts, J. Müller, G. Morel, & B. Vallespir (Eds.), *Enterprise Interoperability: New Challenges and Approaches*, Springer Verlag, London, UK, (pp. 137-147).

Luna-Reyes, L.F., Gil-Garcia, J.R., & Cruz, C.B. (2007). Collaborative digital government in Mexico: Some lessons from federal web-based interorganizational information integration initiatives. *Government Information Quarterly, 24*, 808-826.

Opdahl, A.L. & Berio, G. (2007). A Roadmap for UEML. In G. Doumeingts, J. Müller, Morel, G., & B Vallespir (Eds.), *Enterprise Interoperability: New Challenges and Approaches*, Springer Verlag, London, UK, (pp. 169-178).

Pedersen, M.K., Fountain, J., & Loukis, E. (2006). Preface to the Focus Theme Section: Electronic Markets and e-Government. *Electronic Markets, 16*(4), 263-273.

Reich, B.H., & Benbasat, I. (2000). Factors that influence the social dimension of alignment between business and information technology objectives. *MIS Quarterly, 24*(1), 81-113.

Sabherwal, R., & Chan, Y.E. (2001). Alignment between business and IS strategies: a study of prospectors, analyzers, and defenders. *Information Systems Research, 12*(1), 11-33.

State Services Commission (2007). *New Zealand E-government Interoperability Framework*, www.e.govt.nz.

Touzi, J., Lorré, J.P., Bénaben, F., & Pingaud, H. (2007). Interoperability through Model-based Generation: The Case of the Collaborative Information System (CIS). In G. Doumeingts, J. Müller, G. Morel, & B. Vallespir (Eds.), *Enterprise Interoperability: New Challenges and Approaches*, Springer Verlag, London, UK, (pp. 407-416).

UN (2008). *United Nations e-Government Survey 2008.* Department of Economics and Social Affairs, Division for Public Administration and Development Management, United Nations, New York.

Walker, L. (2007). IBM business transformation enabled by service-oriented architecture. *IBM Systems Journal, 46*(4), 651-667

Wang, H., Song, Y., Hamilton, A., & Curwell, S. (2007). Urban information integration for advanced e-planning in Europe. *Government Information Quarterly, 24*, 736-754.

Wilson, F., Engers, T., & Peters, R. (2007). Training eGovernment actors: Experience and future trends. *European Journal of ePractice, 1*(1), 36-47.

Chapter III
An Explorative Study of Dynamic Influences on ICT-Led Developmental Impact at Community Level

Md. Mahfuz Ashraf
University of South Australia, Australia

Jo Hanisch
University of South Australia, Australia

Paul Swatman
University of South Australia, Australia

ABSTRACT

While there is hope that ICT interventions will lead to socio-economic development in developing countries, there is a dearth of research concerning ICT-led impact studies aiming to identify either potential or actual development at the community (individual/family/group) level in rural areas. This chapter presents an exploratory and interpretive study that investigates the human development perspective at the centre of the research. The authors present data gathered from a village in rural Bangladesh where an ICT intervention; namely Gonokendra (multi-purpose community access centre), has been incepted. From a thematic analysis of the data, issues such as access to technology/information; skills building; income opportunity; health/legal awareness; and gender implications, have emerged. This chapter concludes that development at the community level is a dynamic process emerging from the complex social interaction of actors' (for eg individual, family/group and society) interests. The authors uncover that the interactions are further influenced by other dominant forces, including social constraints over individuals or family interests and decision making.

INTRODUCTION

It is argued that Information and Communication Technology (ICT) can contribute to development, especially in developing countries. Bearing this in mind, developing countries are implementing various ambitious ICT projects (also known as ICT for development/ICT4D projects) in rural areas, aiming to foster the socio-economic development of actual beneficiaries. However, the question remains unanswered: *What are the influences of ICT4D projects on the socio-economic development of the actual beneficiaries in rural areas of developing countries?* Unfortunately, little emphasis has been given to understanding the impact side (for example, users' willingness and capacity to acquire/use services) compared with implementing the project (Ashraf, Hanisch & Swatman, 2006; Heeks, 2002). Few attempts have been undertaken to investigate impact (Harris, 2005; Madon, 2003; Sein & Harindranath, 2004; Selhofer & Hüsing, 2002; UNDP, 2004; UNESCO, 2005; Young, 1997) especially at national and organizational level, leaving a gap in understanding at the community or micro level.

This research is an attempt to fill this gap by addressing the above question in a particular social context of Bangladesh; one of the most densely populated developing countries in the World. The first National ICT policy, 2002 in Bangladesh had a clear vision and an agenda with regard to the national and rural socio-economic development, as described '...promote and facilitate use of ICT in all sectors of the economy for transparency, good governance and efficiency improvement' (Gazette, 2002, section, 2.2.4).

Since then the Government of Bangladesh, along with donor agencies and NGOs, have initiated various ICT4D projects in rural areas. Therefore, it is important to understand the impact of such projects at the micro level in order to analyze the current status of such projects, providing guidance for future effort. This research seeks to contribute to this body of knowledge by understanding one particular ICT4D project namely 'Gonokendra' (multi-purpose community access centre) in a particular village of Bangladesh. Having established the rationale of this research, we turn to present a brief literature review of ICT4D that provides the foundations of this chapter.

ICT for Development (ICT4D): Literature Review

The objective of this section is to analyze some aspects of the evolution of development (concepts and perspectives) and the interaction between ICT and relevant dimensions of development. 'ICT for Development' is a relatively broad concept which requires thorough discussion. Hence, the section is broken into three sub-sections – including (1) the core concept of development; (2) some perspectives of development; and (3) how ICT interacts with development, providing a mechanism to address the research question.

Understanding Development

Development may be viewed with regard to any or all of a list of national goals or values in the economic and social life (McGranahan, 1972). Though there was a tendency to interchange development with growth, such identification came under criticism in 1960 (Szirmai, 2005). Simply put, development considers human resource and infrastructure improvement, whereas growth considers only per capita national income (Yah, 1991). Further, Yah (1991) has differentiated development and growth in terms of long-run and short-run perspective of production, technological change, literacy and so on.

Identifying *per capita* Gross National Product (GNP) is the ultimate intention of defining development from the economic perspective. Some such indicators are production, investment, consumption and government purchase (McGranahan, 1972). This viewpoint has been criticized by many authors (Hettne, 1990; Peet, 1995; Sen,

1999) as it is narrow and not the way the word 'development' is understood in today's society (McGranahan, 1972; Qureshi, 2003). According to Szirmai (2005),

> *...development should not be viewed in terms of economics only. One should also pay attention to changes in family structures, attitudes and mentalities, cultural change, demographic development, political change and nation building, the transformation of rural societies and process of urbanization* (Szirmai, 2005, p.7)

Apart from economic indicators, there are non-economic or social indicators that measure the process of development indirectly (Szirmai, 2005). It is difficult to study non-economic or social indicators in isolation from economic indicators. In the long run, a stagnated national income will reflect social indicators negatively; hence, social indicators are simply a value addition of economic growth (McGranahan, 1972). However, the interplay between economic and non-economic/social indicators gives a better understanding of development as a whole. Therefore, this research focuses all the relevant dimensions of development ranging from economic to social. We focus now on some important perspectives of development, prior to establishing the link between ICT and development.

Some Perspectives of Development

In this sub-section, we briefly describe three important perspectives of development; (1) modernization, (2) dependency, and (3) human-development perspective.

The modernization perspective of development implies that developing countries or poor countries need to follow the footsteps of industrialized or developed countries in economic, technological advancement, political and cultural terms (Szirmai, 2005).

The modernization or westernization perspective of development has been criticized by some economists, as this viewpoint ignores developing countries' different paths for attaining development (Szirmai, 2005). It is not necessarily desirable to blindly copy the same westernized developmental path for each developing nation due to unique circumstances, values, norms and patterns of consumption of host countries compared with developed countries (Larrain, 1989).

Since the 1960s with the decline of the modernization perspective of development, the dependency perspective of development (Szirmai, 2005) has emerged. Although the dependency perspective of development considers local values and context in particular, it also maintains some continuity with the modernization perspective (Sein & Harindranath, 2004; Szirmai, 2005). According to this perspective, developing countries were 'forced' into manufacturing for the benefit of rich nations (Sein & Harindranath, 2004) which is reminiscent of the colonial exploitation of British in Asia and other parts in the World.

The third notable progress towards a perspective on development is the human development perspective. Apart from the traditional measure of economic progress, the GNP, the human development perspective accounts for 'a systematic investigation of a wealth of information about how human beings in each society lives' (Sen, 2000a, p.18). In this perspective, human capacity or capability to development is indicative as success of a nation's development. Human development has enjoyed a relatively high priority from the mid-1980s when Sen (1999) developed his 'capability approach' theory (Cam, 2004). Sen's (1999) theory maintains that development is enabling, and the core of national development is 'the enlargement of people's choice'. For example, the choice of leading a healthy life, the choice to be educated, the choice to be able to access a good standard of living and so on (Soeftestad & Sein, 2003). This human development viewpoint from

Sen's (1999) work inspired the United Nations Development Programme (UNDP) to evaluate nations in terms of social welfare, social equity, democracy, empowerment and sustainable development (UNDP, 2002).

In the next section, we link the above-mentioned three development perspectives with ICT.

Linking ICT with Development in Developing Countries

The literature relating to ICT4D in developing countries appears to be sharply classified into two categories: (1) the optimistic and (2) the pessimistic. The optimistic viewpoint suggests that ICT can act as a catalyst of development by making information exchange faster, more frequent and available at a reduced cost. This viewpoint supports the core idea of modernization where developing countries do not have sufficient skills, knowledge and/or the ability of production. To become developed, developing countries need to seek assistance (capital, technology, skilled workforce) and apply concepts from western countries (Soeftestad & Sein, 2003). For example, Telecenters/Information Kiosks in poor countries are similar to cyber-cafés in western countries. In developing countries, Telecenters and Information Kiosks enable the poor to access information about their government, market price, health, education and so on. This alternative means of providing ICT services to the poor community helps them to become active citizens of a country (Prakash, 2005; Soeftestad & Sein, 2003).

On the other hand, the pessimistic viewpoint expresses little hope of a connection between ICT and national development in developing countries because the competitive advantage of ICT in Western countries enables them to enjoy a superior level of economic growth at the cost of poor countries (Sein & Ahmad, 2001). For example, the offshore software industry is mainly feeding rich nations. This view is consistent with the dependency perspective of development (Krishna & Madon, 2003; Sein & Harindranath, 2004). Moreover, the deep-rooted problem of poverty, poor telecommunication infrastructure, and the lack of IT investment in developing countries makes it difficult to concentrate ICT on development programs such as poverty alleviation (IDRC, 2003; UN, 2005).

The above two schools of thought take extreme positions on two core issues. The optimistic school of thought, inspired by modernization perspective of development, postulates on the global agenda of development, while the pessimistic camp, inspired by the dependency perspective of development, concentrates on local issues above the global context. This discourse of ICT4D in developing countries has been shaped by an alternative perspective of development thought; human development. Another group of researchers emphasizes the social factors apart from technological factors (similar to the economic indicators) while studying Information Systems/Information Technology in developing countries (Avgerou, 2003; Harris & Bhatarai, 2003; Heeks & Kenny, 2002; Kling, 1999; Krishna & Madon, 2003; Madon, 2000; Sein & Ahmad, 2001). According to these researchers, the important challenge is to assess/transform information to meaningful knowledge by using social resources, rather than providing only technology to a particular community (Johnston, 2003; Mansell & When, 1998; RIRDC, 1997). Here, assess/transformation of information requires peoples' capabilities to access and assess data and the capability to acquire and share knowledge. From this point of view, the human development perspective has become crucial for ICT4D research in developing countries. Aligning with the human development perspective, Heeks (1998) and Gigler (2004) emphasise the understanding and study of the users' actual capabilities rather than concentrating only on technology for ICT4D research. For example, computer training cannot bring benefits to the poor people in developing countries unless it addresses or enhances their

Table 1. Perspectives and approach to ICT led development

Perspectives of Development on ICT	**Key issue**	**Approach to ICT led development**
Modernization/ Westernization	Adoption of technology.	Hiring concepts/technologies from Western nations and apply in developing countries (Larrain, 1989; Szirmai, 2005). For example: establishing Multipurpose access centre, Telecenter and Information Kiosks for providing universal access to information in rural areas.
Dependency	Manufacturing and production of IT.	Developing countries manufacture product solely to benefit of rich nations (Larrain, 1989; Sein & Harindranath, 2004). For example: offshore software industry mainly feeding Western nations.
Human development	Individual human capability development.	Develop human capability by providing enabling social settings for the poor people (Sanchez, 2000; Sen, 2000b). Human capability includes capability to get and share knowledge, participate and talk in the society, free from fear and threats (Sen, 2000b; Fukuda-Parr, Lopes & Malik, 2002). For example: enhance individual capability to use ICT by providing sufficient training, resources and opportunity to local users in developing countries.

capability. Such enhanced capacity would transfer knowledge or skills to the real world. Here, the capability could be the level of literacy rate, social power and socio-cultural influence.

In principal, this perspective (human development) provides our research a comprehensive way to understand ICT-led developmental impact. Table 1 summarizes the above discussion:

RESEARCH DESIGN

This research employs an interpretive approach with the qualitative tradition for data collection and analysis. The interpretive approach (Walsham, 1995) suits when the research is about understanding the human behaviour within the surrounding's context where phenomena and contexts are difficult to isolate.

According to Kaplan and Duchon,

Interpretive researchers attempt to understand the way others construe, conceptualize, and understand events, concepts, and categories, in part because these are assumed to influence individual behavior (Kaplan & Duchon, 1998, p.572).

The nature of this research is explorative because little research has been undertaken within the socio-economic context of rural Bangladesh. While conducting the empirical study, we focused on complex social actions in order to understand ICT-led development from the actual beneficiaries' perspectives. Further, understanding ICT-led development was subject to social interpretation by different groups in different ways. Hence, an interpretive approach is appropriate for this research.

We adopted qualitative tradition based on the type of research question, which seeks answers from 'how' or 'what' types of questions (Creswell, 1998), which matched the interests of this research. For an exploratory study, qualitative methods work well when variables cannot be easily identified, theories are not available or theories need to be development (Creswell, 1998). Inadequacy of previous studies in the area of impact of ICT in a particular social context of Bangladesh and the lack of data made qualitative research an appropriate method to deploy. Finally, qualitative research methods enabled us to study individuals or participants in their own natural setting, thereby avoiding contrived findings that are out of context (Creswell, 1998). In this research, we explored ICT led developmental impact within the participant's own natural settings by staying in one particular village in Bangladesh. As this research requires understanding ICT led development from participants' points of view, separation of the participants from the village might not provide such a clear picture within the social contexts.

The interpretive researcher investigates complex human processes considering the surrounding social context (Evert, 2003; Myers & Avison, 2002; Walsham, 2002). The aim of this data collection was to gain knowledge as a social construction (Macome, 2002; Walsham, 1995) through the data collection techniques. These techniques provided more opportunity for us to focus our research interests, ask directive/non directive questions, and capture the subject's perspectives within their surrounding social settings (Evert, 2003; Taylor & Bogdan, 1984; Walsham, 1993).

Table 2 presents sources, types and categories/features of data in this research, which were collected through personal interviews, focus group discussions (FGDs) with participants, and observations of one particular ICT4D project's (Gonokendra) activities. The purposive sampling procedure was applied to select the village for the ICT4D project and to draw respondents. The village was selected on the basis of ICT program availability, the length of time in operation (minimum 5 years) and convenience. Respondents included the librarian/trainer (in-charge of operations), trainees, trainees' guardians and general local people (aware of the presence and activities of the ICT4D project). The sample size was not pre-determined; however, data were gathered from the above participants and secondary sources (official records, reports and statistics from the local public offices) during the month long stay in Bawpara village, forming a rich data set.

The ICT4D project's Gonokendra's librarian/trainer was the key informant who assisted the researchers to identify potential interviewees, who were then invited to participate in the research.

Table 2. Data collection (type/source/category) in this research

Data Type	Sources of Data	Category/feature of the participants
Primary data	Observation	Gonkendra premises and daily operation, and Village meeting places in three (different villages such as shops, market places to understand villagers life style.
	In-depth interview (unstructured)	Trainee, Librarian/trainer, Guardian, General people, and Official.
	Focus Group Discussion (separate for male/female group)	Trainee, Librarian/trainer, Guardian, General people, and Official.
Secondary data	Documentation (Reports & CDs) from Gonokendra and its surrounding local public offices	Gonokendra, Local Government offices, and Bureau of Statistic, Government of Bangladesh.

Common characteristics of the participants were:

- The trainee successfully completed the computer training program or finished at least one basic computing courses and attended few (at least 10) multi-media sessions at Gonokendra,
- The trainees' guardian who attended multi-media sessions once a month,
- The librarian/trainer who had at least two years working experience, and
- The general people who were informed about the presence and functions of Gonokendra in their village.

Generally, we interviewed one librarian/trainer, eight trainees, six trainees' guardians and six general local people in the village. Further, two non-participant/on-site observations and five focus group discussions were conducted. The researcher acted as a mediator of in-depth interviews and focus group discussions. Data collection techniques included open-ended/unstructured questionnaires and checklists for focus group discussions, in-depth interviews and observations. Though there were few predefined questions, the discussions during the interviews and focus group were centered the ICT4D project's activities and effects on the participants' development at their community level.

In-depth interviews, through an unstructured questionnaire (Creswell, 1998; Gillham, 2005; Miles & Huberman, 1994), enabled the participants to explore their views and opinions regarding an ICT4D project in their areas and its implication on development. The contexts of those in-depth interviews were the affectivity of the ICT program, facilities offered, and the influence in socio-cultural development and so on. Non-participant observation (Maykut & Morehouse, 1994; Miles & Huberman, 1994) was required to realize the participants' feelings, interest, socio-cultural conditions of the villagers and progress towards ICT-led development.

It is reported in previous research that rural females are uneasy about expressing their opinion in presence of male participants (Sen, 1992); hence, we separated males from females in the FGDs. Generally FGDs are organized open-ended group discussion with specific goals, structures, time frames and procedures (Gillham, 2005; Miles & Huberman, 1994; Ritchie & Lewis, 2003). In this research, FGDs concentrated on the implementation and implication issues of the ICT4D project for the participants' socio-economic development. Further, FGDs enabled our participants to freely react to each other's responses.

A variety of documents was collected from secondary sources in order to draw inference and were treated as clues worthy of further investigation (Yin, 1984). In general, we gathered data including cost of computer courses, duration of computer courses, computer training materials, content of multi-media program (CDs) and socio-economic background (statistical data) of people in the study site.

Interviews were tape-recorded in the local language of Bangla. All interviews were transcribed in Banlga and then translated into English by the researcher. To ensure accuracy, the interviews were also translated by someone outside the research group. In this research, thematic analysis (Boyatzis, 1998) was undertaken to identify the issues or themes that emerged from interview transcripts. Stake (1995) and Miles and Huberman (1994) support this form of analysis as it focuses on identifiable themes and patterns of living and behaviour. The aim of thematic analysis is to find themes or regularities from data, seek out more data to support or qualify these emerging themes, and then draw inference from the links with other new data segments (Patton, 1980). Thematic analysis (Miles & Huberman, 1994) enabled this research to identify themes from data which then form story lines of our findings.

Further, we present some vignettes derived from our interview data as evidence in support of our findings.

Triangulation of the various data collection techniques and data sources on this research increased the reliability of the data, and reduced the chance of bias. The range of data collection (in-depth interview, focus group discussion, observation, document review) from different participant groups enabled cross checking for multiple perspectives of the same event.

GONOKENDRA IN BAWPARA VILLAGE

In 1999, the Bangladesh Rural Advancement Committee (BRAC) introduced the community-based ICT program, Gonokendra (multi-purpose community access centre) in village areas of Bangladesh (BRAC, 2004) . The primary objectives of the Gonokendra were to 1) increase familiarity with computers in rural communities, 2) promote computer training in rural areas, 3) create access to ICT education and learning through skills, and 4) capacity building of villagers to face future challenges. Previously, Gonokendra was known as rural library, which was then converted for the purposes of computer training and multi-media based information dissemination sessions. Gonokendra is a collaborative effort between BRAC and the community. The community provides a room (400-500 square feet) for the Gonokendra premises free of cost, and must sign up a body of local members contributing a minimum of Taka 50,000 (US$ 1=68 taka). BRAC provides an equal matching grant to create a reserve fund for the Gonokendra (BRAC, 2003). The total amount (at least Taka 100,000) is then deposited on a fixed term basis in the name of a Trustee Board in a recognized financial institution (BRAC, 2003).The Gonokendra's recurring expenses, such as the librarian's salary, electricity and stationery are paid from the monthly interest on this investment.

Gonokendra has two core activities; 1) computer training program and 2) multi-media based information dissemination session. Computer training consists of different computer courses for various age groups in village areas depending on the duration and capacity of the trainer who was the Gonokendra's librarian. The librarian must successfully complete an initial 12 day training session before returning to her Gonokendra to initiate computer courses as the instructor . Each Gonokendra has a set of 15 to 20 CDs containing different educational and social awareness issues, including general knowledge, health/legal information, subject rhymes and games (PACE, 2005). The villagers attend multi-media sessions in a group once or twice a week. Further, one can come alone to watch the CDs at Gonokendra depending on the availability of the computer.

Bawpara village is 48 km north-west of the capital city, Dhaka. The Gonokendra established on 21 October, 2000 is half a kilometre from the highway. This Gonokendra, 300-400 square feet in a two-storied building, is situated at the compound of an academic institution building. The Gonokendra premise is spacious and it has sufficient lights and fans but the electricity continues barely 4-5 hours in a day. There is a partitioned room covered with glass where two computers, one printer and an uninterrupted power supply (UPS) are kept. The trainees attend the computer-training program and multi-media based information dissemination session in this room. Apart from the trainees, their guardians and non-members are also welcome in multi-media session.

Figure 1 represents the village map of Bawpara, which indicates that the majority of the settlements are located at northern part of the village. The village is mostly covered with cultivate land and forest to the south. The total population of the village is 3,420, of which 52.40 % are male and 47.60% are female (Census, 2001). It is evident that the population distribution is skewed towards the older age group. It is noticeable that 1,867 people are within the age band of 18 to 59 years which is 54.60 % of the population (Census, 2001). The major occupations of villagers are agriculture, industry, small business, construction and transportation. Females are engaged in household activities including paddy hustling, vegetable growing and chicken rearing. Almost 168 people are involved in trading and 89 people are working in industry. There are 758 households (approx.) in this village.

Most of the houses are tin shed, and brick built houses are very rare in this village. There is no bank; however there are two government-operated banks located 50 km from the village. One of them is the public commercial bank called *Janata* Bank and other one is the specialized bank called *Krishi* Bank (for facilitating agriculture).Of the total population only four people belong to Buddhist

Figure 1. Bawpara village map

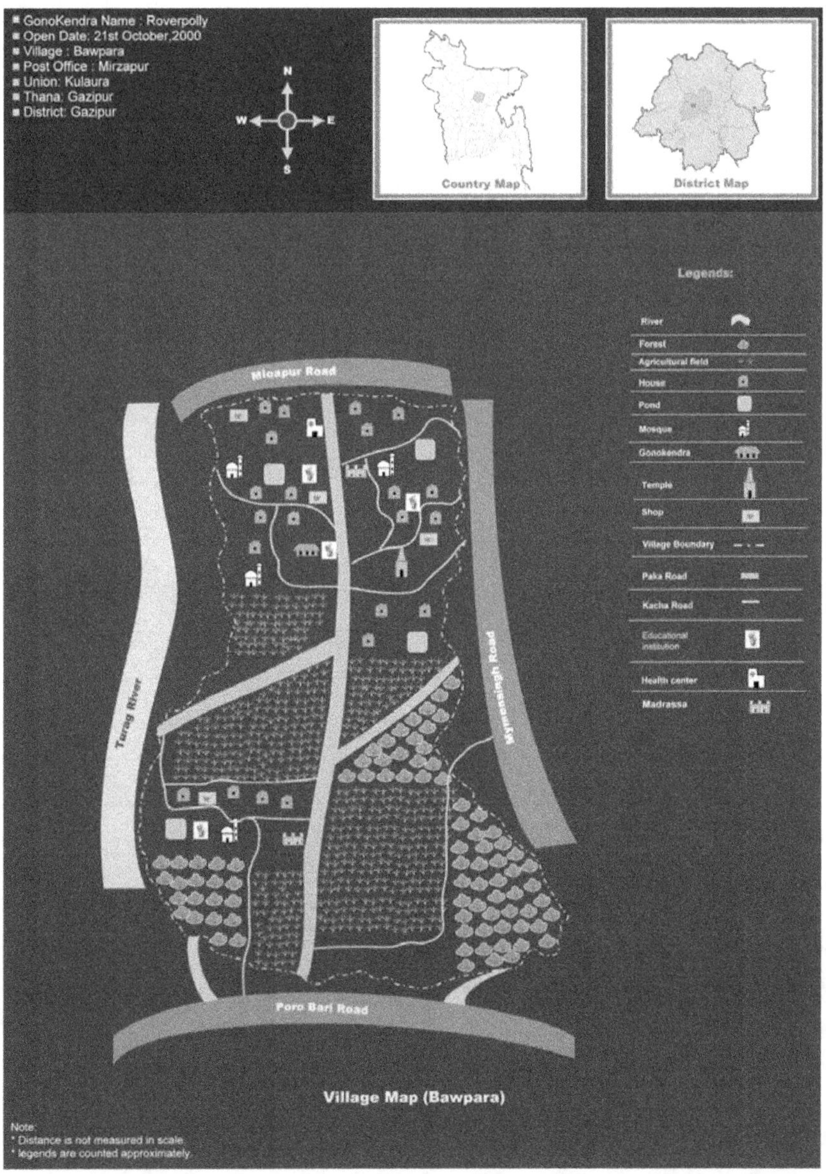

religion, 521 people belong to Hindu religion and 2,895 people are from Islam religion.

Table 3 presents some facts of Bawpara village and its Gonokendra.

RESULTS FROM THE FIELD STUDY

In this section, we discuss some key findings emerging from the month long data collection of Bawpara Gonokendra in Bawpara village. The findings are based on the participants' perspectives towards Gonoekendra's activities conducive to their development at the community level. The findings are now presented for each category of interviewee in the Gonokendra. These include the (1) librarian/trainer, (2) trainees, (3) general rural people (who aware about the activities of Gonokendra in their village) and (4) trainees' guardians.

Librarian/Trainer

The female librarian/trainer experiences self-respect, self-sufficiency and self-reliance; even

Table 3. Fact sheet of Bawpara Gonokendra in Bawpara village

Gonokendra	Gonokendra in Bawpara village
Characteristics	
Village Name	Bawpara
Open date	21st October, 2000
Location	Adjacent to an academic institution
Space size	300-400 square feet
Number of computer	2
Village Name	Bawpara Village
Characteristics	
Total population	3,420 (Male 52.40% and Female 47.60%)
Distance from the capital city	48 kilo meter
Road condition	Majority are raised dirt road, only few concrete roads.
Number of households	758
Average number of person per household	4.51
Availability of health services	No hospital except one primary health care unit.
Occupation	Agriculture, industry, small business, construction and transportation.
Industry wage rate	Industrial wage rate:Female:US$21(monthly) and Male: US$57 (monthly).
Attitude towards education	Both male and female are reluctant in pursuing higher education and female dropout is present after the age of 18.
Electricity availability	4-6 hours (approx) in a day
Temperature	Summer: 30-35°C, Winter: 10-15°C
Common natural disaster	Drought

though she only has achieved the Higher School Certificate (HSC) level of education, her role as the librarian/trainer makes her feel she is given the same respect as a qualified teacher. She says: *'everyone knows me and respects me like school teachers in our village'*. As the librarian/ trainer was a salaried job, she contributed to her family financially and participating in the important role of family decision-making. She adds further,

'It is always embarrassing to seek their (husband or parents) kind to get money for my personal expenses. Now I do not have to do this. I became an important person as I can financially support my self as well as the family'.

The following Vignette 1 demonstrates how a participant of Gonokendra enhanced her family's economic condition from poverty and distress to prosperity.

Vignette 1: Art of Improving Quality of Life
There are very few people in rural Bangladesh who struggle to overcome the difficulties of life, strive for a better lifestyle, and actually make it happen. But that is the story of Malobika Shaha, 26, once a poverty-stricken housewife and now self-reliant, who changed her life by running a computer training centre with the assistance of Gonokendra.

Malobika was a very poor Hindu girl. She always wanted to do something to improve her standard, so she went to Gonokendra for computer training, where she learned software like MSWord and MSExcel. During her training sessions, Malobika met a Muslim boy named Raju; they fell deeply in love and married without their parents' consent. As their society did not permit marriage between different religions, Malobika's family was hostile towards her and told her to leave either them or Raju; eventually they were abandoned by their families. Intense conflict and humiliation drove them into hardship. Raju was unemployed and they had neither shelter nor any means of livelihood. The heartbreaking news came to Malobika one day that her husband had lost one of his legs in an accident: this disaster forced the realisation upon her that *she* must urgently obtain employment. She saw that she might get some form of livelihood from utilising her knowledge of computing, obtained from Gonokendra.

Malobika took a loan from BRAC bank, started her own computer training centre in Gasipur district and began earning money. Now she has completely changed her family's standard of living.

While asking about the multi-media program and its relevance with socio-economic progress or development, the librarian/trainer stressed the importance of learning and knowing health and legal information from Gonokendra which enabled a person to lead a better standard of life. In her family life, she practiced a good healthy life and she influenced others to follow such practice. She added,

We organized a fair in last Eid (muslim) festival at the school playground. I was surprised to see that few attendants of the multi-media session requested others to wash their hand before eating foods at lunch time. They leant such practices from Gonokendra's health related multi-media sessions.

Apart from multimedia-based programs, she emphasises the importance of computer training programs for gaining employment, or even in helping to apply for it. When asked about the merits/disadvantages of Gonokendra, she identifies the lack of electricity as a major obstacle for Gonokendra operation, ultimately hampering trainee learning and practice. She says they have to keep a generator for backup. Despite this limitation, she emphasises that villagers are now accessing technology and information that would not have been possible without Gonokendra. Further, she highlights the positive that poor people have free access to all Gonokendras.

Trainee

The trainees realise that Gonokendra's computer training is an opportunity for them to build their skills. They are interested in receiving the training themselves, and to inspire their classmates to be trained. As they consider that computer literacy might add value to their career, they are interested in attending computer training courses at Gonokendra. According to one trainee,

I am a student of class ten and I have a computer literacy subject. In school, I only get the theoretical knowledge of this subject but from Gonokendra's computer-training program I can also get the practical knowledge.

Further, as it is located close to the school/college, the teachers help influence trainees to attend their Gonokendra. When asked about the implications of computer training and multimedia sessions for development, they illustrate different cases where they implemented their acquired knowledge and learning of different legal, health and environmental issues from multimedia sessions. One trainee states:

We do learn things related to human well-being though Gonokendra's multi-media sessions. Apart from this, the computer training program is an opportunity to create computer literate workforce for the country. A number of ex-trainees from Gonokendra stated to earn their living hood by using their knowledge of computer. As you have seen that we have a market near this village where a small computer shop exists. The owner of that shop is an ex-trainee of Gonokendra....

When discussing the difficulties of training at the Gonokendra, the trainees mention that the social constraints in their villages are difficult to overcome. Some of the social constraints mentioned by trainees are (1) confining females to their home or under *purdah* (veil), (2) women's limited ability to make decisions about their own marriages and educational attainments, and (3) some traditional health practices.

As one female trainee replied, '*...my parents say it is unethical for girls to go to the formal court for legal assistance. People do not want to expose their wives or daughters in public*'.

General Rural People

In the village of the Bawpara Gonokendra, the local rural populace in our study expressed their positive attitudes towards education and considered the Gonokendra ICT programme as a source of learning, skill-building and employment for their community. They also expressed their gratitude to BRAC and to the school teachers of the adjacent Gonokendra for their continuing support and encouragement of the students participating in computer training and multimedia sessions. They believed that participating in those sessions increased their knowledge in basic health and legal practices so that they can live better lives. According to one respondent,

...the multi-media based information dissemination session has created different kinds of social awareness amongst the villagers. Though such information is basic but important for a healthy life.

Regarding health issue, they became aware of AIDS, family planning, giving vaccinations to children, using a sanitary latrine and drinking pure water for their family safety, and so on. According to one respondent,

'*...From the Gonokendra I learned things like the use of sanitary latrines, drinking pure water from safe tubewells, the importance of breast-feeding for newborn babies and the proper care of pregnant women*'.

On legal issues, the locals have become aware of their rights; these include solving legal problems in court rather than through the traditional village *salish*, the legal aspects of women's rights, the cessation of the practice of dowry and the stopping the early marriages of their children. As one respondent said, '*...People were not aware of various legal issues; now we know about some basic legal procedures. For example, people wanting to register their land take a photo, whereas they bought or sold land on verbal commitment only, a while ago.*

And on environmental issues, they have become aware of different types and levels of pollution and the consequences of using excessive chemical fertilisers to cultivate their land. They try to utilise the new knowledge and awareness that has developed through Gonokendra multimedia sessions. According to one respondent:

Gonokendra also teaches and demonstrates the use of organic fertilizer so that the agricultural lands' productivity increases. This information enables our illiterate and poor farmers to increase their agricultural production.

Guardian

All guardians show great interest in and are conscious of their children's education in general, and the Gonokendra ICT program in particular. Investing in their children's careers is one of their major family priorities. The guardians generally send their children to Gonokendra without hesitation. According to one:

...computer training course fee at Gonokendra is as cheap as buying 5 kilo of rice for my family. My son, who is attending the computer course here, found tremendous interest on learning computer. Now he wants to become computer engineer in future.

However, some mothers require their daughters' assistance in household work, so they are not as willing to send their daughters to school or to the Gonokendra, sometimes. According to one guardian, *'It helps the family if she (daughter) stays at home and does household works'.* The problem is a social one. But people's attitudes towards female education are changing; and the guardians believe that an educated female can also contribute to her family, as one respondent replied, *'We would like to equally contribute in our society like men'.*

Some guardians imply that while they have become aware of issues like basic hygiene, the matter of dowry payments and early marriage, and seeking assistance from formal courts, they do not see a huge impact's being made in their village. For example, dowry payments are still quite prevalent as a custom for the rich, whilst compulsory for poor, as per one respondent added, *'...arranging daughters' marriage means giving dowry'.* In reply, another group differed and they believed that literacy could be a remedial measurement for changing people traditional perceptions and attitude towards gender dimensions, dowry and early marriage. They added that the situation has improved due to the presence of Gonokendra

Vignette 2 presents an illustration demonstrating how a rural carpenter of Gonokendra participants motivated others through his knowledge acquired from Gonokendra's multi-media session.

Vignette 2: Stopping EARLY MARRIAGE, Saving teenager's LIFE

When Nasima was only 14, her father, an illiterate farmer, was about to force her to marry a 27-year-old man; but Md. Anwar, 32, a carpenter by profession and brother-in-law of Nasima's father, put a stop to this early marriage. He was a semi-literate carpenter, and aware of the unlawfulness of the practice and of its dire consequences through the Gonokendra multimedia programs. Though Nasima's brothers and sister were educated, they didn't raise their voices against their father's decision, for they were financially dependent on him. But Md. Anwar did a noble job by calling the police immediately, despite the possibility of breaking the good relationship with his brother-in-law. The early marriage was stopped and Md. Anwar saved a teenager's life from the possibly devastating consequences.

Table 4 demonstrates some issues which emerged in our findings from the actual beneficiaries' perspective.

DISCUSSION AND CONCLUSION

Access to ICT is argued to be an effective way to narrow the gap between the rich and the poor; between rural and urban populations; and between being isolated in a poor village with very little access to the outside world and being able to participate in an increasingly technological global village (Raul & Royal, 2002). In short, an ICT intervention can bridge the digital-divide. The World Bank (1998, p.9) concurs, '*This new technology greatly facilitates the acquisition of knowledge, offering developing countries unprecedented opportunities to enhance educational systems...and widen the range of opportunities for business and the poor'.* Therefore, focus has been extended from technology to information conducive to knowledge and capacity building (Cecchini & Scott, 2003; Compaine, 2001; Dixit, 2006; Heeks, 1999; Heeks, 2005a, 2005b) .

By addressing the challenge of providing access to technology/information, Gonokendra has been actively responding the challenges of 'ICT for development' in Bawpara village. Our findings

Table 4. Some emergent issues from the perspective of participants

Category of respondents	Emergent issues
Librarian/Trainer	Librarian felt self-respect, self-sufficient and self-reliant. Importance of learning and knowing of health and legal information. Computer skill as a pre-requisite to get job. Access to 'technology' and 'information' for all groups.
Trainee	Opportunity to expand their choices of job/career. Showing interest to be trained. Teachers inspired them and they inspired their classmates to be trained at Gonokendra. Applying the knowledge of health and environmental issues in world. Presence of social constraints e.g. *Purdah*, limited decision making power etc.
General rural People	Computer training program for learning, skill building and employment of their community. Community supports and participation, Awareness of Health issues e.g. AIDS, family planning, drinking pure water and so on. Awareness of legal issue e.g. moving to formal court, stopping early marriage and so on. Awareness of environmental issue e.g. usages of organic fertilizer.
Trainees' guardian	Investing on children career in their first priority. Daughters might need to stay at home to assist mothers. People attitude towards female group was changing. Awareness and practices of health and legal issues.

demonstrate that the presence of the computer training courses enables the villagers to become literate and to obtain jobs, consequently, improving their financial and social status. Further, the multi-media based information dissemination sessions provide valuable information related to health, legal and environmental awareness to the villagers. In reality, such information reminds and directs the participants to act in their real world. Therefore, information becomes the core of the participants' actions conducive to their development. Our findings are summarized in the illustration based on Checkland's (1981) and Checkland and Holwell's (1998) holistic, soft systems methodology approach, and presented in Figure 2. Here, we conceptualize development as 'improved situation' through the interaction and influence of individual, family or group and society at community level. The illustration contains two major parts.

The first part refers to the implementation of ICT in rural community. In brief, the ICT/ICT4D intervention (Gonokendra) is implemented through a collaborative effort between BRAC, a local NGO, and the community. The rural community is the owner of this project where the community people actively participate in the operations. Two major activities of the ICT program, the computer-training courses and the multi-media sessions were the focus of this research.

The second part of the illustration contains the implication of the ICT program in the participants' real world conducive to their economic and social development. The area of ICT led developmental impact is denoted as 'issues of development' in Figure 2. Our data reveals a hierarchy towards conceptualizing 'improved situation' where society dominates over the action(s) of the individual and the family/group. For example, the society permits dowry practice at individual and family/group level despite knowing it is illegal. On the other hand, the family dominates over individual action(s). For instance, despite trainees' interests in attending Gonokendra's ICT program, their family bindings/obligations may restrict them in fulfilling their desire/interest. Further, it remains a challenge to obtain parents' permission to move outside the home, especially for females. The society is dominated and influenced by a few stakeholders such as politicians, teachers, senior citizens, and religious leaders who play a critical role to form and influence social constraints. Our field data concludes that development (improved situation) at community level is a dynamic process emerges from a complex social interaction of actor's (individual, family/group and society) interest and influences of many forces (social constraints) as presented in Figure 2.

In this chapter, we present the voices of the actual beneficiaries in regard to ICT-led developmental impact in the Bawpara village of Bangladesh. There is an ongoing debate concerning how far ICT interventions can impact on the development of human beings, especially in rural areas of developing countries (Harris, 2005; Heeks, 2002; Sein & Ahmad, 2001; Sein & Harindranath, 2004). This explorative research provides some useful insights and path-ways to link ICT with development at the individual, group level and within the society of the actual beneficiary at village level.

Since it has been an accepted practice with IS researchers drawing theory from other disciplines such as Actor Network Theory and Structuration Theory from Sociology (Walsham & Sahay, 2006), the human development perspective from development studies and economics in this research is proposed as a worthwhile challenge for IS/ICT4D researchers in developing countries.

Although some research studies—by Madon (2003), Giger (2004), and Garai and Sahadrach (2006), for instance—have used Sen's theory (Walsham & Sahay, 2006), ICT4D impact research at the micro or community level in village areas of Bangladesh is almost non-existent. Therefore, this research has potential to contribute knowledge of ICT4D research in a particular social context of Bangladesh in terms of theory/concept. Bear-

Figure 2. Illustration of implementation and implication of the ICT4D (Gonokendra) intervention

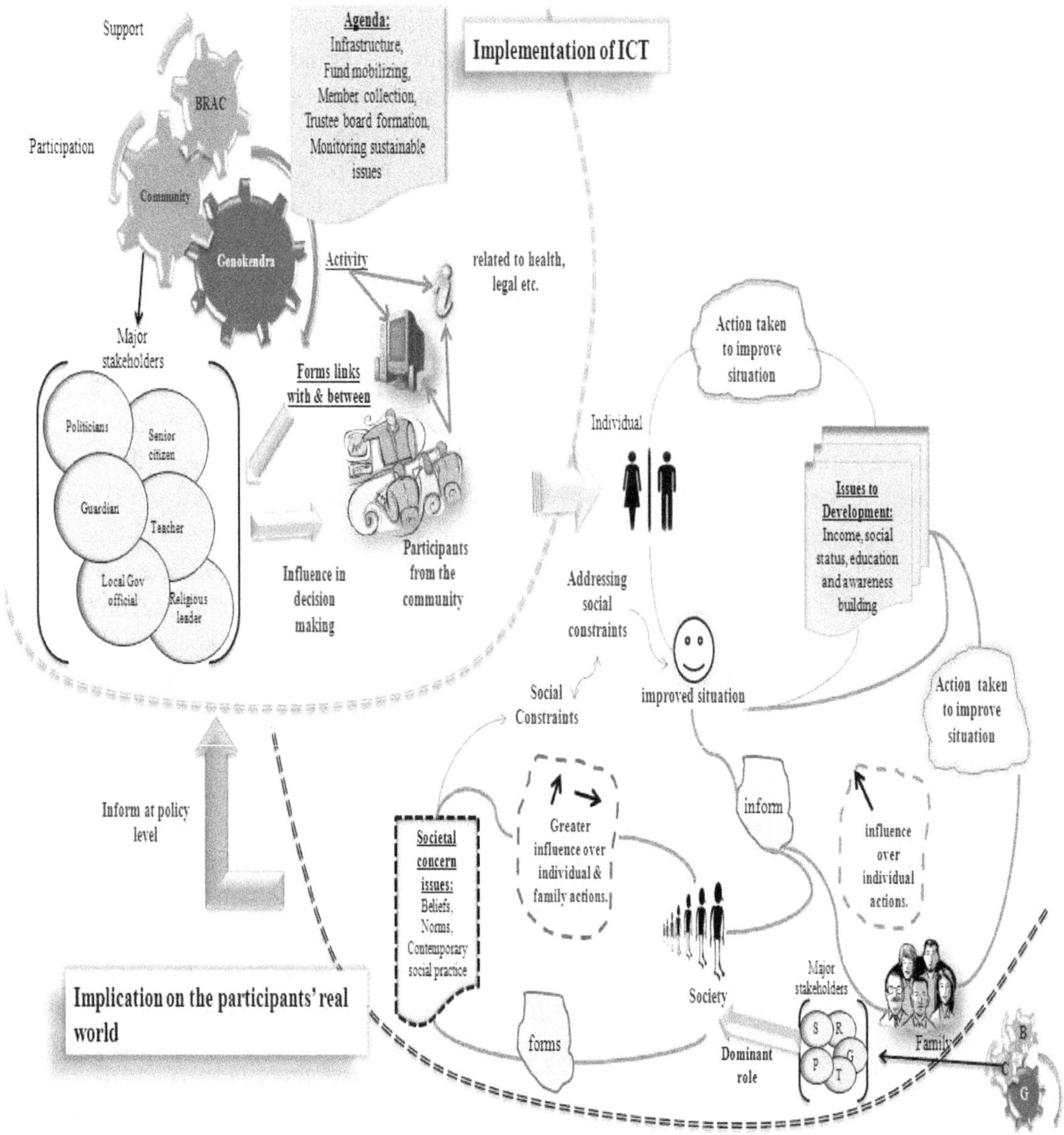

ing the human development perspective in mind, this chapter concludes that an ICT4D project has significant impact on economic and social development at the community level. However, the process of ICT-led developmental impact is dynamic rather than static.

REFERENCES

Ashraf, Md. M., Hanisch, J. & Swatman, P. (2006). ICT Intervention Towards Development In The Third World Countries: some perspectives of IS research. In *Proceedings of the 9th Interna-*

tional Conference on Computer and Information Technology(ICCIT), Dhaka, Bangladesh, 21-23 December.

Avgerou, C. (2003). The link between ICT and economic growth in the discourse of development. In M. Korpela, R. Monetealerge, & K. Poulymenakou (Eds.), *Organizational information systems in the context of globalization,* (pp. 373-386).

Bank, W. (1998). *World Development Report*, Washington, DC.

Boyatzis, R.E. (1998). *Transforming qualitative information : thematic analysis and code development*, Sage Publications, Thousand Oaks, CA.

BRAC (2004). *BRAC annual report: 2004.* Dhaka, Bangladesh.

BRAC (2003). *BRAC Project proposal: 2004-2009.* Bangladesh Rural Advancement Committee (BRAC), Dhaka, Bangladesh.

Cam, C.N. (2004). A conceptual framework for socio-techno centric approach to sustainable development. *International Journal of Technology Management & Sustainable Development, 3*(1), 59-66.

Cecchini, S., & Scott, C. (2003). Can information and communications technology applications contribute to poverty reduction? Lessons from rural India? *Information Technology for Development, 10*(2), 73-84.

Census, P. (2001). *Population Census in Bangladesh.* Dhaka.

Checkland, P. (1981). *Systems thinking, systems practice.* New York: J. Wiley.

Checkland, P., & Holwell, S. (1998). *Information, systems and information systems: making sense of the field.* New York: J. Wiley.

Compaine, B.M. (2001). *The digital Divide- Facing a crisis or creating a myth?* Massachusetts: MIT press.

Creswell, J.W. (1998). *Qualitative inquiry and research design : choosing among five traditions.* Thousand Oaks, USA: Sage Publications.

Dixit, K. (2006). *Does information technology really promote knowledge?* Third World Network Features, Retrieved 10 July, 2006 from <http://sade.sdnp.undp.org/rc/forums/mgr/sdnpmgrs/msg01283.html>.

Evert, G. (2003). All research is interpretive! *Journal of Business & Industrial Marketing, 18*(6/7), 482 - 492.

Fukuda-Parr, S., Lopes, C., & Malik, K. (2002). *Capacity for Development: New Solutions to Old Problems.* London: Earthscan Publications.

Garai, A., & Sahadrach, B. (2006). *Taking ICT to every Indian village: opportunities and challenges.* South Asia, New Delhi: One World.

Gazette, B. (2002). *National Information and Communication Technology (ICT) Policy.* Ministry of Science and Information & Communication Technology Government of the People's Republic of Bangladesh., Dhaka, <http://www.bccbd.org/html/itpolicy.htm#3.3>.

Gigler, B-S. (2004). Including the Excluded - Can ICTs empower poor communities? In *Proceedings of the 4th International Conference on the Capability Approach*, Italy, 5-7 September, 2004.

Gillham, B. (2005). *Research interviewing: the range of techniques.* Open University Press, Maidenhead.

Harris, R., & Bhatarai, M. (2003). *Fact-Finding Review of ICT in Development in a Rural-Urban Setting.* UN-HABITAT and Roger Harris Associates. Rural-Urban Partnerships Programme (RUPP) under Support Services Policy and Programme Development (SPPD).

Harris, R.W. (2005). Explaining the success of rural Asian telecentres. In R.M. Davison, R.W. Harris, S. Qureshi, D.R. Vogel & G-Jd. Vreede

(Eds.), *Information systems in developing countries: theory and practice*. City University of Hong Kong Press, Hong Kong, (pp. 83-100).

Heeks, R. (1998). Foundation of ICTs in Development: Pushing and Pulling, *Information Technology in Developing Countries Newsletter, 4*(I), 1-2.

Heeks, R. (1999). Information and communication technologies, poverty and development. *Working Paper Series,* 5, (June), 1-19.

Heeks, R. (2002). Information Systems and Developing Countries: Failure, Success, and Local Improvisations.' *Information Society, 18*(2), 101-112.

Heeks, R. (2005a). Foundation of ICTs in Development: The information chain. *eDevelopment Briefing,* 3(1), 1-2.

Heeks, R. (2005b). Foundation of ICTs in Development: The Onion Ring Model. *eDevelopment Briefing, 4*, 1-2.

Heeks, R., & Kenny, C. (2002). ICTs and development: Convergence or divergence for developing countries? In *Proceedings of the Norwegian Association for Development Research Conference*, Trondheim, Norway, 14-15 November 2002.

Hettne, B. (1990). *Development theory and the three worlds*. Essex, England: Harlow.

IDRC (2003). *A Dialogue on ICTs and Poverty: The Harvard Forum*. IDRC, Harvard, Retrieved 10 October, 2005 from <http://web.idrc.ca/ev_en.php?ID=46261_201&ID2=DO_TOPIC>.

Johnston, J. (2003). *The Millennium Development Goals and Information and Communications Technology*. United Nations Information and Communication Technologies Task Force, Berlin.

Kaplan, B., & Duchon, D. (1998). Combining Qualitative and Quantitative Methods in Information Systems Research: A Case Study. *MIS Quarterly, 12*(4), 571-586.

Kling, R. (1999) *What is Social Informatics and Why Does it Matter?* Manchester, Retrieved 12th September 2005 from, <http://www.dlib.org/dlib/january99/kling/01kling.html>.

Krishna, S., & Madon, S. (Eds) (2003). *Digital Challenge: Information Technology in the Development Context*. ASHGATE, Aldershot.

Larrain, J. (1989). *Theories of Development: Capitalism, Colonialism and Dependency*. Cambridge, UK: Polity Press

Macome, E. (2002). *The dynamics of the adoption and use of ICT-based initiatives for development: results of a field study in Mozambique*. Faculty of Engineering, Built Environment and Information Technology, Unpublished PhD thesis, University of Pretoria.

Madon, S. (2000). The Internet and socio-economic development: exploring the interaction. *Information Technology & People, 13*(2), 85-101.

Madon, S. (2003). Studying the developmental impact of e-governance initiatives. In *Proceedings of the Internationals Federation of Information Processing, IFIP* , Working Group 8.2 and 9.4, Athens, Greece, 15-17 June 2003.

Mansell, R., & Wehn, U. (1998). *Knowledge societies: information technology for sustainable development*. Published for and on behalf of the United Nations by Oxford University Press, Oxford ; New York.

Maykut, P.S., & Morehouse, R. (1994). *Beginning qualitative research : a philosophic and practical guide*. London ; Washington, D.C.: Falmer Press.

McGranahan, D. (1972). Development Indicators and Development Models. *Journal of Development Studies, 8*(3), 91.

Miles, M.B., & Huberman, A.M. (1994). *Qualitative data analysis: an expanded sourcebook*, (2nd ed.). Thousand Oaks, CA: Sage Publications.

Myers, M.D., & Avison, D. (2002). An introduction to qualitative research in information systems, In M.D. Myers & D. Avison, (Eds.), *Qualitative research in information systems: a reader*(pp. 3-12). London: Sage..

PACE (2005). *ICT in Multi-purpose community learning centres/Gonokendras*. Bangladesh Rural Advancement Committee (BRAC), Dhaka, Bangladesh.

Patton, M.Q. (1980). *Qualitative evaluation methods*. London: Sage publication.

Peet, R. (1995). *Theories of Development*. NY, USA: Guildford Press.

Prakash, G. (2005). Leapfrogging into the Knowledge Era: Use of ICT for Development. *IIMB Management Review, 17*(3), 47-56.

Qureshi, S. (2003). Movement in the information technology for development debate: How can it meet the challenges of global competition? *Information Technology for Development, 10*(3), 147-149.

Raul, R., & Royal. D.C. (2002). *Themes and Issues in Telecentre Sustainability*. Institute for Development Policy and Management, Manchester, Retrieved 10 October, 2005 from, <http://www.man.ac.uk/idpm/idpm_dp.htm#devinf_wp>.

RIRDC (1997). *A framework for developing regional communications initiatives*. Melbourne.

Ritchie, J. & Lewis, J. (2003). *Qualitative research practice: a guide for social science students and researchers*, first edn. London: Sage Publication.

Sanchez, O.A. (2000). *The Legacy of Human Development: a tribute to Mahbub ul Haq*. (pp. 9-16). Routledge.

Sein, M., & Ahmad, I. (2001). A Framework to Study the Impact of Information and Communication Technologies on Developing Countries: The Case of Cellular Phones in Bangladesh. In *Proceedings from the BITWORLD 2001*, Cairo, Egypt.

Sein, M., & Harindranath, G. (2004). Conceptualizing the ICT Artifact: Toward Understanding the Role of ICT in National Development. *Information Society, 20*(1), 15-24.

Selhofer, H., & Hüsing, T. (2002). The digital divide index- a measure of social inequalities in the adoption of ICT, In *Proceedings of the ST 2002 Conference*, Copenhagen, November 2002.

Sen, A. (1999). *Development as freedom*, 1st. edn. New York: Knopf.

Sen, A. (2000a). A Decade of Human Development. *Journal of Human Development, 1*(1), 17-23.

Sen, A. (2000b). *Development as freedom*, (1st. ed.). New Delhi: Oxford University Press.

Sen, R. (1992). *Social constraints for working women: notes from a rural area of Jamalpur*, 75. Mohakhali, Dhaka-1212, Bangladesh.

Soeftestad, L.T., & Sein, M.K. (2003). ICT and Development: East is East and West is West and the Twain may yet Meet. In S. Krishna & S. Madon (Eds), *Digital Challenge: Information Technology in the Development Context*, ASHGATE, (pp. 63-83).

Stake, R.E. (1995). *The art of case study research*. Thousand Oaks, CA: Sage Publications.

Szirmai, A. (2005). *The Dynamics of Socio-Economic Development: An Introduction*, (1st Ed.). Cambridge University Press.

Taylor, S.J., & Bogdan, R. (1984). *Introduction to qualitative research methods: the search for meanings*, (2nd Ed). New York: Wiley.

UN (2005). *The World Summit on the Information Society (WSIS).* Geneva, Retrieved 25 November-2005, from, <http://www.itu.int/wsis/>.

UNDP (2004). *Bridging the gender digital divide.* UNDP regional centre for Europe and the CIS and UNIFEM Central and Eastern Europe, Solvak Republic.

UNDP (2002). *Human development report 2002.* New York: Oxford University Press, Inc..

UNESCO (2005). *Evaluation of UNESCO's Community Multimedia Centres.* United Nations Educational, Scientific and Cultural Organization.

Walsham, G. (1993). *Interpreting information systems in organizations.* England: J. Wiley.

Walsham, G. (1995). 'The Emergence of Interpretivism in IS Research. *Information Systems Research, 6*(4), 376-394.

Walsham, G. (2002). Interpretive case studies in IS research: Nature and method, In D.E .Avison & M.D. Myers (Eds.), *Qualitative research in information systems: a reader*, (pp. 101-113). SAGE, London.

Walsham, G., & Sahay, S. (2006). Research on information systems in developing countries: current landscape and future prospects. *Information Technology for Development, 12*(1), 7-24.

Yah, L.C. (1991). *Development and underdevelopment.* Longman Jurong Town.

Yin, R.K. (1984). *Case study research: design and methods.* CA: Sage Publications.

Young, V. (1997). *ICTs and Development: Testing a framework for Evaluation.* Canada: Canadian International Development Agency.

Section II
E-Governance, Digital Divide and Rural Development

Chapter IV
Tracking the Digital Divide:
Studying the Association of the Global Digital Divide with Societal Divide

Marc Holzer
Rutgers, The State University of New Jersey, USA

Aroon Manoharan
Rutgers, The State University of New Jersey, USA

ABSTRACT

The chapter is based on a study of global municipal Web portals conducted through a collaboration between the E-Governance Institute at Rutgers-Newark, USA, and the Global e-Policy e-Government Institute at Sungkyunkwan University in Seoul, South Korea. The joint study ranked municipalities worldwide based on their scores in five e-governance categories of security and privacy, usability, content, services and citizen participation. Crucial trends in the development of the municipal Web portal indicate a growing digital divide between cities belonging to the OECD and non-OECD nations. This chapter attempts to understand the correlates of this divide, by exploring the association of this digital divide to other divides - social, political, economic and literacy divides among nations, particularly those between OECD and non-OECD nations.

INTRODUCTION

The dawn of the information age and the growth of Internet have led to governments increasingly computerizing their services to citizens around the globe. Governments are transforming into e-governments with public information and services increasingly offered online. This phenomenon is broadly referred to as e-government. "E-government, the application of ICT within public administration to optimise its internal and external functions, provides government and business with a set of tools that can potentially transform the way in which interactions take place, services are delivered,.... and citizens participate in governance..." (UNDESA, 2003, 1). According to Liikanen (2003, 5) e-government is defined as "the use of information and communication technology in public administrations combined with organizational change and new skills in order to improve public services and democratic processes and strengthen support for public policies". Norris defines e-government as "....the delivery of services and information, electronically, to businesses and residents, 24 hours a day, seven days a week" (2001, 5). There are three stages in introducing e-government: (1) publishing government information online; (2) interacting, where ICTs are used to encourage civic participation in government decision making; and (3) transacting, where government services are accessed online (CDT & infoDev, 2002). The internet is also a convenient mechanism for government to conduct citizen-participation exercises, with the potential to decentralize decision-making. ICTs help citizen groups to "do research on the Web, build links with online communities, host their own Websites to post reports, and make use of email to connect with their peers" (Bridges.org, 2002b).

As the use of e-government became popular, academicians have conducted research on the potential effects of e-government. A Pew Internet & American Life Project study examining how Americans contact their government found that e-government is an increasingly popular tool for online users to get information and send messages to their public officials (Horrigan, 2004). Another study by Gant & Gant (2001) finds that in a span of five years, from 1995 to 2000, the number of both public and private Web portals across the globe rose from less than 20,000 to more than 10 million.

Much of this research on the performance of e-government has focused primarily on the public agency, with less consideration of the societal impact of providing services online. Traditional methods of measuring government service, both online and offline have focused on the public official or administrative tool as the central element. Behn's "three big questions of public management" consider the public bureaucrat as the framework of measurement and improvement, thus ignoring the social consequences of public administration in a democratic society (Kirlin, 1996). In this context, an important consequence of the growing use of computers is the growing digital divide among nations and also within nations both developed and developing. Digital divide is not just a divide that applies to people but it can also be applicable on a larger scale to countries and states. Some countries are ranked higher while some are ranked lower on the scale measuring the degree of digital divide leading to an uneven level of participation in a networked society. Thus "the network society is creating parallel communications systems: one for those with income, education and literally connections, giving plentiful information at low cost and high speed; the other for those without connections, blocked by high barriers of time, cost and uncertainty and dependent upon outdated information" (UNDP, 1999, 63). This chapter attempts to understand the correlates of this divide, by exploring the association of this digital divide to other divides - social, political, economic and literacy divides among nations, particularly those between OECD and non-OECD nations.

BACKGROUND

The term digital divide may imply more than one meaning. In simple terms, it refers to the "gap between those people who have access to digital technologies and information on the internet, and those who do not" (Singh, 2002, 7). This refers to the "gap between individuals, households, businesses and geographic areas at different socio-economic levels with regard both to their opportunities to access information and communication technologies (ICTs) and to the use of the internet for a wide variety of activities" (OECD, 2001). Keniston (2004) classifies the divide into four categories in his book *Experience in India: Bridging the Digital Divide*. The first category is a "massive digital divide based on income, related to education and urban residence, and correlated with economic, political and cultural power" (13). The second divide is linguistic implying the advantage of English speaking nations of US, UK Canada, New Zealand, Australia and nations with large English populations like India, South Africa, Singapore and Hong Kong. The author refers this as the "Anglo-Saxon linguistic and cultural hegemony" (16). The third divide is related to the digital gap between the Northern nations that are information-rich and the Southern nations that are information-poor. The fourth divide refers to the creation of new professional elite, made up of computer engineers who have reaped huge benefits from the IT revolution (17).

According to Won Kim (2003), digital divide widens differentially at each stage and it becomes necessary to "devise countermeasures at every stage" (88). The author provides the solutions of "density of information service providers, number of hosting servers and internet users' internet permeation rate" (88) and concludes that the public sector should initiate the process of bridging the divide. Perhaps the most severe effect of the digital divide would be the further division of the society and creation of the fourth world as Castells had predicted in the *End of Millennium*. The fourth world is that section of the population which would not be able to have access to technology and would be burdened with inequality, poverty and disempowerment (Castells, 2000).

Jones (2003) states that digital divide has implications in different dimensions: social divide between the information rich and information poor; global divide between developed and developing nations; democratic divide between those who use internet for civic participation and those who do not. When the term digital divide was initially used in the development circles, it simply referred to the physical access to the computer and internet. However it soon began to encompass various other factors, including access to education, income, gender etc. Jones concludes by stating that digital divide depends on three main aspects; "access to information and communication technologies, access to appropriate content and geopolitical aspects" (138). "Segments of the population with higher socio-economic status tend to acquire information at a faster rate than the lower segments so that the gap in knowledge in these tends to increase rather than decrease" (Tichenor et al., 1970). There are many factors that can be attributed towards the digital divide, such as the structure of opportunities resulting from the public policies in each country, public and private initiatives towards IT education and training, investment in science and technology, the costs of ISP services, and the regulation of telecommunications (Norris 2001).

Some authors consider the digital divide more of an effect than a cause for the problems of the "have-nots". The divide that exists today between the "haves" and "have-nots" is merely an extension of the existing inequalities between the two in terms of standard of living, education, employment levels, access to infrastructure and expertise both with regards to people and nations. Jan van Djk (2005) regards the digital divide as a "social and political problem, not a technological one." He draws a parallel between the digital divide and the internet hype of the 1990's that the new technological innovation would solve all social, political problems. The term digital divide is just like old wine in a new bottle- the divide that has not been sufficiently distinguished from the older inequalities. He quotes the question of the famous moral economist Amartya Sen "equality of what?" – inequalities of opportunities, life chances, freedom, capital, resources, positions, capabilities or skills? Are there people who exist on the higher scale on some factors and lower scales on others? Perhaps the ability of the English language to manipulate a metaphor has encouraged the use of the word "divide" to create an illusion of a deep divide between" haves and have-nots".

The author suggests that instead of any extreme bipolar divide, there actually exist a "tripartite distribution" of the society with different levels of internet use.

Linda Bernnan and Victoria Johnson (2004) recognize that the term digital divide was originally intended to represent the differences in access to technology among the population of a particular nation or community. The transition of the meaning of the term to signify a so-called global problem still lacks much literature. They state that there is actually "no digital divide" to solve and that the difference in physical access is negligible to be considered in decision making. Various solutions are being offered to the growing digital divide but few elaborate exactly on the "problems of inequalities in access to technology. Computer and internet facilities have become very cheap that in many cases, accessibility is not the issue rather; it is the frequency of use of these computers. Purchase of computers and internet would be more expensive to the "have-nots" but they are more unwilling to buy those due to lack of frequent use rather than affordability.

So, is the divide that exists today between the "haves" and "have-nots" merely an extension of the existing inequalities between the two in terms of standard of living, education, employment levels, access to infrastructure and expertise both with regard to population and nations? To examine this proposition, it is important to research the literature on measuring the digital divide and explore the association of this divide to other divides - social, political, economic and literacy divides among nations, particularly those between OECD and non-OECD nations.

Measuring the provision and impact of e-government would need to encompass societal consequences, to shed light on the larger problems like digital divide. In 2003, the Digital Governance in Municipalities Survey was conducted by the E-Governance Institute at Rutgers-Newark, USA and the Global e-Policy e-Government Institute at Sungkyunkwan University in Seoul. The study ranked municipalities worldwide based on their scores in five e-governance categories of security and privacy, usability, content, services and citizen participation. The survey was repeated in 2005 to assess the longitudinal trends in municipal e-governance across the most wired nations of the world and the results indicate a growing digital divide among the cities evaluated. Overall, the average score for OECD nations in 2005 was 44.35 while that of the non-OECD nations was 26.50, thus resulting in a gap of 17.85 points. This gap increased from 12.08 points in the 2003 survey.

To understand the factors associated with digital divide, it would be appropriate to use an overall approach rather than focusing on specific indicators. Nations are often measured on an economic scale using measures like per capita income. If the wealth is concentrated in the hands of a few, the quality of life of the majority of the population may be lower than the perception from its per capita income. A nation with a lesser per capita income which is more spread out would enable its citizens to experience a better quality of life (Kosack, 2002). There is a growing emphasis across the world to understand and assess the factors affecting e-government from a societal perspective.

METHODOLOGY

In this chapter, digital divide is defined as the differences in the average e-governance scores between the cities belonging to the OECD and non-OECD nations among those evaluated in the Digital Governance in Municipalities Worldwide Survey 2003 and 2005. The OECD consists of 30 nations and the largest municipality in each nation was evaluated including those of the 51 non-OECD nations.

This digital divide is then compared to the divides in five different factors – education level, GDP, life expectancy, number of online users and number of computers among OECD and non-

OECD nations. These divides are assessed for the years 2003 and 2005 to determine if they had increased along with the digital divide or decreased as the digital divide increased between OECD and non-OECD nations. The measures for education level, life expectancy and GDP are obtained from the UN Development Report (UNDR, 2007), which ranks nations based on a combination of three important factors – healthy life, access to knowledge and standard of living. These factors are measured by life expectancy, literacy rates, and enrollment at primary, secondary and tertiary level of education and GDP per capita. The life expectancy measures are obtained from the World Population Prospects: 1950-2050, prepared biannually by the United Nations Department of Economic and Social Affairs Population Division. The adult literacy rate is based on the statistics from the United Nations Educational, Social and Cultural Organization (UNESCO).

The measures for number of online users and number of computers in each nation are obtained for 2003 and 2005 from the International Telecommunication Union (ITU), an organization affiliated with the United Nations (UN). The Rutgers-SKKU E-Governance Survey focused on cities worldwide and considered their population size and the total number of online users in the nation overall. The top 100 municipalities were selected using the ITU data from a total of 196 countries for which telecommunications data was reported. Those nations with an online population over 160,000 were identified as the top 100 wired nations, and the most populated cities in these nations were surveyed. Of the 100 cities, 81 were included in the overall rankings, excluding the 19 municipalities where no official Web portals were available.

RESULTS

The scores of the municipal Web portals are correlated with the education level, life expectancy and GDP values obtained from the UN Human Development Report; the number of online users per 100 inhabitants and number of computers per 100 inhabitants obtained from the ITU Report for 2003 and 2005.

Overall, the average score for OECD nations in 2005 was 44.35 while that of the non-OECD nations was 26.50, thus resulting in a gap of 17.85 points. This gap increased from 12.08 points in the 2003 survey. Compared to this digital divide, the human development gap actually decreased with non-OECD nations bridging the gap towards their OECD counterparts. While the digital divide between the OECD and non-OECD nations increased by 1.47%, the overall HDI divide decreased by 0.88%. Among the human development indicators, the education gap seems to have bridged the most with 0.8 %, while GDP index recorded the lowest decrease in the gap.

However the increase in digital divide was matched with an increase in the divide in the number of online users and the number of

Box 1.

Year	Divide between OECD & non-OECD	Digital	Human Development	Life Expectancy	Education Index	GDP Index	Users per 100 inhabitants	Computers per 100 inhabitants
2005	Divide	17.84	0.155	0.128	0.116	0.219	26.69	29.64
2003	Divide	12.08	0.175	0.146	0.145	0.233	24.65	26.21
	Change (%)	**1.47**	**0.88**	**0.87**	**0.80**	**0.94**	**1.08**	**1.13**

computers per 100 inhabitants between the two categories of nations. The average number of online users per 100 inhabitants in OECD nations in 2003 was 38.79, which increased to 45.92 in 2005 while number of online users per 100 inhabitants in non-OECD nations increased from 14.4 in 2003 to 19.23 in 2005. Overall, divide in the number of online users per 100 inhabitants increased from 24.65 in 2003 to 26.65 in 2005 at a rate of 1.08%. Similarly the average number of computers per 100 inhabitants in OECD nations in 2003 was 38.79, which increased to 45.92 in 2005 while the average number of computers per 100 inhabitants in non-OECD nations increased from 14.4 in 2003 to 19.23 in 2005. Overall, divide in the number of computers per 100 inhabitants increased from 26.21 in 2003 to 29.64 in 2005 at a rate of 1.13%.

Thus the digital divide among the OECD and non-OECD nations is more closely related with the number of online users and the number of computers, more specifically with computer education and infrastructure. In the following section, some suggestions are provided to help in bridging the gap between the OECD and non-OECD nations and in general, between the developed and developing nations.

RECOMMENDATIONS

Access to ICT is intertwined in a complex network of physical, social, economical, and political factors. The Former UN Secretary General Kofi Anan had stated in his speech at the Telecom 99 conference in Geneva, Switzerland that excluding the world's poor from the information revolution could turn out more disastrous than expected -"People lack many things: jobs, shelter, food, health care and drinkable water. Today, being cut off from basic telecommunications services is a hardship almost as acute as these other deprivations, and may indeed reduce the chances of finding remedies to them" (as quoted in Norris 2001).

A vocal push for bridging the digital divide has been from the developed nations. The G-8 has formed a special task force - Digital Operating Task Force (DOT) to provide strategic solutions to bridge the digital divide existing in the developing nations. DOT Force was quick to implement its plans and had proposed a network among nations to provide the developing nations with expertise on the policies and regulatory frameworks for bridging the divide (DOT, 2002). According to a report prepared by the OECD (OECD, 2004), any effort to bridging the digital divide should focus on sustaining the infrastructure especially in the telecommunications sector. It suggests that a strong telecommunication infrastructure is vital for sustaining the access to internet and in order to ensure an effective telecommunication market, regulatory reforms need to be implemented in developing nations

The concept of real access to ICT, made up of twelve interrelated factors, was soon proposed by a development based non-profit organization – Bridges (Bridges.org, 2002a). These factors are:

- **Physical access:** Is technology available and accessible to people and organizations?
- **Appropriate technology:** Is the available technology appropriate to local needs and conditions? What is the appropriate technology according to how people need and want to put technology to use?
- **Affordability:** Is technology affordable for people to use?
- **Capacity and training:** Do people have the training and skills necessary for effective technology use? Do they understand how to use technology and its potential uses?
- **Relevant content:** Is locally relevant content available, especially in terms of language?
- **Integration into daily routines:** Is technology use a burden to peoples' lives or is it integrated into daily routines?
- **Socio-cultural factors:** Are people limited in their use of technology based on gender, race, or other socio-cultural factors?

- **Trust in technology:** Do people have confidence in technology and understand the implications of the technology they use, for instance in terms of privacy, security, or cyber-crime?
- **Legal and regulatory framework:** Do laws and regulations limit technology use? Are changes needed to create an environment that fosters its use?
- **Sustainability and the local economic environment:** Is there a local economic environment favourable to technology use? Is technology part of local economic development? What is needed to make it a part?
- **Macro-economic environment:** Is technology use limited by the macro-economic environment in the country or region, for example, in terms of deregulation, investment, and labour issues?
- **Public support and political will:** Is there political will in government to do what is needed to enable the integration of technology throughout society, and public support for government decision-making?

Based on the findings of the research on bridging the digital divide, there are five factors that need to be addressed immediately in the effort to bridge the digital divide: infrastructure; appropriate computer hardware and software; computer education.

Infrastructure

Infrastructure is vital to the sustainability of the project. Many developing nations have good infrastructure that cater only to a minority of the population. Massive efforts are needed to expand the infrastructure to benefit all sections of the society. In the drive to provide computers and technology infrastructure, governments may succumb to the arguments of the private sectors on the impending effects of the divide and would readily award contracts to private business to supply the infrastructure. Thus governments need to consider the opinion of all sections of the society especially theorists and academicians to understand the depth of the issue and thus be able to effectively plan on bridging the divide on a long-term basis.

The telecommunication network in any country or region is a good indicator of the feasibility of providing internet facilities. To enable a wider reach of ICT among the region and to sustain the networked world, it is important to focus more effort on improving tele-connectivity. Apart from providing internet connectivity, telephones are also an important factor in improving communications and providing opportunities for tele-working.

Appropriate Use of Computer Hardware and Software

In the effort to bridge the digital divide, the cost of providing computers can be reduced by using refurbished computers along with open source software. According to Guy Anthony Halse (2005), the latest software programs require the latest hardware facilities. The effort of bridging the digital divide can reduce major costs by avoiding the commercial software and by adopting open source software.

In the year 2005, Microsoft had offered to provide free access to selected Microsoft software that would save millions of Rands to the Government of South Africa in their effort to bridge the digital divide (Halse, 2005, 1). But according to Halse, many computers that had been provided to schools to bridge the digital divide were used-computers that had already been discarded about 3-4 years ago. Buying the latest software may force administrators to buy the latest hardware facilities and such a situation may become a financial obstacle to the effort in the long term. The problem is how to use the latest software on the existing hardware system. Thus the author proposes the use of open-sourced software and reduction in the use of commercial software (Halse, 2005).

CONCLUSION

E-Government is a growing phenomenon across the globe, with many governments providing services online at federal, state and local levels. Providing online public service should focus more on its impact on society rather than operational features of public organizations and such focus would shed more light on the growing digital divide between the developed and developing nations. Access to ICT is intertwined in a complex network of physical, social, economical, and political factors. Based on the study's research, the digital divide among the OECD and non-OECD nations is more closely associated with the number of online users and the number of computers, more specifically with computer education and infrastructure. Any effort in bridging the digital divide should focus on sustaining the infrastructure especially the telecommunication sector and developing human capital in terms of providing appropriate computer education at in schools. A strong telecommunication infrastructure is vital for sustaining the access to internet and in order to ensure an effective telecommunication market, regulatory reforms need to be implemented in developing nations. Administrators and policy makers involved in addressing the digital divide need to thoroughly understand the dynamics of the divide. Rather than viewing the phenomenon as a bipolar split between the "haves" and "have-nots", the different levels of the divide should be recognized since there actually exists a "tripartite distribution" of the society with different levels of internet use.

While it is true that access to computers places one at an advantage, the "have-nots" also have many more impending problems to solve before switching on the computer. Nations should reframe their school curriculum with more focus on computer skills since the future will be dominated by knowledge and ICT based employment sector in which unskilled workers would not stand to gain with the new technologies. Moreover the digital divide may refer to different factors in developed and developing nations – in the developed world, digital divide may simply imply access to internet whereas in developing nations, this divide may refer to access to basic infrastructure like telephone, electricity etc. Therefore developing nations and non-OECD nations should strive to develop indigenous models for bridging the digital divide and introducing e-government models based on the existing social, political, financial and infrastructural conditions in the region without blindly following external models in their effort to leapfrog the years of digital development.

REFERENCES

American Customer Satisfaction Index (2004). *E-Government Satisfaction Index.* Retrieved: July 30th, 2007, from http://www.fcg.gov/pdf/e-gov_comm_092004.pdf

Bridges.org (2002b). *Taking stock and looking ahead: Digital divide assessment of the city of Cape Town, 2002.* Retrieved: Retrieved: August 5, 2007 at: http://www.bridges.org/capetown.

Castells, M. (2000). *End of millennium: The rise of the fourth world: capitalism, poverty and social exclusion,* (p. 168), Second Edition. Oxford: Blackwell.

Center for Democracy and Technology & infoDev (2002). *E-Government Handbook for Developing Countries.* Retrieved: August 5, 2007 at: http://www.cdt.org/egov/handbook/

Cloete, F. (2003). Assessing governance with electronic policy management tools. *Public Performance & Management Review, 26*(3), 276-290.

Digital Opportunities task Force (2002). *Digital Opportunities for All. Sommet Kananaskis Sum-*

mit 2002. Report Card Retrieved 12/02/2005 from http://e-com.ic.gc.ca/epic/internet/inecic-ceac.nsf/vwapj/DOT_General-Report_e.pdf/$file/DOT_General-Report_e.pdf

Economic Commission for Africa. (2002). *Economic Report on Africa 2002: Tracking Performance and Progress*, (p. 74).

Finquelievich, S., Mudhai, O., & Parmar, V. (2004). *Addressing the Digital Divide: A Non-Governmental Organization Sector Perspective.* Retrieved 12/07/2005 from http://www.ssrc.org/programs/itic/publications/knowledge_report/memos/digitaldividepaper.pdf

Gant, J. P., & Gant, D.B. (2001). Web Portal Functionality and State Government E-Service. *Proceedings of the 35th Annual Hawaii International Conference on System Science,* (pp. 1587-1596).

Halse, G., & Terzoli, A. (2005). *Open Source in South African Schools: Two Case Studies.* Centre for Excellence in Distributed Multimedia, Rhodes University.

Horrigan, J.B. (2004). *How Americans get in touch with government: Internet users benefit from the efficiency of e-government, but multiple channels are still needed for citizens to reach agencies and solve problems.* Washington, DC: Pew Internet & American Life Project.

Howard, M. (2001). e-Government across the globe: How will "e" change Government? *Government Finance Review,* (August) 6-9.

Human Development Report (2007). Fighting climate change: Human solidarity in a divided world. Retrieved: April 2, 2008, from http://hdr.undp.org/en/media/hdr_20072008_en_complete.pdf

International Telecommunication Union (2004). *Africa, ICT Indicators, 2003.* Retrieved 10/21/2005 from http://www.itu.int/ITU-D/ict/statistics/at_glance/main04.pdf

Jan A.G.M van Djk. (2005). The Deepening Divide: Inequality in an Information society. Sage publications.

Jones, S. (2003). *Encyclopedia of New Media* (pp. 139). Sage Publications.

Jussawalla, M., & Taylor, R. (2003). Information Technology Parks of the Asia-Pacific: Lessons for the Digital Divide, (p. 259). M.E.Sharpe.

Keniston, K., & Kumar, D. (2004). *Experience in India: Bridging the digital divide, (pp.13-20).* Sage Publications Inc.

Kim, W., Ling, T-W., Lee, Y-J., & Park, S.S. (2003). *The Human Society and the Internet* (p. 88). Springer-Verlag Berlin Heidelberg New York.

Kirlin, J. (2001). Big questions for a significant public administration. *Public Administration Review, 61*(2), 140-143.

Kirlin, J. (1996). What government must do well: Creating value for society, *Journal of Public Administration Research and Theory: J-PART, 6*(1).

Korac-Kakabadse, A., & Korac-Kakabadse, N. (1999). Information technology's impact on the quality of democracy: Reinventing the 'democratic vessel.' In R. Heeks, (Ed.), *Reinventing government in the information age: International practice in IT-enabled public sector reform.* London: Routledge.

Kosack, S. (2003). Effective aid: How democracy allows development aid to improve the quality of life. *World Development, 31*(1), 22.

Linda Bernnan, L., & Johnson, V. (2004). *Social, Ethical and Policy Implications of Information Technology,* (p. 32). Idea group Inc.

Liikanen, E. (2003). *EGovernment for Europe's public services of the future.* Accessed online 04/12/05 from http://www.uoc.edu/inaugural03/eng/article/20336.pdf

Moon, J., Li, J.P., Jo, S., & Sanders, L. (2006). Improving quality of life via blogs and development of a virtual social identity? *Journal of Information Technology Management, 15*(3).

Pippa, N. (2001). *Digital Divide?: Civic Engagement, Information Poverty, and the Internet Worldwide, 1.* New York, NY: Cambridge University Press.

Singh, A. (2002). *Bridging the digital divide: Role of universities in getting South Africa closer to the global information society.* University of Durban Westville. Retrieved 12/02/2005 from http://citte.nu.ac.za/papers/id7.pdf

Schneider, M. (1976). The "quality of life" and social indicators research. *Public Administration Review, 36*(3), 297-305.

Spilker, B., & Revicki, D.A. (1999). Taxonomy of Quality of Life. In B. Spilker (Ed.), *Quality of life and Pharmacoeconomics in Clinical Trials*, (pp. 25–32). Philadelphia: Lippincott-Raven.

Tichenor, P.J., Olien, C.N., & Donahue, G.A. (1970). Mass media flow and differential growth in knowledge. *Public Opinion Quarterly, 34*, 159-170.

The International Bank for Re-construction and Development/World Bank (2000). *Can Africa claim the 21st Century?, 56.*

UNDP(1999). *Human Development Report 1999.* NY: UNDP/Oxford.

United Nations Department of Economic and Social Affairs 2003, *e-Government Readiness Assessment Survey.* Retrieved: August 2, 2007, from http://www.cabinet.gov.jm/docs/pdf/eGov_Readiness_Intro.pdf

Ventura, J. (2003). *Non-Governmental Organizations and the Digital Divide* (p. 9). Retrieved 12/05/2005 from http://www.uweb.ucsb.edu/~jventura/ngo.pdf

APPENDIX A.

Table 1. E-governance performance measures

E-governance Category	Key Concepts	Raw Score	Weighted Score	Keywords
Security/ Privacy	18	25	20	Privacy policies, authentication, encryption, data management, and use of cookies
Usability	20	32	20	User-friendly design, branding, length of homepage, targeted audience links or channels, and site search capabilities
Content	20	48	20	Access to current accurate information, public documents, reports, publications, and multimedia materials
Service	20	59	20	Transactional services involving purchase or register, interaction between citizens, businesses and government
Citizen Participation	20	55	20	Online civic engagement, internet based policy deliberation, and citizen based performance measurement
Total	98	219	100	

Table 2. E-governance scale

Scale	Description
0	Information about a given topic does not exist on the Website
1	Information about a given topic exists on the Website (including links to other information and e-mail addresses)
2	Downloadable items are available on the Website (forms, audio, video, and other one-way transactions, popup boxes)
3	Services, transactions, or interactions can take place completely online (credit card transactions, applications for permits, searchable databases, use of cookies, digital signatures, restricted access)

continued on following page

APPENDIX A. CONTINUED

Table 3. Overall e-governance rankings (2005)

Ranking	City	Country	Score
1	Seoul	Republic of Korea	**81.70**
2	New York	United States	**72.71**
3	Shanghai	China	**63.93**
4	Hong Kong	Hong Kong	**61.51**
5	Sydney	Australia	**60.82**
6	Singapore	Singapore	**60.22**
7	Tokyo	Japan	**59.24**
8	Zurich	Switzerland	**55.99**
9	Toronto	Canada	**55.10**
10	Riga	Latvia	**53.95**
11	Warsaw	Poland	**53.26**
12	Reykjavik	Iceland	**52.24**
13	Sofia	Bulgaria	**49.11**
14	Prague	Czech Rep.	**47.27**
15	Luxembourg	Luxembourg	**46.58**
16	Amsterdam	Netherlands	**46.44**
17	Paris	France	**45.49**
18	Macao	Macao	**45.48**
19	Dublin	Ireland	**44.10**
20	Bratislava	Slovak Republic	**43.65**

Table 4. Average score by e-governance categories in 2005 and 2003

	Usability	Content	Service	Privacy & Security	Citizen Participation
2005 Average Scores	12.42	7.63	5.32	4.17	3.57
2003 Average Scores	11.45	6.43	4.82	2.53	3.26
% Increase in Score	8.47	18.66	10.37	64.82	9.5

Chapter V
Making ICT more Meaningful for Governance in the Rural Areas:
Role of the Community Knowledge Systems

Charru Malhotra
Indian Institute of Public Administration (IIPA), India

V.M. Chariar
Indian Institute of Technology Delhi, India

L.K. Das
Indian Institute of Technology Delhi, India

ABSTRACT

The speed and outreach enabled by information and communication technologies (ICT) have improved mechanisms of delivery of information, services and products to the public. ICT as an enabler of governance, christened as e-governance, is seen as means of attaining good governance. The millennium development goals (MDG) of targeting the poor, listening to the poor and learning from the poor seem to be more within the reach through the use of ICT. However the sustainability of majority of rural ICT interventions has not been very encouraging. The study of literature attributes this negligible success rate to several factors including neglect of traditional indigenous knowledge in the projects designed for rural masses. Authors of this study propose that by defining a proper framework and by use of proper methodologies, community knowledge systems (CKS) of a rural region, when incorporated in an e-governance initiative can assist various actors and processes of governance to attain good governance. Projects based on the proposed CKS based G2C2G framework are expected to be more sustainable and effective for ushering development in the rural areas. However, implementation of such projects would however require synergistic efforts between the government functionaries, aid agencies, non-profit organizations and the rural citizens. The prime hypothesis is that the assimilation, improvisation and dissemination of the traditional community knowledge systems (CKS) using ICT initiatives for rural governance, would help to liberate local ingenuity to catalyse sustainable rural development.

INTRODUCTION

Sustainable Rural Development can make a powerful contribution to four critical goals of: Poverty Reduction, Wider shared growth, Household, national, and global food security and Sustainable natural resource management (World Bank, 1997).

Development is a dynamic process that is entirely an aftermath of human decisions and multiplicity of choices available to them (Sen, 1987). Modern goals of development have laid emphasis on poverty reduction to provide people with better means and resources (for details see Leys, 1996; Rahnema and Victoria, 1997). Emergence of **ICT** has accelerated development towards its goals and led to economic growth and social empowerment of people in the developing countries (Nandi, 2002). Rural economies too can be benefited from ICT by focusing on social production, social consumption and social services to be rendered in the villages (Malhotra, 2001). Any improvement, in the social or economic status of rural areas would not just directly benefit rural poor but would also bring down the migration-pressures on cities and contribute by positive ripple effect in global stride towards Development. Rural Development is the prime concern of governance in the global context.

The chapter is divided in three sections. In the first section of the chapter titled 'Governance for Rural Development using **ICT**', the authors examine the changing paradigm of governance to usher rural development. The chief focus of Governance stays on economic growth and social empowerment of the rural communities that can be enabled by implementation of new-technologies. Several thinkers have therefore studied application of Information and Communication technologies (ICT) in the processes of governance some of which are summarised in this section. The authors also define and demarcate between the popular terms like **'e-Government'** and **'e-Governance'** and further tapers to the issues confronting ICT implementation in rural governance. Research studies indicate that not all ICT initiatives have been successful in improving the quality of life of the rural poor. Some remedial considerations such as 'Inputs to ICT from Community Knowledge' and 'Design of rural **e-Governance** Projects using Systems Approach' have been delineated in the subsequent section titled 'An Alternative Design Strategy'. The review of literature puts forth that the improvement of the quality of life in the rural areas, particularly the poor and socially disadvantaged sections of society is possible by prudent use of Information Communication Technologies (**ICT**) especially if fused with the prevailing **Community Knowledge Systems** (**CKS**) of the region. On basis of this, the final section suggests 'An Integrated Approach to Rural **e-Governance** Projects'. In its first part titled 'The Proposed **CKS** based G2C2G framework' the authors propose a Systems-based, inclusive framework by the same name. The next part of the section referred as 'Projects Based on **CKS** based G2C2G Framework', the authors summarise the goal, objectives, phases of the project **lifecycle**, suggested methodology as well as the key deliverables and benefits that are expected of the projects emanating from the proposed framework. The chapter concludes after putting forth the 'Future Directions' for implementation of such projects that are based on **CKS** based G2C2G framework.

SECTION I: GOVERNANCE FOR RURAL DEVELOPMENT USING ICT

"*Rural* Development *is a strategy to enable a specific group of people, poor rural women and men, to gain for themselves and their children more of what they want and need*" (Chambers, 1983). It involves use of physical, financial and human resources for economic growth and social development (Burkey, 1993) and improvement in the quality of life (Singh, 1999) of rural people in villages. The goal of governance "should be to develop capacities that are needed to realise development that gives priority to the poor, … and creates needed opportunities for employment and other livelihoods" (World Bank, 1992; UNDP, 1994).

ICT is an integral part of development strategies employed by various actors of governance. Application of ICT in processes of governance can be considered in two categories *viz.* for improving government processes and secondly for building interaction with and within civil society. Automation of services managed by Government, such as dissemination of public information, grievance redressal mechanisms, utility payments and billing services, are examples of intervention of ICT in public domain referred to as ***e-Government*** (Mitra and Gupta, 2003). When ICT is used to enhance the mechanisms of civil society participation in the governing process then such ICT based applications applied in the systems of governance are classified as ***e-Governance***. **e-Governance** permits new ways of involvement of citizens and communities for debating issues of public concern (Taylor and Williams, 1994 ;Rogers and Shukla, 2001; Gupta *et al.*, 2004; Heeks, 2004). This in turn, is expected to strengthen government's initiatives towards effective governance and increase transparency to manage a country's social and economic resources for development (Castells, 1996). **e-Governance** has a greater scope and connotation than **e-Government**, even though ordinarily the terms are used interchangeably (Andersen and Henriksen, 2006; Sahu, 2004)

ICT can catalyse progress of rural economies and can serve as means for ushering economic Development, social empowerment, and poverty-alleviation for rural communities. "The cases (of use of ICT for rural societies) range from successful use of ICT in governance, to ICT solutions for improved profits to ICT in micro finance"(Mathur and Ambani, 2005). ICT can improve living standards in remote and rural areas by providing important commercial, social and educational benefits (Share, 1993; Madden *et al.*, 1997; Singh, 2006), especially in the instances of reaching out to the marginalized sections living in remote areas by use of electronic service centres (Singh, 2000). Similarly rural **e-Governance** can provide timely information to the citizens and have the potential to spawn innovative means of wealth generation in rural context (Kaushik and Singh, 2004; Singh, 2004; Malhotra *et al.*, 2006). There is another side of the same coin. Emerging studies show that many of the claims that are being made about the potential of ICT for development are not supported, and point to the possible counter-productive effects of the use of ICT (Gomez *et al.*, 1999). As observed by Galloway and Mochrie (2005), "*there is a lag in rural uptake of ICTs and that the reasons for this include both supply and demand failures*", Wilson (2000) attributes the reason for it to "*purely technology centric approach*", whilst Ray (2005) attributes it to "*slack institutional mechanisms*". Dossani *et al* (2005) while reviewing nine ICT based projects in rural parts of **India** emphasized on **Community participation** for creation of digital content. The report emphatically points out, "… *Other problems, such as high deployment costs and widespread user perception of irrelevant content are partly indicative of insufficient understanding of technology, of local capabilities,* *poor use of partnerships, and poor regulation. But these problems also exist because the strengths of the different* ***stakeholders*** *are not being used optimally*".

Studies like this unmistakably indicate out that the majority of such initiatives have been developed only from the perspective of trends, or institutions, or because of preferences of the aid agencies or administrators. This kind of 'limited-perspective-approach', based on **reductionism**, tends not just to ignore the cascading nature of consequences on other subsystems but also fails to account for expectations of all the **stakeholders**. Therefore projects designed with such constrained approach do not sustain in longer run or fail to get to the far end of the local governance issues. It is therefore important to evolve an alternative strategy for design of rural **e-Governance** projects that would ensure more broad based **Community participation** and hence ensure creation of sustainable projects.

SECTION II: AN ALTERNATIVE DESIGN STRATEGY

Section IIa: Inputs to ICT from Community Knowledge

A common belief prevalent amidst social thinkers and development workers is that the social processes in rural regions need to be integrated in a holistic manner with the prevalent governance model to ensure development (Kanungo, 2004; Pande, 2003). Several gaps are associated with deployment of the information village projects when the larger goals of empowerment, dignity and "*preservation of traditional technologies*" are not considered (Annamalai and Rao, 2003). Heeks (2002) proposes that establishing linkages with local strengths and encouraging **indigenous** development of **e-Governance** initiatives would positively contribute towards achievement of development objectives of a country. Wolfram (2004) too emphasises on the need to supply globally competitive products emerging from Community Knowledge of the region. On a comparable note, Garai and Shadrach (2006) vocalise an urgent need to recognize the role of local knowledge in sustainable development. They latter argue that interactions between community based local bodies and development worker need to be enhanced to affirm success of the development process. International development circles too have adequately stressed incorporation of indigenous knowledge in prevailing models of governance. Misra and Vijayadita (2006) also bring out the importance of community-focused approach for ensuring success **ICT** initiatives for Rural Governance. These afore mentioned discussions and research propositions (see also for instance Jhunjhunwala, *et al.*, 2006) confirm that the business model for rural development should be based on collective partnerships and must incorporate the Community Knowledge available within local area.

CKS includes informal systems incorporating prevalent **indigenous** knowledge structures, skills and resources available at the grass roots. Incorporation of **Community Knowledge Systems** (**CKS**) would ensure involvement and ownership of the rural beneficiaries themselves, which is crucial for the success of any project. Since communities are the closest to grassroots' problems, they are the best judges to evaluate technology alternatives and provide innovative solutions for the problems of their respective areas. This "from the inside out" and "bottom up" perspective to technology has been supported by several social thinkers. (see for instance Lee, 2001). Such form of governance has always been preferred one and is referred as 'community governance' (Toole and Burdess, 2002).

There are several successful case studies to support this proposition. Konstadakopulos (2005) points out through a case study of artisan development in Vietnam that formulation of clusters helped to avail benefits of technology for small-scale entrepreneurs. **Community participation** has been pointed out by Yerramsetti (2005) as a key component of success of telecentres in ushering development and social change in rural areas. In the Indian rural context, there are already several encouraging examples such as "Honey Bee Network" which is a database of **grass root innovations** and technologies and serves as an effective solution to problems of local development .

Section IIb: Design of Rural E-Governance Projects Using Systems Approach

To design successful and sustained **ICT** based projects for rural governance with eqi-participation of all the **stakeholders** especially the citizens/ community, it is important to consider the system as a "whole" rather than dismembering it in isolated units. This would require an interdisciplinary systems approach where interests and inputs of all; especially of the citizens, are considered in harmony with the other stakeholders. Theoretical support for systems approach comes from the General **Systems theory** (GST) proposed by Bertalanffy (1968). It states that behavior of the system as a whole, and often of the individual parts, is a complex aggregation of the interactions of all the parts. The theory also puts forth that a system must be adaptable, it must have a purpose and should strive towards a goal. Such systems are 'self-organizing' and 'self-evolving' with formation of new (or 'emergent') properties, which cannot be predicted (Emmeche *et al.*, 1997).

Corning (2001) applies the concept of emergence in organizational context and insists on self-organizing organisational systems for growth. No matter how effectively an organisation meets the initial needs of its **stakeholders**, it must remain constantly alert and responsive to its citizens continuing needs else the environmental-changes will erode the early advantages of this organisation. In a fast changing global environment, Governance too needs to develop competitiveness through innovative response mechanisms. This requires a mindful balance between global demands and local priorities as well as a balancing of needs of various **stakeholders**' that are embedded in the processes of the governance. By adoption of a holistic approach in design of ICT interventions for governance using **Systems theory**, such conflicting priorities may be easily resolved and needs of various stakeholders can be satisfied.

SECTION III: AN INTEGRATED APPROACH TO RURAL E-GOVERNANCE PROJECTS

Section IIIa: The Proposed CKS Based G2C2G Framework

The authors propose that apart from the already existing Government to Citizen (G2C) interactions that are designed from the perspective of all **stakeholders** other than the citizens (Figure-1: Existing Approach To Design of ICT Initiatives Applied for Rural Governance), the inculcation of a Citizen-to-Government (C2G) and Citizen-to-Citizen (C2C) interface (Figure-2: The Proposed **CKS** based G2C2G **e-Governance** Model for Rural Governance) in rural ICT initiatives would make rural **e-Governance** projects more acceptable to the local communities. Therefore using Systems Approach as the guiding principle, and **Community Knowledge Systems (CKS)** as the prime source of input for establishing a meaningful interface between "Citizen to Government" (C2G) and " Citizen to Citizen" (C2C), a self-evolving framework, termed as ***"CKS based G2C2G framework"***, is proposed (refer Figure-2). The vision of the proposed integrated framework is resolution of local governance issues and improvement in the quality of life, particularly for the poor and socially disadvantaged sections of the rural society by prudent use of Information Communication Technologies (ICT). The main

hypotheses, derived from the review of literature, on which this framework is based, are encapsulated as follows:

- Rural e-Governance projects could lead to rural development only if they are customized as per the needs of the local communities.
- Community participation is critical for customization of e-Governance projects.
- Incorporation of CKS would confirm adequate Community participation in the design of the rural e-Governance projects.
- Incorporation of CKS in the proposed e-Governance projects would address local governance issues in a better manner.

C2G and C2C interactions are ordained by amalgamation of modern and traditional systems. The strength of the proposed framework also lies in its strong feedback loop.

The two variables of the framework, as indicated in Figure-2 (The Proposed CKS Based G2C2G e-Governance Model for Rural Governance) are ICT initiatives and Community Knowledge Systems (CKS), that are blended with each other and then interlinked with the processes of governance using systems approach. These variables are elaborated herewith:

Information Communication Technologies (ICTs) are electronic means of capturing processing, storing and communicating information. ICTs are digital technologies comprising of computer hardware, software and networks. They also include intermediate technologies like radio and television, literate technologies like books and newspapers.. ICT initiatives can benefit all the components of Rural Development (RD) directly or indirectly. Direct ICT initiatives for rural-development refer to the front-end use of computing, networking and Internet technologies for rural communities. Examples are data-base systems, Web portals or Community Service Centers (CSC) at block or village level to address rural concerns such as local governance issues, land records management, supply-chain management, augmenting processes of rural markets or agriculture, and so on. Indirect ICT initiatives for the rural sector would be using ICT in background as a tool for education, weather forecasting and so on. All ICT initiatives, direct or indirect, in rural context have to be designed using an integrated and self-evolving approach.

The central premise of the study is that to make these ICT initiatives sustainable, on-going **Community participation** is essential. The study further submits that **Community participation** can serve as a meaningful design tool only if **indigenous Community Knowledge (CK)** available with these communities is captured and used by designers of ICT initiatives and by other actors of governance such as government bodies, aid agencies and non-profit organisations. **Community Knowledge Systems** or Traditional knowledge systems refer to the unique knowledge, values and technical capabilities existing within and developed around the specific conditions of communities indigenous to a particular geographic area (Chariar, 2005). Community knowledge is also referred as 'local knowledge', 'Traditional Knowledge (TK)', or 'Indigenous Knowledge' (IK), 'People's Knowledge' referred as 'Community Knowledge' (CK) in this study. Assimilation, improvisation and dissemination of the traditional **Community Knowledge Systems (CKS)** using ICT, through means of rural **e-Governance** would help to unlock and utilise local ingenuity to catalyse sustainable rural development .

CKS represents the prevalent practices, skills, resources, systems, techniques, indigenous knowledge or components, existing at grassroots. It is maintained and developed over a long period of time and is a result of close interaction within communities and its intimate eco-system. The knowledge encapsulated in **CKS** is usually not documented or published anywhere and travels in

Figure 1. Existing approach to design of ICT initiatives applied for rural governance

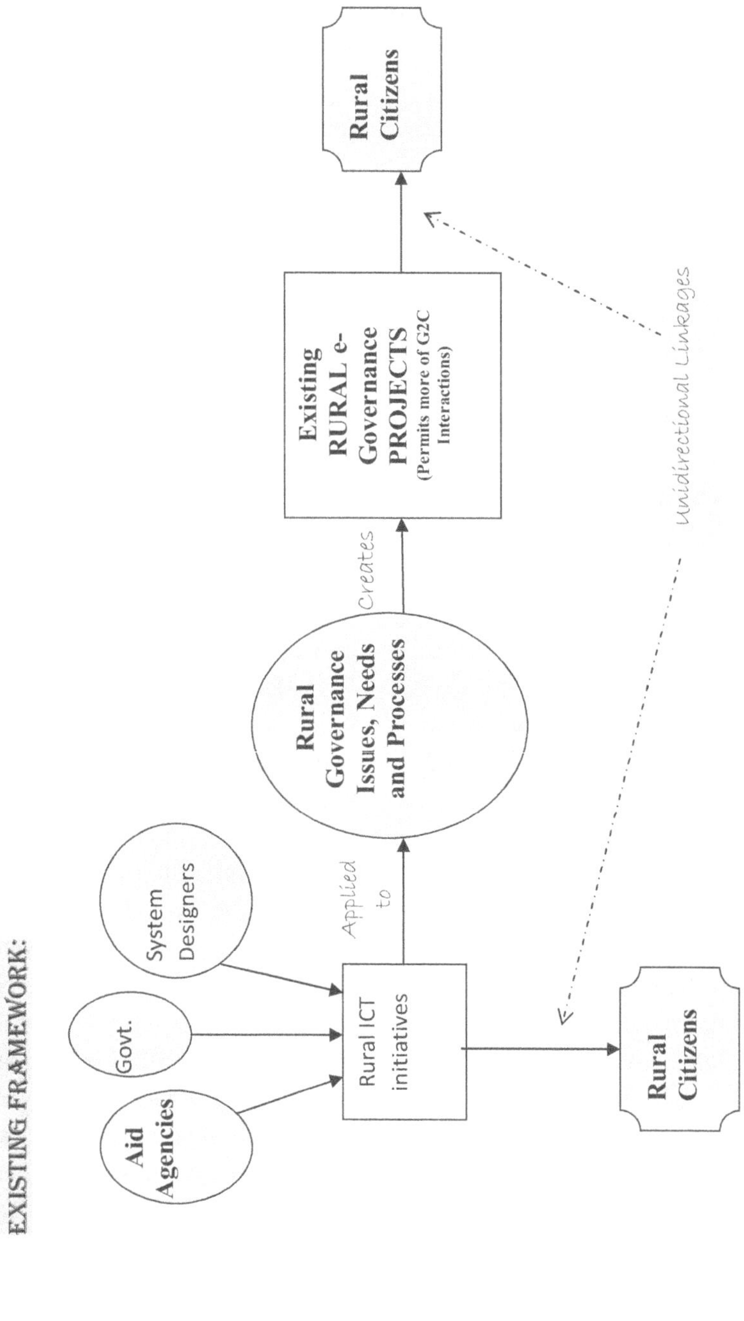

narrative form, as community memory or as an areas' identity or as practices followed by people over millennia. Handed over from generations to generations with modifications dictated by the needs of the time, it gets innovated over a period of time to preserve the social, economic and environmental balance of the region. Another strength of **CKS** is that it persists within local communities, therefore it also possess an inherent inbuilt coping mechanisms to resolve the local

Figure 2. The proposed CKS based G2C2G e-governance model for rural governance

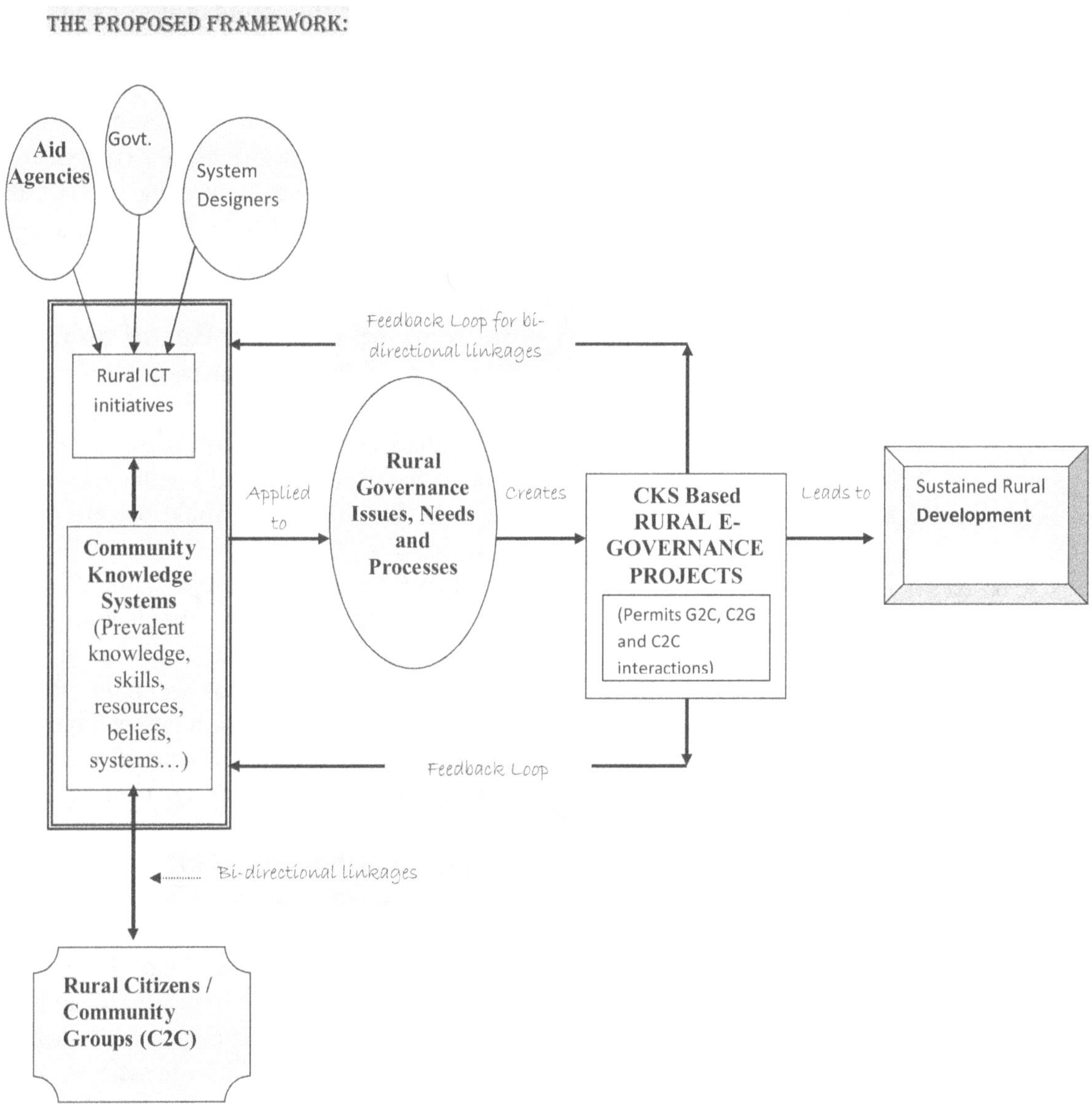

issues with available resources, processes and skills. Due to such special characteristics, these informal bodies of knowledge and systems enable the ease of decision-making processes which relate to fundamental issues concerning communities' day-to-day subsistence and governance. **CKS** therefore refer to the complete system or space of the community defined by prevailing local knowledge along with rules, processes, resources, skills and people required to maintain these informal bodies of information. **CKS** reflect adaptation of existing knowledge to social changes and hence very context specific. Some examples of vocations or areas with inherent **CKS** are:

1. **Traditional vocations** such as pottery, blacksmiths, crafts and artisan communities still use their own styles, methods and raw materials.
2. **Farmer community** could have its own system related to agriculture for cultivation techniques, pest control, crop diversity, and seed varieties.
3. Traditional options of **human healthcare** relying on natural herbs, traditional methods and medicinal plants using home made medicines for special ailments, post delivery care.
4. CK based systems in **veterinary sciences** comprise of ethno veterinary medicines, animal healthcare, animal production
5. CK systems exist in certain tribal communities using traditional techniques for the use and **management of natural resources** like soil conservation, irrigation, rain-water harvesting, water management, food processing and so on.
6. Even in the field of **education** oral traditions and languages could be found in specific ecological zones all over India.

The "CKS based G2C2G framework" propounds that the ICT initiatives designed to resolve governance issues should try to store, process, edit (if desired) and disseminate CK to solve local problems using local solutions. Acceptance of CKS in ICT based initiatives would customize the governance related projects to be adaptable to the local needs. All inputs in the framework are bi-directional, as ICT initiatives may be designed to provide support to local governance as well as should be able to react to queries generated by local needs of the communities/citizens. These inputs are collated in the processes of governance established by institutions, processes, policies and information. In accordance to its title, the e-Governance projects based on this framework are not just 'Government to Citizen' (G2C) but would also have a 'Citizen to Government' (C2G) component. In addition to this, the term G2C2G echoes the importance of keeping the 'C', the Citizen, as the central focus in all technology-based initiatives.

Section IIIb: Projects Based on CKS Based on G2C2G Framework

ICT initiatives designed to resolve local governance rural issues based on the framework proposed in the chapter would be referred as 'CKS based G2C2G e-Governance projects for rural development '. Such projects would not just deliver governance services or products to people but also 'listen' and change as per the people's expectations. This way, rural communities can develop a sense of ownership for such projects, which when integrated with the processes of governance would lead to design of customized, and flexible rural e-Governance systems. Projects based on this CKS based G2C2G framework would guarantee equitable participation, transparency and accountability in local rural governance, which is a cornerstone of Good Governance. The ultimate goal of such projects should be to provide opportunities for employment, lead to creative involvement of the large majority of the rural population and ensure sustainable wealth generation in rural areas. The major objectives of the projects based on this framework would be:

- To implement Information Communication Technologies (**ICT**) based projects for resolving local governance issues to lead to sustainable development of the rural areas.
- To promote and support people's participation in design of ICT initiatives.

- To identify **CKS** as indigenous solutions available within the community for addressing local problems of the rural-areas.
- To use ICT as a tool for development , storage, retrieval and promotion of appropriate rural technologies including **CKS**.

The lifecycle of such a project includes Identification of regional issues and local needs of the community through observation, semi-formal interviews and informal discussions (termed as phase-I), followed by capturing of community knowledge, local skills and resources that has been prevalent in the region for addressing these local needs and issues (termed as phase-II). Relevant community knowledge is identified and recorded by special methodologies and tools and techniques that are normally employed in ethnographic studies such as Participatory Rural Appraisal (PRA), Participant observer, focussed group discussions, household survey, structured and semi-structured questionnaires and so on. The project would therefore liberally resort to participatory research methods, categorised under category of development research titled humanism-based approach (Desai and Potter, 2006). Once the community knowledge has been identified, it could be validated through discussions with experts or community elders, enhanced (if desired) and then integrated with the **ICT** initiatives for storage and further diffusion, as per the community needs. The project **lifecycle** culminates in development of an ICT based governance solution that incorporates community knowledge components attained in phase-III as one of its prime inputs. After the accomplishment of the project, the **deliverables** expected of such a project are:

- Creation, Improvement and Dissemination of a Community Knowledge data bank for the specified rural area in which such a project is implemented.
- Increased footfall to the ICT/ **e-Governance** initiative established in the rural area.

The anticipated tangible **benefits** of this **CKS** based ICT project for governance are innumerable. It would build community awareness on critical development issues related to the regions and promote appropriate rural technologies including ICT in the field-areas. It would provide optimum solutions to basic governance issues afflicting the rural areas. Some employment opportunities and sustainable economic self-reliance and is expected to materialize through the project. Such a project could serve as a valuable tool for social empowerment as it would ensure inclusion of marginalized groups including women and disadvantaged communities in the process of development . Such an innovative approach suggesting the use of ICT amalgamated along with **indigenous** wisdom of communities, and **Community participation** can help to achieve Rural Development in a sustainable manner.

CONCLUSION

Based on review of literature, preliminary assessment and practical presumptions this chapter advocates adoption of a more systematic approach for integrating **Community Knowledge Systems (CKS)** and **ICT** inputs to address local governance issues in the rural context. The examination of literature related to rural development and **e-Governance** has indicated various issues impeding the success of such projects. The main issue is the lack of acceptance of prevailing **Community Knowledge Systems (CKS)** as means of addressing the local issues. The study therefore suggests the use the systems-approach to integrate the relevant **CKS** along with ICT initiatives in the design of **e-Governance** systems for rural development . **CKS** based G2C2G framework originates from 'bottoms-up' participatory approach and applies principles of General System Theory. Projects based on this framework would require synergetic efforts of not just the government functionaries or non-profit based organizations but also adequate participation of rural citizens. The chapter provides future directions for researchers, critical policy inputs to technocrats and innovative options for designers of **e-Governance** projects.

FUTURE DIRECTIONS

The impact of an **e-Governance** project that uses **CKS** based G2C2G framework could be measured by using several governance indicators, on a control group, before and after introduction of the rural **e-Governance** project based on **CKS** or by comparing the economic-status between one cluster using the proposed **CKS** based rural **e-Governance** project and the another cluster that has similar socio-economic status but uses an existing rural **e-Governance** project. This research study could be done using a Case-Study method or Quasi-Experimental pre-test and post-test design. Some of the governance-indicators that could be surveyed are, socio-economic status of the village, per capita income, health indices and the literacy level of the villagers. Similarly any change in the economic production of the region could be assessed by measuring the increase in agricultural productivity or by increased market access of rural community groups. The quality of governance in terms of its effectiveness could be gauged by the eight characteristics of good governance converted to four quantifiable variables *viz.* Citizen Participation Index, Government Orientation Index, Social Development Index and Economic Development Index (Huther and Shah, 1998).

REFERENCES

Andersen, K.V., & Henriksen, H.Z. (2006). E-Government Maturity Models: Extension of the Layne and Lee model. *Government Information Quarterly*, *23*(2), 236-248.

Annamalai, K., & Sachin. R. (2003). *What Works: ITC's e-Choupal and Profitable Rural Transformation Web-Based Information And Procurement Tools For Indian Farmers.* Jointly published as "*What Works Case Study*" by World Resources Institute, Digital Dividend and University of Michigan, (August 2003) (accessed in March, 2005 from <http://www. digitaldividend.org / pdf/ echoupal_case.pdf> , via Google, http://www. google.com).

Bertalanffy, L.v. (1968). *General System Theory: Foundations.* Development *Applications.* New York: George Braziller.

Castells, M. (1996). *Rise of the Network Society: The Information Age, Economy, Society and Culture.* U.S.A.: Oxford: Blackwell Publishers.

Chambers, R. (1983). *Rural* Development*: Putting The Last First*, 147. Robert Chambers. London: Longman.

Chariar, V.M. (2005). *Rejuvenating Community Knowledge Systems of India.* (unpublished).

Corning, P.A. (2001). Devolution as an Opportunity to Test the Synergism Hypothesis and a cybernetic theory of Political Systems. *Systems Research & Behavioral Science* ABI/ INFORM.

Desai, V., & Potter, R.B. (2006). The Raison d'etre of Doing Development Research. In V. Desai & R. B. Potter (Eds.), *Doing Development Research, 8.*. New-Delhi, India: Sage Publications.

Dossani Rafiq, D.C., Misra, R.J. (2005). *Enabling ICT for Rural India.* A Project Report by Asia-Pacific Research Center, Stanford University and National Informatics Centre (NIC), November 2005. Accessed from iis-db.stanford.edu/ pubs/20972/ICT_full_Oct05 on July 10, 2008

Emmeche, C., Simo, K., & Stjernfelt, F. (1997). Explaining Emergence: - towards an ontology of levels. *Journal for General Philosophy of Science, 28*(1997), 83-119. accessed in October, 2006 from

<http:// www.nbi.dk/ ~emmeche/ coPubl/97e. EKS/ emerg.html>

Galloway, L., & Mochrie, R. (2005). The Use of ICT in Rural Firms: A Policy-Oriented Literature Review. *Info-The Journal of Policy, Regulation and Strategy for Telecommunications, 7*(3), 33-46. The Emerald Group Publishing Limited.

Garai, A., & Shadrach, B. (2006). Processes and Appropriation of ICT in Human Development in Rural India: Bridging the Research and Practice Gaps. In A. Garai & B. Shadrach (Eds.), *Taking ICT To Every Village*, (pp.1-35). New Delhi: Oneworld South Asia, 2006. Accessed in February, 2006 from http://www.dgroups.org/ groups/oneworld/ OneWorldSA/docs/TICTEIV_pdf.pdf

Gomez, R., Hunt, P., & Lamoureux, E. (1999). *Enchanted by Telecentres: A Critical look at Universal Access to Information Technologies for International Development.* Paper presented at the conference New IT and Inequality, University of Maryland, February 16-17.

Gupta, M.P., Prabhat, K., & Jaijit, B. (2004). New Paradigms and Value Propositions in e-Governance. In M.P. Gupta, P. Kumar, & J. Bhattacharya (Eds.)m *Government Online*: *Opportunities and Challenges*, (p. 77). New-Delhi, India: Tata McGraw Hill.

Heeks, R. (2002). i-Development and not e-Development , Special Issues on ICTs and Development. *Journal of International* Development, (pp. 141-151).

Heeks, R. (2004). Success and Failure Rates of e-Government in Developing/Transitional Countries: An Overview. Accessed in December, 2004 from http://www. egov4dev. org/sfoverview. htm) .

Jhunjhunwala, A., Anuradha, R., & Sangamitra, R. (2006, February). Connecting Rural India: Taking a Step Back for Two Forward. *Information Technology in Developing Countries, 16*(1). Telecommunications and Computer Networks Group, Madras, IIT-Madras. Accessed in December, 2006 from http://www.iimahd.ernet.in/ egov/ifip/ feb2006/articlel.htm.

Kanungo, S. (2004b). Research Directions for Studying ICT Interventions in Poor and Rural Areas in Developing Countries. In M.P. Gupta (Ed.), *Towards* ***E-Government,*** (pp. 155-171). New Delhi: Tata McGraw Hill.

Kaushik, P.P., & Nirvikar S. (2004). Information Technology and Broad based Development : Preliminary lessons from North India. *World* Development, *32*(4), 591-607.

Konstadakopulos, D. (2005). From Public Loudspeakers to the Internet: The Adoption of Information and Communication Technologies (ICTs) by Small Enterprises Cluster in Vietnam. *Information Technologies and International Development*, *2*(4), 31-39.

Lee, R. (2001, November). *Community Development and the Internet" Brussels: Research Centre `Communication for Social Change' (CSC).* Paper prepared for presentation at the International Conference on Information Technology, Communications and Development in Kathmandu, Nepal..

Leys, C. (1996). *The Rise and Fall of Development Theory.* EAEP and Indiana University Press, Nairobi and Bloomington.

Madden, G., Savage, S., & Simpson, M., (1997). Regional information access: the use of telecentres to meet universal service obligations. *Telematics and Informatics, 14*(3), 273-288.

Malhotra, C. (2001). Rural Informatics and Information Technology Policies for Rural Development in India in emerging institutions. In S.P. Jain (Ed.), *Proceedings of NIRD Foundation Day Seminar for Decentralised Rural Development*, (pp. 223-250). Hyderabad: NIRD, Hyderabad, India, January 7-8.

Malhotra, C., Chariar, V.M., & Das, L.K. (2006). 'e' as an enabler for *Shubh-Labh* for Local Governance in Rural India. In *National Conference on Smart Governance for Rural Development by ITM,* Gurgoan at New Delhi, India on 18th February.

Mathur, A., & Dhirubhai, A. (2005, December). ICT and rural societies: Opportunities for growth. *The International Information & Library Review, International Information Issues: Selected Papers from the American Society for Information Science and Technology, Special Interest Group on International Information Issues International Paper Contests, 37*(4), 345-351.

Misra, D.C., & Vijayaditya, N. (2006, February). Development Informatics: Reaching the Rural India: Role of NIC. *International Journal for Development 16*(1). Accessed in March, 2006 from http://www.iimahd.ernet.in/egov/ifip/feb2006/feb2006.htm

Mitra, R.K., & Gupta, M.P. (2003, August). Evolution of e-Governance in India: Learning from Select Cases. *Indian Management. A Journal of All India Management Association*, New Delhi, India.

Nandi, B. (2002). Role of Telecommunications in Developing Countries in the 21st century. *14th Biennial Conference Seoul: International Telecommunications Society (ITS).*

Pande, A.S. (2003, December). An Emergent Complex Systems Perspective on E-Governance. International Conference on E-Governance (ICEG2003). New Delhi: IIT Delhi.Rahnema, M., & Bawtree, V. (Ed.), (1997). *The Post Development Reader.* University Press Limited, Dhaka.

Ray, I. (2005, January). Good Governance and the Dilemma of Development : What lies Beneath? *Global Socio-Economic Review ABI/INFORM* (pp. 43-59).

Rogers, E., & Shukla, P. (2001). The Role of Telecentres in Development and the Digital Divide. *Journal of* Development *Communication, 12*(2), 26-31.

Sahu, G.P. (2004). A Study of e-Governance Acceptance in India. *A Research Plan on e-Governance , IIT-Delhi, 8.*

Sen, A. (1987). Commodities and Capabilities. Monograph of Professor Dr. P. Hennipman Lectures in Economics, 1982 delivered at the University of Amsterdam, Oxford University Press.

Share, P. (1993). Telecommunication and rural remote Development. *Rural Society, 3*(16).

Singh, K. (1999). *Rural* Development*: Principles, Policies and Management, Katar Singh (*Second Edition), *21.* New-Delhi, India: Sage Publications.

Singh, S.H. (2000). Ways and Means of Bridging the Gap between Developed and Developing Countries. Accessed in October, 2004 from http://www.mit.gov.in.

Singh, N. (2004). *Information Technology and Rural Development in India, 34.* Paper 563, Department of Economics, University of California, Santa Cruz.

Singh, N. (2008). ICTs and Rural Development in India. October 16, 2006. Available at SSRN: http://ssrn.com/abstract=950322, Accessed in May 2008.

O'Toole, K. & Burdess, N. (2002, October). Governance in Rural Communities: The case of Victoria. Presented at the Jubilee conference of the Australasian Political Studies Association Australian National University, Canberra. Accessed in February, 2006 from http://www. auspsa.anu.edu.au/ proceedings/2002/ otoole+burdess.pdf) .

UNDP. (1994). *Initiatives for Change.* http://www.mirror.undp.org/magnet/policy/chapter1.htm, accessed on May 25, 2007.

Wilson, M. (2000). *Understanding the International ICT and Development Discourse: Assumptions and Implications.* Paper is based on research conducted for the author's M.Phil in Development Studies thesis at Oxford, U.K.

Wolfram, E. (2004). The New Economy: Complexity coordination and a Hybrid governance approach. *International Journal of Social Economics,31*(11/12), 1029-1049.

The World Bank Report. (1992). *Governance and Development.* Washington D.C.

The World Bank Report. (1997). *Rural* Development*: From Vision to Action – A Sector Strategy.* Washington D.C.

Yerramsetti, S. (2005). *Role of Information Technology for Rural Development – A Case Study of Rural e-Seva Project in West Godavari District.* Mphil Dissertation at Jawaharlal Nehru University (JNU), New Delhi: 126.

Chapter VI
Impact of E-Government Implementation on Poverty Reduction in Rural India:
Selected Case Studies

Sandeep Kaur
PSG College of Arts and Science, India

N. Mathiyalagan
PSG College of Arts and Science, India

ABSTRACT

ICTs in general and e-governance in particular offer tremendous opportunities for improving demand-driven transparent and accountable service delivery targeting the underprivileged. The objective of this chapter is to examine the effects of E-government implementation in the context of widespread poverty in India through an extensive secondary data analysis on selected pro-poor initiatives in reducing poverty and improving rural livelihoods. Analysis also includes various contexts in which these ICT based interventions operate. Specific recommendations are made to involve the socially excluded groups in the design, implementation and access to e-government services. Governments to design appropriate public policies in implementing socially inclusive e-government strategies in the emerging information society draw the conclusion.

1. INTRODUCTION

The new information and communications technologies are among the driving forces of globalization. They are bringing people together, and bringing decision makers unprecedented new tools for development. At the same time, however, the gap between information 'haves' and 'have-nots' is widening, and there is a real danger that the world's poor will be excluded from the emerging knowledge-based global economy. (Kofi Annan, Secretary-General, 2002).

Mahatma Gandhi's vision of the true India in its villages has led several central and state governments to emphasize on grassroots governance for bridging a growing rural-urban digital divide. ICT impact on the poor is at an early stage, but the potential is being demonstrated at the micro, intermediate and macro levels (Hanna, 2003), thus providing enormous opportunities in remote areas in health care, education, other forms of public services.

India is home to 22% of the World's poor with 35% of its billion plus population living on less than US $1 per day; more than 900 million people surviving on incomes less than US $2 per day and poverty being more concentrated among SCs/STs (24 % of the total population of India - 252 million people). Thus, poverty reduction is considered fundamental for the achievement of international goals (Planning Commission, 10th Five Year Plan [2002-2007], Chapter 3.2, Page No 293). The Human Development Report (2005) ranked India 127th among 177 countries; 58th among 103 developing countries on the Human Poverty Index (HPI-1). This call for an extensive and continued efforts from government and international agencies in terms of sound macroeconomic policies; open trade relations; increases in human and physical capital; good governance; sound legal, incentives and regulatory frameworks; an adequately regulated and supervised financial sector; health, education and social services that reach the poor, women effectively; quality infrastructure and public services to promote rural development and livable cities; and policies to promote environmental and human sustainability, thereby, helping in the delivery of social and economic benefits across a broader base of the populace.

Indian ICT sector is witnessing a rapid expansion in telecom markets in the world with a target of 500 million telephone subscribers by 2010; PC penetration of 65 per 1,000 (from the existing 14 per 1,000) by 2008. **ICTs empower the people at the grassroots level to access information and service delivery effectively** is the underlying philosophy of the National e-Governance Action Plan of India (2003-2007) launched by the Central Government at a cost of Rs.12,400 crore ($1.3 billion) to connect 600,000 villages through 100,000 broadband-enabled multipurpose computer kiosks or CSCs by March 2008 through participation by states, government agencies and corporates. This will enable services like e-learning, e-teaching, ehealth, telemedicine, e-farming, e-tourism, e-entertainment and e-commerce in all of India's 600000 villages (Chandrasekhar, 2006).

Country has witnessed an explosive growth in E-governance projects to nearly $1,300 million in 2007 with increase in the government's IT expenditure to over Rs. 5,000 cr. in 2007 (Second Skoch E-governance report, 2005). UN E-governance Readiness Report (2008) ranked India 113th with an E-government Readiness Index Score of 0.3814 against a World Index of 0.4514. According to E-government Readiness Data (2005), India had a Web Index Measure (0.4783), Infrastructure Index (0.0435) and Human Capital Index (0.6195). India ranked 49 in terms of E-participation Index (0.2500). Indian ICT sector is marching towards achieving the MDGs in areas such as literacy, education, gender equity and employment to benefit larger sections of the population. But the basic service delivery challenges include limited access to social services; economic opportunities to rural poor; lack of efficient local service delivery; lack of budgets for services in rural and remote areas; lack of information about entitlements and availability of services; lack of effective communication channels; lack of accountability and transparency.

A country's overall progress in E-government closely correlates with its social, political or economic composition. Weak governance structure of a nation seriously obstructs poverty reduction towards achieving development goals (Country governance assessment for the Asian Development Bank, Asia Foundation, 2003-04). Countries such as India could benefit from E-government if literacy and basic infrastructure can be improved (UN Study, 2003). Only a few developing countries have implemented pro-poor E-governance strategies depending on the government's willingness to develop and design content relevant usable for the rural fabric.

Considering ICTs' potential to alleviate poverty, this chapter overviews the impact of ICT4D projects towards effective governance of rural areas in India by examining secondary data resources on selected pro-poor e-governance initiatives that have impacted the underprivileged and the marginalized in the milieu of extensive poverty in India. To map the effects among rural poor, this chapter studies six innovative E-governance projects that have contributed significantly to poverty reduction, irrespective of its success or failure, thereby resulting in income generation; increasing productivity; generating employment opportunities. Besides involving the poor in the design and execution of these initiatives, this chapter also emphasizes upon their social, technological, economic and political contexts of operations for enhancing rural livelihood strategies. Conclusion will help the government to free up public funding for use in the pro-policy implementation over a long-term sustenance.

2. LITERATURE REVIEW

The principal cause of poverty is the income and consumption in the globalized economy coupled with inefficient service delivery due to poor communication between the central government and decentralized units; and between urban and rural areas. Problems of accountability, large-scale corruption and abuse of public funds obstruct the transfer of allocated funds for education and health to the target beneficiaries. ICT through strengthening decentralized units and financial flows will make basic needs more accessible by the poor by reducing deprivation, inequality and regional bias in trade and development. A well planned ICT network will enhance participation and knowledge sharing among the poor, thereby empowering them by making commerce, knowledge and information accessible to all irrespective of their age, gender, religion or ethnicity.

New ICTs have tremendous potential to address the developmental challenges by reaching the un-reached and alleviating poverty in terms of increasing opportunity, enhancing empowerment, and improving security (The World Development Report 2000/01: Attacking Poverty). IT in India is still in its infancy in terms of socio-economic development due to lack of a long term vision and sustained efforts to support the government's plan and policy. Research reports reveal that the benefits of the globalization for the poor are particularly strong in the cases where inequality is stable or declining. Michael Bailey (2000) suggests long-term domestic strategies and policies that would enable poor farmers in developing countries to benefit from international trade, thereby contributing to rural poverty reduction and achievement of international development targets. International experience has demonstrated the direct relationship between agricultural growth and rural poverty reduction (Timmer, 1997; Hazell & Ramaswamy, 1991).

The Government's Working Group on Information Technology for Masses (2000) identified the following IT relevant applications that could have a profound effect on poverty reduction: e-governance; enabling literacy and education for masses; fulfilling local information needs of the people; and enabling a better economic condition of people. Rural penetration of ICTs enhances pro-poor access to markets, health, and education with a few success stories resulting in delivering desirable social, economic and government services to rural populations by increasing their efficiency and productivity; improving their livelihood and also helping them voice their concerns, demand their rights and participate in decision-making processes.

ICTs and E-government play a critical role in strengthening the linkages between policymakers and the poor and between the poor and the service providers as well as between the policymakers and the service providers (Bestle, 2004). Effective E-governance applications can minimize some of the vital causes of poverty (overpopulation, lack of education, uneven distribution of resources, deep-rooted corruption) through easy information access to the poor, thus resulting in transparency, accountability and responsiveness in service delivery. Such applications aid the poor to reach policymakers with feedback information about the progress contributing to the transparency and accountability in government services. Sustenance of such a system largely depends on a strong political commitment, administrative support and managerial cooperation to successfully implement E-governance for tackling poverty.

ICT has enabled governments to reach out to rural communities, meet citizens' expectations by providing E-government services, thereby improving their quality of life and empowering them through their participation in the political process, and also reaching out to them in order to deliver much-needed public goods and services (UNDP/APDIP, 2004). Effectual pro-poor e-governance delivery strategies necessitates uncomplicated accessibility and availability of user-driven services to proficiently elevate its quality; reduce socio-cultural, political, economic, technological and legal barriers; broaden the range of service providers; empower the users; decentralization and local governance. Such a stratagem always confine to the internal efficiency rather than service deliverance; is urban focused; pilots with established impact on poverty cutback being rarely simulated with minimal focus on the poor or MDG targets; lack understanding of the ICT demand in rural areas with varied access points for service, content, and the nature of needs of vulnerable groups.

Considered as "a powerful engine of rural development and a preferred instrument in the fight against poverty (World Bank, 2005 cited in IDRC 1999), telecenters are now emerging as vital catalysts for disseminating information and knowledge for developing socio-economic prospects for rural communities. ICTs are better served through telecenters to maximize time, effort and resources for bringing relevant information to rural villages, understanding their information needs and capabilities and to deploy future telecenter initiatives to benefit the poor (Duncombe, 2006; Chapman et al, 2004). These can, under certain conditions, help improve the living conditions of rural poor through better and more sustainable livelihood strategies (UN, 2004: 2-3). But accessibility of rural telecenter does not assure its use by the rural poor to elevate poverty. The incorporation and effectiveness of ICTs depend on the acceptance of individuals and organizations (Rivera, 2003). Though a few technology-mediated telecenter models have proven successful in empowering rural communities, the failure and massive under-use of some telecenters set up in developing countries have raised doubts over their relevance for poverty reduction and sustainability (Heeks, 2005). As stated by the Group of Eight Digital Task Force (G8 DOT Force) "efforts to increase access to ICTs should be rooted in a broader strategy to combat poverty" (Harris, 2004). The following conclusions from the current experiences with rural telecenters (Bhatnagar, 2004) are:

- Rural populations are willing to pay a fee for systems that have clear business potential and benefits for them.
- The uptake of electronic services depend on whether significant added value is delivered in comparison with existing ways of receiving information and services.
- Intermediaries are often needed to respond to the specific information needs of rural citizens, and to interpret and disseminate knowledge from public documents.
- Poor telecom and power infrastructure in rural areas can affect the economic viability of rural kiosks.

Four pillars that need to be addressed for bridging the digital divide can be identified, as follows (Bhatnagar, 2004):

- Applications that draw a large clientele that pays for the service ensuring economic viability of the kiosks.
- Content that empowers rural citizens and enables the formation of communities.
- NGOs and grass-roots organizations that encourage and manage the community-building process.
- Technology that makes rural access inexpensive and robust.

The socio-economic impact of ICT on Poverty Alleviation brings forth enormous qualitative benefits such as e-education; e-marketing; better access to healthcare; e-governance; enhanced transparency; reduced corruption; direct and indirect job creation; increased income for village phone operators and telecommunications operators; marketing opportunities for individual producers and small businesses; access to information relevant to livelihood and production of work; increased access to education and training; empowerment of women through entrepreneurial activity; reduced costs of social and other communications; quality of life for individual users and encouraging the development of local poverty reduction indicators and targets.

Despite the developmental potential of E-governance, few developing countries have implemented pro-poor E-governance strategies depending largely on the Government's willingness to develop and design content relevant and usable for them. The 10th Five-Year Plan (2002-2007) in India had made scant reference to ICT intervention in poverty reduction due to paucity of government efforts at both central and state levels. A comprehensive UNDP-APDIP study by Roger Harris and Rajesh Rajora (2006) titled *"Empowering the Poor Information and Communications Technology for Governance and Poverty Reduction: A Study of Rural Development Projects in India"* examined the application of large-scale approaches to the use of ICTs for E-governance and poverty reduction. The study expressed concern over the factors that hold back the wider rollout of ICTs for poverty reduction in spite of all its technical and human resources at the state and national levels. It was found that such initiatives are not promisingly benefiting the rural populace. Successful projects were mostly expanded into more economically active areas with a stable technology and power infrastructure, leaving behind poorer sections of the population that are more in need. The study suggested a more generalized approach to information and service delivery system applicable for communities with highly varying socio-economic characteristics.

The United Nations Department of Economic and Social Affairs (UNDESA) estimates more than 60 percent of e-government projects in developing countries as failures due to poor understanding of the barriers in the design, implementation and development of E-government systems. These Barriers are the real or perceived characteristics of the social, technological, legal and institutional context that hinder E-government development either through hampering demand by the citizens and businesses for E-government services or through obstructing supply of E-government services by the public sector. E-government services have a variety of economic, social and cultural causes that hinder access to and the effective use of E-government services such as lack of confidence, illiteracy, training, trust, language and citizens' low expectations with respect to the government resulting in the limited use of online information and services (Helen Margetts & Patrick Dunleavy, 2002). E-government does not provide a timely opportunity in the decision-making process for people living in poverty. Being the most frequent users of government services, low-income groups require more information on social policies and programs, but experience greater difficulty in accessing the benefits of E-government. Thus, lack of considerable government efforts in making relevant information reach the poor deprives them from access to e-government services.

The digital divide is one of the crucial global barriers to E-government adoption. India records low Internet and personal computer (PC) penetration rates. World Information Society Report (2006, 2007) reports growth in Infrastructure in India from 0.04 in 2005 to 0.05 in 2006. Digital Opportunity Index (2006) ranks India 124 out of 180 countries surveyed in terms of eleven core ICT indicators. (http://www.itu.int/osg/ spu/statistics/DOI/doi-guide.pdfT.) Several developing countries have attempted to overcome the digital divide problems through programs promoting PC ownership and the provision of public Internet access points. Nonetheless, computer illiteracy, low Internet and PC penetration are still widespread. E-government in many developing nations inadequately represent or lack appropriate strategies and objectives to enhance digital inclusion. Enhancing the reach and effectiveness of services provided to socially excluded groups do reap considerable efficiency gains. Therefore, social inclusion must be a priority in the future development of E-government to reap full benefits of digital transformation.

3. RESEARCH PREROGATIVE

The potential of E-governance as a development tool hinges upon a minimum threshold level of technological infrastructure; human capital and e-connectivity for all. E-government strategies will be effective and "include all" people only if, at the very minimum, all have functional literacy and education, which includes knowledge of computer and internet use; all are connected to a computer and all have access to the Internet. The primary challenge of E-governance for development therefore, is how to accomplish this. Diverse Pro-poor E-governance initiatives are undertaken by Indian government. Six such projects are chosen for this chapter based on extensive secondary data resources fulfilling the following criteria:

a. Analysis of projects based on its duration, objectives, targets, implementers, stakeholders (supply-side in general and demand-side in particular) and current status
b. Contextual examination of poverty-driven e-government projects through STEP analysis (social, technological, economic and political)
c. Scaling up and sustenance of these projects articulating with the stakeholder needs and participation in government-to-citizen interfaces, thereby enhancing their livelihood

Reasons for selection of projects are shown in Table 1.

4. FINDINGS FROM STEP ANALYSIS OF SELECTED CASE STUDIES

Analysis of the selected projects demonstrates the value of projects targeting the poor, the outcome of which serves as models for replication into nationwide approaches and to attain the sustainability of rural telecentres. Development of socially inclusive E-government by identifying relevant context-specific, need-based applications is crucial to the success and sustainability of these initiatives. A suitable technology, the community's development capacity, national policy and infrastructure need to be addressed to make rural telecenters a viable option for poverty alleviation. The study found that e-governance is limited to e-government or e-services with little participation by the beneficiaries in decision-making processes. Few have empowered socially and economically underprivileged groups. Benefits to the women from such initiatives are very few and little effort is made to encourage its use by women as most kiosks are operated by men. Content and

Table 1.

Initiative	*Initiation*	*Objective*	*Agencies involved*	*Status*
AGMARKNET	-One of the farmer--centric Mission Mode Projects of Govt of India to computerize market-related information (market fees, market charges, better market access and price realization by the farming community) ensuring data reliability; operational and pricing efficiency in agricultural marketing system -Intended beneficiaries include farmers, traders, exporters, processors, planners / decision makers, researchers -Farmers benefit from new and improved agricultural practices, to have weather-forecast-based guidance for timely agricultural operations, to be alerted by satellite surveys of pests and diseases, and to access crop-output forecasting and marketing strategies for domestic and for export trade	-To enhance decision-making processes of the farmers in marketing their produce -To enable poor farmers in developing countries to benefit from international trade, thereby contributing to rural poverty reduction and achievement of international development targets	-Directorate of Marketing & Inspection (DMI); NIC;State Agri Marketing Boards / Directorates; and Mandis (APMCs)	-XI plan strategy predicts expansion of 3700 wholesale markets with an emphasis on ensuring regular reporting of prices and arrivals data by all market nodes -This network has Server Access nodes at 35 State Agricultural and Cooperative Departments, and 600 District Agricultural and Cooperative Offices
DISK	-IT-based initiative to streamline the milk production in the country and to organize milk producers at the grassroots level	-To automate milk collection procedures at the collection centres; reduce the time required in collecting milk; use electronic technology to weigh the milk and measure its fat content; automatically calculates the amount payable to each milk collector; maintain regular records at the Dairy Cooperative Societies (DCS) -To promote local entrepreneurship and support pro-poor market development by setting up information kiosks with strong collaboration at the local level	-GCMMF,local village cooperatives and active participation from farmers	-Nearly 600 such systems in operation in the Kheda district in Gujarat with over 700 locations in India -Out of 70,000 village societies in India, 3,500 milk collection centers have been computerized -More than 10.7 million farmers and laborers benefited

continued on following page

Table 1. continued

ITC e-Choupal	-Introduced by the International Business Division (IBD) of ITC Limited in June 2000 and covers over 35,000 villages in the states of Madhya Pradesh, Uttar Pradesh, Maharashtra, Karnataka, Andhra Pradesh, Rajasthan, Haryana and Uttaranchal providing millions of farmers with critical information on farming and to address the fallacies in procurement of agri products such as soybeans in a country where nearly two-thirds of the population's workforce is employed within the agricultural industry, thus bringing about enhanced knowledge sharing, convergence, transparency and trust -Intended beneficiaries are wheat, rice, and pulses farmers	-To demonstrate the role of computers and Internet access in rural farming villages in order to recognize markets and efficiently and effectively increase the agricultural system to benefit and empower the marginalized groups, such as illiterate farmers and women --To catalyze rural transformation to help alleviate rural isolation, create more transparency for farmers, and improve their productivity and incomes	-IBD Group is responsible for procuring, processing, and exporting of agricultural commodities; ITC Ltd finances the establishment of e-Choupals in villages to supplement the traditional mandi system in operation in rural areas	-6,500 eChoupals till date -ITC adding 7 new eChoupals a day and plans to scale up to 20,000 eChoupals by 2012 covering 100,000 villages in 15 states, servicing 15 million farmers - Transactions through these eChoupals may rise to about US $ 2.5 billion by 2010
IVRP	-Initiated in 1998 in Pondicherry, (a centrally administered territory in Southern India), by the MSSRF, a nonprofit organization for sustainable agriculture and rural development -Intended beneficiaries include rural communities for fostering development, social change, cultural values, solidarity, political awareness, community organization and participation	-To enable rural families to access modern ICTs through easy rural access to information related to health, credit, input price and availability, transportation, pest surveillance and agronomic practices -To create awareness in poor communities of the government programmes and entitlements that are available for them from a database of more than 100 such entitlements	-Funded, supported by the IDRC, Canada and the Canadian International Development Agency (CIDA); government partners the project and bears the initial cost of setting up information centers in villages -Implementers are MSSRF and local fishermen colony	-14 out of the 18 Village Knowledge Centres (VKCs) are functional now

continued on following page

Table 1. continued

TARAHaat	-Initiated in 2000 in the resource-deficient and commercially-poor city of Jhansi in the Bundelkhand region followed by kendras in the Bathinda district in the state of Punjab in 2001 to bring computer and Internet technology to rural regions and plans to use these technologies to create revenue streams leading to financial viability for itself and its franchisees -Social objectives include creation of sustainable rural livelihoods; enrichment of the rural Indian economy through improved information flows; education; direct job creation; address issues pertaining to women's health, education, governance, and resource conservation, primarily by providing relevant and easily accessible information on its Web site -Intended beneficiaries are rural folks and students	-Empowermentthroughaccess to information and improved access to government services to rural consumers via the Internet to uplift the social rural fabric in India	-Partnership between Development Alternatives (DA), an NGO focused on promoting sustainable development in India, and its rural marketing arm, Technology and Action for Rural Advancement(TARA) as a franchise-based business enterprise	-Has 22 centres presently
Warana Wired Project	-"Bring the world's knowledge at the doorstep of villagers through the Internet" is the stated goal of the Warana "Wired Village" project, being launched in 1998 by the Government of India, the Government of Maharashtra and Kolhapur Sugar Cooperative on a cost-sharing basis demonstrating not only an increase in the efficiency and productivity of the sugar cane cooperative, but also to provide a wide range of information and services in accelerating socioeconomic development of 70 villages around Warana Nagar in the Kolhapur and Sangli districts of the state of Maharashtra -Intended beneficiaries include villagers to access sources of both local and global knowledge and help provide transparency in administration	- to utilize IT to increase the efficiency and productivity of the existing cooperative enterprise; provide agricultural, medical, educational, communication facilities to villagers at facilitation booths in their villages; provide distance education to both primary and higher educational institutes; and establish a Geographic Information System (GIS) of the surrounding 70 villages leading to greater transparency in administration especially in land related matters	-Jointly funded and supported by government of India (50%), government of Maharashtra (40%), Warana Cooperative (10%)	-The sugarcane cooperative is serving about 70,000 farmers across 75 villages

Table 2. STEP analysis of e-governance initiatives for poverty reduction in India

Initiative	Social	Technological	Economic	Political
AGMARKNET	-Location-specific e-Government model for the Poor to foster agricultural growth; poverty reduction -Computerization of market related information such as market fees, market charges, etc., ensure data reliability and efficiency in agro markets, better market access and price realization by the farming community -Help farmers to improve their labor productivity, increase their yields, realize a better price for their produce, cut transaction cost -Farmers benefit from new improved agro practices, weather-forecast-based guidance for timely agro operations, alert by satellite surveys of pests and diseases, crop-output forecasting	-Server Access nodes at 35 State Agricultural and Cooperative Departments, 600 District Agricultural and Cooperative Offices to make rural infrastructure reach upto 6.5 lakhs villages - NIC and IT through DISNIC-AGRIS Project, and AGRISNET seeks to reach all agricultural districts and blocks through its massive Gateway Networks	-Existence and dissemination of complete and accurate marketing information is the key to achieve both operational and pricing efficiency in the marketing system.	-Need for long-term domestic strategies; policies to would enable poor farmers in developing countries benefit from international trade, thereby contributing to rural poverty reduction and achievement of international development targets -Improves the present agro marketing by linking vital agricultural produce markets in the country, the State Agricultural Marketing Boards & Directorates and DMI for effective information exchange. The dissemination of market information is a common function of Agricultural Produce Market Committee (APMC) that maintains the statistics of arrival, sales, prices etc. Prices prevailing in the market are displayed on the notice boards through various media and supplied to State & Central Government -Highly scalable, planned through bottom-up process, and implemented through active involvement and collaboration of agricultural market committee

continued on following page

Table 2. continued

Dairy Information & Services Kiosk	-Over 700 locations in India -Increased transparency; faster processing; immediate payments to farmers -Remarkable business success for private entrepreneurs -Farmers benefited in earnings due to accurate measurement of fat content and weight -Cooperative societies benefited with a fewer employees to manage daily accounts; automatic daily printing of payment slips helps easier communicate with the farmers -Active grassroots participation circulates thousands of liters of milk nationwide everyday; Number of farmers selling to their local cooperative milk collection centre varies from 100 to 1,000; daily milk collection varies from 1,000 to 10,000 litres; collects 700,000 - 800,000 litres of milk every day from milk societies in Anand and Kheda districts -Farmers contribute to the dairy development across the country, subsequently to the national economy -Milk producers no longer exploited by middlemen -Illiterate villagers access information on animal husbandry practices, health and hygiene of cattle, veterinary care, cattle insurance; download government forms, receive documents, order supplies and agricultural inputs from manufacturers -Women's Dairy Cooperative Leadership Program (WDCLP) extended to 50 district unions that include 2,062 cooperative societies; 90,000 women participants. Women's Dairy Cooperative Societies (WDCSs) and Women's Thrift Groups (WTGs) enhanced women's participation --Accurate and up-to-date records reduced fraud or corrupt practices -Reduction in under-payment to farmers, shorter queues at the milk collection centres save considerable time -Increased productivity through extensive education program to reach millions of farmers and dairy workers	-Maintenance of daily computerized accounts reduced chances of errors; fraud -Poor ICT infrastructure, frequent power breakdowns major impediments in its functioning -Building useful content in local languages is absolutely necessary -Necessary to build effective partnerships among development organizations, telecom companies, small IT service companies, and government agencies -Role of intermediary between the computer screen and the rural farmer is extremely important -Larger part of its success is attributed to the use of appropriate technology -Connectivity to a Dairy Portal serve information-transactional needs -DISK and dairy portal have improved delivery of artificial insemination, veterinary services, functional education about the dairy sector	-Cost a major impediment as milk vending system costs around $2,000 per centre, adapted milk-testing machine costs $500 as compared to $4,000 from the original manufacturer -Socio-economic empowerment through a steady, secure flow of income to more than 10.7 million landless laborers and marginal or small farmers -Promoted local entrepreneurship; supported pro-poor market development -Poor financial position of most of DCSs is the biggest stumbling block -Computerized profit and loss accounts and balance sheets also enforce accountability in the system.	-Increased accountability evident from training sessions, workshops, computerized centers. -Cooperative organizational structure enabled the daily milk collection from millions of illiterate, poor, vulnerable farmers across the country -Local organizational capacity of WTGs mobilize the savings of the women members to facilitate loans for animal maintenance or for the purchase of new livestock

continued on following page

Table 2. continued

ITC e-Choupal	-Established a network of 5,100 local computer kiosks in villages to provide access to real-time information to 6,50,000 farmers; plans to cover 15 states, 1,00,000 villages, 10 million farmers in 20,000 kiosks in coming years -Enhances rural social fabric by improving farmers' productivity; crop quality; livelihoods; e-commerce -Solved the problem of farmers' low income; difficulty in accessing credit limits on agro opportunities by partnering with financial institutions -Provides non-cash loans for farm inputs; loans to sanchalak; direct loans to farmers based on sanchalak recommendation; insurance & risk management services etc -Farmers involvement in local content creation helps customize information, develops local leadership quality -Delivers real-time information; customized knowledge to farmer's decision making ability in securing better quality & price, higher incomes -Farmers reimbursed for transport to the procurement hub of e-choupal -Direct marketing channel to eliminate intermediation, multiple handling, reducing transaction cost, making logistics efficient	-Links agricultural research centers; universities; other agencies in developing technologies to overcome the rural technological gap -Technology helps resolve distortion of information; distance to markets	-Impacts the agro chain from seed to money in the bank; incomes from farming risen by about 10% in 2004 alone; support services risen by over 38% since 2000 -Economic empowerment of farmers by connecting to markets and information on agro inputs; products; services to enhance farm productivity; scientific farming practices; market prices of crops (home-abroad); weather broadcast in local (Hindi) language	-Inefficiencies in serving the farmers; agriculture trading companies; the Mandi system under the Agricultural Produce Marketing Act (APMA) -Faces regulatory barriers from prohibited procurements from outside the mandis; waiving the mandi tax on the produce procured through the eChoupal -Government operates these kiosks as per the nature and requirement of the Act to benefit both the market and farmers -ITC continues paying the tax rather than risking the relationships with the government and the mandis
IVRP	-Provides e-knowledge delivery to the poor' -Awareness in poor communities of the govt programmes, entitlements from a database of more than 100 such entitilements -Promotes development, social change, cultural values, solidarity, political awareness, community organization, participation -Information on crop prices and the prices of inputs help farmers to improve their negotiating power against price-fixing middlemen -Creation and updation of relevant local content on agro practices help farmers market their produce more profitably -Enhances Entrepreneurial activity of women and *Dalit* landless labourers -Procurement of paddy seeds and timely paddy price information result in saving time and money to farmers -Eliminated exploitation of agricultural labourers -Gender sensitivity in the context of participation, content creation, and assessment of information needs facilitates the participation of women (about 50%) in operating the centers and disseminating information -Women gain information on issues relating to reproductive health, income-generating activities	-Proactive intermediaries in the village KCs have contributed to its success. -ICTs intervention in a rural setting has empowered the marginalized groups, such as women and the underprivileged. -Building content is a resource-intensive activity and has implications for the sustainability of such projects	-MSSRF helped in mobilizing financial resources for the project, coordinating the villagers to identify their own information requirements and building an information system responding to their information needs	-Citizens' charter data base provides information from government departments, such as current activities and procedures to obtain various entitlements resulting in greater transparency in governance, increasing accountability of officials, minimizing bureaucracy and corruption

continued on following page

Table 2. continued

TARAHaat	-Leading supplier of online information; services; market opportunities; computer-enabled education to the rural Indians -Created sustainable rural livelihoods -TARAhaat.com primarily transmits information; interactive online services such as health, government schemes, livelihoods, agriculture, education, e-governance, entertainment, matrimony, astrology, land records, grievances redressal, complaints to local government officials, local jobs, daily local commodity prices -Improved employment prospects for students; generated confidence among rural children about their future prospects -Women empowerment as both users and operators -Farmers benefited through weather forecasting, procurement services, sales negotiations; younger generation benefit through career counseling, entertainment, educational, career opportunities	-Connectivity and bandwidth are continuing challenge to the venture -Diesel-powered generator as part of the franchise infrastructure adds considerably to costs and maintenance needs	-Need for the franchise model to harness the entrepreneurial drive; local knowledge through a stronger, more resourceful, more locally-responsive network of kendras	-Local governance reforms towards greater democratic participation and clear regulations on Citizen's Charters are an important prelude to ICT applications
Warana Wired Project	-Computerization in the dairy and sugar industries has brought transparency; improved service delivery; permited efficiency gains to accelerate socioeconomic development of 70 villages around Warana Nagar in the Kolhapur and Sangli districts of the state of Maharashtra -Provision of agro-marketing information, health, educational, communication, government procedure, automated assistance in completing applications for government certificates (ration cards, land records, birth and death certificates),crop information, bus and railway services, grievance redressal benefit the villages -Generates employment opportunities for local population as computer operators -Increased the efficiency and productivity of the existing sugar cane cooperative enterprise, directly impact livelihood -Provides distance education to both primary and higher educational institutes -Computerization result in time and money savings by the farmers on administrative transactions	-Level of human development is relatively high in the sugar cane belt of Maharashtra -Good infrastructure and local organizational capacity is praise worthy	-Socio-economic challenges are still predominant faced by the WGC in terms of low sugar prices and lack of coordination, efficiency and transparency among the cooperatives -Fertilizer stock inventories are now better managed with savings of about US$750,000 to the cooperative -Empowered community adopting ICT to bring efficiency and transparency gains to its main economic activity	-Establishment of a GIS of the surrounding 70 villages lead to greater transparency in administration especially in land related matters -Lack of local staff participation in software development, implementation process -Irregular updation of information on sugar cane growing and agricultural prices since 1998 by local staff -Provide transparency in administration -Access to government services through the Internet benefit people with currently grievances about government services solved through the local village committees (panchayats). Thus, its been perceived useful in terms of sending grievances, downloading government forms, and accessing land records

services are more geared towards needs of men rather than women. Most initiatives suffer from problems such as power cuts or lack of adequate power, and low-quality connectivity.

Economic liberalization and globalization has resulted in extensive agricultural marketing in India with70% of its population live in villages and depend on agriculture as their main occupation. **AGMARKNET** has succeeded in filling a gap by providing access to information at reasonable cost. This case demonstrates the need to sensitize farmers to respond to new challenges in agricultural marketing by using ICT as a vehicle of extension. Some of the constraints are connectivity in rural areas; training the stakeholders; ensuring data updation in real time frame coupled with erratic power supply; frequent transfers of market personnel trained for reporting data; nontransparent auctions in markets. Regional language content needs to be generated for the benefit of farmers by regularly analyzing data for needed market intelligence.

In order to streamline the production of milk in the country by organizing milk producers at the grassroots level, **computerized milk collection centers** demonstrate that useful content and services from the government and other institutions can be delivered effectively to poor rural populations through information kiosks. It has increased the efficiency and effectiveness of the services delivered to rural farmers. Rural farmers are now willing to invest in technology as useful content and services from the government and other institutions can be delivered to poor rural populations through information kiosks. The effort required for motivating rural communities to use IT, and the logistical problems of maintaining communication links and hardware and software can be mitigated through extensive knowledge creation of local dialects and conditions. The role of small private sector and the committed volunteer is also extremely important. In the dairy sector the district unions are willing to spend because they stand to gain as the system described above increases the efficiency and effectiveness of the services delivered by them to rural farmers. Even though the existing application was very successful, careful analysis provided several opportunities to enhance the value of the system by extending the data base and the capacity to analyze the data. A larger part of the effort went into understanding the needs of the farmers and collection center staff, and in building the content on the portal. The effort required for motivating rural communities to use IT, and the logistical problems of maintaining communication links and hardware and software generally keep the large companies away from such rural ventures. Successful venture of this initiative is attributed to the use of appropriate technology. Building useful content in local languages is absolutely necessary. To enhance the efficiency and effectiveness of the services delivered to rural farmers, it is necessary to build partnerships among development organizations, telecom companies, small IT service companies, and government agencies. The role of the committed intermediaries is also extremely important as most of the current success of rural kiosks has been built around the enthusiasm of the same. Intensive training in operating this system and maintenance of the IT systems need to be enhanced. Although AMCS is priced competitively, the cost and poor financial position is the biggest stumbling block in fast replication. Knowledge of local dialects and conditions can help to mitigate these problems. It is recommended to maintain a database of milch cattle, decision support systems, information on veterinary related issues and innovations to benefit the poor.

E-Choupal is a catalyst in rural transformation by providing easy access to agro information; developing local leadership; creating a profitable distribution; alleviating rural isolation; improving productivity and income; creating transparency for farmers. E-Choupal case have shown that provision of ICT services in rural areas enhances the quality of life of the rural Indians and make profit for the service providers, both these companies and their local partners. Local content with appropriate software development, regular updates of prices, local ownership and participation ensure long term sustenance. This system has tackled the challenges posed by the unique features of Indian agriculture, characterized by fragmented farms, weak infrastructure and the involvement of numerous intermediaries. ICT interventions enabled ITC to directly negotiate product sale by making farmers obtain information on mandi prices, good farming practices and place orders for agricultural inputs like seeds and fertilizers. There is a recorded rise in their income levels, improvement in quality of output and a fall in transaction costs. Customized knowledge is disseminated to the farmers free of cost. This case has successfully eliminated non-value adding activities by differentiating product through identity preservation; value added products traceable to farm practices;e-market place and support services to future exchange. Critical factors in its apparent success are managerial competence to execute a complex project and manage cost and ITC's extensive knowledge of agriculture in order to retain existing production system, including maintenance of local partners, the company's commitment to transparency, and the respect and fairness with which both farmers and local partners are treated. Infrastructure creation and maintenance to eliminate market inefficiencies by creating valued services delivered to hitherto underserviced markets will drive its long term sustenance. Some of the constraints are poor telecom infrastructure in villages, ICT illiteracy, low trust on electronic system, selection of an appropriate sanchalak, improper knowledge about rural market, vicious circle of intermediaries, improper and complex user interface on e-choupal, lack of rules and regulation related to electronic choupal, mistrust about inspection, testing and weighing of produce on centres.

IVRP demonstrates the perceived role of ICTs in sustainable agriculture and rural development through e-knowledge delivery to the poor. Replication of such projects require the backing of facilitating conditions as the rural population lack necessary expertise to demand and design a knowledge center on its own. Analysis reveals that villages are not interested in the technology, but in accurate, dynamic and customized information. Building content is a resource-intensive activity and has implications for the sustainability of such projects.

TARAhaat has succeeded in empowering the rural poor; inspiring confidence and higher aspirations among rural children; enabling farmers to gain market information and substantially higher prices for their crops besides harnessing local entrepreneurial energies. Human capacity constraints, pose a challenge. Illiteracy; limited technology experience and low disposable income among its intended users pose continuing challenge to its business strategy. TARAhaat's operational challenges broadly relate to infrastructure development at the franchise level, product development at the enterprise level, and management skills required at both levels. The franchise model should harness the entrepreneurial drive and local knowledge of franchisees through a stronger, more resourceful, and more locally-responsive network of kendras. Understanding and delivering products as per the needs of rural customer base is vital for its long term sustenance. TARAhaat's unique combination of commercial and NGO characteristics is mandatory and depends on societal and environmental factors for its success and replicability. Effective training and management support to its network of franchised TARAkendras will help in providing standardized services. Lack of government support; lack of motivation of farmers; miniscule returns from the rural kiosks compared to the investments made by private entrepreneurs; lack of appropriate content and services; heavy dependence on e-commerce activities pose serious challenges to its organizational, social and financial sustainability. Poor back-up arrangements coupled with lack of backward integration has made this financially viable rural network redundant. This case strongly recommends that the financial viability for the project partners and private entrepreneurs is crucial for kiosk expansion. Functional relationships need to be built with government departments through which numerous e-government services can be delivered to the masses. e-Education and e-health services needs to be outsourced. It is recommended that more community practitioners than technologist be employed in the project.

Warana kiosk case demonstrates the need for community information need as a crucial factor while conceptualizing e-government applications to directly impact the rural livelihood. Effective coordination with the local self government agencies has impacted G2C service delivery through these kiosks. Some of the constraints are lack of women's involvement wherein women generally visit information kiosks to obtain sugar factory services; but only men using the Internet. Warana information kiosks are mostly accessed by farmers who own their land. Non-relevant content for a majority leads to further marginalization wherein the poorest, landless labourers are excluded in their access to e-government as they were unconnected with sugar cane growing and harvesting. Warana has improved the standard of living of the community, especially of rural youth by providing employment opportunities. Providing necessary incentives can enable grassroots operators to become ICT champions in their villages, easing access to information for farmers, providing training to children, and creating new economic opportunities through software development. This case calls for motivated and skilled grassroots intermediaries in bringing e-government to rural communities.

5. TOWARDS SOCIALLY INCLUSIVE/ PRO-POOR E-GOVERNANCE STRATEGY IN INDIA

Implementing pro-poor e-governance is a complex phenomenon. Most e-government for development projects fail, particularly large scale e-government projects with high costs, due to enormous gaps between project design and on-the-ground reality, known as "design-reality gaps" (Heeks, 2003), besides the lack of a supporting organizational and institutional reform as well as poor strategic planning and implementation. Pro-poor strategy in India enhances opportunities for local service delivery to the poor as part of the national poverty reduction strategy and a way towards achieving the MDGs. Successful implementation of E-government initiatives for the poor depend on building trust, a sense of ownership, ensuring transparency, accountability and commitment and building networks. Strategic collaborative planning focuses on how different stakeholders can interact more effectively to add value, ensure that there are no gaps in service delivery, minimize duplication and enhance synergy (ESCAP 2004).

Capacity building, participatory planning for civil servants, local government and communities is vital in designing, implementing and utilizing pro-poor E-governance services. The intended impact on the poor and the vulnerable need to be examined by regular monitoring and evaluation of the existing projects and programmes as well as planning future interventions followed by a feedback mechanism for stakeholders and beneficiaries of the projects. This helps to create and sustain the accountability, transparency and effectiveness of service delivery. Visions and goals should be clearly articulated in terms of socio-economic development and quality of life enhancement for all members of society, including the marginalized poor. Stakeholders are a valuable resource for a sustained E-government function.

6. POLICY RECOMMENDATIONS FOR SOCIALLY INCLUSIVE E-GOVERNMENT

Technology is most effectively deployed in pursuit of some predefined developmental outcome, rather than as an outcome itself. A well-conceived project will be more likely to deliver useful benefits to its target audience in a sustainable manner. Confidential information provided to the study team from a recent project for the Organisation for Economic Co-operation and Development (OECD) found that E-government initiatives targeted on, or particularly useful to, socially excluded groups achieved the highest returns on investment amongst E-government initiatives for citizens. Considering lack of E-government strategies for socially excluded, following recommendations are drawn:

- For socially excluded groups to benefit from digital transformation, local government needs to seize the opportunities that ICT provides by:
    - Making better use of information and data to understand the distribution and magnitude of social exclusion problems and to use this knowledge to underpin social inclusion strategies
    - Greater legal clarity and promotion of the benefits of information sharing between public organizations
    - Making better use of information, ensuring that key staff who work with these individuals/groups are informed and trained so they understand and therefore use their knowledge more effectively to target initiatives and to provide personalized services
- Central government objectives and goals need to emphasize the role of technology and E-government in meeting the needs of socially excluded groups. Action is required to ensure:
    - Social inclusion is a priority in the future development of the E-government agenda
    - Central government develops clearer objectives to support and guide the use of technology to enhance social inclusion
    - Goals for E-government emphasize the provision of better quality services for users as well as increased efficiency for service providers

ICT driven poverty reduction and E-governance projects need to remain financially sustainable. The closer that it comes to self-financing sustainability, the better incentives need to be generated to stimulate people living in poverty to use and benefit from E-government.

7. CONCLUDING REMARKS

This chapter examined the effects of E-government implementation in the context of widespread poverty in India through an analysis of six ICT initiatives in rural areas. Findings call for E-government strategies to target poverty for efficiently serving those who lack access to relevant information and are less likely to participate in government. Lack of integrated E-government strategies will provide less opportunity for these communities to indirectly or directly participate in government, consequently widening the digital divide affecting the development of democracy and its institutions. Equitable access and use of E-government services requires a broader perspective by strengthening the strategies to include socially excluded. Government agencies should creatively extend the use of their information networks and replace current perspectives with a more decentralized focus that translates into the broader reach of their services. Government organizations should implement innovations to explore how citizens use and perceive Internet.

High rate of access to technological devices (e.g., cellular phones) in rural areas must be considered by government to integrate strategies that incorporate the use of other devises to encourage increased use of e-government services to make E-governance a reality in India.

REFERENCES

2007 Asia - Telecoms, Mobile and Broadband in India: http://www.researchandmarkets.com/reportinfo.asp? report_id = 481013

ADB (2003). *Toward E-Development in Asia and the Pacific: A Strategic Approach to Information and Communication Technology*, www.adb.org, accessed 27 May 2007.

Akula, V.B. (2000). *Putting Technology to Work for Poverty Alleviation: A Draft Proposal for $151,030 to Develop Smart Cards for Microfinance,* Swayam Krishi Sangam, Hyderabad.

Asia-Pacific Journal on Information, Communication and Space Technology: Reviews and Updates. First Issue – 2006, Economic and Social Commission for Asia and the Pacific

Baramati Initiatives (2001). *SKS-Smart Cards: Case Study*. www.baramatiinitiatives. com/cases/case10.htm.

Best, M., & Maclay, C.M. (2002). *Community Internet Access in Rural Areas: Solving the economic sustainability puzzle*. The Global Information Technology Report 2001-2002: Readiness for the networked world, ed., Geoffrey Kirkman (Oxford University Press, 2002). Available online at http://www.cid.harvard.edu /cr/gitrr_030202 .html (May 20, 2007)

Bhatnagar, S. (2000). Empowering Dairy Farmers through a Dairy Information & Services Kiosk. Washington, DC: World Bank.

Bhatnagar, S. (2004). *E-government: from vision to implementation – a practical guide with case studies*. New Delhi: Sage Publications (pp. 17, 53, 54, 73).

Bhatnagar, S., & Schware, R. (Eds.) (2000). *Information and Communication Technology in Rural Development. Case Studies from India*. Washington, DC: World Bank.

Bhatnagar, S., & Vyas, N. (2001). Gyandoot: Community-Owned Rural Internet Kiosks. Washington, DC: World Bank.

Cecchini, S. (2001). *Back to Office Report: Information and Communications Technology for Poverty Reduction in Rural India, Mimeo*. Washington, DC: World Bank.

Cecchini, S. (2002). *Back to Office Report: Evaluation of Gyandoot and Bhoomi and International Conferences on ICT for Development, Mimeo*. Washington, DC: World Bank.

Cecchini, S., & Raina, M. (2002, April). Warana: *The Case of an Indian Rural Community Adopting Information and Communications Technology in Information Technology in Developing Countries, 12*(1). www.iimahd.ernet.in/egov/ifip/apr2002/apr2002.htm.

Cecchini, S., & Shah, T. (2002). Information and Communications Technology as a Tool for Empowerment in Empowerment and Poverty Reduction: A Sourcebook. Washington, DC: World Bank. www.worldbank.org/poverty/empowerment/

Centre of E-governance. (2003, June). IIM Ahmedabad, Evaluation Studies by the Centre for E-Governance. Indian Institute of Management, Ahmedabad (CEG-IIMA). *Information Technology in Developing Countries, 13*(1). Available online at http://www.iimahd.ernet.in/egov/ifip/jun2003/ article6.htm

CRISP Group (2003, July). National Informatics Centre, Department of IT, Ministry of Communications & IT, Government of India, Information Needs Assessment for Rural Communities- An

Indian Case Study. Available online at http://ruralinformatics.nic.in/files/4_12_0_229.pdf

Critical Success Factors for Rural ICT Projects in India: A study of n-Logue kiosk projects at Pabal and Baramati. Submitted in partial fulfillment of the requirements for the degree of Master of Management By Vivek Dhawan, IIT Bombay.

Edwin, L. (2003, November). Project Leader, OECD E-Government Project. Challenges for E-Government Development. *5th Global Forum on Reinventing Government*, Mexico City.

Gartner estimate rates India as the fourth largest IT spender. The Economic Times, 13 July 2003. http://www. infochangeindia .org/archivesl.jsp?secno=9&monthname=September&year=2003&detail=T

Handbook on Implementing E-Government with basic introduction to E-Commerce: Developed by D.Net - Development through Access to Network Resources.

Harris, R.W. (2004). Information and Communication Technology for Poverty Alleviation. *E-primers for the Information, Economy, Society and Polity*, Kuala Lumpur (UNDP-APDIP), (pp. 21, 35).

Heeks, R. (1999). *Information and Communication Technologies, Poverty and Development, Development Informatics Working Paper Series, Paper No. 5.* www.idpm.man.ac.uk/idpm/di wp5.htm

Heeks, R. (2003). *Most e-Government-for-Development Projects Fail: How Can Risks be Reduced*? University of Manchester, United Kingdom: IDPM. Accessed from http://www.egov4dev.org.

http://dinkaunc.blogspot.com/2004/09/impact-of-ict-on-poverty-reduction.html

International Telecommunication Union, Global Survey on Rural Communications. (2004, June). *ITU News, No. 5.* www.itu.int/itunews, Accessed 28 May 2007.

James, J. Pro-Poor. (2000). *Modes of Technical Integration into the Global Economy in Development and Change, 31*, 765–783.

Kaur, S. & Mathiyalagan, N. (2007, December 28-30). Adoption of e-governance: Social dimensions of e-government: Poverty perspective. In *Proceedings of the 5th International Conference on E-Governance,* Hyderabad, India.

Keniston, K. (2000). *The Four Digital Divides.* Available online at http://web.mit.edu/~kken/Public/ PDF/Intro_Sage_1_.pdf (May 11, 2007)

Keniston, K. (2002). *Grassroots ICT Projects in India: Some Preliminary Hypotheses ASCI Journal of Management, 31*(1&2). Available online at http://web.mit.edu/~kken/Public/PDF/ASCI _Journal_Intro __ASCI_ version_. pdf (May 11, 2007)

Keniston, K. (2007). *IT for Masses: Hope or Hype*? Available online at http://web.mit.edu /~kken/Public/PDF/EPW_paper.pdf (May 11, 2007)

Kenny, C., Navas-Sabater, J., & Quiang, C. (2001). *Information and Communication Technologies and Poverty in World Bank Poverty Reduction Strategies Sourcebook.* www.worldbank.org/poverty/ strategies/ict/ict.htm

Margetts, H., & Dunleavy, P. (2002). Cultural Barriers to EGovernment, published by the National Audit Office, April 4, 2002 (HC 704-III) in conjunction with the Value for Money report "Better Public Services Through EGovernment."

McNamara, K.S. (2003). *Information and Communication Technologies, Poverty and Development; Learning from Experience.* A background paper for the InfoDev Annual Symposium. The World Bank.

Milestones in India's Internet Journey (2007). http://www.amitranjan.com/category/5/

Mission 2007 India http://www.mission2007.org/

OECD (2005). *The contribution of ICTs to Achieving the Millennium Development Goals (MDGs).* Forthcoming. Good Practice Paper on ICTs for Economic Growth and Poverty Reduction. http://www.oecd.org/dataoecd/15/38/34662239.pdf, accessed 23 May 2007.

Recommendation (2004). *Record of the Committee of Ministers to member states on electronic governance.* Adopted by the Committee of Ministers on December 15, 2004 at the 909th meeting of the Ministers' Deputies.

Singh, S. H.(2000, September 26). Ways and Means of Bridging the Gap between Developed and Developing Countries. High-Level Panel on Information Technology and Public Administration, United Nations, New York.

Sociocultural Barriers to E-Government: An Analysis from a Poverty Perspective: María Inés Salamancal, FLACSO Chile, DIRSI (Regional Dialogue on the Information Society), funded by the IDRC.

Sood, A.D. (2003, May-June). The Kiosk Networks: Information nodes in the rural landscape, I(1). Available online at http://www.i4donline.net/issue/may03/aditya_full.htm

Spence, R. (2003). *Information and Communications Technologies (ICTs) for Poverty Reduction: When, Where and How?* OECD International Development Rese arch Cen ter (IDRC). http://network.idrc.ca/uploa ds/user-S/ 10618469203RS_ICT-Pov_18_July.pdf

The E-Government Divide: Mutual Effects of Digital Divide and E-Government. (2003, October 12-19). *World Congress on Engineering and Digital Divide*, Tunis.

UNDP (2006). *Human Development Report.* India.

UNDP-APDIP (2004). *ICT for Development: A Sourcebook for Parliamentarians* (p. 39), New Delhi: Elsevier.

World Bank (2003). *ICTs and MDGs: A World Bank Perspective.* www.worldbank.org, accessed 26 May 2007.

World Bank Group (2004). *World Development Report 2004: Making Services Work for Poor People* (p. 7). Washington, D.C., World Bank.

World Bank. (2001). *World Development Report 2000/01: Attacking Poverty.* Oxford University Press. www.worldbank.org/poverty/wdrpoverty/.

WEB SITES

www.ejisdc.org/ojs2/index.php/ejisdc/article/view/462/230

http://www.eapf.net/ casestudies/in/agmarket.asp

www.digitalopportunity.org/article/view/113259/

http://www.unapcict.org/ecohub/case-studies/anand-milk-collection-centres-anand-gujarat

http://web.worldbank.org/WBSITE/EXTERNAL/TOPICS/EXTINFORMATIONANDCOMMUNICATIONANDTECHNOLOGIES/EXTEGOVERNMENT/0,,contentMDK:20486020~menuPK:1767268~pagePK:210058~piPK:210062~theSitePK:702586,00.html

http://poverty2.forumone.com/library/view/14655/

www.apdip.net/resources/case/in16/view

http://www.digitaldividend.org/case/case_echoupal.htm

http://www.expresscomputeronline.com/20070702/management02.shtml

http://www.thehindu.com/2007/11/28/stories/2007112862051900.htm

unpan1.un.org/intradoc/groups/public/documents/UN/UNPAN028607.pdf

www.igidr.ac.in/~susant/PDFDOCS/Thomas2003_commoditiesmkts_wb.pdf

download.microsoft.com/download/0/5/d/05dd56a0-1fec-4490-84da-ff2c30974152/Agmarknet.doc

www.patelcenter.usf.edu/assets/doc/IPSA-Singh.doc

India targets PC penetration of 6.5% by 2008: http://mungee.org/archives/2005/05/19/india-targets-pc-penetration-of-65-by-2008/.

India: e-governance market to have an explosive growth by 2007: http://www.digitalopportunity.org/article /view/125575/1/

Chapter VII
E-Governance:
Tool for E-Democracy and Citizen Empowerment in the Horizon of Information Technology Era in Developing Society in India, Nepal and Bangladesh

Subhajit Choudhury
Indian Institute of Technology Guwahati, India

Sudhir Kumar
Vikram University, India

ABSTRACT

The chapter introduces information communication technology and its importance with respect to digital divide. Digital divides is the connotation of three terms global divide, social divide, democratic divide. Further, it discusses the role of United Nations and United Nation's Millennium Development Goals for bridging digital divide amongst the under develop and developing nations. It also relates e-democracy with citizen empowerment. Some projects related to e-governance in developing society in India, Nepal, and Bangladesh have been discussed. The Library and Information Centres have been given utmost priority to maintain the e-governance projects so that these projects can better be maintained with proper information and become more citizen-centric.

INTRODUCTION

Science and technology have undergone revolutionary changes in past century. Only a few decades ago, all telecommunications services were delivered over copper wires. More recently, the world has witnessed the exponential growth of mobile telephony and the widespread commercial deployment of the Internet. Today, the dazzling array of new technologies, services and applications has led to a digital age of information communications technology (ICT) in which access has become a key component of peoples' lives. These changes hold so much promise. The convergence of technologies, its rapid rate of change and its importance in the development of the economic, social, financial and educational sectors, is opening new opportunities from e-commerce & e-governance to Tele-education and Tele-medicine.

The alarming rate of development of ICT the world is being changed into information oriented. The country which is rich in information is regarded as rich in every aspect. Information communication technologies (ICT) can eliminate many of the obstacles of time and space and help overcome gaps in regional development. However the arrangement of advantages brought by ICT is uneven, and this is what gives rise to the phenomenon of a "digital divide".

The concept of the digital divide grows more complex as the phrase becomes shorthand for every conceivable disparity relating to online access. The multi-dimensionality of the concept has been framed by Norris (2000) into three distinct aspects:

a. **Global divide:** Divergence of Internet access between industrialized and developing countries;
b. **Social divide:** Gap between information rich and information poor in each nation; and,
c. **Democratic divide:** Difference between those who do and those who do not use the new technologies to further political participation (Norris, 2000).

The worry internationally is that a widening digital divide between countries could lead to a widening economic divide. In fact, the economic considerations driving the concerns about the digital divide underlie most of the concerns within a country as well as between countries. As economists have observed, however, we are in such early stages of the communications revolution that evidence on the question of the economic impact of differences in connectivity worldwide is very inconclusive.

INTERNATIONAL TELECOMMUNICATION UNION, WSIS AND UNITED NATIONS AND E-DEMOCRACY

International Telecommunication Union is the only international organization whose primary focus is communications. Telecommunication operators make up ITU's core constituency. While today's economy has witnessed a boom in Internet start-up companies—many of which have joined ITU—traditional telecommunication operators remain the world's most important Internet backbone providers and Internet Service Providers. ITU has a unique opportunity to work with these key Internet players. Moreover, one of the main purposes of ITU is to promote the extension of the benefits of the new ICTs to all the world's inhabitants. ITU is mandated to foster and offer technical assistance to developing countries and to promote the mobilisation of the material, human and financial resources needed to implement these goals. Some of the countries that have become today's leading global telecommunications players—Malaysia, Korea and Singapore—were beneficiaries of ITU technical co-operation programmes. ITU's mandate further includes promoting international co-operation and partnerships between government Members and the growing number of private sector members who have joined ITU. ITU Electronic Commerce for Developing Countries (EC-DC) programme, is a shining example of the benefits such partnerships bring to the world's poorest economies. ITU has been playing a leadership role in bridging the digital divide under the four-year strategic Valletta Action Plan (VAP) adopted by the ITU World Telecommunication Development Conference (WTDC) in 1998. VAP is a six-point action plan that address the key elements needed to bridge the digital divide: sector reform, access to new technologies, gender issues, rural development and universal service/access, finance and economics, partnerships with the private sector and human resource development. VAP also includes a special programme to take into consideration the needs of Least Developed Countries (LDCs).

ITU Statistics: ICT in Developed and Developing Countries

The ICT penetration in developed countries is very high as technological development takes place in those countries with the pace of time. Secondly economically it is viable for them to have access those technology. The excessive growth and development of ICT has widened the divide between a developed and developing society. Tables 1 to 5 show the ICT penetration in developed versus countries in transition (i.e. developing countries).

Table 1. Distribution of population, fixed telephone subscribers, personal computers and internet users in percentage (Source: International Telecommunication Union, Report 2006)

Year 1992					
Country	**Population**	**Fixed Telephone**	**Mobile**	**PC**	**Internet Users**
Developed	21	79	88	90	97
Developing	79	21	12	10	3
Year 2002					
	Population	Fixed Telephone	Mobile	PC	Internet Users
Developed	19	55	54	73	66
Developing	81	45	46	27	34

Table 2. Fixed telephone line per 100 inhabitants (Source: International Telecommunication Union, Report 2006)

	1992	2002
Developed	39.1	50
Developing	2.9	9.9
World	10.6	17.7

Table 3. Mobile telephone line per 100 inhabitants (Source: International Telecommunication Union, Report 2006)

	1992	2002
Developed	1.8	52.2
Developing	0.1	10.7
World	0.4	18.7

Table 4. Personal computer per 100 inhabitants (Source: International Telecommunication Union, Report 2006)

	1992	2002
Developed	10.9	36.2
Developing	0.4	3.3
World	3.1	9.8

Table 5. Internet users per 100 inhabitants (Source: International Telecommunication Union, Report 2006)

	1992	2002
Developed	0.7	33.3
Developing	0.02	4.1
World	0.3	9.8

Figure 1. A comparison of digital divide between developed versus developing countries (Data source from Tables 1 to 5)

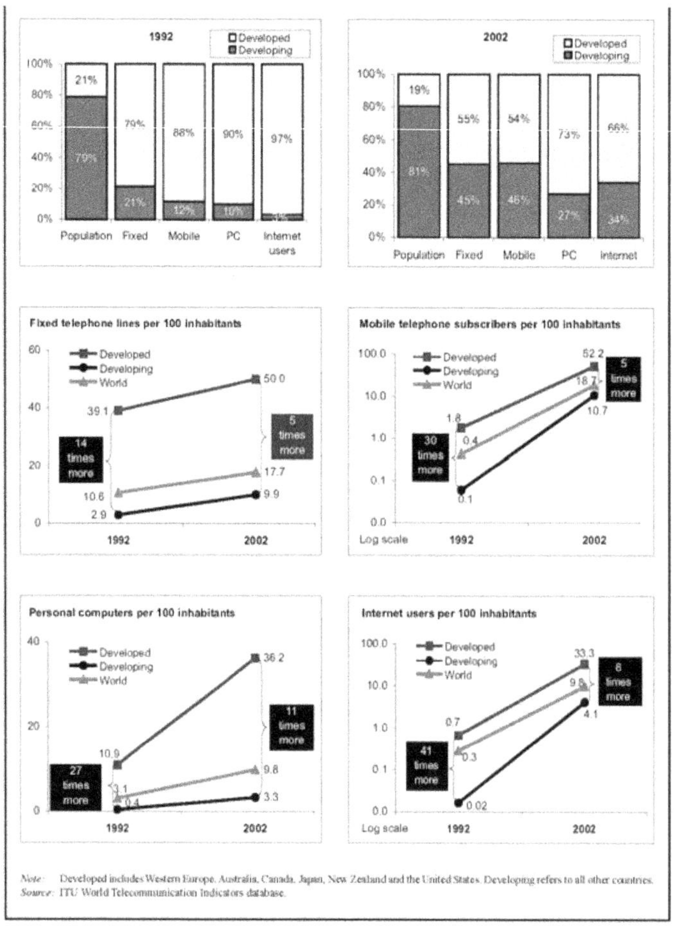

DIGITAL ACCESS WORLD-WIDE

This section is on digital access country-wise. Various parameters of Digital Access Index have been taken for discussion to know the difference between developed and developing nations. As far as High Access is concern Sweden is at the top followed by Denmark and so on. Talking about upper access Ireland being the top with 0.69 rate and in medium category Belarus is on top, while India is in 54th. Nepal and Bangladesh are in low access category with 12th and 13th position respectively (Table 6). Table 6 shows statistics on digital access country-wise.

Top five economies by DAI categories as per ITU World Telecommunication Indicator database 2006. These are shown in Tables 7-13.These tables of various parameters show the position of developing and developed countries.

The data presented in Tables 6-13 shows how undemocratic towards use of electronic access from develop, developing and underdeveloped nations. However, under the leadership of the ITU and with the support and participation of other United Nations Agencies, governments and private sector, a World Summit on the Information Society (WSIS) was scheduled for 2003. In addition to its work under the VAP and programmes approved at the 1998 ITU Plenipotentiary Conference, ITU is collaborating with the UN and other multilateral organisations, financial institutions, NGOs and other entities involved in poverty eradication in a further effort to bridge the digital divide.

World Summit on Information Society in its declaration has made a common vision of the information society which read as "We declare our common desire and commitment to build a people-centred, inclusive and development-oriented Information Society, where everyone can create, access, utilize and share information and knowledge, enabling individuals, communities and peoples to achieve their full potential in promoting their sustainable development and improving their quality of life (International Telecommunication Union Report 2007).

So with the vision of United Nations along with other world bodies the countries through out the world are united with various initiatives at local level to join hand at national level and finally at international level.

E-DEMOCRACY AND CITIZEN EMPOWERMENT

E-Democracy is mostly associated with electronic voting, but it is also associated with citizen participation in the processes of policy making, promoting and preserving the democratic values and successful implementation of Information (Wikipedia, 2007). E-democracy innovations aim to use ICT to engage citizens in the decision-making process. Examples include e-voting, e-consultation, e-representatives, online deliberative polling, e-petitions, e-referendum etc.

The term democracy connotes of three aspects of government i) by the people, ii) of the people and iii) for the people. Whereas, E-Democracy refers to the processes and structures that encompasses all forms of electronic interaction between the government (elected) and the citizen (electorate). E-government is a form of e-Business in governance and refers to the processes and structures needed to deliver electronic services to the public (citizens and businesses), collaborate with business partners and to conduct electronic transactions within an organizational entity. E-Governance is defined as the application of electronic means in the interaction between government and citizens and government and businesses, to simplify and improve democratic, government and business aspects of Governance.

Democratic process incorporates not only voting but also citizen participation and engagement in government. It is this second aspect which most readily offers the opportunity for empowerment by encouraging citizens to care about issues

Table 6. Digital Access Index 2006

HIGH ACCESS		UPPER ACCESS		MEDIUM ACCESS		LOW ACCESS	
Sweden	0.85	Ireland	0.69	Belarus	0.49	Zimbabwe	0.29
Denmark	0.83	Cyprus	0.68	Lebanon	0.48	Honduras	0.29
Iceland	0.82	Estonia	0.67	Thailand	0.48	Syria	0.28
Korea (Rep.)	0.82	Spain	0.67	Romania	0.48	Papua New Guinea	0.26
Norway	0.79	Malta	0.67	Turkey	0.48	Vanuatu	0.24
Netherlands	0.79	Czech Republic	0.66	TFYR Macedonia	0.48	Pakistan	0.24
Hong Kong, China	0.79	Greece	0.66	Panama	0.47	Azerbaijan	0.24
Finland	0.79	Portugal	0.65	Venezuela	0.47	S. Tomé & Principe	0.23
Taiwan, China	0.79	UAE	0.64	Belize	0.47	Tajikistan	0.21
Canada	0.78	Macao, China	0.64	St. Vincent	0.46	Equatorial Guinea	0.20
United States	0.78	Hungary	0.63	Bosnia	0.46	Kenya	0.19
United Kingdom	0.77	Bahamas	0.62	Suriname	0.46	Nicaragua	0.19
Switzerland	0.76	Bahrain	0.60	South Africa	0.45	Lesotho	0.19
Singapore	0.75	St. Kitts and Nevis	0.60	Colombia	0.45	Nepal	0.19
Japan	0.75	Poland	0.59	Jordan	0.45	Bangladesh	0.18
Luxembourg	0.75	Slovak Republic	0.59	Serbia & Montenegro	0.45	Yemen	0.18
Austria	0.75	Croatia	0.59	Saudi Arabia	0.44	Togo	0.18
Germany	0.74	Chile	0.58	Peru	0.44	Solomon Islands	0.17
Australia	0.74	Antigua & Barbuda	0.57	China	0.43	Cambodia	0.17
Belgium	0.74	Barbados	0.57	Fiji	0.43	Uganda	0.17
New Zealand	0.72	Malaysia	0.57	Botswana	0.43	Zambia	0.17
Italy	0.72	Lithuania	0.56	Iran (I.R.)	0.43	Myanmar	0.17
France	0.72	Qatar	0.55	Ukraine	0.43	Congo	0.17
Slovenia	0.72	Brunei Darussalam	0.55	Guyana	0.43	Cameroon	0.16
Israel	0.70	Latvia	0.54	Philippines	0.43	Ghana	0.16
		Uruguay	0.54	Oman	0.43	Lao P.D.R.	0.15
		Seychelles	0.54	Maldives	0.43	Malawi	0.15
		Dominica	0.54	Libya	0.42	Tanzania	0.15
		Argentina	0.53	Dominican Rep.	0.42	Haiti	0.15

continued on following page

Table 6. continued

	Trinidad & Tobago	0.53	Tunisia	0.41	Nigeria	0.15
	Bulgaria	0.53	Ecuador	0.41	Djibouti	0.15
	Jamaica	0.53	Kazakhstan	0.41	Rwanda	0.15
	Costa Rica	0.52	Egypt	0.40	Madagascar	0.15
	St. Lucia	0.52	Cape Verde	0.39	Mauritania	0.14
	Kuwait	0.51	Albania	0.39	Senegal	0.14
	Grenada	0.51	Paraguay	0.39	Gambia	0.13
	Mauritius	0.50	Namibia	0.39	Bhutan	0.13
	Russia	0.50	Guatemala	0.38	Sudan	0.13
	Mexico	0.50	El Salvador	0.38	Comoros	0.13
	Brazil	0.50	Palestine	0.38	Côte d'Ivoire	0.13
			Sri Lanka	0.38	Eritrea	0.13
			Bolivia	0.38	D.R. Congo	0.12
			Cuba	0.38	Benin	0.12
			Samoa	0.37	Mozambique	0.12
			Algeria	0.37	Angola	0.11
			Turkmenistan	0.37	Burundi	0.10
			Georgia	0.37	Guinea	0.10
			Swaziland	0.37	Sierra Leone	0.10
			Moldova	0.37	Central Af. Rep.	0.10
			Mongolia	0.35	Ethiopia	0.10
			Indonesia	0.34	Guinea-Bissau	0.10
			Gabon	0.34	Chad	0.10
			Morocco	0.33	Mali	0.09
			India	0.32	Burkina Faso	0.08
			Kyrgyzstan	0.32	Niger	0.04
			Uzbekistan	0.31		
			Viet Nam	0.31		
			Armenia	0.30		

Note: On a scale of 0 to 1 where 1 = highest access. DAI values are shown to hundreds of a decimal point. Countries with the same DAI value are ranked by thousands of a decimal point.[**Source:** ITU 2006]

Table 7. Top 5 economies by fixed telephone subscribers per 100 inhabitants

1	Sweden	65.25
2	United States	65.02
3	Cyprus	62.44
4	Canada	61.30
5	Taiwan, China	57.45

Table 8. Top 5 economies by mobile cellular subscribers per 100 inhabitants

1	Taiwan, China	106.5
2	Luxembourg	105.4
3	Israel	95.5
4	Italy	92.5
5	Hong Kong, China	91.6

Table 9. Top 5 economies by Internet tariff as percentage of per capita income

1	Hong Kong, China	0.19
2	United States	0.51
3	Singapore	0.64
4	Denmark	0.68
5	Canada	0.68
Note: Calculated as cheapest price for 20 hours of Internet use per month divided by per capita income from the World Bank. Source: ITU		

Table 10. Top economies by UNDP Education index

	Literacy	**School enrolment**	**Education index**
Australia	99	114	0.99
Belgium	99	107	0.99
Denmark	99	98	0.99
Finland	99	103	0.99
Netherlands	99	99	0.99
New Zealand	99	99	0.99
Norway	99	98	0.99
Sweden	99	113	0.99
United Kingdom	99	112	0.99
Note: The Education index is calculated as (2/3) times the literacy rate and (1/3) the school enrolment. Countries are shown in alphabetical order. The methodology and data are from the UNDP.			

Table 11. Top 5 economies by broadband Internet subscribers per 100 inhabitants

1	Korea (Rep.)	21.9
2	Hong Kong, China	14.6
3	Canada	11.1
4	Taiwan, China	9.4
5	Belgium	8.4

Table 12. Top 5 economies by International Internet bandwidth (bits) per inhabitant

1	Denmark	20'284
2	Sweden	10'611
3	Netherlands	10'327
4	Switzerland	8'991
5	Belgium	8'121

Table 13. Top 5 economies by Internet users per 100 inhabitants

1	Iceland	64.9
2	Sweden	57.3
3	Korea (Rep.)	55.2
4	United States	55.1
5	Japan	54.5

within their community and providing them with a feeling of ownership. When citizens feel that their views are respected and contribute to the decision-making process, then it might reasonably be expected to have an impact on voting turnout at elections.

Where technology can contribute is by increasing the opportunity and choice of channels for engagement with Government. This issue of choice is crucial. When using electronic channels such as online discussion forums, email, etc., traditional methods must not be forgotten. An interesting challenge for government in this context is the expectation of immediate response to electronic communication.

Offering electronic services, designed round the needs of the citizens, is another way to empower citizens, increasing their control over when and where they transact with the Council. Research in Glasgow and throughout Scotland shows that the telephone remains the preferred means of contacting government and this must be respected even while encouraging the convenience of online transaction.

What is particularly important is to build confidence in the security of electronic channels particularly where sharing of confidential data takes place. This applied equally to service transactions and to consultation.

E-GOVERNANCE IN INDIA, NEPAL AND BANGLADESH

There are various electronic initiatives which are the step towards e-democracy in these countries some of them have been discussed in this section.

India

The Ministry of Communications and Information Technology has formulated the National e-Governance Plan which aims to bring all government services to the doorstep of each citizen by making the services citizen centric and ensuring that the right people get the benefits. The gap of information amongst various strata of the people (urban and rural, farmers & professionals etc.) can be bridged to a great extent. To further accelerate the drive towards efficient and transparent governance, the Right to Information Act was passed in late 2005 (National Informatics Centres, 2005).

Gyandoot E-Governance project is the first of its kind initiated in Dhar district of Madhya Pradesh as role model of E-Governance project in India. Some e-governance initiatives are:

a. **e-Seva (electronic Seva):** The electronic seva (e-Seva) is the improved version of the TWINS project launched in 1999, in the twin cities of Hyderabad and Secunderabad in Andhra Pradesh.
b. **Bhoomi:** The Department of Revenue in Karnataka State has computerized 20 million records of land ownership of 6.7 million farmers in the State. Farmers of the Village Accountant to get a copy of Record of Rights, Tenancy and Crops (RTC) – a document needed for many tasks such as obtaining bank loans.
c. **CARD:** The Computer-aided Administration of Registration Department - CARD in Andhra Pradesh is designed to eliminate the maladies affecting the conventional registration system by introducing electronic delivery of all registration services. CARD was initiated to meet objectives to demystify the registration process, bring speed, efficiency, consistency and reliability, substantially improve the citizen interface etc.
d. **FRIENDS:** Fast, Reliable, Instant, Efficient Network for the Disbursement of Services is part of the Kerala State IT Mission. FRIENDS counters handle 1,000 types of payment bills originating out of various PSUs. The payments that citizens can make include utility payments for electricity and water, revenue taxes, license fees, motor vehicle taxes, university fees, etc.
e. **LOK MITRA:** Lok Mitra is the first of its own kind of Electronic service in the state of Rajasthan. It aims to deploy Information Technology for the benefit of the masses. It is a, citizen friendly computerized centre located in the heart of the city at Government Hostel, Jaipur. It has facility of making payments through Internet using Credit Card.
f. **SETU:** A bridge for facilitation between Citizen & Government: The Integrated Citizen Facilitation Centres (SETU) is an approach in this direction. At present there are multiple points of interaction between the citizen and individual departments spread over so many different Government offices. The aim is to lay the foundation for e-governance, create visible impact of the intention of the Government in this direction, and facilitate the interaction of the citizens with the Government to make it more transparent, pleasant and satisfying.
g. **Jan Mitra:** Jan Mitra is an Integrated e-platform through which rural population of Rajasthan can get desired information and avail services related to various government departments at kiosks near their doorsteps. To achieve this end, a system has been integrated using IT tools.
h. **Drishtee's software** platform enables e-governance and provides information about and access to education and health services, market-related information, and private information exchanges and transactions. It aims to be the 'window to the

world' for Indian villagers. Drishtee kiosks provide viable employment opportunities for unemployed rural youths and help stem rural-urban migration. Drishtee is capable of enabling the creation of approximately 50,000 Information Kiosks all over India within a span of six years. This communication backbone has been supplemented by a string of rural services for example, Avedan, Land Records, Gram Daak (mailing software), Gram Haat (virtual market place), Vaivahiki (Matrimonial), Shikayat (online grievance redressal), Mandi.

i. **WebCITI:** An e-Governance project for building citizen-IT interface for services offered by district administration at Fatehgarh Sahib in Punjab and also provides complete workflow automation in District Commissioner's office. WebCITI provides web based interface to citizens seeking services from district administration which includes issuance of certificates such as death/birth, caste, rural area etc; licenses such as arms license, permission for conferences/rallies etc and benefits from socio-economic schemes.

j. **Aarakshi** is an Intranet based system that has been developed and implemented for Jaipur City Police. This innovative system enables the city police officers to carry out on-line sharing of crime & criminal data bases, carry out communication and perform monitoring activities.

k. **FAST:** The 'Fully Automated Services of Transport' an e-governance, implemented in the cities of Andhra Pradesh. It is to provide on-line services to the public covering all gamut of services of Transport Department like Issue of Driving Licenses, Registration of Motor Vehicles, Issue Permits, Collection of Motor Vehicle Taxes, etc. All the offices in the state would have inter-connectivity through APSWAN.

l. **VOICE:** It is made to deliver municipal services such as building approvals, and birth and death certificates, to the people of Vijayawada. It also handles the collection of property, water and sewerage taxes. The VOICE system uses five kiosks located close to the citizens.

m. **MUDRA (MUnicipal corporation towards Digital Revenue Administration):** The system is for the Holding owners, Tax collectors, officials at headquarter levels and Circle levels. It is designed to computerize the over all functions of tax collection system of Patna Municipal Corporation. Revenue management is the key to economic stability and development of urban infrastructure.

n. **KHAJANE:** The online treasury project, KHAJANE, computerises all the 216 treasury offices in Karnataka and is connected to a central server at the State Secretariat through VSAT (Very Small Aperture Terminal). It provides regular updates regarding the State expenditure and receipts to the central server. KHAJANE aims to bring about a more transparent and accountable system of financial transactions and also discipline in operations and management, resulting in efficiency and cost savings for the government.

o. **eCops (e-Computerised Operations for Police Services):** This project was launched as part of the VISION 2020, the state's focus on modernization of police administration takes the shape of eCOPS. It helps police stations reduce paperwork and automate the maintenance of registers, report generation, data analysis, planning and co-ordination, enable the speedy detection of crime and monitor prosecutions. For citizens, the project will lead to online interaction with the police department over the Internet.

p. **OLTP (OnLine Transaction Processing):** The project connects 16 government departments in Andhra Pradesh on a single network. The project seeks to serve the Government department users and citizens in ten villages of Shadnagar mandal, one village each in Bijnepally and Jadcherla Mandals, Mahaboobnagar District. Citizens in these pilot locales will be able to conduct government department service transactions efficiently through specially designed internet-enabled kiosks. These transactions can be carried out in English as well as Telugu interfaces. These services include access to information such as income verification and income certificates of citizens, land cultivation details, agriculture marketing, tele-veterinary services, registration of small farmers, birth and death records, house numbering, first information reports, occupation details of residents, drinking water details and irrigation sources, etc.

q. **TARAhaat:** This project, named "TARAhaat" after the all-purpose haat (meaning a village bazaar), comprises a commercially viable model for bringing relevant information, products and services via the Internet to the unserved rural market of India from which an estimated 50% of the national income is derived. TARAhaat combines a mother portal, TARAhaat.com, supported by franchised networks of village cybercafes and delivery systems to provide a full range of services its clients, which includes, TARAdhaba, TARAbazaar, TARAdak, TARAguru, TARAscouts / TARAreporter, TARAvendor, and TARAcard.

r. **Mahiti Shakti:** The portal operates with a single window through which the citizens can access information related to all aspects of the government's functioning, various benefit schemes and services ranging from obtaining ration cards to getting sanction for old age pension.

s. **Warana Wired Villages:** The Warna Wired Village provides agricultural, medical, and educational information in the local language to villages around Warana Nagar in the Kolhapur and Sangli Districts of Maharashtra.

t. **Community Information Center:** The Prime Minister of India dedicated to the people of the eight North-Eastern states a new structure of localised governance called Community Information Centres. Basic services to be provided by CICs include Internet access and e-mail, printing, data entry and word processing and training for the local populace.

u. **Gramsampark:** This is a flagship ICT product of the state of Madhya Pradesh. A complete database of available resources, basic amenities, beneficiaries of government programmes and public grievances in all the 51,000 villages of Madhya Pradesh can be obtained by accessing the website. Gramsampark has three sections-Gram Paridrashya (village scenario), Samasya Nivaran (grievance redress) and Gram Prahari (village sentinel), which includes untouchability-eradication, women's empowerment, water conservation and campaigns for sanitation.

v. **Bharat Nirman Plan:** The Govt. of India has launched a massive rural infrastructure development programme, called 'Bharat Nirman Plan' which is designed to provide a new deal to Rural India in the areas of irrigation, roads, communication, healthcare, education, markets etc. Under the Bharat Nirman Plan the Department of Telecommunications has the responsibility of providing telecom connectivity to 66, 822 villages (out of total 6,38,365 villages in India), which are uncovered by Village Public Telephones (VPTs), will be covered by November 2007. The mission further works towards establishment of knowledge centres that will cater to each and every panchayat, village and hamlet.. This will bridge the divide between urban India and rural Bharat.

w. **Village Knowledge Centre:** Village Knowledge Centre (Anonymous 2007) is the out come of World Summit on Information Society under the Mission 2007 in India. Under this India Mission 2007 by August 2007 all village in India will have knowledge centre. In this regard The Honorable President of India, Dr. A. P. J. Abdul Kalam states that "India has approximately 2.3 lakh Village Panchayats. I visualize establishment of village knowledge centers in these Panchayats to empower the villagers with the knowledge and to act as a nodal center for knowledge connectivity for the villagers."

Village Knowledge Centre should have a computer terminal, wireless (Wi-Max) connections or fibre broadband or satellite connectivity with the nodal knowledge centres at the district level, and equipped with peripherals to function as a self sustained knowledge centre. The knowledge centre should have facility for reading the text with an audio output so that people, who are unable to read, can also benefit. The knowledge center can also be used for collection, digital storage and dissemination of village specific information pertaining to agriculture, craftsmanship, arts, artisan techniques, informal judicial system practiced in village based on values, local remedies for simple ailments, village stories with moral values, village history, village folk songs, village cultural traditions, traditional medicinal practices followed in villages and village marketing information and methods. In nutshell, all good side of village life should be available in the knowledge centre. Such information presently is being transmitted through word of mouth and with changing generation, it is being lost. Apart from providing tele-education and tele-medicine facilities, commercial transactions and administrative issues can also be integrated.

The elections have concluded in six states in India. For the first time voting was entirely electronic and carried out on India made machines. No yard long-ballots stuffed in boxes to be manually counted. People everywhere took to it with ease and are convinced 'poll riggers' would soon be extinct. Results were announced within three hours of beginning the software driven 'counting'.

Over and above, the National Knowledge Commission (National Knowledge Commission Report, 2007) has been made, a high level advisory body to the Prime Minister of India, with the objective of transforming India into a knowledge society. It covers sectors ranging from education to e-governance in the five focus areas of the knowledge paradigm namely (1) access (easy access to knowledge), (2) concepts(all levels & forms of education) (3)creation (effective creation of knowledge), (4) applications (applications of knowledge systems) and (5) services (services like e-governance). The knowledge commission has recommended to strengthen existing library and Information Centres (LIC) and to open new LICs in village areas.

Nepal

The Information Technology Policy of Nepal, 2000, aims to build a knowledge-based society and establish knowledge-based industries. The plan is to make ICTs accessible to the general public and to provide employment in the ICT sector. The government has developed a strategy and action plan that includes private sector participation, infrastructure development, provision of technology to rural areas and the creation of an enabling environment for private sector investment in ICT-related service industries, such as e-commerce, e-education and e-health.

a. **Bharatpur Municipality:** Bharatpur Municipality has tried to introduce the concept of urban e-governance by utilizing available resources. All 14 wards of the municipality are equipped with computers and trained staff. People will be provided with computerized services for taxation, employment exchange, building permits, property valuation and other transactions. Services, which used to be available only at the main municipality office, now be delegated to the ward level. The people may request for information via e-mail. The website of the municipality provides information on the city profile, land use, the Local Governance Act, regulations, important decisions of the municipality, population, land records, tourist information, registration of complaints etc[1]. The municipality orients its efforts towards e-governance as the first step, promote the use of computers and expand computerized services in the second step, and utilize electronic means for governance to the full extent in the third step. The vision of e-governance in Bharatpur Municipality may be a catalyst to initiate e-governance in the Kingdom of Nepal at the local levels.

b. **DoCSI:** Department of Cottage and Small Scale Industry is an e-governance projects started in July 2005. The services available are permission and registration of CSI (Cottage and Small Scale Industry), renewal, amendment, technical administrative consultancy, skill and entrepreneurship development, etc. The main objective of DoCSI is to cater the need of grass-root level entrepreneurs to reach to local, national and international market[2].

c. **E-procurement (Bolpatra):** Bolpatra is the central source for public procurement opportunities within Nepal. The site provides easy-to-use Internet access to all publicly available bidding opportunities with a facility to submit electronic responses online. The site also provides details of His Majesty's Government and Public Corporations awarded contracts for goods, services and works. Bolpatra is designed to help you to find information on government and public sector procurement by providing links and a search engine that can be used to search for notices issued by public bodies across Nepal[3].[9]

d. **Inland Revenue Department:** Inland Revenue Department has all the facilities through its portal to make it free from corruption. The citizens are accessing for e-value added tax system, for filing any application (e-Filing) module, permanent account number (e-PAN), and Tax Deducting at Source (e-TDS). This department has expanded to all its offices phase-wise.

e. **Nepali e-Haat Bazaar:** Nepali e-Haat Bazaar is the National Business to Business (B2B) e-Commerce Market Place as a single electronic gateway to promote the market linkages within the country and with the international markets. The B2B e-Commerce web site is implemented with the objective of using ICTs to reduce poverty in the country. This is a joint initiation of Rural Urban Partnership Programme (MLD/UNDP) and High Level Commission for Information Technology and Agro Enterprise Center/Federation of Nepalese Chamber of Commerce & Industries[4].

f. **E-Post:** The department of post has its electronic service to the citizen such as e-delivery, tracking of mail, electronic money order etc. It has intra departmental module to monitor and maintain staff and administrative set up. E-post is functioning since 2005.

g. **Women Empowerment through ICT:** Having identified the root cause of social crime as poverty and lack of education, the group Advancing Girls and Women in Nepal (AGWN) initiated this project with the belief that by working with women as learners the family will ultimately benefit. In the first phase the goal was to achieve 10,000 computer literate women in Nepal. After one week of computer training, self-help groups were established to enhance the women's learning with the hope they might design instructional materials or set up their own businesses[5].

h. **Digital Broadcast Initiative:** An international non-governmental organization (NGO), is working in conjunction with the United Nations Development Programme (UNDP) on a comprehensive initiative to provide critical information on a range of development issues important to the people of Nepal. Out of this, the Digital Broadcast Initiative (DBI) was created. It is a broad partnership of several groups working with the continuing support of government through three project teams: Content Development, Outreach and Assessment. The teams work collaboratively on determining the information needs of underserved communities; writing and producing relevant and engaging audio and multimedia programmes to address these needs; broadcasting these programmes directly to communities via satellite and FM rebroadcast; integrating broadcast programming into existing outreach work being done by partner community organizations; collecting ongoing feedback and input directly from communities and including it in programming; and monitoring and assessing the overall impact and effectiveness of the initiative[6]. A wide range of programmes are broadcasted, including a Nepali Language Service.

Bangladesh

In Bangladesh, the ICT and its inception has taken some time than other countries in South East Asia. The government has passed its IT policy in 2001 with emphasis on all the sectors for digital inclusion. Here some of initiatives have been discussed.

a. **Electronic Birth Registration System:** Electronic Birth Registration System was introduced by The Rajshahi City Corporation (RCC) and the Local Government Division of the Ministry of Local Government with technical and financial support from UNICEF. The system also doubles as an immunization management system. Once registered, the system also generates an immunization schedule for every child. The system generated ID is also used to get admission in the public schools of the city[7].

b. **Financial Management System:** Ministry of Finance has gradually and surely the ministry of Finance now have developed a quality MIS system that is successfully used for budget planning, sensitivity analysis, impact analysis, financial projections and other core processes of the ministry.

c. **Government Forms Online:** Accessing government forms online is made possible by the Prime Minster's Office of Bangladesh though a project funded by UNDP Bangladesh. This not only saves time but also the cost and hassles associated with the travelling to the government offices located at a distance.

d. **Hajj Web Site:** The Ministry of Religious Affairs, Government of Bangladesh introduced the Hajj Web Site in 2002 to service ten and thousands of pilgrims who go to Mecca to perform holy Hajj. During the Hajj, the website also acts as an important information portal for the family members of the pilgrims and other interested persons and organizations. One of the best examples of a Public-Private Partnership project, the site provides timely and reliable information to a large segment of the population.

e. **MIS for Project Management and Transparency:** Department of Roads and Highways, Ministry of Communication, Government of Bangladesh, developed this MIS as a component of a World Bank funded project for the institutional development of RHD. The e-Governance initiative of RHD involved the launch of a website that provides a variety of information, data and notices to users. Website users include the private sector, related government offices, ordinary citizens, and donor agencies.

f. **National Board of Revenue:** Several development projects like Asian Development Bank funded 'Customs Administration Modernization Project', International Development Agency funded 'Excise, Taxes & Customs (ETAC) Data Computerization Project', World Bank funded 'Modernization and Automation Project' etc. much of the core processes of NBR and some of its citizen services has already been computerized and implemented successfully.

g. **Personnel Database:** The Personnel Management system (more of a database with some analytical reporting) of the Ministry of Establishment is probably the oldest e-government initiative that is still is in use and in demand. The database in maintained by the technical personnel with in the ministry and maintains the personal information card for each government employ of the 'Administration' cadre including their respective annual confidential reports.

h. **GHAT:** Rural ICT Centre (RIC) Digital Equity Network (DEN) runs the RICs with support from KATALYST, a multi-donor consortium working in Bangladesh. Three RICs were launched in 2006. The RICs each have basic ICT facilities (phone, computers, printer, scanner, internet connectivity, digital camera etc.). The RIC mission is to develop and promote ICT services to meet the needs of micro, small and medium enterprises (MSMEs) in rural Bangladesh. D.Net and MART, India conducted market research for this project. As a result, content based information service received attention. RICs disseminate business information for the local businesses in selected sectors (e.g., poultry, fisheries, potato etc) dominant in the localities of each centre. The centres are also a source of various social, health, education, and government information.

i. **Agro-Ecological Zone (AEZ):** AEZ a national database was successfully developed in Bangladesh. The database contains information on the country's land resources including physiography, soils, climate, hydrology, cropping systems, and crop suitability. The database is housed in the Bangladesh Agricultural Research Council (BARC) computer center at Dhaka, Bangladesh, and has been used to generate readily accessible information on the physical land resources of the country for use by researchers, extension workers, and decision makers in land and agricultural resources management as well as agricultural development planning. The AEZ database constitutes the foundation for a new effort to develop a comprehensive multi-scale GIS-based Land Resources Information System (LRIS). This updated system is designed to better deal with the intricacies of land resource planning under the complex environmental conditions that prevail in large parts of Bangladesh. The LRIS includes additional databases and procedures, in particular data on socioeconomic and demographic factors influencing agricultural production. The system is being implemented by BARC with financial support from the United Nations Development Programme (UNDP) and technical support from the United Nations Food and Agriculture Organization (FAO). The technology being used to establish the LRIS includes ArcView GIS; the ArcView Spatial Analyst and Dialog Designer extensions; and Avenue, ArcView GIS software's programming language; as well as multi criteria analysis tools.

j. **GrameenPhone Community Information Centres** GrameenPhone is rolling out Community Information Centers (GPCIC) across rural Bangladesh, giving up to 20 million people the chance to use the Internet and email for the first time. GrameenPhone has already set up with local entrepreneurs more than 500 centers in communities throughout the country by the end of 2006. The GPCICs are designed to be run independently as small businesses by local entrepreneurs. The GPCICs are set up on shared premises in select rural areas around the country. The computers in the 16 centers of the pilot phase were used by an average of 30 people a day, who pay a small fee to access email or Web pages. Currently there are 80 CICs operating in as many upazilas of the country. GrameenPhone trains the entrepreneurs so that they become aware of the full potential of business through GPCIC. Community Information Centers also provide local people with other GrameenPhone services, such as payphones (again using GrameenPhone's mobile network) and electronic recharges for prepaid mobile accounts. Through GPCIC from the Government websites, access to passport forms, birth and death certificates forms and other related information are available. Market prices of agricultural produce are also available through the website of the Agricultural Extension Department. The GPCICs are also of help to students and professionals. Health and medical information will also be made available through the GPCICs soon. In addition, other useful content will also be added gradually. The ranges of services that are available at GPCICs are i)Internet surfing and e-mailing, ii)Chatting with Voice, Picture, iii)Video conferencing, iv)Computer Composing, v) Scanning, Printing, vi)Commercial Mobile Call, vi)E-governance services, vii)GP value added services such as FlexiLoad, Ring tones downloading etc., viii)Fax, ix) CD Writing, x)Telemedicine services, xi) Content on health, agriculture etc., xii) Multimedia education for children[8].

PROBLEMS OF E-GOVERNANCE IN INDIA, NEPAL AND BANGLADESH

The various e-initiatives are emerging in these countries but these initiatives are yet to reach all levels in society. The problem related to e-initiatives in these countries are many, however, some key issues are **Lack of ICT Professionals**: Apart from India in Nepal and Bangladesh there are dearth of ICT professionals, securing sufficient work force is the key fact for implementing E-governance. **Lack of Integrated Services:** Most of the e-Governance Services being offered are not integrated. This can mainly be attributed to ***Lack of Communication between different Departments.*** So the information that resides with one department has no or very little meaning to some other department of Government. **Lack of Key Persons:** e-Governance projects lack key persons, not only from technological aspect, but from other aspects as well. **Population:** This is probably the biggest challenge. Apart from being an asset to the country it offers some unique issues, an important one being **Establishing Person Identities.** There is no unique identity of a person in India. Apart from this, measuring the population, keeping the database of all Indian nationals (& keeping it updated) are some other related challenges. **Different Languages:** A challenge due to the diversity of the country. It enforces need to do governance, in local languages. Ensuring e-Governance in local language is a big task to achieve. **Electricity**: rural electricity is also one of the vital factors for the success of e-initiatives in these countries. **Information illiteracy** is another cause for the failure of e-governance in India, Nepal and Bangladesh. **Lack of proper Infrastructure** is also another setback for e-governance in these countries.

CONCLUSION

E-governance is the use of information and communication technology to promote more efficient and effective government, facilitate more accessible government services, allow greater public access to information and make government more accountable to citizens. One of the early initiatives taken up by nations embarking on a major e-government program is the launching of a country portal. Information illiteracy is the only handicap in the e-governance system in India, Nepal and Bangladesh. Thus, e-governance applications have to be designed and operated in such a way that they are easily and equally accessible to the literacy-challenged users. These electronic governance projects are also working as a tool of teaching of Information Literacy. However, these projects are in always found to be in trial mode, consistency and successful deployment of the projects are yet to go a long way. These e-governance projects are manned by the inexperience and information illiterate personnel. It is important to educate people at all levels, the various benefits and advantages of e-enabling the system should be right at the beginning to ensure popular support, which will lead to greater chances of success.

Citizen empowerment in true sense with e-democracy in a developing society like India, Nepal and Bangladesh is possible when people are information literate. In these countries where, the general and functional literacy is in developing stage, 65% literacy in India, 53% literacy in Nepal and 54% in Bangladesh. To compensate with such condition the simple literacy is not sufficient. Information literacy needs to be replaced with literacy. Information literacy itself makes oneself self-sufficient and self reliable. Further, for economic development, the empowerment through e-governance and other knowledge centres can mobilize the self-help efforts of the poor, rather than providing them with social welfare.

The various initiatives right from the grass-root to the level of higher education the e-democracy is to be inculcate to reap the benefit of new inventions of Information Communication Technology. These initiatives will empower the citizen, creating an environment where others are equipped and encouraged to make decisions in autonomous ways and to feel that they are in control of the outcomes for which they have accepted responsibility. However, empowering leaders invite an atmosphere of inclusion across all levels of the organization by making sure that everyone has a voice and that their voice is heard. This is in contrast to those leaders who include in the decision-making process only people who are like themselves and exclude those who are different. While the disempowering leader fears dissent, empowering leaders see it as a source of objectivity and innovation. They understand that they cannot become a learning organization unless new ideas are allowed to penetrate the decision-making processes. Such leaders resist the urge to exercise their positional authority to "resolve" tensions created by conflicting ideas. For them, power is not a tool to be used upon others; rather, it is understood as "reciprocal forces within a tension-filled network of relations". In reference again to that higher principle, these leaders believe that the process itself will eventually resolve the tension but with a solution far superior to one that could have been declared through the use of positional power.

To strengthen and propagate e-democracy in India, Nepal Bangladesh the community information centres (CICs) should be entrusted the responsibilities of handling e-governance projects, Village Knowledge Cenctres etc. These CICs are public/rural libraries. According to IFLA's (International Federation of Library Associations and Institutions) recommendations in order to make informed citizen there should be one library per one thousand people (*Bhattacharjee, 2002*), according to this, in India, there should be more than 3,30,000, however, right now there are only 60000 public libraries out of which Raja Rammohan Library Foundation has covered only 31,365 libraries. In Nepal there are very few public libraries and in Bangladesh there are only 1671 public libraries which are below the norms. First and foremost public/rural libraries are need to be set up with proper infrastructure so that they can handle E-governance and other such initiatives with proper aims and objectives. Secondly, information literacy needs to be launched at all levels of education putting them into across the curricula. Information literacy at community level for general awareness should be made on regular interval to strengthen the e-governance which will lead to better use of electronic information (Kumar S. et al., 2004). Further, The Internet penetration in three countries is very low owing to English language illiteracy. In India English language literacy is around 18% and in Nepal it is 6% and in Bangladesh is 7%. The content of the web page are in English almost 89% of the content through out of the world. So, basic literacy in English needs to be taken care into account to increase. Here also the English language divide are found in rural and towns. The local language webpage development should be given a primary emphasis but exceptionally in India there are many more languages and have control on these language is a great problem in such cases only option remains either literacy in English or National language Hindi should be made compulsory as basic literacy to be competent with ICT enabled environment. Standardization of local content in the web page should also be taken into concern.

Equality and equity of access can be ensured to one and all, only if the government commits to it by adopting a suitable library and information policy. The ICTs and the Internet are capable of creating a mental space in which there is a continuous conflict between the 'hegemonic forces' on the one hand and the ethnic minorities on the other. As such, the ICTs should be used only to promote the culture tolerance and respect for difference. The libraries and information networks can also play a leading role in promoting mutual understanding and peaceful co-existence.

REFERENCES

Anonymous (2007). *Village knowledge centres vital for rural development.* Available at http://www.thehindubusinessline.com/bline/2005/07/12/stories/2005071200770300.htm, Accessed on 12/07/2007

Bhattacharjee, R. (2002). IFLA: Country Report, India. *Public Library Services in India: Systems and Deficiencies. Available at* <www.ifla.org/VII/s8/anuual/cr02-in.htm> accessed on 21/06/2007 at 4.55 pm

International Telecommunication Union Report (2007). Available at <http://www.itu.int/ITU-D/ict/publications/wtdr_03/index.html> accessed on 11/06/2007

Kumar, S., Choudhury, S., & Shah, L. (2004). Information Literacy Mission in Digital environment- Prospects and Plans for developing Society in India. *70th IFLA conference*, Beunos Aires, Argentina, 22nd to 27th August, 2004. available at <http://www.ifla.org/IV/ifla70> accessed on 15/07/07

National Informatics Centres (2005). *Good Governance through ICT.* NIC, New Deli, 2005 <http:://home.nic.in> access on 14/07/07

National Knowledge Commission Report (2007). People's Access to Knowledge can Transform India. *Digital learning, III*(2), February 2007, (pp 22-24).

Norris, P (2000). Digital Divide. Available at http://Ksghome.Harvard.Edu/~Pnorris/Acrobat/Digitalch1.Pdf. Accessed On 13/10/2006

Wikipedia (2007). *E-Democracy.* Available at <http://en.wikipedia.org/wiki/E-democracy> accessed on 17/07/2007 at 3.23 pm

ENDNOTES

1 Bharatpur municipality e-governance portal, Nepal, Available at http://www.bharatpur-mun.org.np accessed on 14/06/2007

2 Department of Cottage and Small Scale Industry, Nepal, Available at http://www.docsi.gov.np accessed on 15/07/2007

3 E-procurement, Bolpatra, Nepal, Available at http://www.bolpatra.gov.np accessed on 15/07/2007

4 Nepal e-Market prices, Available at <http://www.b2b.com.np/new/index.php> accessed on 15/07/2007

5 Women empowerment through ICT, Available at <www.lbef.org/we.htm> accessed on 12/06/2007

6 Digital Broadcast Initiative, Available at <www.equalaccess.org/programs/nepal/index.htm> Accessed on 17/06/2007

7 El-Governance, Bangladesh, Available at <http://topics.developmentgateway.org/egovernment/rc/> accessed on 15/07/2007 at 7.34 pm

8 GrameenPhone Community Information Centres, Available at http://www.grameenphone.com/index.php?id=86 accessed on 15/05/2007

Section III
E-Governance and Online Services

Chapter VIII
Application of Natural Language Processing (NLP) Techniques in E-Governance

Siddhartha Ghosh
G. Narayanamma Institute of Technology & Sc., India

ABSTRACT

E-governance is the public sector's use of information and communication technologies (ICT) with the aim of improving information and service delivery, encouraging citizen participation in the decision-making process and making government more accountable, transparent, and effective. Effective and efficient e-governments deploy information and communication technology systems to deliver services through multiple channels that are accessible, fast, secure, reliable, seamless, and coherent. To implement better government-to-government (G2G), government-to-business (G2B), government-to-enterprise (G2E) and government-to-citizen (G2C) services a good governance should not only utilize ICT, it has to be also serious about implementing natural language processing (NLP) Techniques to reach up to the masses and make e-governance successful one. This chapter shows the need of applying NLP technologies in the field of e-governance and also tries to focus on the issues, which can be resolved very easily with the help of these modern technologies. It also shows the advantages of applying NLP in e-governance.

INTRODUCTION

Good governance is an act of balancing the interests that cut across community, space and time. The task is multi-dimensional and requires the employment of tools that can articulate the process through meaningful participation of the common man. Once we talk about the common man we should also think about how they communicate and how they understand

If the major aims of e-governance are:

- To strengthen and upgrade the present infrastructure of information technology in the ministry. It may also introduce the ICT for the first time in governance if it is not there till date.
- To bring in transparency the functioning by placing the information, to the extent possible, in the public domain. Public should not just wait for a Right for Information acts. They should be available just with a mouse click.
- To interlink the functioning of different offices to bring about synergy in the aspirations and enable effective and timely decision-making. Because the offline process are time consuming and tough to monitor.
- To develop public grievances and complaint system and eliminate the need of personal visits to offices by the public. This is the area where lot of work has to be done. There are lots of issues with public, which needs to be answered. Government cannot close their eye for a long time.
- To make available forms and information on the Internet and the facility of filling the applications from remote rural areas-Web enabled application system. Here the application of natural language processing (NLP) system can just totally change the face of a government.

Then the next major point should be:

- Application of modern technologies by the e-governance (i.e. NLP techniques) to make a governance good governance, to make good governance a better one and then the best. And most important issue is to hold that position for a long time with making citizens happy.

What is Natural Language Processing (NLP)?

According to Wikipedia Natural language processing is a sub-field of **artificial intelligence** and linguistics. It studies the problems of automated generation and understanding of natural human languages. Natural language generation systems convert information from computer databases into normal-sounding human language, and natural language understanding systems convert samples of human language into more formal representations that are easier for computer programs to manipulate.

ORIGINS

The idea of using digital computers in NLP is 'old', possibly because one of the first uses of computers was in breaking military codes in the Second World War. Some computer scientists appear to have reflection that Russian (for example) is just English in a different code. In which case, since codes can be broken, so can Russian. This idea assumes there is a common 'meaning base' to all natural languages, apart from of their surface differences. The overwhelming harmony among linguists is that this is simply not true.

'Artificial Language Processing', in the form of compilers and interpreters for programming languages, was a key element in the success of digital computers from their earliest days. This success indisputably expectanted research into NLP (and also encouraged an optimistic approach).

There have been cycles of sanguinity and pessimism in the field of NLP (we are possibly in a more optimistic phase at present); although some very real advances have been made, the target of a general NLP system remains intangible. Historically, computer scientists have often been far too over-optimistic about NLP, probably for some of the reasons noted above.

It is also important to note that there are differences between natural languages. More work has probably been done on English than on any other language, largely because of the importance of American researchers, although there are very active workers in Europe and Japan. However, English is in some ways an untypical language, as it uses few inflections and relies heavily on word order. Textbooks and other introductory sources written in English rarely contain satisfactory discussions of NLP for languages with markedly different grammatical structures. Very less work is done in other languages in Asian countries like India, Iran, China and some others in comparison to USA.

We can distinguish at least three discrete 'levels' in processing NL:

- **Sounds/Speech:** If these three words are considered, spoken by a native English speaker from the south of England: input, intake, income. It's clear that all three words contain the element in with the same meaning. To input is to put something in; the intake of a water pump is the place where water is taken in; one's income is the money that he earn, i.e. that comes in. Is the element in pronounced the same in all three words (by the specified speaker)? Careful listening will show that it is not. The word input is pronounced as if spelt imput, whereas intake is pronounced as spelt. If N stands for the sound usually spelt ng in English (e.g. in words like sing or singer), then income is pronounced iNcome.
- **Grammar:** Grammar in this context refers to both the structure of words (morphology) and the structure of sentences (syntax).
- **Meaning:** Meaning can be subdivided in many ways. A simple division is between semantics, referring to the meaning of words and thus the meaning of sentences formed by those words[3] and pragmatics, referring to the meanings intended by the originator of the words. Note the meaning of sentences depends not only on the meaning of the words, but also on rules about the meaning of word combinations, word orders, etc.

NLP includes -

SPEECH SYNTHESIS (SS)

Although this may not at first sight appear very 'intelligent', the synthesis of natural-sounding speech is technically complex and almost certainly requires some 'understanding' of what is being spoken to ensure, for example, correct intonation.

Speech synthesis is the artificial production of human speech. A computer system used for this purpose is called a speech synthesizer, and can be implemented in software or hardware. A text-to-speech (TTS) system converts normal language text into speech; other systems render symbolic linguistic representations like phonetic transcriptions into speech.

Synthesized speech can be created by concatenating pieces of recorded speech that are stored in a database. Systems differ in the size of the stored speech units; a system that stores phones or diphones provides the largest output range, but may lack clarity. For specific usage domains, the storage of entire words or sentences allows for high-quality output. Alternatively, a synthesizer can incorporate a model of the vocal tract and other human voice characteristics to create a completely "synthetic" voice output.

The quality of a speech synthesizer is judged by its similarity to the human voice, and by its ability to be understood. An intelligible text-to-speech program allows people with visual impairments or reading disabilities to listen to written works on a home computer. Many computer operating systems have included speech synthesizers since the early 1980s.

SPEECH RECOGNITION (SR)

Basically this is the reduction of continuous sound waves to discrete words. Speech recognition (also known as automatic speech recognition or computer speech recognition) converts spoken words to machine-readable input (for example, to the binary code for a string of character codes). The term voice recognition may be imprecisely used to refer to speech recognition, but more precisely refers to speaker recognition, which attempts to identify the person speaking, as opposed to what is being said.

Speech recognition applications include voice dialing (e.g., "Call home"), call routing (e.g., "I would like to make a collect call"), domotic appliance control and content-based spoken audio search (e.g., find a podcast where particular words were spoken), simple data entry (e.g., entering a credit card number), preparation of structured documents (e.g., a radiology report), speech-to-text processing (e.g., word processors or emails), and in aircraft cockpits (e.g., Direct Voice Input).

NATURAL LANGUAGE UNDERSTANDING (NLU)

Natural language understanding (NLU) is a key component in a dialog system. Particularly in a spoken dialog system. It uses Natural language processing techniques.

Steps of NLU:

- General Natural language processing
- Named Entity identification
- Part-of-speech tagging
- Parsing
- Semantic slot extraction
- Dialog act identification

NATURAL LANGUAGE GENERATION (NLG)

Generating appropriate NL responses to unpredictable inputs. Natural Language Generation (NLG) is the natural language processing task of generating natural language from a machine representation system such as a knowledge base or a logical form.

Some people view NLG as the opposite of natural language understanding. The difference can be put this way: whereas in natural language understanding the system needs to disambiguate the input sentence to produce the machine representation language, in NLG the system needs to make decisions about how to put a concept into words.

STAGES OF NLG

The process to generate text can be as simple as keeping a list of canned text that is copied and pasted, possibly linked with some glue text. The results may be satisfactory in simple domains such as horoscope machines or generators of personalized business letters. However, a sophisticated NLG system needs to include stages of planning and merging of information to enable the generation of text that looks natural and does not become repetitive. Typical stages are:

- **Content determination:** Determination of the salient features that are worth being said. Methods used in this stage are related to data mining.
- **Discourse planning:** Overall organization of the information to convey.
- **Sentence aggregation:** Merging of similar sentences to improve readability and naturalness. For example, the sentences "The next train is the Caledonian Express" and "The next train leaves Aberdeen at 10am" can be aggregated to form "The next train,

which leaves at 10am, is the Caledonian express".

- **Lexicalisation:** Putting words to the concepts.
- **Referring expression generation:** Linking words in the sentences by introducing pronouns and other types of means of reference.
- **Syntactic and morphological realization:** This stage is the inverse of parsing: given all the information collected above, syntactic and morphological rules are applied to produce the surface string.
- **Orthographic realization:** Matters like casing, punctuation, and formatting are resolved.

MACHINE TRANSLATION (MT)

Translating one NL into another. Machine translation, sometimes referred to by the acronym MT, is a sub-field of computational linguistics that investigates the use of computer software to translate text or speech from one natural language to another. At its basic level, MT performs simple substitution of words in one natural language for words in another. Using corpus techniques, more complex translations may be attempted, allowing for better handling of differences in linguistic typology, phrase recognition, and translation of idioms, as well as the isolation of anomalies.

Current machine translation software often allows for customization by domain or profession (such as weather reports) — improving output by limiting the scope of allowable substitutions. This technique is particularly effective in domains where formal or formulaic language is used. It follows then that machine translation of government and legal documents more readily produces usable output than conversation or less standardized text.

Improved output quality can also be achieved by human intervention: for example, some systems are able to translate more accurately if the user has unambiguously identified which words in the text are names. With the assistance of these techniques, MT has proven useful as a tool to assist human translators, and in some cases can even produce output that can be used "as is". However, current systems are unable to produce output of the same quality as a human translator, particularly where the text to be translated uses casual language.

MAJOR TASKS IN NLP

- Automatic summarization
- Foreign Language Reading Aid
- Foreign Language Writing Aid
- Information extraction
- Information retrieval
- Machine translation
- Named entity recognition
- Natural language generation
- Optical Character Recognition
- Question answering
- Speech recognition
- Spoken dialogue management
- Text simplification
- Text to speech
- Text-proofing

In the next couple of points we will try to focus on how some of the above mentioned techniques could be utilized to enhance e-governance services. Before that we will have a look in to the major e-governance projects for any country.

MAJOR E-GOVERNANCE RELATED ACTIVITIES

1. Creation of Country Portal
2. Creation of State Portals
3. EDI
4. eBiz
5. eProcurement

Country Portal

Country portal is a one-stop shop to all Government Business in any country. There are various governments departments and ministries in the Centre and various agencies. The Country portal is a single link to all the departments and agencies and also the state/sub governments.

Services Those are Offered Under this Category

- Forms (Downloading)
- Directory Services (For E-Mail, telephones, Addresses, Contact Personnel of all Government Offices)
- Government Schemes
- Links to all other Government sites
- Links to Education
- Health Services
- Survey Reports
- Parliamentary Discussions
- Trade related Queries
- Legal sub-portal
- Grievance Handling
- File Monitoring
- State Government Links
- Employment
- Who's who of Government
- News etc

State Portals

State portals are the single window Government entry points of various States. On lines of the National portal the State portals incorporates all most the same solutions mentioned above as well as link to central Govt. resources.

EDI

Electronic Data Processing can be implemented in every level of central and state governments. Electronic Data Interchange (EDI) is a set of standards for structuring information that is to be electronically exchanged between and within businesses, organizations, government entities and other groups. The standards describe structures that emulate documents, for example purchase orders to automate purchasing. The term EDI is also used to refer to the implementation and operation of systems and processes for creating, transmitting, and receiving EDI documents.

Electronic Data Interchange (EDI) can be formally defined as 'The transfer of structured data, by agreed message standards, from one computer system to another without human intervention'. Most other definitions used are variations on this theme.

Despite being relatively unheralded, in this era of technologies such as XML Web services, the Internet and the World Wide Web, EDI is still the data format used by the vast majority of electronic commerce transactions in the world.

e-Biz

The e-Biz project is a single window for all Government to Business services. The proposed E-BIZ can incorporate the following services:

- Information about laws, regulation, codes and procedures involved in running businesses in the country
- Filing of taxation, returns, claims and refunds
- The registration and start up of a Company/ Business/ SME or any form of Organization
- Issue of Licenses, permits & certification
- Renewal of Licenses, permits & certification
- To facilitate the FDI
- Filing of reports, compliance of statutory provisions
- Availability of facilities like telephone, water, electricity, transport, posts

- Window for all Procurement by the Government
- Interactions with the Stock Exchange, SEBI and other regulatory bodies
- Recruitment of skilled manpower
- Feedback on various initiatives / Discussion forums thereof
- Source of funding (banking & FI's)
- Obtaining Land and building approvals
- Compliance of labor laws and interaction with trade unions
- Issues related to IPR
- Technology transfer from R& D institutions to industry
- Getting feedback on market trends (market research)
- To act as the interface to international agencies

E-Procurement

Each Government Department, Agency, State Government at time procures material. With the use of ICT in procurement process, the procurement overhead cost will go down. There had been examples in the west wherein Governments have reduced their costs by over 50% by choosing E-Procurement.

NLP Techniques in E-Governance and How ?

NLP based e-governance systems are already in use some countries. As for example Natural Language Based Information Retrieval System of India Anveshak (The Questioner) is a Natural Language based Information Retrieval system, which can efficiently and accurately provide explicit information in natural language text to the question intended to be queried on a certain document, developed by CDAC, India.

More initiative has to be taken in various level of state and central govt. to implement NLP based e-governance models or systems in every country. And mainly when it is matter of multi

Figure 1. A multi lingual e-governance portal of USA government

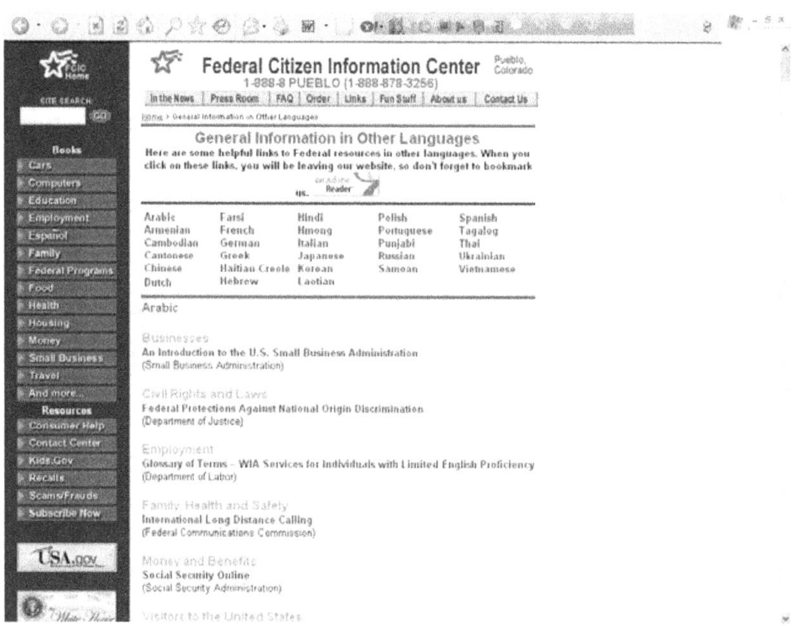

lingual countries like India then NLP may be the black horse of the e-governance.

As all of us know that e-governance is not only for educated people its for every one. Starting from a Govt. employee , up to a simple farmer in village any one can utilize the facilities offered by e-governance systems. Now lets us take an example – a farmer want to put the prices for his rice to sell through the kiosks available in village. If he is an educated person he can use the kiosk or internet connected computer, which is kept in the gram panchayet (village court) office, very easily. If he is not educated then a speech recognition (speech to text converter) system may be just work for him as the best friend.

As well as, if the **speech recognition system** is also enhanced with a speech translation system the even though the person may use his mother language like Gujrati and can quote the price in English. The NLP based machine translation system will be used here as a human friend.

Blind people can use speech recognition based systems very easily. They can do form fill up for any govt. job application, death and birth registration, online application for including name in voter list etc. They can just utter the sentences; words and the system will help them to feed it in the required places.

USE OF NATURAL LANGUAGE IN GOVERNMENT WEBSITES

As government Websites are full of information, forms, data etc. it is the major vehicle of offering e-governance services. In this context the use of multilingual Web portals, providing, e-governance services, can change the face of any govt. as well as it helps in overall development of any country or state. In India along with the central govt. so many state govt. offers multi lingual Websites or local language based Websites. In this regard we can name few of them which have already become very popular for their services.

Some good effort has been made or initiative has been taken form India Govt. side like the Hindi Website of Ministry of Home Affairs (HA). Such effort is not found from smaller states level.

Figure-2. Hindi Web site of Ministry of HA, India

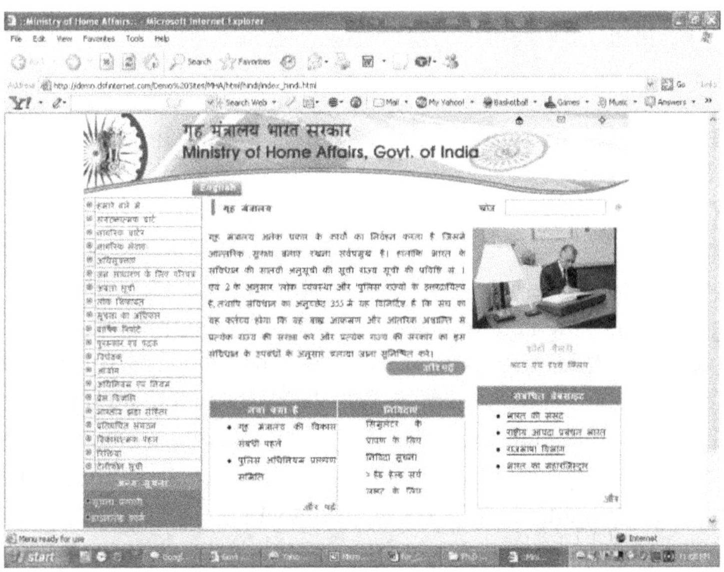

Figure-3. Official Tamil Web site of government of Tamilnadu

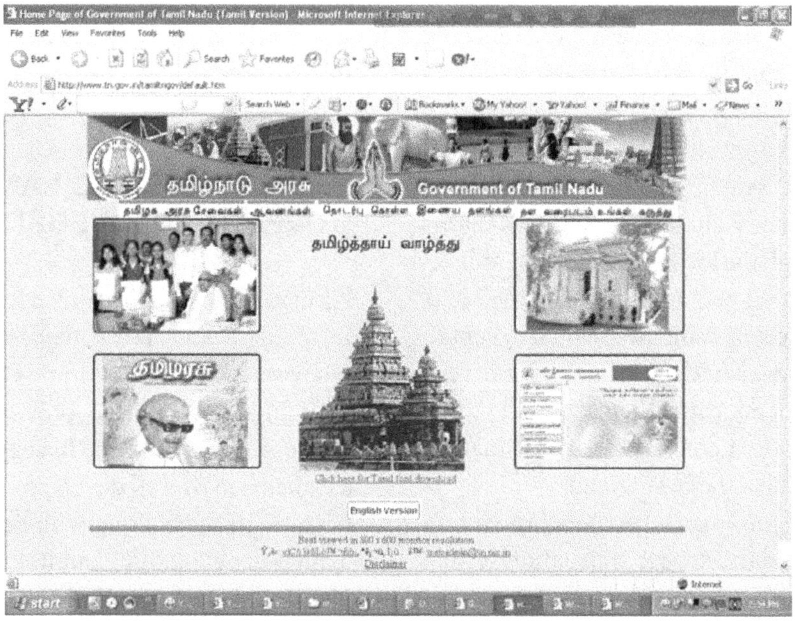

Where as Govt. of Andhra Pradesh, Tamilnadu, Karnataka, and West Bengal have made good effort in this direction. A major reason may be the unavailability of the funds in this direction for all the states. But the Time has come when we should take up the issue of using local languages for developing Websites for various purposes, like starting from basic information distribution to writing online exams in local languages.

NATURAL LANGUAGE GENERATION SYSTEMS IN E-GOVERNANCE

Natural Language Generation is a sub field of Computational Linguistics and language-oriented Artificial Intelligence research devoted to studying and simulating the production of written or spoken discourse. The study of human language generation is a multidisciplinary enterprise, requiring expertise in areas of linguistics, psychology, engineering and computer science. One of the central goals is to investigate how computer programs can be made to produce high-quality natural language text from computer-internal representations of information.

Natural language generation often is characterized as a process that has to start from the communicative goals of the writer or speaker and needs to employ some sort of planning to progressively convert them into written or spoken words. In this view, the general aims of the language producer are refined into goals that are increasingly linguistic in nature, culminating in low-level goals to produce particular words. Usually, a modularization of the generation process is assumed which roughly distinguishes between a strategically (deciding what to say) and a tactical (deciding how to say it) part. This strategy-tactics distinction is partly mirrored by a distinction between text planning and sentence generation. Text planning is concerned with working out the large-scale structure of the text to be produced and may also comprise content selection. The result of this sub process is commonly taken to be a tree-like discourse structure, which has at each leaf an instruction to produce a single sentence. These instructions are then passed in turn to a sentence generator, whose task can be further subdivided into sentence planning, i.e. organizing the content of each sentence, and the final step of surface realization, i.e. converting sentence-sized chunks of representation into grammatically correct sentences.

Any e-governance system, which uses natural language generation techniques, can provide better service as a part of e-governance. As for example – a natural language generation based e-governance system can help the people to listen to the text as an audio files once any one selects them. Now the person may be educated but not familiar with that text but he can understand and speak or for blind people it can read news, information, process, job vacancies information etc. For elderly people having short sight this tool will be a useful one.

The NLP based question answer systems can just help the people like anything. A farmer who can not read text properly can even get help from a Website, like how to use fertilizer in filed. How to grow new crop and how to water them using new techniques. Govt. institutions like India railway and Air India etc can utilize such systems for common people to make the services much people friendly.

CONCLUSION

Moving house, having a baby, setting up a business... there are numerous reasons why citizens or companies contact public administrations, and local government are under increasing pressure to improve the quality and speed of service delivery. More than offering just Web-based information, Time has come to give citizens personalized assistance and solutions to enquiries, entered entirely using natural language processing techniques. Its not a new concept but as the same time still now, we fill, these techniques are adopted by so many good e-governance providers. Time has come more R&D work has to be initiated in govt. level to take up this issue much seriously and making e-governance a common man's friend.

REFERENCES

Baweja, Y. (2005, August). Does E-Governance means Good governance? *Yojana, 49.*

Ghosh, S., & Fatima, S.S. (2007). A Web Based English to Bengali Text Converter. *In the 3rd Indian International Conference on Artificial Intelligence (IICAI-07)*, Pune, India, December 17-19.

Ghosh, S., & Fatima, S.S. (2007). Retrieval of XML data to support NLP applications. ICAI'07- *The 2007 International Conference on Artificial Intelligence Monte Carlo Resort*, Las Vegas, Nevada, USA ,June 25-28.

Ghosh, S., & Fatima, S.S. (2007, June). Use of local languages in Indian portals. CSI Communication, (pp 4-12).

Khitoliya, R.K., & Tanwar, N. (2005, October). *E-Governance: An aid to the development of Isolated Rural Communities in Developing Countries, Agriculture Today.*

Khitoliya, R.K., Moudgil, G., & Bansal, M. (2003). Potential application of IT based Techniques in Residential/Institutional Buildings. *Seminar of Information Technology in built environment, 141,* Bangalore, November 28-29.

Raushina, A. (2005, March). E-governance for good Governance-The national E-governance Action Plan, *Kurukshetra, 53*(5).

Sachdeva, S (2002, December). *e-Governance Action Plan for India.*

WEB SITES

http://egovstandards.gov.in/localisation_wg/localisation_std

http://portal.unesco.org/ci/en/ev.php-URL_ID=3038&URL_DO=DO_TOPIC&URL_SECTION=201.html

http://www.cdac.in/html/aai/anvesh.asp

http://www.pueblo.gsa.gov/multilanguage/multi-lang.htm?urlnet99

http://www.egovjournal.com/journal_archive_voli_issue1.htm

Chapter IX
Assessing E-Governance Online-Service Quality (EGOSQ)

Anand Agrawal
Researcher and Consultant, India

ABSTRACT

A primary goal of e-governance is providing online-services to citizens over the internet (Web portals) to facilitate government-to-citizen (G2C) and citizen-to-government (C2G) interactions and transactions. This chapter provides a perspective on the users' perceptions of the attributes which determine e-governance online-service quality. The research based approach is used to first develop the discussion on the needs of quality "e-governance online services" (EGOS) and then a research study is used to demonstrate development of measurement instrumentation to measure online service quality from the users' perspective. The presented method and the instrument can be adopted in any country/state with minor contextual modifications. The limitations and future directions for scholars and researchers to facilitate the knowledge in measuring and thus, improving in e-governance online service quality is also presented at the end of the chapter.

INTRODUCTION

Governments all over the world, especially in developed nations are facing enormous pressures to create and deliver high quality services for their citizens. As a result of the rapid development in information and communication technology, e-governance initiatives provided online interaction using electronic means like internet. E-governance is defined as 'the application of electronic means in the interaction between government and citizens and government and businesses, as well as in internal government operations, to simplify and improve democratic, government and business aspects of Governance' (Backus, 2001). This chapter focuses on methods and approaches of assessing e-governance online-service quality (EGOSQ)[1] from the perspective of users of such services (Citizens). Existing studies from the domains of service quality measurement, e-service quality, technology adoption model, system quality and self service technology form the background of the chapter in order to present the conceptual understanding of online service quality parameters. The following sections deal with method to devise the instrument that can be used to measure online e-governance service (EGOSQ). This chapter is aimed to demonstrate the development of quality instrumentation to measure e-governance online service quality.

NEED TO MEASURE E-GOVERNANCE ONLINE SERVICE QUALITY

E-governance should not be seen as a vehicle to deliver information over the internet, but should facilitate citizens to participate in decision making process, reflecting their wants and welfare. "UNESCO and COMNET-IT define governance as the process by which society steers itself."[2] Citizens' awareness level, acceptance level and hopes and fears about the e-governance can be the important factors determining the success of e-governance initiatives (Agrawal and Fuloria, 2003). A high quality of online-service delivery by government will ensure high acceptance level and fewer fears. But, at present, most of the existing studies on e-governance service quality focus on the governments' (service provider) perspective. Such studies are limited to discussions on the need to develop, and to conform the quality standards (Tawil and Sait, 2002), with focus on engineering or system dimensions, or, organizing and streamlining administrative and organizational processes. Though, most of the government institutions in developing nations and government agencies till now have been ill-prepared for the dramatic changes in information technology and human knowledge, yet citizens increasingly expect the same level of service from governments as they do from the private sector. Most of the citizens and institutions perceive all government functions inward looking and self-oriented. This is analogous to the product concept in Marketing where firms try to improve their products without involving customers and without knowing customers' preferences. The results of such approach are drastically negative as customer does not adopt such products/services rapidly.

Globally, workshops and the conferences for developing quality standards for e-governance have realized the need for a separate approach for developing 'beneficiary oriented,' standards, but still, Action Plans generally emphasize IT enabled services management standards, technical standards and mere complaint management standards (E-Governance Standards Workshop, Hyderabad, Andhra Pradesh, September 20-21, 2006).

According to e-governance maturity model, provision of information and enabling transactions are regarded as completion of first/second stage of e-governance implementation (as suggested by Gartner e-governance maturity model). Many government web portals are already providing information and enabling transactions. However, the issue arises now is how to find the success of these stages? Is mere these provisions means success? In fact, until and unless majority of citizens adopt the e-governance and use government portals extensively, the success of e-governance will not be realized. Once, the citizen users are satisfied with the e-services, the word of mouth is the fastest vehicle for rapid adoption of these services by other citizens. Therefore, there is a need to understand e-governance users' perceptions, specifically, what constitutes a high quality e-governance online service quality to ensure the acceptance, and participation of citizens in the governance.

UNDERSTANDING E-GOVERNANCE ONLINE SERVICES

There are eight related domains which can help in understanding online services. These are: Service Quality Measurement, e-Service Quality Measurement, System Quality, Information Quality, Technology Adoption Model (TAM), End user satisfaction, Self Service Technologies and e-governance assessment models. Earlier many researchers have studied these domains to develop instrumentations to measure e-service quality (Agrawal, 2007). E-service refers to electronic service – where the service is delivered through electronic means like mobile, telephone, ATMs or internet etc. This chapter uses the term online services, that denotes essentially electronic services delivered through internet sites.

Studying these domains helps in getting conceptual understanding of online services, thus, providing a number of constructs which can be included in online service quality measurement instrument. Service Quality Measurement literature indicates the aspects of service to measure-like 'what to measure' and 'how to measure.' e-Service Quality Measurement literature helps in exploring the impact of delivery of service using technology on service quality perceptions. TAM provides the direction to analyze the motivational aspect of use of e-service. End user satisfaction is useful for understanding the behavioural aspects. Self Service Technologies (SSTs) help in exploring the behavioural orientations towards the internet use as a technology and system quality explains the engineering and operational aspects of technology. In addition, e-governance assessment models provide attributes related specific to e-governance services. A combined and integrated view of all these concepts provide the initial understanding of online-services, essential to proceed further towards developing e-governance online service quality measurement instrument.

A. Service Quality Measurement

Service quality measurements literature describes two major dimensions of service quality - Core Dimensions/Outcome aspects concerning 'What is delivered' and Relational Dimensions/Process aspects concerning 'How it is delivered' (Gronroos 1982; McDougall and Levesque 1992; Parasuraman et al.1991, Dabholkar, Thorpe & Rentz, 1996). In late 1990s, research studying the impact of environment on service quality was started, largely after the Bitner's (1992) seminal work on physical environment's effect on the service quality. The most widely known instrument to measure service quality consists of twenty-two statements (SERVQUAL) in which measure performance across five dimensions of Service Quality (Parasuraman, Zeithaml, and Berry, 1985). SERVQUAL measures the difference between expectations and perceptions of performance levels of the service attributes. It considers service quality as the degree and direction of discrepancy between consumers' perception of performance and expectations, where expectations are viewed as desired or what consumers feel a service provider should offer, and the perception of performance denotes what the service providers are actually delivering. Bolton and Drew (1991) suggested that service quality is a function of consumers' residual perception of the service quality from the prior period and his or her level of (dis)satisfaction with the current level of service performance. Later, Cronin and Taylor (1992) suggested that SERVPERF scale, based on performance perceptions alone provides a better measure for service quality as compared to the measures based on the discrepancy between expectation and perception. The attributes in SERVPERF scale were kept same as SERVQUAL. Though, the core dimensions concern two aspects of service quality measurement –'what is delivered' and 'how it is delivered.' SERVQUAL and SERVPERF measures seem to measure just one aspect of it, i.e. 'how it is delivered.' Brady and

Cronin (2001) argued that SERVQUAL attributes do not suggest measure which aspects of service should be measured, more specifically, if the reliability is perceived as a dimension contributing to service quality, then which aspects of service quality should be reliable? Therefore, there is a need to focus on not only 'how the service is delivered' but also on 'what is to be delivered.' Parasuraman and Grewal (2000) suggested that research is needed on whether "the definitions and relative importance of the five service quality dimensions change when customers interact with technology rather than with service personnel."

B. E-Service Quality Measurement

Several dimensions of e-service quality are identified by various studies Table 1 shows the dimensions. Thee is a lack of consistency is the proposed dimensions by various researchers. Other problem is that most of the e-services quality measurement research is limited to e-retailing only. Another set of research exist that aimed to measure the website quality (Loiacono et al, 2000; Yoo and Donthu, 2001). There is a lack of substantial research providing a generalized scale developed using a variety of e-service industry. Also, comparative studies to find the best approach (discrepancy/gap, or, perception based) to measure e-service quality are also non existent (Agrawal, 2007). There is a predominance of perception based measurement approach in e-service quality measurement research. But, the comparative study by Agrawal (2007) suggests that discrepancy/gap based approach is superior to the perception based approach in measuring e-service quality.

C. Technology Adoption Model (TAM)

Davis (1989) model is one of the most widely used to predict technology adoption. TAM, is a modified form of Theory of Reasoned Action (TRA) that incorporates technology into the model to explain the usage behaviour of Technology. TRA (Fishbein & Ajzen, 1975) suggests that behavioural intention is the primary determinant of an individual's behaviour. TAM identifies the causal linkages between an individual user's attitudes and perceptions toward technology and the actual adoption of technology. The theory emphasizes that perceptions about 'how useful is this for me' and 'how easy it is' to use are the determinants that influence technology adoption. The first construct, "Perceived Usefulness", is defined as "the prospective user's subjective probability that using a specific application system will increase his or her job performance." The second construct, "Perceived Ease of Use", is the "degree to which the prospective user expects the target system to be free of effort." The use of online-services can be viewed as similar to the new technology adoption, therefore, the two constructs: 'Perceived Ease of Use', and 'perceived usefulness' seem important in assessing online-services quality (Yang and Fang, 2004). Several key dimensions of online-services quality like: customization, content, reliability, and response are found to have significant effect on perceived ease of use and perceived usefulness, which in turn influence attitude towards usage and re-usage of websites also. (Lin and Wu, 2002).

D. System Quality

Shannon and Weaver (1949), Mason (1978) and Deleon and McLean (1992) suggested three levels of information which yield six categories, namely, System Quality, Information Quality, Use, User Satisfaction and Individual and Organizational Impacts. For online service quality assessment study, System quality, Information Quality and User satisfaction are relevant.

(a) System Quality

System Quality research focuses on the engineering-oriented performance characteristics. Table 2 shows empirical measures of system quality.

Table 1. Proposed dimensions of e-service quality by previous researchers

Kaynama and Black (2000) *"E-QUAL"*	**Zeithaml et al (2001)**	**Liljander et al (2001)**	**Loiacono et al. (2000) *"WEBQUAL"***
1. Responsiveness, 2. Content and Purpose, 3. Accessibility, 4. Navigation, 5. Design and Presentation, 6. Background, 7. Personalization and customization	1. Reliability, 2. Responsiveness, 3. Access, 4. Flexibility, 5. Ease of navigation, 6. Efficiency, 7. Assurance/trust, 8. Security/privacy, 9. Price knowledge, 10. Site aesthetics 11. Customization / personalization.	1. User Interface, 2. Responsiveness, 3. Reliability, 4. Customization 5. Assurance	1. Information fit to task, 2. Interaction, 3. Trust, 4. Response time, 5. Design, 6. Intuitiveness, 7. Visual appeal, 8. Innovativeness 9. Flow (Emotional appeal), 10. Integrated communication, 11. Business processes, 12. Substitutability
Lin and Wu (2002)	**Zeithaml (2002)**	**van Riel et al (2004)**	**Yang, Jun and Peterson (2004)**
1. Information content, 2. Customization, 3. Response rate	***Core e-SQ*** Efficiency, Reliability, Fulfilment Privacy. ***Recovery-SQ*** Responsiveness, Compensation, Contact	1. Usability, 2. E-Scape Design, 3. Customization, Assurance 4. Responsiveness.	1. Reliability 2. Responsiveness 3. Competence 4. Easer of Use 5. Product Portfolio 6. Security
Yoo and Donthu (2001) SITE-QUAL	***Li, Tan and Xie (2002)***	**Zeithaml, Parasuraman and Malhotra (2005) "e-SQUAL"**	**Agrawal (2007)**
1. Ease of Use 2. Processing Speed 3. Aesthetic Design 4. Interactive Responsiveness	1. Website Design 2. Customer Service 3. Reliability 4. Privacy	1. Tangibility 2. Reliability 3. Responsiveness 4. Integration of Communication 5. Assurance 6. Quality of Information 7. Empathy	1. Information 2. Interaction 3. Integration 4. Access 5. Corporate Image 6. Emotional engagement 7. Active Service Recovery 8. Assurance

(b) Information Quality

Information Quality research focuses on the quality of the information system output. Bailey and Pearson (1983) suggested 39 system related items to measure user satisfaction. The most important items are: Information accuracy, Output timeliness, Reliability, Completeness, Relevance, Precision and Currency. Many information quality criteria are included within the area of 'User Information Satisfaction' (Iivari 1987; Iivari and Koskela 1987). The constructs used are: "informativeness", consisting of relevance, comprehensiveness, recentness, accuracy and credibility, "accessibility", consisting of convenience, timeliness and interpretability; and "adaptability.". Table 3 summarizes the attributes found by the researches on information quality.

(c) End User Satisfaction

Doll and Torkzadeh (1988) suggested 12 items with five dimensions to measure end-user satisfaction: Content, Accuracy, Format, Ease of Use and Timeliness. E-services users are the end users of the computer programs –a part of the online-

Table 2. Empirical measures of system quality (Deleon and McLean, 1992)

Authors	Description Of Study	Type	Description of Measure(s)
Bailey and Pearson (1983)	Overall I/S, (8 organizations, 32 managers)	Field	1. Convenience of access 2. Flexibility of System 3. Integration of Systems 4. Response Time
Conklin, Gotterer and Rickman (1982)	Transaction Processing: (one organization)	Lab	Response time
Franz and Rokey (1986)	Specific I/S, 34 organizations, (118 user managers)	Field	Perceived usefulness of I/S (12 items)
Mahmood (1987)	Specific I/S, (61 managers)	Field	Flexibility of system
Srinivisan (1985)	Computer Based modelling System, (29 firms)	Field	1. Response Time 2. System Reliability 3. System accessibility

Table 3. Empirical measures of information quality (deLeon and McLean, 1992)

Authors	Description Of Study	Type	Description of Measure(s)
Bailey and Pearson (1983)	Overall I/S, (8 organizations, 32 managers)	Field	1. Accuracy 2. Precision 3. Currency 4. Timeliness 5. Reliability 6. Completeness 7. Conciseness 8. Format 9. Relevance
King and Epstein (1983)	Overall I/S (2 firms, 76 managers)	Field	Information 1. Currency 2. Sufficiency 3. Understanding 4. Freedom from Bias 5. Timeliness 6. Reliability 7. Relevance 8. Comparability 9. Quantitativeness

service design. The goals of the I/S are to help in conducting transactions, to keep the records and to help consumers to seek desired product and service information through websites.

The literature review suggests that technology adoption model provides the conceptual clarification about the basic motivational reasons of using technology. TAM attributes can provide valuable insights to the customers' assessment of e-governance online-services quality. Moreover, the attributes of the system quality, information quality and end using computing categories overlap.

E. Self Service Technologies

According to Meuter et al (2000), "*Self-service technologies (SSTs) are technological interfaces that enable customers to produce a service independent of direct service employee involvement*". Automated teller machines (ATMs), telephone banking, and services over the Internet, such as Federal Express package tracking and online brokerage services are examples of self services." SST is advantageous as it can be utilized by customers to get customization and flexibility of service offerings, recovery from service failures, and, instant spontaneous delight. Meuter et al (2000) found major factors leading to a satisfactory evaluation of an SST experience - SST's ability to bail customers out of immediate or troubling situations due to SSTs' pervasive nature and relatively easy accessibility, customers' perception of the relative advantage they get from using an SST in comparison with interpersonal service delivery alternatives and the perception that technology does what it intends to do effectively, i.e. "the novelty of the technology and its ability to perform these services may be satisfying" On the other hand dissatisfying incidents were found to be caused by process failures -due to the breakdown at some point after the SST encounter has occurred but before the service consumption was completed, poor design, and, customer-driven failure where customers are willing to take some of the blame when dissatisfying encounters with SSTs occur. Feeling of enjoyment and control ownership by consumers are also found as important factors for satisfaction.

DESIGNING THE MEASUREMENT INSTRUMENTATION

To develop the instrumentation to measure, referred in this chapter as e-Governance Online Service Quality (EGOSQ), a two stage research needs to be done. The first stage is to conduct a qualitative research consisting of focus groups and in-depth interviews, the second stage comprises of questionnaire survey. This is the basic methodology to develop any quality measurement instrumentation. A measurement scale developed by combining the exploratory and the empirical study provides the best result. Therefore, in order to develop EGOSQ, a pool of forty eight attributes, conceptualized in seven dimensions was formed as a result of the literature survey on eight related domains mentioned above. This pool was refined using the qualitative techniques of focus groups and in-depth interviews. The focus groups' participants were registered users of e-sevaonline.com (a web-portal by Andhra Pradesh government of India, providing online services to citizens). The groups were balanced in terms of gender. Total three focus groups were organized to find out the relevance of the dimensions extracted by the literature review. The resulting pool of dimensions and items was further refined through in-depth interviews of ten registered users of e-sevaonline.com. This pool of items was further elaborated to a panel of experts, academicians and researchers to get their feedback. The result of the qualitative study was a pool of twenty six items spread across proposed seven overlapping dimensions (See Table 4). These 26 items are cast into questions described below.

Pre-Test and Data Collection

The questionnaire survey was administered to the registered users of esevaonline.com. The respondent's profiles ranging from college students, housewives to industry executives and academicians. Face validity of the measures was validated by group of experts or judges, who looked at the scale and measures to decide whether it measures what its name suggests (Judd et al. 1991, p. 54). After the feedback from six academics and four professionals who are expert in online-service, some items were modified. Then, the questionnaire was forwarded through email to more than

100 online e-sevaonline.com registered users to get their critique. After getting the feedback from 16 respondents, the questionnaire was further revised.

Measures

The questionnaire after the pre-test consisted of:

- Twenty Six e-service quality items, each item cast into two set of statements. First statement reflects the expectation of the customer about the levels of e-governance online-services that should be offered, and second reflecting the perception of the customers of the level of e-governance online-services they are getting, Five point Likert Scale was used ranging from Completely Disagree to Completely Agree for these statements. (Refer table 4 for all items of questionnaires)
- Set of three questions on overall service quality, two questions on use satisfaction and two questions on behavioural satisfaction. Five point Likert Scale was used for these questions (Refer table 5 for these questions)
- Set of eleven demographic and online-service usage related questions (Refer table 5 for these questions)

Data Collection and Analysis

Convenience and snowballing sampling was used due to lack of access to database of e-sevaonline.com users. Sixty five valid responses were obtained after a month of survey. As the study takes into consideration both of the approaches of quality measurement (Perception and discrepancy/gap-perceptions minus expectations), data analysis was done using both the scores separately as separate sets of data. For profile of the respondents refer Table 6.

After data collection, for each of the proposed dimensions, scale reliability analysis was done for both sets of data, which provided vague results. Therefore, an exploratory factor analysis was carried out to get a fresh look into the dimensional structure of the data. As, the principal component analysis in both sets of data could not provide any pattern, principal axis factoring with oblique rotation (factors were found correlated with each other) provided better results. The perception score data provided four dimensions, with 16 items in total. The discrepancy score data provided seven dimensions with 22 items in total. Scale items reduction was done using the criteria of corrected item-total correlation in SPSS. Dimensions with less than coefficient value of 0.5 were discarded. Table 7 provides the results of factor analysis and coefficient of alpha values of the dimensions extracted from factor analysis. Good consistency in the results was observed in case of both approaches of measurement as 16 similar items were retained in the questionnaires after the statistical reduction of items. Even, in terms of factor loadings, similar loading patterns emerged in two measurement approaches.

The relationship between the overall online-service quality and dimensions of EGOSQ (using both measurement approaches) was analysed by using regression analysis. In gap based scores; three dimensions (Reliability, Assurance and Resourceful) were found significantly impacting overall online-service quality (with 10% level of statistical significance). The regression model was found significant and R^2 value was 0.327. In the perception based scores; three out of four dimensions (Reliability, Assurance and Resourceful) were found significant. Regression model was found significant and R^2 value was 0.322. Relationship between users' satisfaction and EGOSQ dimensions & behavioural intentions were not found significant.

Table 4. Pool of EGOSQ items

A. Information
1. Accurate information*
2. Reliable information
3. Comprehensive information*
4. Useful information
5. Timely information
6. Easy to retrieve and use information
7. Easy to comprehend information
8. Information in concise format
9. Information not easy to get otherwise form other sources (exclusive information)
10. Updated information
B. Interaction
11. Friendly and courteous interaction by employees
12. Employees understand my needs
13. Availability of easy to use various online contact options
14. Employees behave empathetically
15. Employees respond in time
16. Employees take prompt actions to address my needs
17. Employees demonstrated their willingness to help me
18. Employees know their jobs well
19. Employees have enough knowledge to answer my questions
20. Employees appear concerned always
C. Integration
21. Features can be customized according to my needs
22. Wide range of services through a single website
23. Ease of use of all e-service features.
24. Personalization of WebPages/services possible
25. Various payment options
26. Provides confirmations on my email/phone
D. Accessibility
27. Availability of online-services on all days and at all time
28. Fast navigation without jams
29. Impressive looking interface (website)
30. Well designed and organized interface (website)
31. Simple and easy to navigate website
32. Quick response to my actions (clicks) in website
33. Web pages load quickly
34. The website does not crash often
E. Emotional Engagement
35. Provides opportunities to contact other users (through blogs/discussions forums)
36. Using esevaonline.com is exciting*
37. Using esevaonline.com provides fun and enjoyment
F. Active Service Recovery
38. Getting fair compensation in case of loss in the event of service failures/ faults by e-firm*
39. Government accepting responsibility and taking control in the event of service failure/ fault.
40. Shows concern about the problem in case of service failure*
41. Describe me why the service had failed
42. Always get a chance to raise my concerns in case of service failure
43. Excellent complaint handling procedures to satisfy my needs in case of service failure
G. Assurance
41. Getting things done right the first time
42. Financial security during the online transactions.
43. Protection of personal information and privacy
44. Getting things done within the expected time frame.
45. Takes appropriate precautionary measures to prevent frauds
46. Honest to deal with
47. Transparent in all transactions
48. Maintenance of accurate records
(The Questionnaire contains 26 items which are presented in bold letters; 5 items (marked) were further dropped during data analysis. Final instrument contains 16 items in perception based and 22 items in gap based questionnaire see table 7 for details on final questionnaire)*

Table 5. Items to measure overall online-service quality, satisfaction, behavioural intentions

Items used to measure overall service quality
1. Excellent overall online-service
2. Online-service service of very high quality
3. A high standard of online-service
Items used to measure satisfaction
1. The overall experience with online-service (very pleasant/ extremely terrible)
2. Feeling with online-service as user (absolutely delighted /absolutely terrible)
Items used to measure behavioural intention
1. Intention to continue use the online-service
2. Intention to recommend others

Table 6. Profile of the respondents

	Percentage (n=65)
	22
Unmarried	78
Male	62
Female	38
Age group	
16-24	51
25-34	46
35-44	3
Income	
Under Rs. One lac	0
Rs One lac to Two lac	0
Rs Two lac to Three lac	0
Rs Three lac to Four lac	12
Rs Four lac to Five lac	37
Rs Five lacs & over	51
Internet Usage	
Less than 1year	0
1-3 Years	0
3-6 Years	22
6 Years & over	78

continued on following page

Table 6. continued

Average Usage of internet	
1-5 times a month	0
1-5 times a week	0
1-5 times day	43
More than that	57
Internet Usage-Hours per week	
5-10 Hours	3
10-15 Hours	40
15-20 Hours	48
20-40 Hours	9
1-5 Hours	0
Above 40	0

DISCUSSION & IMPLICATIONS

The dimensions which were found common to both the approaches in the study were: Reliability, Resourceful and Utility. It implies that users consider these dimensions to assess the quality of e-governance online-service quality (EGOSQ). Reliability refers to attributes of protection of personal information and privacy, getting things done within the expected time frame, getting things done right the first time, fast navigation in the website without frequent jams and, availability of online-services on all days and at all time. It suggests that the governments have to ensure apart from 24X7 availability of online-services, ensuring performance of the services right always. Users don't expect slow navigations and frequent jams while surfing the sites. Users also expect the service performance within the expected time frame. Therefore, governments should clearly suggest the users the time required to fulfil the service request online.

The dimension labelled as "Resourceful" contains attributes - getting updated information and getting useful information. It means governments have to provide useful information to users and have to update the information frequently. Users expect the websites to be a resourceful website having all the information they need. The dimension of utility consists of attributes- availability of easy to use various online contact options, friendly and courteous interaction by employees, availability of wide range of services through a single website and availability of customizable features according to the users needs. Contact options include email, telephone, online chatting etc. Presence of these options will improve the perception of the quality of online-services provided by the government. Moreover, users expect friendly and courteous interactions too. In addition, a wide range of services should be offered through the web portal so that customers perceive a high level of utility of such online-services.

Another dimension that is up to a large extent common to both measurement approaches is Assurance. Users expect transparency from online service providers in all transactions and want prompt actions to address their needs. Users also expect options to contact other users (through blogs/discussions forums) so that they can share

Table 7. Reliability and factor analysis results

	Using Gap Scores (P-E)				**Using Perception Scores**		
S. No	**Items & Factors**	**Loadings**	**(Coefficient of Alpha)**	**S.No**	**Items & Facotrs**	**Loadings**	**(Coefficient of Alpha)**
	Reliability		0.899		**Reliability**		0.904
1	Protection of personal information and privacy	0.959		1	Protection of personal information and privacy	0.957	
2	Getting things done within the expected time frame	0.842		2	Getting things done within the expected time frame	0.891	
3	Getting things done right the first time	0.684		3	Getting things done right the first time	0.669	
4	Fast navigation without jams	0.81		4	Fast navigation without jams	0.822	
5	Availability of online-services on all days and at all time	0.723		5	Availability of online-services on all days and at all time	0.734	
	Resourceful		0.708		**Resourceful**		0.676
6	Getting Updated information	0.783		6	Getting Updated information	0.72	
7	Getting Useful information	0.865		7	Getting Useful information	0.877	
	Utility		0.625		**Utility**		0.646
8	Availability of easy to use various online contact options	0.377		8	Availability of easy to use various online contact options	0.552	
9	Friendly and courteous interaction by employees	0.497		9	Friendly and courteous interaction by employees	0.381	
10	Wide range of services through a single website	0.622		10	Wide range of services through a single website	0.639	
11	Features can be customized according to my needs	0.764		11	Features can be customized according to my needs	0.717	
	Assurance		0.732		**Assurance**		0.77
12	Transparent in all transactions	0.776		12	Transparent in all transactions	0.571	
13	Employees take prompt actions to address my needs	0.649		13	Employees take prompt actions to address my needs	0.846	
14	Provides opportunities to contact other users (through blogs/discussions forums)	0.677		14	Provides opportunities to contact other users (through blogs/discussions forums)	0.621	
				15	Financial security during the online transactions	0.572	
				16	Getting Timely information	0.58	
	Accountability		0.642				
15	Government accepting responsibility and taking control in the event of service failure/ fault.	0.454					
16	Financial security during the online transactions	0.683					
17	Shows concern about the problem in case of service failure	0.672					
	Convenience		0.589				
18	Getting Timely information	0.833					
19	Getting Reliable Information	0.517					
20	Easy to retrieve and use information	0.454					
	Appealing website		0.708				
21	Well designed and organized interface (website)	0.627					
22	Impressive looking interface (website)	0.785					

*Table 8. Regression results**

	Using Gap Scores		Using Perception Scores
Dimensions	**t-value**	**Dimensions**	**t-value**
Reliability	2.439	Reliability	2.538
Assurance	1.828	Assurance	2.196
Resourcefulness	1.803	Resourcefulness	1.908
R^2 value	0.327	**R^2 value**	0.322
F value (ANOVA Table)	3.954	**F value (ANOVA Table)**	7.130
Sig	0.001	**Sig**	0.000

* *Other variables were insignificant and not shown in the results.*

their views. In India, most of the e-governance online-service portals lack this feature, which if is included can help in a more rapid adoption of e-governance i.e. use of online-service by users for most of the transactions. Two other related attributes were financial security during the online transactions and getting timely information. However, these attributes appear in separate dimensions in the gap based approach of measurement, it seems that users are quite concerned about these attributes in their quality perceptions. Though in terms of expectations, they expect the financial security as a feature of accountability and timely information as convenience.

Other dimensions which exist in case of the gap based approach are convenience, accountability and appealing website. Users expect that government service providers should accept responsibility and take control in the event of service failure/ fault, and, the government should show concern about the problems users face in case of service failure. Availability of reliable information to enable users to take quick decisions in an easy to retrieve and use form is also expected by the users. A well designed and organized website with impressive looking was also found important attribute adding to the quality perception.

CONCLUSION

The chapter presented a study to demonstrate development of a quality measurement instruments to measure e-governance online-service quality (EGOSQ). The study used literature survey into eight domain areas related to Service Quality Measurement, e-Service Quality Measurement, System Quality, Information Quality, Technology Adoption Model (TAM), End user satisfaction, Self Service Technologies and e-governance assessment models. The qualitative study resulted into seven dimensions of EGOSQ. The quantitative study using factor analysis later extracted seven dimensions in case of perception minus expectation (discrepancy/gap) based approach of measurement and four dimensions in case of perception based approach. Consistency was found in the instrument evident from the similar pattern of factor loadings in both of the approaches. Though, the sample size (n=65) is too small for any conclusive results, but, the reliability analysis and the factor analysis results suggest possibly good factor structure of the instrument. Regression analysis suggested validity of the instrument. In addition, comparisons with few studies already present on e-governance provide support to the findings. Information delivery is regarded as one of the most important role of e-governance initiatives. The research report of IICD Research brief (Backus, 2001) emphasized importance of information, interaction and involving users to get success in e-governance initiatives. The result suggests one point of contact for users to provide convenience. Convenience is one of the factors regarded as critical in another report pertaining to New Zealand e-governance initiatives (E-government Unit Research paper, 2004). The report brings out other important attributes as ready access to information, wide range of services by single website, ease of contact by users, integrated services, assurance factors, interaction using multiple means, website design, privacy and security concerns. End to end responsibility of service delivery and trust concerns are elaborated in other study also (Al-Omani & Al-Omani, 2006; Tawil & Sait, 2002).

LIMITATIONS & FUTURE DIRECTIONS

The development of quality instrumentation or any other research may have a number of limitations. The study presented in this chapter had similar limitations. However, a good research in spite of such limitations provides future research directions. The foremost limitation of the study was the sample size. Due to small sample size, the results of the study should be viewed with caution. However, high reliability coefficients of dimensions suggest the rigour with which the questionnaire is developed. Factor analysis provides better results with large sample sizes (about 5 times the number of variables used). Other related limitation is perhaps somewhat biased sample of high internet usage group, more experienced users of internet, high income group and relatively younger age of the sample. These characteristics of sample need to be taken into consideration. Another limitation is the absence of dependant variables which should be used to test the predictive validity of the proposed measurement instrument. The dependant variables used in this study are derived from the related field of e-service, which represent commercial businesses. There is a need to conduct more exploratory research to find out the variables which impact e-governance online-service quality. Qualitative studies involving the users of such online-services will provide more insights in this field. There is a need to study more about the users of the services, their behaviours while availing online-services, their preferences and expectations and their dispositions to understand them better. This will definitely result into a more rapid acceptance and adoption of government online-services by the users.

ACKNOWLEDGMENT

The author thanks following for assistance in the research study presented in the chapter Pragya Shah and Varun Wadhwa, students IBS Hyderabad Batch of 2008.

REFERENCES

Agrawal, A. (2007). *Assessing Service Quality in e-Services: Building up on the Quality Instrumentation.* PhD Dissertation, submitted to ICFAI University.

Agrawal, A., & Fuloria, S. (2003). A Study of Interest, Awareness Level, Perception & Acceptability of E-governance by Indian Citizens. In M.P. Gupta (Ed.), *Promise of E-Governance: Operational Challenges* (pp, 49-56). New Delhi: Tata McGraw Hill.

Al-Omani, A., & Al-Omani, H. (2006). E-governance Readiness Assessment Model. *Journal of Computer Science, 2*(11), 841-845.

Al-Tawil, K.M., & Sadiq, S.M. (2002). *E-governance- Where We Stand?* Available at: http://www.worldbank.org/wbi/mdf/mdf4/papers/altawil-sait.pdf. Accessed July 28, 2007.

Backus, M. (2001, March). *E-governance in Developing Countries.* IICD Research Brief - No 1. Available at: http://www.ftpiicd.org/files/research/briefs/brief1.doc. Accesses July 28, 2007.

Bailey, J.E., & Pearson, S.W. (1983). Development of a Tool for Measuring & Analyzing Computer User Satisfaction. *Management Science, 29*(5), 530-545.

Bitner, M.J. (1992). Servicescapes: The impact of Physical Surroundings on Customers & Employees. *Journal of Marketing, 56* 57-71.

Bolton, R.N., & Drew, J. (1991). A Longitudinal Analysis of the Impact of Service Changes on Customer Attitudes. *Journal of Marketing, 55,* 1-9.

Brady, K.M., & Cronin, Jr. J.J. (2001). Some New Thoughts on Conceptualizing Perceived Service Quality: A Hierarchical Approach. *Journal of Marketing, 65*(July), 34-43.

Cronin, J.J., & Taylor, S.A. (1992, July). Measuring service quality: A re-examination & extension. *Journal of Marketing, 56*, 55-68.

Dabholkar, P.A., Thorpe, D.I., & Rentz, J.O. (1996). A measure of Service Quality for Retailing Stores: Scale Development & Validation. *Journal of the Academy of Marketing Science, 24*(1). 3-16.

DeLeone, W.H., & McLean, E.R. (1992). Information Systems Success: The Quest for the Dependent Variable. *Information Systems Research, 3*(1), 60-95.

Doll, W.J., & Torkzadeh G. (1988, June). The Measurement of End-User Computing Satisfaction. *MIS Quarterly, 12*(2), 259- 274.

E-government Unit Research paper (2004). *Achieving e-government 2004: A report on progress towards the New Zealand E-government Strategy.* Available at: http://www.e.govt.nz/resources/research/research/ready-access-2004/. Accessed July 28, 2007.

Fishbein, M., & Ajzen, I. (1975). *Belief, Attitude, Intention & Behavior: An Introduction to Theory & Research.* Reading, MA: Addison-Wesley.

Gronroos, C. (1982). *Strategic Management & Marketing in the Service Sector.* Helsingfors; Swedish School of Economics & Business Administration Hoffman. K. D.

Iivari, J., & Koskela, E. (1987, September). The PIOCO Model for Information Systems Design. *MIS Quarterly, 11*(3), 401-419.

Judd, C.M., Smith E.R., & Kidder L.H. (1991). *Research methods in social relations.* Sydney: Harcourt Brace Jovanovich College Publishers .

Kaynama, S.A., & Black, C.I. (2000). A Proposal to Assess the Service Quality of Online Travel Agencies. *Journal of Professional Services Marketing, 21*(1), 6368.

King, W., & Epstein B. (1983). Assessing information value: an experimental study. *Decision Sciences, 14,* 34-35.

Liljander, V., van Riel A.C.R., & Minna, P. (2001). Customer Satisfaction with E-Services: The Case of an Online Recruitment Portal, In Bruhn. M. & B. Stauss, Eds. Yearbook of Services Management - 2002-E-Services.

Lin, C.S., & Wu, S. (2002). Exploring the impact of online service quality on portal site usage. *Proceedings of the 35th Hawaii International Conference on System Science.*

Lociacono, E., Watson, R.T., & Goodhue, D.L. (2002). *WebQual: a measure of Web site quality.* Working paper, Terry College of Business.

Mahmood, M.A. (1987). Systems development methods – a comparative investigation. *MIS Quarterly, 11*(3), 293-311.

Mason, R.O. (1978). Measuring Information Output: A Communication Systems Approach. *Information & Management, 1*(5), 219-234.

McDougall, G., & Levesque, T. (1992). The measurement of service quality: some methodology issues. 2eme. Seminaire Internationale de Recherché en Management des *Activites de Service,* (pp. 411-30).

Meuter, M.L., Ostrom, A.L., Roundtree, R.I., & Bitner, M.J. (2000, July). Self-service technologies: understanding customer satisfaction with technology-based service encounters. *Journal of Marketing, 64*, 50-64.

Parasuraman, A., Berry, L.L., & Zeithaml, V.A. (1991). Refinement & Reassessment of the SERVQUAL Scale. *Journal of Retailing, 67*(4), 420-50.

Parasuraman, A., & Grewals, D. (2000). The Impact of Technology on the Quality-Value-Loyalty Chain: A Research Agenda. *Journal of the Academy of Marketing Science, 28*(1), 168–74.

Parasuraman, A., Zeithaml, V.A., & Berry, L.L. (1985). A conceptual model of service quality & its implications for future research. *Journal of Marketing, 49*(Fall), 41-50.

Parasuraman, A., Zeithaml, V.A., & Berry, L.L. (1988). SERVQUAL: A multiple item scale for measuring consumer perceptions of service quality. *Journal of Retailing, 64*(1), 12-40.

Parasuraman, A., Zeithaml, V.A., & Malhotra A. (2005). E-S-QUAL: A Multiple-Item Scale for Assessing Electronic Service Quality. *Journal of Service Research, 7*(3), 213-233.

van Riel, A.C.R., Lemmink, J., Streukens, S., & Liljander, V. (2004). Boost customer loyalty with online services: the case of mobile telecoms providers. *International Journal of Internet Marketing & Advertising, 1*(1), 4–23.

Yang, Z., & Fang, X. (2004). Online Service Quality Dimensions & their Relationship with Satisfaction. *International Journal of Service Industry Management, 15*(3).

Yang, Z., Jun, M., & Robin, P.T. (2004). Measuring customer perceived online service quality, International Journal of Operations & Production Management, 24, (11), 1149.

Li, Y.N., Tan, K.C., & Xie, M., (2002). Factor analysis of service quality dimension shifts in the information age. *Managerial Auditing Journal, 18*(4), 297.

Yoo, B., & Naveen, D. (2001). Developing a Scale to Measure the Perceived Quality of Internet Shopping Sites (SITEQUAL). *Quarterly Journal of Electronic Commerce, 2*(1). 31-47.

Zeithaml, V.A. (2002). Service Excellence in Electronic Channels. *Managing Service Quality, 12*(3), 135-139.

ENDNOTES

1. EGOSQ is used in this paper as an abbreviation to e-governance online-service quality. And, also as suggested name for the proposed quality measurement instrumentation
2. http://www.openit.co.za/cgi-bin/fccgi.exe?w3exec=showArticle&ArticleID=00013

Chapter X
The Success Model of Evolution from Government to E-Governance

Sundresan Perumal
University Utara Malaysia, Malaysia

ABSTRACT

As the world is streaming into an electronic world there are still huge communities that don't understand the evolution government into the era of e-government. Many still do not understand what is meant by e-government and e–governance. At the same time they don't understand how the actual transmission between the old government and the new e-government framework model works. This chapter develops a model to understand e-governance better and at the same time to help avoid possible problems during the period of transition from traditional government to e-government. Towards introducing the new model, we will also identify a few unique cases of e-government. As the heat of the business to consumer e-commerce (B2C) sector grows, public services are entering the frame whereby government-to-business (G2B) and government-to-citizen (G2C) services are becoming popular at local, regional, national, or even supranational level, albeit at a comparatively slower rate. Further, the concept of the traditional government model is a more conservative entity, slower to change into new initiatives, than operators in the commercial field.

INTRODUCTION

As the world is streaming into the electronic world there are still large number of communities that don't understand the revolution of traditional government into the era of E-government. The concept of the traditional government is a more conservative entity, slower to change into new initiatives, than operators in the commercial field. Due to this consideration e-government movement is now building with a number of national governments taking extensive measure to engage the extreme transformation of their portfolio. In this chapter we are going to look and illustrate a transition model from the traditional government to the e-government process. The actual positive idea to develop this model is to understand e-governance better and at the same time this will avoid possible problems during the period of transition. Towards introducing the new model, we will also identify a few unique cases of e-government. In this chapter we are going to look at how "Improved public management" works and at the same time how e-government is implemented in various communities worldwide. Then we introduce the models of e-government maturity as well as the strategic alignment model of Henderson and Venkodraman (1993). Through previous readings, we explore the transition process of government to e-government and offer implications to the model introduced in the chapter. If we look at few years back there was very little literature that discussed the theme of public management (Bevir et al., 2003) and the reinvention of government that in many ways lay's the groundwork for e-government initiatives that were to follow. In the context of e-government, Osbourne and Gaebler (1992) suggested considering citizens as a customer and that the entire government service should be focused on customer's needs. But Mintzberg (1996) has come out with another powerful point challenging Osbourne and Gaebler saying that we do not need to identify the citizen as a customer because customer buy product's, clients buy services, but citizen have rights and the priority for them is more than a customer or client in the government sector. This does not however imply that the necessity to reinvent government is not there, but highlights the extent to which the nomenclature of B2C relationship parallels that of G2C relationships.

TRADITIONAL GOVERNMENT

The stereotypical image of a Government is of a slow-moving bureaucracy, unwilling or unable to change and years behind other industry sectors in its use of new technology and new business models (Accenture, 2000). In this model, citizens and businesses engage with government in many areas, creating vast amounts of paperwork – an inconvenient and confusing process. Stereotypes are by nature unspecific – there are always exceptions. Yet the image here is one that will be familiar to many citizens who do not have access to e-government.

THE OPPORTUNITIES OF E-GOVERNMENT

A public sector organization planning to adopt an e-government initiative and formulate its IT strategies must evaluate its business models and select appropriate technology solutions that deliver on central government policy. Although there are significant differences in the composition of organizations, there are a number of technologies and systems infrastructure that many organizations need to adopt in common to provide facilities for the integration of their systems in a way that enables them to build a platform for sharing their knowledge resources. For example, an E-government portal requires a common and integrated architecture framework that allows different organizations, provinces, and municipalities to share and exchange data, independent of formats, devices and underlying architecture (Sharma and Gupta, 2002). Therefore, organization must have a clear understating of architecture frameworks from both the technical and information management level. The e-government architecture defines the standards, infrastructure components, applications, technologies, business model and guidelines for electronic commerce among and between organizations that facilitates the interaction of the government and promotes group productivity. Since e-government is a relatively new research area, its architecture and adoption strategy have not been widely discussed. Therefore the concepts from other relevant areas such as e-business, e-services, and e-commerce notwithstanding, a number of studies have discussed the architecture or components of e-government, such as Cabinet Office(2000), Heeks (2001), Sharma and Gupta (2002), Office of Information Technology (2001) and Daniels (2002). However, these studies did not address the aspect of business management model and how it is aligned with the IT infrastructure. Since e-government goes beyond the IT infrastructure, the significance of integration technologies have been discussed and classified under the e-business layer section since these technologies and approaches are often and need to be used in e-government projects.

FRAMEWORK LAYERS OF E-GOVERNMENT

The reason is that they are designed to support e-business and e-commerce applications. The framework is structured into four layers connected through two-direction arrows which present the hierarchical level of e-government implementation and portray the logical connection of each relevant layer that allow two-way transmission of data and services. The top level of the framework represents the access layer that illustrates who might use the government services and what are the channels of access. Throughout these channels, the e-government portal should integrate all government information and services from disparate departments and Organizations, which represent the e-government layer. In connection to the e-government layer, the e-business layer is emerged to manipulate and integrate government data sources across government bodies and make information and services available to the e-government portal in real-time. In the bottom level of the framework, the ICT infrastructure of e-government should be built to reach out all parts of government and hence, support the e-government operation and provide Effective and reliable e-government services. This section now discusses the architecture that forms the framework of e-government architecture project. Figure 1 show the architecture framework of e-government which is divided into our Layers: access layer, e-government layer, e-business layer, and infrastructure layer.

Early adopters of Web-enabled technology applications tended to automate existing business processes, with little redesign or innovation. Typical approaches involved automation of the front-end Web presence so as to spark e-commerce activity, but failed to integrate and redesign the business as a whole in order to make it truly Web-centric. The same was true of early e-government initiatives – there was a scramble to get as many services or Web pages up with little regard to quality, service level or appropriateness for the citizenship. However, as Burn and Robins observe," Government is not just about putting forms and services online. It provides the Opportunity to rethink how the government provides services and how it links them in a way that is tailored to the users' needs". This rethinking must necessarily include disavowal of the "build it and they will use it" mentality that infiltrates much Web-enabled thinking. The failure of many dot. coms to garner business, and indeed the proverbial failure of the horse to drink the water proffered, should alert governments to the risk that e-government initiatives may also go hideously wrong. Consequently, "government must develop a far more sophisticated view of the people it is there to serve and devolve real power as an integral part of its approach to e-government And provide more freedom of information" (Burn and Robins, 2003). If the governments can achieve this radical new conception of their role, then there is the po-

Figure 1. Show the architecture framework of e-government (Criado and Ramilo 2003)

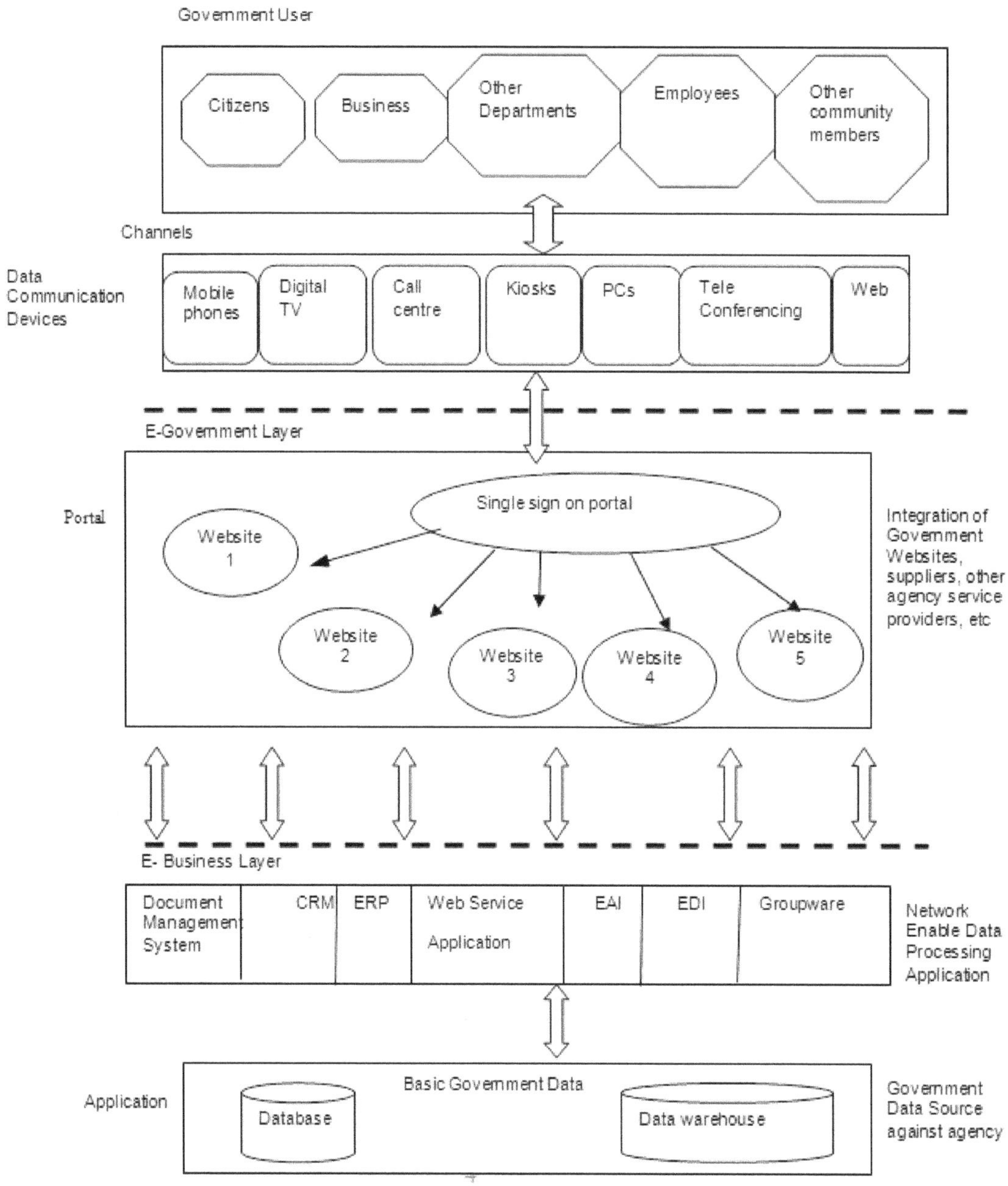

tential for e-government to transform "not only the way in which most public services are delivered, but also the fundamental relationship between government and citizen. This implies, of course, not only e-government but also e-governance – if real power is really to be devolved to citizens.

There are many opportunities for e-government applications, whether they involve the provision of information, handling complaints and queries electronically, processing applications for permits/ licenses electronically, paying taxes, duties, and fees electronically.

THE LIMITATION OF E-GOVERNMENT

Themistocleous and Irani (2001) and Shung and Seddon (2000) propose a model to classify the limitation that derived from IT infrastructure such as ERP. These models are considered adaptable for the classification of e-government limitation, since the main purposes of e-government adoption is to automate business processes and integrates IT infrastructures in public sector organizations. *Figure 2 analyses e-government limitation and then classifies them accordingly in order to provide a comprehensive insight to those barriers restricting the adoption of e-government.* Many e-government initiatives are in their strategic phase of implementation (infancy), however, some key problems and limitation are already beginning to emerge. There are a number of limitations experienced in public sector organizations that prevent the realization of anticipated benefits and degrade successful adoption of e-government projects. This section analyses and summarizes the limitation of e-government adoption experienced in public sector organisations.Technology itself would not guarantee success with e-government but, it is necessary that any e-government initiative must ensure that it has sufficient resources, adequate infrastructure, management support, capable IT staff, and effective IT training and support. Despite the cost of IT going down, an adequate IT infrastructure still represents the key limitation for e-government adoption. The infrastructure is composed of hardware and software that will provide secure electronic services to citizens, businesses, and employees. Bonham et al. (2001), Bourn (2004), Dillon and Pelgrin (2004), McClure (2000) and National Research Council (2005), in their research, agree that governments view a lack of technical infrastructure as a significant barrier to the development of government organizations' capabilities to provide online services and transactions. They also agree that unreliable IT infrastructure in public sector organizations will degrade e-government performance. Practically, Layne and Lee (2001) and Dillon and Pelgrin (2002) emphasize the importance of network capacity and communication infrastructure layer) as an important foundation for integrating information systems across Government organizations. It should be in place before e-government services can be offered reliably and effectively to the public (McClure, 2000). Therefore, the key to success in an e-government strategy is to implement an adequate IT infrastructure that will support a users' experience of easy and reliable electronic access to government. For example, as discussed in earlier section, intranet and extranet should be maintained in public sector organization to provide reliable groundwork for required information systems and applications. As *Figure 2 illustrates, many examples of limitation exists that associate with IT infrastructure*, and as discussed in earlier section that LAN, reliable server, and internet connections are important to build a strong foundation for e-government infrastructure. A barrier frequently cited is the need to ensure adequate security and privacy in an e-government strategy (Daniels, 2002; James, 2000; Joshi et al., 2001; Lambrinoudakis et al., 2003; Layne and Lee, 2001; Sanchez et al., 2003). Bonham et al. (2001) and Gefen et al. (2002) agree that one of the most significant limitations for implementing e-government applications is computer security, privacy and confidentiality of the personal data. One of the sophisticated applications of e-government is e-voting, which uses electronic ballots that allow voters to transmit their vote to election officials over the internet. This application requires extensive security approaches to secure the voting process and protect the voter personal data. In addition, government organizations at all levels use, collect, process, and disseminate a wide range of sensitive information on personal, financial, and medical aspects. Hence, IT departments in organizations should aware that security and privacy are not only critical for the availability and delivery of government services

Figure 2. Analyses e-government limitation (Criado, J.I. and Ramilo, M.C. (2003))

Dimension	Examples
IT skills	Lack of IT training programmes in government Shortage of well-trained IT staff in market Lack of employees with integration skills Developing Web site by unskilled staff Unqualified project manager Shortage of salaries and benefits in public sector Flow of IT specialist staff
Operational cost	Cultural issues Resistance to change by high-level management Time consuming for reengineering business process in public organizations Operational cost Main supply come from central government Shortage of financial recourses in public sector organizations High cost of IT professionals and consultancies IT cost is high in developing countries Cost of installation, operation and maintenance of e-government systems Cost of training and system development
IT infrastructure	Shortage of reliable networks and communication Inadequate network capacity or bandwidth Lack resources standards and common architecture policies and definitions Existing systems are incompatible and complex Existing internal systems have restrictions regarding their integrating capabilities Lack of integration across government systems Integration technologies of heterogeneous databases are confusing Lack of knowledge regarding e-government interoperability High complexity in understanding the processes and systems in order to redesign and integrate them Lack of enterprise architecture Availability and compatibility of software, systems and applications
Organizational	Lack of coordination and cooperation between departments Lack of effective leadership support and commitment amongst senior public officials Unclear vision and management strategy Complex of business processes Politics and political impact
Operational Cost	Main supply come from central government Shortage of financial recourses in public sector organizations High cost of IT professionals and consultancies IT cost is high in developing countries Cost of installation, operation and maintenance of e-government systems Cost of training and system development.
Organizational	Lack of coordination and cooperation between departments Lack of effective leadership support and commitment amongst senior public official's Unclear vision and management strategy Complex of business processes Politics and political impact

but also to build citizen confidence and trust in the online services and transactions

Analyses of E-Government Limitation Concept

Open the transition process from the government to e-government transition process offers the government a unique opportunity to enhance not only their operational transparency, clarity of purpose and responsiveness to citizens (Marche and McNiven, 2003), but also their own internal efficiency and effectiveness, important concerns in times of economic downturn and increasing public pressure for internal accountability. However, achieving transparency requires significant "internal process redesign that hides the internal complexity of transactions" (Marche and McNiven, 2003) from citizens who really don't care which department provides a particular service, or who they are paying, so long as they can get it. This transparency is likely to increase citizen empowerment they will be able to access information of their own choosing, rather than merely accepting whatever explanation is provided (if any) by the (in)competent authorities. There are both similarities and differences between .com and .gov, both of which bear closer attention. Individual B2C customers will have a general experience of the 24/7 world where they can do anything, any time and anywhere. As citizens, it is likely that they will expect a similar level of service from e-government a one-stop shop service that is simple and capable of personalization .Achieving such a service requires changes in the way government functions it needs significant inter-departmental cooperation. Citizens are more likely to develop loyalty towards those e-government portals that are citizen-centric, that are designed to address their needs. The Australian Centrelink.gov.au is a good example of an early portal that did integrate across agencies within government. A key difference between e-government and e-business concerns loyalty businesses have tried to develop customer loyalty with customer relationship management (CRM) so as to encourage customers to return time and again to buy their services or products. So long as customers need to buy, they may indeed return.

However, with e-government, loyalty is rather different. E-governments should encourage digital loyalty, i.e. the preference of citizens to use digital services over other forms (e.g. counter, mail, fax, telephone), since digital services should be much cheaper to provide. Yet at the same time, since governments by definition operate as a monopoly, they may perceive that they don't need to spend extra effort to compete with other providers. That said, some government services such as the Post Office (not a government service in all countries) may well face private-sector competition in the form of courier and parcel delivery firms, so it is unwise to assume absolute monopoly status. At a higher level, a government can also be considered to be in competition (e.g. for investment or human resources) with neighboring governments, whether in nearby cities, regions or countries. In this sense, Singapore and Hong Kong compete with each other for international business: the quality and extent of their e-government services are part of the competitive environment. Nevertheless, e-government services should be designed so as to help citizens get in, find their information or transact their business, and then get out as efficiently as possible. It is useful here to refer to "stickiness". In an e-business context, "stickiness" suggests keeping a customer on a Web site as long as possible, in the hope that the customer will buy something. In consequence, Web sites are often designed to be maximally sticky. In contrast, few e-government Web sites need such levels of adhesiveness. In most cases, it is more appropriate that the citizen can easily access the service, complete a transaction, and get out. This suggests that optimal stickiness rather than maximal stickiness is desirable.

E-GOVERNMENT MATURITY MODELS

Accentor started its annual surveys of e-government development in 2000, characterizing e-government progression via a multi-stage "publish, interact, transact" model. Later, the model was extended to incorporate the notion of the transformation of government – redesigning processes so as to put the citizen at the centre (Accenture, 2004). This transformation involves structural and cultural change within government. In 2003, the model was further revised to five stages:

1. Online presence;
2. Basic capability;
3. Service availability;
4. Mature delivery; and
5. Service transformation.

Considering the transitions between stages, Accenture (2003) commented we find that at the start of each stage countries make large steps and, often, rapid development. As each plateau is approached, the limitation to further progress become apparent and the rate of development slows. In moving to the highest stage of e-government (i.e. service transformation), Canada demonstrated its ability to apply leading-edge practices, such as involving customers in service development and identifying/focusing on high-value services. A similar staged development model was articulated by Chen (2002), who argues that e-government delivers its content and services through the continuum of the four levels of interaction:

- *By enabling information search by citizens via the internet;*
- *By evolving into providers of two-way communication services such as simple groupware functionalities like Web forms, e-mail and bulletin boards;*
- *By facilitating transaction services for businesses and citizens; and*
- *By transforming practices and services from government to the agents and the* community (e.g. e-voting or opinion poll).

He further argues that most e-government initiatives are moving upwards continuously. Both these development models focus on the service delivery or "e-commerce" side. However, another transformation model (Hodgkinson, 2002) suggests that e-government progresses through a learning curve for its back-end (e-business) activities, similar to the learning curve of data processing maturity of a six-stage growth model (Nolan 1979). While these staged models tend to help identify "where you are", they usually fail to "guide you to the next stage". This requires a more comprehensive maturity model, such as Galliers and Sutherland's (1991) six-stage model (i.e. adhocracy, starting the foundations, centralized dictatorship, democratic dialectic and cooperation, entrepreneurship opportunity, and integrated harmonious relationships), which associates the characteristics of each of the stages with the seven "S" framework (i.e. strategy, structure, systems, staff, style, skills and super-ordinate goals). Similarly, the strategic alignment maturity matrix proposed by Luftman (2000) consists of five conceptual levels (i.e. initial, committed process, established focused process, improved/managed process, and optimized process) and six IT business alignment maturity criteria (i.e. communication, competency/value measurement, governance, partnership, scope, and architecture and skills). As Hodgkinson (2002) observes, reports from various knowledge management initiatives suggest that islands of automation can exist long after databases have been established within the various agencies, and that cultural issues will hinder interoperability long after technological interoperability has become feasible In the end, mature e-government is characterized by high levels of capability and performance on multiple dimensions. Performance dimensions include the government's ability to offer the vast maturity of suitable services with an e-delivery option, and a large number of citizens and organizations making use of them. Capabilities include the ability to share data and information across government units, reduce process times through workflow and ERP systems, and the ability to capture and share knowledge of government employees. It also includes the ability to assess performance, through monitoring systems such as a balanced scorecardA mature e-government will also differ from a less mature one in other areas, such as IT management by senior CIOs, an effective management structure, regular planning and re-engineering activities to determine areas for improvement and making the changes to capitalize on the improvement potential, and by an IT (ICT) architecture that fosters integration, enables government-wide standardization, and offers the above-mentioned performance.

E-GOVERNANCE AND E-GOVERNMENT

There is an important distinction to be made between "government" and governance". Government is the institution itself, whereas governance is a broader concept describing forms of governing which are not necessarily in the hands of the formal government. Corporate governance, for example, refers to how the private sector structures its internal mechanisms to provide for accountability to its stakeholders: while government may be involved in this through company law, there are aspects which it does not control. According to Keohane and Nye (2000) governance means the processes and institutions, both formal and informal that guide and restrain the collective activities of a group. Government is the subset that acts with authority and creates formal obligations. Governance need not necessarily be conducted exclusively by governments. Private firms, associations of firms, nongovernmental organizations (NGOs), and associations ofNGOs all engage in it, often in association with governmental bodies, to create governance; sometimes without governmental authority.

E-GOVERNANCE IN DEVELOPING COUNTRIES

Implications of e-governance are slightly different for developing countries. Where Public sector reforms or the NPM movement in industrialized countries was internally driven (as in the UK, USA, etc.), in most developing countries the public sector reforms were externally driven, through the World Bank and other donor institutions (McGill, 1997) in some countries such as Turkey, there were no pressures to accept these reforms (Sozen and Shaw, 2002). Consequently, in spite of economic restructuring in many developing countries (such as India), public administration is still continued to remain highly bureaucratized and extremely centralized (Saxena, 1996). Another difference between e-governance in industrialized and developing a country is in the available ICT infrastructure. The e-governance movement in industrialized countries was largely triggered by the availability of internet technology, through which it became possible to access government agencies remotely and inexpensively. But, for their internal operations, government organizations were already using ICT-based systems. However, in the case of developing countries, ICT use in the public sector was very small, and therefore they had poor ICT infrastructure, if any (Bhatnagar and Bjorn-Andersen, 1990; Yong, 2003).Consequently for developing countries, e-government's first stage was the computerization of internal operations and services. Thus, for many government departments, "e-governance" was a significant, expensive, infrastructural change, as they had to plan switching from totally paper-based systems and services to totally computer- and internet-based systems and services. But e-governance is not a shortcut to economic development, budget savings or clean, efficient government. Instead, e-governance is an evolutionary process and often a struggle that presents costs and risks, both financial and political (Pacific Council on International Policy, 2002). These risks can be significant (Heeks, 2003). Therefore, if e-government initiatives are not well conceived and implemented, they can waste resources, fail in their promise to deliver useful services, and thus increase public frustration with government. Moreover, e-government in developing countries must accommodate certain unique conditions, needs and obstacles (Heeks, 2001). For instance, developing countries may have poor infrastructure, corruption, weak educational systems, and unequal access to technology.

THE MEANING OF EXCELLENT E-GOVERNANCE (E2-GOVERNANCE)

Excellence in organizations has been perceived to have the following attributes (Emersen and Harvey, 1996) purpose-driven (i.e. goal-centric) Customer (i.e. citizen)-centric, Process-oriented and Structure-supported. To some extent this is confirmed by the definition of "e-government" used by the Ministry of Labour and Government Administration (1999) that defines excellence in governance in terms of fulfillment of the following goals. Efficient and result-oriented administration Government administration shall, to the greatest extent possible, achieve "results" in accordance with stipulated goals, and these goals shall be attained without any unnecessary use of resources.

Thus, excellence involves goal-centricity or is purpose-driven provide user (citizen) oriented administration. Government administration should acquaint itself with the needs and desires of the users (citizens), and adapt its way of working whenever possible in accordance with their desires. Open and democratic administration under the rule of law Government administration under the rule of law shall contribute to ensuring predictability and equal treatment, and emphasizing openness and the right of access to information or decision-making in government activities. This statement again ensures that in addition to being purpose-driven, this purpose itself should be governance-centricity to have excellence. Politically manageable administration Government administration shall be an adaptable and flexible tool for implementing Government's policies. Though not explicitly, but this statement attempts to ensure that the processes and the structure of government (which constitute "administration") should support implementation of Government's policies, i.e. should be "outcome-driven". Thus, excellence in e-governance is characterized by exploitation of governance processes, structure and technology to provide an administration, which is efficient, effective (outcome-driven), politically manageable, and open and democratic (governance-centricity). This is essentially what we have called as "governance-centric" e-governance.

ISSUES IN BRINGING EXCELLENCE TO E-GOVERNMENT APPLICATIONS

Bringing a governance-centric focus, though very much desirable, is often difficult as it requires addressing a number of critical issues, some of which are given below. Defining a citizen-centric or governance-centric vision for the e-governance projects. Often e-governance projects lack a clear vision in terms of their effectiveness focus, and are treated merely as "computerization" projects for service efficiency. Developing a process-oriented view of government work. Government work is generally performed through vertical and rigid "silos" of departments (or agencies), that get on with their jobs without any collaboration between them. Such a fragmented view of government work results in mere computerization of individual or a few of the activities in individual departments rather than of the end-to-end integrated work process which is necessary to promote effectiveness and governance-centricity. Developing a performance management system for efficient and effective service delivery, which continuously measures and monitors service performance. Since such a measurement system also focuses on service effectiveness, it also ensures that the service outcome is aligned with the governance-centric vision. Defining a flexible technology architecture that is secure, provides easy access to users, and is scalable for high-volume operations as well as being cost-effective for the government. Many of the vendor-driven solutions for e-governance are rigid and/or poor in one or more of these dimensions and therefore not appropriate in the long run. Thus, implementing "excellent e-governance" is a reform process, and not merely the computerization of government operations. Only in this way will it contribute to building an "information society" in which the lives of citizens are empowered and enriched by access to information and the social, economic and political opportunities that it offers. Consequently excellence in e-governance is rapidly becoming a key national priority for all countries, rich or poor, developed or developing.

CONCLUDING REMARKS

The transition from government to e-government appears to be inevitable for many governments around the world. In this chapter, we have developed and illustrated a layer of the government to e-government transition process. This incorporates a number of preferred and less preferred transition strategies. We suggest that future research should assess the extent to which this model is validated by e-government reality, in particular the way in which e-government develops from initial rhetorical intentions through strategic planning, systems development, integration and finally transformation. It may well be that a post-transformation stage will emerge, since strategic planners are unlikely to be content with any current position: it is in their blood to be generative, to conjure up new services, new dynamics, and new forms of transformation, new ways of involving citizen participation. Such innovations may well change government as we know it today, though this may be little more than wishful thinking in the case of the more authoritarian governments that do not tolerate political opposition. Nevertheless, we expect that the increased dissemination of information that is inevitably associated with e-government can only have a positive.

REFERENCES

Aichholzer, G., & Schmutzer, R. (2000). *Organisational challenges to the development of electronic government.* Paper presented at 11th International Workshop on Database and Expert Systems Applications, IEEE Computer Society, London.

Bonham, G., Seifert, J., & Thorson, S. (2001). *The transformational potential of e-government: the role of political leadership.* Paper presented at 4th Pan European International Relations Conference, University of Kent.

Burn, J., & Robins, G. (2003). Moving towards e-government: a case study of organizational change processes. *Logistics Information Management, 16*(1), 25-35.

Chen, H. (2002) Digital government: technologies and practices. *Decision Support Systems, 34*(3), 223-227.

Chen, M. (2003). Factors affecting the adoption and diffusion of XML and Web services standards for e-business systems. *International Journal of Human-Computer Studies, 58*(3), 259-79.

Chesher, M., & Kaura, R. (2003). *Electronic Business & Commerce*, Springer, London.

Ciborra, C.U. (2003). *Unveiling e-government and development: governing at a distance in the new war.* Working Paper 126, London School of Economics and Political Science, London, available at: http://is.lse.ac.uk/wp/pdf/WP126.PDF.

Criado, J.I., & Ramilo, M.C. (2003). E-government in practice: an analysis of Web site orientation to the citizens in Spanish municipalities. *The International Journal of Public Sector Management, 16*(3), 191-218.

Dillon(2004). The importance of usability in the establishment of organizational software standards for end user computing. *International Journal of Human-Computer Studies, 45*,243-258.

Galliers, R.D., & Sutherland, A.R. (1991). Information systems management and strategy formulation: the 'stages of growth' model revisited. *J. of Information Systems, 1*, 89-114.

Heeks, R. (2003). *Most egovernment-for-development projects fail: how can risks be reduced?* Paper no. 14, i-Government Working Paper Series, Institute for Development Policy and Management, University of Manchester, Manchester.

Hodgkinson, C. (2002). *Equations towards a general logic of administration.* Paper presented at the 7th Annual Values and Leadership Conference, Toronto, Canada.

Henderson, J., & Venkatraman, N. (1993). Strategic Alignment: A model for organizational transformation through information technology,

Transforming Organisations, Oxford University Press.

Ho, A.L. (2003, January). EO allots 1-2% of RP budget to e-government spending. *Inquirer News Service.*

Hong Kong Special Administrative Region (2004). *Digital 21 Strategy: Sustainability and Opportunities, March, Government of the Hong Kong Special Administrative Region*, Hong Kong.

Keohane, R.O., & Nye, Jr., J.S. (2000). Globalization: What's New? What's Not? (And So What?) *Foreign Policy, 118*, 104-120.

Layne, K., & Lee, J. (2001). Developing Fully Functional E-government: A four-stage model. *Government Information Quarterly, 18*(2), 122-136.

Lambrinoudakis, C., & Gritzalis, S. et al. (2003). Security requirements for e-government services: a methodological approach for developing a common PKI-based security policy. *Computer Communications*, *26*(16), 1873-83.

Marche, S., & McNiven, J.D. (2003). E-government and e-governance: TheFuture isn't what it used to be, *Canadian Journal of Administrative Science,* 20(1).

Mintzberg. (1996). *Population pressure, economic stagnation and deforestation in Costa Rica and the Philippines.* Paper to IUSP Seminar on Population and Deforestation in the Humid Tropics, Sao Paulo Brazil.

Osbourne, D., & Gaebler, E. (1992). *Reinventing Government: How the entrepreneurial spirit is transforming the Public Sector.* Tampa, FL.

Saxena, N.C. (1996). *The Saga of Participatory Forest Management in India.* Center For International Forestry Research (CIFOR), Bogor.

Sikka, B.K., Sharma, M.L., Singh, S., & Narula, S.A. (2005). On E-Marketing of Apples in Uttaranchal Conference Proceedings of Indian Society of Agricultural Marketing, Pantnagar. In *Indian Journal of Agricultural Marketing, 19*(2), Conference Spl., May-August.

Themistocleous, M., & Irani, Z. (2001). Benchmarking the benefits and barriers of application integration. *Benchmarking: An International Journal*, *8*(4), 317–331.

Shang, S., & Seddon, P. (2002). Assessing and managing the benefits of enterprise systems: the business manager's perspective. *Information Systems Journal*, *20*(12), 271–299.

Sozen, S., & Shaw, I. (2002). The international applicability of "new" public management: lessons from Turkey. *International Journal of Public Sector Management, 15*(4), 475-86.

Chapter XI
Technology Acceptance of Free Wireless Internet Park Initiatives

Shafi Al-Shafi
Brunel University, UK

Vishanth Weerakkody
Brunel University, UK

ABSTRACT

This chapter examines the adoption of free wireless internet parks (iPark) by Qatari citizens as means of accessing electronic services from public parks. The Qatari government has launched free wireless internet parks concept under their national electronic government (e-government) initiative with a view of providing free internet access for all citizens while enjoying the outdoors. By offering free wireless internet access, the Qatari government hopes to increase accessibility of e-government services and encourage their citizens to actively participate in the global information society with a view of bridging the digital divide. The adoption and diffusion of iPark services will depend on user acceptance and availability of wireless technology. This chapter examines an extended technology acceptance model (TAM) that proposes individual differences and technology complexity to determine perceived usefulness and perceived ease of the iPark initiative by using a survey based study. The chapter provides a discussion on the key findings, research implications, limitations, and future directions for the iPark initiative in Qatar.

INTRODUCTION

The Qatari free-wireless-internet-park (iPark) concept was launched in 2007 under the banner of e-government to make public services more accessible to citizens. The iPark initiative is implemented in a number of public parks and provides free connection to the citizens' Internet ready devices such as, laptop and PDA's any time of day. The first such initiative was launched in the city of Doha in Qatar and it is the first of its kind in the Western Asia region. The primary goal of the initiative is to increase internet usage by establishing "hot spots" in public parks (IctQATAR, 2007). There are currently three designated wireless internet hotspots throughout selected public parks in the city (ibid). This chapter explores citizens' acceptance of the iPark concept as part of the e-government initiative in Qatar.

The Qatari e-government initiative was launched in 2000. In global terms the UN E-government readiness report (2008) ranked Qatar's e-government project as number 53 worldwide. As in many countries, the national e-government focus in Qatar is to achieve the highest performance in executing governmental transactions electronically, through streamlined business processes and integrated information technology solutions (IctQATAR, 2007). Moreover, the Qatari government hopes that free internet access offered through the iPark concept will encourage more citizens to use e-government services and help bridge the digital divide.

The Internet while being the primary mode of access to e-government services has not been adapted globally at the same time or rate; some countries are considered as leaders (such as the US, UK and Singapore) and others simply follow (i.e. the Arabian Gulf region) (Gupta and Gupta, 2005). More recently, wireless technologies have become a useful means of internet connectivity and access to electronic services (e-services). Wi-Fi for 'Wireless Fidelity' is a set of standards for wireless local area networks (WLAN) and provides wireless access to the Internet (Lehr and McKnight, 2003). Hotspots providing such access include Wi-Fi-cafes where services may be free to customers. In fact, a hotspot need not be limited to a confined location; as illustrated in this chapter, public parks can be used to offer free wireless internet access to citizens.

In particular, Wi-Fi has opened up new opportunities for electronic commerce (e-commerce) and e-government by allowing citizens to build connectivity 24/7. Moreover, it helps to increase accessibility of services and to expand social, government and business networks. The European Commission estimated Wi-Fi users to be around 125 million worldwide in the year 2006, and that there will be more than 500 million Wi-Fi users worldwide by 2009 (JiWire, 2006). However, wireless security remains mostly important factor that challenges wireless internet hot spots. As Wi-Fi grows the security threat also increases rapidly and therefore the need to protect information becomes imperative (Peikari and Fogie, 2003). The security risk remains largely from hackers, who are individuals, that access into the system without any authorization and for personal gain.

Given the above context, the rationale for this research is to gain a better understanding about the free wireless internet park "iPark" initiative in Qatar. Using a pilot survey questionnaire, this study aims to explore the intention of citizens to use iPark services in Qatar. This is achieved by examining their perceptions of 'ease of use' and 'usefulness' in relation to internet access in the iPark. To pursue this line of inquiry, this research uses the technology acceptance model (TAM). TAM theorizes that an individual's behavioral intention to use a technology is determined by two factors: perceived usefulness and perceived ease of use (Gardner and Amoroso, 2004).

The chapter is structured as followed. In the next section the national Qatari e-government background is presented then a literature perspective of e-government is offered followed by an outline of the theoretical model used for the research. Then the empirical background to the research is presented. This is followed by the methodology used for the research and a presentation of the empirical results. Finally the chapter concludes by analysing the empirical results, discussing the research implications and identifying areas for future research.

E-GOVERNMENT IN THE STATE OF QATAR

The State of Qatar is a peninsula with a strategic position at the centre of the west coast of the Arabian Gulf. The total land area is approximately 11,437 sq km. The population estimated to be around 1,500,000 (The Peninsula, 2008; Al-Shafi and Weerakkody, 2008b); however, only a minority of the population is citizens by birth, while the rest are residents who live or work in Qatar and are not Qatari's by birth (Al-Shafi and Weerakkody, 2008a).

E-government was launched in Qatar in July 2000 and the initial period of strategy formulation and implementation was laggard compared to e-government efforts during the same period in developed countries. However, with the establishment of ictQATAR in 2004 and their consequent takeover of the national e-government initiative a year later resulted in accelerated progress in the last three years. Parallel programmes were introduced in key areas such as health, interior affairs and education. The vision of ictQATAR states "....Serve as independent and fair regulator, protecting consumers and businesses from unfair practices as Qatar transitions to a competitive telecoms market, lead the government's ICT strategy, nurture innovative technologies to benefit those who live and work in Qatar, and help make people from all walks of life become comfortable with technology" (ictQATAR, 2008).

The Qatari e-government site offers many services, ranging from student registration and paying traffic violations to applying online for visas and permits (Al-Shafi and Weerakkody, 2007). In global terms the UN Global E-government readiness report (2008) ranked Qatar's e-government project as number 53 worldwide, where as in 2005 it was ranked as number 62worldwide (Al-Shafi and Weerakkody, 2007). In addition to this, the UN (2005) report considered the Qatari e-government project to be regional (West Asia) best practice. This implies that major improvements and developments have been made during recent times. As part of Qatar government's ongoing efforts to increase accessibility to e-government services and bridge the digital divide, free wireless internet access in public parks – (iPark) initiative was launched in March 2007; this concept provides "Broadband for all" and aims to foster a knowledge based society. The primary goal of the initiative is to increase internet usage by establishing "hot spots" in public parks (IctQATAR, 2007). There are currently three designated wireless internet hotspots throughout selected public parks in the city; these parks are targeting visitors who have internet access available on their laptops, PDAs, and other internet-ready devices (The Peninsula, 2007).

E-GOVERNMENT ADOPTION AND DIFFUSION: A LITERATURE PERSPECTIVE

With the popularity of e-government growing, various researchers have offered different definitions to explain the concept (Seifert and Petersen, 2002). However, these definitions differ according to the varying e-government focus and are usually centered on technology, business, citizen, government, process, or a functional perspective. (Wassenaar, 2000; Wimmer and Traunmuller, 2000; Bonham *et al.*, 2001; Seifert and Petersen, 2002; Zhiyuan, 2002; and Irani *et al.*, 2006). The definition considered to be most suitable for the purpose of this chapter is one that defines e-government as making full use of the potential of technology to help put its citizens at the centre of the e-services provided and which makes its citizens its intention (Waller *et al.*, 2001)

Like e-business, e-government promises to deliver a number of benefits to citizens, businesses and governments. The most significant benefits of e-government, according to the literature, are delivering electronic and integrated public services through a single point of access to public services 24 hours a day, seven days a week (Reffat, 2003); bridging the digital divide so that every citizen in society will be offered the same type of information and services from government (InfoDev, 2002); rebuilding customer relationships by providing value-added and personalised services to citizens (Davison et al., 2005); fostering economic development and helping local businesses to expand globally; and creating a more participative form of government by encouraging online debating, voting and exchange of information (Reynolds and Regio, 2001; Bonham et al., 2001; InfoDev, 2002; and Davison, et al., 2005).

Like any other new technology or organisational concept, the introduction of e-government to a country will also result in a number of challenges for the citizens and the government alike (Margetts and Dunleavy, 2002; Seifert and Petersen, 2002; Zakareya and Irani, 2005). Lack of access to e-services (Chircu and Lee, 2005), security concerns (Harris and Schwartz, 2000), trust (Al-Sebie and Irani, 2005), individual differences (Reffat, 2003) and digital divide (Carter and Bèlanger, 2005; Chen et al., 2006) are challenges that can impact on participation and thereby obstruct the further take-up of e-government services.

From the aforementioned, this research will focus particularly on the influence that Wi-Fi technology complexity and attitudes have on the intention to use a new technology, in this instance iPark. Similarly it will also examine perceived usefulness, ease of use and attitude of iPark services and the influence that a citizen's individual differences have on the intention to use such services.

In terms of adoption and diffusion, several studies have explored e-government acceptance in the United States (Carter and Belanger, 2005) and the U.K (Choudrie and Dwivedi, 2005). However, no studies exist that examine factors that influence Qatari citizens' adoption of e-government services. In this respect Lee et *al.*, (2005) state that cross-national research on e-government is sparse in the literature and Dwivedi et *al.*, (2006) highlights the need for studies that investigate the adoption rate and behaviour of e-services. Given this context, this study attempts to address this gap in a Qatari perspective by integrating the aforementioned constructs from the Technology Acceptance Model.

TECHNOLOGY ADOPTION: THE THEORETICAL BACKGROUND

Researchers in the field of Information Systems and Technology have for long been interested in investigating the theories and models that have the power in predicting and explaining behaviour (Venkatesh et al, 2003). For example these theories and models include, Theory Of Reasoned Action (TRA), Theory Of Planned Behaviour (TPB), Innovation Diffusion Theory (IDT) (Rogers, 1995), Unified Theory Of Acceptance and Use of Technology (UTAUT), and Technology Acceptance Model (TAM) (Venkatesh et al., 2003).

The Technology Accepted Model is adapted from the Theory of Reasoned Action (TRA) to the field of information systems. Davis developed TAM in 1989 (Davis, 1989) and uses TRA as a theoretical basis for specifying the linkages between two key beliefs: perceived usefulness and perceived ease of use and users' attitudes, intentions and actual usage behaviour. According to Davis et al., (1989) the main goal of the model is to give an explanation of the determinants of computer acceptance which resulted to an explanation of user behaviour across a broad range of end-user computing technologies and user populations (Davis et al., 1989). In addition, another key focus of TAM (figure 1) is to provide a base for determining or exposing the impact of external variables on internal beliefs, attitudes, and intentions.

During previous years, TAM has received extensive support through validation, applications, and replications for its power to predict

Figure 1. Technology acceptance model (Source: Davis, 1989)

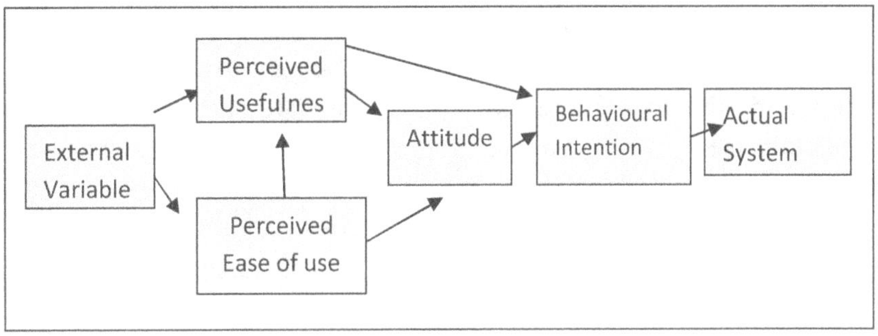

use of information systems (Cheng *et al.,* 2006). Also, Davis et al., (1989), Venkatesh and Davis (2000) and Chau (1996) claimed that TAM is the most influential model in explaining IS/IT adoption behaviour. In this study, TAM will be used as the theoretical basis for examining user intention to use the iPark concept in Qatar. We have extended the TAM model to include two other relevant constructs, technology complexity in terms of Wireless Internet response time, and individual differences that includes age, gender, and qualifications.

CONCEPTUAL MODEL AND HYPOTHESIS

Attitude has been defined as a cause of intention (June et *al.*, 2003). According to Fishbein and Ajzen's (1975) attitude is classified into two constructs: attitude toward the object and attitude toward the behaviour. Investigation of the attitude construct toward using iPark services and examining its relationship with intention to use is appropriate for predicting usage behaviour.

According to Davis (1989) the perceived usefulness in TAM relates to productivity, performance, and effectiveness. This is an important construct as it provides a clear indication of how user attitude toward using and intention to use are influenced by perceived usefulness; perceived usefulness also has an indirect affect on intention to use via attitude (Davis et al,. 1989; June et al., 2003).

Perceived ease of use is another important determinant of attitude in TAM (June *et al.,* 2003). According to Davis's (1989) perceived ease of use is the individual's assessment of the level of effort involved in using the given system. Few authors confirmed the affect of ease of use on attitude toward use (Al-Gahtani and King, 1999; Venkatesh and Davis, 1996).

TAM primarily focuses on the development and identification of two key constructs, 'perceived usefulness' and 'perceived ease of use'. However, the original TAM does not include any moderating affects, and research suggests incorporating these moderators to include gender and age into the original TAM in order to make better predictions and explanations associated with user behaviour for a particular technology (Venkatesh and Davis, 2000; Morris and Venkatesh, 2000). Furthermore, research has found that gender (Venkatesh *et al.,* 2003; June *et al.,* 2003) and educational background (Agarwal and Prasad, 1999) significantly moderates the influence of the determinants on behaviour intention.

The adoption and diffusion of Wireless hotspots will depend very much on the speed of Internet connection. Moreover, according to Pew Internet and American Life Project (2006), Wifi has the potential to reshape customers' needs and conversely customers can reshape the technology.

Based on the aforementioned and the theoretical context offered, this chapter will test the strength of the hypothesized relationships mentioned in the theoretical model outlined in Figure-2 (and Table 1) and the appropriateness of the model in predicting users' intention to use iPark in the State of Qatar.

RESEARCH METHODOLOGY

To explore the argument set out above and understand the context of the iPark initiative in Qatar, brief informal open-ended interviews (Yin, 1994) were conducted with three citizens and one Academic in the last quarter of 2007. The interviews lasted around 30 minutes and provided the context to formulate a detailed survey questionnaire that was to be used to investigate the citizens' perceptions of iPark in Qatar.

After the questionnaire was designed, a limited testing was done using one researcher and four practitioners. This was important to improve the questions and to test respondents' comprehension and clarity before the actual survey was

Figure 2. Factors influencing iPark adoption

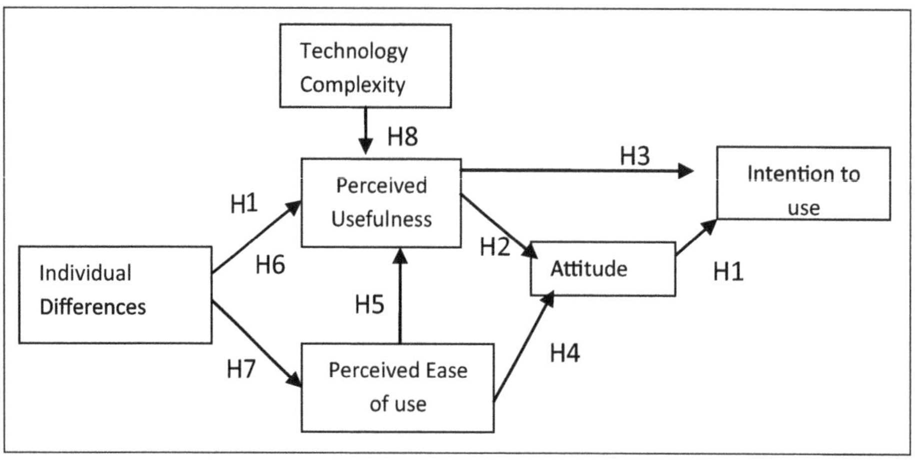

Table 1. Research hypothesis

NO.	Hypothesis
H1:	Attitude toward iPark may have a significant positive affect on intentions to use iPark.
H2:	Perceived usefulness of iPark may have a significant positive affect on attitude toward using iPark
H3:	Perceived usefulness of iPark may have a significant positive affect on intention to use iPark.
H4:	Perceived ease of use of iPark may have a significant positive affect on attitude toward using iPark.
H5:	Perceived ease of using iPark may have a significant positive affect on Perceived usefulness of iPark
H6:	Individual differences may have a significant positive affect on perceived ease of using iPark in terms of gender, age and qualification.
H7:	Individual differences may have a significant positive affect on perceived ease of using iPark in terms of gender, age and qualification
H8:	Technology complexity may have a positive significant affect on perceived usefulness of iPark in terms of Wireless Internet Speed.

administered (Saunders *et al.,* 2002). The pilot testing led to the removal of one question and modification to another.

The protocol followed for data collection was as follows. First, one of the researchers approached the iPark users, identified himself and provided a brief description of the research and the main purpose of the questionnaire. Then, the process of completing the questionnaire began by distributing the questionnaire to users and briefly explaining the contents of the questionnaire. Thereafter the questionnaires were collected after a period of around 20 to 30 minutes.

The survey questionnaire was distributed to a total of 55 iPark users between the period of November and December 2007; 54 usable responses were obtained. Overall, a survey questionnaire approach was selected as it is inexpensive, less time consuming and has the ability to provide both quantitative scale and qualitative data from a large research sample (Cornford and Smithson, 1997). The questionnaire used had 26 closed-ended questions and used likert scale type (5-point scale) questions (Saunders et al., 2002).

Data Analysis

The proposed research model consists of seven dependant and independent variables: (2) individual differences in terms of age, gender and qualifications; (2) perceived usefulness; (3) perceived ease of use; (4) attitude; (5) intention to use; and (6) technology complexity in terms of wireless internet speed.

The authors generated the descriptive statistics (percentage and tables), used reliability of measurements and construct correlations by utilising SPSS (Version 15.0). Descriptive data analysis provides the reader with an appreciation of the actual numbers and values, and hence the scale that researchers are dealing with (Dwivedi and Weerakkody, 2007).

RESEARCH FINDINGS

Of these 54 usable respondents (15%) were females while 85% were males. Also, of the 54 respondents, (74%) had an internet connections in their home/work or both.

When examining the 'ease of use' of iPark services, 85% of the respondents mentioned that they found the service was easy for them, while 15% thought otherwise.

In terms of age, the results revealed that the majority of respondents (38%) were found in the age group of 31-45, followed by the age group of 19-30 constituting around (32%) of the total respondents. In contrast, the younger groups (less than 18) and older age groups (46-60) consisted together of (30%) of the total respondents (see figure 3).

As far as education is concerned, the majority of respondents (38%) hold postgraduate degrees (Masters and PhD), and (36%) hold undergraduate level qualifications and 26% hold secondary school certificates (see figure 3).

Finally, Figure 4 shows that the majority of respondents used iPark for: emails (76%); chat (35%); e-government services (22%); Fun (43%); Research (22%); News (56%); Enquiry (26%); Downloading Information (54%); and other (6%).

As outlined in table-2, the average scores for respondents' perceived ease of use ranged from 4.07 to 4.37. Descriptive statistics show that these scores are quite high. For perceived usefulness, the score ranged from 3.85 and 4.54, which is quite high. Concerning technology complexity, the score ranged 3.70, indicating that the scale is average. In addition, for attitude towards iPark, the score ranged from 4.35 to 4.59, indicating that the scale is uniform. Also, the score ranged from 1.15 to 2.64 for individual differences toward iPark. The last score ranged from 3.30 to 3.72 for intention to use.

Cronbach's coefficient alpha values were chosen to examine the internal consistency of the

Figure 3. Age and qualification of the respondents

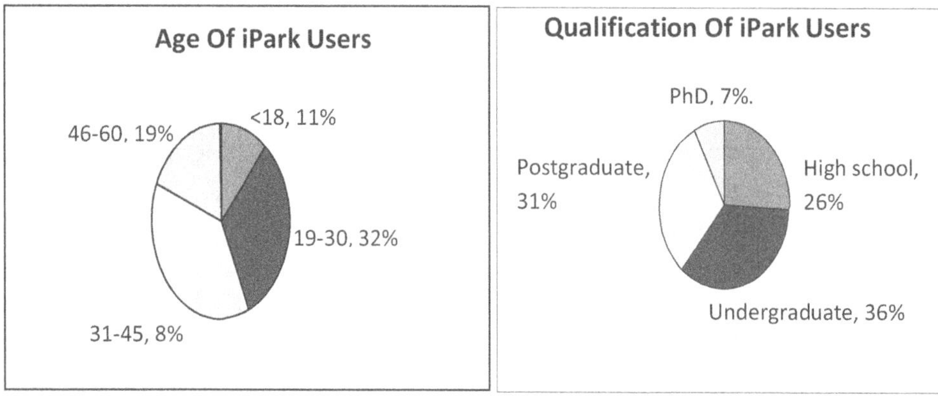

Figure 4. Primary uses of iPark user respondents, November & December, 2007

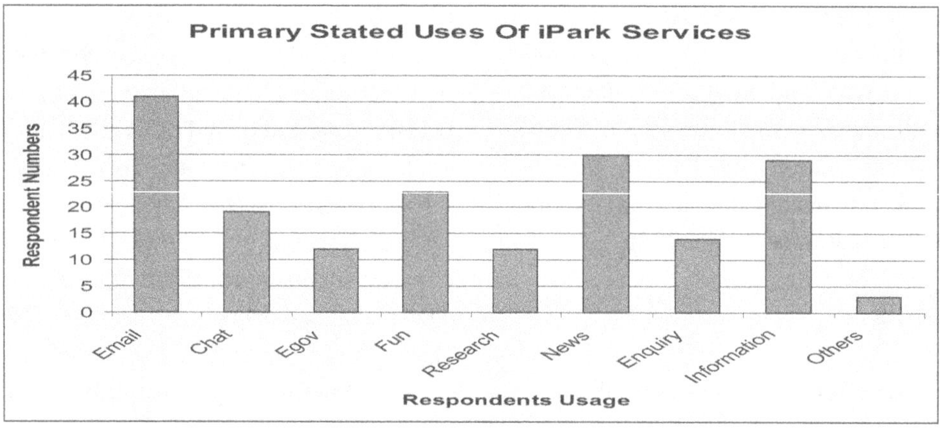

measure (Hinton et al., 2004) (table 3). Cronbach's results varied between 8.26 for the intention to use and 8.60 for the individual constructs.

Hinton et al., (2004) have suggested four different points of reliability, excellent ranges (0.90 and above), high (0.70- 0.90), high moderate (0.50-0.70) and low (0.50 and below). The previous mentioned values in table 3 show that all of the constructs got high reliability. The high Cronbach's values of the constructs means that constructs were internally consistent and the reliability is measuring the same construct.

Table 4 also shows that the correlation is significant for one key factoring as per the hypothesis (H3), *perceived usefulness (0.417), which implies that it is correlated* with intention to use, whereas attitude (0.143) was found to be insignificantly associated with intention to use as per hypothesis (H1).

Table 5 also shows that the correlation is significant for one key factor as per hypothesis (H2), *perceived usefulness (0.286), which implied that it has an* impact on attitude. Whereas, *perceived use of ease* (0.025) was found to have an insignificant

Table 2. Descriptive statistics of iPark usage reliability test

		Std. Deviation
Use iPark frequently	3.43	1.238
Encounter problem frequently in using the iPark	2.70	1.218
Individual Differences		
Gender	1.15	.359
Qualification	2.20	.919
Age	2.64	.922
Perceived Ease Of Use		
Using the iPark service is easy for me	4.07	.949
Interaction with the iPark services is clear and understandable	4.08	.917
Becoming skilful in the use of the iPark services is easy	4.37	.853
Overall, I find the use of the iPark services easy	4.17	1.060
Perceived Usefulness		
Using the iPark would enable me to accomplish my tasks more quickly	3.89	1.144
Using the iPark would make it easier for me to carry out my tasks	3.85	1.139
iPark is useful for me	4.54	.803
Overall, using the iPark is advantageous for me	4.50	.897
Technology Complexity Speed of Internet in the iPark is good	3.70	.964
Attitude		
Using the iPark is a good idea	4.59	.567
Using the iPark is pleasant	4.43	.742
In my opinion, it would be desirable to use the iPark	4.35	.828
In my view, Using free Wireless Internet from public parks is a wise idea	4.42	.936
Intention To Use		
I would Use the iPark channels for my needs.	3.72	1.140
I would use iPark for my e-government services	3.30	1.207

correlation and negative affect on attitude toward using iPark as per hypothesis (H4).

Table 6 also shows that the correlation is significant for the following four key factors: perceived ease of use (0.489) as per the hypothesis (H5); technology complexity in terms of wireless internet speed (0.358) as per hypothesis (H8); individual differences in terms of age (0.478) and Qualification (0.251) as per hypothesis (H6). These results imply that these constructs have a significant impact on perceived usefulness. In contrast, individual difference in terms of gender (0.113) was found to have an insignificant correlation. In addition, individual differences in terms of age and qualification had a negative affect on perceived usefulness toward using iPark as per hypothesis (H6).

Table 7 shows that the correlation is insignificant for one key factor, *individual differences in terms of age (0.*140*)*, gender (0.066) and qualification (0.491) as per hypothesis (H7). This result implies that they have an insignificant impact on the perceived ease of use construct. In addition, individual differences in terms of age and gender

Table 3. Reliability of measurements

Constructs	Number of items	Cronbach's Alpha (a)
Individual Differences	3	0.86
Perceived Ease Of Use	4	0.83
Perceived Usefulness	4	0.83
Technology Complexity	1	0.84
Attitude	4	0.84
Intention To Use	2	0.83

Table 4. Correlations of intention to use construct

Constructs		Intention to use
I would find the iPark useful	Pearson Correlation	.417(**)
	Sig.(1-tailed)	.001
In my view, Using free wireless Internet from public parks is a wise idea	Pearson Correlation	.143
	Sig.(1-tailed)	.155

Table 5. Correlations of attitude

Constructs		ATTITUDE
Overall, I find the use of the iPark services easy	Pearson Correlation	-.025
	Sig.(1-tailed)	.430
I would find the iPark useful	Pearson Correlation	.286(*)
	Sig.(1-tailed)	.021

constructs had a negative affect on perceived ease of using iPark as per hypothesis (H7), whereas the individual's educational background though showed a positive impact on perceived ease of using iPark.

DISCUSSION AND CONCLUSION

E-government is widely accepted and seen as a growing trend worldwide. In the Middle East, most countries have implemented e-government services. However, the growth and adoption of e-government in a country will depend on basic prerequisites such as education, trust, marketing and awareness (Reffat, 2003; Navarra and Cornford, 2003; Bhattacherjee, 2002). The Qatari e-government project serves natural citizens, foreign residents and workers, and business and government agencies. As part of Qatar's wider national e-government program objectives to entice more users to access electronic government services, free wireless internet access in public parks – (iPark) initiative was launched in March 2007.

This chapter discussed the results of a survey targeted towards iPark users in Qatar and it provides a representative account of the citi-

Table 6. Perceived usefulness correlations

Constructs		Perceived Usefulness
Overall, I find the use of the iPark services easy	Pearson Correlation	.489(**)
	Sig.(1-tailed)	.000
I would rate the speed of Internet/ Response time in the iPark is good	Pearson Correlation	.358(**)
	Sig.(1-tailed)	.005
Age	Pearson Correlation	-.478(**)
	Sig.(1-tailed)	.000
Gender	Pearson Correlation	.113
	Sig.(1-tailed)	.212
Level of Education	Pearson Correlation	-.251(*)
	Sig.(1-tailed)	.036
Overall, the iPark is a safe place to transmit sensitive information	Pearson Correlation	.297(*)
	Sig.(1-tailed)	.016

Table 7. Perceived usefulness correlations

Constructs		Perceived ease of use
Age	Pearson Correlation	-.140
	Sig.(1-tailed)	.159
Gender	Pearson Correlation	-.066
	Sig.(1-tailed)	.317
Level of Education	Pearson Correlation	.003
	Sig.(1-tailed)	.491

zens' perceptions of the iPark project. While the availability and use of Wi-Fi networks continue to increase, for users, Wi-Fi facilitates greater mobility, information access, and flexibility in connectivity, improved efficiency, low cost, ease of use, and new applications, which could change the way they access electronic services.

The results of this research showed that individual differences have a negative affect on perceived ease of use (H7) and perceived ease of use has a negative relationship with attitude (H4). The remaining hypotheses showed that they were consistent. This implies that contrary to expectations the citizens' intention to use new technological concepts such as iPark has no link with the individual differences in terms of age and educational background of the citizen in the Qatari context. Given these findings, it can be concluded that the iPark initiative in Qatar has been successful initially in promoting wider access to the Internet. This is encouraging from an e- government perspective. The authors suggest that public parks (iParks) can be used to advertise and market the Qatari e-government national website and raise e-government awareness among Qatari citizens. While the research findings are encouraging from a practical perspective for the Qatari government, from a theoretical perspective these results reconfirm that technology acceptance is influenced by key constructs such as perceived usefulness, attitude, and technology complexity aspects of the services used.

This research describes an early attempt to study the adoption of the iPark initiative by Qatari citizens and thus represents only the views of a limited sample of users (54). To ensure more thorough testing of the hypothesis proposed in this research, the authors have planned future research in the first quarter of 2009 to survey a larger number of iPark users.

REFERENCES

Agarwal, R., & Prasad, J. (1999). Are individual differences germane to the acceptance of new information technologies? *Decision Sciences, 30*(2), 361-91.

AL-Gahtani, S., & King, M. (1999). Attitudes, satisfaction and usage: factors contributing to each in the acceptance of information technology. *Behavior And Information Technology, 18(4), 277-297.*

Al-Shafi, S., & Weerakkody, V. (2007). Implementing and managing e-government in the State of Qatar: a citizens' perspective. *Electronic Government, an International Journal, 4*(4), 436-450.

Al-Shafi, S. and Weerakkody, V. (2008a). Adoption of wireless internet parks: an empirical Study in Qatar. Paper presented at the *Proceedings of the European and Mediterranean Conference on Information systems (EMCIS08),*Dubai, UAE.

Al-Shafi, S. and Weerakkody, V. (2008b). The Use Of Wireless Internet Parks To Facilitate Adoption And Diffusion Of E-Government Services: An Empirical Study In Qatar. Paper presented at the *Proceedings of the 14th Americas Conference on Information Systems (AMCIS 2008)* Toronto, Ontario.

Al-Sebie, M., & Irani, Z. (2005). Technical and organisational challenges facing transactional e-government systems: an empirical study. *Electronic Government, An International Journal, 2*(3), 247–276.

Bonham, G., Seifert, J., & Thorson, S. (2001). *The Transformational Potential of e-Government: The Role Of Political Leadership.* Paper presented at the The 4th Pan European International Relations Conference of the European Consortium for Political Research, University of Kent, Canterbury, U.K.

Carter, L., & Bélanger, F. (2005). The utilization of e-government services: citizen trust, innovation and acceptance factors. *Information Systems Journal, 15*, 5-26.

Chau, P.Y.K. (1996). An Empirical Assessment Of A Modified Technology Acceptance Model. *Journal of Management Information Systems, 13*(2), 185-204.

Chen, C., Tseng, S., & Huang, H. (2006). A comprehensive study of the digital divide phenomenon in Taiwanese government agencies. *International Journal Of Internet And Enterprise Management, 4*(3), 244-256.

Cheng, T., Lam, D., & Yeung, A. (2006). Adoption of internet banking: An empirical study in Hong Kong. *Decision Support Systems, 42*, 1558-1572.

Chircu, A.M., & Lee, D.H-D. (2005). E-government: Key Success Factors For Value Discovery And Realisation. *E-Government, an International Journal, 2*(1), 11-25.

Choudrie, J., & Dwivedi, Y. (2005). A Survey of Citizens Adoption and Awareness of E-Government Initiatives. The Government Gateway: A United Kingdom Perspective. *E-Government Workshop.* Brunel University, West London.

Cornford, T., & Smithson, S. (1997). *Project Research in Information Systems: A Student's Guide.* London: Macmillan Press.

Davis, F.D. (1989). Perceived usefulness, perceived ease of use, and user acceptance of information technology. *MIS Quarterly, 13*(319-340).

Davis, F.D., Bagozzi, R.P., & Warshaw, P.R. (1989). User Acceptance of Computer Technology: A Comparison of Two Theoretical Models. *Management Science, 35*(8), 982-1003.

Davison, R.M., Wagner, C., & Ma, L.C. (2005). From government to e-government: a transition model. *Information Technology & People, 18*(3), 280-299.

Dwivedi, Y., & Weerakkody, V. (2007). Examining the factors affecting the adoption of broadband in the Kingdom of Saudi Arabia. *Electronic Government, an International Journal, 4*(1), 43-58.

Dwivedi, Y., Papazafeiropoulou, A., & Gharavi, H. (2006). *Socio-Economic Determinants of Adoption of the Government Gateway Initiative in the UK, Electronic Government, 3*(4), 404-419.

Fishbein, M., & Ajzen, I. (1975). *Belief, Attitude, Intention and Behaviour: An Introduction to Theory and Research*, Reading, MA: Addison-Wesley.

Gardner, C., & Amoroso, D. (2004). *Development of an Instrument to Measure the Acceptance of Internet Technology by Consumers.* Paper presented at the Proceedings of the 37th Hawaii International Conference on System Sciences, Hawaii, USA.

Gupta, V., & Gupta, S. (2005) Experiments in Wireless Internet Security. *Statistical Methods In Computer Security*

Harris, J.F., & Schwartz, J. (2000). Anti drug website tracks visitors. *Washington Post*, 22 June, (p. 23).

Hinton, P.R., Brownlow, C., McMurvay, I., & Cozens, B. (2004). *SPSS explained.* East Sussex, England: Routledge Inc.

IctQatar. (2007). *Free wireless internet in Qatar's public parks.* from http://www.ict.gov.qa/output/page422.asp

InfoDev. (2002). *The e-Government Handbook for Developing Countries.* from http://www.cdt.org/egov/handbook.

Irani, Z., Al-Sebie, M., & Elliman, T. (2006). *Transaction Stage of e-Government Systems: Identification of its Location & Importance.* Paper presented at the Proceedings of the 39th Hawaii International Conference on System Science, Hawaii.

Jiwire (2006). *JiWire Launches Worldwide Point-of-Connection Wi-Fi Hotspot Advertising Network*, from http://www.jiwire.com/about/announcements/press-advertising-network.htm

June, L., Chun-Sheng, Y., Chang, L., & James, E. (2003). Technology Acceptance Model For Wireless Internet. *Internet Research: Electronic Networking Application And Policy,13*(3), 206-222.

Lee, S.M., Tan, X., & Trimi, S. (2005). *Current practices of leading e-government countries. Communications of the ACM, 48*(10), 99-104.

Lehr, W., & McKnight, L.W. (2003). Wireless Internet access: 3G vs. WiFi? *Telecommunications Policy,* 27, 351-370.

Margetts, H., & Dunleavy, P. (2002). *Cultural Barriers to E-Government* (Working Paper): University Collage of London and London School of Economics for National Audit Office.

Morris, M.G., & Venkatesh, V. (2000). Age differences in technology adoption decisions: implications for a changing work force. *Personnel Psychology, 53*(2), 375-403 .

Peikari, C., & Fogie, S. (2003). *Maximum Wireless Security.* from http://www.berr.gov.uk/files/file9972.pdf.

Pew Internet & American Life Project (2006) Home Broadband Adoption. from http://www.pewinternet.org/pdfs/PIP_Broadband_trends2006.pdf

Reffat, R. (2003). *Developing A Successful E-Government* (Working Paper): University Of Sydney, Australia.

Reynolds, M.M., & Regio-Micro, M. (2001). The Purpose Of Transforming Government-E-Government as a Catalyst In The Information Age. *Microsoft E-Government Initiatives*, from http://www.netcaucus.org/books/egov2001/pdf/EGovIntr.pdf

Rogers, E.M. (1995). *Diffusion of innovations.* New York.

Saunders, M., Lewis, P., & Thornhill, A. (2002). *Research methods for business students* (Third edition). Harlow: Prentice Hall.

Seifert, J., & Petersen, E. (2002). The Promise Of All Things E? Expectations and Challenges of Emergent E-Government. *Perspectives on Global Development and Technology, 1*(2), 193-213.

The Peninsula Newspaper. (2008). *Bursting at the seams,* from http://www.thepeninsulaqatar.com/Display_news.asp?section=Local_News&month=January2008&file=Local_News200801296298.xml.

UN. (2008). *World public sector report: UN E-Government survey, From E-Government To Connected Governance.* New York.

Venkatesh, V., & Davis, F.D. (1996). A model of the antecedents of perceived ease of use: Development and test. *Decision Sci., 27*, 451-481.

Venkatesh, V., & Davis, F.D. (2000). A theoretical extension of the technology acceptance model: Four longitudinal field studies. *Management Science, 46*(2), 186-205.

Venkatesh, V., Morris, M., Davis, G., & Davis, F. (2003). User Acceptance of Information Technology: Toward a Unified View. *MIS Quarterly, 27*(3), 425-478.

Waller, P., Livesey, P., & Edin, K. (2001). e-Government in the Service of Democracy. *ICA Information, 74.*

Wassenaar, A. (2000). E-Governmental Value Chain Models. *DEXA, IEEE Press*, (pp. 289-293).

Wimmer, M., & Traunmuller, R. (2000). *Trends in e-government: managing distributed knowledge.* Paper presented at the Proceedings from 11th International Workshop on Database and Expert Systems Applications, New York.

Yin, R.K. (1994). *Case Study Research - Design And Methods* (Second Edition). London:Sage Publications.

Zakareya, E., & Irani, Z. (2005), E-government adoption: Architecture and barriers. *Business Process Management Journal, 11*(5), 589-611.

Zhiyuan, F. (2002). E-Government in Digital Era: Concepts, Practice and Development. *International Journal Of The Computer, The Internet and Management, 10*(2), 1-22.

Section IV
E-Government Research

Chapter XII
A Bibliometric Analysis of Electronic Government Research

Yogesh K. Dwivedi
Swansea University, UK

ABSTRACT

The main purpose of this chapter is to provide readers an exhaustive list of references focused upon electronic government related issues.The chapter also presents information on a series of variables which were extracted after conducting a bibliometric analysis of 1,037 articles on various aspects of electronic government research, published in 19 peer reviewed journals between 1986 and 2008. Results of this research may have implications for authors/researchers, journal and book editors, reviewers and universities.

INTRODUCTION

It has been argued that the electronic government concepts and applications are varied and ranges from facilitating regular interaction and transactions of citizens with local and federal/national Governments to managing the unforeseen calamities and anti-social behaviour (Irani and Dwivedi, 2008). It has also been argued that electronic government research is truly multi-disciplinary in nature and required theories and methods from various disciplines to understand and explain the issues related with its conception, design, implementation, adoption, use and impact (Irani and Dwivedi, 2008). Many scholars suggest electronic government research still in emerging state but others argues that e-government research currently moving towards initial maturity. Since it's a relatively new area of investigation, there are only few academic outlets (*Electronic Gov-*

ernment, An International Journal, International Journal of Electronic Government Research and *Transforming Government: People, Process and Policy (TGPPP)*) dedicated solely to publish research on e-government (Dwivedi 2009). This indicates that electronic government research may have opening in various journals and conferences from its reference disciplines (such as information systems, electronic commerce, public administration etc.). However, such wide distribution of the research publications on electronic government poses problems to potential researchers searching publications sparsely located across various disciplines. Such challenges become more severe if researchers unfortunately do not have access to academic search databases representing various reference disciplines. A thorough literature search and analysis critical for establishing research gap and providing basis for new research and to identify relevant theoretical and methodological approaches. Considering the wide distribution of the electronic government research and critical role of accessibility of published research, it was felt important to undertake an analysis of published research in this area as hardly any published research has made such attempt.

Therefore, the main purpose of this chapter is to provide electronic government researchers an exhaustive list of references focused upon electronic government related issues. Utilising identified references the chapter also attempts to create a profile of electronic government research on following dimensions: subject categories; source titles publishing most articles on electronic government; the general trends on electronic government research according to the year of publication; and countries and institutions (and hence areas of greatest activity) with the largest number of publications on electronic government; authors active in the area of electronic government.

In order to realise aforementioned aim, a Bibliometric analysis of 1037 articles published during the period 1986-2008 was conducted. The remainder of this chapter is structured as follows. In Section 2 a discussion of the method employed in this analysis is presented. Findings are presented and discussed in Section 4 and finally, Section 5 presents conclusions from this work and the limitation to the approach.

METHODOLOGY

The method utilised in this study is adapted from previous studies which have employed Bibliometrics approach to analyse literature on specific topics (Dwivedi et al. 2008abc). In line with previous studies (Dwivedi et al. 2008abc) this research also made use of the academic journals database provided by Thomson Scientific (previously known as the Institute for Scientific Information (ISI)). The Web of Science® product provides two main search-techniques i.e. 'General Search' and 'Advanced Search'. The search-technique used within this research exercise was the 'General Search'. The main reason for employing a 'General Search' approach was simply that its easy to use characteristics facilitate the repetition of searches without any confusion, henceforth is straightforward to obtain consistent results in repetitive searches provided the same search criteria are applied (Dwivedi et al. 2008abc).

In order to identify publications specific to the electronic government area, following search-terms were sought after in this study: "Electronic government" OR "egovernment" OR "e-government" OR "e-gov" OR "egov" OR "transformational government" OR "online government" OR "e-democracy". The search was restricted to occurrences of any of these keywords appearing in the article title in order to avoid locating publications where any of these keywords might have been used as casual words in the main text. However, if one of these words appeared in the article title, it suggested that the main focus of the article is electronic government related issues in some form. The search using the aforementioned keywords resulted in 1037 conference and journal research and review publications on e-government. All 1037 items were then examined manually to crosscheck and confirm the relevance of the search results.

A number of analyses were then conducted on the search output employing the various analysis tools available in the Web of Science®. Count and percentage data was generated for the assorted variables utilised to categorise the search output. Variables analysed included subject category, journal in which an article appeared, year of publication, author, author's institution, and the country in which the research was conducted.

FINDINGS

Electronic Government Studies According to Subject Category

Table 1 illustrates that a total of 28 Web of Science® Subject Categories have published five

Table 1. Electronic government studies according to subject category

Subject Area	Count	% of 1037
Computer Science, Information Systems	379	36.55%
Computer Science, Theory & Methods	342	32.98%
Computer Science, Interdisciplinary Applications	214	20.64%
Information Science & Library Science	196	18.90%
Business	142	13.69%
Computer Science, Artificial Intelligence	107	10.32%
Political Science	90	8.68%
Public Administration	84	8.10%
Management	82	7.91%
Telecommunications	74	7.14%
Computer Science, Software Engineering	63	6.08%
Engineering, Electrical & Electronic	62	5.98%
Operations Research & Management Science	61	5.88%
Social Issues	56	5.40%
Economics	27	2.60%
Engineering, Industrial	27	2.60%
Computer Science, Hardware & Architecture	26	2.51%
Business, Finance	18	1.74%
Computer Science, Cybernetics	17	1.64%
Communication	16	1.54%
Social Sciences, Interdisciplinary	16	1.54%
Education & Educational Research	14	1.35%
Planning & Development	11	1.06%
Automation & Control Systems	8	0.77%
Engineering, Multidisciplinary	7	0.68%
Engineering, Manufacturing	5	0.48%
Imaging Science & Photographic Technology	5	0.48%
Mathematics, Applied	5	0.48%

or more articles on electronic government, the largest number of articles (379) appearing within the 'Computer Science, Information Systems' category. This is followed by the 'Computer Science, Theory & Methods' category (342), and then the 'Computer Science, Interdiscipilanry Applications' category (214). Three categories 'Engineeing, Manufacturing', 'Imaging Science & Photographic Technology' and 'Mathematics, Applied' contributed equal and lowest number of articles (5) presented in Table 1. A range of other categories that published electronic government research includes business, political science, public administration, management, telecommunications, social issues, economics, planning & development, education and communication. This clearly illustrates true multidisipilanary nature of electronic government research.

Electronic Government Studies According to Document Type

It emerged from the analysis that a large number of search results were research papers published within conference proceeding (802, 77.34%) followed by journal articles (231, 22.28%) and only four (0.39%) classified as review articles.

Electronic Government Studies According to Source Titles (Journals/Conferences)

Table 2 presents the breakdown of the search output according to the source titles in which the articles on electronic government appeared. A total of 47 source titles have published five or more articles on electronic government. Table 2

Table 2. Electronic government studies according to source titles (Journals/Conferences)

Source Title	Count	% of 1037
Lecture Notes in Computer Science	249	24.01%
Electronic Government, Proceedings	141	13.60%
Government Information Quarterly	59	5.69%
International Federation for Information Processing (Ifip)	56	5.40%
Electronic Govenment, Proceedings	43	4.15%
7th European Conference on E-Government, Proceedings	28	2.70%
ICEG 2007: Proceedings of the 3rd International Conference on E-Government	22	2.12%
Lecture Notes in Artificial Intelligence	15	1.45%
12th International Workshop on Database and Expert Systems Applications, Proceedings	14	1.35%
E-Government: Towards Electronic Democracy, Proceedings	14	1.35%
Eadoption and the Knowledge Economy: Issues, Applications, Case Studies, Pts 1 And 2	14	1.35%
Information and Communication Technologies and the Knowledge Economy Series	14	1.35%
International Conference on Politics and Information Systems: Technologies and Applications, Vol 2	14	1.35%
Seventh International Conference on Electronic Commerce, Vols 1 and 2, Selected Proceedings	14	1.35%
Sixth Wuhan International Conference on E-Business, Vols 1-4	13	1.25%
Innovations Through Information Technology, Vols 1 And 2	12	1.16%
Knowledge Management in Electronic Government, Proceedings	11	1.06%
International Conference on Politics and Information Systems: Technologies and Applications, Proceedings	10	0.96%
Knowledge Management in Electronic Government	10	0.96%

continued on following page

Table 2. continued

Public Administration Review	10	0.96%
Towards The E-Society: E-Commerce, E-Business, And E-Government	10	0.96%
3rd International Conference On Politics And Information Systems: Technologies And Applications, Proceedings	9	0.87%
Integration And Innovation Orient To E-Society, Vol 2	9	0.87%
11th International Workshop On Database And Expert Systems Application, Proceedings	8	0.77%
Social Science Computer Review	8	0.77%
European Journal Of Information Systems	7	0.68%
Wirtschaftsinformatik	7	0.68%
American Review Of Public Administration	6	0.58%
Challenges Of Expanding Internet: E-Commerce, E-Business, And E-Government	6	0.58%
Fourth Wuhan International Conference On E-Business: The Internet Era & The Global Enterprise, Vols 1 And 2	6	0.58%
Information Management In The Networked Economy: Issues & Solutions	6	0.58%
Journal Of Strategic Information Systems	6	0.58%
Proceedings Of 2003 International Conference On Management Science & Engineering, Vols I And Ii	6	0.58%
Building The E-Service Society: E-Commerce, E-Business, And E-Government	5	0.48%
Certification And Security In E-Services: From E-Government To E-Business	5	0.48%
Decision Support Systems	5	0.48%
Electrical And Computer Engineering	5	0.48%
Electronic Commerce Research And Applications	5	0.48%
Fifth Wuhan International Conference On E-Business, Vols 1-3	5	0.48%
First International Conference On Availability, Reliability And Security, Proceedings	5	0.48%
Information Management In The Modern Organizations: Trends & Solutions, Vols 1 And 2	5	0.48%
Information Systems Journal	5	0.48%
International Conference On Management Of E-Commerce And E-Government, Proceedings	5	0.48%
Internet & Information Systems In The Digital Age: Challenges And Solutions	5	0.48%
Journal Of Global Information Management	5	0.48%
Journal Of Government Information	5	0.48%
On Line Citizenship: Emerging Technologies For European Cities	5	0.48%

illustrates that the largest number of articles (249) on electronic government appeared in the journal *Lecture Notes in Computer Science* and the least number (5) of articles resulting from the search activities appeared in 14 journals. Other source titles that have published a significant number of articles on electronic government include *Electronic Government, Proceeding* (141), *Government Information Quarterly* (59), *IFIP* (56), *Public Administration Review, European Journal of Information Systems* (7) and Information Systems Journal (5). Our findings further reveal that of the source titles publishing the highest numbers of articles on electronic government, only few appeared within academic journals which follow more stringent review process than conferences.

This could be due to the fact that early research on electronic government were exploratory in nature and have utilised very weak theory and less rigrous methodological approach therefore comparatively fewer numbers crossed rigrous revoew process of journals than publication in conferences which follow less rigrous approaches to allow publication of early research to allow academic debate and discussion on early ideas.

Electronic Government Studies According to Publication Year

Findings (illustrated in Table 3) reveal that the number of articles published on electronic government has constantly increased from 2000 (when 12 papers were published) to 2007 (which has so far seen 221 papers to appear). To date, the largest number of articles (221) appeared in 2007, followed by 2004 with a total count of 163 articles. Prior to 2000, a low number of articles appeared in each year, with no articles at all appearing in our selected journals during some years. This clearly indicates that althought e-government concept originated in late 1980s and early 1990s, main academic interest generated from year 2000 onwards.

Authors Actively Involved in Publishing Electronic Government Research

Table 4 lists the authors actively involved in conducting and publishing electronic government related research. It appears that the most productive author in electronic government research is Traunmuller, R with 112 articles, closely followed by Wimmer, M.A. with 98 articles each. A total

Table 3. Electronic government studies according to publication year

Field: Publication Year	Record Count	% of 1037
2007	221	21.31%
2004	163	15.71 %
2005	153	14.75 %
2008	126	12.15 %
2006	125	12.05 %
2003	121	11.66 %
2002	63	6.07 %
2001	39	3.76 %
2000	12	1.15 %
1992	4	0.38 %
1999	3	0.28 %
1986	1	0.09 %
1988	1	0.09%
1990	1	0.09 %
1994	1	0.09 %
1996	1	0.09 %
1997	1	0.09%
1998	1	0.09 %

Table 4. Authors actively involved in publishing electronic government research

Author	Count	% of 1037	Author	Count	% of 1037
Traunmuller, R	112	10.80%	Yang, X	9	0.87%
Wimmer, Ma	98	9.45%	Alzobaidie, A	8	0.77%
Remenyi, D	51	4.92%	Ieee Comp Soc	8	0.77%
Gronlund, A	50	4.82%	Mentzas, G	8	0.77%
Carrasquero, JV	39	3.76%	Corradini, F	7	0.68%
Welsch, F	37	3.57%	Nardelli, E	7	0.68%
Lenk, K	33	3.18%	Pan, Sl	7	0.68%
Scholl, HJ	33	3.18%	Polzonetti, A	7	0.68%
Andersen, KV	31	2.99%	Sabucedo, LA	7	0.68%
Traumuller, R	31	2.99%	Talamo, M	7	0.68%
Oropeza, A	29	2.80%	Tambouris, E	7	0.68%
Tjoa, AM	28	2.70%	Tang, Zw	7	0.68%
Ieee	23	2.22%	Wang, YZ	7	0.68%
Wagner, RR	23	2.22%	Chung, JY	6	0.58%
Soliman, KS	21	2.03%	Funabashi, M	6	0.58%
Scholl, J	19	1.83%	Grzech, A	6	0.58%
Khosrowpour, M	18	1.74%	Janssen, M	6	0.58%
Li, Q	16	1.54%	Li, M	6	0.58%
Tschammer, V	16	1.54%	Malpica, F	6	0.58%
Ferro, E	15	1.45%	Niehaves, B	6	0.58%
Bohlen, M	14	1.35%	Riedl, R	6	0.58%
Cunningham, M	14	1.35%	Rifon, LA	6	0.58%
Cunningham, P	14	1.35%	Stephanidis, C	6	0.58%
Filipe, J	14	1.35%	Xu, LD	6	0.58%
Gamper, J	14	1.35%	Amarger, S	5	0.48%
Lan, H	14	1.35%	Becker, J	5	0.48%
Liang, TP	14	1.35%	Chaudhry, SS	5	0.48%
Polasek, W	14	1.35%	Chen, Y	5	0.48%
Alfred University	13	1.25%	Cheung, W	5	0.48%
Duserick, FG	13	1.25%	Chutimaskul, W	5	0.48%
Callaos, N	12	1.16%	Dimaria, E	5	0.48%
Cordeiro, J	11	1.06%	Gouscos, D	5	0.48%
Li, Yh	10	0.96%	Henriksen, HZ	5	0.48%
Schmid, B	10	0.96%	Huang, W	5	0.48%
Stanoevskaslabeva, K	10	0.96%	Ieee Computer Society	5	0.48%
Tso, CD	10	0.96%	Lamersdorf, W	5	0.48%
Urrea, C	10	0.96%	Li, X	5	0.48%
Yan, L	10	0.96%	Liao, GQ	5	0.48%
Chen, J	9	0.87%	Macintosh, A	5	0.48%

continued on following page

Table 4. continued

Duan, Z	9	0.87%	Micelli, S	5	0.48%
Flueier, T	9	0.87%	Posadziejewski, S	5	0.48%
Jaeger, PT	9	0.87%	Stojanovic, L	5	0.48%
Li, HX	9	0.87%	Tarabanis, K	5	0.48%
Li, Y	9	0.87%	Wan, CX	5	0.48%
Wang, W	9	0.87%	Zhang, S	5	0.48%

of 90 authors who contributed 5 or more publications on electronic government are listed in Table 4. Comparatively large number articles by first few authors may be due to the fact that they might be editors of conference proceedings. However, this is just an assumption, true reasons can only be discovered by undertaking further analysis of publications of individual authors.

Electronic Government Studies According to Institutions

Table 5 identifies the institutions apparently most active in the area of electronic government research. The overall number of contributions from each university varies from 1 to 17. Clearly National Technical University (with 17 publications) has contributed the largest number and can therefore be seen one of the leading centre of electronic government related research followed by National University of Singapore (with 12 publications) and Shanghai Jiao Tong University (with 11 outputs). Table 5 presents 41 active institutions with five or more publications.

Electronic Government Studies According to Country

Findings (illustrated in Table 6) disclose that the research presented in the 1037 publications identified on electronic government was conducted in a total of 68 countries. Almost equal amount of published activity has taken place in the China and USA, with a number of others countries (including the Germany, Italy, UK, Greece, Spain, and Austria) also being the location of a substantial amount of research activity which has resulted in publications that appeared in the search results. A number of countries (including Portugal, Slovakia, South Africa, Emirates, Hungry, Philippines, Poland and Israel) have been the location of research which has resulted in a low number of publications (less than five papers), and given the overall level of research activity in such countries, and indeed the supposed high-profile of ICT in country such as Philippines, this is perhaps a surprising result and indicates that there is opportunity for additional research based in such counties to take place in order to further expand the existing knowledge base (Dwivedi et.al. 2008ab).

Electronic Government Studies According to Language

Table 7 illustrate that electronic government research published in a total of seven languages. However, very few articles published in the languages other than English (Table 7).

CONCLUSION

This chapter has intended to provide an overview of the current state of electronic government research by presenting the results of a Bibliometric analysis of 1037 articles published during the period 1986-2008. Findings are presented along a series of dimensions including the source titles

Table 5. Electronic government studies according to institutions

Institution Name	Count	Institution Name	Count
Natl Tech Univ Athens	17	City Univ Hong Kong	6
Natl Univ Singapore	12	Erasmus Univ	6
Shanghai Jiao Tong Univ	11	S China Univ Technol	6
Dalian Univ Technol	10	Syracuse Univ	6
Univ Elect Sci & Technol China	10	Univ Aegean	6
Univ Linz	10	Univ Athens	6
Univ Manchester	10	Univ Karlsruhe	6
Univ Illinois	9	Univ Ljubljana	6
Univ Maryland	9	Univ New S Wales	6
Univ Zurich	9	Xian Jiaotong Univ	6
Wuhan Univ	9	Agder Univ Coll	5
Florida State Univ	8	Harbin Inst Technol	5
Suny Albany	8	Huazhong Univ Sci & Technol	5
Univ Twente	8	Jiangxi Univ Finance & Econ	5
Univ Zaragoza	8	Napier Univ	5
Brunel Univ	7	Univ Milan	5
Delft Univ Technol	7	Univ Nebraska	5
Univ Camerino	7	Univ Orebro	5
Univ Munster	7	Univ Texas	5
Univ Washington	7	Univ Vigo	5
Wuhan Univ Technol	7		

most often publishing articles on electronic government, authors most active in the subject area (in terms of articles published), institutions, countries and languages. Purpose of conducting this analysis was to provide a useful and usable resource for future researchers. This study has achieved this by providing an exhaustive list of references (1037 references) listed at the end of this chapter. Since electronic government research is mutidiscipilnary in nature and sources falls within several subject categories, it is difficult for interested researchers to search multiple databases in order to find relevant litearature. Therefore, this chapter will form a useful initial source for anyone interested in undertaking e-government research. Other contribution of this chapter is to help researchers to find journals and conferences engaged in or sympathetic publishing electronic government research. Similarly, this chapter provides useful resource for researchers, editors, conference organisers who wish to find research active individuals in this area.

It is important to acknowledge that this study has some limitations, and readers should be aware of these and indeed interpret the material presented in this paper within the context of these limitations. Firstly, our search activities were restricted to occurrences of the keywords in the article titles only, and study fully acknowledge that there may be numerous studies which lack all utilised keywords in the title, but still focus upon electronic government in the main text (Dwivedi et al. 2008ab). A further limitation is the overall number of journals considered. This study

Table 6. Electronic government studies according to country

Country/Territory	Count	% of 1037	Country/Territory	Count	% of 1037
Peoples R China	172	16.59%	South Africa	4	0.39%
USA	171	16.49%	U Arab Emirates	4	0.39%
Germany	67	6.46%	Wales	4	0.39%
Italy	65	6.27%	Argentina	3	0.29%
England	63	6.08%	Hungary	3	0.29%
Greece	52	5.01%	Jordan	3	0.29%
Spain	42	4.05%	Morocco	3	0.29%
Austria	41	3.95%	Philippines	3	0.29%
Netherlands	35	3.38%	Poland	3	0.29%
Australia	28	2.70%	Tunisia	3	0.29%
Switzerland	21	2.03%	Chile	2	0.19%
Brazil	20	1.93%	Croatia	2	0.19%
Canada	18	1.74%	Cyprus	2	0.19%
South Korea	18	1.74%	Indonesia	2	0.19%
France	15	1.45%	Israel	2	0.19%
Singapore	15	1.45%	Lebanon	2	0.19%
Sweden	15	1.45%	North Ireland	2	0.19%
Belgium	14	1.35%	Azerbaijan	1	0.10%
Scotland	11	1.06%	Barbados	1	0.10%
Taiwan	11	1.06%	Botswana	1	0.10%
Denmark	10	0.96%	Egypt	1	0.10%
Japan	10	0.96%	Iran	1	0.10%
Ireland	9	0.87%	Jamaica	1	0.10%
Norway	9	0.87%	Lithuania	1	0.10%
India	8	0.77%	Luxembourg	1	0.10%
Slovenia	7	0.68%	Macedonia	1	0.10%
Thailand	7	0.68%	Malaysia	1	0.10%
Czech Republic	5	0.48%	Mauritius	1	0.10%
Finland	5	0.48%	Mexico	1	0.10%
Romania	5	0.48%	Nigeria	1	0.10%
Turkey	5	0.48%	Oman	1	0.10%
Estonia	4	0.39%	Russia	1	0.10%
Portugal	4	0.39%	Sudan	1	0.10%
Slovakia	4	0.39%	Uzbekistan	1	0.10%

limited the search to the source titles indexed in Web of Science®, but there are many well known journals and conferences dedicated entirely on publication of electronic government research but they are not indexed in this product, and this clearly will have limited the ability to identify

Table 7. Electronic government studies according to language

Language	Count	% of 1037
English	1018	98.17%
German	7	0.68%
French	4	0.39%
Spanish	4	0.39%
Turkish	2	0.19%
Chinese	1	0.10%
Norwegian	1	0.10%

all relevant articles. Author believe that further comprehensive research is required in order to reduce the impact of the identified limitations in order to provide a greater understanding of the domain of electronic government research and include analysis on other variables such as research methods and topics.

REFERENCES

Irani, Z., & Dwivedi, Y.K. (2008). Editorial. *Transforming Government: People, Process and Policy*, 2(4), 221-224.

Dwivedi, Y.K. (2009). An analysis of e-government research published in Transforming Government: People, Process and Policy (TGPPP). *Transforming Government: People, Process and Policy*, 3 (1).

Dwivedi, Y.K., Williams, M.D., Lal, B., & Schwarz, A., (2008a). Profiling Adoption, Acceptance, and Diffusion Research in the Information Systems Discipline. In proceedings of the *16th European Conference on Information Systems*, 2008b, Galway, Ireland, June 9th-11th 2008.

Dwivedi, Y.K., Williams, M.D., & Lal, B. (2008b). The Diffusion of Research on the Adoption and Diffusion & Diffusion of Information Technology. In proceedings of the *IFIP8.6 Conference*, (eds. Gonzalo, L., Bernardos, A., Casar, J., Kautz, K., and DeGross, J.), Boston: Springer, Madrid, Spain, October 2008.

Dwivedi, Y.K., Williams, M.D., Lal, B., and Dwivedi, A., (2008c). A Profile of Research on Adoption and Diffusion of ICT/IT/IS in the Consumer/Household/Residential Context. In Proceedings of the Fourteenth Americas Conference on Information Systems, Toronto, ON, Canada August 14th-17th 2008.

ADDITIONAL READINGS

Abdelghaffar, H., & Kamel, S. (2008). *The impact of eReadiness on eGovernment in developing nations - Case of universities and colleges admission services.* Paper presented at the 9th International-Business-Information-Management-Association Conference (IBIMA), Marrakech, MOROCCO.

Abramowicz, W., Bassara, A., Wisniewski, M., & Zebrowski, P. (2008). *Interoperability governance for e-government.* Paper presented at the 2nd International United Informational Systems Conference, Klagenfurt, AUSTRIA.

Abusin, M. (2007). *Government of Sudan e-Government initiative: Challenges and opportunities.* Paper presented at the 7th European Conference on e-Government (ECEG 2007), The Hague, NETHERLANDS.

Adeshara, P., Juric, R., Kuljis, J., Paul, R., & Ieee (2004). *A survey of acceptance of e-government services in the UK.* Paper presented at the 26th International Conference on Information Technology Interfaces, Cavtat, CROATIA.

Affisco, J. F., & Soliman, K. S. (2007). *Guiding the implementation of service delivery strategy in an e-government environment.* Paper presented at the 8th International-Business-Information-Management-Association Conference (IBIMA), Dublin, IRELAND.

Aichholzer, G. (2005). *Service take-up and impacts of e-government in Austria.* Paper presented at the 4th International Conference on Electronic Government (EGOV 2005), Copenhagen, DENMARK.

Aichholzer, G. (2007). *Opening the black box: Economic and organisational effects of e-Government.* Paper presented at the 3rd International Conference on e-Government, Montreal, CANADA.

Aichholzer, G., & Schmutzer, R. (2000). *Organizational challenges to the development of electronic government.* Paper presented at the 11th International Workshop on Database and Expert Systems Applications, London, England.

Aichholzer, G., & Sperlich, R. (2001). *Electronic government services for the business sector in Austria.* Paper presented at the 12th International Conference on Database and Expert Systems Applications (DEXA), Munich, Germany.

Aidemark, J. (2003). *A knowledge perspective on e-democracy.* Paper presented at the 2nd International Conference on Electronic Government (EGOV 2003), Prague, Czech Republic.

Akramov, F., & Khudoyberganov, B. (2007). *The e-Government in Uzbekistan: On a way to information society.* Paper presented at the 3rd International Conference on e-Government, Montreal, CANADA.

Akther, M. S., Onishi, T., & Kidokoro, T. (2005). *E-government practice: What one country could learn from other.* Paper presented at the 4th International Conference on Electronic Government (EGOV 2005), Copenhagen, DENMARK.

Al-Ahmad, W., & Al-Kaabi, R. (2008). *An extended security framework for e-government.* Paper presented at the IEEE International Conference on Intelligence and Security Informatics (ISI 2008), Taipei, TAIWAN.

Al-Kindi, A., Al-Gharbi, K., & Al-Salti, Z. (2007). *E-government initiative in the Sultanate of Oman.* Paper presented at the 8th International-Business-Information-Management-Association Conference (IBIMA), Dublin, IRELAND.

Al-Sarayreh, K. T., & Al-Qutaish, R. E. (2008). *Enhancing the security of e-government portals using biometric voice along with a traditional password.* Paper presented at the 7th WSEAS International Conference on Artificial Intelligence, Knowledge Engineering and Data Bases, Cambridge, ENGLAND.

Alexander, C. J. (2001). Wiring the nation! Including First Nations? Aboriginal Canadians and Federal e-government initiatives (Canada). *Journal of Canadian Studies-Revue D Etudes Canadiennes, 35*(4), 277-296.

Alexopoulos, P., Kafentzis, K., Benetou, X., Tagaris, T., & Georgolios, P. (2007). *Towards a generic fraud ontology in e-government.* Paper presented at the 2nd International Conference on e-Business (ICE-B 2007), Barcelona, SPAIN.

Alfonso, C., Caballer, M., Carrion, J. V., & Hernandez, V. (2006). *gCitizen: Using grids for creating an integrated view of the citizen in an eGovernment framework.* Paper presented at the 15th IEEE International Workshop on Enabling Technologies - Infrastructure for Collaborative Enterprises (WET ICE 2006), Manchester, ENGLAND.

Algermissen, L. (2004). *Realigning public administrations with the concept of electronic government: How to prepare process oriented reorganization projects.* Paper presented at the International Conference of the Information-Resources-Management-Association, New Orleans, LA.

Alkhatib, G., Bataineh, E., Fraihat, H., & Maamar, Z. (2007). *An intelligent integrated e-Government framework: The case of Jordan.* Paper presented at the 7th European Conference on e-Government (ECEG 2007), The Hague, NETHERLANDS.

Allan, J. D. O., Rambajun, N., Sood, S. P., Mbarika, V., Agrawal, R., Saquib, Z., et al. (2006). *The eGovernment concept: A systematic review of research and practitioner literature.* Paper presented at the Innovations in Information Technology Conference 2006, Dubai, U ARAB EMIRATES.

Altameem, T., Zairi, M., Alshawi, S., & Ieee (2006). *Critical success factors of E-government: A proposed model for E-government implementation.* Paper presented at the Innovations in Information Technology Conference 2006, Dubai, U ARAB EMIRATES.

Amato, F., Mazzeo, A., Penta, A., & Picariello, A. (2008). *Knowledge representation and management for e-government documents.* Paper presented at the 20th World Computer Congress, Milan, ITALY.

Andersen, K. V., & Henriksen, H. Z. (2006). E-government maturity models: Extension of the Layne and Lee model. [Article]. *Government Information Quarterly, 23*(2), 236-248.

Andersen, K. V., & Medaglia, R. (2008). *eGovernment Front-End Services: Administrative and Citizen Cost-Benefits.* Paper presented at the 7th International Conference on Electronic Government, Turin, ITALY.

Anderson, S., Bohman, P. R., Burmeister, O. K., & Sampson-Wild, G. (2004). *User needs and e-Government accessibility: The future impact of WCAG 2.0.* Paper presented at the 8th ERCIM Workshop on User Interfaces for All, Vienna, AUSTRIA.

Anderson, S., Felici, M., & Soc, I. C. (2005). *How democratic will e-Democracy be?* Paper presented at the 29th Annual International Computer Software and Applications Conference, Edinburgh, SCOTLAND.

Andrew, A. M. (2008). Cybernetics and e-democracy. *Kybernetes, 37*(7), 1066-1068.

Ansari, M. Z. A., & Khan, M. I. (2008). *Utilizing Owl-S in Multi-Agent Based Architecture for Semantic E-Government Services.* Paper presented at the International Symposium on Information Technology, Kuala Lumpur, MALAYSIA.

Anthopoulos, L. G., Siozos, P., & Tsoukalas, L. A. (2007). Applying participatory design and collaboration in digital public services for discovering and re-designing e-Government services. *Government Information Quarterly, 24*(2), 353-376.

Antovski, L., & Gusev, M. (2007, Jun 21-22). *Model for mobile and ubiquitous e-government.* Paper presented at the 7th European Conference on e-Government (ECEG 2007), The Hague, NETHERLANDS.

Anttiroiko, A. V. (2003). Building strong E-democracy - The role of technology in developing democracy for the information age. *Communications of the Acm, 46*(9), 121-128.

Anwar, M., Nadeem, M., Ali, M. Z., & Raza, S. (2006). *Multi-agent based semantic e-government web service architecture using extended WSDL.* Paper presented at the IEEE/WIC/ACM International Conference on Web Intelligence and Intelligent Agent Technology (WI-IAT 2006), Hong Kong, PEOPLES R CHINA.

Apostolou, D., Stojanovic, L., Lobo, T. P., Miro, J. C., & Papadakis, A. (2005). *Configuring e-Government services using ontologies.* Paper presented at the 5th IFTP Conference on E-Commerce, E-Business, and E-Government, Poznan, POLAND.

Apostolou, D., Stojanovic, L., Lobo, T. P., & Thoenssen, B. (2005). *Towards a semantically-driven software engineering environment for eGovernment.* Paper presented at the International Conference on E-Government (TCGOV 2005), Bolzano, ITALY.

Arcieri, F., Cappadozzi, E., Nardelli, E., & Talamo, M. (2001). *SIM: a working example of an e-government service infrastructure for mountain communities.* Paper presented at the 12th International Conference on Database and Expert Systems Applications (DEXA), Munich, Germany.

Arcieri, F., & Giaccio, R. (2002). *E-government services: Certification and security overlay.* Paper presented at the 17th World Computer Congress, Montreal, Canada.

Arcieri, F., Medideo, G., Nardelli, E., & Talamo, M. (2002). *Experiences and issues in the realization of e-government services.* Paper presented at the 12th International Workshop on Research Issues in Data Engineering - Engineering E-Commerce/E-Business Systems, San Jose, Ca.

Arendsen, R., & van Engers, T. M. (2004). *Reduction of the administrative burden: An e-government perspective.* Paper presented at the 3rd International Conference on Electronic Government (EGOV 2004), Zaragoza, SPAIN.

Aris, S. R. S., Mohamed, A., & Arshad, N. H. (2007). *Preliminary study on risk management in E-Government outsourcing projects.* Paper presented at the 6th WSEAS International Conference on E-ACTIVITIES, Puerto de la Cruz, SPAIN.

Ask, A., & Gronlund, A. (2008). *Implementation Challenges: Competing Structures When New Public Management Meets eGovernment.* Paper presented at the 7th International Conference on Electronic Government, Aug 31-Sep 05, Turin, ITALY.

Auksztol, J., & Przechlewski, T. (2004). *Towards flexible geographic information infrastructure for e-government.* Paper presented at the 3rd International Conference on Electronic Government (EGOV 2004), Aug 30-Sep 03, Zaragoza, SPAIN.

Avny, A. B. (2005). *Promises, perils & prospects of E-Government.* Paper presented at the 3rd International Conference on Politics and Information Systems - Technologies and Applications/International Symposium on Social and Organizational Informatics and Cybernectics, Jul 14-17, Orlando, FL.

Awan, M. A. (2003). *E-government: Assessment of GCC (Gulf Co-Operating Council) countries and services provided.* Paper presented at the 2nd International Conference on Electronic Government (EGOV 2003), Sep 01-05, Prague, Czech Republic.

Axelsson, K., & Melin, U. (2008). *Citizen Participation and Involvement in eGovernment Projects: An Emergent Framework.* Paper presented at the 7th International Conference on Electronic Government, Aug 31-Sep 05, Turin, ITALY.

Azad, B., & Faraj, S. (2008). Making e-Government systems workable: Exploring the evolution of frames. *Journal of Strategic Information Systems, 17*(2), 75-98.

Backhouse, J. (2007). *e-Democracy in Australia: The challenge of evolving a successful model.* Paper presented at the 7th European Conference on e-Government (ECEG 2007), Jun 21-22, The Hague, NETHERLANDS.

Baida, Z., Liu, J. W., & Tan, Y. H. (2007). *Towards a methodology for designing e-Government control procedures.* Paper presented at the 6th International Conference on Electronic Government, Sep 03-07, Regensburg, GERMANY.

Baier, H., & Ruppert, M. (2004). *Interoperable and flexible digital signatures for e-government and e-commerce.* Paper presented at the International Conference on Human Perspectives in the Internet Society, Sep 06-10, Cadiz, SPAIN.

Baines, S., Gannon-Leary, P., & Wilson, R. (2005, Oct 28-30). *Practitioner buy-in and resistance to e-enabled information sharing across agencies - The case of an e-government project to join up local services in England.* Paper presented at the 5th IFTP Conference on E-Commerce, E-Business, and E-Government, Poznan, POLAND.

Baldoni, R., Fuligni, S., Mecella, M., & Tortorelli, F. (2008, May 19-21). *The Italian e-Government Enterprise architecture: A comprehensive introduction with focus on the SLA issue.* Paper presented at the 5th International Service Availability Symposium (ISAS 2008), Tokyo, JAPAN.

Balimann, C., & Zimmermann, F. (2005, Jul 14-17). *Inter-governmental e-Government processes: Comparison of different solution approaches - Based on examples from Switzerland/Europe.* Paper presented at the 3rd International Conference on Politics and Information Systems - Technologies and Applications/International Symposium on Social and Organizational Informatics and Cybernectics, Orlando, FL.

Ballardini, L., Germagnoli, F., Pagani, M., Picchi, M., Stoppini, A., & Cristiani, P. (2004, Sep 07-11). *Putting e-government to work in healthcare environment: a Multiregional project funded by the Italian innovation & technology ministry.* Paper presented at the 11th World Congress on Medical Informatics, San Francisco, CA.

Bannister, F. (2007). The curse of the benchmark: an assessment of the validity and value of e-government comparisons. [Article]. *International Review of Administrative Sciences, 73*(2), 171-188.

Baptista, C. D., Leite, F. L., da Silva, E. R., & Paiva, A. C. (2004, Aug 30-Sep 03). *Using open source GIS in e-Government applications.* Paper presented at the 3rd International Conference on Electronic Government (EGOV 2004), Zaragoza, SPAIN.

Barbosa, A., Junqueira, A., Diniz, E., & Prado, O. (2007, Sep 27). *Electronic government in Brazil: A historical perspective of its development based on a structured model of analysis.* Paper presented at the 3rd International Conference on e-Government, Montreal, CANADA.

Barnes, S. J., & Vidgen, R. T. (2006). Data triangulation and web quality metrics: A case study in e-government. [Article]. *Information & Management, 43*(6), 767-777.

Barnum, G. (2002). Availability, access, authenticity, and persistence: Creating the environment for permanent public access to electronic government information. [Article]. *Government Information Quarterly, 19*(1), 37-43.

Bartels, U., & Steimke, F. (2004, Aug 30-Sep 03). *How to modernize the people registration process. Experiences in the leading e-government project in Germany.* Paper presented at the 3rd International Conference on Electronic Government (EGOV 2004), Zaragoza, SPAIN.

Baskoy, T. (2007, Sep 27). *The European union and e-democracy: Interactive policy-making initiative (IPM).* Paper presented at the 3rd International Conference on e-Government, Montreal, CANADA.

Batini, C., Barone, D., Garasi, M. F., & Viscusi, G. (2006, Nov 06-09). *Design and use of ER repositories: Methodologies and experiences in eGovernment initiatives.* Paper presented at the 25th International Conference on Conceptual Modeling, Tucson, AZ.

Baumgartner, I., & Green, P. (2008, Sep 07-10). *Adoption of Service Oriented Computing from the IT professionals' perspective: An e-Government case study.* Paper presented at the IFIP TC 8 Information Systems Conference held at the 20th World Computer Congress, Milan, ITALY.

Bavec, C., & Vintar, M. (2007, Sep 03-07). *What matters in the development of the e-government in the EU?* Paper presented at the 6th International Conference on Electronic Government, Regensburg, GERMANY.

Becker, J., Algermissen, L., & Niehaves, B. (2003, Sep 01-05). *Processes in E-government focus: A procedure model for process oriented reorganisation in public administrations on the local level.* Paper presented at the 2nd International Conference on Electronic Government (EGOV 2003), Prague, Czech Republic.

Becker, J., Niehaves, B., Algermissen, L., Delfmann, P., & Falk, T. (2004, Aug 30-Sep 03). *E-government success factors.* Paper presented at the 3rd International Conference on Electronic Government (EGOV 2004), Zaragoza, SPAIN.

Becker, J., Niehaves, B., Algermissen, L., Falk, T., & Delfmann, P. (2005, Aug 14-17). *Selecting processes for co-designing eGovernment services.* Paper presented at the 14th International Conference on Information Systems Development - Bridging the Gap between Academia and Industry (ISD 2005), Karlstad, SWEDEN.

Becker, J., Niehaves, B., Bergener, P., & Rackers, M. (2008, Aug 31-Sep 05). *Digital Divide in eGovernment: The eInclusion Gap Model.* Paper presented at the 7th International Conference on Electronic Government, Turin, ITALY.

Becker, S. A. (2004). E-government visual accessibility for older adult users. [Article]. *Social Science Computer Review, 22*(1), 11-23.

Beddie, L., Macintosh, A., & Malina, A. (2001, Oct 03-05). *E-democracy and the Scottish Parliament.* Paper presented at the 1st IFIP International Conference on E-Commerce, E-Business, and E-Government (I3E 2001), Zurich, Switzerland.

Bednar, P., Furdik, K., Kleimann, M., Klischewski, R., Skokan, M., & Ukena, S. (2008, Aug 31-Sep 05). *Semantic integration of eGovernment services in Schleswig-Holstein.* Paper presented at the 7th International Conference on Electronic Government, Turin, ITALY.

Beer, D., Kunis, R., Runger, G., & Soc, I. C. (2006, Apr 20-22). *A component based software architecture for e-government applications.* Paper presented at the 1st International Conference on Availability, Reliability and Security, Vienna, AUSTRIA.

Bekkers, V. (2005, Aug 22-26). *The governance of back office integration in e-government: Some Dutch experiences.* Paper presented at the 4th International Conference on Electronic Government (EGOV 2005), Copenhagen, DENMARK.

Bekkers, V. (2006). Flexibility of information architecture in e-government chains *Electronic Government, Proceedings* (Vol. 4084, pp. 243-255). Berlin: Springer-Verlag Berlin.

Bekkers, V., & Homburg, V. (2007). The myths of E-government: Looking beyond the assumptions of a new and better government. [Article]. *Information Society, 23*(5), 373-382.

Belanger, F., & Carter, L. (2008). Trust and risk in e-government adoption. [Article]. *Journal of Strategic Information Systems, 17*(2), 165-176.

Bellman, B. (2003, Jul 31-Aug 02). *The role & function of enterprise architecture in e-Government.* Paper presented at the International Conference on Politics and Information Systems - Technologies and Applications (PISTA 03), Orlando, FL.

Bellman, B., & Rausch, F. (2004, Aug 30-Sep 03). *Enterprise Architecture for e-Government.* Paper presented at the 3rd International Conference on Electronic Government (EGOV 2004), Zaragoza, SPAIN.

Benamou, N., Busson, A., & Keravel, A. (2004, Aug 30-Sep 03). *Impact of e-Government interoperability in local governments.* Paper presented at the 3rd International Conference on Electronic Government (EGOV 2004), Zaragoza, SPAIN.

Benamou, N., Guarnieri, D., Mantovani, S., & Savoldelli, A. (2004, Oct 27-29). *QUALEG - Quality of service & legitimacy in eGovernment.* Paper presented at the eChallenges e-2004 Conference, Vienna, AUSTRIA.

Benelli, G., Marzucchi, B., Piroli, I., Pratelli, G., & Ieee (2005, Sep 05-07). *An innovative approach to E-government geo-based services on packet-switched mobile networks.* Paper presented at the 2nd International Symposium on Wireless Communications Systems (ISWCS 2005), Siena, ITALY.

Berce, J., Bianchi, A., Centeno, C., Osimo, D., Millard, J., & Shahin, J. (2006, Sep 04-08). *The organisation and coordination of European e-government research for the EU in 2010.* Paper presented at the 5th International Conference on Electronic Government (EGOV 2006), Cracow, POLAND.

Bertot, J. C., Jaeger, P. T., Langa, L. A., & McClure, C. R. (2006). Drafted - I want you to deliver e-government. [Article]. *Library Journal, 131*(13), 34-37.

Bettahar, F., Moulin, C., & Barthes, J. P. A. (2005, 2005). *Ontologies supporting eGovernment services.* Paper presented at the Portuguese Conference on Artificial Intelligence, Covilha, PORTUGAL.

Beynon-Davies, P. (2005, 2004). *Constructing electronic government: The case of the UK inland revenue.* Paper presented at the European Conference on Information Systems, Turku, FINLAND.

Bezzazi, E. H. (2006, Aug 31-Sep 02). *On some inferences based on stratified forward chaining: An application to E-Government.* Paper presented at the 15th International Conference on Information Systems Development, Budapest, HUNGARY.

Biasiotti, M. A., & Nannucci, R. (2004, Aug 30-Sep 03). *Teaching e-government in Italy.* Paper presented at the 3rd International Conference on Electronic Government (EGOV 2004), Zaragoza, SPAIN.

Bicking, M. (2007, Oct 10-12). *Roadmapping future e-government research.* Paper presented at the 7th IFIP International Conference on e-Business, e-Service, and e-Society, Wuhan, PEOPLES R CHINA.

Bin, H. C., Yewei, Chen, Z. J., Ling, H. F., & Chen, G. H. (2006, Oct 28-29). *Research on the implementation mechanism of spatial data services in land resources e-government platform - art. no. 642119.* Paper presented at the 14th International Conference on Geoinformatics, Wuhan, PEOPLES R CHINA.

Bin, X., & Bin, P. (2007, Dec 15-19). *Appraisal research of the government achievements based on electronic government affairs angle.* Paper presented at the International Conference on Computational Intelligence and Security, Harbin, PEOPLES R CHINA.

Bishop, S., & Savoury, S. (2004, May 23-26). *Towards e-government in a small state: An AGILE framework.* Paper presented at the International Conference of the Information-Resources-Management-Association, New Orleans, LA.

Bochicchio, M. A., Celentano, M. G., & Longo, A. (2004, Aug 30-Sep 03). *Innovation needs in the e-government scenario: A survey.* Paper presented at the 3rd International Conference on Electronic Government (EGOV 2004), Zaragoza, SPAIN.

Boden, C., Fischer, J., Herbig, K., & Spierling, U. (2006, Dec 04-06). *CitizenTalk: aPplication of chatbot infotainment to E-democracy.* Paper presented at the 3rd International Conference on Technologies for Interactive Digital Storytelling and Entertainment (TIDSE 2006), Darmstadt, GERMANY.

Bof, F., & Previtali, P. (2007, Sep 27). *Is e-Government on the agenda of small municipalities? Empirical evidence from an Italian case study.* Paper presented at the 3rd International Conference on e-Government, Montreal, CANADA.

Bolici, F. (2004, Aug 30-Sep 03). *Knowledge and boundaries in e-Government.* Paper presented at the 3rd International Conference on Electronic Government (EGOV 2004), Zaragoza, SPAIN.

Bolici, F., Cantoni, F., Sorrentino, M., & Virili, F. (2003, Sep 01-05). *Cooperating strategies in e-government.* Paper presented at the 2nd International Conference on Electronic Government (EGOV 2003), Prague, Czech Republic.

Bolivar, M. P. R., Perez, C. C., & Hernandez, A. M. L. (2007). E-government and public financial reporting - The case of Spanish regional governments. [Article]. *American Review of Public Administration, 37*(2), 142-177.

Bonacin, R., Baranauskas, M. C. C., & Dos Santos, T. M. (2007, Jun 12-16). *A semiotic approach for flexible e-government service oriented systems.* Paper presented at the 9th International Conference on Enterprise Information Systems (ICEIS 2007), Funchal, PORTUGAL.

Borthwick, L. (2004, Oct 27-29). *The evolution of an eGovernment identity management architecture.* Paper presented at the eChallenges e-2004 Conference, Vienna, AUSTRIA.

Bose, R. (2004, Apr 05-07). *Information technologies for education & training in e-government.* Paper presented at the International Conference on Information Technology - Coding and Computing, Las Vegas, NV.

Botterman, M., Ettedgui, E., Graafland, I., & Ligtvoet, A. (2003, Sep 01-05). *Citizens and e-government: An international comparison of the demand-side of e-government.* Paper presented at the 2nd International Conference on Electronic Government (EGOV 2003), Prague, Czech Republic.

Bouaziz, F. (2006, Dec 14-16). *Managing e-government projects failure and risks.* Paper presented at the 7th International-Business-Information-Management-Association Conference (IBIMA), Brescia, ITALY.

Bouguettaya, A., Medjahed, B., Rezgui, A., Ouzzani, M., Liu, X. M., & Yu, Q. (2004, Nov 08-12). *WebDG - A platform for e-government Web services.* Paper presented at the ER 2004 Workshops held in Conjunction with the 23rd International Conference on Conceptual Modeling, Shanghai, PEOPLES R CHINA.

Bresciani, P., Donzelli, P., Ferrari, S., & Sannicolo, F. (2004, May 17-19). *Knowledge elicitation and modeling for E-government a practical approach.* Paper presented at the 5th IFIP Interenational Working Conference on Knowledge Management in Electronic Government, Krems, AUSTRIA.

Bresciani, P., Donzelli, P., & Forte, A. (2003, May 26-28). *Requirements engineering for knowledge management in eGovernment.* Paper presented at the 4th Annual International Working Conference on Knowledge Management in Electronic Government, Rhodes, Greece.

Breu, R., Hafner, M., Weber, B., & Novak, A. (2005, Mar 02-04). *Model driven security for inter-organizational workflows in e-government.* Paper presented at the International Conference on E-Government (TCGOV 2005), Bolzano, ITALY.

Brewer, G. A., Neubauer, B. J., & Geiselhart, K. (2006). Designing and implementing e-government systems - Critical implications for public administration and democracy. [Article]. *Administration & Society, 38*(4), 472-499.

Brown, C. (2004). Knowing where they're going: Statistics for online government document access through the OPAC. [Article]. *Online Information Review, 28*(6), 396-409.

Brown, D. (2005). Electronic government and public administration. [Article]. *International Review of Administrative Sciences, 71*(2), 241-254.

Brown, M. M. (2007). Understanding E-government benefits - An examination of leading-edge local governments. [Article]. *American Review of Public Administration, 37*(2), 178-197.

Brown, W. R. (1999). Federal initiatives to promote access to electronic government information: The impact on the federal depository library program. [Article]. *Law Library Journal, 91*(2), 291-303.

Bruggemeier, M., Dovifat, A., & Kubisch, D. (2005). Micropolitical innovation arenas as a tool for analyzing innovation processes in the context of electronic government. [Article]. *Wirtschaftsinformatik, 47*(5), 347-355.

Brunschwig, C. (2002, Sep 02-06). *Legal design and e-Government: Visualisations of cost & efficiency accounting in the wif! e-learning environment of the Canton of Zurich (Switzerland).* Paper presented at the 1st International Conference on Electronic Government (EGOV 2002), Aix Provence, France.

Brunschwig, C. R. (2003, Jul 31-Aug 02). *Good Practice in Swiss e-Government? How the Swiss authorities pay lip service to the multi-coding potential of the new information and communication technologies.* Paper presented at the International Conference on Politics and Information Systems - Technologies and Applications (PISTA 03), Orlando, FL.

Bu, D. (2005, Aug 15-17). *The application study on Chinese e-government construction.* Paper presented at the 7th International Conference on Electronic Commerce (ICEC 2005), Xian, PEOPLES R CHINA.

Bus, J., & Soc, I. C. (2005, Jul 26-28). *Position statement: How democratic wiH e-Democracy be?* Paper presented at the 29th Annual International Computer Software and Applications Conference, Edinburgh, SCOTLAND.

Busson, A., & Keravel, A. (2004, Oct 27-29). *Strategies used to reach eGovernment interoperability: An initial evaluation.* Paper presented at the eChallenges e-2004 Conference, Vienna, AUSTRIA.

Cabri, G., Ferrari, L., & Leonardi, L. (2005). A role-based mobile-agent approach to support e-democracy. [Article]. *Applied Soft Computing, 6*(1), 85-99.

Cairns, G., Wright, G., Bradfield, R., van der Heijden, K., & Burt, G. (2004). Exploring e-government futures through the application of scenario planning. [Article]. *Technological Forecasting and Social Change, 71*(3), 217-238.

Caituiro-Monge, H., Rodriguez-Martinez, M., & Society, I. C. (2004, Jul 06-09). *Net Traveler: A framework for autonomic web services collaboration, orchestration and choreography in e-government information systems.* Paper presented at the IEEE International Conference on Web Services (ICWS 2004), San Diego, CA.

Cao, J. T., & Che, Z. (2007, Oct 14-16). *Applications of ICT services for e-government.* Paper presented at the 2nd International Conference on Research and Practical Issues of Enterprise Information Systems, Beijing, PEOPLES R CHINA.

Cap, C. H., & Maibaum, N. (2001, Oct 03-05). *Digital identity and its implication for electronic government.* Paper presented at the 1st IFIP International Conference on E-Commerce, E-Business, and E-Government (I3E 2001), Zurich, Switzerland.

Capek, J., & Komarkova, J. (2003, Jul 31-Aug 02). *E-Government from Regional point of view.* Paper presented at the International Conference on Politics and Information Systems - Technologies and Applications (PISTA 03), Orlando, FL.

Carenini, M., Whyte, A., Bertorello, L., & Vanocchi, M. (2007). Improving communication E-democracy using natural language processing. [Article]. *Ieee Intelligent Systems, 22*(1), 20-27.

Carratta, T., Dadayan, L., & Ferro, E. (2006, Sep 04-08). *ROI analysis in e-government assessment trials: The case of sistema piemonte.* Paper presented at the 5th International Conference on Electronic Government (EGOV 2006), Cracow, POLAND.

Carter, L., & Belanger, F. (2004, Jan 05-09). *The utilization of e-government services: citizen trust, innovation and acceptance factors.* Paper presented at the HICSS 2004 Conference, Hi.

Carter, L., & Weerakkody, V. (2008). E-government adoption: A cultural comparison. [Article]. *Information Systems Frontiers, 10*(4), 473-482.

Carvalho, A., Rocha, A., & Oliveira, M. A. (2003, Sep 01-05). *SINUP: Using GIS to support e-democracy.* Paper presented at the 2nd International Conference on Electronic Government (EGOV 2003), Prague, Czech Republic.

Castelnovo, W. (2008, Sep 07-10). *E-Government for small local government organizations.* Paper presented at the 20th World Computer Congress, Milan, ITALY.

Castelnovo, W., & Simonetta, M. (2007, Sep 20-21). *A public value evaluation of e-Government policies.* Paper presented at the European Conference on Information Management and Evaluation, Montpellier, FRANCE.

Cava, I., & Guijarro, L. (2003, Sep 01-05). *Interoperability issues of Shared Infrastructures for e-Government.* Paper presented at the 2nd International Conference on Electronic Government (EGOV 2003), Prague, Czech Republic.

Cegarra Navarro, J. G., Dewhurst, F. W., & Briones Penalver, A. J. (2007). Factors affecting the use of e-Government in the telecommunications industry of Spain. [Article]. *Technovation, 27*(10), 595-604.

Chadwick, A. (2003). Bringing e-democracy back in - Why it matters for future research on e-governance. [Article]. *Social Science Computer Review, 21*(4), 443-455.

Chadwick, A., & May, C. (2001, Aug 30-Sep 02). *Interaction between states and citizens in the age of the internet: "e-government" in the United States, Britain, and the European Union.* Paper presented at the 97th Annual Meeting of the American-Political-Science-Association, San Francisco, California.

Chamberlain, J., & Castleman, T. (2002, Jun 09-11). *E-government business strategies and services to citizens.* Paper presented at the 2nd Working Conference on E-Business, Copenhagen, Denmark.

Chan, C. M. L., Lau, Y. M., & Pan, S. L. (2008). E-government implementation: A macro analysis of Singapore's e-government initiatives. [Article]. *Government Information Quarterly, 25*(2), 239-255.

Chan, C. M. L., & Pan, S. L. (2008). User engagement in e-government systems implementation: A comparative case study of two Singaporean e-government initiatives. [Article]. *Journal of Strategic Information Systems, 17*(2), 124-139.

Chao, Y. F., & Tong, F. (2005, Aug 15-17). *The problems in the implementation of E-government administration, the analysis and strategies.* Paper presented at the 7th International Conference on Electronic Commerce (ICEC 2005), Xian, PEOPLES R CHINA.

Chappelet, J. L. (2004, Aug 30-Sep 03). *e-government as an enabler of public management reform: The case of Switzerland.* Paper presented at the 3rd International Conference on Electronic Government (EGOV 2004), Zaragoza, SPAIN.

Chappelet, J. L., & Kilchenmann, P. (2005, Mar 02-04). *Interactive tools for e-democracy: Examples from Switzerland.* Paper presented at the International Conference on E-Government (TCGOV 2005), Bolzano, ITALY.

Charalabidis, Y. (2008, Mar 26-28). *Ontological support in eGovernment interoperability through service registries.* Paper presented at the 4th International Conference on Interoperability for Enterprise Software and Applications (I-ESA 2008), Berlin, GERMANY.

Charalabidis, Y., Askounis, D., Gionis, G., Lampathaki, F., & Metaxiotis, K. (2006, Sep 04-08). *Organising municipal e-government systems: A multi-facet taxonomy of e-services for citizens and businesses.* Paper presented at the 5th International Conference on Electronic Government (EGOV 2006), Cracow, POLAND.

Charalabldis, Y., Lampathaki, F., Sarantis, D., Sourouni, A. M., Mouzakitis, S., Gionis, G., et al. (2008, Aug 28-30). *The Greek Electronic Government Interoperability Framework: Standards and Infrastructures for One-Stop Service Provision.* Paper presented at the 12th Pan-Hellenic Conference on Informatics, Samos Isl, GREECE.

Charif, H., & Ramadan, M. (2003, May 26-28). *E-government attempts in ESCWA member countries.* Paper presented at the 4th Annual International Working Conference on Knowledge Management in Electronic Government, Rhodes, Greece.

Chatfield, A. T., & Al Hujran, O. (2007, Jun 21-22). *The role of strategic leadership in driving transformative e-government: A comparative analysis of the Arab states in the Middle East.* Paper presented at the 7th European Conference on e-Government (ECEG 2007), The Hague, NETHERLANDS.

Chatzidimitriou, M., Koumpis, A., & Int Assoc, E. (2007, Jul 02-04). *Matters of conceptualization and security in the building of one-stop-shop e-Government solutions in europe: Experiences from the European OneStopGov project.* Paper presented at the World Congress on Engineering 2007, London, ENGLAND.

Chen, D. L., Nie, G. H., Liu, P. F., & Alfred, U. (2007, May 26-27). *Research on knowledge sharing of E-government based on automatic ontology mapping.* Paper presented at the 6th Wuhan International Conference on E-Business, Wuhan, PEOPLES R CHINA.

Chen, E. T., Hu, G., & Hu, J. (2002, Jul 14-18). *The opportunities and challenges facing e-government.* Paper presented at the 6th World Multi-Conference on Systemics, Cybernetics and Informatics (SCI 2002)/8th International Conference on Information Systems Analysis and Synthesis (ISAS 2002), Orlando, Fl.

Chen, F. J., & Yang, S. L. (2003, Aug 15-17). *Research on information integration framework based on XML for public-oriented service in e-government.* Paper presented at the International Conference on Management Science and Engineering, Atlanta, Ga.

Chen, F. J., & Yang, S. L. (2004, Aug 08-10). *Research on personalized information service based on data mining in e-government.* Paper presented at the International Conference on Management Science and Engineering, Harbin, PEOPLES R CHINA.

Chen, J., & Shao, P. J. (2006, May 27-28). *The support ability of government websites to G2B E-Government.* Paper presented at the 5th Wuhan International Conference on E-Business, Wuhan, PEOPLES R CHINA.

Chen, L. L., Tang, Z. W., & Alfred, U. (2007, May 26-27). *Study on the E-government construction investment of centre government and local government with game theory.* Paper presented at the 6th Wuhan International Conference on E-Business, Wuhan, PEOPLES R CHINA.

Chen, X. X. (2002, Sep 02-06). *The E-GOV action plan in Beijing.* Paper presented at the 1st International Conference on Electronic Government (EGOV 2002), Aix Provence, France.

Chen, Y. C., & Gant, J. (2001, Mar). *Transforming local e-government services: the use of application service providers.* Paper presented at the Workshop on Foundations of Electronic Government in Americas Cities, Chicago, Illinois.

Chen, Y. C., & Thurmaier, K. (2005, Nov 10-12). *Advancing e-government: Financing challenges and opportunities.* Paper presented at the Annual Conference of the Association-for-Budgeting-and-Financial-Management, Washington, DC.

Chen, Y. N., Chen, H. M., Huang, W., & Ching, R. K. H. (2004, Dec). *E-government strategies in developed and developing countries: An implementation framework and case study.* Paper presented at the 1st International Symposium of IS/IT in Asia-Pacific (ISAP 2004), Washington, DC.

Cheng, J. J., Cheng, S. C., & Yang, M. J. (2007, Oct 10-12). *Evaluating the E-government based on BSC.* Paper presented at the 7th IFIP International Conference on e-Business, e-Service, and e-Society, Wuhan, PEOPLES R CHINA.

Cheng, X. R., Li, M., & Zhao, H. L. (2007, Aug 14-17). *Information security evaluation of e-government systems.* Paper presented at the International Symposium on Distributed Computing and Applications to Business, Engineering and Science, Yichang, PEOPLES R CHINA.

Chernov, S., Larichev, A., & Chernova, T. (2007, Sep 27). *e-Government in Russia: Obstacles on the way to improve public management in a federal state.* Paper presented at the 3rd International Conference on e-Government, Montreal, CANADA.

Chiang, J. K., Huang, K., & Yen, E. (2007, Dec 02-05). *e-Government reform and shared services in Taiwan.* Paper presented at the IEEE International Conference on Industrial Engineering and Engineering Management, Singapore, SINGAPORE.

Chou, H. C., Sun, Y. A., Chen, J., & Alfred, U. (2007, May 26-27). *Investigating on the government employees' decision style in the environment of e-government.* Paper presented at the 6th Wuhan International Conference on E-Business, Wuhan, PEOPLES R CHINA.

Chou, T. C., Chen, J. R., & Pu, C. K. (2005, Jul). *Exploring the collective actions of public servants in e-government development.* Paper presented at the 9th Pacific Asia Conference on Information Systems (PACIS 2005), Bangkok, THAILAND.

Chun, A. H. W. (2007a, Jun 22-26). *An AI framework for the automatic assessment of e-government forms.* Paper presented at the Conference on Innovative Applications Artificial Intelligence, Vancouver, CANADA.

Chun, A. H. W. (2007b, Apr 15-17). *Automatic rule-based assessment of e-government application forms.* Paper presented at the 6th WSEAS International Conference on Applied Computer Science (ACOS 07), Hangzhou, PEOPLES R CHINA.

Chutimaskul, W. (2003, Sep 01-05). *E-government requirement elicitation.* Paper presented at the 2nd International Conference on Electronic Government (EGOV 2003), Prague, Czech Republic.

Chutimaskul, W., & Chongsuphajaisiddhi, V. (2004, May 17-19). *A framework for developing local e-government.* Paper presented at the 5th IFIP Interenational Working Conference on Knowledge Management in Electronic Government, Krems, AUSTRIA.

Chutimaskul, W., & Funilkul, S. (2004, Aug 30-Sep 03). *The framework of e-Democracy development.* Paper presented at the 3rd International Conference on Electronic Government (EGOV 2004), Zaragoza, SPAIN.

Chutimaskul, W., & Wangpipatwong, S. (2004, Jul 21-25). *e-Government information quality (e-GIQ) framework.* Paper presented at the International Conference on Politics and Information Systems, Orlando, FL.

Ciborra, C., & Navarra, D. D. (2003, Jun 15-17). *Good governance and development aid - Risks and challenges of e-government in Jordan.* Paper presented at the Working Conference on Information Systems Perspectives and Challenges in the Context of Globalization, Athens, Greece.

Civilka, M. (2004, Jul 21-25). *Situation of e-government in Lithuania and principles of regulation.* Paper presented at the International Conference on Politics and Information Systems, Orlando, FL.

Collins, N., & Butler, P. (2001, Oct 03-05). *Under some delusion: Considerations on the limits of e-democracy.* Paper presented at the 1st IFIP International Conference on E-Commerce, E-Business, and E-Government (I3E 2001), Zurich, Switzerland.

Cong, S. Q., Fang, Z. Y., Zhang, C., Liu, X. N., & Zhang, Y. R. (2006, May 03-05). *A CA-based security e-government system.* Paper presented at the 10th International Conference on Computer Supported Cooperative Work in Design, Nanjing, PEOPLES R CHINA.

Connolly, R. (2007, Mar 03-06). *Citizen trust in e-government in Ireland - The role of website service quality.* Paper presented at the 3rd International Conference on Web Information Systems and Technologies, Barcelona, SPAIN.

Connolly, R., & Bannister, F. (2006a, Dec 14-16). *Electronic government & online service quality: Methodological considerations.* Paper presented at the 7th International-Business-Information-Management-Association Conference (IBIMA), Brescia, ITALY.

Connolly, R., & Bannister, F. (2006b, Jun 19-21). *The revenue Online service in Ireland: The relationship between website service quality & consumer trust in eGovernment.* Paper presented at the 6th International-Business-Information-Management-Association Conference (IBIMA), Bonn, GERMANY.

Contenti, M., Mecella, M., Termini, A., & Baldoni, R. (2005, Mar 02-04). *A distributed architecture for supporting e-Government cooperative processes.* Paper presented at the International Conference on E-Government (TCGOV 2005), Bolzano, ITALY.

Cook, I., & Horobin, G. (2006). Implementing eGovernment without promoting dependence: Open source software in developing countries in Southeast Asia. [Article]. *Public Administration and Development, 26*(4), 279-289.

Coombs, P. (1999). The crisis in electronic government record keeping - A strategy far long-term storage. [Article]. *Library Computing, 18*(3), 196-202.

Cordella, A. (2007). E-government: towards the e-bureaucratic form? [Article]. *Journal of Information Technology, 22*(3), 265-274.

Corradini, F., De Angelis, F., Nepi, S., & Polzonetti, A. (2005, Dec). *Dynamic services modeling for e-government applications.* Paper presented at the ITI 3rd International Conference on Information and Communications Technology (ICICT 2005), Cairo, EGYPT.

Corradini, F., Marcantoni, F., Polzonetti, A., & Re, B. (2007, Jun 25-28). *A formal model for quality of service measurement in e-government.* Paper presented at the 29th International Conference on Information Technology Interfaces, Cavtat, CROATIA.

Corradini, F., Meschini, G., Polzonetti, A., & Riganelli, O. (2007, Jun 21-22). *Business Rules and their use in an e-government scenario.* Paper presented at the 7th European Conference on e-Government (ECEG 2007), The Hague, NETHERLANDS.

Corradini, F., Paganelli, E., Polzonetti, A., Forastieri, L., & Settimi, D. (2006, Jun 19-22). *Smart card distribution for e-Government digital identity promotion: Problems and solutions.* Paper presented at the 28th International Conference on Information Technology Interfaces, Cavtat, CROATIA.

Corradini, F., Polzonetti, A., Pruno, R., & Forastieri, L. (2006, Sep 04-08). *Document exchange methodology for collaborative work in e-Government.* Paper presented at the 17th International Conference on Database and Expert Systems Applications, Cracow, POLAND.

Corradini, F., Polzonetti, A., & Riganelli, O. (2005, Jun 20-23). *Small administrations: eGovernment in disadvantaged environments.* Paper presented at the 27th International Conference on InformationTechnology Interfaces, Cavtat, CROATIA.

Corradini, F., Sabucedo, L. A., Polzonetti, A., Rifon, L. A., & Re, B. (2007, Sep 03-07). *A case study of semantic solutions for citizen-centered web portals in eGovernment: The tecut portal.* Paper presented at the 6th International Conference on Electronic Government, Regensburg, GERMANY.

Costake, N. (2002, Sep 02-06). *Some specific e-government management problems in a transforming country.* Paper presented at the 1st International Conference on Electronic Government (EGOV 2002), Aix Provence, France.

Costake, N. (2003, Sep 01-05). *Anti-corruption information systems and e-Government in transforming countries. A point of view.* Paper presented at the 2nd International Conference on Electronic Government (EGOV 2003), Prague, Czech Republic.

Costilla, C., Palacios, J. P., Cremades, J., & Vila, J. (2005, Mar 02-04). *e-government: A legislative ontology for the 'SIAP' parliamentary management system.* Paper presented at the International Conference on E-Government (TCGOV 2005), Bolzano, ITALY.

Cotterill, S., & King, S. (2007, Sep 03-07). *Public sector partnerships to deliver local e-government: A social network study.* Paper presented at the 6th International Conference on Electronic Government, Regensburg, GERMANY.

Coursey, D., & Norris, D. F. (2008). Models of e-government: Are they correct? An empirical assessment. [Article]. *Public Administration Review, 68*(3), 523-536.

Cresswell, A. M., Pardo, T. A., & Canestraro, D. S. (2006, Sep 04-08). *Digital capability assessment for eGovernment: A multi-dimensional approach.* Paper presented at the 5th International Conference on Electronic Government (EGOV 2006), Cracow, POLAND.

Cruse, P., & Jahns, C. (1996). GPO GATE - University of California, San Diego's new gateway to electronic government information. [Article]. *Journal of Government Information, 23*(4), 403-410.

Csetenyi, A. (2000, Sep 04-08). *Electronic government: Perspectives from E-commerce.* Paper presented at the 11th International Workshop on Database and Expert Systems Applications, London, England.

D'Elia, I. (2004, Aug 30-Sep 03). *e-Government and information society: The first regional law in Italy.* Paper presented at the 3rd International Conference on Electronic Government (EGOV 2004), Zaragoza, SPAIN.

da Cunha, A. M., & Costa, P. M. (2004, Aug 22). *Towards key business process for e-government.* Paper presented at the 4th International Conference on E-Commerce, E-Business and E-Government held at the 18th World Computer Congress, Toulouse, FRANCE.

Daddieco, R. J. (2004, May 17-19). *Retrieving knowledge in E-government: The prospects of ontology for regulatory domain record keeping systems.* Paper presented at the 5th IFIP Interenational Working Conference on Knowledge Management in Electronic Government, Krems, AUSTRIA.

Danielson, M., & Ekenberg, L. (2004, Oct 27-29). *A method for decision support in e-democracy.*

Paper presented at the eChallenges e-2004 Conference, Vienna, AUSTRIA.

Daskapan, S., & Soc, I. C. (2006, Apr 20-22). *Building governments in e-government: settlement of trusted e-oligarchy.* Paper presented at the 1st International Conference on Availability, Reliability and Security, Vienna, AUSTRIA.

Davenport, D. D., Richey, J., & Westbrook, L. (2008). E-government access to social service information: State web resources for domestic violence survivors. [Article]. *Journal of the American Society for Information Science and Technology, 59*(6), 903-915.

Dawes, S. S., Pardo, T. A., & Cresswell, A. M. (2004). Designing electronic government information access programs: a holistic approach. [Article]. *Government Information Quarterly, 21*(1), 3-23.

Dawkins, F. (2002, Sep 02-06). *e-Government observatory.* Paper presented at the 1st International Conference on Electronic Government (EGOV 2002), Aix Provence, France.

De Bernardis, L., Ferrari, G., Nasi, S., & Nunziata, E. (2004, Jul 21-25). *A socio-technical approach for change management due to the introduction of new egovernment solutions in public sector.* Paper presented at the International Conference on Politics and Information Systems, Orlando, FL.

De Meo, P., Quattrone, G., Terracina, G., & Ursino, D. (2005, Sep 19-22). *A multi-agent system for the management of e-government services.* Paper presented at the International Conference on Intelligent Agent Technology, Compiegne, FRANCE.

De Meo, P., Quattrone, G., & Ursino, D. (2006, Sep 27-29). *Using intelligent agents in e-government for supporting decision making about service proposals.* Paper presented at the 16th International Symposium on Methodologies for Intelligent Systems, Bari, ITALY.

De Meo, P., Quattrone, G., & Ursino, D. (2008a). A decision support system for designing new services tailored to citizen profiles in a complex and distributed e-government scenario. [Article]. *Data & Knowledge Engineering, 67*(1), 161-184.

De Meo, P., Quattrone, G., & Ursino, D. (2008b). A multiagent system for assisting citizens in their search of e-government services. [Article]. *Ieee Transactions on Systems Man and Cybernetics Part C-Applications and Reviews, 38*(5), 686-698.

De Petra, G., & De Pietro, L. (2003, May 30-31). *The Italian approach to local e-government.* Paper presented at the International Conference On Line Citizenship, Venice, ITALY.

De, R. (2005, Aug 22-26). *E-government systems in developing countries: Stakeholders and conflict.* Paper presented at the 4th International Conference on Electronic Government (EGOV 2005), Copenhagen, DENMARK.

De, R. (2006, Sep 04-08). *Evaluation of e-government systems: Project assessment vs development assessment.* Paper presented at the 5th International Conference on Electronic Government (EGOV 2006), Cracow, POLAND.

De, R., & Sen, C. (2004, Aug 30-Sep 03). *The complex nature of e-government projects: A case study of Bhoomi, an initiative in Karnataka, India.* Paper presented at the 3rd International Conference on Electronic Government (EGOV 2004), Zaragoza, SPAIN.

De Saulles, M. (2007, Jun 21-22). *e-government and patterns of innovation in the public sector.* Paper presented at the 7th European Conference on e-Government (ECEG 2007), The Hague, NETHERLANDS.

Debnath, N., Dasso, A., Funes, A., Uzal, R., Paganini, J., & Ieee (2007, May 13-16). *E-government services offerings evaluation using continuous logic.* Paper presented at the 5th IEEE/ACS International Conference on Computer Systems and Applications, Amman, JORDAN.

Debnath, N., Felice, L., Montejano, G., & Riesco, D. (2008, Apr 07-09). *A feature model of e-government systems integrated with formal specifications.* Paper presented at the 5th International Conference on Information Technology - New Generations, Las Vegas, NV.

Decman, M. (2003, Sep 01-05). *Trust in e-government: Digital signatures without time stamping?* Paper presented at the 2nd International Conference on Electronic Government (EGOV 2003), Prague, Czech Republic.

Della Valle, E., Cerizza, D., Celino, I., Estublier, J., Vega, G., Kerrigan, M., et al. (2007, Jun 03-07). *SEEMP: An semantic interoperability infrastructure for e-government services in the employment sector.* Paper presented at the 4th European Semantic Web Conference, Innsbruck, AUSTRIA.

Denes, T., & Andersson, K. E. (2004, Aug 30-Sep 03). *Framework for the e-government jigsaw puzzle, a policy implementation of infra-e-service on national basis.* Paper presented at the 3rd International Conference on Electronic Government (EGOV 2004), Zaragoza, SPAIN.

Denman-Maier, E., & Parycek, P. (2003, Sep 01-05). *Cross-cultural factors in global e-Government.* Paper presented at the 2nd International Conference on Electronic Government (EGOV 2003), Prague, Czech Republic.

Devadoss, P. R., Pan, S. L., & Huang, J. C. (2003). Structurational analysis of e-government initiatives: a case study of SCO. [Article]. *Decision Support Systems, 34*(3), 253-269.

Di Maria, E., & Rizzo, L. S. (2003, May 30-31). *E-democracy: The participation of citizens and new forms of the decision-making process.* Paper presented at the International Conference On Line Citizenship, Venice, ITALY.

Dias, G. P., & Rafael, J. A. (2007). A simple model and a distributed architecture for realizing one-stop e-government. [Article]. *Electronic Commerce Research and Applications, 6*(1), 81-90.

Diez, C., & Prenafeta, J. (2002, Sep 02-06). *e-Government applied to judicial notices and inter-registrar communications in the European Union: The AEQUITAS Project.* Paper presented at the 1st International Conference on Electronic Government (EGOV 2002), Aix Provence, France.

Dimitrova, D. V., & Chen, Y. C. (2006). Profiling the adopters of e-government information and services - The influence of psychological characteristics, civic mindedness, and information channels. [Article]. *Social Science Computer Review, 24*(2), 172-188.

Ding, J. L., Le, Z. J., & Zhou, P. (2008, Oct 17-19). *A Collaborative Framework for developing E-Government Emergency System.* Paper presented at the 2nd International Conference on Management of e-Commerce and e-Government, Nanchang, PEOPLES R CHINA.

Dong, Y. M., Rui, Y. N., Shuai, D. X., & Ieee, I. (2003, Oct 12-15). *The researching of constructing a convenient, safe, credible, new e-government system.* Paper presented at the 6th IEEE International Conference on Intelligent Transportation Systems, Shanghai, Peoples R China.

Donzelli, P., & Bresciani, P. (2003, Jun 16-20). *Goal-oriented requirements engineering: A case study in e-Government.* Paper presented at the 15th International Conference on Advanced Information Systems Engineering, Velden, Austria.

Dorfler, A. (2003, May 26-28). *Business process modelling and help systems as part of KM in e-government.* Paper presented at the 4th Annual International Working Conference on Knowledge Management in Electronic Government, Rhodes, Greece.

dos Santos, I. J. G., & Madeira, E. R. M. (2007, Jun 12-16). *e-Government and grid computing - Potentials and challenges towards Citizen-centric Services.* Paper presented at the 9th International Conference on Enterprise Information Systems (ICEIS 2007), Funchal, PORTUGAL.

dos Santos, I. J. G., Madeira, E. R. M., & Tschammer, V. (2005, Oct 28-30). *Towards dynamic composition of e-Government services - A policy-based approach.* Paper presented at the 5th IFTP Conference on E-Commerce, E-Business, and E-Government, Poznan, POLAND.

Doty, P., & Erdelez, S. (2002). Information micro-practices in Texas rural courts: methods and issues for E-government. [Article]. *Government Information Quarterly, 19*(4), 369-387.

Dovifat, A., Kubisch, D., Bruggemeier, M., Lenk, K., & Reichard, C. (2004, Aug 30-Sep 03). *Explaining successes and failures of e-government implementation with micropolitics.* Paper presented at the 3rd International Conference on Electronic Government (EGOV 2004), Zaragoza, SPAIN.

Dridi, F., Fischer, M., & Pernul, G. (2003, May 26-28). *CSAP - An adaptable security module for the e-government system webocrat.* Paper presented at the 18th International Conference on Information Security, Athens, Greece.

Du, J. P., & Ye, K. P. (2005, Aug 15-17). *A study on the development and tactics of E-government construction of Jiangxi province.* Paper presented at the 7th International Conference on Electronic Commerce (ICEC 2005), Xian, PEOPLES R CHINA.

Du, R. J., Tang, Z. W., & Gao, T. P. (2005, Jun 04-05). *The risk analysis of E-government information system based on ISM.* Paper presented at the 4th Wuhan International Conference on E-Business - Global Business Interface, Wuhan, PEOPLES R CHINA.

Dugan, R. E., & Cheverie, J. F. (1992). ELECtronic Government Information And The Depository Library Program - Paradise Found. [Article]. *Government Information Quarterly, 9*(3), 269-289.

Dugdale, A., Daly, A., Papandrea, F., & Maley, M. (2005). Accessing e-government: challenges for citizens and organizations. [Article]. *International Review of Administrative Sciences, 71*(1), 109-118.

Dunleavy, P., Margetts, H., Bastow, S., & Tinkler, J. (2008). Australian e-government in comparative perspective. [Article]. *Australian Journal of Political Science, 43*(1), 13-26.

Durrant, F. (2002, Sep 02-06). *e-government and the Internet in the Caribbean: An initial assessment.* Paper presented at the 1st International Conference on Electronic Government (EGOV 2002), Aix Provence, France.

Dzhumalieva, S., & Helfert, M. (2008, Apr 22-25). *A conceptual framework for handling complex administrative processes in e-government.* Paper presented at the 2nd International United Informational Systems Conference, Klagenfurt, AUSTRIA.

Ebbers, W. E., Pieterson, W. J., & Noordman, H. N. (2008). Electronic government: Rethinking channel management strategies. [Article]. *Government Information Quarterly, 25*(2), 181-201.

Ebbers, W. E., & van Dijk, J. (2007). Resistance and support to electronic government, building a model of innovation. [Article]. *Government Information Quarterly, 24*(3), 554-575.

Eddowes, L. A. (2005, Mar 02-04). *Good practice in e-Government: Management over methods?* Paper presented at the International Conference on E-Government (TCGOV 2005), Bolzano, ITALY.

Edmiston, K. D. (2003). State and local e-government - Prospects and challenges. [Article]. *American Review of Public Administration, 33*(1), 20-45.

Eka, M. I. (2008, May 04-07). *E-government in Africa - Strengthening it through European co-operation.* Paper presented at the 4th International Conference on Web Information Systems and Technologies, Funchal, PORTUGAL.

Ekelin, A. (2003, Jul 31-Aug 02). *It takes more than two to TANGO co-constructing situated accountability through a local e-government arena.* Paper presented at the International Conference on Politics and Information Systems - Technologies and Applications (PISTA 03), Orlando, FL.

Elayoubi, M. (2008, Jan 04-06). *E-government and marketing communication strategies of Moroccan public institutions: basis and implications.* Paper presented at the 9th International-Business-Information-Management-Association Conference (IBIMA), Marrakech, MOROCCO.

Elovaara, P., Eriksen, S., Ekelin, A., Hansson, C., Nilsson, M., & Winter, J. (2004, Aug 30-Sep 03). *Educational programs in e-government - An active, practice- and design-oriented network?* Paper presented at the 3rd International Conference on Electronic Government (EGOV 2004), Zaragoza, SPAIN.

Elsas, A. (2003a, Jul 31-Aug 02). *E-government in Germany: Status quo and perspectives.* Paper presented at the International Conference on Politics and Information Systems - Technologies and Applications (PISTA 03), Orlando, FL.

Elsas, A. (2003b, Sep 01-05). *Integration of E-Government and E-Commerce with Web services.* Paper presented at the 2nd International Conference on Electronic Government (EGOV 2003), Prague, Czech Republic.

Elsas, A. (2006, Jun 19-21). *Economic benchmarking of e-government.* Paper presented at the 6th International-Business-Information-Management-Association Conference (IBIMA), Bonn, GERMANY.

Eriksen, S., Dittrich, Y., Fiedler, M., & Aurell, M. (2003, Sep 01-05). *It takes more than two ... developing a TANGO arena for regional cooperation around e-government.* Paper presented at the 2nd International Conference on Electronic Government (EGOV 2003), Prague, Czech Republic.

Eriksen, S., Ekelin, A., Elovaara, P., Dittrich, Y., Hansson, C., & Winter, J. (2004, Aug 30-Sep 03). *What have we learned from the TANGO arena for regional cooperation around e-government in Southern Sweden?* Paper presented at the 3rd International Conference on Electronic Government (EGOV 2004), Zaragoza, SPAIN.

Esteves, J. (2007, Jun 21-22). *A semiotic analysis of Spanish local e-government websites.* Paper presented at the 7th European Conference on e-Government (ECEG 2007), The Hague, NETHERLANDS.

Esteves, J., & Joseph, R. C. (2008). A comprehensive framework for the assessment of eGovernment projects. [Article]. *Government Information Quarterly, 25*(1), 118-132.

Estevez, E., & Janowski, T. (2007a, Apr 10-13). *Building a dependable messaging infrastructure for Electronic Government.* Paper presented at the 2nd International Conference on Availability, Reliability and Security, Vienna, AUSTRIA.

Estevez, E., & Janowski, T. (2007b, Sep 24-25). *Programmable messaging for electronic government - Building a foundation.* Paper presented at the Symposium on Formal Methods and Hybrid Real-Time Systems held in Honour of Dines Bjorner/Zhou Chaochen, Macao, PEOPLES R CHINA.

Evangelidis, A., Akomode, J., Taleb-Bendiab, A., & Taylor, M. (2002, Sep 02-06). *Risk assessment & success factors for e-Government in a UK establishment.* Paper presented at the 1st International Conference on Electronic Government (EGOV 2002), Aix Provence, France.

Evangelidis, A., Macintosh, A., & Davenport, E. (2004, Aug 30-Sep 03). *FRAMES towards risk modelling in e-government services: A UK perspective.* Paper presented at the 3rd International Conference on Electronic Government (EGOV 2004), Zaragoza, SPAIN.

Evans, D., & Yen, D. C. (2005). E-government: An analysis for implementation: Framework for understanding cultural and social impact. [Article]. *Government Information Quarterly, 22*(3), 354-373.

Evans-Cowley, J., & Conroy, M. M. (2006). The growth of E-government in municipal planning. [Article]. *Journal of Urban Technology, 13*(1), 81-107.

Facis, R., Torres, C. A. N., & de Vasconcelos, J. B. (2007, Sep). *Sao Paulo state e-gov: LabIHC and e-poupatempo's experience.* Paper presented at the 11th IFIP International Conference on Human-Computer Interaction, Rio de Janeiro, BRAZIL.

Fan, J., Zhang, P., & Alfred, U. (2007, May 26-27). *A conceptual model for G2G information sharing in e-government environment.* Paper presented at the 6th Wuhan International Conference on E-Business, Wuhan, PEOPLES R CHINA.

Fang, L., Tang, S. Q., Xiao, R. L., Li, L., Deng, X. U., Yu, Y., et al. (2007, May 26-27). *On change management using meta-ontology in the E-government.* Paper presented at the 6th Wuhan International Conference on E-Business, Wuhan, PEOPLES R CHINA.

Farahmand, F., Navathe, S. B., Sharp, G. P., & Enslow, P. H. (2004, Jun 21-24). *Data confidentiality in e-government and e-commerce.* Paper presented at the International Conference on Security and Management, Las Vegas, NV.

Favier, L., & Mekhantar, J. (2004, Aug 30-Sep 03). *Trade unions in e-democracy.* Paper presented at the 3rd International Conference on Electronic Government (EGOV 2004), Zaragoza, SPAIN.

Feng, F. J. (2002, May 23-26). *The research of e-government model construction.* Paper presented at the International Conference on E-Business (ICEB2002), Beijing, Peoples R China.

Feng, Y. Q., Huang, F. Y., Li, C. H., Zhang, H. W., & Lu, P. Y. (2006, Oct 05-07). *Analysis on public economics characteristics of E-government as a kind of public goods.* Paper presented at the 13th International Conference on Management Science and Engineering, Lille, FRANCE.

Feng, Y. Q., & Li, Y. (2002, Oct 22-24). *Research on E-government and its development in China.* Paper presented at the International Conference on Management Science and Engineering, Moscow, Russia.

Feng, Y. Q., Li, Y., & Xin, B. L. (2003, Aug 15-17). *Appling intelligent collaborative agent to workflow management system on one-stop e-government.* Paper presented at the International Conference on Management Science and Engineering, Atlanta, Ga.

Fernandez, E., Fernandez, I., Jimenez, S., & Salvador, J. (2006). E-government for water management in Spain. The case of Hispagua. [Article]. *Profesional De La Informacion, 15*(2), 99-113.

Ferro, E., Cantanmessa, M., & Paolucci, E. (2004, Aug 30-Sep 03). *Economies of scale in e-government: Time for evidence.* Paper presented at the 3rd International Conference on Electronic Government (EGOV 2004), Zaragoza, SPAIN.

Figueiredo, A., Mendes, M. D., Kamada, A., Borelli, J. R., Rodrigues, M. A., Damasceno, L. L., et al. (2004, Aug 30-Sep 03). *Applying MDA concepts in an e-government platform.* Paper presented at the 3rd International Conference on Electronic Government (EGOV 2004), Zaragoza, SPAIN.

Fischmann, L., Jakisch, G., & Riedel, R. (2001, Sep 03-07). *E-Vienna living situation based eGovernment and eDemocracy.* Paper presented at the

12th International Conference on Database and Expert Systems Applications (DEXA), Munich, Germany.

Flak, L. S., Moe, C. E., & Saebo, O. (2003, Sep 01-05). *On the evolution of e-Government: The user imperative.* Paper presented at the 2nd International Conference on Electronic Government (EGOV 2003), Prague, Czech Republic.

Flak, L. S., Sein, M. K., & Saebo, O. (2007, Sep 03-07). *Towards a cumulative tradition in e-Government research: Going beyond the gs and cs.* Paper presented at the 6th International Conference on Electronic Government, Regensburg, GERMANY.

Folstad, A. (2008, May 04-07). *Improving the user-centredness of e-Government projects.* Paper presented at the 4th International Conference on Web Information Systems and Technologies, Funchal, PORTUGAL.

Foster, J. (2001, Oct 03-05). *Towards a democratic education for e-government - A study of deliberative decision-making via information and communications technology.* Paper presented at the 1st IFIP International Conference on E-Commerce, E-Business, and E-Government (I3E 2001), Zurich, Switzerland.

Fotinea, S. E., & Efthimiou, E. (2008, Jul 09-11). *Tools for deaf accessibility to an eGOV environment.* Paper presented at the 11th International Conference on Computers Helping People with Special Needs, Linz, AUSTRIA.

Franzel, J. M., & Richardson, C. A. (2003, Jul 31-Aug 02). *Urban electronic government - Innovation, adoption, and metropolitan characteristics.* Paper presented at the International Conference on Politics and Information Systems - Technologies and Applications (PISTA 03), Orlando, FL.

Fraser, J., Adams, N., Macintosh, A., McKay-Hubbard, A., Lobo, T. P., Pardo, P. F., et al. (2003, May 26-28). *Knowledge management applied to e-government services: The use of an ontology.* Paper presented at the 4th Annual International Working Conference on Knowledge Management in Electronic Government, Rhodes, Greece.

Freeman, R. (2007, Jun 21-22). *Evaluation and distribution of e-government services.* Paper presented at the 7th European Conference on e-Government (ECEG 2007), The Hague, NETHERLANDS.

French, S. (2004, Sep 22-24). *Web-enabled strategic GDSS, e-democracy and Arrow's theorem: A Bayesian perspective.* Paper presented at the 15th Mini-EURO Conference on Managing Uncertainty in Decision Support Models, Coimbra, PORTUGAL.

Freya, K. N., & Holden, S. H. (2005). Distribution channel management in e-government: Addressing federal information policy issues. [Article]. *Government Information Quarterly, 22*(4), 685-701.

Fu, X. F., Peng, D., Xu, H. S., Lu, Y. S., & Xiao, S. T. (2005, May 24-26). *Research of E-government information portal applications based on grid technology.* Paper presented at the 9th International Conference on Computer Supported Cooperative Work in Design, Coventry, ENGLAND.

Fu, X. F., Peng, D., Xu, H. S., Lu, Y. S., & Zhan, Y. W. (2005, May 24-26). *Research and implementation of E-Government information portal based on grid technology.* Paper presented at the 9th International Conference on Computer Supported Cooperative Work in Design, Coventry, ENGLAND.

Fugini, M. (2007, Apr 10-13). *A security model and architecture for multichannel E-Government systems.* Paper presented at the 2nd International Conference on Availability, Reliability and Security, Vienna, AUSTRIA.

Futo, I. (2006, Jun 19-22). *A general purpose front-office system for eGovernment communications.*

Paper presented at the 28th International Conference on Information Technology Interfaces, Cavtat, CROATIA.

Gaaloul, K., Charoy, F., Schaad, A., & Lee, H. (2007, Dec 03). *Collaboration for human-centric eGovernment workflows.* Paper presented at the 8th International Conference on Web Information Systems Engineering (WISE 2007), Nancy, FRANCE.

Gadda, L., & Savoldelli, A. (2002, Sep 02-06). *The local e-government best practice in Italian country: The case of the centralised desk of "area berica".* Paper presented at the 1st International Conference on Electronic Government (EGOV 2002), Aix Provence, France.

Galindo, F. (2000, Sep 04-08). *Electronic government: From the theory to the action.* Paper presented at the 11th International Workshop on Database and Expert Systems Applications, London, England.

Galindo, F. (2001, Sep 03-07). *Public key certification providers and e-government assurance agencies. An appraisal of trust on the Internet.* Paper presented at the 12th International Conference on Database and Expert Systems Applications (DEXA), Munich, Germany.

Galindo, F. (2002, Sep 02-06). *Self-regulation in e-Government: A step more.* Paper presented at the 1st International Conference on Electronic Government (EGOV 2002), Aix Provence, France.

Gallemore, C. (2005). Of lords and (cyber)serfs: eGovernment and poststructuralism in a neomedieval Europe. [Article]. *Millennium-Journal of International Studies, 34*(1), 27-55.

Gan, X. H. (2008, Oct 17-19). *Research on Risk Aversion of E-government Network Security.* Paper presented at the 2nd International Conference on Management of e-Commerce and e-Government, Nanchang, PEOPLES R CHINA.

Gant, D. B., & Gant, J. P. (2004, May 23-26). *Providing access for all or all of those who have access: Do e-government information policies matter for the accessibility of government web portals?* Paper presented at the International Conference of the Information-Resources-Management-Association, New Orleans, LA.

Gao, G. W., Wang, Y. Z., Li, H. M., Ding, F., & Weng, C. (2004, Aug 08-10). *The research of E-government application integration based on integrated service portal.* Paper presented at the International Conference on Management Science and Engineering, Harbin, PEOPLES R CHINA.

Gao, G. W., Wang, Y. Z., Wang, N., Li, H. M., & Wang, D. J. (2006, Dec 18-22). *An intelligent and cooperative information system for the dynamic management of E-government services in inter-administration.* Paper presented at the IEEE/WIC/ACM International Conference on Web Intelligence and Intelligent Agent Technology (WI-IAT 2006), Hong Kong, PEOPLES R CHINA.

Gao, X. R., & Liu, W. (2005, Jun 13-15). *Incentives for information sharing across branches in e-government.* Paper presented at the International Conference on Service Systems and Service Management, Chongqing, PEOPLES R CHINA.

Garcia, A. C. B., Maciel, C., & Pinto, F. B. (2005, Aug 22-26). *A quality inspection method to evaluate e-Government sites.* Paper presented at the 4th International Conference on Electronic Government (EGOV 2005), Copenhagen, DENMARK.

Garcia, T., Pomar, C., & Hoeschl, H. C. (2004, Aug 22). *Democracy in the electronic government era.* Paper presented at the 4th International Conference on E-Commerce, E-Business and E-Government held at the 18th World Computer Congress, Toulouse, FRANCE.

Garcia, T. H. B., Theiss, I., Zimath, P., Hoeschl, H. C., Donatti, F., Loureiro, G. M., et al. (2003, Sep 01-05). *Consumer-SC: An E-gov portal for consumers rights protection in Brazil.* Paper presented at the 2nd International Conference on Electronic Government (EGOV 2003), Prague, Czech Republic.

Garcia-Martinez, G., Romero Civera, A., Segui Mas, E., & Villalonga Granana, I. (2006, Dec 14-16). *Corporative e-government in the digital era : empirical study of rural Spanish cashiers.* Paper presented at the 7th International-Business-Information-Management-Association Conference (IBIMA), Brescia, ITALY.

Garcia-Sanchez, F., Sabucedo, L. A., Martinez-Bejar, R., Rifon, L. A., Valencia-Garcia, R., & Gomez, J. M. (2008, May 12). *A knowledge technologies-based multi-agent system for eGovernment environments.* Paper presented at the International Workshop on Service-Oriented Computing - Agents, Semantics, and Engineering (SOCASE 2008), Estoril, PORTUGAL.

Garimella, S., & Vanka, S. (2004, Jul 21-25). *E-government in the developing context - The Indian experience.* Paper presented at the International Conference on Politics and Information Systems, Orlando, FL.

Garofalakis, J., Koskeris, A., & Vopi, A. (2007, Jun 21-22). *An e-government application for integrated, multi-level management of large scale resources of the Greek primary and secondary education.* Paper presented at the 7th European Conference on e-Government (ECEG 2007), The Hague, NETHERLANDS.

Germanakos, P., Christodoulou, E., & Samaras, G. (2007, Sep 03-07). *European perspective of e-Government presence - Where do we stand? The EU-10 case.* Paper presented at the 6th International Conference on Electronic Government, Regensburg, GERMANY.

Gil-Garcia, J. R., Chengalur-Smith, I., & Duchessi, P. (2007). Collaborative e-Government: impediments and benefits of information-sharing projects in the public sector. [Article]. *European Journal of Information Systems, 16*(2), 121-133.

Gil-Garcia, J. R., & Martinez-Moyano, I. J. (2004, Dec 12-15). *Understanding the evolution of e-government: The influence of systems of rules on public sector dynamics.* Paper presented at the International Conference on Information Systems, Washington, DC.

Gil-Garcia, J. R., & Pardo, T. A. (2005). E-government success factors: Mapping practical tools to theoretical foundations. [Review]. *Government Information Quarterly, 22*(2), 187-216.

Gisler, M., & Spahni, D. (2000, Sep 04-08). *eGovernment experiences of the Swiss Federal Institute of Intellectual Property.* Paper presented at the 11th International Workshop on Database and Expert Systems Applications, London, England.

Glassey, O., & Chappelet, J. L. (2003, Sep 01-05). *From e-Government to e-Governance: A survey of the federal and cantonal e-Policies in Switzerland.* Paper presented at the 2nd International Conference on Electronic Government (EGOV 2003), Prague, Czech Republic.

Goh, B. H. (2007, Oct 14-16). *E-government for construction: The case of Singapore's CORENET project.* Paper presented at the 2nd International Conference on Research and Practical Issues of Enterprise Information Systems, Beijing, PEOPLES R CHINA.

Goh, D. H. L., Chua, A. Y. K., Luyt, B., & Lee, C. S. (2008). Knowledge access, creation and transfer in e-government portals. [Article]. *Online Information Review, 32*(3), 348-369.

Gomez-Perez, A., Ortiz-Rodriguez, F., & Villazon-Terrazas, B. (2006). Legal ontologies for the Spanish e-Government *Current Topics in Artificial Intelligence* (Vol. 4177, pp. 301-310). Berlin: Springer-Verlag Berlin.

Gonzalez, R., Gasco, J., & Llopis, J. (2007). E-government success: some principles from a

Spanish case study. [Article]. *Industrial Management & Data Systems, 107*(5-6), 845-861.

Gortmaker, J., & Janssen, M. (2004, May 23-26). *Business process orchestration in e-government: A gap analysis.* Paper presented at the International Conference of the Information-Resources-Management-Association, New Orleans, LA.

Gortmaker, J., Janssen, M., & Wagenaar, R. W. (2005, Mar 02-04). *Towards requirements for a reference model for process orchestration in e-government.* Paper presented at the International Conference on E-Government (TCGOV 2005), Bolzano, ITALY.

Goudos, S. K., Loutas, N., Peristeras, V., & Tarabanis, K. (2007, Jul 09-13). *Public Administration domain ontology for a semantic Web services e-government framework.* Paper presented at the IEEE International Conference on Services Computing, Salt Lake City, UT.

Gouscos, D., Kalikakis, M., Legal, M., & Papadopoulou, S. (2007). A general model of performance and quality for one-stop e-Government service offerings. [Article]. *Government Information Quarterly, 24*(4), 860-885.

Gouscos, D., Lambrou, M., Mentzas, G., & Georgiadis, P. (2003, Sep 01-05). *A methodological approach for defining one-stop E-government service offerings.* Paper presented at the 2nd International Conference on Electronic Government (EGOV 2003), Prague, Czech Republic.

Gouscos, D., Laskaridis, G., Lioulias, D., Mentzas, G., & Georgiadis, P. (2002, Sep 02-06). *An approach to offering one-stop e-Government services - Available technologies and architectural issues.* Paper presented at the 1st International Conference on Electronic Government (EGOV 2002), Aix Provence, France.

Gouscos, D., Mentzas, G., & Georgiadis, P. (2001, Sep 03-07). *PASSPORT - A novel architectural model for the provision of seamless cross-border e-government services.* Paper presented at the 12th International Conference on Database and Expert Systems Applications (DEXA), Munich, Germany.

Grandi, F., Mandreoli, F., Martoglia, R., Ronchetti, E., Scalas, M. R., & Tiberio, P. (2005, Aug 22-26). *Personalized access to multi-version norm texts in an eGovernment scenario.* Paper presented at the 4th International Conference on Electronic Government (EGOV 2005), Copenhagen, DENMARK.

Grandi, F., Mandreoli, F., Martoglia, R., Ronchetti, E., Scalas, M. R., & Tiberio, P. (2006, Nov 06-09). *Semantic Web techniques for personalization of eGovernment services.* Paper presented at the 25th International Conference on Conceptual Modeling, Tucson, AZ.

Grant, G., & Chau, D. (2005). Developing a generic framework for e-government. [Article]. *Journal of Global Information Management, 13*(1), 1-30.

Grimsley, M., & Meehan, A. (2007a, Jun 21-22). *Attaining social value from electronic government.* Paper presented at the 7th European Conference on e-Government (ECEG 2007), The Hague, NETHERLANDS.

Grimsley, M., & Meehan, A. (2007b). e-Government information systems: Evaluation-led design for public value and client trust. [Article]. *European Journal of Information Systems, 16*(2), 134-148.

Grimsley, M., Meehan, A., Green, G., & Stafford, B. (2003, May 28-30). *Social capital, community trust, and E-government services.* Paper presented at the 1st International Conference on Trust Management, Iraklion, Greece.

Gronlund, A. (2003, Sep 01-05). *Framing e-gov: e=mc3.* Paper presented at the 2nd International Conference on Electronic Government (EGOV 2003), Prague, Czech Republic.

Gronlund, A. (2004, Aug 30-Sep 03). *State of the art in e-Gov research - A survey.* Paper presented at the 3rd International Conference on Electronic Government (EGOV 2004), Zaragoza, SPAIN.

Gronlund, A., & Andersson, A. (2006, Sep 04-08). *e-gov research quality improvements since 2003: More rigor, but research (perhaps) redefined.* Paper presented at the 5th International Conference on Electronic Government (EGOV 2006), Cracow, POLAND.

Gross, T. (2000, Sep 04-08). *Technological support for e-democracy: History and perspectives.* Paper presented at the 11th International Workshop on Database and Expert Systems Applications, London, England.

Groznik, A., Kovacic, A., Jaklic, J., & Ieee, I. (2003, Jun 16-19). *Simulation modeling in practice - Towards e-government.* Paper presented at the 25th International Conference on Information Technology Interfaces, Cavtat, Croatia.

Groznik, A., & Vicic, D. (2005, Jun 01-04). *Towards E-government: Business renovation of public sector in Slovenia.* Paper presented at the 19th European Conference on Modelling and Simulation (ECMS 2005), Riga, LATVIA.

Grunden, K. (2007, Jun 21-22). *Back-office implementation of e-Government - A learning process.* Paper presented at the 7th European Conference on e-Government (ECEG 2007), The Hague, NETHERLANDS.

Guijarro, L. (2004, Aug 30-Sep 03). *Analysis of the interoperability frameworks in e-government initiatives.* Paper presented at the 3rd International Conference on Electronic Government (EGOV 2004), Zaragoza, SPAIN.

Guijarro, L. (2005, Aug 22-26). *Policy and practice in standards selection for e-government interoperability frameworks.* Paper presented at the 4th International Conference on Electronic Government (EGOV 2005), Copenhagen, DENMARK.

Guijarro, L. (2007). Interoperability frameworks and enterprise architectures in e-government initiatives in Europe and the United States. [Article]. *Government Information Quarterly, 24*(1), 89-101.

Guijarro-Coloma, L. (2005, Sep 21-23). *Standards and iteroperability in e-government initiatives.* Paper presented at the 4th International Conference on Standardization and Innovation in Information Technology, Geneva, SWITZERLAND.

Gunter, B. (2004). The prospects for e-government on digital television. [Article]. *Aslib Proceedings, 56*(4), 222-233.

Guo, X. T., & Lu, J. (2004, Sep 01-03). *Intelligent e-government services with personalized recommendation techniques.* Paper presented at the 6th International FLINS Conference on Applied Artificial Intelligence, Blankenberge, BELGIUM.

Gupta, M. P., & Jana, D. (2003). E-government evaluation: A framework and case study. [Article]. *Government Information Quarterly, 20*(4), 365-387.

Hackney, R., Jones, S., & Losch, A. (2007). Towards an e-Government efficiency agenda: the impact of information and communication behaviour on e-Reverse auctions in public sector procurement. [Article]. *European Journal of Information Systems, 16*(2), 178-191.

Hadzilias, E. A. (2005, Mar 02-04). *A methodology framework for calculating the cost of e-Government services.* Paper presented at the International Conference on E-Government (TCGOV 2005), Bolzano, ITALY.

Halaris, C., Magoutas, B., Papadomichelaki, X., & Mentzas, G. (2007). Classification and synthesis of quality approaches in e-government services. [Article]. *Internet Research, 17*(4), 378-401.

Halaris, C., & Verginadis, G. (2004, Aug 30-Sep 03). *e-Government: A strategy for deploying social security related electronic services.* Paper presented at the 3rd International Conference on Electronic Government (EGOV 2004), Zaragoza, SPAIN.

Halchin, L. E. (2002). Electronic government in the age of terrorism. [Article]. *Government Information Quarterly, 19*(3), 243-254.

Halchin, L. E. (2004). Electronic government: Government capability and terrorist resource. [Article]. *Government Information Quarterly, 21*(4), 406-419.

Han, J., Liu, X. D., Huai, J. P., Lin, X. L., Ma, X. X., & Li, X. (2007, Jul 11-13). *InfoXP: An e-government information eXchange platform based on overlay network.* Paper presented at the 6th IEEE/ACIS International Conference on Computer and Information Science in Conjunction with 1st IEEE/ACIS International Workshop on e-Activity, Melbourne, AUSTRALIA.

Han, S. J., Wang, N., & Yu, M. (2005, Apr 04-06). *Research on role-network model for E-Government Affairs.* Paper presented at the International Conference on Information Technology - Coding and Computing, Las Vegas, NV.

Handzic, M. (2004, May 17-19). *The role of knowledge mapping in electronic government.* Paper presented at the 5th IFIP Interenational Working Conference on Knowledge Management in Electronic Government, Krems, AUSTRIA.

Hao, P., Wu, H. R., & Zhao, L. (2007, Oct 26-29). *Application of CVS in small town E-government system.* Paper presented at the 4th International Symposium on Intelligent Information Technology in Agriculture, Beijing, PEOPLES R CHINA.

Hardy, C. A., & Williams, S. P. (2008). E-government policy and practice: A theoretical and empirical exploration of public e-procurement. [Article]. *Government Information Quarterly, 25*(2), 155-180.

Harrison, C., & Petrie, H. (2006, Sep 11-15). *Severity of usability and accessibility problems in eCommerce and eGovernment websites.* Paper presented at the 20th Annual Conference of the British-HCI-Group, London, ENGLAND.

Hart, T., Yan, L., & Alfred, U. (2007, May 26-27). *Government with a plug useful and less useful approaches to E-government and its regulatory environment.* Paper presented at the 6th Wuhan International Conference on E-Business, Wuhan, PEOPLES R CHINA.

Hashim, H. R. H., Roslin, R. M., & Jamaludin, A. (2007, Jun 21-22). *The transition to e-government for local governments: A conceptual framework on issues in Ict implementation.* Paper presented at the 7th European Conference on e-Government (ECEG 2007), The Hague, NETHERLANDS.

He, W., Lu, P., Zhou, C., & Lin, X. L. (2006, Sep 16-18). *Web based E-Government information sharing system.* Paper presented at the IEEE International Conference on Information Reuse and Intergration (IRI 2006), Waikoloa, HI.

Heck, U., & Rogger, A. (2004, May 17-19). *Knowledge management for E-service-delivery - A conceptual approach within E-government.* Paper presented at the 5th IFIP Interenational Working Conference on Knowledge Management in Electronic Government, Krems, AUSTRIA.

Heeks, R., & Bailur, S. (2007). Analyzing e-government research: Perspective, philosophies, theories, methods, and practice. [Article]. *Government Information Quarterly, 24*(2), 243-265.

Heeks, R., & Stanforth, C. (2007). Understanding e-Government project trajectories from an actor-network perspective. [Article]. *European Journal of Information Systems, 16*(2), 165-177.

Heinderyckx, F. (2002, Sep 02-06). *Assessing e-government implementation processes: A pan-European survey of administrations officials.* Paper presented at the 1st International Conference on Electronic Government (EGOV 2002), Aix Provence, France.

Heindl, P., Prosser, A., & Krimmer, R. (2003, Sep 01-05). *Constitutional and technical requirements for democracy over the Internet: E-democracy.* Paper presented at the 2nd International Conference on Electronic Government (EGOV 2003), Prague, Czech Republic.

Henman, P. (2003, Jul 31-Aug 02). *E-government and the electronic transformation of modes of rule: The case of partnerships.* Paper presented at the International Conference on Politics and Information Systems - Technologies and Applications (PISTA 03), Orlando, FL.

Henriksen, H. Z., & Damsgaard, J. (2006, Jun 07-10). *The rise and descent of visions for e-government.* Paper presented at the International Working Conference on Transfer and Diffusion of Information Technology for Organization Resilience, Galway, IRELAND.

Henriksen, H. Z., & Damsgaard, J. (2007). Dawn of e-government - an institutional analysis of seven initiatives and their impact. [Article]. *Journal of Information Technology, 22*(1), 13-23.

Hilton, S. (2006). Developing local e-democracy in Bristol - From information to consultation to participation and beyond. [Article]. *Aslib Proceedings, 58*(5), 416-428.

Hinkelmann, K., Thonssen, B., & Probst, F. (2005). Reference modelling for E-Government services. [Article]. *Wirtschaftsinformatik, 47*(5), 356-366.

Ho, A. T. K. (2002). Reinventing local governments and the e-government initiative. [Article]. *Public Administration Review, 62*(4), 434-444.

Ho, A. T. K., & Ni, A. Y. (2004). Explaining the adoption of e-government features - A case study of Iowa County treasurers' offices. [Article]. *American Review of Public Administration, 34*(2), 164-180.

Hoegler, T., & Schuster, T. (2002, Sep 02-06). *Quo vadis e-Government? - A trap between unsuitable technologies and deployment strategies.* Paper presented at the 1st International Conference on Electronic Government (EGOV 2002), Aix Provence, France.

Hoeschl, H. C., Bueno, T. C. D., Bortolon, A., Mattos, E. S., Ribeiro, M. S., Theiss, I., et al. (2004, Aug 22). *An intelligent search engine for electronic government applications for the resolutions of the united nations security council.* Paper presented at the 4th International Conference on E-Commerce, E-Business and E-Government held at the 18th World Computer Congress, Toulouse, FRANCE.

Hof, S. (2002, Sep 02-06). *Arguments for a holistic and open approach to secure e-Government.* Paper presented at the 1st International Conference on Electronic Government (EGOV 2002), Aix Provence, France.

Hof, S. (2003, Sep 01-05). *Security aspects within e-Government.* Paper presented at the 2nd International Conference on Electronic Government (EGOV 2003), Prague, Czech Republic.

Hof, S., & Reichstadter, P. (2004, Aug 30-Sep 03). *Securing e-government.* Paper presented at the 3rd International Conference on Electronic Government (EGOV 2004), Zaragoza, SPAIN.

Holden, S. H. (2002, May 19-22). *Electronic authentication initiatives in the IRS e-file program: Enabling e-government through electronic signatures.* Paper presented at the International Conference of the Information-Resources-Management-Association, Seattle, Wa.

Holden, S. H., & Millett, L. I. (2005). Authentication, privacy, and the federal E-Government. [Article]. *Information Society, 21*(5), 367-377.

Holliday, I. (2002). Building E-government in East and Southeast Asia: Regional rhetoric and national (in)action. [Article]. *Public Administration and Development, 22*(4), 323-335.

Holliday, I., & Kwok, R. C. W. (2004). Governance in the information age: building e-government in Hong Kong. [Article]. *New Media & Society, 6*(4), 549-570.

Holliday, I., & Yep, R. (2005). E-government in China. [Article]. *Public Administration and Development, 25*(3), 239-249.

Hollosi, A., Leitold, H., & Posch, R. (2002, Sep 26-27). *An open interface enabling secure e-Government - The approach followed with the Austrian citizen card.* Paper presented at the 6th IFIP Working Conference on Communications and Multimedia Security, Portoroz, Slovenia.

Hollosi, A., Naber, L., & Liehmann, M. (2004, Oct 27-29). *Personal identity and proxy identities in Austria's eGovernment.* Paper presented at the eChallenges e-2004 Conference, Vienna, AUSTRIA.

Homburg, V. M. F. (2004, May 23-26). *New public management and e-government: Trajectories of a marriage between managerial and technological reform in government.* Paper presented at the International Conference of the Information-Resources-Management-Association, New Orleans, LA.

Hong, G. H., Lee, J. H., Kim, T. H., Park, S. C., Rho, H. M., & Jang, D. S. (2005, Jul 27-29). *Intelligent Web information service model for minimizing information gap among people in e-government.* Paper presented at the 5th International Conference on Web Engineering, Sydney, AUSTRALIA.

Hoogwout, M. (2003, Sep 01-05). *Super pilots, subsidizing or self-organization: Stimulating E-government initiatives in Dutch local governments.* Paper presented at the 2nd International Conference on Electronic Government (EGOV 2003), Prague, Czech Republic.

Hornfeldt, J., Heumann, M., Wilson, W. P., & Ieee, I. (1998, Oct 11-14). *CommBridge - An enterprise application integration architecture for electronic government.* Paper presented at the 23rd Annual Conference on Local Computer Networks (LCN 98), Lowell, Ma.

Hornung, H., Baranauskas, M. C. C., & Tambascia, C. A. (2008, Jun 12-16). *Assistive Technologies And Techniques For Web Based Egov In Developing Countries.* Paper presented at the 10th International Conference on Enterprise Information Systems, Barcelona, SPAIN.

Horst, M., Kuttschreuter, M., & Gutteling, J. M. (2007). Perceived usefulness, personal experiences, risk perception and trust as determinants of adoption of e-government services in The Netherlands. [Article]. *Computers in Human Behavior, 23*(4), 1838-1852.

Horton, F. W. (2001). The message of the medium - The risks and opportunities of migrating pre-electronic government information products to the Internet. [Article]. *Journal of Government Information, 28*(1), 1-20.

Hoshino, H., Zhong, N., & Soc, I. C. (2007, Nov 02-05). *Dynamic hybrid Type mining in an intelligent e-government model.* Paper presented at the IEEE/WIC/ACM International Conference on Intelligent Agent Technology and Web Intelligence, Fremont, CA.

Hu, Y., Xiao, J. H., Pang, J. F., & Xie, K. (2005, Aug 15-17). *Research on the appraisal framework of E-government project success*.* Paper presented at the 7th International Conference on Electronic Commerce (ICEC 2005), Xian, PEOPLES R CHINA.

Huang, C. (2006, Oct 23-26). *Analysis on the construction of management modes of e-government information exchange in China.* Paper presented at the 7th International Conference on Web Information Systems Engineering, Wuhan, PEOPLES R CHINA.

Huang, J. H., & Shyu, S. H. P. (2008). E-government web site enhancement opportunities: a learning perspective. [Article]. *Electronic Library, 26*(4), 545-560.

Huang, W., D' Ambra, J., & Bhalla, V. (2002). An empirical investigation of the adoption of eGovernment in Australian citizens: Some unexpected research findings. [Article]. *Journal of Computer Information Systems, 43*(1), 15-22.

Huang, Z. Y. (2007). A comprehensive analysis of US counties' e-Government portals: development status and functionalities. [Article]. *European Journal of Information Systems, 16*(2), 149-164.

Huffer, M. E. (2000, Aug 20-24). *The legal and policy framework for electronic reporting of environmental compliance reports: Challenges of E-Government: Maintaining effective stewardship of the environment.* Paper presented at the Symposium on Capturing and Reporting Electronic Date, Washington, D.C.

Hui, P., Tao, L., Yujuan, S., & Yilei, W. (2007, Aug 16-18). *Application on the E-government of the personal information service based on the multi-agent.* Paper presented at the 8th International Conference on Electronic Measurement and Instruments, Xian, PEOPLES R CHINA.

Huijboom, N., & Hoogwout, M. (2004, Aug 30-Sep 03). *Trust in e-government cooperation.* Paper presented at the 3rd International Conference on Electronic Government (EGOV 2004), Zaragoza, SPAIN.

Hung, S. Y., Chang, C. M., & Yu, T. J. (2006). Determinants of user acceptance of the e-Government services: The case of online tax filing and payment system. [Article]. *Government Information Quarterly, 23*(1), 97-122.

Hussein, R., & Mohamed, N. (2006, Jun 19-21). *The roles of management support and proactive technological orientation: Managing end-user satisfaction in the e-government context.* Paper presented at the 6th International-Business-Information-Management-Association Conference (IBIMA), Bonn, GERMANY.

Huysmans, X. (2007, Aug 04-10). *Privacy-Friendly Identity Management in eGovernment.* Paper presented at the Joint Conference of the International-Federation-for-Information-Processing Working Group/3rd International Summer School on the Future of Identity in the Information Society, Karlstad, SWEDEN.

Hwang, S. D., Choi, Y., & Myeong, S. H. (1999). Electronic government in South Korea: Conceptual problems. [Article]. *Government Information Quarterly, 16*(3), 277-285.

Ilie-Nemedi, I., & Zota, R. D. (2007, Jun 20-22). *Cooperative framework for e-Government.* Paper presented at the 8th International-Business-Information-Management-Association Conference (IBIMA), Dublin, IRELAND.

Imai, H., & Nakagawa, K. (2004, Jul 21-25). *Coordination problems in e-government.* Paper presented at the International Conference on Politics and Information Systems, Orlando, FL.

Imai, H., & Yamagishi, A. (2000, Dec 03-07). *CRYPTREC project - Cryptographic evaluation project for the Japanese electronic government.* Paper presented at the 6th International Conference on the Theory and Application of Cryptology and Informnation Security (ASIACRYPT 2000), Kyoto, Japan.

Insua, D. R., Fernandez, E., & Rios, J. M. (2004, Jul 21-25). *Beyond e-government: Towards e-democracy.* Paper presented at the International Conference on Politics and Information Systems, Orlando, FL.

Intissar, B. D. S., Elissar, T., & St-Amant, G. (2006, Dec 14-16). *Proposal of evolution typology in the G to C relationship in the context of e-government development.* Paper presented at the 7th International-Business-Information-

Management-Association Conference (IBIMA), Brescia, ITALY.

Ioannidis, A., Spanoudakis, M., Priggouris, G., Eliopoulou, C., Hadjiefthymiades, S., & Merakos, L. (2002, Sep 02-06). *EURO-CITI security manager: Supporting transaction services in the E-Government domain.* Paper presented at the 1st International Conference on Electronic Government (EGOV 2002), Aix Provence, France.

Iovan, A. A., & Iovan, S. (2005, Jul 14-17). *e-Government in Romania; Methodological and legal aspects.* Paper presented at the 3rd International Conference on Politics and Information Systems - Technologies and Applications/International Symposium on Social and Organizational Informatics and Cybernectics, Orlando, FL.

Iovan, S., Feher, A. A., & Iovan, A. A. (2005, Jul 14-17). *e-Government in Romania; Theoretical and practical aspects.* Paper presented at the 3rd International Conference on Politics and Information Systems - Technologies and Applications/International Symposium on Social and Organizational Informatics and Cybernectics, Orlando, FL.

Irani, Z., & Dwivedi, Y.K. (2008). Editorial. *Transforming Government: People, Process and Policy*, 2(4), 221-224.

Irani, Z., Love, P. E. D., Elliman, T., Jones, S., & Themistocleous, M. (2005). Evaluating e-government: learning from the experiences of two UK local authorities. [Article]. *Information Systems Journal, 15*(1), 61-82.

Irani, Z., Love, P. E. D., & Jones, S. (2008). Learning lessons from evaluating eGovernment: Reflective case experiences that support transformational government. [Article]. *Journal of Strategic Information Systems, 17*(2), 155-164.

Iribarren, M., Concha, G., Valdes, G., Solar, M., Villarroel, M. T., Gutierrez, P., et al. (2008, Aug 31-Sep 05). *Capability Maturity Framework for eGovernment: A Multi-dimensional Model and Assessing Tool.* Paper presented at the 7th International Conference on Electronic Government, Turin, ITALY.

Iriberri, A., & Leroy, G. (2007, Aug 13-15). *Natural language processing and e-Government: Extracting reusable crime report information.* Paper presented at the IEEE International Conference on Information Reuse and Integration, Las Vegas, NV.

Jackson, P., & Curthoys, N. (2001, Sep 03-07). *E-Government: Developments in the US and UK.* Paper presented at the 12th International Conference on Database and Expert Systems Applications (DEXA), Munich, Germany.

Jaeger, P. T. (2003). The endless wire: E-government as global phenomenon. [Article]. *Government Information Quarterly, 20*(4), 323-331.

Jaeger, P. T. (2004). Beyond Section 508: The spectrum of legal requirements for accessible e-government Web sites in the United States. [Article]. *Journal of Government Information, 30*(4), 518-533.

Jaeger, P. T. (2005). Deliberative democracy and the conceptual foundations of electronic government. [Article]. *Government Information Quarterly, 22*(4), 702-719.

Jaeger, P. T. (2006). Assessing Section 508 compliance on federal e-government Web sites: A multi-method, user-centered, evaluation of accessibility for persons with disabilities. [Article]. *Government Information Quarterly, 23*(2), 169-190.

Jaeger, P. T., & Fleischmann, K. R. (2007). Public libraries, values, trust, and e-government. [Article]. *Information Technology and Libraries, 26*(4), 34-43.

Jaeger, P. T., Shneiderman, B., Kenneth, R. F., Preece, J., Qu, Y., & Wu, P. F. (2007). Community response grids: E-government, social networks, and effective emergency management. [Article]. *Telecommunications Policy, 31*(10-11), 592-604.

Jaeger, P. T., & Thompson, K. M. (2003). E-government around the world: Lessons, challenges and future directions. [Article]. *Government Information Quarterly, 20*(4), 389-394.

Jaeger, P. T., & Thompson, K. M. (2004). Social information behavior and the democratic process: Information poverty, non-native behavior, and electronic government in the United States. [Article]. *Library & Information Science Research, 26*(1), 94-107.

Jaklic, J., Groznik, A., & Kovacic, A. (2003, Oct 26-29). *Towards e-government - The role of simulation modeling.* Paper presented at the 15th European Simulation Symposium, Delft, NETHERLANDS.

Jansen, A. (2006, Sep 04-08). *What role has Scandinavian IS tradition in eGovernment implementations.* Paper presented at the 5th International Conference on Electronic Government (EGOV 2006), Cracow, POLAND.

Janssen, M., Huizer, A., van der Duin, P., & Wagenaar, R. (2007, Jun 21-22). *The results of a scenario building and road mapping workshop for e-government in 2020.* Paper presented at the 7th European Conference on e-Government (ECEG 2007), The Hague, NETHERLANDS.

Janssen, M., Kuk, G., & Wagenaar, R. W. (2005, Aug 15-17). *A survey of e-government business models in the Netherlands.* Paper presented at the 7th International Conference on Electronic Commerce (ICEC 2005), Xian, PEOPLES R CHINA.

Janssen, M., Kuk, G., & Wagenaar, R. W. (2008). A survey of Web-based business models for e-government in the Netherlands. [Article]. *Government Information Quarterly, 25*(2), 202-220.

Janssen, M., & Versteegt, C. (2002, Oct 23-26). *Towards an e-government lab.* Paper presented at the 14th European Simulation Symposium, Dresden, Germany.

Jensen, K. L. (2001). Providing access to online government documents in an academic research library collection: A case study in the geosciences. [Article]. *Science & Technology Libraries, 20*(2-3), 15-25.

Jho, W. (2005). Challenges for e-governance: protests from civil society on the protection of privacy in e-government in Korea. [Article]. *International Review of Administrative Sciences, 71*(1), 151-166.

Jia, X. M., & Tang, Z. W. (2006, May 27-28). *A research on constructive strategy for E-government in towns.* Paper presented at the 5th Wuhan International Conference on E-Business, Wuhan, PEOPLES R CHINA.

Jiang, L. Q., Chi, Z. R., Wu, R. M., & Li, Y. (2005, Nov 04-06). *Research framework on relations among E-government, E-commerce & E-community.* Paper presented at the Conference of System Dynamics and Management Science, Shanghai, PEOPLES R CHINA.

Jiang, L. Q., Tian, P., Li, Y., Wu, R. M., Wang, H. C., Gu, W. J., et al. (2004, Jul 19-21). *Research on service quality management for E-government.* Paper presented at the International Conference on Service Systems and Service Management, Beijing, PEOPLES R CHINA.

Jiang, L. Q., Wu, R. M., Li, Y., & Wang, H. C. (2005, Jun 13-15). *Citizen-oriented community E-government service platform.* Paper presented at the International Conference on Service Systems and Service Management, Chongqing, PEOPLES R CHINA.

Jiang, M. W., Tang, B. Y., & Alfred, U. (2007, May 26-27). *An ontology-based e-Government services architecture.* Paper presented at the 6th Wuhan International Conference on E-Business, Wuhan, PEOPLES R CHINA.

Jiang, Y., & Dong, H. (2008, Sep 14-19). *Towards Ontology-Based Chinese E-Government Digital Archives Knowledge Management.* Paper presented at the 12th European Conference on Research and Advanced Technology for Digital Libraries, Aarhus, DENMARK.

Jin, M. L., Wang, Y. H., & Orient Academic Forum Press, O. A. F. P. (2001, Oct 20-30). *Based on governance theory and E-Government researching the organization structure and reformation of government.* Paper presented at the International Conference on Management Science and Engineering, Sydney, Australia.

Jin, M. Z., & Jiang, X. P. (2004, Dec 05-09). *Benefit evaluation model of e-government procurement.* Paper presented at the 4th International Conference on Electronic Business (ICEB 2004), Beijing, PEOPLES R CHINA.

Ju, C. H., Liang, Y., & Liu, D. S. (2006, Oct 24-26). *A kind of E-government website evaluation method based on Neural Network.* Paper presented at the IEEE International Conference on e-Business Engineering, Shanghai, PEOPLES R CHINA.

Ju, C. H., Zhang, C. H., & Ieee Computer, S. O. C. (2008, Aug 03-05). *A Collaboration Model for E-government Based on Semantics and Multi-agent.* Paper presented at the International Symposium on Electronic Commerce and Security, Guangzhou, PEOPLES R CHINA.

Jung, H., & Kim, S. (2003, Jul 31-Aug 02). *The value of a city-owned broadband network for e-Government: The case of e-Seoul Net.* Paper presented at the International Conference on Politics and Information Systems - Technologies and Applications (PISTA 03), Orlando, FL.

Justice, J. B., Melitski, J., & Smith, D. L. (2006). E-government as an instrument of fiscal accountability and responsiveness - Do the best practitioners employ the best practices? [Article]. *American Review of Public Administration, 36*(3), 301-322.

Kahraman, C., Demirel, N. C., & Demirel, T. (2007). Prioritization of e-Government strategies using a SWOT-AHP analysis: the case of Turkey. [Article]. *European Journal of Information Systems, 16*(3), 284-298.

Kaiser, S. (2004, Aug 30-Sep 03). *Qualification requirements in e-government: The need for information systems in public administration education.* Paper presented at the 3rd International Conference on Electronic Government (EGOV 2004), Zaragoza, SPAIN.

Kaiser, S., Mayer, A., Meyer, U., & Troitzsch, K. G. (2003). A comparative discussion of new books on E-Government. [Article]. *Wirtschaftsinformatik, 45*(5), 560-566.

Kaliontzoglou, A., Sklavos, P., Karantjias, T., & Polemi, D. (2005). A secure e-Government platform architecture for small to medium sized public organizations. [Article]. *Electronic Commerce Research and Applications, 4*(2), 174-186.

Kalja, A., Kindel, K., Kivi, R., & Robal, T. (2007, Aug 05-09). *eGovernment services: How to develop them, how to manage them?* Paper presented at the Conference of the Portland-International-Center-for-Management-of-Engineering-and-Technolo gy (PICMET 2007), Portland, OR.

Kalja, A., Reitsakas, A., & Saard, M. (2005, Jul 31-Aug 04). *eGovernment in Estonia: Best practices.* Paper presented at the Portland International Conference on Management of Engineering and Technology, Portland, OR.

Kalloniatis, C., Kavakli, E., & Gritzalis, S. (2004, Aug 30-Sep 03). *Security requirements engineering for e-Government applications: Analysis of current frameworks.* Paper presented at the 3rd International Conference on Electronic Government (EGOV 2004), Zaragoza, SPAIN.

Kalu, K. N. (2007). Capacity building and IT diffusion - A comparative assessment of E-government environment in Africa. [Article]. *Social Science Computer Review, 25*(3), 358-371.

Kamada, A., & Mendes, M. (2005, Oct 28-30). *A business rule engine applied to egovernment services integration.* Paper presented at the 5th IFTP Conference on E-Commerce, E-Business, and E-Government, Poznan, POLAND.

Kampen, J. K., & Snijkers, K. (2003). E-democracy - A critical evaluation of the ultimate e-dream. [Article]. *Social Science Computer Review, 21*(4), 491-496.

Kampen, J. K., Snijkers, K., & Bouckaert, G. (2005). Public priorities concerning the development of e-government in Flanders. [Article]. *Social Science Computer Review, 23*(1), 136-139.

Karyda, M., Balopoulos, T., Dritsas, S., Gymnopoulos, L., Kokolakis, S., Lambrinoudakis, C., et al. (2006, Apr 20-22). *An ontology for secure e-government applications.* Paper presented at the 1st International Conference on Availability, Reliability and Security, Vienna, AUSTRIA.

Katzy, B. R., Van Den Hoven, J., & Igl, G. (2004, Oct 27-29). *In principle: Towards an open architecture for eGovernment identity management.* Paper presented at the eChallenges e-2004 Conference, Vienna, AUSTRIA.

Kawalek, P. (2002, Aug 25-29). *The remaking of public services: an international review of the potential of e-government.* Paper presented at the 10th European Conference on Health Records, Dublin, Ireland.

Kawalek, P., Wastell, D., & Newman, M. (2003, Sep 01-05). *Problematisation and obfuscation in E-government.* Paper presented at the 2nd International Conference on Electronic Government (EGOV 2003), Prague, Czech Republic.

Kaylor, C., Deshazo, R., & Van Eck, D. (2001, Mar). *Gauging e-government: A report on implementing services among American cities.* Paper presented at the Workshop on Foundations of Electronic Government in Americas Cities, Chicago, Illinois.

Ke, W. L., & Wei, K. K. (2004). Successful e-government in Singapore - How did Singapore manage to get most of its public services deliverable online? [Article]. *Communications of the Acm, 47*(6), 95-99.

Kendall, S. L., Bakke, C., & McDaniels, L. (2006). Tracking usage of e-government publications. [Article]. *Serials Librarian, 50*(3-4), 295-303.

Kettani, D., & Ghailani, M. (2004, Jul 21-25). *E-Government for better governance: Morocco's first pilot experience.* Paper presented at the International Conference on Politics and Information Systems, Orlando, FL.

Kettani, D., & Maghraoui, D. (2003, Jul 31-Aug 02). *Practicing E-government in Morocco.* Paper presented at the International Conference on Education and Information Systems - Technologies and Applications (EISTA 03), Orlando, FL.

Kettani, D., Moulin, B., & El Mahdi, A. (2008, Jan 23-25). *Proposition of a method for the development and deployment of e-Government systems that emphasize good governance.* Paper presented at the 3rd International MCETECH Conference on eTechnologies, Montreal, CANADA.

Kim, H. J., Pan, G., & Pan, S. L. (2007). Managing IT-enabled transfonnation in the public sector: A case study on e-government in South Korea. [Article]. *Government Information Quarterly, 24*(2), 338-352.

Kim, J. (2008). A model and case for supporting participatory public decision making in e-democracy. [Article]. *Group Decision and Negotiation, 17*(3), 179-193.

Kim, J. W., Kim, K. T., & Choi, J. U. (2006). Securing e-government services. [Article]. *Computer, 39*(11), 111-112.

Kim, S., & Lee, H. (2004, May 17-19). *Organizational factors affecting knowledge sharing capabilities in e-government: An empirical study.* Paper presented at the 5th IFIP Interenational Working Conference on Knowledge Management in Electronic Government, Krems, AUSTRIA.

Kim, S. T. (2001, Jul 04-06). *Leapfrogging from traditional government to e-government.* Paper presented at the 1st International Conference on Human Society and the Internet, Seoul, South Korea.

Kim, T. H., Im, K. H., & Park, S. C. (2005, Aug 22-26). *Intelligent measuring and improving model for customer satisfaction level in e-government.* Paper presented at the 4th International Conference on Electronic Government (EGOV 2005), Copenhagen, DENMARK.

Kim, Y. S., & Icact (2006, Feb 20-22). *Challenges and barriers in implementing e-government: Investigation on NEIS of Korea.* Paper presented at the 8th International Conference on Advanced Communication Technology, Phoenix Pk, SOUTH KOREA.

King, S., & Cotterill, S. (2007). Transformational government? The role of information technology in delivering citizen-centric local public services. [Article]. *Local Government Studies, 33*(3), 333-354.

Kita, T., & Murakami, T. (2006, Jul 16-19). *A colaborative approach for the next generation of "e-government" in Japan.* Paper presented at the 10th World Multi-Conference on Systemics, Cybernetics and Informatics/12th International Conference on Information Systems Analysis and Synthesis, Orlando, FL.

Klein, M. R., & Dang, J. (2002, Sep 02-06). *e-learning for e-government.* Paper presented at the 1st International Conference on Electronic Government (EGOV 2002), Aix Provence, France.

Klischewski, R. (2003, Sep 01-05). *Semantic Web for e-government.* Paper presented at the 2nd International Conference on Electronic Government (EGOV 2003), Prague, Czech Republic.

Klischewski, R., & Ukena, S. (2008, Aug 31-Sep 05). *Test Strategies for Evaluation of Semantic eGovernment Applications.* Paper presented at the 7th International Conference on Electronic Government, Turin, ITALY.

Klischewski, R., & Wetzel, I. (2001, Oct 03-05). *XML-based process representation for e-government serviceflows.* Paper presented at the 1st IFIP International Conference on E-Commerce, E-Business, and E-Government (I3E 2001), Zurich, Switzerland.

Klumpp, D. (2002, Sep 02-06). *From websites to e-government in Germany.* Paper presented at the 1st International Conference on Electronic Government (EGOV 2002), Aix Provence, France.

Koga, T. (2003). Access to government information in Japan: a long way toward electronic government? [Article]. *Government Information Quarterly, 20*(1), 47-62.

Koh, C. E., & Prybutok, V. R. (2003). The three ring model and development of an instrument for measuring dimensions of E-government functions. [Article]. *Journal of Computer Information Systems, 43*(3), 34-39.

Koh, C. E., Ryan, S., & Prybutok, V. R. (2005). Creating value through managing knowledge in an e-government to constituency (G2C) environment. [Article]. *Journal of Computer Information Systems, 45*(4), 32-41.

Kolsaker, A. (2005, Mar 02-04). *Third way e-government: The case for local devolution.* Paper presented at the International Conference on E-Government (TCGOV 2005), Bolzano, ITALY.

Kolsaker, A., & Lee-Kelley, L. (2006, Sep 04-08). *'Mind the Gap': e-government and e-democracy.* Paper presented at the 5th International Conference on Electronic Government (EGOV 2006), Cracow, POLAND.

Kolsaker, A., & Lee-Kelley, L. (2007, Sep 03-07). *'Mind the gap II': e-Government and e-Governance.* Paper presented at the 6th International Conference on Electronic Government, Regensburg, GERMANY.

Kong, M., Su, X. N., & Zhu, Y. F. (2003, Nov 28-30). *E-Government Application Framework (EGAF).* Paper presented at the International Conference on Management of e-Commerce and e-Government, Nanchang, PEOPLES R CHINA.

Kong, W. C., & Chen, S. F. (2005, Aug 15-17). *The characteristics, problems and solutions of e-government in China.* Paper presented at the 7th International Conference on Electronic Commerce (ICEC 2005), Xian, PEOPLES R CHINA.

Korhonen, J., Pajunen, L., & Puustjarvi, J. (2003, Sep 01-05). *Requirements for using agent-based automation in distributed E-government applications.* Paper presented at the 2nd International Conference on Electronic Government (EGOV 2003), Prague, Czech Republic.

Korteland, E., & Bekkers, V. (2007, Sep 03-07). *Diffusion of e-government innovations in the dutch public sector: The case of digital community policing.* Paper presented at the 6th International Conference on Electronic Government, Regensburg, GERMANY.

Kral, J., & Zemlicka, M. (2001, Sep 03-07). *Electronic government and software confederations.* Paper presented at the 12th International Conference on Database and Expert Systems Applications (DEXA), Munich, Germany.

Kral, J., & Zemlicka, M. (2006, Jul 17-21). *Engineering education promotion and e-government.* Paper presented at the 5th Global Congress on Engineering Education, Brooklyn, NY.

Krebs, I. (2006, Jul 03-06). *eGovernment in small administrative departments - obstacles and potentials.* Paper presented at the 7th International Baltic Conference on Databases and Information Systems, Vilnius, LITHUANIA.

Kumar, R., & Best, M. L. (2006). Impact and sustainability of e-government services in developing countries: Lessons learned from Tamil Nadu, India. [Article]. *Information Society, 22*(1), 1-12.

Kunis, R., Runger, G., & Schwind, M. (2007, Jun 21-22). *A new model for document management in e-government systems based on hierarchical process folders.* Paper presented at the 7th European Conference on e-Government (ECEG 2007), The Hague, NETHERLANDS.

Kunstelj, M., Jukic, T., & Vintar, M. (2007, Sep 03-07). *Analysing the demand side of e-government: What can we learn from slovenian users?* Paper presented at the 6th International Conference on Electronic Government, Regensburg, GERMANY.

Kutsikos, K. (2007, Jun 21-22). *Distribution-collaboration networks (DCN): A systems-based model for developing collaborative e-government services.* Paper presented at the 7th European Conference on e-Government (ECEG 2007), The Hague, NETHERLANDS.

Lagzian, M., & Wood-Harper, T. (2006, Jun 19-21). *From the traditional bureaucratic paradigm to E-government: visible and invisible Barriers.* Paper presented at the 6th International-Business-Information-Management-Association Conference (IBIMA), Bonn, GERMANY.

Lahteenmaki-Smith, K., & Steineke, J. M. (2004, Jul 21-25). *Between e-government and e-governance: From enabling to mobilizing civic participation.* Paper presented at the International Conference on Politics and Information Systems, Orlando, FL.

Lai, J. J., Xu, Y., & Li, Y. H. (2006, Apr 06-07). *Constructing Intranet for the security E-*

government based on ArcIMS. Paper presented at the International Conference on Intelligent Systems and Knowledge Engineering, Shanghai, PEOPLES R CHINA.

Lam, T. M. (2008, Jul 26-29). *The private and public partnership strategy in e-government ESDlife in Hong Kong.* Paper presented at the International Conference on e-Business (ICE-B 2008), Oporto, PORTUGAL.

Lambrinoudakis, C., Gritzalis, S., Dridi, F., & Pernul, G. (2003). Security requirements for e-government services: a methodological approach for developing a common PKI-based security policy. [Article]. *Computer Communications, 26*(16), 1873-1883.

Lambrou, M. A., & Ieee, I. (2003, Nov 02-04). *Advancing the one-stop shop e-government paradigm.* Paper presented at the IEEE International Engineering Management Conference, Albany, La.

Lampathaki, F., Charalabidis, Y., Sarantis, D., Koussouris, S., & Askounis, D. (2007, Sep 03-07). *E-Government services composition using multi-faceted metadata classification structures.* Paper presented at the 6th International Conference on Electronic Government, Regensburg, GERMANY.

Lan, L. (2004, May 17-19). *E-government: A catalyst to good governance in China.* Paper presented at the 5th IFIP Interenational Working Conference on Knowledge Management in Electronic Government, Krems, AUSTRIA.

Lan, L. (2005, Mar 02-04). *Enhancing e-democracy via fiscal transparency: a discussion based on china's experience.* Paper presented at the International Conference on E-Government (TCGOV 2005), Bolzano, ITALY.

Lan, Z. Y., & Falcone, S. (1997). Factors influencing Internet use - A policy model for electronic government information provision. [Article]. *Journal of Government Information, 24*(4), 251-257.

Lankhorst, M. M., & Derks, W. L. A. (2007, Oct 15-19). *Towards a service-oriented architecture for demand-driven e-government.* Paper presented at the 11th IEEE International Enterprise Distributed Object Computing Conference, Annapolis, MD.

Larsen, B., & Milakovich, M. (2005, Aug 22-26). *Citizen Relationship Management and E-government.* Paper presented at the 4th International Conference on Electronic Government (EGOV 2005), Copenhagen, DENMARK.

Lassnig, M., & Markus, M. (2003, Sep 01-05). *Usage of e-government services in European regions.* Paper presented at the 2nd International Conference on Electronic Government (EGOV 2003), Prague, Czech Republic.

Latre, J. L. B. (2003, Sep 01-05). *Implementing E-Government in Spain.* Paper presented at the 2nd International Conference on Electronic Government (EGOV 2003), Prague, Czech Republic.

Lau, T. Y., Aboulhoson, M., Lin, C., & Atkin, D. J. (2008). Adoption of e-government in three Latin American countries: Argentina, Brazil and Mexico. [Article]. *Telecommunications Policy, 32*(2), 88-100.

Lay, K., Alam, M. S., & Phu, H. E. L. (2007, Dec 05-06). *Different stages of developing e-government between Cambodia and japan.* Paper presented at the 4th International Conference on Innovation and Management, Ube, JAPAN.

Layne, K., & Lee, J. W. (2001). Developing fully functional E-government: A four stage model. [Article]. *Government Information Quarterly, 18*(2), 122-136.

Lee, E. J., Han, Y. T., Park, H. S., Lee, Y. S., & Etri (2008, Feb 17-20). *A novel bandwidth estimation model for e-government communication network.* Paper presented at the 10th International Conference on Advanced Communication Technology, Phoenix Pk, SOUTH KOREA.

Lee, J., & Kim, J. (2007). Grounded theory analysis of e-government initiatives: Exploring perceptions of government authorities. [Article]. *Government Information Quarterly, 24*(1), 135-147.

Lee, S., & Cho, J. E. (2007, Jul 22-27). *Usability evaluation of Korean e-Government portal.* Paper presented at the 4th International Conference on Universal Access in Human-Computer Interaction held at the HCI International 2007, Beijing, PEOPLES R CHINA.

Lee, S., Kim, B. G., & Kim, J. G. (2007, Jul 22-27). *Accessibility evaluation of Korean e-Government.* Paper presented at the 4th International Conference on Universal Access in Human-Computer Interaction held at the HCI International 2007, Beijing, PEOPLES R CHINA.

Lee, S. M., Tan, X., & Trimi, S. (2005). Current practices of leading e-government countries. [Article]. *Communications of the Acm, 48*(10), 99-104.

Leitner, C., & Kreuzeder, M. (2005, Aug 22-26). *Organisational changes, skills and the role of leadership required by eGovernment.* Paper presented at the 4th International Conference on Electronic Government (EGOV 2005), Copenhagen, DENMARK.

Lemon, W. F., Holden, S. H., & Preece, J. J. (2003, May 18-21). *A descriptive framework for federal electronic government: A necessary step prior to field research.* Paper presented at the International Conference of the Information-Resources-Management-Association, Philadelphia, PA.

Lenk, K., & Traunmuller, R. (2000, Sep 04-08). *A framework for electronic government.* Paper presented at the 11th International Workshop on Database and Expert Systems Applications, London, England.

Lenk, K., & Traunmuller, R. (2002, Sep 02-06). *Electronic Government: Where are we heading?* Paper presented at the 1st International Conference on Electronic Government (EGOV 2002), Aix Provence, France.

Lepouras, G., Sotiropoulou, A., Theotokis, D., & Vassilakis, C. (2004, May 23-26). *Tailorability in the context of e-government information systems: An approach.* Paper presented at the International Conference of the Information-Resources-Management-Association, New Orleans, LA.

Leung, T. P. Y., Chiu, D. K. W., & Society, I. C. (2006, Dec 12-15). *Alert-driven e-government service management: A case study on road maintenance management system.* Paper presented at the IEEE Asia-Pacific Services Computing Conference (APSCC 2006), Guangzhou, PEOPLES R CHINA.

Leutgeb, A., Utz, W., Woitsch, R., & Fill, H. G. (2007, Jun 12-16). *Adaptive processes in E-government - A field report about semantic-based approaches from the EU-project „FIT".* Paper presented at the 9th International Conference on Enterprise Information Systems (ICEIS 2007), Funchal, PORTUGAL.

Levillain, P., Jourdan, A., & Hill, N. (2005). E-government: The new collaborative environment for user-centric public administrations. [Article]. *Alcatel Telecommunications Review*(1), 84-87.

Li, B. L. (2005, Aug 15-17). *On the Barriers to the development of e-government in China.* Paper presented at the 7th International Conference on Electronic Commerce (ICEC 2005), Xian, PEOPLES R CHINA.

Li, C. M. (2007, Aug 26-27). *Research on the construction and characteristics of small towns E-government system.* Paper presented at the 2nd International Workshop on Information Systems for Crisis Response and Management, Harbin, PEOPLES R CHINA.

Li, F., Qi, Z. Y., Ma, Y. F., & Wang, Z. (2005, Jun 04-05). *E-government: A dissipative structure.* Paper presented at the 4th Wuhan International Conference on E-Business - Global Business Interface, Wuhan, PEOPLES R CHINA.

Li, H. G., Fan, B., Zheng, X. X., & Alfred, U. (2007, May 26-27). *The top layer design theory and its revelations on the application of e-government in China.* Paper presented at the 6th Wuhan International Conference on E-Business, Wuhan, PEOPLES R CHINA.

Li, H. L., & Le, Z. J. (2008, Oct 17-19). *E-government Evaluation based on Binary Relative Performance.* Paper presented at the 2nd International Conference on Management of e-Commerce and e-Government, Nanchang, PEOPLES R CHINA.

Li, J. H. (2003, Aug 15-17). *Mechanisms of electronic service delivery in electronic government.* Paper presented at the International Conference on Management Science and Engineering, Atlanta, Ga.

Li, J. H. (2004, Jul 19-21). *Analysis of electronic service delivery processes in electronic government: A view of business process reengineering.* Paper presented at the International Conference on Service Systems and Service Management, Beijing, PEOPLES R CHINA.

Li, L., Tang, S. Q., Fang, L. N., Xiao, R. L., Deng, X. G., Xu, Y. W., et al. (2007, Jul 25-27). *Rule-based semantic-enabled e-government services evolution.* Paper presented at the 2nd International Conference on Computer Science and Education, Wuhan, PEOPLES R CHINA.

Li, L. Z. (2008, Oct 17-19). *Research on the E-Government Scheme based on Multi-Technologies and Bi-directional Authentication.* Paper presented at the 2nd International Conference on Management of e-Commerce and e-Government, Nanchang, PEOPLES R CHINA.

Li, M. Y., Wu, H. R., Zhao, C. J., Zhu, H. J., Sun, X., & Yang, B. Z. (2007, Oct 26-29). *Research and implementation of model for E-Government on Lightweight Web Framework.* Paper presented at the 4th International Symposium on Intelligent Information Technology in Agriculture, Beijing, PEOPLES R CHINA.

Li, T., Zhao, Z. Q., & Wang, H. C. (2002, Oct 22-24). *Study on management pattern of electronic government under information environment.* Paper presented at the International Conference on Management Science and Engineering, Moscow, Russia.

Li, Y., & Cao, Y. K. (2007, Aug 26-27). *The analysis and design of the requirement of urban green supervising information system under e-government affairs.* Paper presented at the 2nd International Workshop on Information Systems for Crisis Response and Management, Harbin, PEOPLES R CHINA.

Li, Y., & Ieee (2006, Jun 21-23). *Evaluation of public service maturity of e-government: A case in Chinese cities.* Paper presented at the IEEE International Conference on Service Operations and Logistics and Informatics, Shanghai, PEOPLES R CHINA.

Li, Y., Li, M. L., & Chen, Y. (2005, Mar 02-04). *Towards building E-government on the grid.* Paper presented at the International Conference on E-Government (TCGOV 2005), Bolzano, ITALY.

Li, Z. C. (2004, Dec 05-09). *Achievements and future trends of e-government service implications from the SARS outbreak.* Paper presented at the 4th International Conference on Electronic Business (ICEB 2004), Beijing, PEOPLES R CHINA.

Liang, Y., Ju, C. H., & Liu, D. S. (2006, Oct 12-15). *Evaluative research into E-government sites based on BP neural network.* Paper presented at the International Symposium on Distributed Computing and Applications to Business, Engineering and Science, Hangzhou, PEOPLES R CHINA.

Liao, S. H., & Jeng, H. P. (2005). E-government implementation: Business contract legal support for Taiwanese businessmen in Mainland China. [Article]. *Government Information Quarterly, 22*(3), 505-524.

Lienesch, M. (1992). WO(E)BEGON(E) DEMOCRACY. [Article]. *American Journal of Political Science, 36*(4), 1004-1014.

Lim, J. H., & Tang, S. Y. (2008). Urban e-government initiatives and environmental decision performance in Korea. [Review]. *Journal of Public Administration Research and Theory, 18*(1), 109-138.

Lim, S., & Song, Y. (2003, Sep 01-05). *Secure Online Internet Reservation of e-Government Service (ORGS) using Java Card Applications Toolkit (J-CAT).* Paper presented at the 2nd International Conference on Electronic Government (EGOV 2003), Prague, Czech Republic.

Lin, T., Huang, L., & Peng, Y. Q. (2006, Aug 12-14). *The design and realization of E-Government system based on the framework of lightweight J2EE (ID : 8-045).* Paper presented at the 13th International Conference on Industrial Engineering and Engineering Management, Weihai, PEOPLES R CHINA.

Lin, T. Y., & Ieee Computer Society, I. C. S. (2003, Nov 03-06). *Information flows in E-Government.* Paper presented at the 27th Annual International Computer Software and Applications Conference, Dallas, Tx.

Lind, N. S., Otenyo, E. E., & Smith, B. M. (2003, Jul 31-Aug 02). *PKI Enabled E-Government.* Paper presented at the International Conference on Politics and Information Systems - Technologies and Applications (PISTA 03), Orlando, FL.

Lindblad-Gidlund, K. (2008, Aug 31-Sep 05). *Driver or Passenger? An Analysis of Citizen-Driven eGovernment.* Paper presented at the 7th International Conference on Electronic Government, Turin, ITALY.

Lines, L., Ikechi, O., & Hone, K. S. (2007, Jul 22-27). *Accessing e-Government services: Design requirements for the older user.* Paper presented at the 4th International Conference on Universal Access in Human-Computer Interaction held at the HCI International 2007, Beijing, PEOPLES R CHINA.

Liu, H. L., & Tian, Z. H. (2006, Nov 08-20). *Research on application of web usage mining in e-government personalized information system.* Paper presented at the International Conference on Management Science and Engineering, Wuhan, AUSTRALIA.

Liu, J. W., Derzsi, Z., Raus, M., & Kipp, A. (2008, Aug 31-Sep 05). *eGovernment Project Evaluation: An Integrated Framework.* Paper presented at the 7th International Conference on Electronic Government, Turin, ITALY.

Liu, M. S., Sun, S. J., Yin, X. H., & Ieee (2008, Jul 12-15). *Research on the evaluation of security risk for e-government information system.* Paper presented at the 7th International Conference on Machine Learning and Cybernetics, Kunming, PEOPLES R CHINA.

Liu, W. Y., & Wang, J. L. (2007, Aug 18-20). *The enlightenment to China of e-government application in rural areas from Japan, South Korea and India.* Paper presented at the 1st International Conference on Computer and Computing Technologies in Agriculture (CCTA 2007), Wuyishan, PEOPLES R CHINA.

Liu, Y., Zhu, L., & Gorton, I. (2007, Jul 09-11). *Performance assessment for e-government services: An experience report.* Paper presented at the 10th International Symposium on Component-Based Software Engineering, Medford, MA.

Liu, Y. B., & Liu, J. (2004, Jun 04-07). *How e-government helps combat corruption in developing countries.* Paper presented at the 3rd Wuhan International Conference on E-Business - Global Business Interface, Wuhan, PEOPLES R CHINA.

Love, J. P. (1992). The Marketplace And Electronic Government Information. [Article]. *Government Publications Review, 19*(4), 397-412.

Lowe, C. (2003, Sep 01-05). *Experiences of take-up of e-Government in Europe.* Paper presented at the 2nd International Conference on Electronic Government (EGOV 2003), Prague, Czech Republic.

Lowe, C. (2004, Oct 27-29). *eGovernment learning journeys: Knowledge management in action.* Paper presented at the eChallenges e-2004 Conference, Vienna, AUSTRIA.

Lu, L. L., & Liu, Y. F. (2008, May 15-17). *Public-oriented Land Information Service frame in E-government.* Paper presented at the International Conference on Informational Technology and Environmental System Science, Jiaozuo, PEOPLES R CHINA.

Lu, L. M., Zhu, G. J., & Chen, J. X. (2004a, Dec 16-18). *A collaborative work framework for joined-up e-government web services.* Paper presented at the 1st International Symposium oncomputational and Information Science, Shanghai, PEOPLES R CHINA.

Lu, L. M., Zhu, G. J., & Chen, J. X. (2004b, Sep 15-18). *An enfrastructure for e-government based on semantic web services.* Paper presented at the IEEE International Conference on Services Computing, Shanghai, PEOPLES R CHINA.

Lu, X. (2007, Jul 30-Aug 01). *Distributed secure information sharing model for e-government in China.* Paper presented at the 8th ACIS International Conference on Software Engineering, Artificial Intelligence, Networking and Parallel/Distributed Computing/3rd ACIS International Workshop on Self-Assembling Wireless Networks, Qungdao, PEOPLES R CHINA.

Luo, Y. L., Tang, Y. Y., & Luo, Y. D. (2005, Jun 04-05). *Data exchange of E-Government.* Paper presented at the 4th Wuhan International Conference on E-Business - Global Business Interface, Wuhan, PEOPLES R CHINA.

Lutz, G., & Moukabary, G. (2004, Aug 30-Sep 03). *The challenge of inter-administration e-government.* Paper presented at the 3rd International Conference on Electronic Government (EGOV 2004), Zaragoza, SPAIN.

Ma, H., & Li, J. H. (2005, Oct 20-24). *E-Government coordination system base on service-oriented workflow technology.* Paper presented at the International Symposium on Computer Science and Technology, Ningbo, PEOPLES R CHINA.

Ma, L., Li, Y. J., & Huang, F. Y. (2003, Aug 15-17). *The research on knowledge management implemented in electronic government of China.* Paper presented at the International Conference on Management Science and Engineering, Atlanta, Ga.

Ma, L. J., Chung, J. P., & Thorson, S. (2005). E-government in China: Bringing economic development through administrative reform. [Article]. *Government Information Quarterly, 22*(1), 20-37.

Maciel, C., Nogueira, J. L. T., & Garcia, A. C. B. (2005, Sep 12-16). *An X-ray of the Brazilian e-Gov Web sites.* Paper presented at the International Conference on Human-Computer Interaction, Rome, ITALY.

Madon, S., Sahay, S., & Sudan, R. (2007). E-government policy and health information systems implementation in Andhra Pradesh, India: Need for articulation of linkages between the macro and the micro. [Article]. *Information Society, 23*(5), 327-344.

Maggipinto, A., & Visconti, E. (2008, Sep 07-10). *A normative approach to democracy in the electronic government framework.* Paper presented at the 20th World Computer Congress, Milan, ITALY.

Magoutas, B., Halaris, C., & Mentzas, G. (2007, Sep 03-07). *An ontology for the multi-perspective evaluation of quality in e-government services.* Paper presented at the 6th International Conference on Electronic Government, Regensburg, GERMANY.

Mahrer, H., & Krimmer, R. (2005). Towards the enhancement of e-democracy: identifying the notion of the 'middleman paradox'. [Article]. *Information Systems Journal, 15*(1), 27-42.

Maibaum, N., Sedov, I., & Cap, C. H. (2002, Sep 02-06). *A citizen digital assistant for e-government.* Paper presented at the 1st International Conference on Electronic Government (EGOV 2002), Aix Provence, France.

Makhera, N., Moloisane, A., & Busler, M. (2004, Aug 14-17). *Lesotho's migration path to e-government.* Paper presented at the International Conference on Computing, Communications and Control Technologies (CCCT 2004), Austin, TX.

Makolm, J. (2002, Sep 02-06). *Best practice in e-Government.* Paper presented at the 1st International Conference on Electronic Government (EGOV 2002), Aix Provence, France.

Makolm, J. (2005, Jul 14-17). *Holistic approach and stakeholder integration: The Austrian way to successful e-Government applications.* Paper presented at the 3rd International Conference on Politics and Information Systems - Technologies and Applications/International Symposium on Social and Organizational Informatics and Cybernectics, Orlando, FL.

Mambrey, P. (2004, Aug 30-Sep 03). *Networked ICT to foster e-Democracy?* Paper presented at the 3rd International Conference on Electronic Government (EGOV 2004), Zaragoza, SPAIN.

Mandalianos, I., Kourgiantakis, M., & Migdalas, A. (2005, Aug 19-20). *Prometheus: A web based system focusing on local E-government.* Paper presented at the 4th International Conference on Management of Technological Changes, Chania, GREECE.

Mandreoli, F., Martoglia, R., Grandi, F., & Scalas, M. R. (2006, Apr 11-13). *Efficient management of multi-version XML documents for e-government applications.* Paper presented at the 2nd International Conference on Web Information Systems and Technologies, Setubal, PORTUGAL.

Manouselis, N., Kastrantas, K., Tzikopoulos, A., Costopoulou, C., & Sideridis, A. (2008, Sep 24-26). *Implementing an e-Government Observatory for rural SMEs.* Paper presented at the 1st World Summit on the Knowledge Society (WSKS 2008), Athens, GREECE.

Mansar, S. L., & Ieee (2006, Nov 19-21). *E-government implementation: Impact on business processes.* Paper presented at the Innovations in Information Technology Conference 2006, Dubai, U ARAB EMIRATES.

Mantymaki, M. (2008, Sep 24-26). *Does e-government trust in e-commerce when investigating trust? A review of trust literature in e-commerce and e-government domains.* Paper presented at the 8th IFIP International Conference on e-Business, e-Service, and e-Society, Tokyo, JAPAN.

Manuela, W. S., & Tiglao, N. M. C. (2006, Dec 14-16). *E-government applications in the Philippines.* Paper presented at the 7th International-Business-Information-Management-Association Conference (IBIMA), Brescia, ITALY.

Marche, S., & McNiven, J. D. (2003). E-government and e-governance: The future isn't what it used to be. [Article]. *Canadian Journal of Administrative Sciences-Revue Canadienne Des Sciences De L Administration, 20*(1), 74-86.

Marchese, M., & Ieee Computer Society, I. C. S. (2003, Jan 27-31). *Service oriented architectures for supporting environments in eGovernment applications.* Paper presented at the International Symposium on Applications and the Internet, Orlando, Fl.

Marciano, R., Ludascher, B., Zaslavsky, I., Moore, R., & Pezzoli, K. (2002, Sep 02-06). *Multi-level information modeling and preservation of eGOV data.* Paper presented at the 1st International Conference on Electronic Government (EGOV 2002), Aix Provence, France.

Margetis, G., Ntoa, S., & Stephanidis, C. (2008, Jul 09-11). *Requirements of users with disabilities for e-government services in Greece.* Paper presented at the 11th International Conference on Computers Helping People with Special Needs, Linz, AUSTRIA.

Margetts, H. (2006). E-government in Britain - A decade on. [Article]. *Parliamentary Affairs, 59*(2), 250-265.

Mariagrazia, F., Piercarlo, M., Krysnaia, N., Roberto, B., Mirko, C., & Mario, M. (2008, Sep 07-10). *Why is True eGovernment still difficult to be achieved?* Paper presented at the 20th World Computer Congress, Milan, ITALY.

Marinelli, G., & Russo, P. (2002, Aug 25-30). *Mountain information system: A distributed e-government office.* Paper presented at the 17th World Computer Congress, Montreal, Canada.

Marques, I. C., Lima, D. L. M., & Martins, M. L. C. (2004, Jul 21-25). *E.gov, the government and citizens: a study of the government's official web portal in Brazil.* Paper presented at the International Conference on Politics and Information Systems, Orlando, FL.

Martin, M. L. P., Vasquez, A. C., & Garcia, B. C. (2007). Premises for an electronic government strategy in the management of university virtualization. [Article]. *Revista Venezolana De Gerencia, 12*(40), 572-598.

Martin, R. L., & Montagna, J. M. (2006, Aug 21-24). *Business process reengineering role in electronic government.* Paper presented at the 19th World Computer Congress, Santiago, CHILE.

Martinez-Moyano, I. J., & Gil-Garcia, J. R. (2004, Aug 30-Sep 03). *Rules, norms, and individual preferences for action: An institutional framework to understand the dynamics of e-government evolution.* Paper presented at the 3rd International Conference on Electronic Government (EGOV 2004), Zaragoza, SPAIN.

Masters, Z., Macintosh, A., & Smith, E. (2004, Aug 30-Sep 03). *Young people and e-democracy: Creating a culture of participation.* Paper presented at the 3rd International Conference on Electronic Government (EGOV 2004), Zaragoza, SPAIN.

Maumbe, B. M., Owei, V., & Alexander, H. (2008). Questioning the pace and pathway of e-government development in Africa: A case study of South Africa's Cape Gateway project. [Article]. *Government Information Quarterly, 25*(4), 757-777.

McClure, C. R., & Online, I. N. C. (1990, Nov 05-07). *Access To Electronic Government Information Through The Gpos Depository Library Program - An Update.* Paper presented at the Online / Cd-Rom 90 Conf, Washington, Dc.

McDonagh, J. (2003, May 18-21). *Surfacing occupational threats to electronic government - A neglected role for organization development?* Paper presented at the International Conference of the Information-Resources-Management-Association, Philadelphia, PA.

McFall, B., & Williams, S. (2004). Systems language for e-democracy: Personal resource systems management (PRSM), a model and action research. [Article]. *Systemic Practice and Action Research, 17*(4), 353-371.

McGregor, M. A., & Holman, J. (2004). Communication technology at the federal communications commission: E-government in the public interest? [Article]. *Government Information Quarterly, 21*(3), 268-283.

McKenzie, R., Crompton, M., & Wallis, C. (2008). Use-cases for identity management in E-government. [Article]. *Ieee Security & Privacy, 6*(2), 51-57.

McNeal, R., Schmeida, M., & Hale, K. (2007). E-disclosure laws and electronic campaign finance reform: Lessons from the diffusion of e-government policies in the States. [Article]. *Government Information Quarterly, 24*(2), 312-325.

McPherson, M., & Ramli, R. (2004, May 23-26). *Lessons learned from the implementation of a Malaysian eGovernment project.* Paper presented at the International Conference of the Information-Resources-Management-Association, New Orleans, LA.

Mecella, M., & Batini, C. (2001a, Oct 03-05). *A review of the first cooperative projects in the Italian e-government initiative.* Paper presented at the 1st IFIP International Conference on E-Commerce, E-Business, and E-Government (I3E 2001), Zurich, Switzerland.

Mecella, M., & Batini, C. (2001b). Enabling Italian e-government through a cooperative architecture. [Article]. *Computer, 34*(2), 40-+.

Medjahed, B., & Bouguettaya, A. (2005). Customized delivery of e-government Web services. [Article]. *Ieee Intelligent Systems, 20*(6), 77-82.

Medjahed, B., Rezgui, A., Bouguettaya, A., & Ouzzani, M. (2003). Infrastructure for E-government Web services. [Article]. *Ieee Internet Computing, 7*(1), 58-65.

Meijer, A. J., & Zouridis, S. (2004, May 23-26). *E-government as institutional transformation.* Paper presented at the International Conference of the Information-Resources-Management-Association, New Orleans, LA.

Mele, V. (2007, Apr 03). *Explaining programmes for change: Electronic government policy in Italy (1993-2003).* Paper presented at the 11th International Research Symposium on Public Management, Potsdam, GERMANY.

Melin, U., & Axelsson, K. (2007, Sep 03-07). *Action in action research - Illustrations of what, who, why, where, and when from an e-Government project.* Paper presented at the 6th International Conference on Electronic Government, Regensburg, GERMANY.

Meneklis, B., Kaliontzogiou, A., Douligeris, C., & Polemi, D. (2005, Nov 14-16). *Engineering and technology aspects of an e-Government architecture based on Web Services.* Paper presented at the 3rd European Conference on Web Services (ECOWS 2005), Vaxjo, SWEDEN.

Meneklis, B., Kaliontzoglou, A., Polemi, D., & Douligeris, C. (2005, Mar 02-04). *Applying the ISO RM-ODP standard in E-government.* Paper presented at the International Conference on E-Government (TCGOV 2005), Bolzano, ITALY.

Meneklis, V., Douligeris, C., & Ieee (2007, Sep 03-07). *Extending a distributed system architecture with e-government modelling concepts.* Paper presented at the 18th IEEE International Symposium on Personal, Indoor and Mobile Radio Communication, Athens, GREECE.

Menzel, T., & Reichstadter, P. (2002, Sep 02-06). *The role of citizen cards in e-Government.* Paper presented at the 1st International Conference on Electronic Government (EGOV 2002), Aix Provence, France.

Mezzanzanica, M., & Cesarini, M. (2007, Jun 21-22). *e-Government as decision support system to improve public services provision.* Paper presented at the 7th European Conference on e-Government (ECEG 2007), The Hague, NETHERLANDS.

Micelli, S. (2003, May 30-31). *E-government developmental guidelines.* Paper presented at the International Conference On Line Citizenship, Venice, ITALY.

Miesenberger, K., & Puhretmair, F. (2005, 2005). *Help.gv.at - Accessible e-Government in Austria.* Paper presented at the 8th European Conference for the Advancement of Assistive Technology, Lille, FRANCE.

Millard, J. (2002, Sep 02-06). *e-Government strategies: Best practice reports from the European front line.* Paper presented at the 1st International Conference on Electronic Government (EGOV 2002), Aix Provence, France.

Mineo, S. (2002). Security for electronic government. [Article]. *Nec Research & Development, 43*(3), 218-221.

Mirchandani, D. A., Johnson, J. H., & Joshi, K. (2008). Perspectives of citizens towards e-government in Thailand and Indonesia: A multigroup analysis. [Article]. *Information Systems Frontiers, 10*(4), 483-497.

Mirel, B., Maher, M., & Huh, J. (2006, 2005). *User needs in e-government: Conducting policy analysis with models-on-the-Web.* Paper presented at the 19th Annual Conference of the British-Human-Computer-Interaction-Group, Edinburgh, SCOTLAND.

Mitchell, C. (2007, Sep 27). *The effects of online groups on e-Government.* Paper presented at the 3rd International Conference on e-Government, Montreal, CANADA.

Mitra, R. K., & Gupta, M. P. (2008). A contextual perspective of performance assessment in eGovernment: A study of Indian Police Administration. [Article]. *Government Information Quarterly, 25*(2), 278-302.

Mnjama, N., & Wamukoya, J. (2007). E-government and records management: an assessment tool for e-records readiness in government. [Article]. *Electronic Library, 25*(3), 274-284.

Monks, N. (2004, Oct 27-29). *eGovernment and the feasibility of going online.* Paper presented at the eChallenges e-2004 Conference, Vienna, AUSTRIA.

Monsalve, M. (2007, Nov 08-09). *Managing the QoS of E-Government: Metrics for large scale SOA.* Paper presented at the 26th International Conference of the Chilean-Society-of-Computer-Science, Iquique, CHILE.

Montagna, J. M. (2005). A framework for the assessment and analysis of electronic government proposals. [Article]. *Electronic Commerce Research and Applications, 4*(3), 204-219.

Moody, R. (2007, Sep 03-07). *Assessing the role of GIS in e-government: A tale of e-participation in two cities.* Paper presented at the 6th International Conference on Electronic Government, Regensburg, GERMANY.

Moon, M. J. (2002, 2001). *The evolution of e-government among municipalities: Rhetoric or reality?* Paper presented at the Annual APSA Conference, San Francisco, California.

Moon, M. J., & Norris, D. F. (2003, Mar 26-29). *Does managerial orientation matter? The adoption of reinventing government and e-government at the municipal level.* Paper presented at the Western Political Science Conference, Denver, CO.

Morici, R., Nunziata, E., & Sciarra, G. (2003, May 26-28). *A knowledge management system for e-government projects and actors.* Paper presented at the 4th Annual International Working Conference on Knowledge Management in Electronic Government, Rhodes, Greece.

Morphet, J. (2003). Joining policy with implementation in central government: The approach to e.government. [Article]. *Local Government Studies, 29*(1), 111-116.

Moukdad, H. (2004, Jul 21-25). *Canadian E-government sites: An exploratory study of the political dimensions of disseminating information.* Paper presented at the International Conference on Politics and Information Systems, Orlando, FL.

Moulin, C., Bettahar, F., Barthes, J. P., & Sbodio, M. L. (2007, Nov 25-30). *Ontology based categorization in eGovernment application.* Paper presented at the OTM Confederated International Conference and Workshop, Vilamoura, PORTUGAL.

Moulin, C., Bettahar, F., Barthes, J. P. A., Sbodio, M., & Korda, N. (2006, Jun 05-07). *Adding support to user interaction in eGovernment environment.* Paper presented at the 4th International Atlantic Web Intelligence Conference (AWIC 2006), Beer Sheva, ISRAEL.

Moulsley, H. (2005, Sep 01-03). *Transforming local government services through an e-government modernisation agenda.* Paper presented at the 44th Congress of the Federation-of-Telecommunications-Engineers-of-the-European-Community (FITCE), Vienna, AUSTRIA.

Mousavi, S. A., Pimenidis, E., & Jahankahni, H. (2007, Jun 21-22). *e-business models for use in e-Government for developing countries.* Paper presented at the 7th European Conference on e-Government (ECEG 2007), The Hague, NETHERLANDS.

Mrugalla, C. (2005, Sep 27-29). *The Virtual MailOpening: Usable cryptography in German e-government.* Paper presented at the Information Security Solutions Europe Conference, Budapest, HUNGARY.

Mugellini, E., Khaled, O. A., Chiara, M., & Kuonen, P. (2005, Mar 29-Apr 01). *eGovSM metadata model: Towards a flexible, interoperable and scalable egovernment service marketplace.* Paper presented at the IEEE International Conference on e-Technology, e-Commerce and e-Service, Hong Kong, PEOPLES R CHINA.

Mugellini, E., Pettenati, M. C., Abou Khaled, O., & Pirri, F. (2005, Mar 02-04). *eGovernment service marketplace: Architecture and implementation.* Paper presented at the International Conference on E-Government (TCGOV 2005), Bolzano, ITALY.

Muir, A., & Oppenheim, C. (2002). National Information Policy developments worldwide I: electronic government. [Article]. *Journal of Information Science, 28*(3), 173-186.

Mullner, T., & Grimm, D. (2004, Aug 30-Sep 03). *Applications and interface for e-government.* Paper presented at the 3rd International Conference on Electronic Government (EGOV 2004), Zaragoza, SPAIN.

Muslumov, S. Y. (2005, Jul 14-17). *E-government and eftective social insurance system management.* Paper presented at the 3rd International Conference on Politics and Information Systems - Technologies and Applications/International Symposium on Social and Organizational Informatics and Cybernectics, Orlando, FL.

Naidoo, G. (2007, Sep 27). *e-Government in South Africa: A perspective on issues and challenges.* Paper presented at the 3rd International Conference on e-Government, Montreal, CANADA.

Nedbal, D., & Petz, G. (2008, Jul 09-11). *A software solution for accessible e-Government portals.* Paper presented at the 11th International Conference on Computers Helping People with Special Needs, Linz, AUSTRIA.

Neubauer, T., Weippl, E., Biffl, S., & Soc, I. C. (2006, Apr 20-22). *Digital signatures with familiar appearance for e-government documents: Authentic PDF.* Paper presented at the 1st International Conference on Availability, Reliability and Security, Vienna, AUSTRIA.

Neumann, L., & Sekanina, P. (2007, Jun 21-22). *Strengths and weaknesses of the European interoperability framework related to the real applicationofICT in e-government.* Paper presented at the 7th European Conference on e-Government (ECEG 2007), The Hague, NETHERLANDS.

Ni, A. Y., & Bretschneider, S. (2007). The decision to contract out: A study of contracting for e-government services in state governments. [Article]. *Public Administration Review, 67*(3), 531-544.

Ni, A. Y., & Ho, A. T. K. (2005). Challenges in e-government development: Lessons from two information kiosk projects. [Article]. *Government Information Quarterly, 22*(1), 58-74.

Ni Fhloinn, A. (2004, Oct 27-29). *Resolving interoperability issues for eGovernment identification systems.* Paper presented at the eChallenges e-2004 Conference, Vienna, AUSTRIA.

Ni, J., Zhao, X. L., & Zhu, L. J. (2007, Dec 05-06). *A Semantic Web Service Oriented Architecture for Chinese e-government.* Paper presented at the 4th International Conference on Innovation and Management, Ube, JAPAN.

Nick, M., Gross, S., & Snoek, B. (2003, May 26-28). *How knowledge management can support the IT security of eGovernment services.* Paper presented at the 4th Annual International Working Conference on Knowledge Management in Electronic Government, Rhodes, Greece.

Niehaves, B. (2007, Sep 03-07). *Innovation processes in the public sector - New vistas for an interdisciplinary perspective on e-Government research?* Paper presented at the 6th International Conference on Electronic Government, Regensburg, GERMANY.

Niehaves, B., & Becker, J. (2008, Sep 24-26). *The age-divide in E-Government - Data, interpretations, theory fragments.* Paper presented at the 8th IFIP International Conference on e-Business, e-Service, and e-Society, Tokyo, JAPAN.

Nikolaidou, M., Laskaridis, G., Panayiotaki, A., & Anagnostopoulos, D. (2006, Jul 20-23). *What is the affect of providing e-government services based on existing legacy systems and applications? The case of the Hellenic ministry of economy and finance.* Paper presented at the 4th Int Conf on Education and Information Syst/2nd Int Conf on Social and Organizational Informatics and Cybernetics/4th Int Conf on Politics and Information Syst, Orlando, FL.

Nogueras-Iso, J., Latre-Abadia, M. A., Muro-Medrano, P. R., & Zarazaga-Soria, F. J. (2004, Aug 30-Sep 03). *Building e-government services over spatial data infrastructures.* Paper presented at the 3rd International Conference on Electronic Government (EGOV 2004), Zaragoza, SPAIN.

Norris, D. F. (2004, Aug 30-Sep 03). *e-government impacts at the American grassroots: An initial assessment.* Paper presented at the 3rd International Conference on Electronic Government (EGOV 2004), Zaragoza, SPAIN.

Norris, D. F., & Moon, M. J. (2005). Advancing e-government at the grassroots: Tortoise or hare? [Article]. *Public Administration Review, 65*(1), 64-75.

Notess, G. R. (2000). Finding online government publications. [Article]. *Econtent, 23*(3), 67-+.

Nour, M. A., AbdelRahman, A. A., & Fadlalla, A. (2008). A context-based integrative framework for e-government initiatives. [Article]. *Government Information Quarterly, 25*(3), 448-461.

O'Keefe, T. P., Palmer, T., Miller, G., & Shirazi, F. (2004, Jun 04-07). *Characteristics of rural citizens in an electronic government environment.* Paper presented at the 3rd Wuhan International Conference on E-Business - Global Business Interface, Wuhan, PEOPLES R CHINA.

Oberer, B. J. (2002, Jul 14-18). *Guidelines for implementing electronic government.* Paper presented at the 6th World Multi-Conference on Systemics, Cybernetics and Informatics (SCI 2002)/8th International Conference on Information Systems Analysis and Synthesis (ISAS 2002), Orlando, Fl.

Ogurlu, Y. (2007, Jun 21-22). *e-Government applications and its effects on public service in Turkey.* Paper presented at the 7th European Conference on e-Government (ECEG 2007), The Hague, NETHERLANDS.

Oikonomidis, N., Tcaciuc, S., & Ruland, C. (2005, Sep 19-21). *An architecture for secure policy enforcement in E-government services deployment.* Paper presented at the 9th International Conference on Communications and Multimedia Security, Salzburg, AUSTRIA.

Olbrich, S., & Simon, C. (2007, Jun 21-22). *Process modelling towards e-Government - Visualisation of process-like legal regulations.* Paper presented at the 7th European Conference on e-Government (ECEG 2007), The Hague, NETHERLANDS.

Oleskow-Szlapka, J., & Przybylska, J. (2008, Sep 08-10). *E-government in Poland against the background of other EU countries.* Paper presented at the 9th Working Conference on Virtual Enterprises, Poznan, POLAND.

Oliveira, M. A., Carvalho, A., & Bartolo, L. (2004, Aug 30-Sep 03). *Public discussion of Oportos municipal master plan: An e-Democracy service supported by a geographical information system.* Paper presented at the 3rd International Conference on Electronic Government (EGOV 2004), Zaragoza, SPAIN.

Olphert, W., & Damodaran, L. (2004, Jul 21-25). *Dialogue with citizens - the missing link in delivering e-government?* Paper presented at the International Conference on Politics and Information Systems, Orlando, FL.

Olphert, W., & Damodaran, L. (2007). Citizen participation and engagement in the design of e-government services: The missing link in effective ICT design and delivery. [Article]. *Journal of the Association for Information Systems, 8*(9), 491-507.

Omura, H. (2000). Information technology (IT) for e-Government. [Article]. *Fujitsu Scientific & Technical Journal, 36*(2), 232-235.

Oostveen, A. M., & Van den Besselaar, P. (2001, Oct 03-05). *Linking databases and linking cultures - The complexity of concepts in international e-government.* Paper presented at the 1st IFIP International Conference on E-Commerce, E-Business, and E-Government (I3E 2001), Zurich, Switzerland.

Orita, A., & Soc, I. C. (2006, Apr 20-22). *Designing mutual-aid model for RAQ (Rarely Asked Question) in e-Government: Practical use of anonymity.* Paper presented at the 1st International Conference on Availability, Reliability and Security, Vienna, AUSTRIA.

Orr, N. (2000). COINS - eGovernment becomes reality. [Article]. *Bt Technology Journal, 18*(2), 100-106.

Ostergaard, S. D. (2007, Jul 12-15). *From eGovernment to eSociety - Challenges and opportunities.* Paper presented at the International Multi-Conference on Society, Cybernetics and Informatics, Orlando, FL.

Ostermann, H., & Staudinger, R. (2005). Benchmarking E-Government - Formal aspects of applicability regarding differentiated objectives. [Article]. *Wirtschaftsinformatik, 47*(5), 367-377.

Otjacques, B., Hitzelberger, P., & Feltz, F. (2007). Interoperability of e-government information systems: Issues of identification and data sharing. [Article]. *Journal of Management Information Systems, 23*(4), 29-51.

Ou, Y. Y., Guo, H. Q., & Su, J. D. (2005, Jun 04-05). *Orchestration of web service in e-government.* Paper presented at the 4th Wuhan International Conference on E-Business - Global Business Interface, Wuhan, PEOPLES R CHINA.

Ouyang, Z. H. (2005, Aug 15-17). *The epitome of middle city's e-government in China: Quanzhou.*

Paper presented at the 7th International Conference on Electronic Commerce (ICEC 2005), Xian, PEOPLES R CHINA.

Pacheco, A., & Serrao, C. (2007, 2006). *Developing secure web-applications - Security criteria for the development of e-Democracy web-applications.* Paper presented at the International Conference on Telecommunications and Networking (TeNe)/ International Conference on Industrial Electronics, Technology and Automation (IETA), Electr Network.

Padilla, C. (2008). Using e-government websites for research: Content and quality. [Article]. *Online, 32*(3), 18-22.

Palkovits, S., & Wimmer, M. A. (2003, Sep 01-05). *Processes in E-government - A holistic framework for modelling electronic public services.* Paper presented at the 2nd International Conference on Electronic Government (EGOV 2003), Prague, Czech Republic.

Palkovits, S., Woitsch, R., & Karagiannis, D. (2003, May 26-28). *Process-based knowledge management and modelling in E-government - An inevitable combination.* Paper presented at the 4th Annual International Working Conference on Knowledge Management in Electronic Government, Rhodes, Greece.

Pan, F., & Chen, F. (2005, Jul 20-21). *Property right management of enterprises based on electronic government.* Paper presented at the 12th International Conference on Management Science and Engineering, Incheon, SOUTH KOREA.

Pan, G., Pan, S. L., Newman, M., & Flynn, D. (2006, 2004). *Escalation and de-escalation of commitment: a commitment transformation analysis of an e-government project.* Paper presented at the European Conference on Information Systems, Turku, FINLAND.

Pan, S. L., Tan, C. W., & Lim, E. T. K. (2006). Customer relationship management (CRM) in e-government: a relational perspective. [Article]. *Decision Support Systems, 42*(1), 237-250.

Panayiotou, P. (2007, Sep 27). *e-Government in Cyprus: The reality and the perspective.* Paper presented at the 3rd International Conference on e-Government, Montreal, CANADA.

Papadomichelaki, X., Magoutas, B., Halaris, C., Apostolou, D., & Mentzas, G. (2006, Sep 04-08). *A review of quality dimensions in e-government services.* Paper presented at the 5th International Conference on Electronic Government (EGOV 2006), Cracow, POLAND.

Papantoniou, A., Hattab, E., Afrati, F., Kayafas, E., & Loumos, V. (2001, Sep 03-07). *Change management, a critical success factor for e-government.* Paper presented at the 12th International Conference on Database and Expert Systems Applications (DEXA), Munich, Germany.

Pappa, D., & Makropoulos, C. (2004, May 17-19). *Designing a brokerage platform for the delivery of e-Government services to the public.* Paper presented at the 5th IFIP Interenational Working Conference on Knowledge Management in Electronic Government, Krems, AUSTRIA.

Paraiso, E. C., & Barthes, J. P. A. (2005, Jan 24-28). *A voice-enabled assistant in a multi-agent system for e-Government services.* Paper presented at the 5th International School and Symposium on Advanced Distributed Systems, Guadalajara, MEXICO.

Paralic, J., & Sabol, T. (2001, Sep 03-07). *Implementation of e-government using knowledge-based system.* Paper presented at the 12th International Conference on Database and Expert Systems Applications (DEXA), Munich, Germany.

Paralic, J., Sabol, T., & Mach, M. (2002, Sep 02-06). *A system to support e-democracy.* Paper presented at the 1st International Conference on Electronic Government (EGOV 2002), Aix Provence, France.

Paralic, J., Sabol, T., & Mach, M. (2003, May 26-28). *Knowledge enhanced e-Government portal.* Paper presented at the 4th Annual International Working Conference on Knowledge Management in Electronic Government, Rhodes, Greece.

Parent, M., Vandebeek, C. A., & Gemino, A. C. (2005). Building citizen trust through e-government. [Article]. *Government Information Quarterly, 22*(4), 720-736.

Paris, M. (2005). Local E-government and devolution: Electronic service delivery in Northern Ireland. [Article]. *Local Government Studies, 31*(3), 307-319.

Paris, M. (2006). Local e-government and devolution: Electronic service delivery in Northern Ireland. [Article]. *Local Government Studies, 32*(1), 41-53.

Parisopoulos, K., Tambouris, E., & Tarabanis, K. (2007, Sep 27). *Analyzing and comparing European e-Government strategies.* Paper presented at the 3rd International Conference on e-Government, Montreal, CANADA.

Parvez, Z. (2003, Sep 01-05). *Local democracy shaping e-democracy.* Paper presented at the 2nd International Conference on Electronic Government (EGOV 2003), Prague, Czech Republic.

Parycek, P., & Risku, H. (2004, May 17-19). *Intercultural E-government.* Paper presented at the 5th IFIP Interenational Working Conference on Knowledge Management in Electronic Government, Krems, AUSTRIA.

Pasic, A., Diez, S., & Espinosa, J. A. (2002, Sep 02-06). *IMPULSE: Interworkflow model for e-Government.* Paper presented at the 1st International Conference on Electronic Government (EGOV 2002), Aix Provence, France.

Pasic, A., Sassen, A. M., & Garcia, A. (2004, Aug 30-Sep 03). *e-Government intermediation.* Paper presented at the 3rd International Conference on Electronic Government (EGOV 2004), Zaragoza, SPAIN.

Pelaez, J. I., Dona, J. M., La Red, D. L., & Brys, C. R. (2008, Sep 21-24). *A linguistic model for citizen participation in electronic government.* Paper presented at the 8th International Conference on Fuzzy Logic and Intelligent Technologies in Nuclear Science, Madrid, SPAIN.

Peled, A. (2001). Centralization or diffusion? Two tales of online government. [Article]. *Administration & Society, 32*(6), 686-709.

Peng, J., Ding, Z. Y., Guo, H., & Liu, J. D. (2002, May 23-26). *Research and design for the territorial eGovernment system based on middleware.* Paper presented at the International Conference on E-Business (ICEB2002), Beijing, Peoples R China.

Peng, L. F., & Chen, Y. (2005, Aug 15-17). *Research on objective orientation of e-government system.* Paper presented at the 7th International Conference on Electronic Commerce (ICEC 2005), Xian, PEOPLES R CHINA.

Perez, C. C., Bolivar, M. P. R., & Hernandez, A. M. L. (2008). e-Government process and incentives for online public financial information. [Article]. *Online Information Review, 32*(3), 379-400.

Peristeras, V., & Tarabanis, K. (2005, Aug 22-26). *Providing Pan-European e-Government services with the use of semantic Web services technologies: A generic process model.* Paper presented at the 4th International Conference on Electronic Government (EGOV 2005), Copenhagen, DENMARK.

Petrakaki, D. (2008, Aug 10-13). *E-government and changes in the public sector: The case of Greece.* Paper presented at the International Working Conference on Information Technology in the Service Economy - Challenges and Possibilities for the 21st Century, Toronto, CANADA.

Petralkaki, D., Hayes, N., & Introna, L. (2007, Jun 21-22). *e-government and the joing-up of the Greek Public Sector.* Paper presented at the 7th European Conference on e-Government (ECEG 2007), The Hague, NETHERLANDS.

Petrovic, O. (2002, Sep 02-06). *The immanent fields of tension associated with e-government.* Paper presented at the 1st International Conference on Electronic Government (EGOV 2002), Aix Provence, France.

Pfaff, D., & Simon, B. (2002, Sep 02-06). *New services through integrated e-Government.* Paper presented at the 1st International Conference on Electronic Government (EGOV 2002), Aix Provence, France.

Phang, C. W., Kankanhalli, A., & Ang, C. (2008). Investigating organizational learning in eGovernment projects: A multi-theoretic approach. [Article]. *Journal of Strategic Information Systems, 17*(2), 99-123.

Phang, C. W., Sutanto, J., Kankanhalli, A., Li, Y., Tan, B. C. Y., & Teo, H. H. (2006). Senior citizens' acceptance of information systems: A study in the context of e-government services. [Article]. *Ieee Transactions on Engineering Management, 53*(4), 555-569.

Phippen, A., & Lacohee, H. (2006). eGovernment - issues in citizen engagement. [Article]. *Bt Technology Journal, 24*(2), 205-208.

Picci, L. (2006). The quantitative evaluation of the economic impact of e-government: A structural modelling approach. [Article]. *Information Economics and Policy, 18*(1), 107-123.

Pirog, M. A., & Johnson, C. L. (2008). Electronic Funds and Benefits Transfers, E-Government, and the Winter Commission. [Article]. *Public Administration Review, 68*, S103-S114.

Plaisent, M., Diallo, A., & Bernard, P. (2007, Sep 27). *Can e-Government improve charities effectiveness, efficiency and communication?* Paper presented at the 3rd International Conference on e-Government, Montreal, CANADA.

Podgayetskaya, T., & Stucky, W. (2005, Oct 28-30). *Hypr&A - A security model for the support processes in eGovernment.* Paper presented at the 5th IFTP Conference on E-Commerce, E-Business, and E-Government, Poznan, POLAND.

Podgayetskaya, T., Stucky, W., & ieee computer, s. (2004, Aug 30-Sep 03). *A model of business process support system for e-government.* Paper presented at the 15th International Conference on Database and Expert Systems Applications (DEXA 2004), Zaragoza, SPAIN.

Pollard, P. (2003, Sep 01-05). *Spatial Data Infrastructure and e-government: A case study of the UK.* Paper presented at the 2nd International Conference on Electronic Government (EGOV 2003), Prague, Czech Republic.

Pontico, F., Farenc, C., & Winckler, M. (2006, Oct 23-24). *Model-based support for specifying eService eGovernment applications.* Paper presented at the 5th International Workshop on Task Models and Diagrams for Users Interface Design, Hasselt, BELGIUM.

Poostchi, M., & Grant, G. (2002, May 19-22). *Implementing E-government: Impact on business processes and organizational structure.* Paper presented at the International Conference of the Information-Resources-Management-Association, Seattle, Wa.

Posch, R., & Leitold, H. (2002, Aug 25-30). *Identification and confidentiality for e-government.* Paper presented at the 17th World Computer Congress, Montreal, Canada.

Povalej, R., Horvatek, R., & Tomicic, M. (2007, Jun 20-22). *Trainings courses in eGovernment for civil servants in Croatia: The EU project eGovCRO - An actual overview.* Paper presented at the 8th International-Business-Information-Management-Association Conference (IBIMA), Dublin, IRELAND.

Pribil, J., Sumpikova, M., & Nemec, J. (2005, Jul 14-17). *Effective public finance: Can e-government help to improve public administration?* Paper presented at the 3rd International Conference on Politics and Information Systems - Technologies and Applications/International Symposium on Social and Organizational Informatics and Cybernectics, Orlando, FL.

Priebe, T., Muschall, B., Dobmeier, W., & Pernul, G. (2004, Aug 30-Sep 03). *A flexible security system for enterprise and e-government portals.* Paper presented at the 15th International Conference on Database and Expert Systems Applications (DEXA 2004), Zaragoza, SPAIN.

Pries-Heje, J. (2005, Aug 22-26). *eGovernment and structural reform on Bornholm: A case study.* Paper presented at the 4th International Conference on Electronic Government (EGOV 2005), Copenhagen, DENMARK.

Prosser, A., Guo, Y., Lenhart, J., & Insticc (2006, May 23-27). *The attitude towards e-democracy - Empirical evidence from the Viennese population.* Paper presented at the 8th International Conference on Enterprise Information Systems (ICEIS 2006), Paphos, CYPRUS.

Prosser, A., & Muller-Torok, R. (2002). E-democracy: a new dimension in democratic decision making. [Article]. *Wirtschaftsinformatik, 44*(6), 545-556.

Prybutok, V. R., Zhang, X. N., & Ryan, S. D. (2008). Evaluating leadership, IT quality, and net benefits in an e-government environment. [Article]. *Information & Management, 45*(3), 143-152.

Qi, M., & Ma, Q. M. (2003, Oct 24-27). *The six most important relations in E-government.* Paper presented at the 3rd International Conference on Electronic Commerce Engineering, Hangzhou, Peoples R China.

Qi, M., & Wei, B. B. (2005, Aug 15-17). *Design and analysis of administrative approval act based electronic government evaluation system.* Paper presented at the 7th International Conference on Electronic Commerce (ICEC 2005), Xian, PEOPLES R CHINA.

Qing, C. (2007, Dec 05-06). *One-stop e-government services integration.* Paper presented at the 4th International Conference on Innovation and Management, Ube, JAPAN.

Qiu, J. N., Tian, J., & Wang, Y. Z. (2007, Oct 14-16). *A research on the authorization model based on organizational management in e-gov.* Paper presented at the 2nd International Conference on Research and Practical Issues of Enterprise Information Systems, Beijing, PEOPLES R CHINA.

Qiu, J. N., Yao, Y. X., Wang, Y. Z., & Wang, X. H. (2006, Dec 18-22). *Research of E-government knowledge navigation system based on XTM.* Paper presented at the IEEE/WIC/ACM International Conference on Web Intelligence and Intelligent Agent Technology (WI-IAT 2006), Hong Kong, PEOPLES R CHINA.

Rawal, R., & Nixon, P. (2007, Sep 27). *How cyberterrorism challenges e-Government and its successful implementation.* Paper presented at the 3rd International Conference on e-Government, Montreal, CANADA.

Reddick, A. (2004, Mar 28-29). *Leveraging of social science and applied science for e-government applications.* Paper presented at the 14th International Workshop on Research Issues on Data Engineering - Web Services for E-Commerce and E-Government Applications, Boston, MA.

Reddick, C. G. (2004). A two-stage model of e-government growth: Theories and empirical evidence for US cities. [Article]. *Government Information Quarterly, 21*(1), 51-64.

Reddick, C. G. (2005). Citizen interaction with e-government: From the streets to servers? [Article]. *Government Information Quarterly, 22*(1), 38-57.

Reddick, C. G. (2006). Information resource managers and E-government effectiveness: A survey of Texas state agencies. [Article]. *Government Information Quarterly, 23*(2), 249-266.

Reddick, C. G., & Frank, H. A. (2007). The perceived impacts of e-government on US cities: A survey of Florida and Texas City managers. [Article]. *Government Information Quarterly, 24*(3), 576-594.

Reichstadter, P. (2003, Sep 01-05). *E-signatures for delivery in e-government.* Paper presented at the 2nd International Conference on Electronic Government (EGOV 2003), Prague, Czech Republic.

Reichstaedter, P. (2004, Oct 27-29). *E-delivery - Based on the Austrian eGovernment law.* Paper presented at the eChallenges e-2004 Conference, Vienna, AUSTRIA.

Reiss, D., Rumpe, B., Schulze-Quester, M., & Stein, M. (2008, Apr 22-25). *Evolving and implanting web-based e-government-systems in universities.* Paper presented at the 2nd International United Informational Systems Conference, Klagenfurt, AUSTRIA.

Reitz, J. C. (2006, Jul). *E-government.* Paper presented at the 17th Congress of the International-Academy-of-Comparative-Law, Utrecht, NETHERLANDS.

Relyea, H. C. (2001). E-gov: The Federal overview. [Article]. *Journal of Academic Librarianship, 27*(2), 131-148.

Relyea, H. C. (2002). E-gov: Introduction and overview. [Article]. *Government Information Quarterly, 19*(1), 9-35.

Ren, Z. T., & Zhang, R. (2007, Aug 20-22). *Analysis of e-government services outsourcing and incentive scheme.* Paper presented at the 14th International Conference on Management Science and Engineering, Harbin, PEOPLES R CHINA.

Resca, A. (2004, May 17-19). *How to develop e-Government: The Italian case.* Paper presented at the 5th IFIP Interenational Working Conference on Knowledge Management in Electronic Government, Krems, AUSTRIA.

Riad, A. M., Fahmy, M. M., & El-Sharkawy, M. A. (2005, Dec). *An architecture for Mining the Egyptian E-Government Network Traffic for Intrusion Detection.* Paper presented at the ITI 3rd International Conference on Information and Communications Technology (ICICT 2005), Cairo, EGYPT.

Riedl, R. (2001a, Aug 06-09). *Interdisciplinary engineering of interstate e-government solutions.* Paper presented at the 4th International Conference on Cognitive Technology - Instruments of Mind, Coventry, England.

Riedl, R. (2001b, Sep 03-07). *Limitations for interstate e-government and for interdisciplinary projects.* Paper presented at the 12th International Conference on Database and Expert Systems Applications (DEXA), Munich, Germany.

Riedl, R. (2003, Sep 01-05). *Affordances in e-government.* Paper presented at the 2nd International Conference on Electronic Government (EGOV 2003), Prague, Czech Republic.

Riedl, R. (2004, Aug 22). *Rethinking trust and confidence in European E-government - Linking the public sector with post-modern society.* Paper presented at the 4th International Conference on E-Commerce, E-Business and E-Government held at the 18th World Computer Congress, Toulouse, FRANCE.

Riedl, R., & Juen, M. (2006, Sep 04-08). *IT auditing in e-government.* Paper presented at the 5th International Conference on Electronic Government (EGOV 2006), Cracow, POLAND.

Riedl, R., & Maibaum, N. (2002, Sep 02-06). *FASME - From smartcards to holistic IT-architectures for interstate e-government.* Paper presented at the 1st International Conference on Electronic Government (EGOV 2002), Aix Provence, France.

Rios, O. L., & Lechuga, M. (2007, Jun 21-22). *Fair e-government strategies for digital illiterate population.* Paper presented at the 7th European Conference on e-Government (ECEG 2007), The Hague, NETHERLANDS.

Riquelme, H., & Buranasantikul, P. (2004, Aug 30-Sep 03). *e-government in Australia: A citizen's perspective.* Paper presented at the 3rd International Conference on Electronic Government (EGOV 2004), Zaragoza, SPAIN.

Robins, G., & Burn, J. (2001, Oct 03-05). *Building value into e-government: An Australian case study.* Paper presented at the 1st IFIP International Conference on E-Commerce, E-Business, and E-Government (I3E 2001), Zurich, Switzerland.

Rodger, J., & Pendharkar, P. (2007, Sep 27). *Lessons learned from testing, analyzing and problem solving an online Military Watchboard Medical Decision Support System (MWMDSS) application: Potential implications for civilian and e-Government organizations.* Paper presented at the 3rd International Conference on e-Government, Montreal, CANADA.

Rohde, M., Schmidt, A., & Hauschild, T. (2002, Oct 07-09). *IT security - A crucial success factor for e-government!* Paper presented at the 2nd IFIP Conference on E-Commerce, E-Business, E-Government (13E 2002), Lisbon, Portugal.

Rosiyadi, D., Nuryani, & Waskita, D. (2007, Sep 27). *The development of e-Government framework based on open source in Indonesia.* Paper presented at the 3rd International Conference on e-Government, Montreal, CANADA.

Ross, P., Hutton, N., Peng, L. M., & Lei, J. (2004). Revolutionary e-Government strategies across Asia-Pacific. [Article]. *Alcatel Telecommunications Review*(3), 332-337.

Rotthier, S. (2004, Aug 30-Sep 03). *e-Government policies, strategies and implementation: e-Government in the federal country Belgium.* Paper presented at the 3rd International Conference on Electronic Government (EGOV 2004), Zaragoza, SPAIN.

Rupp, C. (2004, Oct 27-29). *The Austrian eGovernment initiative - Good practice in European eAdministration.* Paper presented at the eChallenges e-2004 Conference, Vienna, AUSTRIA.

Ryan, S. M. (1994). UNCLE-SAM ONLINE - GOVERNMENT INFORMATION ON THE INTERNET. [Article]. *Communication Education, 43*(2), 151-158.

Saarenpaa, A. (2003, Sep 01-05). *A legal framework for e-government.* Paper presented at the 2nd International Conference on Electronic Government (EGOV 2003), Prague, Czech Republic.

Sabucedo, L. A., & Anido, L. (2004, Aug 30-Sep 03). *A review of current e-government initiatives in Spain.* Paper presented at the 3rd International Conference on Electronic Government (EGOV 2004), Zaragoza, SPAIN.

Sabucedo, L. A., & Rifon, L. A. (2005, Aug 22-26). *A proposal for a semantic-driven eGovernment service architecture.* Paper presented at the 4th International Conference on Electronic Government (EGOV 2005), Copenhagen, DENMARK.

Sabucedo, L. A., & Rifon, L. A. (2006, Sep 18-22). *Life event oriented architecture for eGovernment solutions.* Paper presented at the IEEE Services Computing Workshops, Chicago, IL.

Sabucedo, L. A., & Rifon, L. A. (2007, Mar 03-06). *Semantic life event environment for egovernment services - Towards a holistic support to host eGovernment services in a scalar manner.* Paper presented at the 3rd International Conference on Web Information Systems and Technologies, Barcelona, SPAIN.

Sabucedo, L. A., Rifon, L. A., & Perez, R. M. (2008, Sep 24-26). *A Practical Approach to a Semantic-Based eGovernment Platform: The PLEDGE project.* Paper presented at the 1st World Summit on the Knowledge Society (WSKS 2008), Athens, GREECE.

Sacco, G. M. (2005, Mar 02-04). *No (e-)democracy without (e-)knowledge.* Paper presented at the International Conference on E-Government (TCGOV 2005), Bolzano, ITALY.

Sadok, M., & Djemaiel, Y. (2007, Sep 27). *Leading factors to assess and conduct effective e-government deployment: Modelling, analysis, and practice.* Paper presented at the 3rd International Conference on e-Government, Montreal, CANADA.

Saebo, O. (2006, Aug 31-Sep 02). *How to identify objectives and genres in E-Democracy projects: Learning from an action case study.* Paper presented at the 15th International Conference on Information Systems Development, Budapest, HUNGARY.

Salem, J. A. (2003). Public and private sector interests in e-government: a look at the DOE's PubSCIENCE. [Article]. *Government Information Quarterly, 20*(1), 13-27.

Salhofer, P., Ferbas, D., Janser, G., & Meyer, B. (2007, Sep 27). *Towards the e-Government Shop: Applying the e-Shop paradigm to e-Government.* Paper presented at the 3rd International Conference on e-Government, Montreal, CANADA.

Salzano, G., Guemeida, A., & Jeansoulin, R. (2007, Sep 27). *Quality-aware agents for e-Government information systems architecture.* Paper presented at the 3rd International Conference on e-Government, Montreal, CANADA.

Sanati, F., & Lu, J. (2008, Apr 07-09). *Semantic web for e-government service delivery integration.* Paper presented at the 5th International Conference on Information Technology - New Generations, Las Vegas, NV.

Sandoz, A., Eudes, J. R., & Prevot, R. (2008, Jan 23-25). *Public-private partnership in e-government: a case implementation.* Paper presented at the 3rd International MCETECH Conference on eTechnologies, Montreal, CANADA.

Sannarnes, M. K., Henriksen, H. Z., & Andersen, K. V. (2006, Sep 04-08). *The e-government melting pot: Lacking new public management and innovation flavor?* Paper presented at the 5th International Conference on Electronic Government (EGOV 2006), Cracow, POLAND.

Santos, J. M. V., & Alonso, A. I. (2006, Jun 12-14). *E-democracy and citizen's empowerment: a case study of the city of Madrid.* Paper presented at the 2nd International Conference on the Internet Society, New Forest, ENGLAND.

Sardy, S., Asvial, M., & Jamal, A. (2007, Jul 12-15). *E-government and FOSS policies in Indonesia.* Paper presented at the International Multi-Conference on Society, Cybernetics and Informatics, Orlando, FL.

Savvas, I., Pimenidis, E., & Sideridis, A. (2007, Jun 21-22). *Proposing a high-level requirements mapping framework for testing implementation compatibility in e-government projects.* Paper presented at the 7th European Conference on e-Government (ECEG 2007), The Hague, NETHERLANDS.

Schedler, K., & Scharf, M. C. (2001, Oct 03-05). *Exploring the interrelations between electronic government and the new public management - A managerial framework for electronic government.* Paper presented at the 1st IFIP International Conference on E-Commerce, E-Business, and E-Government (I3E 2001), Zurich, Switzerland.

Schedler, K., & Summermatter, L. (2007, 2005). *Customer orientation in electronic government: Motives and effects.* Paper presented at the Annual Meeting of the European-Group-of-Public-Administration, Berne, SWITZERLAND.

Scherlis, W. L., & Eisenberg, J. (2003). It research, innovation, and e-government. [Article]. *Communications of the Acm, 46*(1), 67-68.

Scholl, H. J. (2001, Oct 03-05). *Applying stakeholder theory to e-government: Benefits and limits.* Paper presented at the 1st IFIP International Conference on E-Commerce, E-Business, and E-Government (I3E 2001), Zurich, Switzerland.

Scholl, H. J. (2003, Sep 01-05). *Electronic government: Make or buy?* Paper presented at the 2nd International Conference on Electronic Government (EGOV 2003), Prague, Czech Republic.

Scholl, H. J. (2004, Aug 30-Sep 03). *Electronic government: Scope and scale of process change.* Paper presented at the 3rd International Conference on Electronic Government (EGOV 2004), Zaragoza, SPAIN.

Scholl, H. J. (2005, Aug 22-26). *Organizational transformation through e-Government: Myth or reality?* Paper presented at the 4th International Conference on Electronic Government (EGOV 2005), Copenhagen, DENMARK.

Scholl, H. J. (2006a). Electronic government: Information management capacity, organizational capabilities, and the sourcing mix. [Article]. *Government Information Quarterly, 23*(1), 73-96.

Scholl, H. J. (2006b, Sep 04-08). *Is e-government research a flash in the pan or here for the long shot?* Paper presented at the 5th International Conference on Electronic Government (EGOV 2006), Cracow, POLAND.

Scholl, H. J., Fidel, R., Liua, S., Paulsmeyer, M., & Unsworth, K. (2007, Sep 03-07). *E-government fieldforce automation: Promises, challenges, and stakeholders.* Paper presented at the 6th International Conference on Electronic Government, Regensburg, GERMANY.

Schweighofer, E. (2003, Sep 01-05). *E-government in the European Commission.* Paper presented at the 2nd International Conference on Electronic Government (EGOV 2003), Prague, Czech Republic.

Schweighofer, E. (2004, Aug 30-Sep 03). *An e-government intercface for the director-general - Or: How to support decision makers with an electronic chief secretary?* Paper presented at the 3rd International Conference on Electronic Government (EGOV 2004), Zaragoza, SPAIN.

Seaton, J. (2005). The Scottish Parliament and e-democracy. [Article]. *Aslib Proceedings, 57*(4), 333-337.

Sebek, J. (2003, Sep 01-05). *Delivering e-Government services to citizens and businesses: The government gateway concept.* Paper presented at the 2nd International Conference on Electronic Government (EGOV 2003), Prague, Czech Republic.

Sedaghat, S., Pieprzyk, J., & Seltsikas, P. (2007, Jun 21-22). *The management of citizen identity in electronic government.* Paper presented at the 7th European Conference on e-Government (ECEG 2007), The Hague, NETHERLANDS.

See-To, E., & Kiwango, P. (2007, Jun 21-22). *Strategic e-government planning: Lessons from direct applications of standard SISP methodologies.* Paper presented at the 7th European Conference on e-Government (ECEG 2007), The Hague, NETHERLANDS.

Seel, C., Guengoez, O., & Thomas, O. (2004, May 23-26). *Towards an integrated e-government.* Paper presented at the International Conference of the Information-Resources-Management-Association, New Orleans, LA.

Seel, C., & Thomas, O. (2005, Jul 14-17). *Process performance measurement for E-Government - Concept and application.* Paper presented at the 3rd International Conference on Politics and Information Systems - Technologies and Applications/International Symposium on Social and Organizational Informatics and Cybernectics, Orlando, FL.

Seel, C., Thomas, O., Kaffai, B., & Matheis, T. (2005, Oct 28-30). *Evaluating E-Government.* Paper presented at the 5th IFTP Conference on E-Commerce, E-Business, and E-Government, Poznan, POLAND.

Segaard, S. B. (2008). E-Democracy Project As Organizational Change. [Article]. *Tidsskrift for Samfunnsforskning, 49*(3), 375-407.

Segovia, R., & Jennex, M. E. (2006, Aug 31-Sep 02). *Improving trust in E-government through paralingual web design.* Paper presented at the 15th International Conference on Information Systems Development, Budapest, HUNGARY.

Sell, D., Cabral, L., Goncalves, A., Motta, E., & Pacheco, R. (2004, Oct 05-08). *A framework to improve semantic web services discovery and integration in an E-gov knowledge network.* Paper presented at the 14th International Conference on Knowledge Engineering and Knowledge Management, Whittlebury, ENGLAND.

Sepic, R., & Kase, K. (2002). The National Biological Information Infrastructure as an e-government tool. [Article]. *Government Information Quarterly, 19*(4), 407-424.

Serra, T. (2003, May 30-31). *Telecities: The role of city networks in e-government processes.* Paper presented at the International Conference On Line Citizenship, Venice, ITALY.

Shackleton, P., Fisher, J., & Dawson, L. (2003, Aug 29-31). *E-government services - One local government's approach.* Paper presented at the 12th International Conference on Information Systems and Development, Melbourne, AUSTRALIA.

Shan, Z. G., Li, X. Y., Wang, Z. M., & Ning, J. J. (2004, Sep 13-15). *Policies and practice of E-government construction in China.* Paper presented at the IEEE International Conference on E-Commerce Technology for Dynamic E-Business, Beijing, PEOPLES R CHINA.

Sharifi, H., & Zarei, B. (2004). An adaptive approach for implementing e-government in IR Iran. [Article]. *Journal of Government Information, 30*(5-6), 600-619.

Shen, Y., Yu, F., Zhang, L. F., Liao, G. P., Zhou, T., & Ieee (2006, Aug 07-10). *Research on distributed access control by security E-government.* Paper presented at the 25th Chinese Control Conference, Harbin, PEOPLES R CHINA.

Shi, Y., & Ieee (2007, Aug 27-29). *Improving e-government services should start with domain names: A longitudinal study of chinese e-government domain names.* Paper presented at the IEEE International Conference on Service Operations and Logistics and Informatics, Philadelphia, PA.

Shi, Y. Q. (2006). E-government web site accessibility in Australia and China - A longitudinal study. [Article]. *Social Science Computer Review, 24*(3), 378-385.

Shill, H. B. (1992). Information Publics And Equitable Access To Electronic Government Information - The Case Of Agriculture. [Article]. *Government Information Quarterly, 9*(3), 305-322.

Shuler, J. A. (2001). XML, UDDI, and SOAP: The "verbs" and "nouns" of "semantic electronic government information". [Article]. *Journal of Academic Librarianship, 27*(6), 467-469.

Shuler, J. A. (2002). Of Web portals, E-gov, and the public's prints. [Article]. *Journal of Academic Librarianship, 28*(6), 410-413.

Siau, K., & Long, Y. (2004, May 23-26). *A stage model for e-government implementation.* Paper presented at the International Conference of the Information-Resources-Management-Association, New Orleans, LA.

Siau, K., & Long, Y. (2005). Synthesizing e-government stage models - a meta-synthesis based on meta-ethnography approach. [Article].

Industrial Management & Data Systems, 105(3-4), 443-458.

Siau, K., & Long, Y. A. (2004, Dec). *Using social development lenses to understand e-government development.* Paper presented at the 1st International Symposium of IS/IT in Asia-Pacific (ISAP 2004), Washington, DC.

Siau, K., & Shen, Z. X. (2002, May 19-22). *Constituent relationship management and e-government.* Paper presented at the International Conference of the Information-Resources-Management-Association, Seattle, Wa.

Siegfried, T. (2002, Sep 02-06). *The experience of German local communities with e-government - Results of the MEDIA@ Komm project.* Paper presented at the 1st International Conference on Electronic Government (EGOV 2002), Aix Provence, France.

Siegfried, T., Grabow, B., & Druke, H. (2003, Sep 01-05). *Ten factors for success for local community e-government.* Paper presented at the 2nd International Conference on Electronic Government (EGOV 2003), Prague, Czech Republic.

Silcock, R. (2001). What is e-Government? [Article]. *Parliamentary Affairs, 54*(1), 88-+.

Simmons, S. (2004, Oct 27-29). *Democracy in action - Open source in eGovernment.* Paper presented at the eChallenges e-2004 Conference, Vienna, AUSTRIA.

Simurina, J., Hruska, D., & Markovic, M. (2007, Dec 14-16). *E-government in Croatia.* Paper presented at the 6th WSEAS International Conference on E-ACTIVITIES, Puerto de la Cruz, SPAIN.

Singh, S., Lubbe, S., Naidoo, G., & Klopper, R. (2007, Jun 21-22). *Towards a hypothetical e-government solution: A South African perspective.* Paper presented at the 7th European Conference on e-Government (ECEG 2007), The Hague, NETHERLANDS.

Slack, F., & Rowley, J. E. (2004). Challenges in the delivery of e-government through kiosks. [Article]. *Journal of Information Science, 30*(4), 369-377.

Smith, D. H. (1988). Online Government Databases - Into The Maelstrom. [Article]. *Database, 11*(3), 56-62.

Smith, E., & Macintosh, A. (2003, Sep 01-05). *E-voting: Powerful symbol of E-democracy.* Paper presented at the 2nd International Conference on Electronic Government (EGOV 2003), Prague, Czech Republic.

Smith, S., & Jamieson, R. (2006). Determining key factors in E-government information system security. [Article]. *Information Systems Management, 23*(2), 23-32.

Sneed, H. M. (2005, Sep 26). *Testing an E-Government web site.* Paper presented at the 7th International Symposium on Web Site Evolution, Budapest, HUNGARY.

Soliman, K. S., & Affisco, J. F. (2003, May 18-21). *Key factors in establishing successful e-government services.* Paper presented at the International Conference of the Information-Resources-Management-Association, Philadelphia, PA.

Sorgaard, P. (2003, Oct 06-08). *Co-ordination of e-government - Between politics and pragmatics.* Paper presented at the Working Conference on the Diffusion and Adoption of Networked Information Technologies, Copenhagen, DENMARK.

Sorrentino, M. (2007, Sep 03-07). *Interpreting e-government: Implementation as the moment of truth.* Paper presented at the 6th International Conference on Electronic Government, Regensburg, GERMANY.

Sorrentino, M., & Ferro, E. (2008, Aug 31-Sep 05). *Does the Answer to eGovernment Lie in Intermunicipal Collaboration? An Exploratory Italian Case Study.* Paper presented at the 7th

International Conference on Electronic Government, Turin, ITALY.

Sorrentino, M., & Virili, F. (2003, Sep 01-05). *Socio-technical perspectives on e-Government initiatives.* Paper presented at the 2nd International Conference on Electronic Government (EGOV 2003), Prague, Czech Republic.

Sou, G., & Cstp (2004, Nov 02-06). *e-Government vis-a-vis logistics industry in the Hong Kong special administrative region.* Paper presented at the World Engineers Convention 2004, Shanghai, PEOPLES R CHINA.

Soufi, B., & Maguire, M. (2007, Jul 22-27). *Achieving usability within E-government web sites illustrated by a case study evaluation.* Paper presented at the Symposium on Human Interface and the Management of Information held at HCI International 2007, Beijing, PEOPLES R CHINA.

Sourouni, A. M., Lampathaki, F., Mouzakitis, S., Charalabidis, Y., & Askounis, D. (2008, Aug 31-Sep 05). *Paving the way to eGovernment transformation: Interoperability registry infrastructure development.* Paper presented at the 7th International Conference on Electronic Government, Turin, ITALY.

Spahni, D. (2003, Sep 01-05). *URN : Technology - A building block of the Swiss e-government platform.* Paper presented at the 2nd International Conference on Electronic Government (EGOV 2003), Prague, Czech Republic.

Spremic, M., & Brzica, H. (2008, Apr 06-08). *E-Government and its application in the Republic of Croatia.* Paper presented at the WSEAS Conference on Recent Advances in Systems, Communications and Computers, Hangzhou, PEOPLES R CHINA.

Sriramesh, K., & Rivera-Sanchez, M. (2006). E-government in a corporatist, communitarian society: the case of Singapore. [Article]. *New Media & Society, 8*(5), 707-730.

Srivastava, S. C., & Teo, T. S. H. (2006, Jul 06-09). *E-government payoffs: Evidence from cross-country data.* Paper presented at the 10th Pacific Asia Conference on Information Systems, Kuala Lumpur, MALAYSIA.

Stanziola, E., Espil, M. M., Landoni, L., & Montoya, S. (2006, Sep 04-08). *Hidden negative social effects of poor e-government services design.* Paper presented at the 5th International Conference on Electronic Government (EGOV 2006), Cracow, POLAND.

Stefan, V., & Stefan, A. (2008, May 04-07). *Live services for citizens with live technologies - e-payment in Romania as first step to an effective e-Government.* Paper presented at the 4th International Conference on Web Information Systems and Technologies, Funchal, PORTUGAL.

Steimke, F., & Hagen, M. (2003, Sep 01-05). *A common communications standard for E-government.* Paper presented at the 2nd International Conference on Electronic Government (EGOV 2003), Prague, Czech Republic.

Stemberger, M. I., & Jaklic, J. (2007). Towards E-government by business process change - A methodology for public sector. [Article]. *International Journal of Information Management, 27*(4), 221-232.

Steyaert, J. C. (2004). Measuring the performance of electronic government services. [Article]. *Information & Management, 41*(3), 369-375.

Stoddart, J. (2002, Aug 25-30). *Respecting privacy in e-government.* Paper presented at the 17th World Computer Congress, Montreal, Canada.

Stojanovic, L., Abecker, A., Stojanovic, N., & Studer, R. (2004, Oct 25-29). *On managing changes in the ontology-based E-Government.* Paper presented at the On the Move Confederated International Workshop and Conference, Agia Napa, CYPRUS.

Stojanovic, L., Stojanovic, N., & Ma, J. (2007, Dec 03). *An approach for combining ontology learning and semantic tagging in the ontology development process: eGovernment use case.* Paper presented at the 8th International Conference on Web Information Systems Engineering (WISE 2007), Nancy, FRANCE.

Streib, G., & Navarro, I. (2006). Citizen demand for interactive e-government - The case of Georgia consumer services. [Article]. *American Review of Public Administration, 36*(3), 288-300.

Strejcek, G., & Theil, M. (2003). Technology push, legislation pull? E-government in the European Union. [Article]. *Decision Support Systems, 34*(3), 305-313.

Su, F., & Zhu, H. (2007, Oct 10-12). *Exploring the intelligent and collaborative control for e-government system.* Paper presented at the 7th IFIP International Conference on e-Business, e-Service, and e-Society, Wuhan, PEOPLES R CHINA.

Su, J. D., Guo, H. Q., & Yu, S. S. (2004, Sep 13-16). *Security design model of E-government collaborative platform.* Paper presented at the International Symposium on Distributed Computing and Applications to Business, Engineering and Sciences, Wuhan, PEOPLES R CHINA.

Sukhbaatar, B., Odgerel, U., & Ieee (2005, Nov 09-10). *A study on e-government policy in Mongolia.* Paper presented at the 6th Asia-Pacific Symposium on Information and Telecommunication Technologies, Yangon, MYANMAR.

Sullivan, S. J. (2004, Apr 20-23). *Electronic records management (ERM) electronic government (E-Gov) initiative transferring permanent electronic records to the national archives of the United States.* Paper presented at the 1st IS&T Archiving Conference, San Antonio, TX.

Sun, J., & Chen, J. B. (2007, Oct 14-16). *Research on the "Thematic and Intelligent Portfolio" service of E-government system.* Paper presented at the 2nd International Conference on Research and Practical Issues of Enterprise Information Systems, Beijing, PEOPLES R CHINA.

Sun, W., Ji, C. X., & Alfred, U. (2007, May 26-27). *Design and implementation of e-government topic-focused search engine.* Paper presented at the 6th Wuhan International Conference on E-Business, Wuhan, PEOPLES R CHINA.

Susanto, T. D., & Goodwin, R. (2006, Jun 12-14). *Opportunity and overview of SMS-based e-government in developing countries.* Paper presented at the 2nd International Conference on the Internet Society, New Forest, ENGLAND.

Susanto, T. D., Goodwin, R., & Insticc (2006, May 23-27). *An SMS-based e-government model.* Paper presented at the 8th International Conference on Enterprise Information Systems (ICEIS 2006), Paphos, CYPRUS.

Sweisi, N. A., & Adams, C. (2007, Jun 20-22). *Proposed framework to manage the change to e-Government (lessons from Libya).* Paper presented at the 8th International-Business-Information-Management-Association Conference (IBIMA), Dublin, IRELAND.

Sweisi, N. A., Eldresi, F. Y., & Adams, C. (2007, Sep 27). *e-government services to support vaccination programmes: Libya, a successful implementation.* Paper presented at the 3rd International Conference on e-Government, Montreal, CANADA.

Talamo, M. (2002, Aug 25-30). *E-government services: Certification and security.* Paper presented at the 17th World Computer Congress, Montreal, Canada.

Tambouris, E. (2001, Sep 03-07). *An integrated platform for realising online one-stop government: The eGOV project.* Paper presented at the 12th International Conference on Database and Expert Systems Applications (DEXA), Munich, Germany.

Tambouris, E., & Gorilas, S. (2003, Sep 01-05). *Evaluation of an e-democracy platform for European cities.* Paper presented at the 2nd International Conference on Electronic Government (EGOV 2003), Prague, Czech Republic.

Tambouris, E., Gorilas, S., Kavadias, G., Apostolou, D., Abecker, A., Stojanovic, L., et al. (2004, May 17-19). *Ontology-enabled E-gov service configuration: An overview of the OntoGov project.* Paper presented at the 5th IFIP Interenational Working Conference on Knowledge Management in Electronic Government, Krems, AUSTRIA.

Tambouris, E., Loutas, N., Peristeras, V., & Tarabanis, K. (2007, Nov 21-23). *A semantic approach for discovering eGovernment services.* Paper presented at the 6th WSEAS International Conference on System Science and Simulation in Engineering, Venice, ITALY.

Tambouris, E., Manouselis, N., & Costopoulou, C. (2007). Metadata for digital collections of e-government resources. [Article]. *Electronic Library, 25*(2), 176-192.

Tambouris, E., & Tarabanis, K. (2004, Aug 30-Sep 03). *Overview of DC-based e-Government metadata standards and initiatives.* Paper presented at the 3rd International Conference on Electronic Government (EGOV 2004), Zaragoza, SPAIN.

Tan, C. W. (2005). Managing stakeholder interests in e-government implementation: Lessons learned from a Singapore e-government project. [Article]. *Journal of Global Information Management, 13*(1), 31-53.

Tan, C. W., & Pan, S. L. (2003). Managing e-transformation in the public sector: an e-government study of the Inland Revenue Authority of Singapore (IRAS). [Article]. *European Journal of Information Systems, 12*(4), 269-281.

Tang, Z. W., & Jia, X. M. (2005, Jul 20-21). *An E-government planning framework based on QFD.* Paper presented at the 12th International Conference on Management Science and Engineering, Incheon, SOUTH KOREA.

Tang, Z. W., Jia, X. M., & Alfred, U. (2007, May 26-27). *Citizen oriented e-government planning and case study at county level.* Paper presented at the 6th Wuhan International Conference on E-Business, Wuhan, PEOPLES R CHINA.

Tang, Z. W., Xu, G. D., & Alfred, U. (2007, May 26-27). *Study on the risk evaluation in electronic government system - Based on OCTAVE model.* Paper presented at the 6th Wuhan International Conference on E-Business, Wuhan, PEOPLES R CHINA.

Tang, Z. W., Zhao, S. H., & Chen, L. L. (2006, May 27-28). *The analysis of the structure of e-government theory system in China.* Paper presented at the 5th Wuhan International Conference on E-Business, Wuhan, PEOPLES R CHINA.

Teodosio, A. S. S. (2002, 2002). *Participatory budgeting and e-democracy in Brazil: new strategies, new challenges in the city management.* Paper presented at the 2nd International Conference on the Sustainable City, Segovia, Spain.

Tepandi, J. (2004, Oct 27-29). *Born to co-operate: New communication approaches for eGovernment.* Paper presented at the eChallenges e-2004 Conference, Vienna, AUSTRIA.

Thomas, C. A., LeBlanc, P. D., Mbarika, V. W., & Meso, P. (2004, May 23-26). *E-government in Africa: A new era for better governance in sub-Saharan Africa.* Paper presented at the International Conference of the Information-Resources-Management-Association, New Orleans, LA.

Thomas, J., Shen, Z. M., Paprzycki, M., & Crossland, M. (2003, Nov 28-30). *A mobile location-based framework for secure e-commerce and e-government.* Paper presented at the International Conference on Management of e-Commerce and e-Government, Nanchang, PEOPLES R CHINA.

Thomas, J. C., & Streib, G. (2003). The new face of government: Citizen-initiated contacts in the era of e-government. [Article]. *Journal of Public Administration Research and Theory, 13*(1), 83-101.

Thomas, J. C., & Streib, G. (2005). E-democracy, e-commerce, and e-research. [Article]. *Administration & Society, 37*(3), 259-280.

Thome, R., & Schinzer, H. (2005). Consultative Assistance Systems for eGovernment. [Article]. *Wirtschaftsinformatik, 47*(5), 326-336.

Thompson, C. S. (2002). Enlisting on-line residents: Expanding the boundaries of e-government in a Japanese rural township. [Article]. *Government Information Quarterly, 19*(2), 173-188.

Thompson, D. V., Rust, R. T., & Rhoda, J. (2005). The business value of e-government for small firms. [Article]. *International Journal of Service Industry Management, 16*(3-4), 385-407.

Tian, J., & Tianfield, H. (2003, Sep 03-05). *Object-oriented design of e-government system: A case study.* Paper presented at the 7th International Conference on Knowledge-Based Intelligent Information and Engineering Systems (KES 2003), Oxford, England.

Tian, J., Tianfield, H., & Alfred, U. (2007, May 26-27). *Multi-agent approach to e-government systems development and systems reusability and evolvability.* Paper presented at the 6th Wuhan International Conference on E-Business, Wuhan, PEOPLES R CHINA.

Tiglao, N. M. C., Manuela, W. S., & Verdillo, R. C. (2008, Jan 04-06). *Barriers to e-government maturity: the Philippine experience.* Paper presented at the 9th International-Business-Information-Management-Association Conference (IBIMA), Marrakech, MOROCCO.

Tilli, M., Panhan, A. M., Lima, O., & Mendes, L. S. (2008, Jul 26-29). *A web-based architecture for e-gov application development.* Paper presented at the International Conference on e-Business (ICE-B 2008), Oporto, PORTUGAL.

Tizzo, N. P., Borelli, J. R., Mendes, M. D., Damasceno, L. L., Kamada, A., Figueiredo, A., et al. (2004, Aug 22). *Service composition applied to e-Government.* Paper presented at the 4th International Conference on E-Commerce, E-Business and E-Government held at the 18th World Computer Congress, Toulouse, FRANCE.

Tolbert, C. J., & Mossberger, K. (2006). The effects of e-government on trust and confidence in government. [Article]. *Public Administration Review, 66*(3), 354-369.

Tolbert, C. J., Mossberger, K., & McNeal, R. (2008). Institutions, policy innovation, and e-government in the American states. [Article]. *Public Administration Review, 68*(3), 549-563.

Torres, L., Pina, V., & Acerete, B. (2004, Jul 21-25). *Gauging e-government evolution in EU municipalities.* Paper presented at the International Conference on Politics and Information Systems, Orlando, FL.

Torres, L., Pina, V., & Acerete, B. (2005). E-government developments on delivering public services among EU cities. [Article]. *Government Information Quarterly, 22*(2), 217-238.

Torres, L., Pina, V., & Royo, S. (2005). E-government and the transformation of public administrations in EU countries - Beyond NPM or just a second wave of reforms? [Article]. *Online Information Review, 29*(5), 531-553.

Traunmuller, R., & Wimmer, M. (2001, Sep 03-07). *Directions in e-Government: Processes, portals, knowledge.* Paper presented at the 12th International Conference on Database and Expert Systems Applications (DEXA), Munich, Germany.

Traunmuller, R., & Wimmer, M. A. (2001, Dec 03-06). *Web semantics in e-government: A tour d'Horizon on essential features.* Paper presented at the 2nd International Conference on Web Information Systems Engineering (WISE 2001), Kyoto, Japan.

Trusler, J. (2003, Sep 01-05). *South African e-government policy and practices: A framework to close the gap.* Paper presented at the 2nd International Conference on Electronic Government (EGOV 2003), Prague, Czech Republic.

Tsampoulatidis, I., Tzovaras, D., & Strintzis, M. G. (2004, Oct 25-29). *Ontology-based E-government thematic services based on topic maps.* Paper presented at the On the Move Confederated International Workshop and Conference, Agia Napa, CYPRUS.

Tseng, P. T. Y., Yen, D. C., Hung, Y. C., & Wang, N. C. F. (2008). To explore managerial issues and their implications on e-Government deployment in the public sector: Lessons from Taiwan's Bureau of Foreign Trade. [Article]. *Government Information Quarterly, 25*(4), 734-756.

Tso, C. D. (2003, Jul 31-Aug 02). *E-government as a means of anti-corruption.* Paper presented at the International Conference on Politics and Information Systems - Technologies and Applications (PISTA 03), Orlando, FL.

Tung, L. L., & Rieck, O. (2005). Adoption of electronic government services among business organizations in Singapore. [Article]. *Journal of Strategic Information Systems, 14*(4), 417-440.

Turner, T., & Schwager, A. (2005, Jun 20-23). *Analysing e-Government market segment behaviour.* Paper presented at the International Conference on E-Business, Enterprise Information Systems, E-Government and Outsourcing, Las Vegas, NV.

Usero, J. A. M. (2006). Metadata as a tool to improve knowledge interoperability in e-government services. [Article]. *Profesional De La Informacion, 15*(2), 114-+.

Vahtera, A. (2008, Sep 24-26). *e-government in the Finnish early childhood education: An analysis of current status and challenges.* Paper presented at the 8th IFIP International Conference on e-Business, e-Service, and e-Society, Tokyo, JAPAN.

Vamos, T., & Soos, I. (2003, May 26-28). *Data management and AI in E-government.* Paper presented at the 4th Annual International Working Conference on Knowledge Management in Electronic Government, Rhodes, Greece.

Van Audenhove, L., Jans, G., Staelens, T., Van Attenhove, J., Jacobs, A., Verdegem, P., et al. (2007, Sep 27). *Multichannel e-government. A reality check by way of in-depth user and usability research in Flanders.* Paper presented at the 3rd International Conference on e-Government, Montreal, CANADA.

van Dam, N., Evers, V., & Arts, F. A. (2003, Sep 18-19). *Cultural user experience issues in e-government: Designing for a multi-cultural society.* Paper presented at the 3rd International Digital Cities Workshop, Amsterdam, NETHERLANDS.

van der Vyver, A. G. (2008, Jan 04-06). *Reinventing government communications: Going mobile with e-government.* Paper presented at the 9th International-Business-Information-Management-Association Conference (IBIMA), Marrakech, MOROCCO.

van der Vyver, B. (2007, Jun 20-22). *A South African case study into the use of public Internet facilities for participation in e-democracy and e-governance.* Paper presented at the 8th International-Business-Information-Management-Association Conference (IBIMA), Dublin, IRELAND.

van Deursen, A., van Dijk, J., & Ebbers, W. (2006, Sep 04-08). *Why e-government usage lags behind: Explaining the gap between potential and actual usage of electronic public services in the Netherlands.* Paper presented at the 5th International Conference on Electronic Government (EGOV 2006), Cracow, POLAND.

van Overeem, A., Witters, J., & Peristeras, V. (2006, Jul 20-23). *Semantic Interoperability in pan-European eGovernment services.* Paper presented at the 4th Int Conf on Education and Information Syst/2nd Int Conf on Social and Organizational Informatics and Cybernetics/4th Int Conf on Politics and Information Syst, Orlando, FL.

van Velsen, L., van der Geest, T., ter Hedde, M., & Derks, W. (2008, Aug 31-Sep 05). *Engineering User Requirements for e-Government Services: A Dutch Case Study.* Paper presented at the 7th International Conference on Electronic Government, Turin, ITALY.

van Wamelen, J. P. (2004, May 23-26). *Creating conditions for the realization of e-government.* Paper presented at the International Conference of the Information-Resources-Management-Association, New Orleans, LA.

van Warnelen, J. (2007, Sep 27). *Conditions for creating e-Government.* Paper presented at the 3rd International Conference on e-Government, Montreal, CANADA.

Vanka, S., & Garimella, S. (2005, Jul 14-17). *E-democracy in the developing context - The citizen perspective.* Paper presented at the 3rd International Conference on Politics and Information Systems - Technologies and Applications/International Symposium on Social and Organizational Informatics and Cybernectics, Orlando, FL.

Varavithya, W., & Esichaikul, V. (2003, Sep 01-05). *The development of electronic government: A case study of Thailand.* Paper presented at the 2nd International Conference on Electronic Government (EGOV 2003), Prague, Czech Republic.

Varavithya, W., & Esichaikul, V. (2005, Jul). *Using the composite act frame technique to model 'Rules of Origin' knowledge representations in e-government services.* Paper presented at the 9th Pacific Asia Conference on Informataion Systems (PACIS 2005), Bangkok, THAILAND.

Vassilakis, C., Laskaridis, G., Lepouras, G., Rouvas, S., & Georgiadis, P. (2002, Sep 02-06). *Transactional e-government services: An integrated approach.* Paper presented at the 1st International Conference on Electronic Government (EGOV 2002), Aix Provence, France.

Vassilakis, C., Lepouras, G., & Halatsis, C. (2007). A knowledge-based approach for developing multi-channel e-government services. [Article]. *Electronic Commerce Research and Applications, 6*(1), 113-124.

Vaughan, D. M., Real, C. R., McGuire, T., Swift, J., Peters, A., & Moskovitz, R. (2004, Jul 27-31). *An E-government Web portal for dissemination of geotechnical data.* Paper presented at the Conference on Geotechnical Engineering for Transportation Projects (Geo-Trans 2004), Los Angeles, CA.

Verginadis, G., Gouscos, D., & Mentzas, G. (2004, Aug 30-Sep 03). *Modeling e-government service workflows through recurring patterns.* Paper presented at the 3rd International Conference on Electronic Government (EGOV 2004), Zaragoza, SPAIN.

Vergnolle, S., Amin, N., & Pritchard, H. (2007, Jun 21-22). *Review and contrast of the French and German approaches to e-democracy.* Paper presented at the 7th European Conference on e-Government (ECEG 2007), The Hague, NETHERLANDS.

Verhoosel, J., & Akkersdijk, V. (2004, Oct 27-29). *eGovernment for businesses: Lessons learned from a trajectory for standardization of business information.* Paper presented at the eChallenges e-2004 Conference, Vienna, AUSTRIA.

Virili, F. (2001, Sep 03-07). *The Italian e-government action plan: from gaining efficiency to rethinking goverment.* Paper presented at the 12th International Conference on Database and Expert Systems Applications (DEXA), Munich, Germany.

Viscusi, G., Thevenet, L. H., & Salinesi, C. (2008, Jun 16-20). *Strategic alignment in the context of e-services - An empirical investigation of the INSTAL approach using the Italian eGovernment initiative case study.* Paper presented at the 20th International Conference on Advanced Information Systems Engineering, Montpellier, FRANCE.

Voss, A., Roeder, S., & Marker, O. (2003, May 26-28). *Optimizing cooperation in spatial planning for eGovernment.* Paper presented at the 4th Annual International Working Conference on Knowledge Management in Electronic Government, Rhodes, Greece.

Votis, K., Alexakos, C., & Likothanassis, S. (2008, Sep 24-26). *The Impact of a Service Oriented Approach as an Enabler for E-Government Educational Services for All Citizens.* Paper presented at the 1st World Summit on the Knowledge Society (WSKS 2008), Athens, GREECE.

Vriens, D., & Achterbergh, J. (2003). Planning local E-government. [Article]. *Information Systems Management, 21*(1), 45-57.

Waksberg-Guerrini, A., & Aibar, E. (2007, Sep 03-07). *Towards a network government? A critical analysis of current assessment methods for e-government.* Paper presented at the 6th International Conference on Electronic Government, Regensburg, GERMANY.

Wang, J., Cao, J., Leckie, J. O., & Zhang, S. S. (2004, Sep 14-16). *Managing E-Government IT infrastructure: An approach combining autonomic computing and awareness based collaboration.* Paper presented at the 4th International Conference on Computer and Information Technology, Wuhan, PEOPLES R CHINA.

Wang, J. B., & Wang, H. C. (2007, Dec 05-06). *E-government: Governance mode innovation in a knowledge-based economy.* Paper presented at the 4th International Conference on Innovation and Management, Ube, JAPAN.

Wang, K., Cai, Z., Li, Z. X., & Zhou, L. H. (2005, Dec 05-08). *A disaster recovery system model in an e-Government system.* Paper presented at the 6th International Conference on Parallel and Distributed Computing, Applications and Technologies (PDCAT 2005), Dalian, PEOPLES R CHINA.

Wang, L. H., Qin, Z., & Han, G. (2005, Jul 20-21). *Internet use and e-government performance: A conceptual model.* Paper presented at the 12th International Conference on Management Science and Engineering, Incheon, SOUTH KOREA.

Wang, N., Li, H. M., Ye, X., & Gao, G. W. (2004, Aug 08-10). *The research on the whole structure of information resource conformity in the Comprehensive Service Portal of E-Government Affairs.* Paper presented at the International Conference on Management Science and Engineering, Harbin, PEOPLES R CHINA.

Wang, N., Zhang, W. Y., Wang, X. F., & Liu, L. (2007, Oct 14-16). *A research on dissipative structure of the information resource organization of e-government.* Paper presented at the 2nd International Conference on Research and Practical Issues of Enterprise Information Systems, Beijing, PEOPLES R CHINA.

Wang, R. W., & Chen, J. X. (2008, Aug 12-19). *Querying Web services based on ontology in e-government.* Paper presented at the 7th International Conference on Information and Management Sciences, Urumchi, PEOPLES R CHINA.

Wang, S., Kim, A., & Shin, H. K. (2007, Aug 26-27). *A research on multilateral cooperation system of public crisis management based on the e-government in China.* Paper presented at the 2nd International Workshop on Information Systems for Crisis Response and Management, Harbin, PEOPLES R CHINA.

Wang, S. G., Liu, R., Liu, X. T., Yuan, Y. J., & Li, G. (2008, May 15-17). *A Framework of Developing Web-Based Applications for E-Government.* Paper presented at the International Conference on Informational Technology and Environmental System Science, Jiaozuo, PEOPLES R CHINA.

Wang, X. D., Shang, X. L., & Fan, K. (2007, Oct 10-12). *Research on implementation of E-government integrated information services.* Paper presented at the 7th IFIP International Conference on e-Business, e-Service, and e-Society, Wuhan, PEOPLES R CHINA.

Wang, Y. F., Zhou, H. R., Jing, Z. L., Xiang, L. H., & Cai, W. J. (2006, Oct 21-23). *The exploration of urban gridded management in E-government.* Paper presented at the 5th International Conference on Grid and Cooperative Computing (GCC 2006), Hunan, PEOPLES R CHINA.

Wang, Y. L., Pan, H., Li, T., & Ieee (2007, Mar 20-24). *The data mining of the E-government on the basis on fuzzy logic.* Paper presented at the IEEE International Conference on Integration Technology, Shenzhen, PEOPLES R CHINA.

Wang, Y. L., Song, L. H., Li, T., & Su, Q. T. (2007, Oct 20-22). *The application of E-Government on the correct convergence of the EM algorithm.* Paper presented at the 2nd International Conference on Intelligent Information Management Systems and Technology, Yantai, PEOPLES R CHINA.

Wang, Y. S., & Liao, Y. W. (2006, Jun 14-18). *Assessing e-government systems success: A validation of the DeLone and McLean model of information systems success.* Paper presented at the 11th Annual Conference of the Asia-Pacific-Decision-Sciences-Institute, Kowloon, PEOPLES R CHINA.

Wang, Y. S., & Liao, Y. W. (2008). Assessing eGovernment systems success: A validation of the DeLone and McLean model of information systems success. [Article]. *Government Information Quarterly, 25*(4), 717-733.

Wang, Z. Y., Qi, D. Y., Qiu, S. S., & ieee (2004, Aug 26-29). *Design of finance service platform of E-government architecture in one-station service infrastructure.* Paper presented at the International Conference on Machine Learning and Cybernetics, Shanghai, PEOPLES R CHINA.

Wangpipatwong, S., & Chutimaskul, W. (2005, Aug 15-17). *E-government web quality assessment: A citizen-centric approach.* Paper presented at the 9th IASTED International Conference on Internet and Multimedia Systems and Applications, Honolulu, HI.

Wassenaar, A. (2000, Sep 04-08). *E- governmental value chain models - E-government from a business (modelling) perspective.* Paper presented at the 11th International Workshop on Database and Expert Systems Applications, London, England.

Wastell, D., Kawalek, P., Newman, M., Willetts, M., & Langmead-Jones, P. (2004, Jul 15-17). *Building capacity for E-government: Contradictions and synergies in the dialectics of action research.* Paper presented at the Conference on Relevant Theory and Informed Practice - Looking Foward from a 20-Year Perspective on IS Research, Manchester, ENGLAND.

Wastell, D. G. (2002, Dec 12-14). *Organizational discourse as a social defense: T0aming the tiger of electronic government.* Paper presented at the Working Conference on Global and Organizational Discourse about Information Technology, Barcelona, Spain.

Wauters, P. (2006). Benchmarking e-government policy within the e-Europe programme. [Article]. *Aslib Proceedings, 58*(5), 389-403.

Wei, X. J., & Zhao, J. (2005, Aug 15-17). *Citizens' requirement analysis in chinese e-government.* Paper presented at the 7th International Conference on Electronic Commerce (ICEC 2005), Xian, PEOPLES R CHINA.

Wei, Y. M., Fang, Z. Y., Dai, Z. M., Han, X., & Xu, F. Y. (2006, Nov 21-24). *A MPLS and VPN based eGovernment System.* Paper presented at the 15th International Conference on Computing, Mexico City, MEXICO.

Welch, E. W., Hinnant, C. C., & Moon, M. J. (2005). Linking citizen satisfaction with e-government and trust in government. [Article]. *Journal of Public Administration Research and Theory, 15*(3), 371-391.

Welch, E. W., & Pandey, S. K. (2007). E-government and bureaucracy: Toward a better understanding of intranet implementation and its effect on red tape. [Article]. *Journal of Public Administration Research and Theory, 17*(3), 379-404.

Welp, Y. (2007, Mar 14-15). *Latin America in the e-government era. Analysis of the introduction of new technologies to the improvement of democracy and government.* Paper presented at the International Conference on Direct Democracy in Latin America, Buenos Aires, ARGENTINA.

Wen, J., & Cheng, L. H. (2007, Aug 05-09). *Innovation in e-government initiatives: New website service interfaces and market creation - The Taiwan experience.* Paper presented at the Conference of the Portland-International-Center-for-Management-of-Engineering-and-Technology (PICMET 2007), Portland, OR.

Wescott, C. G. (2004, Jul 21-25). *e-government in the Asia-Pacific region: Progress and challenges.* Paper presented at the International Conference on Politics and Information Systems, Orlando, FL.

West, D. M. (2004). E-government and the transformation of service delivery and citizen attitudes. [Article]. *Public Administration Review, 64*(1), 15-27.

Westbrook, L. (2008). E-government support for people in crisis: An evaluation of police department website support for domestic violence survivors using "person-in-situation" information need analysis. [Review]. *Library & Information Science Research, 30*(1), 22-38.

Westholm, H. (2002, Sep 02-06). *e-democracy goes ahead. The Internet as a tool for improving deliberative policies?* Paper presented at the 1st International Conference on Electronic Government (EGOV 2002), Aix Provence, France.

Whitson, T. L., & Davis, L. (2001). Best practices in electronic government: Comprehensive electronic information dissemination for science and technology. [Article]. *Government Information Quarterly, 18*(2), 79-91.

Wiesmaier, A., Lippert, M., Karatsiolis, V., Raptis, G., & Buchmann, J. (2005, Jun 20-23). *An evaluated certification services system for the German national root CA - Legally binding and trustworthy transactions in e-business and e-Government.* Paper presented at the International Conference on E-Business, Enterprise Information Systems, E-Government and Outsourcing, Las Vegas, NV.

Willemson, J., & Ansper, A. (2008, Mar 04-07). *A secure and scalable infrastructure for inter-organizational data exchange and eGovernment applications.* Paper presented at the 3rd International Conference on Availability, Reliability and Security, Barcelona, SPAIN.

Williams, C. (2007, Sep 27). *24-7 government, the permanent campaign, and e-democracy: An analysis of Massachusetts governor Deval Patrick's interactive website.* Paper presented at the 3rd International Conference on e-Government, Montreal, CANADA.

Williams, M. E. (1986). ONLINE GOVERNMENT DATABASES - AN ANALYSIS. [Article]. *Online Review, 10*(4), 227-236.

Williamson, A., Dawson, A., & Barton, J. (2004, Jul 21-25). *ASPECT: Digital election ephemera to support e-democracy in Scotland.* Paper presented at the International Conference on Politics and Information Systems, Orlando, FL.

Wimmer, M., & Traunmuller, R. (2000, Sep 04-08). *Trends in electronic government: Managing distributed knowledge.* Paper presented at the 11th International Workshop on Database and Expert Systems Applications, London, England.

Wimmer, M., & von Bredow, B. (2001, Sep 03-07). *E-government: Aspects of security on different layers.* Paper presented at the 12th International Conference on Database and Expert Systems Applications (DEXA), Munich, Germany.

Wimmer, M. A., Codagnone, C., & Ma, X. F. (2007, Sep 03-07). *Developing an e-government research roadmap: Method and example from E-GovRTD2020.* Paper presented at the 6th International Conference on Electronic Government, Regensburg, GERMANY.

Wimmer, M. A., & Holler, U. (2002, Oct 24-25). *Applying a holistic approach to develop user-friendly, customer-oriented e-Government portal interfaces.* Paper presented at the 7th ERCIM International Workshop on User Interfaces for All, Paris, France.

Wittmann, G., Breitschaft, M., Krabichler, T., & Stahl, E. (2007, Sep 03-07). *Selection of appropriate payment methods for e-government - Model and application.* Paper presented at the 6th International Conference on Electronic Government, Regensburg, GERMANY.

Wohlers, T. E. (2007, Jul 12-15). *E-government: Trends and sophistication at the local level of government.* Paper presented at the International Multi-Conference on Society, Cybernetics and Informatics, Orlando, FL.

Wolf, P., & Krcmar, H. (2005). Process-oriented E-Government evaluation. [Article]. *Wirtschaftsinformatik, 47*(5), 337-346.

Wolter, C., Plate, H., & Hebert, C. (2007, Sep 03-07). *Collaborative workflow management for eGovernment.* Paper presented at the 18th International Conference on Database and Expert Systems Applications, Regensburg, GERMANY.

Wong, W., & Welch, E. (2004). Does e-government promote accountability? A comparative analysis of website openness and government accountability. [Article]. *Governance-an International Journal of Policy and Administration, 17*(2), 275-297.

Wouters, K., Simoens, K., Lathouwers, D., & Preneel, B. (2008, Mar 04-07). *Secure and privacy-friendly logging for eGovernment services.* Paper presented at the 3rd International Conference on Availability, Reliability and Security, Barcelona, SPAIN.

Wu, J., Hu, B., & Ieee (2007, Dec 09-12). *Modeling and simulation of group behavior in e-government implementation.* Paper presented at the 2007 Winter Simulation Conference, Washington, DC.

Wulf, L. M., Kaylor, C., & Prosperi, D. C. (2004, Jul 21-25). *Local E-government: Concept and correlates.* Paper presented at the International Conference on Politics and Information Systems, Orlando, FL.

Xia, Y., & Huang, C. (2007, Oct 10-12). *Government information access: A decisive factor for e-government.* Paper presented at the 7th IFIP International Conference on e-Business, e-Service, and e-Society, Wuhan, PEOPLES R CHINA.

Xia, Y., Zhang, H., Zhang, L., & Xu, Z. (2008, Jul 27-31). *Application and Research of a New Multi-party Digital Signature Scheme in E-Commerce and E-Government.* Paper presented at the International Symposium on Distributed Computing and Applications to Business, Engineering and Science, Dalian, PEOPLES R CHINA.

Xiang, W. X., Wang, Y. H., Zhang, Z. Y., & Ieee (2008, Apr 06-08). *The research on business continuity planning of E-government based on information security risk management.* Paper presented at the IEEE International Conference on Networking, Sensing and Control, Sanya, PEOPLES R CHINA.

Xiao, J., Chen, H. X., Zhang, P. Z., & Zhou, J. T. (2004, Sep 15-17). *The application of a fast image indexing scheme in E-Government.* Paper presented at the 16th International Conference on Computer Communication (ICCC 2004), Beijing, PEOPLES R CHINA.

Xin, H., & Xue, F. R. (2003, Dec 07-10). *Workflow interoperability - Enabling Online approval in E-government.* Paper presented at the 2nd International Workshop on Grid and Cooperative Computing, Shanghai, PEOPLES R CHINA.

Xin, M. J., Wu, C., & Li, W. H. (2006, Jul 17-19). *An approach to self-adaptive active control mechanism to support E-government based on multi-agent system.* Paper presented at the 5th IEEE International Conference on Cognitive Informatics (ICCI 2006), Beijing, PEOPLES R CHINA.

Xin, X. (2004, Oct). *Analyze comparatively the relationship of e-government and government waste.* Paper presented at the 2nd International Conference of Value Engineering and Technology Innovation of Enterprise, Hangzhou, PEOPLES R CHINA.

Xiong, J. A. (2006). Current status and needs of Chinese e-government users. [Article]. *Electronic Library, 24*(6), 747-762.

Xu, M. J., Zhi, W. T., & Tan, B. L. (2005, Jun 04-05). *Application of QFD for e-government planning at county level.* Paper presented at the 4th Wuhan International Conference on E-Business - Global Business Interface, Wuhan, PEOPLES R CHINA.

Xu, W. H. (2006, May 27-28). *Local e-government in China: A study in the context of administration reformation.* Paper presented at the 5th Wuhan International Conference on E-Business, Wuhan, PEOPLES R CHINA.

Xu, Y., Tang, S. Q., Xu, Y. W., & Li, L. (2007, Jul 25-27). *On tackling changes with aspect oriented technologies for E-Government services.* Paper presented at the 2nd International Conference on Computer Science and Education, Wuhan, PEOPLES R CHINA.

Yammine, A. (2002, Sep 02-06). *A new approach to the phenomenon of e-Government: Analysis of the public discourse on e-Government in Switzerland.* Paper presented at the 1st International Conference on Electronic Government (EGOV 2002), Aix Provence, France.

Yan, L., & Yang, J. M. (2007, Oct 10-12). *Business models of E-government: Research on dynamic E-government based on web services.* Paper presented at the 7th IFIP International Conference on e-Business, e-Service, and e-Society, Wuhan, PEOPLES R CHINA.

Yang, B., Li, Q., & Zuo, M. Y. (2007, Oct 14-16). *Analysis of e-government outsourcing.* Paper presented at the 2nd International Conference on Research and Practical Issues of Enterprise Information Systems, Beijing, PEOPLES R CHINA.

Yang, B., & Shen, F. (2002, May 23-26). *E-government: The case study of Nanhai's e-government practice.* Paper presented at the International Conference on E-Business (ICEB2002), Beijing, Peoples R China.

Yang, D., Tong, L. X., & Ieee (2006, Jun 21-23). *Modeling e-government administrative processes using unified modeling language.* Paper presented at the IEEE International Conference on Service Operations and Logistics and Informatics, Shanghai, PEOPLES R CHINA.

Yang, D., Tong, L. X., Ye, Y., & Wu, H. W. (2006, Sep 03-07). *Applying CommonKADS and semantic web technologies to ontology-based e-government knowledge systems.* Paper presented at the 1st Asian Semantic Web Conference, Beijing, PEOPLES R CHINA.

Yang, D. H., Kim, S., Nam, C., & Lee, I. G. (2004, Aug 30-Sep 03). *The future of e-government: Collaboration across citizen, business, and government.* Paper presented at the 3rd International Conference on Electronic Government (EGOV 2004), Zaragoza, SPAIN.

Yang, D. J., Han, Y. B., & Xiong, J. H. (2007, Oct 10-12). *EGovGrid: A service-grid-based framework for e-government interoperability.* Paper presented at the 7th IFIP International Conference on e-Business, e-Service, and e-Society, Wuhan, PEOPLES R CHINA.

Yang, F., & Wu, M. H. (2006, May 27-28). *RE-SVM: Improving the safety in e-government of China by information retrieval based on SVM.* Paper presented at the 5th Wuhan International Conference on E-Business, Wuhan, PEOPLES R CHINA.

Yang, K. F. (2003). Neoinstitutionalism and e-government - Beyond Jane Fountain. [Article]. *Social Science Computer Review, 21*(4), 432-442.

Yang, L. Q., Lu, Y., & Fu, G. (2005, Aug 15-17). *Study on e-government construction.* Paper presented at the 7th International Conference on Electronic Commerce (ICEC 2005), Xian, PEOPLES R CHINA.

Yang, Q., & Chen, W. J. (2007, Sep 25-26). *Study on public emergency command platform based on E-government network.* Paper presented at the 1st International Conference on Risk Analysis and Crisis Response, Shanghai, PEOPLES R CHINA.

Yang, W. (2003, Nov 28-30). *Study on the Chinese reform and e-government adaptability.* Paper presented at the International Conference on Management of e-Commerce and e-Government, Nanchang, PEOPLES R CHINA.

Yang, X. Y. (2005, Aug 15-17). *Single system, EDI system and H2000 system - Case study of CIQ development in E-Government system.* Paper presented at the 7th International Conference on Electronic Commerce (ICEC 2005), Xian, PEOPLES R CHINA.

Yao, G. G., Qin, Z., & Wu, Z. L. (2005, Apr 23-25). *Assessment on maintenance cost of electronic government: A perspective of system entropy.* Paper presented at the 11th International Conference on Industrial Engineering and Engineering Management, Shenyang, PEOPLES R CHINA.

Yao, X. M., Tan, Y. D., & Qian, Q. Q. (2005, Jun 20-23). *Building an adaptive e-government in a changing environment: a fractal and ADS approach.* Paper presented at the International Conference on E-Business, Enterprise Information Systems, E-Government and Outsourcing, Las Vegas, NV.

Ye, X., Niu, G. X., & Dai, Z. L. (2008, May 23-25). *Research on flexible control on dynamic business process in e-government.* Paper presented at the International Symposium on Information Processing (ISIP 2008)/International Pacific Workshop on Web Mining and Web-based Application (WMWA 2008), Moscow, RUSSIA.

Yidiz, M. (2007). E-government research: Reviewing the literature, limitations, and ways forward. [Review]. *Government Information Quarterly, 24*(3), 646-665.

Yildirim, I., Demir, B., Erturk, S., & Ieee (2006, Apr 16-19). *3-dimensional modelling and visualization of cultural assets for e-government.* Paper presented at the IEEE 14th Signal Processing and Communications Applications, Antalya, TURKEY.

Yildiz, M. (2007). Impact of the international organizatons 39 on the e-government policies of Turkiye. [Article]. *Amme Idaresi Dergisi, 40*(2), 39-+.

Yoo, N. (2008, Aug 19-21). *A SOA-based vulnerability system engineering for E-government solution.* Paper presented at the International Conference on Systems Engineering, Las Vegas, NV.

Yoo, N., Choi, H. A., & Insticc (2006, May 23-27). *A SOA-based system interface control for E-Government.* Paper presented at the 8th International Conference on Enterprise Information Systems (ICEIS 2006), Paphos, CYPRUS.

Yu, C. C. (2008, Aug 31-Sep 05). *Building a Value-Centric e-Government Service Framework Based on a Business Model Perspective.* Paper presented at the 7th International Conference on Electronic Government, Turin, ITALY.

Yu, M., & Wang, Y. Z. (2003, Aug 15-17). *Research on electronic government affairs official system characteristics analysis & the relative reference model.* Paper presented at the International Conference on Management Science and Engineering, Atlanta, Ga.

Yu, N. (2003, Oct 24-27). *E-government promoting the informatization of small and medium-sized enterprises.* Paper presented at the 3rd International Conference on Electronic Commerce Engineering, Hangzhou, Peoples R China.

Yun, H., Guo, S. J., & Liu, Q. Y. (2005, Jun 04-05). *Empirical analysis of the e-government development level of Chinese foreign trade and economic cooperation.* Paper presented at the 4th Wuhan International Conference on E-Business - Global Business Interface, Wuhan, PEOPLES R CHINA.

Zahan, E., & Costake, N. (2007, Sep 27). *Priorities for e-Government in European transforming countries. Example of Romania.* Paper presented at the 3rd International Conference on e-Government, Montreal, CANADA.

Zhang, A. R., & Guo, X. (2008, Oct 17-19). *Study on motivation mechanism of citizens' participation under the conditions of e-government.* Paper presented at the 2nd International Conference on Management of e-Commerce and e-Government, Nanchang, PEOPLES R CHINA.

Zhang, J. H. (2002). Will the government 'serve the people'? The development of Chinese e-government. [Article]. *New Media & Society, 4*(2), 163-184.

Zhang, N., & Alfred, U. (2007, May 26-27). *A framework for government process management under electronic government environment.* Paper presented at the 6th Wuhan International Conference on E-Business, Wuhan, PEOPLES R CHINA.

Zhang, P., & Wang, Y. Z. (2003, Aug 15-17). *Study on the knowledge management system in E-government.* Paper presented at the International Conference on Management Science and Engineering, Atlanta, Ga.

Zhang, P., Wang, Y. Z., & Wang, X. H. (2006, Dec 18-22). *Research on the integration in E-government based on multi-agent.* Paper presented at the IEEE/WIC/ACM International Conference on Web Intelligence and Intelligent Agent Technology (WI-IAT 2006), Hong Kong, PEOPLES R CHINA.

Zhang, P. Z., Xu, F. F., Jiang, L. Q., & Ge, R. Y. (2005, Aug 15-17). *G2C e-government: Shanghai social security and citizen services.* Paper presented at the 7th International Conference on Electronic Commerce (ICEC 2005), Xian, PEOPLES R CHINA.

Zhang, S., Makedon, F., Ford, J., Sudborough, C., Ai, L., Kapidakis, S., et al. (2004, Aug 30-Sep 03). *An international trade negotiation framework for e-government.* Paper presented at the 3rd International Conference on Electronic Government (EGOV 2004), Zaragoza, SPAIN.

Zhang, X., Chi, T. H., Chen, H. B., Zhao, H. R., & Ieee, I. I. (2003, Jul 21-25). *Research on electronic government oriented geographic information service system.* Paper presented at the 23rd International Geoscience and Remote Sensing Symposium (IGARSS 2003), Toulouse, France.

Zhang, X. Y., Han, G. Q., Li, B., Zou, K., & Li, W. (2008, Apr 07-09). *An e-government platform based on multi-tier architecture.* Paper presented at the 5th International Conference on Information Technology - New Generations, Las Vegas, NV.

Zhang, Z. J., Sun, J., Liu, H. L., & Chen, J. Y. (2004, Aug 08-10). *Research and realization on a customized service of E-government system.* Paper presented at the International Conference on Management Science and Engineering, Harbin, PEOPLES R CHINA.

Zhao, G. Q., & Yan, H. (2008, May 15-17). *Inquiry on Information Division in the Electronic Government Information Access.* Paper presented at the International Conference on Informational Technology and Environmental System Science, Jiaozuo, PEOPLES R CHINA.

Zhao, X. Q., & Ye, J. (2008, Aug 04-05). *Analysis of the E-government Operation Services of China in the Present Situation.* Paper presented at the International Colloquium on Computing, Communication, Control, and Management, Guangzhou, PEOPLES R CHINA.

Zheng, Y. X., Lei, L., & Hai, W. (2007, Jul 23-27). *State-based process description model in Chinese E-government affair system.* Paper presented at the 31st Annual International Computer Software and Applications Conference, Beijing, PEOPLES R CHINA.

Zhou, P., & Le, Z. J. (2007, Oct 10-12). *A framework for web usage mining in electronic government.* Paper presented at the 7th IFIP International Conference on e-Business, e-Service, and e-Society, Wuhan, PEOPLES R CHINA.

Zhou, S. D., & Zhang, Z. J. (2006, Nov 08-20). *Applied research on the customized service in the E-government system.* Paper presented at the International Conference on Management Science and Engineering, Wuhan, AUSTRALIA.

Zhu, H. T., & Su, F. L. (2007, Oct 10-12). *An integrated model in e-government based on semantic web, web service and intelligent agent.* Paper presented at the 7th IFIP International Conference on e-Business, e-Service, and e-Society, Wuhan, PEOPLES R CHINA.

Zhu, X. N., & Mao, D. (2006, Oct 05-07). *Deconstruction and reconstruction of the value rationality of E-government in post-modernity linguistic context.* Paper presented at the 13th International Conference on Management Science and Engineering, Lille, FRANCE.

Ziedi, M. J., & Azizi, M. Z. (2008, Jan 04-06). *E-government and business : G to B (Government to Business) - Contribution of e-government to the performance of Tunisian businesses.* Paper presented at the 9th International-Business-Information-Management-Association Conference (IBIMA), Marrakech, MOROCCO.

Zissis, D., Papadopoulou, A. E., & Lekkas, D. (2008, May 04-07). *Enhancing security in the integration of e-Government - The e-School initiative.* Paper presented at the 4th International Conference on Web Information Systems and Technologies, Funchal, PORTUGAL.

Zobel, R. (2003, May 30-31). *E-government: European commission policies and activities.* Paper presented at the International Conference On Line Citizenship, Venice, ITALY.

Section V
E-Government Practice

Chapter XIII
Towards an E-Governance Grid for India (E-GGI):
An Architectural Framework for Citizen Services Delivery

C.S.R. Prabhu
National Informatics Centre, India

ABSTRACT

The National e-Governance Plan (NeGP) proposes citizen service delivery up to the village level through various channels including village kiosks. The citizen services to be delivered are going to be web services (as against the present simply web enabled services) based on the Service Oriented Architecture paradigm. These Web Services expect adequate networking and computing resources for effective and efficient service delivery. Grid computing is the new computing paradigm. According to Gartner, computing (scientific, business and e-governance based) will be completely transformed in this decade by using grid enabled web services to integrate across the Internet to share not only information and application but also computing power. The latest grid computing standard OGSA (Open Grid Services Architecture) integrates the power of the grid with that of the web services – both stateless and stateful, based on Service Oriented Architecture (SOA). Leveraging the power of grid computing for e-governance takes us towards an e-governance grid for India. Towards this objective, the existing computing networks such as NICNET with all its SAN Data Centres connected with each other and also the other state owned Data Centres and SWANs (State Wide Area Networks) are required to be connected with each other to ultimately form the e-Governance Grid of India (e-GGI). Once this is achieved, the web services which offer citizen services will be effectively supported by the powerful resources of this e-ggI, ensuring nonstop, fast and efficient delivery, with all the due backup, mirroring and recovery features in place. Then we can successfully operationalise Web Services Repositories at the District, State and National levels on the e-governance grid of India, thereby delivering citizen services across the country. An architectural framework for citizen services delivery is also proposed based on e-GGI.

INTRODUCTION

The National e-Governance Plan (NeGP) is an ambitious plan to achieve e-governance and deliver citizen services through the 100000 kiosks throughout the country including rural areas. These citizen services will have to be web services based on Service Oriented Architecture. This gigantic effort calls for extensive computing and network infrastructure and resources so as to meet the requirements of NeGP. Conventional technological approaches such as client server model of architecture or the central server model of architecture will not be able to meet the requirements of NeGP. The Storage Area Network (SAN) based Data Centres being set up by NIC and also various state governments will be the first step towards a more recent technological advancement, popularly described as "grid computing". In a "grid" of computer systems all the Data Centres (SAN) will be connected into a grid where in all the computational resources such as the CPUs, disk storage system, specialized software systems, etc., will be shared by all the users connecting to the grid and the users are expected to draw adequate computational power from the grid just like they draw electric power from the Power grid, ubiquitously and unlimited or at least more than adequate required for any authorized user.

According to Gartner, in the current decade all computing (including e-governance) will be completely transformed by using grid enabled web services to integrate across the Internet to share not only information and application (as of now) but also computing power (through grid computing). Sooner or later all the computing function in the world is thus expected to become grid based – to share resources – so as to minimize the cost by optimizing the utilization of the resources. In a country like India, where the government administration is structured in a 3 tier—Central, State and District levels—Web Services Repositories can be launched and operationalized in the same three levels in the grid.

OGSA (OPEN GRID SERVICES ARCHITECTURE): INTEGRATING WEB SERVICES (BASED ON SOA) WITH GRID COMPUTING

While the earlier versions of grid computing technology were supporting predominantly applications of scientific domain and thus were not concerned with the concept of Web Services (based on Service Oriented Architecture), the current grid technology initiatives are based upon the new standard OGSA or Open Grid Services Architecture, wherein the Web Services are integrated with grid technology so as to result in a win-win situation both for the Web Services (by higher resource provision) and grid technology (extending to the commercial or e-governance domain). As Web Services are increasingly becoming standardized, the ability of the "grid" to support Web Services is a key provision for effective delivery of services in any application domain, especially e-governance domain, wherein citizen services are being launched as Web Services over the grid for better and efficient service delivery. In fact, without the grid computing approach, Web Services may not even be possible to be launched at a large scale.

OGSA (Open Grid Services Architecture) is the latest standard evolved by Global Grid Forum (GGF) to integrate Web Services with grid computing. This Architecture integrates the conventional grid computing features such as resource allocation and monitoring, mirroring, etc., with Web Services facility. Citizen services which are basically Web Services, will be supported by grid computing features and facilities to ensure adequate resources and background processes to effectively operationalize them.

OGSA supports WSRF (Web Services Reference Framework) which provides standard architecture for Stateful Web Services (conventionally all Web Services are Stateless). Stateful Web Services will be useful for applications that require reference to data of past transactions, for continuity of processing (if such continuity is not essential, conventional (stateless) web services can be utilised).

GLOBUS TOOLKIT

Globus Toolkit (GT) is an open source, middleware software for the grid. It is the most popular and successful middleware evolved out of various experimental grids in the world. Today, it is almost the standard grid middleware software. Globus Toolkit Versions 1 and 2 did not support Web Services. From Version 3 onwards and the present Version 4 known as Globus Toolkit 4 or GT4 offers full fledged support for Web Services delivery in Java, C and Python. It provides various modules which are essential for grid computing, such as Grid Resource Allocation and Monitoring (GRAM), Grid File Transfer Protocol (GridFTP), data replication and monitoring (mirroring), Authentication and Authorization (through Public Key Infrastructure or PKI), etc. The Globus Toolkit Version 4 (GT4) has been installed and tested for its functionality in NICNET and can be utilized for any grid application in e-governance domain.

E-GOVERNANCE GRID OF INDIA (E-GGI)

The proposed e-Governance Grid of India envisages to design and implement a grid in India for e-governance service delivery across the country. With an objective to implement the National e-Governance Plan (NeGP), SAN Data Centres have been established in all the 35 States/UTs, through NIC, as a part of NICNET or independently by the State Governments. Similarly, State Wide Area Networks (SWANs) are also set up in various States either through NIC, as a part of NICNET or by the State Governments themselves. However, as of now, even through the State SAN Data Centres and SWANs are individually connected there is no concept of grid computing being implemented. The State SAN Data Centres are independently operating without any resource sharing or even without replica/mirroring storage elsewhere (only for Delhi Data Centre, a DRC (Disaster Recovery Centre) is operationalized at Hyderabad). The grid technology implementation, utilizing the middleware (such as Globus Toolkit) software can result in better utilization of the resources, while also providing the backup recovery features along with mirroring and replication services (in the remote sites in the grid). Security is also ensured through authentication and authorization for all users trying to access the grid, using the Public Key Infrastructure (PKI). This will result in overall productivity improvement, in addition to obtaining all the benefits of grid computing.

NATIONAL EGOV PLAN (NEGP)

The Govt. of India, Department of Information Technology, has initiated National e-Governance Plan (NeGP) for the execution of e-governance projects in the country, both at Central and State levels. It had identified "Mission Mode" Projects at both the levels as follows:

A. State Level:

Land Records
Road Transport
Property Registration
Agriculture
Treasuries
Municipalities
Gram Panchayats
Commercial Taxes

Police
Employment Exchanges

B. National Level
Income Tax
Company Affairs
Passport & Immigration
Insurance
National Citizen Database
Central Excise
Pensions
Banking

IMPLEMENTATION STRATEGY AND METHODOLOGY

Clearly, even though efforts are underway, it is a large task to complete the application software development for all these Mission Mode Projects. After the software development is completed, it calls for great efforts of implementation of these projects all over the country.

After the completion of the implementation of all these application software projects, they are required to be converted to web services based on the Service Oriented Architecture (SOA). After the completion of all the services being converted to Web services in the Service Oriented Architecture paradigm, we will have a three tier architectural framework as shown in Fig. 1.

All the sub-district level web services such as e-Panchayat, e-Municipality, e-Land Records, e-Registration will be grouped together under the category of "District level Web Services Repository" to be managed at the District level with District Data Centres.

All the State level applications (both as top level aggregation of district level applications and also independent state level applications) will be managed at the State Level Web Services Repositories located at State Data Centres.

Similarly, the aggregation at the National level and also nation-wide centrally controlled web services will be managed at National level Web Services Repository located at the National Data Centre.

The e-Governance Grid of India (e-GGI), discussed in previous section, will be the backbone IT infrastructure for this purpose.

All the Data Centres will have to be integrated with State Wide Area Networks into a grid (broadband) which will provide access to Internet/Intranet right from the village level. National portals and national web services will also be able to provide access to individual village portals.

As an example, the National Panchayat Portal will be the aggregate level entry point which will permit access to individual Panchayat Portals across the country.

The above action Plan needs to be implemented in a period of atleast five years. After the creation and integration of web services into web services repositories, a workflow interoperability plan can be executed using BPEL (Business Process Execution Language) which can enable process orchestration across diverse web services (based on Service Oriented Architecture.

In the above lines, a pilot attempt is being made in Andhra Pradesh State to integrate diverse web services such as Property Registration (CARD Project) and Land Records (LRMIS Project) with ePanchayat Project.

WEB SERVICES REPOSITORIES

Three Levels of e-governance Services can be identified and accordingly 3 level Web Services Repositories can be established:

a. National level Web Services Repository (NWSR) for National level e-governance initiatives of NeGP
b. State level Web Services Repository (SWSR) for the State level e-governance services, and

c. District (or Sub district) level Web Services Repository (DWSR) for the district and sub-district (taluka or village)

All this will be possible only if adequate computing, network and data infrastructure is made available. What is the appropriate and adequate infrastructure for achieving this? The requisite infrastructure can be categorized into:

a. Computing infrastructure (including software infrastructure)
b. Network infrastructure
c. Data infrastructure

PRE-REQUISITES FOR NATIONAL E-GOVERNANCE ARCHITECTURAL FRAMEWORK

What are the essential requirements for establishing a national framework for e-governance architecture?

The following can easily be identified as the essential pre-requisites:

a. Establishment of nation-wide broad band IP network, right upto the village level (by taking care of all the requirements such as power and bandwidth to form a National e-Governance Grid of India (e-GGI), described in the previous section)
b. A nation-wide unique citizen identification mechanism (using the latest technology such as Iris identification and smart cards)

E-GOVERNANCE ARCHITECTURAL FRAMEWORK

With the above pre-requisites in place (which call for a concerted effort at the national level), the following e-governance architectural framework (Figure 1) can be established:

The action plan for achieving this will be:

Step 1
Development and implementation of web services (based on SOA – Service Oriented Architecture) for all the e-governance applications (such as ePanchayat for Village Panchayats, eMunicipality for Municipalities) at various tiers of the government, as indicated.

Step 2
Establishing web services repositories at three levels

a. District level
b. State level
c. National level

Step 1 above includes the software development and implementation of information systems for various levels such as Villages, Municipalities, Talukas, Districts, State and National levels – all this being converted to web services based on Services Oriented Architecture (SOA). The National e-Governance Plan (NeGP) clearly envisages all these services in all its Mission Mode Projects as indicated above.

All these activities will take place on e-Governance Grid of India, comprising National Data Centre, all State Data Centres and the (proposed) District Data Centres, all connected in a grid of broadband network.

CONCLUSION

In this chapter we have presented the proposed e-Governance Grid of India (e.GGI) to support the Web Services Repositories at National, State and District levels for service delivery to citizens as per the National e-Governance Plan (NeGP).

The architectural framework given in this chapter serves as the blueprint for the effective implementation of National e-Governance

Figure 1. Web services repositories on e-Governance Grid of India (e-GGI)

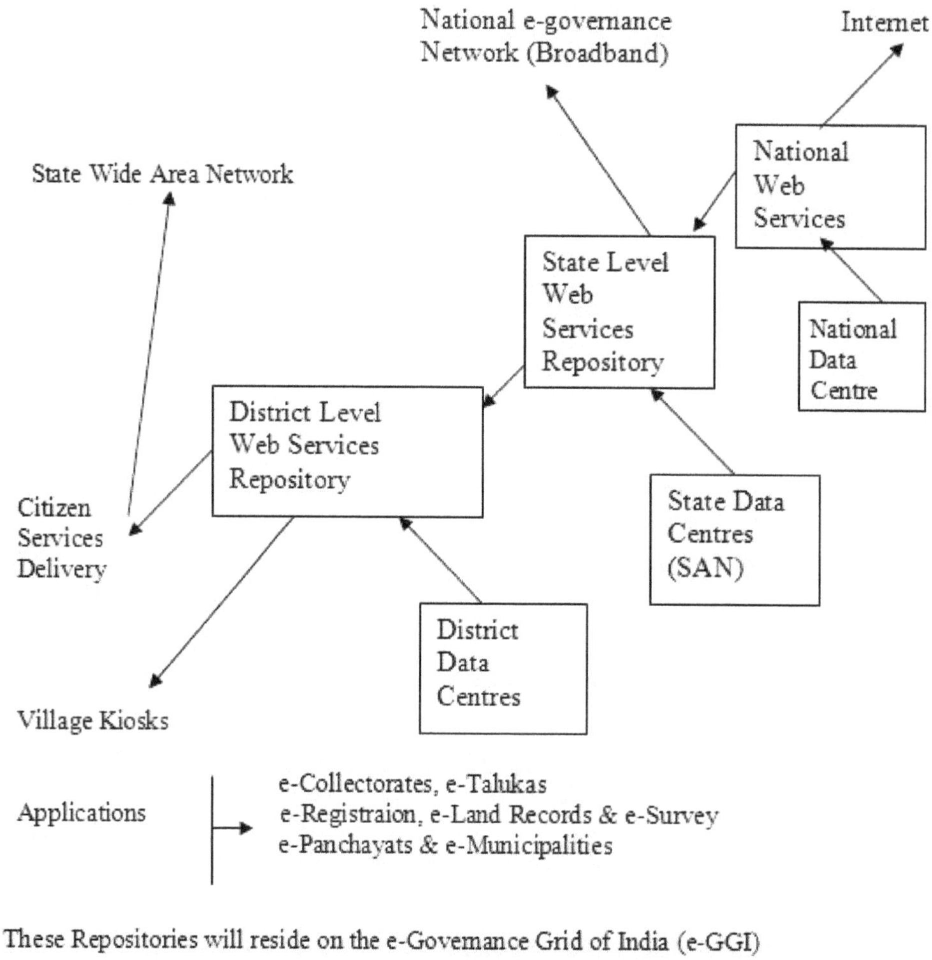

Plan (NeGP) in the country. In fact, without this framework of action and implementation, it may not be possible to implement NeGP to its completion with its large objectives of Citizen Services Delivery. This framework represents the state of the art technological architectural opportunity to implement NeGP. Without this approach (with continued status quo approach) the effective and efficient utilization of national computing resources all over the country will not be possible, thereby making it difficult to achieve the successful implementation of NeGP in its full scope, content and objectives.

In comparison with the successful architectural framework of e-governance in other advanced countries such as the United States and other European Union, it may be noted that the grid technology has not yet been applied to e-governance framework projects in any country in the world. The U.S. Federal Enterprise Architecture (FEA), based on which the bulk of e-governance service delivery (for example FirstGov.gov) has taken place, was built several years ago before the grid computing paradigm could be applied to e-governance. Similarly, in the European Union, the e-governance projects as Eu-Publi.com, e-Gov, FASME have their own architectural frameworks to deliver citizen services across Europe successfully. Even though they are successful projects, grid computing paradigm had not been used even in the European Union, due to the recent nature of grid computing technology and its application to e-governance. (Earlier grid computing technology was applied only in scientific research). In fact, if implemented, the e-governance grid of India will be the first ever national level e-governance grid architectural framework in the world which will leverage the technological benefits and strengths of grid technology for the effective delivery of e-governance services to the citizens at large.

Chapter XIV
E-Halli:
An Opportunity to Become Rural Entrepreneurs

Swamy Tribhuvananda H.V.
Bapuji Institute of Engineering & Technology, India

Gopakumar K.
Bapuji Institute of Engineering & Technology, India

ABSTRACT

ICTs are increasingly being recognized by the people across the globe as essential tools of development – tools that can empower them, enhance skills and increase productivity. Today, the realities have changed. The world is not what it was during their times. Technology, science and other aspects of affluence have widened the gulf between rich and poor. On the other hand, they have also brought the world closer, in terms of connectivity. This has resulted in stupendous growth in terms of information exchange, business, education, agriculture, infotainment, inventions and better contact between places and people. The concept that the authors are about to present represents this very dream of bringing villages, towns, and cities closer, in more ways than tying them by technology. This chapter mainly reviews the conceptual frame work of e-halli. The second section deals with the e-halli as a business perspective.

INTRODUCTION

We need to have a system that coordinates rural knowledge and information networks would be useful in helping get development information circulated on agriculture and non-agricultural subjects. Communications support for rural development is challenged by the need for financial sustainability of the systems established. It is suggested three essentials for rural development through Information systems: one, organize networks of rural knowledge and information centers for rural development that would respond to observed and expressed rural development needs; two, develop appropriate ICT programs, which continually install and maintain new information and communication technologies, especially computers with Internet access; three, establish mechanisms for linkages with public and private sector agencies and organizations, institutes and centers.

The information system (***e-halli***) is intended as a vehicle for sharing ideas, knowledge and information with the various stakeholders addressing the causes, and seeking solutions, for rural development.

ABOUT E-HALLI

Though cities depend on villages for every thing needed for survival like food grains and marketing of every kind of consumer products but they have an edge over information needed for all such activities. The villages are forced to depend on cities to get this information at the time of the need.

This has created an imbalance in the flow of information in the system and is affecting the overall development of our nation. This system has to be balanced in order to bridge the gap between the resources and the end point of the usage.

Based on this thinking, the initiative has been taken to develop a portal which can focus on bridging the gap. In order to bridge this divide, ***e-halli*** (which means electronic village in Kannada) project has been taken up. This ***e-halli*** project is based on the concept PURA (Providing Urban amenities in Rural Area), the dream of taking technology and its benefits to rural areas.

"e-grama" is basically an Intranet Portal, having some static and dynamic pages with Intranet e-mailing facility among different users of the Intranet. The e-halli project implemented at Central part of Karnataka as a pilot project to bring the benefits of Information and Communication Technology (ICT) to all the rural mass.

Before venturing into an unknown world of information flow and its effects, detailed studies were conducted to understand the needs of the rural people. Based on these studies, a more scientific, practical, relevant and state-of-the art project called ***e-halli*** was conceptualized and is being run as a pilot project in about 10 villages across Karnataka.

The ***e-halli*** project is conceptualized and implemented by Yeshaswini Nagara Hagu Grameena Abhivruddhi Parishat (R), a Non Governmental Organization. This IT-enabled project will not only help bridge the growing digital divide, but also increase computer literacy of those living in rural areas. It is also expected to generate more employment opportunities in these regions and reduce migration of educated unemployed youths to cities.

There are four levels of operations:

- Support Network
- Software Network
- Economic Support Network
- Research Support Network

Support Network: The project will be implemented with the basic structure shown in Figure 1.

Software Network: A core team of professionals with expertise in software development are developing the software. The software developed has the capability of providing AT THE POINT DATA ENTRY, a new inventive methodology where a window is provided at different information points like banks, Government offices etc., from where the information is directly entered in the formats and are readily available at the e-halli centers immediately. For ex: the tour program of District Collector (DC), once it is entered in the formats at the source, it can reach every e-halli instantaneously. This process avoids even the slightest delay in information dissipation and becomes more authentic. See Figure 2.

Economic Support Network: A specialized team who take care of supporting the VSP in various forms of revenue generation for the sustainability

Figure 1.

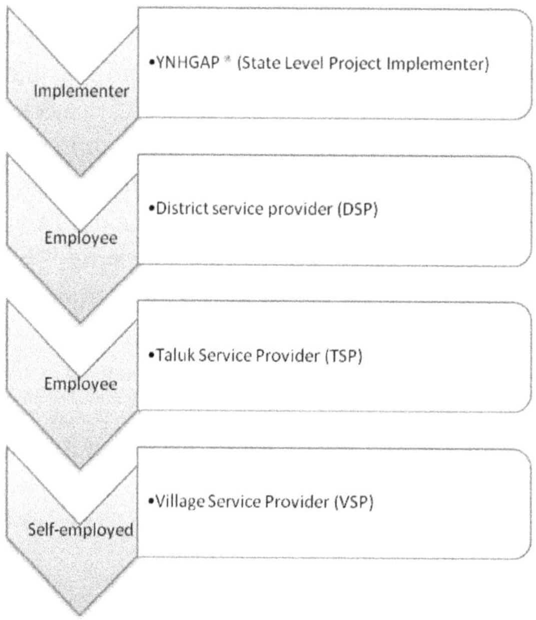

Figure 2.

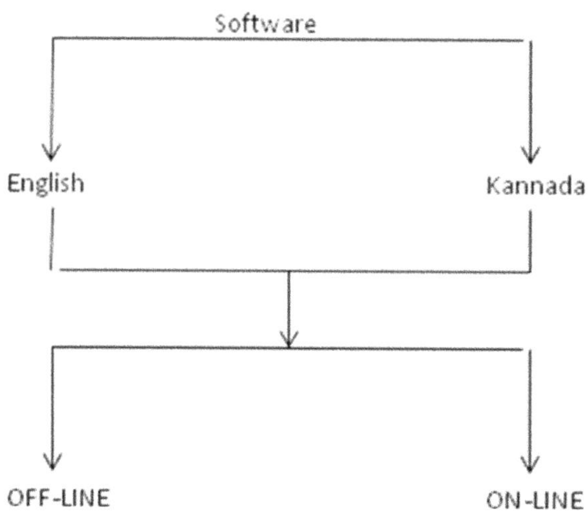

of the village centre. This team finds out the new methods of revenue generation and incorporates it to the use of village service centre.

Research Support Network: This support is established with a leading Management Consultancy which gives a professional and scientific feedback on a regular basis for the improvement of the project. The research team takes care of proper coordination amongst various entities involved in the project like, Government, Public Sector, Banking sector, Private sector and educational Institute.

IDENTIFICATION OF VILLAGE SERVICE PROVIDER

A village is selected and a service provider is chosen amongst the group satisfying the following criteria:

1. He / She should be the resident of the Village
2. He / She should have studied minimum up to 12th Standard.
3. Should have a basic computer knowledge
4. Should be willing work for long hours
5. Should have a good reputation in the village and nearby villages
6. Should be able to independently run the centre
7. Should possess a place to open up the centre at the village which can be accessed by every one
8. Should possess a telephone connection for internet connectivity

FINANCIAL SUPPORT

Selected candidates are helped to obtain a Bank Loan up to Rs. 100000 (Details are provided in the Annexure) from any Nationalized Bank to establish the e-halli centre. The process of tying up a bank for such schemes is underway to help the rural youth. The financial support could be provided either directly from the banks to the individual directly or through a centralized body and later distributed as micro finance. We have two options

- **First option:** Providing the loans directly to the individual, the individual will provide minimum security for such loans with the down payment of Rs. 10000/-. For such loans a tripartite agreement should be reached among the funding agency, YNHGAP and VSP. YNHGAP will take up the responsibility of proper repayment of the loan from the VSP.
- **Second option:** The funding agency can provide micro finance to YNHGAP, which can distribute the same to the VSPs. The collection and the repayment of loans will be done by YNHGAP.

TRAINING

Once a candidate is chosen, he / she will under go an in-house training for 1 month. These include the following:

1. Basic hardware training
2. E-halli software training
3. Entrepreneurship training
4. Business module development training and
5. Practical field training

SETUP

The e-halli centre will comprise of following equipment:

Desktop PC, Digital Camera, LCD Projector, All-in-one Printer, Speakers, Projection Screen, UPS with 5 hours backup, e-halli dual language software, soil testing kit, educational CD's, Internet connectivity with phone, required furniture and PCO phone with package.

SUPPORT

Complete support will be provided to the VSP. All the villages in a taluk are monitored by TSP, employed for the purpose. The TSP will monitor, guide and give all possible support to the VSPs of that taluk. Similarly the DSP will support all the TSPs of the district in coordination with YNHGAP.

REVENUE SHARING

Once the revenue is generated in the VSP, a part of it will be shared amongst YNHGAP, DSP, TSP and VSP.

WORKING MODULE

Unlike other projects which concentrate only on information dissipation, e-halli provides both information as well as the support to execute the information.

1. E-halli membership drive: every family in the village and adjoining village can become members by paying an annual fee of Rs. 90/-. The members have the following benefits
    - Rs. 100000/- accidental insurance for 1 year
    - Free access to any sort of information at the e-halli centre
    - Access to different varieties of information on various products, literatures available in the centre
    - Discount facilities in various hospitals, drug stores etc.
2. Proper information dissipation: the information in the centre is displayed through software, literatures, CDs etc., so all possible ways of information is dissipated. The members can access to any kind of information any time of the day.
3. Practical support for villages: e-halli centre provide support to the villagers to provide support in executing the information. For example, the member only can view the information about train reservations but also can get the reservations done through the network. E-halli provides complete support in opening of bank accounts, sending applications, ticket bookings, currency recharge, bill payments and many more.
4. Emphasis on mass education through state of the art technology: everyday different shows are projected on variety of subjects like education, health care, agriculture and modern technology. Along with the educational programs, e-halli has entered an agreement with various companies for providing details about their products. Such companies are charged on annual basis and the revenue generated is equally shared among all the existing VSPs.
5. Implementation of rural health care: e-halli has tied up with specialized hospitals and is running e-halli rural health care projects. With the specialized team from the hospital, different projects like HIV awareness camps, cancer detection camps for women, general health checkup, blood group and donation camps. Apart from these activities, health awareness film screening is also done.

REFERENCES

Ho, A.L. (2003). EO Allots 1-2% of RP Budget to E-Government Spending. *Inquirer News Service*, January 23. http://www.inq7.net/inf/2003/jan/24/inf_1-1.htm

Ho, J., Schraefel, M.C., & Chignell, M. (2000). Towards an Evaluation Methodology for the Development of Research-Oriented Virtual Communities. *Proceedings of the 9th International Workshops on Enabling Technologies:*

Infrastructure for Collaborative Enterprises, Maryland, (pp. 112-117).

Hodgkinson, S. (2002, November). The Victorian Electronic Records Strategy: Centre of Excellence Executive Briefing. http://www.prov.vic.gov.au/vers/published/versbriefing20021122.pdf

Jones, Q., & Rafaeli, S. (2000). Time to Split, Virtually: 'Discourse Architecture' and 'Community Building' as means to Creating Vibrant Virtual Metropolises. *Electronic Markets*, *10*(4), 214-223.

Karnjanatawe, K. (2003). *Government web sites fail user test – Information is out of date.* Bangkok Post, http://www.bangkokpost.com/290103_Database/29Jan2003_data03.html

Sangita, S.N., & Dash, B.C. (2006). *Electronic Governance and Service Delivery in India: Theory and Practice.* The Institute for Social and Economic Change, Bangalore.

WEB REFERENCES

http://orissagov.nic.in/e-magazine/Orissareview/jan2006/engpdf/e-gram.pdf, browsed on 23.05.2007

http://www.infovisiongroup.com/news/aug16-02.html, browsed on 20.04.2007

http://rural.nic.in/success.htm, browsed on 23.04.2007

ANNEXURE

Table 1. Annual minimum income generation for each VSP

Sl. No.	Particulars	Units	Calculation	No's	Unit Revenue (in Rs.)	Amount Generated	Expenditures		Net Income
							Expenses incurred	DSP Charges	
1	e-halli Memberships	Per individual		1000	90	90000	25000	25000	40000
2	e-halli Students Memberships	Student		2000	60	120000	50000	50000	20000
3	Soil Testing	Per Test		200	70	14000	7200	0	6800
4	Digital Photography	Per Photo	Rs. 100/Day * 365 Days (300 days)	3000	12	36000	18000	0	18000
5	DTP Work	Per page	100/Month * 12 Months	1200	10	12000	4800	0	7200
6	Browsing/Fax/E-mail	Per job		300	12	3600	1200	0	2400
7	Basic Computer Education	Per Student	4 students/Month* 12 Months	48	100	4800	2500	0	2300
8	Education Programs for 8,9 &10 Class	Per Student	100 Students * 9 Months	100	90	9000	1000	0	8000
9	Coin Phone	Per call	50 calls/Day*365 Days	18250	1	18250	10950	0	7300
10	Audio/Video CD Rentals	Per CD/Day	5 CDs/Day*365 Days	1825	10	18250	3650	0	14600
11	E-Produce Registration	Per Member	250 Members*Rs. 10	250	10	2500	750	0	1750
12	Mobile Currency Sales		Rs. 20000*12 Months	20000	12	240000	231600	0	8400
13	Corporate Advertisements	Per Company	(30 Companies * Rs. 8500 PM*12 Months)/240 Centers			12750	1275	0	11475
14	Commissions from others Sources	Per Job	1 Job/Day*365 Days	365	10	3650	730	0	2920

ANNEXURE

Table2. Monthly recurring expenses

Sl. No.	Particulars	Per Month	Annual Expenses
1	Rent	500	6000
2	Electricity Expenses	400	4800
3	Telephone & Internet	1000	12000
4	Bank Loan Repayment EMI/Month (Appx)	5000	60000
			82800
	Average Recurring Expense/Month	6900	
	Total Annual Income	68345	
	Average Monthly Net Income	5695.42	

Chapter XV
E-Government Implementation in Oman:
A Preliminary Investigation

Moaman Al-Busaidy
Brunel University, UK

Vishanth Weerakkody
Brunel University, UK

ABSTRACT

With the advancement of the Internet and supporting information and communication technologies, e-government has emerged as an effective means of delivering government services to citizens. In the recent past, e-government has become popular in many developing countries. Most notably are the Middle Eastern countries that have continued to invest significantly into e-government initiatives in the last five years. The aim of this chapter is to examine e-government activities in the Sultanate of Oman and to identify factors that are currently impeding e-government development and implementation in this country. While issues such as lack of legal frameworks, strategy, project plans, usability issues and information quality are identified in the published literature as impeding e-government progress in Oman, this research suggests that factors such as web accessibility and integration of various government agencies also pose a major challenge for e-government implementation in Oman.

1. INTRODUCTION

While commercial enterprises have been exploiting the business opportunities offered by the Internet for some time by engaging in e-business activities, public sector organizations have until recently failed to capitalize on the potential benefits of e-enabling their services. However, this notion is now beginning to change with many governments initiating e-government projects with a view of offering better and more accessible services to citizens. This shift has been facilitated largely as a result of the availability of innovative and cost effective ICT solutions and the evolution of the Internet. While developed countries have exploited the power of the Internet to successfully e-enable public services and entice citizens, developing countries have been comparatively slow in developing successful e-government strategies (Karunanada and Weerakkody, 2006; Weerakkody et al., 2007) .

With the number of e-government initiatives increasing from three in 1996 to over five hundred national initiatives (Al-Kibsi *et al.*, 2001), the benefits of e-government have been highlighted by many researchers. Given that the public sector is often classified as bureaucratic, inefficient and less technology savvy, e-government can be considered as a revolution that was waiting to happen, particularly in a developing country context. Given this context, e-government has the potential to radically change public sector agencies and offer many benefits that were previously not envisaged (Moulder, 2001).

E-government is the short form for electronic government, and it is also referred to as digital government, online government and even transformational government (Riley, 2003). E-government discusses the manner in which governments make use of the exchange of information and services that are pertinent with regards to citizens, individual businesses, and other governmental agencies to name a few (Welch, 2005). When e-government is implemented successfully, it will ensure that there is improvement in processes within government agencies, efficiency is achieved, and public services are better managed and delivered (Riley, 2003).

However, for e-government implementation to be widespread and successful, exemplary strategies and practices need to be identified in addition to establishing and prioritizing processes to be e-enabled. Furthermore, every e-government programme needs to have a clear idea of the proposed benefits to citizens, what challenges need to be overcome and the level of institutional change that needs to take place for it to be successful in a given context (Hazlett and Hill., 2003). While many developed countries have identified successful strategies and overcome obstacles to pioneer the e-government concept (Jones, 2007), developing countries such as Oman have much to learn in this context. However, there has been little research done to examine, for instance, the reasons for the lack of progress since the initiation of the national e-government project in Oman in 2003. Moreover, there is very little published literature (apart from UN reports) that identifies the issues impeding e-government efforts in Oman. This chapter aims to examine key issues that are currently influencing the implementation of e-government in Oman.

In order to achieve the aforementioned aim, the chapter is structured as follows. The next section briefly examines the benefits and challenges of e-government as published in the literature. This is followed by a brief overview of Oman and e-government implementation efforts in that country in section three. Next, a brief overview of the research approach used for this study is offered. In section five, a preliminary case study of e-government implementation in Oman is offered. The chapter then concludes by discussing the most salient issues currently influencing e-government implementation in Oman.

2. E-GOVERNMENT BENEFITS AND CHALLENGES: A LITERATURE PERSPECTIVE

The purpose of e-government according to Kostopoulos (2003) is to build a digital state where public services and information can be offered to citizens electronically. Choudrie et al., (2004) suggests that e-government has the potential to improve external and internal relationships among the various stakeholders involved in the government services delivery process (including citizens, government employees, external businesses etc) and facilitate sharing of knowledge among these stakeholders. For many governments, particularly in developing countries, reducing expenditure and cutting down the cost of running government institutions is also a major concern (Bwoma and Huang, 2003). For instance, e-government will eliminate the expenditure needed for building more physical premises and agencies around the country to provide government services to citizens. In addition, mismanagement and poor organization, particularly in developing countries is common and affects public expenditure. In this context, e-government can cut costs by making operations constrained online. Moreover, e-government will encourage the improved interaction and communication between governments and its citizens (Kostopoulos, 2003). Furthermore, e-government will also establish an environment where public agencies can remain open for 24/365 to serve their citizens and help establish a new line of services for the citizen (Bwoma and Huang, 2003). This environment will therefore reduce the need for direct contact with government agencies thereby reducing the cost for government and improving services for the citizens (Awan, 2003; Stoltzfus, 2004; Martin, 2000).

The result of the aforementioned developments will affect communication as well as bring about reforms on the terms and conditions for using government services. The use of ICTs will improve the whole process of government; not only how citizen will interact with such services, but also even help create greater trust between the government and their customers (Choudrie and et al., 2004). Moreover, e-government will reduce the time public sector employees have to spend in their offices, help create better polices, and improve the organizational competitiveness within all government sectors. Choudrie and et al., (2004) classifies two broad benefits of e-government, namely, improving government-citizen relationship, which talks about rapport between government and citizens, and gaining e-commerce benefits such as better cost management. As Belanger and Carter (2004) have highlighted the main similarity between e-commerce and e-government is that, in e-commerce, people exchange their goods and similarly in e-government citizens exchange information and services with the government.

Most researchers have mentioned similar type of relationships in e-government which revolve around Government to Government (G2G), Government to Business (G2B), and Government to Citizen (G2C) (Bwoma and Huang, 2003; Stoltzfus, 2004; Ndou, 2004; Chesi et al 2005). However, Bwoma and Huang (2003) noted one more type of relationship G2E, which explain the relation between the government and their employees. One of the most important issues in the G2G, G2C and G2B models is the integration between different government agencies. According to Belanger and Carter (2004) G2G can establish a standard system or network between government agencies for faster and more efficient information exchange between them. Even more, this can be done by using a common or standard computer language under a secure system to save the information within any type of online connection.

Researchers and practitioners also assert that e-government offers many benefits to citizens. Among the greatest benefits of e-government is improving IT infrastructure and reducing logistical costs, based on data integration of various government agencies (Al-Khouri and Bal 2007; United nation, 2003; Ndou, 2004; Chesi, 2005). For example, collecting all data require for citizens in one portal can ensure that citizens have the ability to explore and use all services from home or work. Moreover, there are many other benefits offered by e-government such as, improved business processes, globalization and increased use of the internet (Al-Khouri and Bal 2007).

Although there are vast advantages in implementing e-government, efforts have been obstructed by a number of challenges in developing and implementing e-government systems. Many challenges have been mentioned in different articles published in the last five years. Most common challenges are privacy and authentication (Al-

Khouri and Bal, 2007; Al-Joobri, 2006; Bwoma and Huang, 2003), accessibility (Al-Joobri, 2006; Abanumy et al, 2005; Choudrie and et al, 2004; Chesi 2005), infrastructure (Al-Khouri and Bal, 2007; Bwoma and Huang, 2003; Chesi, 2005), and information mismanagement (Bwoma and Huang, 2003; Chesi, 2005). In addition, Bwoma and Huang (2003) identified integration of technologies between government agencies, as a major obstacle for e-government implementation. In this context, using interoperability standards for building e-government systems will increase the flexibility of integration with other systems (Borras, 2004). However, although there is a real need for a common language to complete this process of integration, still many government agencies have their own regulatory environment and strategic priorities (Borras, 2004).

Furthermore, Abanumy et al., (2005) also note that website accessibility is a good measurement for e-government success, but at the same time serves as a barrier, because web accessibility will mean allowing universal use for the information. Thus, the success of e-government will depends on 'how user-friendly government websites will be' and 'what the website ability is' as well as 'how familiar the users are with various web based technologies' (Kostopoulos, 2003).

Another important issue with e-government development is the technical and software infrastructure requirements. This is one of the most costly aspects of e-government as transferring traditional government processes to an e-enables state where services are reliant on efficient enterprise applications and network infrastructure (i.e. high speed Internet connections) requires huge capital investments (UN, 2008). Moreover, accountability of limited financial resources, particularly in developing countries is an important challenge that governments need to manage well. Therefore, the stance adopted by governments should be one that is geared more towards the effective utilization of relevant resources as well as any foreign aid that is offered to finance e-government related projects (Al-Nahas, 2006).

3. A BRIEF OVERVIEW OF E-GOVERNMENT IN OMAN: CURRENT PROGRESS AND CHALLENGES

Oman is located in the southeast of the Arabian Peninsula next to Saudi Arabia and the United Arab Emirates and is bounded in the northeast by the gulf of Oman and southeast by the Arabian Sea. Oman covers an area of about 119,500 square miles. According to the Ministry of National Economy, in 2003 Oman had a population of 2.34 million people and a growth of around 46800 every year; at the end of 2006 Oman had a population Of 2.577 million people (www.moneoman.gov.om, 2008).

Official e-Government efforts in Oman (referred to as 'e-Oman') started in 2003 with the establishment of a government organization called 'Oman digital'. This organisation is responsible for all e-government and e-commerce services in Oman. Initially, this organization was responsible for identifying the information and technological needs for different government agencies in Oman to participate in e-government. Currently this organization is developing the infrastructure and a national web portal for e-government in Oman, sadly, a process that has taken nearly half a decade to establish.

Research by Abanumy, Al-Badi and Mayhew (2005) suggests that Oman e-government is still in the initial stage of building e-services, which concentrate on supplying information to the users (see Layne and Lee, 2001). The United Nations Economic and Social Commission for Western Asia described Oman's ICT e-participation policies and missions as average when compared with Saudi Arabia, and below average when compared with the United Arab Emirates. In 2008, the UN world e-government readiness survey showed that the Omani e-government efforts improved significantly since the 2005 survey by moving up from 112 to 84 in the rankings. Sadly, though, according to the same survey Oman's e-government project was ranked last among Gulf countries (UN, 2008).

In the light of the discussion presented above, the lack of a legal framework to identify guidelines and regulations regarding the use of electronic data is identified by the UN as one of the main limitations of Oman's e-government concept (UN, 2005). Furthermore, according to United Nations Economic and Social Commission for Western Asia, Oman needs to provide new laws to regulate the Internet, which will control the relations between service providers and users (ESCWA, 2006). In addition, though Oman connected to the internet in 1997 the country still has only one internet provider, which means that not all towns and cities are covered by internet services (ibid). However, since of late with the establishment of 'Oman Digital' the government has ensured the formulation of national ICT strategy to enhance e-services such as e-procurement, e-payment and privacy (UN, 2005; ESCWA, 2006). Nevertheless, sceptics have suggested that Oman lacks clear detailed plans for implementing e-government, which will affect their progress (Al-Jboori et al., 2006). Moreover, there are no software industries, which can grow with Oman's e-government needs. Other researchers have also identified common issues, such as, usability and information quality as factors affecting the efficiency of e-government implementation in Oman (Abanumy et al., 2005).

4. RESEARCH APPROACH

The aim of this chapter is to offer a synopsis of the key factors influencing e-government implementation efforts in Oman through a literature review of relevant publications and a preliminary case study in the capital city of Oman, Muscat. The chapter is a research in progress study and is thus only an initial effort to collate some of the significant factors that are currently impeding the progress of the national e-government initiative in Oman. Therefore, the data collection strategy used for this chapter relied primarily on reviewing published academic literature, other relevant Omani government and United Nations publications, and a preliminary semi-structured interview with the Chief Executive Officer (CEO) of the Information Technology Authority in Oman.

5. E-GOVERNMENT IMPLEMENTATION IN OMAN: A PRELIMINARY CASE STUDY

This section has presented the results of an interview that was conducted in Oman during July and August of 2008 in the Information Technology Authority (ITA). The ITA is the organization that is overall responsible for project managing the Omani e-government initiative. The interview was conducted with the CEO; he has a professional IT background and is responsible for around 200 employees who have similar backgrounds. Using an interview, this chapter hopes to identify key issues that may need to be considered for e-government success from a government's perspective in Oman. By doing so the authors hope to answer one question, 'why the progress of e-government has been slow in Oman'. The interview with the CEO lasted around two hours and provided the context of Omani e-government in practice.

During the last two years, the ITA has moved the Omani government agencies steadily into the digital age. At present, a number of e-services have been implemented in Oman such as e-payments, e-learning and e-billing. According to the CEO, the next big challenge for ITA is to move the country to activate plans for economic diversification. As the CEO states: *"...after 2006, the strategy was devised to introduce e-government and create a 'digital society' in Oman... The vision Oman 2020 (future plans) is focused on developing an improved ICT sector in Oman with an aim to activate the economic diversification plan."*

The Oman e-government strategy evolved through different project implementations. As the CEO of ITA explained: *"...The E-government Services Portal, National e-Payment Gateway, Innovation and Support Centres, Standards Framework, and Information Security Management Framework..."* are a few examples.

To implement these projects, it was crucial to involve five different government ministries who were dealing with citizens frequently (on a daily basis). In addition, the ITA has tried to keep the initial e-government services in Oman 'as simple as possible, to understand and use' in order to create a higher level of citizen satisfaction and awareness. As the CEO stated: *"...In order to improve awareness of e-government services among Omani citizens, we developed a few centres that provide ICT training opportunities; we hope to improve computer literacy through these centres. These centres are called Innovation and Support Centres, Community Knowledge Centres and Government Training Projects"***.** Further, the ITA has developed a plan for the next five years to train number of (approx 93000) employees in various government agencies to improve the skills and performance of civil servants.

The next goal of the ITA is to interconnect all of the government agencies by using various applications and integrating different levels of information to provide better management and usage of different types of e-services, such as e-payment. The CEO of ITA comment that *"... currently the ITA has completed the connections of 120 government websites, established the e-payment gateways and in July 2008 inaugurated the Omani national e-government portal for testing purposes".* The e-payment gateway allows citizens to make payments to different government agencies through a single point of contact. Citizens can link to other government agencies websites through the e-payment gateway, complete information on those websites and for those services that require payments, citizens will be redirected back to the e-payment gateway. While this facility was tested during the period July to October 2008, since November 2008 the service went live for citizens to use. As the CEO stated *"While the initial availability of this e-payment facility will be offered by five (of the 120) government agencies in November 2008, we will add remaining 115 organizations to the portal within a very short time".* The CEO explained that a phased implementation approach would allow the remaining 115 agencies to prepare the necessary IT infrastructure to integrate with the e-payment gateway.

The CEO suggested that one of the critical success factors for citizens' adoption of the e-payment gateway would depend on gaining citizens' trust on using electronic services for financial transactions. In this context, the ITA developed a new project called Information Security Centre (ISC). The ISC will provide a secure environment for the processing of electronic payments and ensure that citizens' personal information and data is protected.

The interview with the CEO also revealed that a lack of appropriate infrastructure, lack of leadership, lack of a good IT teams and the late appointment of the ITA for managing the Omani e-Government initiative were all crucial factors that affected the implementation of e-government in Oman. Nevertheless, since the appointment of the ITA to oversee implementation of e-government in 2006, as indicative from the interview results, steady progress has been made in terms of creating a national e-government web portal and e-enabling key services in Oman.

6. DISCUSSION AND CONCLUSION

This research found that e-government implementation efforts in Oman are still in its initial stages and that the country is faced with a number of challenges. Among the most salient factors identified as posing major challenges to e-government implementation were lack of strategy, leadership, legal and regulatory frameworks and infrastructure related issues. Abanumy et al., (2005) explain that Oman government needs to develop a set of polices and regulations to enhance the development of accessible sites and encourage the use of ICTs that facilitate citizens' needs in the context of e-government. Moreover, researchers such as Kostopoulos (2003) have suggested that e-government awareness in Oman is relatively low when compared with other Gulf countries such as United Arab Emirates and Bahrain. In this respect Mansar (2006) explains that the UAE have used different methods for successfully implementing e-government services in the public sector in that country. At the same time, Mansar (2006) also recognizes that huge improvement have been made in the private sector in several Gulf countries mainly as a result of responding to the investments and improvements made in the context of e-government.

Questions that need to be addressed for implementing e-government, particularly in a developing country context is, whether the ICT infrastructure should be developed according to the country's own polices and guidelines, or should lessons be learnt from other developed countries' experiences and external solutions be introduced accordingly. When reviewing real world experiences though, the latter has caused problems for countries such as Oman where e-government efforts have been stagnating and changing in focus for many years as a result of external involvement and introduction of solutions that do not fit with the socio-cultural values and beliefs of the country. In this respect, some researchers have suggested common strengths and weaknesses that currently influence e-government implementation in Oman (Table 1). As outlined in Table 1, although there are a few encouraging reasons, there are also a number of significant weaknesses relating to ICT infrastructure that can hinder the e-government implementation efforts in the country.

7. RESEARCH LIMITATIONS AND FUTURE RESEARCH

This chapter focused primarily on e-government literature in developing countries in the Gulf re-

Table 1. Strengths and weaknesses of implementing e-government in Oman

Strengths	*Source*
Good economic status and good international relations	*MONE, (2008); ESCWA (2006);*
Stable political system and peaceful society	*MONE, (2008); ESCWA, (2006);*
Government support for private sector collaboration	*MOMP (2008);*
Strategic geographic location	*MONE, (2008); ESCWA, (2006);*
Majority of population between the age group of 15-65 years	*MONE, (2008)*
Weaknesses	*Literature*
Lack of internet services	*ESCWA, (2006);*
Incomplete ICT infrastructure and Lack of a strong IT industry	*MONE, (2008); Kostopoulos (2003)*
Lack awareness of benefits from e-government	*Abanumy.et al, (2005); Kostopoulos. (2003); ESCWA (2006);*
No standard ICT applications among government organizations	*Kostopoulos (2003);*
Lack of clear detailed plans for implementing e-government	*Abanumy et al, (2005); Kostopoulos (2003)*

gion, in particular Oman. The chapter therefore does not provide a comprehensive review of general e-government literature. Furthermore, there is very little published (normative) literature on e-government implementation that has focused on Oman. Therefore, obtaining information about the Omani e-government efforts was challenging. Although a detailed semi-structured interview was conducted with a senior government official responsible for e-government implementation in Oman, this represents one individual's views on e-government implementation. The next steps in this research will be to offer a more comprehensive literature review of e-government in developing Gulf countries, which will be complemented with case-study-based empirical evidence in key Omani government agencies to explore the challenges, issues and complexities of e-government implementation in the country.

REFERENCES

Abanumy, A., Albadi A., & Mayhew, P. (2005). e-Government website Accessibility: In-Depth Evaluation of Saudi Arabia and Oman. *The Electronic Journal of e-Government, 3*(3), 99-106.

Al-Amer, M.A. (2003). *Kingdom of Bahrain: e-Government Program [Internet],* Available from: <http://unpan1.un.org/intradoc/groups/public/documents/UNESCWA/UNPAN015333.pdf> [Accessed Jan 5th, 2008].

Al-Jboori, A. (2006, September). *E-Government in Saudi Arabia: Can It Overcome Its Challenges*? eGovernment Workshop, Brunel University.

Al-Kibsi, G., de Boer, K., Mourshed, M., & Rea, N.P. (2001). *Putting citizens on-line, not in line, McKinzey Quarterly, 2*, 65-73.

Al-Khouri, A., & Bal, J. (2004). Electronic Government in the GCC Countries. *International Journal of Social Sciences*, 1(2), 83-98.

Al-Nahas, N. (2006). The Role of Knowledge and Capability Evaluation in E-Business Strategy: An Integrative Approach and Case Illustration. *SAM Advanced Management Journal, 71.*

Apostolou, D., Mentzas, G., & Stojanovic, N. (2006). *Semantic-enabled Aglie Knowledge-based e-government*, American Association for Artificial Intelligence [online], http://www.imu.iccs.gr/ sweg/papers/SS0606StojanovicN2-sake.pdf [accessed 02/11/2007]

Awan, M. (2003), *E-Government: Assessment of GCC (*Gulf Co-operating Council) Countries and Services Provided, Lecture Notes in Computer Science 2739, (pp. 500-503).

Belanger, F., & Carter, L. (2004). Citizen Adoption of Electronic Government Initiatives. In *Proceedings of the 37th Hawaii International Conference on Systems Sciences.*

Borras, J. (2004). International Technical Standards for e-Government. *Electronic Journal of e-Government, Academic Conferences Limited* [online] http://www.ejeg.com/volume-2/volume2-issue2/v2-i2-borras-pp75-80.pdf [accessed 02/01/08]

Bwoma, P.O., & Huang, Z . (2003). An overview of critical issues of E-government. *Issues of Information Systems, 4*(1), 164-170.

Chesi, F., Pallotti, M., & Oreste, S. (2005). *A Working E-Government Experience: The Citel Project, CMG Poland Annual Conference*, Warsaw, 9-10 May, 2005, [online] Available from <http://www.w3c.it/papers/ cmg2005Poland-egov.pdf > [12th march 2008].

Choudrie. J, & Ghinea, G., & Weerakkody, V. (2004). Evaluating Global e-Government Sites: A view using Web Diagnostic Tools. *Electronic Journal of E-Government, 2*(2), 105-114.

Darwish, A. (2001, February). Bahrain leads the way. *The Middle East* (p. 13).

Hazlett, S., & Hill, F. (2003). *E-government: the realities of using IT to transform the public sector.* Managing Service Quality, *13*(6).

Huang, Z., & Bwoma, O.P. (2003). *An Overview of Critical Issues of E-Government.* Central Michigan University.

Karunanada, A., & Weerakkody, V. (2006, October). E-government Implementation in Sri Lanka: Lessons from the UK. *Proceedings of the 8th International Information Technology Conference (IITC),* Colombo, Sri Lanka.

Weerakkody, V., Jones, S., & Olsen, E. (2007). *E-Government: A Comparison of Strategies in Local Authorities in the UK and Norway. International Journal of Electronic Business, Inderscience,* 5(2), 141-159.

Kostopoulos, G. (2003). *E-Government In The Arabian Gulf: Avision Toward Reality.* American University of Sharjah.

Mansar, L.S. (2006). E-Government Implementation: A comparative evaluation of websites maturity. *Proceedings of the European and Mediterranean Conference on Information Systems (EMCIS),* 6-7 July, 2006, Costa Blanca, Alicante, Spain.

Martin, J. (2000). *E-Commerce Arrives.* The Middle East, April 2000, (p. 34),

Ministry of Manpower (MOMP) (2008). *Self Employment and National Autonomous Development,* [online], http://www.manpower.gov.om/sanad_en.asp, Ministry of Manpower, Muscat.

Ministry of National Economy Oman (MONE) (2008). *Social Indicators [Internet],* Available from:<http://www.moneoman.gov.om/book/syb2007/index_Index.htm> [Accessed Jan 11th 2008].

Moulder, E. (2001). E-Government. *Public Management, 83.*

Ndou, V.D. (2004). E-government for developing countries: opportunities and challenges. *The Electronic Journal on Information Systems in Developing Countries, 18*(1), 1-24.

Oman Telecommunication Company (2003). *Internet Services* [Internet] < http://www.omantel.net.om/services/business/internet> [Accessed March 12th 2008]

Riley, T.B. (2003). *Defining E-Government and E-Governance: Staying the Course.* eGov Monitor.

Siddiqi, A. (2001). *The United Arab Emirates: Financial Report.* The Middle East.

Stoltzfus, K. (2004). *Motivations for implementing E-Government: An Investigation of the Global Phenomenon,* University of California, Santa.

Tigran, G. (2006). *Economic and Social Commission for Western Asia (ESCWA).* United Nation Networking o f Expertise on Foreign Direct Investment in the Member States of the ESCWA. http://www.escwa.un.org/divisions/pptcd/upload/EvaluationDA2.pdf, [last accessed 03/2008]

United Nations (2008). *World Public Sector Report 2003: E-Government at the Crossroads.* United Nations publication. http://unpan1.un.org/intradoc/groups/public/documents/UN/UNPAN012733.pdf [last accessed 03/2008]

United Nations (2008). *Global E-Government Readiness Report 2005 for E-Givernment to E-Inclusion.* http://unpan1.un.org/intradoc/groups/public/ documents/un/unpan021888.pdf United Nations publication. [last accessed 02/2008]

United Nations (2008), *United Nations e-Government Survey 2008.* United Nations publication. http://unpan1.un.org/intradoc/groups/public/documents/UN/UNPAN028607.pdf [last accessed 03/2008].

Wert, J.M.V. (2002). E-Government and Performance: A Citizen-Centered Imperative. *The Public Manager, 31.*

Chapter XVI
Telecentres:
The New Public Spheres?

Vineeta Dixit
Consultant, Department of Administrative Reforms & Public Grievances, Government of India

ABSTRACT

Information communications technologies (ICTs) are one of the major areas of research and investment in developing countries because they seem to serve the cause of democratisation and empowering citizens by extending the public sphere. ICTs and especially Internet are regarded as the new public sphere for they seem to lie outside the market and the State, nurtured by civil society serving the cause of good governance and democratisation and empowering grassroots initiatives, giving them access to critical information, organising political actions, influencing public opinion and policy-making. This chapter examines the 'publicness' of the telecentres in the framework of public sphere as defined by Habermas. The chapter uses telecentres as representative of 'technology mediated public space' created by ICTs and Internet and examines two approaches to the Telecentre movement, analysing whether Telecentres can meet the requirements of the rational-critical discussions and if and what factors influence the extension of the public sphere. The chapter concludes that while the telecentres create opportunities to improve communication and reconnect citizens to the State, offering greater access to information and support for group based discussion, they are likely to support only incremental modifications to the democratic system because the current use of information communication technologies (ICTs) concentrates primarily on information provision, and not linkages that improve the quality of democratic discourse.

INTRODUCTION

Information communications technologies (ICTs) are one of the major areas of research and investment in developing countries not only because technology is deemed instrumental for economic development but also because they seem to serve the cause of democratisation and empowering citizens by extending the public sphere (Clift 2004; UNPAN 2003; UNCTAD 2006; OECD 2001; WB 1999). It has been long argued that there is a close inter-relationship between technology – its capabilities and limitations and creation and functioning of public sphere (Dewey 1927) and that special attention must be paid to the way technologies construct, structure, or pre-empt social dialogue (Sclove 1994). In Habermasian terms, international agencies such as the World Bank (WB) and UNDP regard ICTs and especially Internet as the new public sphere for they seem to lie outside the market and the State, nurtured by civil society serving the cause of good governance and democratisation and empowering grassroots initiatives, giving them access to critical information, organising political actions, influencing public opinion and policy-making.

It is argued that the growing deployment of ICTs creates new channels of communication and exchange resulting in formulation of completely new sets of relationships and characterises the development of mediated interactive communication as a major structural change produced by communications revolution and it is believed that such processes lead to the creation of a Public Sphere albeit mediated by technology that is critical to support the emerging civil society in hitherto non-democratic countries (Baker and Ward 2002; Van Djik 1999).

One critical move in this direction has been the setting up of public-access centres, variously known as Telecentres, Telecottages etc. that are considered to have the capacity for creating a 'public sphere' in which information dissemination and access combined with reasoned dialogue strengthens democracy and community formation (Damiris and Wild 1997; Wei and Kuzmanovic 2000).

This chapter examines the 'publicness' of the telecentres in the framework of public sphere as defined by Habermas.

CONCEPTUAL FRAMEWORK

The multiple conceptual threads that intertwine with the core question required a multidisciplinary approach that included the conceptualisation of the public sphere, elaboration on governance, Telecentres and the factors affecting these elements.

Many scholars have extrapolated from Habermas' work in constructing connections between technology, information and civil society (Wishard, 1994; Boyte and Kari 1996). The conceptual framework used to examine the 'publicness' is based on the Habermasian public sphere and its linkages with the system factor encompassing social, technology and use factors (adapted from Lin, 2003) that shape and re-shape it. The left side of the diagram represents the context and the right side, the universal parameters. It can therefore be adapted to analyse varied contexts against a set of universal parameters.

Diagrammatically, the framework can be represented as shown in Figure 1.

Conceptually, the four factors – system, social, technology and use that form the contextual half of the conceptual framework will now be discussed in turn.

The system factor is based on the open system theory (Buckley, 1967) in which a system is dynamic and system structure and innovations continuously interact to not only bring about change but also to alter the power structures within the social system. It is a combination of regulatory and policy environment, technology culture in the society and market forces that constantly create or close window of opportunities.

Figure 1. Conceptual framework to examine the 'Publicness' (Source: Adapted from Lin, 2003)

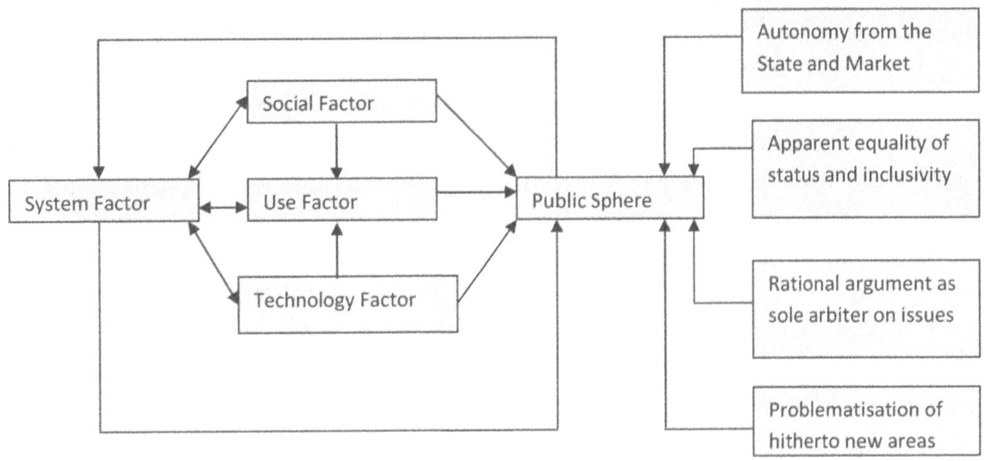

The social factor is determined not only by the social structures and the hierarchies but also by the opinion leaders and the availability of a critical mass of adopters. This factor is highly influenced by political symbolism (Edelman, 1964). The technology factor includes the hardware and the software and critically the essential element of ICTs – interactivity - that is viewed as an attribute of the technological interface (Sundar, 2004); as user experiences and perceptions (Bertz, 1983; Newhagen, Cordes and Levy, 1995; van Djik, 1999); as multi-locational residing in different locations whether as a feature of media system, message exchanges or user perception (Bucy, 2004). Chadwick (2001) gives a new twist to the debate on interactivity by arguing that the information available to citizens is controlled and filtered by government and thus the interaction between the citizen and the State is very much on the terms of the State. The use factor, Lin argues demonstrates varied responses depending upon the expected award associated with the technology use; gratification received from such use; the perceived ability to control such an experience; and user attention and interest generated by the use experience. For Habermas (1989), to defer the face-to-face meeting of minds is to corrupt reason, to open the door for manipulation by politicians. Derrida echoes similar sentiments by claiming that 'parliamentary democracy ….. is exercised with more and more difficulty in a public space profoundly upset by ……. rhythms of information and communication' (ibid 1994:79).

All of these factors contribute to our understanding of the 'publicness' of a technology mediated public sphere, specifically Telecentres.

METHODOLOGY

The methodology uses telecentres as representative of 'technology mediated public space' created by ICTs and Internet and examines two approaches to the Telecentre movement, analysing whether Telecentres can meet the requirements of the rational-critical discussions and if and what system, social, technical and use factors influence the extension of the public sphere. These case studies are chosen because they provide us with the opposing ends of Telecentre discourses - commercially driven and civically oriented. A contrast between the two elucidates alternatives omitted when the analysis is limited to just one type of Telecentre, for if we need to understand the implication of technology mediated spaces, only the comparison of a variety of such actually operating spaces can shed light on these issues (Monberg, 1998). The comparative case study method will focus on four elements of the public sphere to review Telecentre's capacity to create and support "new forms of 'publicness' within public spheres dominated by privately owned and controlled media and the State" (Tsagarousianou, 1998:175 emphasis in original). The paper itself does not examine the conceptualisation, elements and critique of the public sphere in detail. However, the analysis would be incomplete if we do not clarify the contemporary notion of governance driving the Telecentre movement worldwide using the system, social, technological and use factors. Thus, in literature review, the literature on governance, Telecentre and their relationship will also be clarified.

LITERATURE REVIEW: PUBLIC SPHERE, GOVERNANCE AND TELECENTRES

In recent times there has been a growing interest in potential uses of ICTs in the delivery of government services and enhancing government citizen interaction. A large body of literature has focussed on the concept of 'informatisation' that has fired the imagination of theorists, governments, and civil society alike (Hudson, 1999). It is legitimated in terms of a desirable move away from mass communication and back toward forms of interpersonal communication that are seen inherently more desirable and liberating. The theory of 'public sphere' is the basis for current and widespread revival of interest in direct, deliberative or participatory democracy, as an essential complement to representative components of diverse political systems (Garnham, 1992).

The idea of public sphere is not new and can be traced back to the times of Aristotle. However, the most widely acknowledged attempt to elaborate came from Jurgen Habermas who theorized the 'discursive Public Sphere'. In his thesis 'The Structural Transformation of the Public Sphere' (Habermas, 1989), he developed a normative model of the bourgeois public sphere, its creation and its subsequent degradation or corruption and described the public sphere as an "intersubjectively shared space" (ibid, 1996:360) reproduced through communicative rationality in a "domain of social life through which such a thing as public opinion can be formed" (ibid, 1989:231). He contended that the function of the public sphere was to mediate between private concerns of individuals in their familial, economic and social life, and demands and concerns of social and public life. Situated as an interface between the private realm of civil society and the public realm of state authority, "the bourgeois Public sphere was based on the fictitious identity of the two roles assumed by the privatised individuals who came together to form public: the role of property owners and the role of human beings" (Habermas 1989: 56) to put the State in touch with society through the vehicle of public opinion, which was based on rational-critical discourse among these individuals.

Thus, the public sphere can be understood as a space for public dialogue where people meet and discuss socio-political issues of their concern. It is brought to life through various forms of communication, such as, face-to-face interaction to vast structures mediated by communications infrastructures.

Some features in the Habermasian public sphere are crucial to their current relevance to the discourse of democratisation- a kind of social intercourse that, "far from presupposing the equality of status, disregarded status altogether" (Habermas, 1989:36), which is linked to the notion that rational argument was the sole arbiter of any issue; "the problematisation of areas that until then had not been questioned" (Habermas 1989:36); the emerging public established itself as inclusive in principle; and autonomy from state and economic power (Calhoun, 1992; Dahlberg, 2001). "The ideal public sphere calls for social integration to be based on rational-critical discourse" (Calhoun, 1992:29). Integration therefore is founded on communication rather than domination. Communication in this context means not merely sharing information and knowledge and thoughts but also a process of potential transformation in which reason is advanced by debate itself.

While many scholars agree with Habermas concerning the importance of citizen debate for strong democracy, his theory has been criticised from many perspectives (Calhoun 1992; Ku, 2000:223; Eley 1992; Benhabib 1992; Young 1987; Fraser 1992)

However, as Monberg argues that since the role of public in the discussions of the development of ICTs is explicitly framed as apolitical therefore the use of public sphere" as an analytic lens to identify the issues of political consequences is essential ... that highlights aspects that would otherwise remain submerged and depoliticised" (1998: 435)

GOVERNANCE

Governance has become a key concept in the international democratisation debate since 1990s and marks the transformation in focus from micro-level to macro-level issues (Hyden 2004; Rhodes, 1997; Kooiman, 2003) and resonates the policy debates in western democracies and multilateral institutions such as WB. Taylor argues that "whilst governments have taken shape universally through their creation and use of institutional structures of the State,.... the perceived institutional failure of these institutions has established enthusiasm for govern*ance* rather than govern*ment"* (1998: 144, italics in original)

The review of literature suggests that there is little consensus on the meaning of governance and has many theoretical roots (Hyden, 2004; Kjaer, 2004; Kooiman 2003; Stoker 1998; Ahrens 1997; Rhodes 1997; Rosenau 1992; Leftwich; 1993). The different theories in various degrees do however agree that in current context governance is no longer just about government, that it refers to a complex set of inter-related and yet autonomous self-governing institutions and actors resulting in blurring of boundaries of responsibility and accountability for socio-economic development and the role of state is to primarily guide and steer using new tools and techniques (Stoker, 1998) and that it can no longer rely on traditional authority to function.

Adapting Habermasian model of societal development, Broadbent *et al.* (1991) suggest that government, professional and financial institutions are societal steering media that manoeuvre the functioning of the societal systems through steering mechanisms. These systems are, in turn, made up of public, private and voluntary organizations. Both the steering institutions and organizational systems are deemed to have their own distinct lifeworlds, steering media and systems, which guide and direct the behaviours of each.

This paradigmatic shift from provision to more with facilitation, enablement and partnerships in the management and delivery of public services is occurring alongside the rhetoric of the Information Age and the intensive application of ICTs emerging to sustain and support this paradigmatic shift. The two developments put together gave rise to the concept of e-governance. Thus, "e-Governance lies at the heart of two global shifts: the information revolution and the governance revolution" (Heeks, 2001:21) resulting in a paradigmatic shift in the process of the understanding of democratic governance (Becker, 1998:343) and help build new spaces for citizens to participate in their overall development (Gasco, 2003).

TELECENTRE

A Telecentre is typically a building or a room with computers, a telephone line, Internet connection and other office automation equipments such as photocopier and fax. It is a common meeting place where people are exposed to tools, skills, attitudes and values of ICTs (Fuchs, 1998); provide public access to ICTs for personal, social, educational and economic development; offer a range of services and vary in their location and business models. Roman & Colle (2001) identify five basic purposes of a Telecentre – to provide access to rural areas, to reduce marginalisation, to facilitate dialogue between communities and policy makers, to encourage participation in decision making and finally to gain information and resources. Proenza *et al.* (2001) discern two main types of Telecentres. The first type are micro-enterprises typically run by small entrepreneurs generating revenue by offering basic telecommunication services, marketing low cost products and by providing services related to government departments such as payment of electricity bills etc. The second type is meant to facilitate the provision of public and private information based services to support local socio-economic development. International agencies such as IDRC, USAID, ITU, UNESCO, WB, in conjunction with the local or central government supports many of these enterprises (Ernberg, 1998), with a belief that the Telecentres create this public sphere in which information about civic affairs can be subjected to "rational debate and discussion", is "open to inspection by the citizenry" and can be used to form "public opinion" (Webster 1995: 101). For ordinary citizens, computer technology may contribute towards reducing isolation and enabling more informed participation in local management and politics.

In the next section, two case studies from Hungary and India are examined to explore whether and to what extent do Telecentres extend the public sphere.

CASE STUDY: COMPARATIVE ANALYSIS OF THE HUNGARIAN TELECOTTAGE MOVEMENT AND DRISHTEE TELECENTRE INITIATIVE

This section evaluates the Telecentre discourse against some specific parameters of the public sphere developed by Jurgen Habermas using the case studies of the Hungarian Telecottage Movement (HTM) and Drishtee Telecentre Initiative (DTI). While HTM demonstrates how Telecentres can innovatively be structured to approximate the forum for rational-critical discourse and socio-technical and political impediments can be mitigated through innovative thinking, sustained efforts and empathy; DTI is very clearly oriented towards the economic development model that presupposes the democratisation and inclusion process just by its existence. The next two sections provide further details on each of the case study and the final section in this chapter compares them against the requirements of the Habermasian public sphere.

HUNGARIAN TELECOTTAGE MOVEMENT

The **Republic of Hungary** is a country in transition and is attempting to re-integrate itself in the European mainstream. It has a large number of very small villages and towns, of which about 4,500 have fewer than 2,000 residents each. These communities are poorly serviced by state and public service delivery, educational institutions, business services, and offer few job opportunities. Personal computer (PC) penetration is only around 15-17%, while the Internet penetration rate is around 13%. Only 8% of households have Internet access. The idea of telecottage was developed organically to service this neglected population of Hungary. As a result, telecottages are mostly located in small towns and villages and currently more than 500 telecottages across Hungary serve these rural communities.

The telecottages operate under the umbrella of the National Association of Telecottages (Magyar Teleház Szövetség - MTSz). The MTSz was formed to assure the best conditions for the network and the services to expand, to make telecottages sustainable over the long run, to guarantee a high level of operating quality, and to preserve their community-based origins and character. A key player in the HTM, MTSz lobbies the central government for equal rights and equal access to information, education and public resources. It is a key partner in the formulation of the National Telehouse Strategy (Gaspar, 2001).

Each telecottage is an independent, autonomous body, where a local NGO provides legal and business framework for lawful operation. Sometimes, the local government provides support by offering office space, personnel, and financial services and by contracting out work to the telecottages. The operator could often be a private firm that signs a contract with a local NGO. The nature of a telecottage thus incorporates attributes of business, not-for-profit and public administration, creating a highly flexible and hybrid structure (UNDP, 2006), with differing foci such as social problems, children, minorities (generally Roma), small and medium enterprises, computer literacy, NGO support, local democracy, empowerment, etc. As present, the most widespread services (80% and above) are civic service centre, local advertising and information services, public Internet access, office services, public information services, community development and program services, computer games, computer working, and public administration client services (ITU, 2001).

"The explicit goals of the Hungarian telecottage movement are, on the more general level, rural modernisation, economic development, and a strengthening of democracy and civil society" (ITU, 2001:9). They have a six-point operation characteristic defined as minimum that each centre must meet in order to qualify for the telecottage label. These are - Public benefit, "NGO-ness," societal oversight; Open services that constantly adapt to serve the community's changing needs; Community space and memory, a public forum, and a catalyst; Public services for everyone; Responsible, independent, competent manager and servicing organization; and Modern information and communications technology. It is further emphasized that the telecottage must exist at the service of the community. It must investigate and be sensitive to specific needs of local residents, organisations and enterprises. Furthermore, the telecottage must secure a public meeting place and instigate public debate, 'civic virtues' and free access to information. Besides the general operational principles the material also lists ten basic services, namely, civil organisations' service centre; Assistance (with official procedures); Internet access; electronic mail for the citizens; Public information; Local centre for announcements and news; office services; multimedia use; computer games and computer related work. (Adapted from UNDP, 2006)

Although a majority of these services are related to ICTs, notable is the emphasis on civil services organisation, assistance with official procedures and dissemination of local information. While prima facie they may seem innocuous, they are critical to the basic purpose of the telecottage i.e. enhancement of civil society, assistance to citizens dealing with public authorities due to scarcity of information regarding procedures, rules and regulation and provision of more effective and trustworthy information for the only other source of information available to the citizens is a bulletin board in front of the Municipal office, administered by municipality staff (Gaspar, 2001). Telecottages provide information on and organise citizens' dialogues with candidates standing up in local elections, opportunity for telework and source funds for other social activities. 70% of visitors enter telecottages to meet friends and relatives, 62% of visitors believe community life has been changed since the telecottage was set up in the settlement, while only 9% claimed they have not experienced such transformation. Meanwhile 48% thinks the telecottage should organize more community programs. The communal influence of telecottages can be seen in the opinion of 81% of visitors who see the influence of telecottage services expanding towards non-visitors. This compared merely 3% who disagreed and claimed that telecottages did not have influence beyond its immediate sphere. Interestingly, it is citizens between 36 to 55 age group who play the most important part and to encourage other people to use the services (72% of the 36 to 45 age group, and 79% of those aged between 46 and 55) not the younger generation (Molnar, 2000). Telecottages are not merely collections of dispersed best-available technology instead the success of telecottages is due to the public service, community organization, and self-reliance that they provide to often economically depressed and isolated areas.

DRISHTEE TELECENTRE INITIATIVE

In February 2000, Cyber Edge (renamed Drishtee) entered into an agreement with the district administration of Dhar in the Indian State - Madhya Pradesh, to develop e-governance modules for the state's Internet project - "Gyandoot". Encouraged by the experience, in 2000, Drishtee signed an agreement with the administration of a small but prosperous and developed district in the Indian state of Haryana - Sirsa.

The aim of the project was to deliver both governmental and private services efficiently to citizens, provide a forum for interacting with government directly and to generate revenues for financial sustainability of the project by charging fee for these services (IIITB, 2005). The services provided included access to government records, issuance of documents and certificates, market-related information, details of development work under the *Sarkar Aapke Dwar* (Government at your doorstep) Scheme, applications for pensions, filing of grievances and computer training for local businesses. Citizens would come to kiosks and send any of these queries/requests/grievances via the intranet in a standard format. As there was no connectivity at either the district or block level, Drishtee employees at District Rural Development Agency would download and print the forms and send them to appropriate department (Drishtee, 2005).

The business model was a franchisee based three-tier structure and comprised of the management (Drishtee staff), the district operators (hub owners), and the village operators (kiosk owners). Drishtee staff members managed the interface with government and corporate clients, supplied the software, and created and managed the network between the kiosks and their office. The district operators identified and recruited local entrepreneurs at the village level and networked with the local government to access government data for on-time delivery of services. The village operators who marketed and delivered kiosk services to the villagers, paid in addition to a one-time license fee, 20% of all e-governance transactions charged to the citizens, as a commission to Drishtee, and bore the operation cost of running the kiosks. They were permitted to generate additional income by functioning as a petition writer and under a contract between Drishtee and the district administration, act as licensed vendor of government judicial stamps (Drishtee 2005; IIITB, 2005).

In the initial phase, three kiosks were set up and the Additional District Collector took personal ownership and explained in detail the operation of the 'complaint system' to the citizens. In the first year of its operation, the kiosks were a huge success because there was a sense of empowerment amongst citizens who believed that they could now hold government officials accountable. It also built in transparency in the system, as now the citizens understood the processes involved in various transactions. Most importantly, the system allowed the poor and the marginalized to voice their grievances (WB, 2003).

In late 2001, buoyed by the success of the first three kiosks, 25 new kiosks were added. To improve back-end support, at the district administration level, attempts were made to computerize land records, issuance of pension and payroll system and certificates. However, the degree of computerization was limited and therefore nearly all processes remained manual. As a result, while due to the increased outreach of the kiosks, the number of complaints mounted, Drishtee employees found it increasingly difficult to follow up and keep track of the complaints. On the side of the government, the initial enthusiasm was buried under the ever enlarging mountain of applications and grievances and often went pending for further action as they had to follow the manual system as well keep the intranet updated (IIITB, 2005; WB 2004a; WB, 2004b).

The kiosk owners refused the offer of the District Collector to vet the applications as each application was a source of revenue to them. In addition, the budget allocated in each scheme was limited and the same was neither conveyed to the kiosk owner nor to the citizens. As a result, the 'customers' of the kiosks felt cheated because in spite of paying to the kiosk owner, their application was not considered. This problem was further exacerbated due to the fact that the government offices such as the village council and block level offices continued to accept these applications free of charge thereby creating a conflict between the two systems. The citizens therefore started to question the reasons and the efficacy of the charged process. As a result, the kiosk owners stopped taking the applications, as no guarantee for response could be given. In the next two years less than 20% of applications and complaints through Drishtee were addressed.

By end 2002, most of the kiosks were floundering and by 2004, only about half of the kiosks were operational, and none of them offered any e-governance services for which they were originally established. By early 2003, Drishtee also took a cue from the kiosk owners' experience and moved on to private activities such as insurance, computer education and rural newspaper and decided not to pursue its e-governance initiative (IIITB, 2005; WB, 2004c). They however operate on the same model in 8 other Indian states.

ANALYSIS

Drawing from the description of the two case studies and the conceptual framework, this section seeks to establish how does the Telecentre discourse of Telecentre functions in reality and '*whether and to what extent do Telecentres extend the public sphere*?'

System Factor: This is an overarching factor that critically impacts the public sphere and is in turn affected by it. The difference between the two country's policy and regulatory environment is as different as chalk from cheese. While Hungary is making a transition from controlled to free market economy and the government is moving towards democratisation, it is creating space for civil society and other forms of association that encourage experimentation. Also, the civil society discourse is heavily influenced by the western ideologue. The system is still viewed with suspicion and therefore an open and honest way of dealing with the system is welcomed. The Indian environment is on the other hand is a controlled movement towards market economy. The government relinquishes control in piecemeal and both the government as well as the citizen view their roles as that of a provider and receiver respectively. In the changed scenario since 1990s, the market forces are seen as a new conduit for service provision, and the focus is more on efficiency rather than effectiveness or creation of space for further dialogue. The other crucial factor in Indian environment is the power wielded by the politicians who dispense favours in a system that is constantly under pressure and under funded.

Technology mediation in such a scenario is not viewed favourably.

Social Factor: There are two critical factors in Hungary – a large old population that grew up in the communist era, who are still learning to adapt to the new way and a significant young population that takes the current open political structure for granted; and expanding civil society funded aggressively by the West. These two factors encourage interaction and opportunity for dialogue due to presence of divergent views and a need to make the new system work. As Jokay (2003) observes Telecottages are a place for these people to come and interact and debate about local and national issues and it is the older generation that seems eager to exploit the new opportunities presented by the telecottages and explain to the younger generation the value of new found democracy that gives them an opportunity to voice their opinion and be heard. In India on the other hand, due to paternalistic political culture, very little dialogue exists or is encouraged and people are always looking for ways to short-circuit the system to work for them. In such a scenario, information becomes power and as Chadwick (2001) observed, it is often controlled by the government, who do not share full information even in a project initiated by it. It is therefore extremely difficult to build a cohesive social bond and an individualistic pattern in society emerges with every person acting towards his/her own benefit.

Technology Factor: Of the four factors mentioned by Lin (2003), interactivity seems to play the most important role and as Bucy (2004) explained it lies in the perception of the user. In Hungary, the users find Telecottages interactive as it fulfils their need for a community, information, news, mail and much more. In case of India, the interactivity is limited and technology is seen only as a more advanced form of complaint system rather than as an opportunity for a two-way interaction with the government.

Use Factor: The above three factors, determine the Use Factor. In Hungary, due to conducive policy environment, high social interaction and use of telecottages more as a communal space rather than a technology space, the use factor is extremely high. Whereas in India, so long as the citizens were getting responses to their grievances, they used the Telecentres, the moment the number of responses dwindled they were quick to abandon the Telecentres.

Juxtaposing the contextual factor analysis, the HTM and DTI will now be examined against the four universal elements of the public sphere to determine whether and to what extent Telecentres extend the public sphere.

Autonomy from the State and the Market: This parameter defines not just functional autonomy but emphasises that the discourse itself must be driven by citizens rather than by market or the state. The case study evidence demonstrates that it s not a case of simple autonomy form the state and the market, but a case of hybrid forms containing both public and private organisational structures. While the character of HTM cannot be considered truly 'autonomous', the list of the basic minimum requirements set out for their qualification as a telecottage, quite clearly sets them out as independent from both state and market. It is true that they receive funding from both the state as well as the market, but their zeal and dedication to protection of civic virtue remains undiluted. They are not affiliated to any political party or interest group. The MTSz insists on training the new telecottageers in the civic responsibility to ensure freedom including financial sustainability that is often obtained through government contracts and offering its services to citizens for a fee. Nevertheless, it cannot be deemed as commercialisation for if the operating expenses ($20,000 annually) are not met through legitimate means, increased dependence upon government and other sources of funding can have adversely impact on the telecottages. Drishtee Telecentres on the other hand, are not only been promoted with active support of the State are also very clearly influenced by market as the model was based on a public-private partnership ethos (Hunt, 2001), and although Drishtee's original vision incorporated e-governance, its primary focus remained financial viability of its kiosks. Unlike HTM telecottages, it firmly placed itself in the realm of market that eventually resulted in the closer of the majority of the kiosks.

One can therefore cannot but agree with Fraser (1992) who argues that any conception of the public sphere that requires a sharp separation between (associational) civil society and the State will be unable to comprehend and encompass various requirements and configurations of management, inter-public coordination, and political accountability that are essential to democratic and egalitarian society. Thus, although both the movements do not seem to fulfil the conditions of this element of the Habermasian public sphere, under the new context of governance they do extend the public sphere in their own limited manner by involving all three participants – the state, the market and the civil society.

Apparent Equality of Status and Inclusivity: This element is in principle applicable to both the Telecentres. From a system factor perspective, in the process of the commodification of services and treatment of citizens as customers, there must be a balance between promoting entrepreneurship, the services being offered to citizens as well as issues regarding the agency's legal right to charge for services that are and ought to be available free-of-cost from government offices. This principle was judiciously followed by HTM but largely ignored by DTI. Analysing the social and use factor, in case of HTM, the telecottage is open to one and all and does not discriminate against any citizen based on race, class or status and all can participate freely, bracketing their differences. Its guideline of email for all citizens ensures that all members of the community gain access to email through the telecottage and each citizen should have a private mailbox and address that is password protected. In addition, it instructs that the internet needs to be available to all who want to use it, and cannot, or do not want to purchase access at home. Since no demographic data is available, it is not possible to comment on gender or other kinds of discrimination, however, it can be deduced from the wide variety of services provided under the telecottage umbrella that it ensure a comprehensive reach. Some of the telecottages focus on the hitherto neglected Roma community thereby further strengthening the case of equality and inclusivity.

Drishtee's case demonstrated that one of the biggest hurdle while attempting to operationalise an e-governance initiative through a private agency is maintaining equality of service in principle as the goal of universal provision of service because market based mechanisms choose to segment the market to seek maximum profits and need for higher profits eventually drives the agency to seek greener pastures (Ciborra, 2003). Also, "the notion of 'customer' entails a number of market mechanisms, which cannot be completely transferred to a public administration" (ibid:9, emphasis in original). In DTI's case, technically speaking while the kiosks were open to all citizens, only those who were able and willing to pay for the services were entertained. The kiosks also did not keep in mind the need of the citizens and chose not to provide citizens with impartial advise on eligibility under various schemes and were more interested in making profit. From the technological factor point of view, in their different ways, both attempted to make the experience as user-friendly as socially acceptable as possible, focussing more on service than technology. The technological factor plays a key role in HTM's case, for the national telecommunication policy of the State allows it to expand it network. In DTI's case however, the impact is visible only in the disconnect between the citizens and the government, demonstrating that focus on increased citizen interaction through front-end services will not be successful unless it is supported by investing in effective information systems and improved processes at the backend (IIITB, 2005).

Thus, the community patterns at the Telecentres do fulfil this requirement in principle and therefore can be said to extend the public sphere, although in case of DTI, the extension is limited to paying customers only, thereby bringing Fraser's (1992) criticism into focus that the inclusivity although possible but if often limited by other factors especially financial considerations. Therefore, it is critical that although these processes need to become self-sustaining and financially viable over long term, initially they must be protected from market mechanisms and not be driven by it, otherwise these spaces will be available to only those who can afford to pay for access and … allow … little opportunity to create the kind of media content that would allow them to have a voice in debates over public importance" (Monberg, 1998:442)

Rational argument as the sole arbiter on issues: This not fully realised in either of the cases because, while the State uses them successfully for 'informatising' the public, as Chadwick argues the information available to citizens is controlled and filtered by government and thus the interaction between the citizen and the State is very much on the terms of the State. Further, communities have not yet learned how to apply this technology to creating public dialogue about community issues, concerns or capacities because the use of Telecentres for civic purposes takes longer to develop than other functions Pigg (2001). In similar vein, Monberg opines, "for access to be meaningful, individuals must possess the necessary literacy skills and find and interpret information and participate in debates that involve public issues as well as necessary hardware and software" (1998:441). HTM, did attempt to mitigate this deficiency by providing space for political debate about the socio-political and economic issues especially related to local elections and mainstreaming with Europe because providing a forum for public debate, enforcing citizens' rights, and empowering people were considered as critical issues in the transition from socialism to democracy and a free-market economy (UNDP, 2006). Local residents also had the opportunity to recommend new services or programs after due deliberations at the telecottage. The MTSz used the rational critical discourse at the national level by engaging in debates about the role of the telecottages in the various socio-economic sectors. As such, each telecottage serves as a centre of information and debate. Methodological collection and dissemination of national, regional and local information on behalf of local users takes place not only electronically, but also through traditional bulletin boards and newspapers. It provides a coercion-free space for more rational deliberations of local issues.

In DTI's case however, there was no space for rational deliberation or participation. Rational deliberation involving both the administration as well the citizens was limited; the former was viewed as the deliverer of the services and the latter as the client. No debate even amongst citizens was possible regarding government policy, for no information was available. The entire exercise was purely transactional where the citizen filed grievances/applications and the administration chose to respond or not. Unlike HTM associates, the DTI staff did not view the creation of a debating platform as part of their mandate. For them the ability to complain was good enough. Had a rational deliberation through the staff and citizen participation taken place while designing the e-governance solution, they might have pointed out the need for whetting the application at the kiosk level or information sharing regarding the budget constraints or even involvement of the village councils and the block development office to deal with more complex requirements thereby creating a more transparent system. Instead a preconceived solution was foisted on both thereby further muddling an already complex relationship.

Thus, while Telecentres create opportunities to improve communication and reconnect citizens to the State, offering greater access to information and support for group based discussion, they are likely to support only incremental modifications to the democratic system because the current use of ICTs concentrates primarily on information provision, and not linkages that improve the quality of democratic discourse.

Problematisation of hitherto new areas: This element is an eclectic one. From a system factor perspective, does technology-mediation make it a new area or from the social factor perspective, the unveiling of apparent issues connotes new area? Hungary is a country in transition therefore we may contend that every democratic issue is an un-addressed issue. HTM raised many issues - access to information, democratisation, civil rights and most prominently the gap between rural and urban populations in access to information and technology, which the movement argues is increasing the widening economic gap between rural and urban populations - that can be viewed as issues that are new for Hungarian society and polity. With over 15% population over 64 years, it also draws attention to the problem of internalisation of newfound freedom where required and acts as a mediator between the old and young generations and secure a smooth transition to democratic life. These issues are new both from a system as well as social perspective. However, the HTM initiative has not yet created reciprocal response from the government, thus, it has not been able to directly influence the delivery of government, administrative or public services by central agencies and telecottage expansion have not yet proven to be enough for the feedback loop to reach the affected ministries (Jokay, 2002).

In DTI's case, the system factor perspective was solution oriented rather than problematised, for they did not view the service provision as new area. Although from the technical factor perspective it was new for them, for till now they had relied on face-to-face communication. From the social and use factor perspective, although it managed to raise the expectations regarding accountability of public officials to ordinary citizens – an unknown in Indian context, the absence of accountability measures in case the agency fails to deliver the promised services, or when the district administration does not respond to the citizens led to what is termed as blame avoidance or scapegoating (Stoker, 1998) with each actor blaming the other for not keeping its end of the promise. Thus although an unknown issue was problematised, instead of providing solution, the Telecentre further complicated the issue and alienated the population for it never even sought to create a feedback loop.

Thus, for any real transformation to occur, changes at both the government as well as the citizen end must happen simultaneously and feed into each other

For as Kanungo (2004) argues, sustainability of public sphere hinges upon collaborative and discursive frameworks and the process must allow stakeholders to influence and experience the process of value creation, which in turn becomes a process of collective learning and dialogue.

CONCLUSION

The growing deployment of sophisticated ICTs such as the Telecentres permits new modes of communication and information exchange, and the concomitant emergence of an entirely new array of relationships. The creation and maintenance of such opportunities presents tremendous possibilities for communities, as well as for those charged with governance of the polity.

In this paper I have examined whether and to what extent do Telecentres extend the public sphere. By examining the 'publicness' of the ICTs and Internet it may be said that *while they create opportunities to improve communication and reconnect citizens to the State, offering greater access to information and support for group based discussion, they are likely to support only incremental modifications to the democratic system because the current use of Information Communication Technologies (ICTs) concentrates primarily on information provision, and not linkages that improve the quality of democratic discourse. For any real transformation to occur, changes at both the government as well as the citizen end must be concurrent and feed into each other. At the same time, for these processes to become meaningful and self-sustaining over long term, initially they must be protected from market mechanisms and not be driven by it.*

In the literature review, first of all, the concept of the public sphere was clarified to show that although the specific conceptualisation of the Habermasian public sphere may be contested, the concept of public sphere underpins the idea of a space where citizens are able to deliberate in a democratic process and the importance of public sphere lies in its conception of public discourse or communicative action that has the potential to link the state, market and the citizen – the three components of governance in the current context. It is also "useful for understanding the consequences of target marketing technologies .... when the commercial factors determine who is connected to whom and on what terms" (Monberg, 1993, as cited in Monberg, 1998: 431) and repoliticise an issue that is being presented in an essentially apolitical terms for however, technologies do not exist in isolation. The social, political and economic environment conditions the scope of imagination that assigns technology certain roles in our lives, as well its use, acceptance, integration and utility. By introducing the concept of governance and the role of Telecentres in governance, it was established that the public sphere could no longer be viewed as distinct from the State and the market.

In light of the established conceptual framework, two Telecentre case studies were evaluated against four elements of the public sphere against the backdrop of the system, social, technology and use factors. The analysis demonstrated Telecentres could enhance the public sphere only when they are community embedded and oriented. They must therefore, function more as a community space rather than technology space. Also, the public sphere demands an informed, educated, objective and rational polity. Resource availability too plays a key role in a citizen's ability to participate consistently in democratic debates and the government must be sensitised and willing to engage in a fruitful dialogue with the citizens, moving beyond the simple norm of provision public services. It is something that cannot be achieved either overnight or by sheer presence of technology or ability to file a complaint or apply for a grant.

The paper concluded that while Telecentres create opportunities to extend the public sphere, it is unlikely that any major transformation in the system is will result as a consequence of this extension because the current use of ICTs concentrates primarily on information provision, and not linkages that improve the quality of democratic discourse. For any real transformation to occur, changes at both the government as well as the citizen end must be concurrent and inter-related. At the same time, the must be protected from market mechanisms and not be driven by it.

Telecentres can play a crucial role in linking the hitherto unlinked or distant areas to the centre of politics and give the marginalized citizens voice, however akin to the Habermasian public sphere, they cannot ensure if the voice will be heard and acted upon. Habermas observes "whereas the growth of systems and networks multiplies the possible contacts and exchanges of information, it does not lead per se to the expansion of an intersubjectively shared world and to the discursive interweaving of conceptions of relevance, themes, and contributions from which political public spheres arise" (Habermas, 1998:120-121). Therefore, "the extent to which ICTs foreclose or promote community contact is crucial and community centres are shaped by their positions relative to their surrounding region … and local and national economy" (Monberg, 1998:445). Telecentre's role therefore in technology-mediated 'public sphere' may be important but for the moment it is limited.

At the policy level, it implies first, the understanding of the complex weave between technology and context that informs underlying structures and processes; second, efficiency does not always equal effectiveness and transparency does not automatically lead to accountability; third, technology-mediated space must at least correspond in some fashion to the nature of the information infrastructure that would normally be used for civic or community building purposes; and finally, the proponents of technology-mediated public sphere must identify and meet the pre-existing needs of the community member as well as to identify and meet those needs that emerge as community members dynamically interact with one another, otherwise, participation rates decline and the Telecentres runs the risk of becoming irrelevant, and eventually abandoned.

REFERENCES

Ahrens, J. (1997). Prospects of institutional and policy reform in India. *Asian Development Review, 15*(1), 111-146.

Baker, P.M.A., & Ward, A.C. (2002). Bridging temporal and spatial 'gaps': The role of information and communication technologies in defining communities. *Information, Communication & Society, 5*(2), 207–224

Becker, T. (1998). Governance and electronic innovation: A clash of paradigms. *Information, Communication and Society, 1*(3), 339-343.

Benhabib S. (1992). Models of Public Space: Hannah Arendt, the Liberal Tradition, and Jurgen Habermas. In C. Calhoun (Eds.), *Habermas and the Public Sphere.* Cambridge, MA: MIT Press.

Bertz, R. (1983). *Media for Interactive Communication.* Beverly Hills, CA: Sage.

Boyte, H.C., & Kari, N.N. (1996). *Building America: The Democratic Promise of Public Work.* Philadelphia: Temple University Press

Broadbent, J., Laughlin, R., & Read, S. (1991). Recent financial and administrative changes in the NHS: a critical theory analysis. *Critical Perspectives on Accounting, 2*, 1-29

Buckley W. (1967). *Sociology and Modern Systems Theory.* Englewood Cliffs, NJ: Prentice Hall.

Bucy, E.P. (2004). Interactivity in society. *The Information Society, 20*(5) 373-385.

Calhoun, C. (1992). Introduction: Habermas and the Public Sphere. In C. Calhoun (Ed.), *Habermas and the Public Sphere*, Cambridge, MA: MIT Press.

Chadwick, A. (2001). The electronic face of government in the internet age: Borrowing from Murray Edelman. *Information, Communication & Society, 4*(3), 435–457.

Ciborra, C. (2003). Unveiling E-Government and Development: Governing at a Distance in the New War. *Department of Information Systems, LSE,* (no. 126).

Clift, S. L (2004). e-Government and Democracy: Representation and engagement in Information Age. http://publicus.net/e-government Last accessed: 30/06/08.

Dahlberg, L. (2001). The Internet and Democratic Discourse: Exploring the prospects of online deliberative forums extending the public sphere. *Information, Communication & Society, 4*(4), 615-633.

Damiris, N., & Wild, H. (1997). The Internet: A New Agora. In J. Baleur & D. Whitehouse (Eds.), *An Ethical Global Information Society: Culture and Democracy Revisited,* (pp. 307–17). Boston: Kluwer Publishing.

Dewey, J. (1927). *The Public and its Problems.* New York: Henry Holt.

Drishtee (2005). Address: http://www.drishtee.com. Last accessed: 30/06/08

Edelman, M. (1964). *The Symbolic Uses of Politics.* London: University of Illinois Press.

Eley G. (1992). Nations, Publics, and Political Cultures: Placing Habermas in the Nineteenth Century. In C. Calhoun (Ed.), *Habermas and the Public Sphere.*Cambridge, MA: MIT Press.

Ernberg, J. (1998). Integrated Rural Development and Universal Access towards a Framework for Evaluation of Multipurpose Community Telecentre Pilot Projects Implemented by ITU and its Partners. *A Conference at the University of Guelph,* Guelph, Ontario, Canada, October 26 & 27, 1998, www.itu.int/ITU-D-UniversalAccess Last accessed: 30/06/08.

Fraser, N. (1992). Rethinking the Public Sphere: A Contribution to the Critique of Actually Existing Democracy. In C. Calhoun (Ed.), *Habermas and the Public Sphere.* Cambridge, MA: MIT Press.

Fuchs, R. (1998). *Little Engines That Did": Case Histories from the Global Telecentre Movement.* IDRC Study/Acacia Initiative http://info.worldbank.org/etools/docs/library/91628/telecentres/telecentres/workshop/sbt-pdf/otherresouces/engine.pdf Last accessed: 30/06/08

Garnham, N. (1992). The media and the public sphere. In C. Calhoun (Ed.), *Habermas and the Public Sphere.* Cambridge, MA: MIT Press.

Gasco, M. (2003). New Technologies and Institutional Change in Public Administration. *Social Science Computer Review, 21*(1), 6-14.

Gaspar, M. (2001). Telehouse in Hungary. *The Journal of Development Communication, 12*(2).

Habermas, J. (1989). *The Structural Transformation of the Public Sphere: An Inquiry into a Category of Bourgeois Society.* Translated Thomas Burger, Massachusetts: MIT Press.

Habermas, J. (1994). The emergence of the public sphere. In J. Habermas (Ed.), *The Polity Reader in Cultural Theory.* Cambridge: Polity Press.

Habermas, J. (1996). *Between Facts and Norms: Contributions to a Discourse Theory of Law and Democracy.* Translated William Rehg, Cambridge, UK: Polity Press.

Heeks, R.B. (2001). Understanding E-Governance for Development. *Information Systems for Public Sector Management Working Paper Series, IDPM: University of Manchester,* Paper No. 11.

Hudson, H. (1999). Designing research for Telecentre evaluation. In R. Gomez & P. Hunt, (Eds.), *Telecentre Evaluation: A Global Perspective.* Far Hills Inn, Quebec.

Hyden, G., Court, J., & Mease, K. (2004). *Making Sense of Governance: Empirical Evidence from 10 Developing Countries.* London: Lynne Riener.

Indian Institute of Information Technology (2005). *Drishtee Soochana Kendras, Sirsa, Haryana*: Address: http://www.iiitb.ac.in/Complete_report.pdf Last accessed: 30/06/08

ITU (2001). *Telecottages in Hungary* http://www.itu.int/ITU-D/univ_access/casestudies/hun_mct.html Last accessed: 30/06/08

Jokay, K.Z. (2002). Telecottages and the Modernization of Public Services in Hungary: The Case of the Village of Jászkísér. In G. Wright & J. Nemec, (Eds.), *Public Management in the Central and Eastern European Transition: Concepts and Cases, Bratislava,* NISPACEE (link: www.nispa.sk) (pp. 457-471).

Kanungo, S. (2004). *On the Emancipatory Role of Rural Information Systems.* Information Technology & People, *17*(4), 407-422.

Kjaer, A.M. (2004). *Governance.* Cambridge: Polity Press.

Kooiman, J. (2003). *Governing as Governance.* London: Sage.

Ku, A.S. (2000). Revisiting the notion of "public" in Habermas's theory – Toward a theory of politics of public credibility. *Sociological Theory, 18*(2), 216-240

Leftwich, A. (1993). Governance, democracy and development in the Third World. *Third World Quarterly, 14* 605-24.

Lin, C.A (2003). A interactive communication technology adoption model. *Communication Theory, 13*(4), 345-365

Monberg, J. (1998). Making the public count: a cpmparative case study of emergent information technology-based publics. *Communication Theory, 8*(4) *426-454.*

Newhagen, C., & Levy (1995). Nightly@nbc.com: Audience scope and perception of interactivity in viewer mail in the Internet. *Journal of Communication, 45*(3), 164-175

OECD (2001) *Information and Communication Technologies and Rural Development.* http://www.oecd.org.

Pigg, K.E. (2001). Applications of Community Informatics for building Community and enhancing civic society. *Information, Communication & Society, 4*(4), 507–527

Proenza, F.J, Bastidas-Buch, R., & Montero, G. (2001). *Telecentres for Socio-economic and Rural Development in Latin America and the Caribbean.* FAO, ITU and IADB, Washington DC

Roman, R., & Colle, R.D. (2002). *Themes and Issues in Telecentre Sustainability.* Development Informatics Working Paper Series Paper No. 10, IDPM, University of Manchester.

Rosenau, J.N. (1992). Governance, Order and Change in World Politics. In J.N. Rosenau & E-O. Czempiel (Eds.), *Governance without Government: Order and Change in World Politics.* New York: Cambridge University Press.

Rhodes, R.A.W. (1997). *Understanding Governance: Policy Networks, Governance, Reflexivity and Accountability.* Maidenhead: Open University Press.

Sclove, R. (1994). Democratising technology. *The Chronicle of Higher Education, B1-2*

Sundar, S.S. (2004). Theorizing interactivity's effects. *The Information Society, 20*(5), 387-391.

Stoker, G. (1998). Governance as theory: Five propositions. *International Journal of Social Science, 155* 17 - 28.

Taylor, J.A. (1998). Governance and electronic innovation: Whither the information polity' *Information, Communication & Society, 1*(2), 144-162.

Tsagarousianou, R. (1998). Electronic democracy and the public sphere: opportunities and challenges. In R. Tsagarousianou, D. Tambini, & C. Bryan (Eds.), *Cyberdemocracy: Technology, Cities and Civic Networks* eds.. London: Routledge.

UNCTAD (2006). *E-Commerce and Development Report.* available at http://r0.unctad.org/ecommerce/ecommerce_en/ier06_en.htm Last accessed: 30/06/08

UNDP (2006). *http://europeandcis.undp.org/home/show/1EAEB3D3-F203-1EE9-BD-0C279330992AC8* Last accessed: 30/06/08

UNPAN (2007). http://www.unpan.org/Library/MajorPublications/WorldPublicSectorReport/tabid/645/Default.aspx#2007: Last accessed: 30/06/08

Van Dijk, J. (1999). *The Network Society: Social Aspects of New Media.* London: Sage

Webster, F. (1995). *Theories of the Information Society.* London: Routledge.

Wei, S.X., & Kuzmanovic, M. (2000). From representation to performance:responsive public space. *CPSR Newsletter, 18*. Online. Available: http://www.cpsr.org/publications/newsletters/issues/2000/Summer2000/wei-kuzmanovic.html

Wishard, W.V.D. (1994). Global trends reshaping civil society. In D.E. Eberly, (Ed.), *Building a Community of Citizens: Civil Society in the 21st Century*, Lanham, MA: The Commonwealth Foundation, (pp. 57–82).

World Bank (1999). *World Development Report 1998/99.* World Bank http://econ.worldbank.org

World Bank (2003). *Drishtee: Connecting India Village by Village* Address: http://web.worldbank.org/WBSITE/EXTERNAL/OPPORTUNITIES/GRANTS/DEVMARKETPLACE/0,,contentMDK:20208584~menuPK:214469~pagePK:180691~piPK:174492~theSitePK:205098,00.html Last accessed: 18/03/05

World Bank (2004a). *Dm 2003 Project Implementation Progress Report.* Address: http://siteresources.worldbank.org/DEVMARKETPLACE/Resources/DM-2003-Reports/146601.pdf Last accessed: 18/03/05:

World Bank (2004b). h*ttp://Siteresources.Worldbank.Org/Devmarketplace/Resources/205097-1090596582429/1466pcr.Pdf* Last accessed: 18/03/05

World Bank (2004c). *Drishtee Telecenter Initiative* Address: http://poverty.worldbank.org/files/14646_Drishtee-web.pdf Last accessed: 23/04/2005

Young, I.M. (1987). Impartiality and the civic public: Some implications of feminist critiques of moral and political theory. In S. Benhabib & D. Cornell (Eds.), *Feminism as Critique: Essays on the Politics of Gender in Late-Capitalist Societies.* Cambridge: Polity.

Compilation of References

2007 Asia - Telecoms, Mobile and Broadband in India: http://www.researchandmarkets.com/reportinfo.asp?report_id = 481013

Abanumy, A., Albadi A., & Mayhew, P. (2005). e-Government website Accessibility: In-Depth Evaluation of Saudi Arabia and Oman. *The Electronic Journal of e-Government, 3*(3), 99-106.

Accenture. (2004). eGovernment leadership: High performance, maximum value. *The Government Executive Series, May 2004.*

Accenture. (2005). Leadership in customer service: New expectations, new experiences. *The Government Executive Series, April 2005.*

ADB (2003). *Toward E-Development in Asia and the Pacific: A Strategic Approach to Information and Communication Technology*, www.adb.org, accessed 27 May 2007.

Agarwal, R., & Prasad, J. (1999). Are individual differences germane to the acceptance of new information technologies? *Decision Sciences*, *30*(2), 361-91.

Agrawal, A. (2007). *Assessing Service Quality in e-Services: Building up on the Quality Instrumentation.* PhD Dissertation, submitted to ICFAI University.

Agrawal, A., & Fuloria, S. (2003). A Study of Interest, Awareness Level, Perception & Acceptability of E-governance by Indian Citizens. In M.P. Gupta (Ed.), *Promise of E-Governance: Operational Challenges* (pp, 49-56). New Delhi: Tata McGraw Hill.

Ahrens, J. (1997). Prospects of institutional and policy reform in India. *Asian Development Review, 15*(1), 111-146.

Aichholzer, G., & Schmutzer, R. (2000). *Organisational challenges to the development of electronic government.* Paper presented at 11th International Workshop on Database and Expert Systems Applications, IEEE Computer Society, London.

Akula, V.B. (2000). *Putting Technology to Work for Poverty Alleviation: A Draft Proposal for $151,030 to Develop Smart Cards for Microfinance,* Swayam Krishi Sangam, Hyderabad.

Al-Amer, M.A. (2003). *Kingdom of Bahrain: e-Government Program [Internet],* Available from: <http://unpan1.un.org/intradoc/groups/public/documents/UNESCWA/UNPAN015333.pdf> [Accessed Jan 5th, 2008].

AL-Gahtani, S., & King, M. (1999). Attitudes, satisfaction and usage: factors contributing to each in the acceptance of information technology. *Behavior And Information Technology, 18(4), 277-297.*

Al-Jboori, A. (2006, September). *E-Government in Saudi Arabia: Can It Overcome Its Challenges*? eGovernment Workshop, Brunel University.

Al-Khouri, A., & Bal, J. (2004). Electronic Government in the GCC Countries. *International Journal of Social Sciences*, 1(2), 83-98.

Al-Kibsi, G., de Boer, K., Mourshed, M., & Rea, N.P. (2001). *Putting citizens on-line, not in line, McKinzey Quarterly, 2*, 65-73.

Al-Nahas, N. (2006). The Role of Knowledge and Capability Evaluation in E-Business Strategy: An Integrative Approach and Case Illustration. *SAM Advanced Management Journal, 71.*

Al-Omani, A., & Al-Omani, H. (2006). E-governance Readiness Assessment Model. *Journal of Computer Science, 2*(11), 841-845.

Al-Sebie, M., & Irani, Z. (2005). Technical and organisational challenges facing transactional e-government systems: an empirical study. *Electronic Government, An International Journal, 2*(3), 247–276.

Al-Shafi, S., & Weerakkody, V. (2007). Implementing and managing e-government in the State of Qatar: a citizens' perspective. *Electronic Government, an International Journal, 4*(4), 436-450.

Al-Tawil, K.M., & Sadiq, S.M. (2002). *E-governance-Where We Stand?* Available at: http://www.worldbank.org/wbi/mdf/mdf4/papers/altawil-sait.pdf. Accessed July 28, 2007.

American Customer Satisfaction Index (2004). *E-Government Satisfaction Index.* Retrieved: July 30th, 2007, from http://www.fcg.gov/pdf/e-gov_comm_092004.pdf

Andersen, K.V., & Henriksen, H.Z. (2006). E-Government Maturity Models: Extension of the Layne and Lee model. *Government Information Quarterly, 23*(2), 236-248.

Annamalai, K., & Sachin. R. (2003). *What Works: ITC's e-Choupal and Profitable Rural Transformation Web-Based Information And Procurement Tools For Indian Farmers.* Jointly published as "*What Works Case Study*" by World Resources Institute, Digital Dividend and University of Michigan, (August 2003) (accessed in March, 2005 from <http://www. digitaldividend.org / pdf/echoupal_case.pdf> , via Google, http://www.google.com).

Anonymous (2007). *Village knowledge centres vital for rural development.* Available at http://www.thehindubusinessline.com/bline/2005/07/12/stories/2005071200770300.htm, Accessed on 12/07/2007

Apostolou, D., Mentzas, G., & Stojanovic, N. (2006). *Semantic-enabled Aglie Knowledge-based e-government,* American Association for Artificial Intelligence [online], http://www.imu.iccs.gr/ sweg/papers/SS0606StojanovicN2-sake.pdf [accessed 02/11/2007]

Archmann, S., & Kudlacek, I. (2008). Interoperability and the exchange of good practice cases. *European Journal of ePractice, 2*(1), 3-12.

Arcieri, F., Melideo, G., Nardelli, E., & Talamo, M. (2002). Experiences and issues in the realization of e-government services. In *12th International Workshop on Research Issues in Data Engineering: Engineering e-Commerce/ e-Business Systems (RIDE.02).*

Ashraf, Md. M., Hanisch, J. & Swatman, P. (2006). ICT Intervention Towards Development In The Third World Countries: some perspectives of IS research. In *Proceedings of the 9th International Conference on Computer and Information Technology(ICCIT*), Dhaka, Bangladesh, 21-23 December.

Asia-Pacific Journal on Information, Communication and Space Technology: Reviews and Updates. First Issue – 2006, Economic and Social Commission for Asia and the Pacific

Avgerou, C. (2003). The link between ICT and economic growth in the discourse of development. In M. Korpela, R. Monetealerge, & K. Poulymenakou (Eds.), *Organizational information systems in the context of globalization,* (pp. 373-386).

Awan, M. (2003), *E-Government: Assessment of GCC (*Gulf Co-operating Council) Countries and Services Provided, Lecture Notes in Computer Science 2739, (pp. 500-503).

Backus, M. (2001, March). *E-governance in Developing Countries.* IICD Research Brief - No 1. Available at: http://www.ftpiicd.org/files/research/briefs/brief1.doc. Accesses July 28, 2007.

Bailey, J.E., & Pearson, S.W. (1983). Development of a Tool for Measuring & Analyzing Computer User Satisfaction. *Management Science, 29*(5), 530-545.

Baker, P.M.A., & Ward, A.C. (2002). Bridging temporal and spatial 'gaps': The role of information and communication technologies in defining communities. *Information, Communication & Society, 5*(2), 207–224

Bank, W. (1998). *World Development Report*, Washington, DC.

Baramati Initiatives (2001). *SKS-Smart Cards: Case Study*. www.baramatiinitiatives. com/cases/case10. htm.

Becker, T. (1998). Governance and electronic innovation: A clash of paradigms. *Information, Communication and Society, 1*(3), 339-343.

Bekkers, V. (2007). The governance of back-office integration. *Public Management Review, 9*(3), 377-400.

Belanger, F., & Carter, L. (2004). Citizen Adoption of Electronic Government Initiatives. In *Proceedings of the 37th Hawaii International Conference on Systems Sciences*.

Belanger, F., Hiller, J., & Smith, W. (2002). Trustworthiness in electronic commerce: the role of privacy, security, and site attributes. *Journal of Strategic Information Systems, 11*, 245-270.

Benhabib S. (1992). Models of Public Space: Hannah Arendt, the Liberal Tradition, and Jurgen Habermas. In C. Calhoun (Eds.), *Habermas and the Public Sphere*. Cambridge, MA: MIT Press.

Bertalanffy, L.v. (1968). *General System Theory: Foundations*. Development *Applications*. New York: George Braziller.

Bertz, R. (1983). *Media for Interactive Communication*. Beverly Hills, CA: Sage.

Best, M., & Maclay, C.M. (2002). *Community Internet Access in Rural Areas: Solving the economic sustainability puzzle*. The Global Information Technology Report 2001-2002: Readiness for the networked world, ed., Geoffrey Kirkman (Oxford University Press, 2002). Available online at http://www.cid.harvard.edu /cr/gitrr_030202 .html (May 20, 2007)

Beynon-Davies, P. (2007). Models for e-government. *Transforming Government: People, Process and Policy, 1*(1), 7-28.

Beynon-Davies, P., & Williams, M.D. (2003). Evaluating electronic local government in the UK. *Journal of Information Technology, 18*(2), 137-149.

Bhatnagar, S. (2000). Empowering dairy farmers through a dairy information & services kiosk. Washington, DC: World Bank.

Bhatnagar, S. (2002). Egovernment: Lessons from implementation in developing countries. *Regional Development Dialogue, 24*, 164-174.

Bhatnagar, S. (2004). *E-government: from vision to implementation – a practical guide with case studies*. New Delhi: Sage Publications (pp. 17, 53, 54, 73).

Bhatnagar, S., & Schware, R. (Eds.) (2000). *Information and Communication Technology in Rural Development. Case Studies from India*. Washington, DC: World Bank.

Bhatnagar, S., & Vyas, N. (2001). Gyandoot: Community-Owned Rural Internet Kiosks. Washington, DC: World Bank.

Bhattacharjee, R. (2002). IFLA: Country Report, India. *Public Library Services in India: Systems and Deficiencies. Available at* <www.ifla.org/VII/s8/anuual/cr02-in.htm> accessed on 21/06/2007 at 4.55 pm

Bhattacherjee, A. (2001). Understanding information systems continuance: An expectation-confirmation model. *MIS Quarterly, 25*(3), 351-370.

Bhatti, N., Bouch, A., & Kuchinsky, A. (2000). Integrating user-perceived quality into Web server design. *Computer Networks, 33*(1-6), 1-16.

Bitner, M.J. (1992). Servicescapes: The impact of Physical Surroundings on Customers & Employees. *Journal of Marketing, 56* 57-71.

Bolton, R.N., & Drew, J. (1991). A Longitudinal Analysis of the Impact of Service Changes on Customer Attitudes. *Journal of Marketing, 55*, 1-9.

Bonham, G., Seifert, J., & Thorson, S. (2001). *The Transformational Potential of e-Government: The Role Of Political Leadership.* Paper presented at the The 4th Pan European International Relations Conference of the European Consortium for Political Research, University of Kent, Canterbury, U.K.

Borras, J. (2004). International Technical Standards for e-Government. *Electronic Journal of e-Government, Academic Conferences Limited* [online] http://www.ejeg.com/volume-2/volume2-issue2/v2-i2-borras-pp75-80.pdf [accessed 02/01/08]

Boyatzis, R.E. (1998). *Transforming qualitative information : thematic analysis and code development*, Sage Publications, Thousand Oaks, CA.

Boyne, G., Gould-Williams, J., Law, J., & Walker, R. (2002). Plans, performance information and accountability: The case of best value. *Public Administration, 80*(4), 691-710.

Boyte, H.C., & Kari, N.N. (1996). *Building America: The Democratic Promise of Public Work.* Philadelphia: Temple University Press

BRAC (2003). *BRAC Project proposal: 2004-2009.* Bangladesh Rural Advancement Committee (BRAC), Dhaka, Bangladesh.

BRAC (2004). *BRAC annual report: 2004.* Dhaka, Bangladesh.

Brady, K.M., & Cronin, Jr. J.J. (2001). Some New Thoughts on Conceptualizing Perceived Service Quality: A Hierarchical Approach. *Journal of Marketing, 65*(July), 34-43.

Breen, J. (2000). At the dawn of e-Government: The citizen as customer. *Government Finance Review, 16*(5), 15-20.

Bretschneider, S., Gant, J., & Ahn, M. (2003). A general model of e-government service adoption: Empirical exploration. *Public Management Research Conference, Georgetown Public Policy Institute Washington, DC, October*, 9-11.

Bridges.org (2002). *Taking stock and looking ahead: Digital divide assessment of the city of Cape Town, 2002.* Retrieved: Retrieved: August 5, 2007 at: http://www.bridges.org/capetown.

Broadbent, J., Laughlin, R., & Read, S. (1991). Recent financial and administrative changes in the NHS: a critical theory analysis. *Critical Perspectives on Accounting, 2*, 1-29

Buckley W. (1967). *Sociology and Modern Systems Theory.* Englewood Cliffs, NJ: Prentice Hall.

Bucy, E.P. (2004). Interactivity in society. *The Information Society, 20*(5) 373-385.

Burn, J., & Robins, G. (2003). Moving towards e-government: a case study of organizational change processes. *Logistics Information Management, 16*(1), 25-35.

Bwoma, P.O., & Huang, Z . (2003). An overview of critical issues of E-government. *Issues of Information Systems, 4*(1), 164-170.

Cabinet Office (2005). *e-Government Interoperability Framework.* e-Government Unit, Cabinet Office, London, UK.

Cabinet Office (2005). *Geographic Information: An Analysis of Interoperability and Information Sharing in the United Kingdom.* e-Government Unit, Cabinet Office, London, UK.

Cabinet Office. (2000). *Electronic government services for the 21st century.* London.

Calhoun, C. (1992). Introduction: Habermas and the Public Sphere. In C. Calhoun (Ed.), *Habermas and the Public Sphere*, Cambridge, MA: MIT Press.

Cam, C.N. (2004). A conceptual framework for socio-techno centric approach to sustainable development. *International Journal of Technology Management & Sustainable Development, 3*(1), 59-66.

Carter, L., & Bélanger, F. (2005). The utilization of e-government services: citizen trust, innovation and acceptance factors. *Information Systems Journal, 15*(1), 5-25.

Castells, M. (1996). *Rise of the network society: The information age, economy, society and culture.* USA/ Oxford, UK: Blackwell Publishers.

Castells, M. (2000). *End of millennium: The rise of the fourth world: capitalism, poverty and social exclusion,* (p. 168), Second Edition. Oxford, UK: Blackwell.

Cecchini, S. (2001). *Back to office report: information and communications technology for poverty reduction in rural india, mimeo.* Washington, DC: World Bank.

Cecchini, S. (2002). *Back to office report: Evaluation of Gyandoot and Bhoomi and International Conferences on ICT for Development, Mimeo.* Washington, DC: World Bank.

Cecchini, S., & Raina, M. (2002, April). Warana: *The Case of an Indian Rural Community Adopting Information and Communications Technology in Information Technology in Developing Countries, 12*(1). www.iimahd.ernet.in/egov/ifip/apr2002/apr2002.htm.

Cecchini, S., & Scott, C. (2003). Can information and communications technology applications contribute to poverty reduction? Lessons from rural India? *Information Technology for Development, 10*(2), 73-84.

Cecchini, S., & Shah, T. (2002). Information and Communications Technology as a Tool for Empowerment in Empowerment and Poverty Reduction: A Sourcebook. Washington, DC: World Bank. www.worldbank.org/poverty/empowerment/

Census, P. (2001). *Population Census in Bangladesh.* Dhaka.

Center for Democracy and Technology & infoDev (2002). *E-Government Handbook for Developing Countries.* Retrieved: August 5, 2007 at: http://www.cdt.org/egov/handbook/

Centre of E-governance. (2003, June). IIM Ahmedabad, Evaluation Studies by the Centre for E-Governance. Indian Institute of Management, Ahmedabad (CEG-IIMA). *Information Technology in Developing Countries, 13*(1). Available online at http://www.iimahd.ernet.in/egov/ifip/jun2003/ article6.htm

Chadwick, A. (2001). The electronic face of government in the internet age: Borrowing from Murray Edelman. *Information, Communication & Society, 4*(3), 435–457.

Chaffey, D. (2007). *E-business and e-commerce management.* Upper Saddle River, NJ:Prentice-Hall, Inc.

Chambers, R. (1983). *Rural* development*: Putting the last first.* London: Longman.

Chan, Y.E., Huff, S.L., Barclay, D.W., & Copeland, D.G. (1997). Business strategic orientation, information strategic orientation, and strategic alignment. *Information Systems Research, 8*(2), 125-150.

Chariar, V.M. (2005). *Rejuvenating **Community Knowledge Systems** of India.* (unpublished).

Chau, P.Y.K. (1996). An Empirical Assessment Of A Modified Technology Acceptance Model. *Journal of Management Information Systems, 13*(2), 185-204.

Checkland, P. (1981). *Systems thinking, systems practice.* New York: J. Wiley.

Checkland, P., & Holwell, S. (1998). *Information, systems and information systems: making sense of the field.* New York: J. Wiley.

Chen, C., Tseng, S., & Huang, H. (2006). A comprehensive study of the digital divide phenomenon in Taiwanese government agencies. *International Journal Of Internet And Enterprise Management, 4*(3), 244-256.

Chen, H. (2002) Digital government: technologies and practices. *Decision Support Systems, 34*(3), 223-227.

Chen, J., & Stanney, K. (1999). A theoretical model of wayfinding in virtual environments: proposed strategies for navigational Aidiin. *MIT Press, 8*(6), 671-686.

Chen, M. (2003). Factors affecting the adoption and diffusion of XML and web services standards for e-business systems. *International Journal of Human-Computer Studies, 58*(3), 259-79.

Cheng, T., Lam, D., & Yeung, A. (2006). Adoption of internet banking: An empirical study in Hong Kong. *Decision Support Systems, 42*, 1558-1572.

Chesher, M., & Kaura, R. (2003). *Electronic Business & Commerce*, Springer, London.

Chesi, F., Pallotti, M., & Oreste, S. (2005). *A Working E-Government Experience: The Citel Project, CMG Poland Annual Conference*, Warsaw, 9-10 May, 2005, [online] Available from <http://www.w3c.it/papers/cmg2005Poland-egov.pdf> [12th march 2008].

Chircu, A.M., & Lee, D.H-D. (2005). E-government: Key Success Factors For Value Discovery And Realisation. *E- Government, an International Journal, 2*(1), 11-25.

Choudrie, J., & Dwivedi, Y. (2005). A survey of citizens adoption and awareness of e-government initiatives. The Government Gateway: A United Kingdom Perspective. *E-Government Workshop*. Brunel University, West London.

Choudrie. J, & Ghinea, G., & Weerakkody, V. (2004). Evaluating global e-government sites: a view using web diagnostic tools. *Electronic Journal of E-Government, 2*(2), 105-114.

Ciborra, C.U. (2003). *Unveiling e-government and development: governing at a distance in the new war.* Working Paper 126, London School of Economics and Political Science, London, available at: http://is.lse.ac.uk/wp/pdf/WP126.PDF.

City of Cape Town. (2003). *E-government services research project: Initial research to inform the design and development of e-government services.*

Clift, S. L (2004). e-Government and Democracy: Representation and engagement in Information Age. http://publicus.net/e-government Last accessed: 30/06/08.

Cloete, F. (2003). Assessing governance with electronic policy management tools. *Public Performance & Management Review, 26*(3), 276-290.

Collier, J.E., & Bienstock, C.C. (2006). Measuring service quality in e-retailing. *Journal of Service Research, 8*(3), 260.

Compaine, B.M. (2001). *The digital Divide- Facing a crisis or creating a myth?* Massachusetts: MIT press.

Cornford, T., & Smithson, S. (1997). *Project Research in Information Systems: A Student's Guide*. London: Macmillan Press.

Corning, P.A. (2001). Devolution as an Opportunity to Test the Synergism Hypothesis and a cybernetic theory of Political Systems. *Systems Research & Behavioral Science* ABI/INFORM.

Creswell, J.W. (1998). *Qualitative inquiry and research design : choosing among five traditions*. Thousand Oaks, USA: Sage Publications.

Criado, J.I., & Ramilo, M.C. (2003). E-government in practice: an analysis of web site orientation to the citizens in Spanish municipalities. *The International Journal of Public Sector Management, 16*(3), 191-218.

CRISP Group (2003, July). National Informatics Centre, Department of IT, Ministry of Communications & IT, Government of India, Information Needs Assessment for Rural Communities- An Indian Case Study. Available online at http://ruralinformatics.nic.in/files/4_12_0_229.pdf

Critical Success Factors for Rural ICT Projects in India: A study of n-Logue kiosk projects at Pabal and Baramati. Submitted in partial fulfillment of the requirements for the degree of Master of Management By Vivek Dhawan, IIT Bombay.

Cronin, J.J., & Taylor, S.A. (1992, July). Measuring service quality: A re-examination & extension. *Journal of Marketing, 56*, 55-68.

Dabholkar, P.A., Thorpe, D.I., & Rentz, J.O. (1996). A measure of Service Quality for Retailing Stores: Scale Development & Validation. *Journal of the Academy of Marketing Science, 24*(1). 3-16.

Dahlberg, L. (2001). The Internet and Democratic Discourse: Exploring the prospects of online deliberative forums extending the public sphere. *Information, Communication & Society, 4*(4), 615-633.

Damiris, N., & Wild, H. (1997). The Internet: A New Agora. In J. Baleur & D. Whitehouse (Eds.), *An Ethical Global Information Society: Culture and Democracy*

Revisited, (pp. 307–17). Boston: Kluwer Publishing.

Darwish, A. (2001, February). Bahrain leads the way. *The Middle East* (p. 13),

Davenport, T. (1997). *Information ecology: Mastering the information and knowledge environment*. New York: Oxford University Press.

Davis, F.D. (1989). Perceived usefulness, perceived ease of use, and user acceptance of information technology. *MIS Quarterly, 13*(3), 319-340.

Davis, F.D., Bagozzi, R.P., & Warshaw, P.R. (1989). User Acceptance of Computer Technology: A Comparison of Two Theoretical Models. *Management Science, 35*(8), 982-1003.

Davis, W.S., & Benamati, J. (2003). *E-commerce basics: Technology foundations and e-business applications*. Addison-Wesley.

Davison, R.M., Wagner, C., & Ma, L.C. (2005). From government to e-government: a transition model. *Information Technology & People, 18*(3), 280-299.

DeLeone, W.H., & McLean, E.R. (1992). Information Systems Success: The Quest for the Dependent Variable. *Information Systems Research, 3*(1), 60-95.

Deloitte Research. (2000). *Through the portal: Enterprise transformation for e-government*. Deloitte and Touche.

Demchak, C.C., Friis, C., & La Porte, T.M. (2000). Webbing governance: National differences in constructing the public face. In G. Garson (Ed.), *Handbook of public information systems*. New York: Marcel Dekker Inc.

Desai, V., & Potter, R.B. (2006). The Raison d'etre of Doing Development Research. In V. Desai & R. B. Potter (Eds.), *Doing Development Research, 8.*. New-Delhi, India: Sage Publications.

Dewey, J. (1927). *The Public and its Problems*. New York: Henry Holt.

Dholakia, U., & Rego, L. (1998). What makes commercial Web pages popular? *European Journal of Marketing, 32*(7/8), 724-736.

Digital Opportunities task Force (2002). *Digital Opportunities for All. Sommet Kananaskis Summit 2002. Report Card Retrieved 12/02/2005 from http://e-com.ic.gc.ca/epic/internet/inecic-ceac.nsf/vwapj/DOT_General-Report_e.pdf/$file/DOT_General-Report_e.pdf*

Dijkman, R., & Dumas, M. (2007). Service-oriented design: A multi-viewpoint approach. *International Journal of Cooperative Information Systems, 13*(4), 337-368.

Dillon(2004). The importance of usability in the establishment of organizational software standards for end user computing. *International Journal of Human-Computer Studies, 45*,243-258.

Galliers, R.D., & Sutherland, A.R. (1991). Information systems management and strategy formulation: the 'stages of growth' model revisited. *J. of Information Systems, 1*, 89-114.

Dittrich, Y., Ekelin, A., Elovaara, S., & Hansson, C. (2003). *Making e-government happen everyday co-development of services, citizenship and technology*, Hawaii.

Dixit, K. (2006). *Does information technology really promote knowledge?* Third World Network Features, Retrieved 10 July, 2006 from <http://sade.sdnp.undp.org/rc/forums/mgr/sdnpmgrs/msg01283.html>.

Doll, W.J., & Torkzadeh G. (1988, June). The Measurement of End-User Computing Satisfaction. *MIS Quarterly, 12*(2), 259- 274.

Dossani Rafiq, D.C., Misra, R.J. (2005). *Enabling ICT for Rural India*. A Project Report by Asia-Pacific Research Center, Stanford University and National Informatics Centre (NIC), November 2005. Accessed from iis-db.stanford.edu/pubs/20972/ICT_full_Oct05 on July 10, 2008

Drigas, A., & Koukianakis, L. (2004). E-government application for supporting a network of distributed public administration units. *WSEAS Transactions on Computers, 6*.

Drishtee (2005). Address: http://www.drishtee.com. Last accessed: 30/06/08

Dwivedi, Y., & Weerakkody, V. (2007). Examining the factors affecting the adoption of broadband in the Kingdom of Saudi Arabia. *Electronic Government, an International Journal, 4*(1), 43-58.

Dwivedi, Y., Papazafeiropoulou, A., & Gharavi, H. (2006). *Socio-Economic Determinants of Adoption of the Government Gateway Initiative in the UK, Electronic Government, 3*(4), 404-419.

Dwivedi, Y.K. (2009). An analysis of e-government research published in Transforming Government: People, Process and Policy (TGPPP). *Transforming Government: People, Process and Policy*, 3 (1).

Dwivedi, Y.K., Williams, M.D., & Lal, B. (2008). The diffusion of research on the adoption and diffusion & diffusion of information technology. In proceedings of the *IFIP8.6 Conference*, (eds. Gonzalo, L., Bernardos, A., Casar, J., Kautz, K., and DeGross, J.), Boston: Springer, Madrid, Spain, October 2008.

Dwivedi, Y.K., Williams, M.D., Lal, B., & Schwarz, A., (2008). Profiling adoption, acceptance, and diffusion research in the information systems discipline. In proceedings of the *16th European Conference on Information Systems*, 2008b, Galway, Ireland, June 9th-11th 2008.

Dwivedi, Y.K., Williams, M.D., Lal, B., and Dwivedi, A., (2008). A profile of research on adoption and diffusion of ict/it/is in the consumer/household/residential context. In Proceedings of the Fourteenth Americas Conference on Information Systems, Toronto, ON, Canada August 14th-17th 2008.

Ebrahim, Z., & Irani, Z. (2005). E-government adoption: Architecture and barriers. *Business Process Management Journal, 11*(5), 589-611.

Eckman, B.A., Bennett, C.A., Kaufman, J.H., & Tenner, J.W. (2007). Varieties of interoperability in the transformation of the health-care information infrastructure. *IBM Systems Journal, 46*(1), 19-41.

Economic Commission for Africa. (2002). *Economic Report on Africa 2002: Tracking Performance and Progress*, (p. 74).

Edelman, M. (1964). *The Symbolic Uses of Politics.* London: University of Illinois Press.

Edwin, L. (2003, November). Project Leader, OECD E-Government Project. Challenges for E-Government Development. *5th Global Forum on Reinventing Government*, Mexico City.

Egan, J. (2004). *Relationship marketing.* Harlow, UK: Prentice Hall.

E-government Unit Research paper (2004). *Achieving e-government 2004: A report on progress towards the New Zealand E-government Strategy.* Available at: http://www.e.govt.nz/resources/research/research/ready-access-2004/. Accessed July 28, 2007.

Eley G. (1992). Nations, Publics, and Political Cultures: Placing Habermas in the Nineteenth Century. In C. Calhoun (Ed.), *Habermas and the Public Sphere.*Cambridge, MA: MIT Press.

Elmagarmid, A., & McIver, W. (2001). The ongoing march toward digital government. *IEEE Computer, 34*(2), 32-38.

Emmeche, C., Simo, K., & Stjernfelt, F. (1997). Explaining Emergence: - towards an ontology of levels. *Journal for General Philosophy of Science, 28*(1997), 83-119. accessed in October, 2006 from <http:// www.nbi.dk/ ~emmeche/ coPubl/97e.EKS/ emerg.html>

Ernberg, J. (1998). Integrated Rural Development and Universal Access towards a Framework for Evaluation of Multipurpose Community Telecentre Pilot Projects Implemented by ITU and its Partners. *A Conference at the University of Guelph,* Guelph, Ontario, Canada, October 26 & 27, 1998, www.itu.int/ITU-D-UniversalAccess Last accessed: 30/06/08.

Evert, G. (2003). All research is interpretive! *Journal of Business & Industrial Marketing, 18*(6/7), 482 - 492.

Fang, Z. (2002). E-government in digital era: Concept, practice, and development. *International Journal of The Computer, The Internet and Management, 10*(2), 1-22.

Fedorowicz, J., Gogan, J.L., & Williams, C.B. (2007). A collaborative network for first responders: Lessons from the CapWIN case. *Government Information Quarterly, 24*, 785-807.

Finquelievich, S., Mudhai, O., & Parmar, V. (2004). *Addressing the Digital Divide: A Non-Governmental Organization Sector Perspective.* Retrieved 12/07/2005 from http://www.ssrc.org/programs/itic/publications/knowledge_report/memos/digitaldividepaper.pdf

Fishbein, M., & Ajzen, I. (1975). *Belief, attitude, intention & behavior: An introduction to theory & research.* Reading, MA: Addison-Wesley.

Fountain, J.E. (2001). *Building the virtual state.* Washington, DC: Brookings Institution Press.

Fraser, N. (1992). Rethinking the Public Sphere: A Contribution to the Critique of Actually Existing Democracy. In C. Calhoun (Ed.), *Habermas and the Public Sphere.* Cambridge, MA: MIT Press.

Fuchs, R. (1998). *Little Engines That Did": Case Histories from the Global Telecentre Movement.* IDRC Study/Acacia Initiative http://info.worldbank.org/etools/docs/library/91628/telecentres/telecentres/workshop/sbt-pdf/otherresouces/engine.pdf Last accessed: 30/06/08

Fukuda-Parr, S., Lopes, C., & Malik, K. (2002). *Capacity for Development: New Solutions to Old Problems.* London: Earthscan Publications.

Furuli, K., & Kongsrud, S. (2007). Mypage and Borger.dk - A case study or two government service Web portals. *The Electronic Journal of e-Government*, *5*(2), 165-176.

Galloway, L., & Mochrie, R. (2005). The Use of ICT in Rural Firms: A Policy-Oriented Literature Review. *Info-The Journal of Policy, Regulation and Strategy for Telecommunications, 7*(3), 33-46. The Emerald Group Publishing Limited.

Gant, J., & Gant, D. (2002). Web portal functionality and state government e-service. In *Proceedings of the 35th Annual Hawaii International Conference on System Sciences, 2002. HICSS* (pp. 1627-1636).

Garai, A., & Sahadrach, B. (2006). *Taking ICT to every Indian village: opportunities and challenges.* South Asia, New Delhi: One World.

Garai, A., & Shadrach, B. (2006). Processes and Appropriation of ICT in Human Development in Rural India: Bridging the Research and Practice Gaps. In A. Garai & B. Shadrach (Eds.), *Taking ICT To Every Village*, (pp.1-35). New Delhi: Oneworld South Asia, 2006. Accessed in February, 2006 from http://www.dgroups.org/ groups/oneworld/OneWorldSA/docs/TICTEIV_pdf.pdf

Gardner, C., & Amoroso, D. (2004). *Development of an Instrument to Measure the Acceptance of Internet Technology by Consumers.* Paper presented at the Proceedings of the 37th Hawaii International Conference on System Sciences, Hawaii, USA.

Garnham, N. (1992). The media and the public sphere. In C. Calhoun (Ed.), *Habermas and the Public Sphere.* Cambridge, MA: MIT Press.

Gartner estimate rates India as the fourth largest IT spender. The Economic Times, 13 July 2003. http://www.infochangeindia .org/archives1.jsp?secno=9&monthname=September&year=2003&detail=T

Gartner Group. (2000). *Gartner's four phases of e-government model.* Retrieved from http://www.gartner.com.

Gasco, M. (2003). New Technologies and Institutional Change in Public Administration. *Social Science Computer Review, 21*(1), 6-14.

Gaspar, M. (2001). Telehouse in Hungary. *The Journal of Development Communication, 12*(2).

Gazette, B. (2002). *National Information and Communication Technology (ICT) Policy.* Ministry of Science and Information & Communication Technology Government of the People's Republic of Bangladesh., Dhaka, <http://www.bccbd.org/html/itpolicy.htm#3.3>.

Ghinea, G., & Thomas, J. (1998). *QoS impact on user perception and understanding of multimedia video clips.* pp. 49 - 54, Bristol, U.K.

Ghosh, S., & Fatima, S.S. (2007). A Web Based English to Bengali Text Converter. *In the 3rd Indian International Conference on Artificial Intelligence (IICAI-07)*, Pune, India, December 17-19.

Ghosh, S., & Fatima, S.S. (2007). Retrieval of XML data to support NLP applications. ICAI'07- *The 2007 International Conference on Artificial Intelligence Monte Carlo Resort*, Las Vegas, Nevada, USA ,June 25-28.

Ghosh, S., & Fatima, S.S. (2007, June). Use of local languages in Indian portals. CSI Communication, (pp 4-12).

Gigler, B-S. (2004). Including the Excluded - Can ICTs empower poor communities? In *Proceedings of the 4th International Conference on the Capability Approach*, Italy, 5-7 September, 2004.

Gillham, B. (2005). *Research interviewing: the range of techniques.* Open University Press, Maidenhead.

Goings, D., Young, D., & Hendry, S. (2003). Critical factors in the delivery of e-government services: Perceptions of technology executives. *Communications of the International Information Management Association*, *3*(3), 1-15.

Gomez, R., Hunt, P., & Lamoureux, E. (1999). *Enchanted by Telecentres: a critical look at universal access to information technologies for international development.* Paper presented at the conference New IT and Inequality, University of Maryland, February 16-17.

Gouscos, D., Kalikakis, M., Legal, M., & Papadopoulou, S. (2007). A general model of performance and quality for one-stop e-government service offerings. *Government Information Quarterly*, *24*, 860-885.

Government CIO (2007). *The HKSARG interoperability framework.* Office of the Government Chief Information Officer, The Government of the Hong Kong Special Administrative Region, www.ogcio.gov.hk.

Grant, G., & Chau, D. (2005). Developing a generic framework for e-government. *Journal of Global Information Management*, *13*(1), 1-30.

Grefen, P., Ludwig, H., & Angelov, S. (2003). A three-level framework for process and data management of complex e-services. *International Journal of Cooperative Information Systems*, *12*(4), 487-531.

Greiner, U., Lippe, S., Kahl, T., Ziemann, J., & Jäkel, F.W. (2007). Designing and Implementing Cross-Organizational Business Processes - Description and Application of a Modeling Framework. In G. Doumeingts, J. Müller, G. Morel, & B. Vallespir (Eds.), *Enterprise Interoperability: New Challenges and Approaches*, Springer Verlag, London, UK, (pp. 137-147).

Griffin, D., & Halpin, E. (2005). An exploratory evaluation of UK local e-government from an accountability perspective (pp13-28). *Electronic Journal of e-Government*, *3*(1).

Grönlund, Å. (2005). What's in a field-exploring the e-goverment domain. *System Sciences, 2005. HICSS'05. Proceedings of the 38th Annual Hawaii International Conference on*, 125a-125a.

Gronroos, C. (1982). *Strategic Management & Marketing in the Service Sector.* Helsingfors; Swedish School of Economics & Business Administration Hoffman. K. D.

Gupta, M.P., Prabhat, K., & Jaijit, B. (2004). New Paradigms and Value Propositions in e-Governance. In M.P. Gupta, P. Kumar, & J. Bhattacharya (Eds.)m *Government Online: Opportunities and Challenges*, (p. 77). New-Delhi, India: Tata McGraw Hill.

Gupta, V., & Gupta, S. (2005) Experiments in Wireless Internet Security. *Statistical Methods In Computer Security*

Habermas, J. (1989). *The structural transformation of the public sphere: An inquiry into a category of bourgeois society.* Translated Thomas Burger, Massachusetts: MIT Press.

Habermas, J. (1994). The emergence of the public sphere. In J. Habermas (Ed.), *The Polity Reader in Cultural Theory.* Cambridge: Polity Press.

Habermas, J. (1996). *Between facts and norms: Contributions to a discourse theory of law and democracy.* Translated William Rehg, Cambridge, UK: Polity Press.

Halse, G., & Terzoli, A. (2005). *Open Source in South African Schools: Two Case Studies.* Centre for Excellence in Distributed Multimedia, Rhodes University.

Handbook on Implementing E-Government with basic introduction to E-Commerce: Developed by D.Net - Development through Access to Network Resources.

Harris, J.F., & Schwartz, J. (2000). Anti drug Website tracks visitors. *Washington Post*, 22 June, (p. 23).

Harris, R., & Bhatarai, M. (2003). *Fact-finding review of ict in development in a rural-urban setting.* UN-HABITAT and Roger Harris Associates. Rural-Urban Partnerships Programme (RUPP) under Support Services Policy and Programme Development (SPPD).

Harris, R.W. (2004). Information and Communication Technology for Poverty Alleviation. *E-primers for the Information, Economy, Society and Polity*, Kuala Lumpur (UNDP-APDIP), (pp. 21, 35).

Harris, R.W. (2005). Explaining the success of rural Asian telecentres. In R.M. Davison, R.W. Harris, S. Qureshi, D.R. Vogel & G-Jd. Vreede (Eds.), *Information systems in developing countries: theory and practice.* City University of Hong Kong Press, Hong Kong, (pp. 83-100).

Hazlett, S., & Hill, F. (2003). *E-government: the realities of using IT to transform the public sector.* Managing Service Quality, *13*(6),

Heeks, R. (2004). Success and Failure Rates of e-Government in Developing/Transitional Countries: An Overview. Accessed in December, 2004 from http:// www. egov4dev. org/sfoverview. htm) .

Heeks, R. (1998). Foundation of ICTs in Development: Pushing and Pulling, *Information Technology in Developing Countries Newsletter, 4*(I), 1-2.

Heeks, R. (1999). *Information and Communication Technologies, Poverty and Development, Development Informatics Working Paper Series, Paper No. 5.* www. idpm.man.ac.uk/idpm/di wp5.htm

Heeks, R. (2001). Understanding e-governance for development. *I-Government Working Paper Series*, Institute for Development Policy and Management., *11.*

Heeks, R. (2002). i-Development and not e-Development, Special Issues on ICTs and Development. *Journal of International* Development, (pp. 141-151).

Heeks, R. (2002). Information systems and developing countries: Failure, success, and local improvisations.' *Information Society, 18*(2), 101-112.

Heeks, R. (2003). *Most e-government-for-development projects fail: how can risks be reduced?* Paper no. 14, i-Government Working Paper Series, Institute for Development Policy and Management, University of Manchester, Manchester.

Heeks, R. (2005). Foundation of ICTs in Development: The information chain. *eDevelopment Briefing,* 3(1), 1-2.

Heeks, R. (2005). Foundation of ICTs in Development: The Onion Ring Model. *eDevelopment Briefing, 4*, 1-2.

Heeks, R. (2006). *Implementing and managing e-government: An international text.* Sage.

Heeks, R., & Kenny, C. (2002). ICTs and development: Convergence or divergence for developing countries? In *Proceedings of the Norwegian Association for Development Research Conference*, Trondheim, Norway, 14-15 November 2002.

Heeks, R.B. (2001). Understanding e-governance for development. *Information Systems for Public Sector Management Working Paper Series, IDPM: University of Manchester,* Paper No. 11.

Henderson, J., & Venkatraman, N. (1993). Strategic Alignment: A model for organizational transformation through information technology, *Transforming Organisations,* Oxford University Press.

Hettne, B. (1990). *Development theory and the three worlds.* Essex, England: Harlow.

Hiller, J., & Belanger, F. (2001). Privacy strategies for electronic government. In *E-Government 2001.* Oxford, UK: Rowman and Littlefield Publishers.

Hinton, P.R., Brownlow, C., McMurvay, I., & Cozens, B. (2004). *SPSS explained.* East Sussex, England: Routledge Inc.

Ho, A.L. (2003). EO Allots 1-2% of RP Budget to E-Government Spending. *Inquirer News*

Ho, A.L. (2003, January). EO allots 1-2% of RP budget to e-government spending. *Inquirer News Service.*

Ho, J., Schraefel, M.C., & Chignell, M. (2000). Towards an evaluation methodology for the development of research-oriented virtual communities. *Proceedings of the 9th International Workshops on Enabling Technologies: Infrastructure for Collaborative Enterprises*, Maryland, (pp. 112-117).

Hodgkinson, C. (2002). *Equations towards a general logic of administration.* Paper presented at the 7th Annual Values and Leadership Conference, Toronto, Canada.

Hodgkinson, S. (2002, November). The Victorian electronic records strategy: Centre of Excellence Executive Briefing. http://www.prov.vic.gov.au/vers/published/versbriefing20021122.pdf

Hong Kong Special Administrative Region (2004). *Digital 21 Strategy: Sustainability and Opportunities, March, Government of the Hong Kong Special Administrative Region*, Hong Kong.

Horrigan, J.B. (2004). *How Americans get in touch with government: Internet users benefit from the efficiency of e-government, but multiple channels are still needed for citizens to reach agencies and solve problems.* Washington, DC: Pew Internet & American Life Project.

Howard, M. (2001). e-Government across the globe: How will "e" change Government? *Government Finance Review*, 17(4) 6-9.

http://dinkaunc.blogspot.com/2004/09/impact-of-ict-on-poverty-reduction.html

http://poverty2.forumone.com/library/view/14655/

http://web.worldbank.org/WBSITE/EXTERNAL/TOPICS/EXTINFORMATIONANDCOMMUNICATIONANDTECHNOLOGIES/EXTEGOVERNMENT/0,,contentMDK:20486020~menuPK:1767268~pagePK:210058~piPK:210062~theSitePK:702586,00.html

http://www.digitaldividend.org/case/case_echoupal.htm

http://www.eapf.net/ casestudies/in/agmarket.asp

http://www.expresscomputeronline.com/20070702/management02.shtml

http://www.thehindu.com/2007/11/28/stories/2007112862051900.htm

http://www.unapcict.org/ecohub/case-studies/anand-milk-collection-centres-anand-gujarat

Huang, Z., & Bwoma, O.P. (2003). *An overview of critical issues of e-government.* Central Michigan University.

Hudson, H. (1999). Designing research for Telecentre evaluation. In R. Gomez & P. Hunt, (Eds.), *Telecentre Evaluation: A Global Perspective.* Far Hills Inn, Quebec.

Human Development Report (2007). Fighting climate change: Human solidarity in a divided world. Retrieved: April 2, 2008, from http://hdr.undp.org/en/media/hdr_20072008_en_complete.pdf

Hyden, G., Court, J., & Mease, K. (2004). *Making Sense of Governance: Empirical Evidence from 10 Developing Countries.* London: Lynne Riener.

IctQatar. (2007). *Free wireless internet in Qatar's public parks.* from http://www.ict.gov.qa/output/page422.asp

IDRC (2003). *A Dialogue on ICTs and Poverty: The Harvard Forum.* IDRC, Harvard, Retrieved 10 October, 2005 from <http://web.idrc.ca/ev_en.php?ID=46261_201&ID2=DO_TOPIC>.

Iivari, J., & Koskela, E. (1987, September). The PIOCO Model for Information Systems Design. *MIS Quarterly, 11*(3), 401-419.

India targets PC penetration of 6.5% by 2008: http://mungee.org/archives/2005/05/19/india-targets-pc-penetration-of-65-by-2008/.

India: e-governance market to have an explosive growth by 2007: http://www.digitalopportunity.org/article / view/125575/1/

Indian Institute of Information Technology (2005). *Drishtee Soochana Kendras, Sirsa, Haryana*: Address:

http://www.iiitb.ac.in/Complete_report.pdf Last accessed: 30/06/08

InfoDev. (2002). *The e-Government Handbook for Developing Countries.* from http://www.cdt.org/egov/handbook.

International Telecommunication Union (2004). *Africa, ICT Indicators, 2003.* Retrieved 10/21/2005 from http://www.itu.int/ITU-D/ict/statistics/at_glance/main04.pdf

International Telecommunication Union Report (2007). Available at <http://www.itu.int/ITU-D/ict/publications/wtdr_03/index.html> accessed on 11/06/2007

International Telecommunication Union, Global Survey on Rural Communications. (2004, June). *ITU News, No. 5.* www.itu.int/itunews, Accessed 28 May 2007.

Irani, Z., & Dwivedi, Y.K. (2008). Editorial. *Transforming Government: People, Process and Policy*, 2(4), 221-224.

Irani, Z., Al-Sebie, M., & Elliman, T. (2006). *Transaction Stage of e-Government Systems: Identification of its Location & Importance.* Paper presented at the Proceedings of the 39th Hawaii International Conference on System Science, Hawaii.

ITU (2001). *Telecottages in Hungary* http://www.itu.int/ITU-D/univ_access/casestudies/hun_mct.html Last accessed: 30/06/08

Jaeger, P. (2003). The endless wire: E-government as global phenomenon. *Government Information Quarterly, 20*(4), 323-331.

Jaeger, P., & Thompson, K. (2003). E-government around the world: Lessons, challenges, and future directions. *Government Information Quarterly, 20*(4), 389-394. doi: Article.

James, J. Pro-Poor. (2000). *Modes of Technical Integration into the Global Economy in Development and Change, 31*, 765–783.

Jan A.G.M van Djk. (2005). The Deepening Divide: Inequality in an Information society. Sage publications.

Janssen, D., & Rotthier, S. (2003). How are they doing elsewhere? Trends and consolidations in e-government implementation. *Annual EGPA Conference, Oeiras.*

Jhunjhunwala, A., Anuradha, R., & Sangamitra, R. (2006, February). Connecting Rural India: Taking a Step Back for Two Forward. *Information Technology in Developing Countries, 16*(1). Telecommunications and Computer Networks Group, Madras, IIT-Madras. Accessed in December, 2006 from http://www.iimahd.ernet.in/egov/ifip/ feb2006/article1.htm.

Jiwire (2006). *JiWire Launches Worldwide Point-of-Connection Wi-Fi Hotspot Advertising Network*, from http://www.jiwire.com/about/announcements/press-advertising-network.htm

Johnston, J. (2003). *The Millennium Development Goals and Information and Communications Technology.* United Nations Information and Communication Technologies Task Force, Berlin.

Jokay, K.Z. (2002). Telecottages and the Modernization of Public Services in Hungary: The Case of the Village of Jászkísér. In G. Wright & J. Nemec, (Eds.), *Public Management in the Central and Eastern European Transition: Concepts and Cases, Bratislava*, NISPACEE (link: www.nispa.sk) (pp. 457-471).

Jones, Q., & Rafaeli, S. (2000). Time to Split, Virtually: 'Discourse Architecture' and 'Community Building' as means to Creating Vibrant Virtual Metropolises. *Electronic Markets, 10*(4), 214-223.

Jones, S. (2003). *Encyclopedia of New Media* (pp. 139). Sage Publications.

Judd, C.M., Smith E.R., & Kidder L.H. (1991). *Research methods in social relations.* Sydney: Harcourt Brace Jovanovich College Publishers .

Jul, S., & Furnas, G. (1997). Navigation in electronic worlds. *CHI Æ97 Workshop ACM SIGCHI Bulletin, 29*(4), 44-49.

June, L., Chun-Sheng, Y., Chang, L., & James, E. (2003). Technology Acceptance Model For Wireless Internet. *Internet Research: Electronic Networking Application And Policy,13*(3), 206-222.

Jussawalla, M., & Taylor, R. (2003). Information Technology Parks of the Asia-Pacific: Lessons for the Digital Divide, (p. 259). M.E.Sharpe.

Kalakota, R., & Whinston, A. (1996). *Frontiers of electronic commerce*. Reading, MA: Addison-Wesley.

Kanungo, S. (2004). *On the Emancipatory Role of Rural Information Systems*. Information Technology & People, *17*(4), 407-422.

Kanungo, S. (2004). Research Directions for Studying ICT Interventions in Poor and Rural Areas in Developing Countries. In M.P. Gupta (Ed.), *Towards E-Government,* (pp. 155-171). New Delhi: Tata McGraw Hill.

Kaplan, B., & Duchon, D. (1998). Combining Qualitative and Quantitative Methods in Information Systems Research: A Case Study. *MIS Quarterly, 12*(4), 571-586.

Karnjanatawe, K. (2003). *Government web sites fail user test – Information is out of date.* Bangkok Post, http://www.bangkokpost.com/290103_Database/29Jan2003_data03.html

Karunanada, A., & Weerakkody, V. (2006, October). E-government Implementation in Sri Lanka: Lessons from the UK. *Proceedings of the 8th International Information Technology Conference (IITC),* Colombo, Sri Lanka.

Kaushik, P.P., & Nirvikar S. (2004). Information Technology and Broad based Development : Preliminary lessons from North India. *World* Development, *32*(4), 591-607.

Kaynama, S.A., & Black, C.I. (2000). A Proposal to Assess the Service Quality of Online Travel Agencies. *Journal of Professional Services Marketing, 21*(1), 6368.

Kelly, J. (2003). The audit commission: Guiding, steering and regulating local government. *Public Administration, 81*(3), 459-476.

Kendrick, A. (1998). Promotional products vs price promotion in fostering customer loyalty: A report of two controlled field experiments. *Journal of Services Marketing, 12*(4), 312-326.

Keniston, K. (2000). *The Four Digital Divides.* Available online at http://web.mit.edu/~kken/Public/ PDF/Intro_Sage_1_.pdf (May 11, 2007)

Keniston, K. (2002). *Grassroots ICT Projects in India: Some Preliminary Hypotheses ASCI Journal of Management, 31*(1&2). Available online at http://web.mit.edu/~kken/Public/PDF/ASCI _Journal_Intro __ASCI_version_. pdf (May 11, 2007)

Keniston, K. (2007). *IT for Masses: Hope or Hype*? Available online at http://web.mit.edu /~kken/Public/PDF/EPW_paper.pdf (May 11, 2007)

Keniston, K., & Kumar, D. (2004). *Experience in India: Bridging the digital divide, (pp.13-20).* Sage Publications Inc.

Kenny, C., Navas-Sabater, J., & Quiang, C. (2001). *Information and Communication Technologies and Poverty in World Bank Poverty Reduction Strategies Sourcebook.* www.worldbank.org/poverty/ strategies/ict/ict.htm

Keohane, R.O., & Nye, Jr., J.S. (2000). Globalization: What's New? What's Not? (And So What?) *Foreign Policy, 118*, 104-120.

Khitoliya, R.K., & Tanwar, N. (2005, October). *E-Governance: An aid to the development of Isolated Rural Communities in Developing Countries, Agriculture Today.*

Khitoliya, R.K., Moudgil, G., & Bansal, M. (2003). Potential application of IT based Techniques in Residential/Institutional Buildings. *Seminar of Information Technology in built environment, 141,* Bangalore, November 28-29.

Kim, W., Ling, T-W., Lee, Y-J., & Park, S.S. (2003). *The Human Society and the Internet* (p. 88). Springer-Verlag Berlin Heidelberg New York.

King, W., & Epstein B. (1983). Assessing information value: an experimental study. *Decision Sciences, 14,* 34-35.

Kini, A., & Choobineh, J. (1998). Trust in electronic commerce: Definition and theoretical considerations. *In Hawaii: IEEE Computer Society.*

Kirlin, J. (1996). What government must do well: Creating value for society. *Journal of Public Administration Research and Theory: J-PART, 6*(1).

Kirlin, J. (2001). Big questions for a significant public administration. *Public Administration Review, 61*(2), 140-143.

Kjaer, A.M. (2004). *Governance.* Cambridge: Polity Press.

Kling, R. (1978). Value conflicts and social choice in electronic funds transfer developments. *Communications of the ACM, 21*(8), 642-657.

Kling, R. (1999) *What is social informatics and why does it matter?* Manchester, Retrieved 12th September 2005 from, <http://www.dlib.org/dlib/january99/kling/01kling.html>.

Konstadakopulos, D. (2005). From Public Loudspeakers to the Internet: The Adoption of Information and Communication Technologies (ICTs) by Small Enterprises Cluster in Vietnam. *Information Technologies and International Development, 2*(4), 31-39.

Kooiman, J. (2003). *Governing as Governance.* London: Sage.

Korac-Kakabadse, A., & Korac-Kakabadse, N. (1999). Information technology's impact on the quality of democracy: Reinventing the 'democratic vessel.' In R. Heeks, (Ed.), *Reinventing government in the information age: International practice in IT-enabled public sector reform.* London: Routledge.

Kosack, S. (2003). Effective aid: How democracy allows development aid to improve the quality of life. *World Development, 31*(1), 22.

Kostopoulos, G. (2003). *E-Government In The Arabian Gulf: Avision Toward Reality.* American University of Sharjah.

Kraemer, K., & King, J. L. (2006). Information technology and administrative reform: Will e-government be different? *International Journal of Electronic Government Research, 2*(1), 1-20.

Krishna, S., & Madon, S. (Eds) (2003). *Digital challenge: Information technology in the development context.* ASHGATE, Aldershot.

Ku, A.S. (2000). Revisiting the notion of "public" in Habermas's theory – Toward a theory of politics of public credibility. *Sociological Theory, 18*(2), 216-240

Kulviwat, S., Guo, C., & Engchanil, N. (2004). Determinants of online information search: a critical review and assessment. *Internet Research: Electronic Networking Applications and Policy, 14*(3), 245-253.

Kumar, S., Choudhury, S., & Shah, L. (2004). Information Literacy Mission in Digital environment- Prospects and Plans for developing Society in India. *70th IFLA conference*, Beunos Aires, Argentina, 22nd to 27th August, 2004. available at <http://www.ifla.org/IV/ifla70> accessed on 15/07/07

Lambrinoudakis, C., & Gritzalis, S. et al. (2003). Security requirements for e-government services: a methodological approach for developing a common PKI-based security policy. *Computer Communications, 26*(16), 1873-83.

Larrain, J. (1989). *Theories of Development: Capitalism, Colonialism and Dependency.* Cambridge, UK: Polity Press

Laudon, K.C., & Traver, C.G. (2001). *E-commerce: Business. technology, society.* Boston: Addison-Wesley Longman Publishing Co., Inc.

Layne, K., & Lee, J. (2001). Developing fully functional e-government: A four stage model. *Government Information Quarterly, 18*(1), 122-136.

Lee, J. (2003). A model for monitoring public sector Web site strategy. *Internet Research: Electronic networking application and policy, 13*(4), 259-266.

Lee, R. (2001, November). *Community Development and the Internet" Brussels: Research Centre `Communication for Social Change' (CSC).* Paper prepared for presentation at the International Conference on Information Technology, Communications and Development in Kathmandu, Nepal..

Lee, S.M., Tan, X., & Trimi, S. (2005). *Current practices of leading e-government countries. Communications of the ACM, 48*(10), 99-104.

Leftwich, A. (1993). Governance, democracy and development in the Third World. *Third World Quarterly, 14* 605-24.

Lehr, W., & McKnight, L.W. (2003). Wireless Internet access: 3G vs. WiFi? *Telecommunications Policy,* 27, 351-370.

Leys, C. (1996). *The Rise and Fall of Development Theory.* EAEP and Indiana University Press, Nairobi and Bloomington.

Li, Y.N., Tan, K.C., & Xie, M., (2002). Factor analysis of service quality dimension shifts in the information age. *Managerial Auditing Journal, 18*(4), 297.

Liikanen, E. (2003). *EGovernment for Europe's public services of the future.* Accessed online 04/12/05 from http://www.uoc.edu/inaugural03/eng/article/20336.pdf

Liljander, V., van Riel A.C.R., & Minna, P. (2001). Customer Satisfaction with E-Services: The Case of an Online Recruitment Portal, In Bruhn. M. & B. Stauss, Eds. Yearbook of Services Management - 2002-E-Services.

Lin, C.A (2003). A interactive communication technology adoption model. *Communication Theory, 13*(4), 345-365

Lin, C.S., & Wu, S. (2002). Exploring the impact of online service quality on portal site usage. *Proceedings of the 35th Hawaii International Conference on System Science.*

Lin, J., & Lu, H. (2000). Towards an understanding of the behavioural intention to use a Web site. *International journal of information management, 20*(3), 197-208.

Linda Bernnan, L., & Johnson, V. (2004). *Social, Ethical and Policy Implications of Information Technology,* (p. 32). Idea group Inc.

Loiacono, E.T., Watson, R.T., & Goodhue, D.L. (2002). WebQual: A measure of Web site quality. *2002 Marketing Educators' Conference: Marketing Theory and Applications, 13,* 432-437.

Luna-Reyes, L.F., Gil-Garcia, J.R., & Cruz, C.B. (2007). Collaborative digital government in Mexico: Some lessons from federal web-based interorganizational information integration initiatives. *Government Information Quarterly, 24,* 808-826.

Macintosh, A., Robson, E., Smith, E., & Whyte, A. (2003). Electronic democracy and young people. *Social Science Computer Review, 21*(1), 43-54.

Mack, R., Ravin, Y., & Byrd, R. (2001). Knowledge portals and the emerging digital knowledge workplace. *IBM System Journal, 21,* 54-80.

Macome, E. (2002). *The dynamics of the adoption and use of ICT-based initiatives for development: results of a field study in Mozambique.* Faculty of Engineering, Built Environment and Information Technology, Unpublished PhD thesis, University of Pretoria.

Madden, G., Savage, S., & Simpson, M., (1997). Regional information access: the use of telecentres to meet universal service obligations. *Telematics and Informatics, 14*(3), 273-288.

Madon, S. (2000). The Internet and socio-economic development: exploring the interaction. *Information Technology & People, 13*(2), 85-101.

Madon, S. (2003). Studying the developmental impact of e-governance initiatives. In *Proceedings of the Internationals Federation of Information Processing, IFIP* , Working Group 8.2 and 9.4, Athens, Greece, 15-17 June 2003.

Mahmood, M.A. (1987). Systems development methods – a comparative investigation. *MIS Quarterly, 11*(3), 293-311.

Malhotra, C. (2001). Rural Informatics and Information Technology Policies for Rural Development in India in emerging institutions. In S.P. Jain (Ed.), *Proceedings of NIRD Foundation Day Seminar for Decentralised Rural Development,* (pp. 223-250). Hyderabad: NIRD, Hyderabad, India, January 7-8.

Malhotra, C., Chariar, V.M., & Das, L.K. (2006). 'e' as an enabler for *Shubh-Labh* for Local Governance in Rural India. In *National Conference on Smart Governance for Rural Development by ITM,* Gurgoan at New Delhi, India on 18th February.

Malta e-Government White-Paper. (2001). *Vision and strategy for the attainment of e-government, Malta.*

Mansar, L.S. (2006). E-Government Implementation: A comparative evaluation of websites maturity. *Proceedings of the European and Mediterranean Conference on Information Systems (EMCIS)*, 6-7 July, 2006, Costa Blanca, Alicante, Spain.

Mansell, R., & Wehn, U. (1998). *Knowledge societies: information technology for sustainable development.* Published for and on behalf of the United Nations by Oxford University Press, Oxford ; New York.

Marche, S., & McNiven, J.D. (2003). E-government and e-governance: The future isn't what it used to be'. *Canadian Journal of Administrative Sciences, 20*(1), 74-86.

Margetts, H., & Dunleavy, P. (2002). *Cultural barriers to e-government* (Working Paper): University Collage of London and London School of Economics for National Audit Office.

Margetts, H., & Dunleavy, P. (2002). Cultural Barriers to EGovernment, published by the National Audit Office, April 4, 2002 (HC 704-III) in conjunction with the Value for Money report "Better Public Services Through EGovernment."

Martin, B., & Byrne, J. (2003). Implementing e-government: Widening the lens. *Electronic Journal of e-Government, 1*(1), 11-22.

Martin, J. (2000). *E-Commerce Arrives.* The Middle East, April 2000, (p. 34),

Mason, R.O. (1978). Measuring Information Output: A Communication Systems Approach. *Information & Management, 1*(5), 219-234.

Mathur, A., & Dhirubhai, A. (2005, December). ICT and rural societies: Opportunities for growth. *The International Information & Library Review, International Information Issues: Selected Papers from the American Society for Information Science and Technology, Special Interest Group on International Information Issues International Paper Contests, 37*(4), 345-351.

Maykut, P.S., & Morehouse, R. (1994). *Beginning qualitative research : a philosophic and practical guide.* London ; Washington, D.C.: Falmer Press.

McClure, D. (2000). *Electronic Government: Federal Initiatives Are Evolving Rapidly But They Face Significant Challenges.* Washington: US General Accounting Office.

McDougall, G., & Levesque, T. (1992). The measurement of service quality: some methodology issues. 2eme. Seminaire Internationale de Recherché en Management des *Activites de Service,* (pp. 411-30).

McGranahan, D. (1972). Development Indicators and Development Models. *Journal of Development Studies, 8*(3), 91.

McNamara, K.S. (2003). *Information and Communication Technologies, Poverty and Development; Learning from Experience.* A background paper for the InfoDev Annual Symposium. The World Bank.

McNeal, R., Tolbert, C., Mossberger, K., & Dotterweich, L. (2003). Innovating in digital government in the American states. *Social Science Quarterly, 84*(1), 52-70.

Meijer, A.J. (2003). Transparent government: Parliamentary and legal accountability in an information age. *Information Polity, 8*(1), 67-78.

Meuter, M.L., Ostrom, A.L., Roundtree, R.I., & Bitner, M.J. (2000, July). Self-service technologies: understanding customer satisfaction with technology-based service encounters. *Journal of Marketing, 64*, 50-64.

Miles, M.B., & Huberman, A.M. (1994). *Qualitative data analysis: an expanded sourcebook,* (2nd ed.). Thousand Oaks, CA: Sage Publications.

Milestones in India's Internet Journey (2007). http://www.amitranjan.com/category/5/

Ministry of Manpower (MOMP) (2008). *Self Employment and National Autonomous Development,* [online], http://www.manpower.gov.om/sanad_en.asp, Ministry of Manpower, Muscat.

Ministry of National Economy Oman (MONE) (2008). *Social Indicators [Internet],* Available from:<http://

www.moneoman.gov.om/book/syb2007/index_Index.htm> [Accessed Jan 11th 2008].

Mintzberg. (1996). *Population pressure, economic stagnation and deforestation in Costa Rica and the Philippines.* Paper to IUSP Seminar on Population and Deforestation in the Humid Tropics, Sao Paulo Brazil.

Misra, D.C., & Vijayaditya, N. (2006, February). Development Informatics: Reaching the Rural India: Role of NIC. *International Journal for Development 16*(1). Accessed in March, 2006 from http://www.iimahd.ernet.in/egov/ifip/feb2006/ feb2006.htm

Mission 2007 India http://www.mission2007.org/

Mitra, R.K., & Gupta, M.P. (2003, August). Evolution of e-Governance in India: Learning from Select Cases. *Indian Management. A Journal of All India Management Association*, New Delhi, India.

Mohammad, R., Fisher, R., Jaworski, B., & Paddison, G. (2004). *Internet marketing: Building advantage in a networked economy* (2nd ed., p. 743). McGraw Hill.

Monberg, J. (1998). Making the public count: a cpmparative case study of emergent information technology-based publics. *Communication Theory, 8*(4) *426-454.*

Moon, J., Li, J.P., Jo, S., & Sanders, L. (2006). Improving quality of life via blogs and development of a virtual social identity? *Journal of Information Technology Management, 15*(3).

Moon, M.J. (2002). The evolution of e-government among municipalities: Rhetoric or reality? *Public Administration Review, 62*(4), 424-433.

Moon, M.J., & Norris, D.F. (2005). Does managerial orientation matter? The adoption of reinventing government and e-government at the municipal level. *Information Systems Journal, 15*(1), 43-60. doi: Article.

Morris, M.G., & Venkatesh, V. (2000). Age differences in technology adoption decisions: implications for a changing work force. *Personnel Psychology, 53*(2), 375-403 .

Moulder, E. (2001). E-Government. *Public Management, 83.*

Myers, M.D., & Avison, D. (2002). An introduction to qualitative research in information systems, In M.D. Myers & D. Avison, (Eds.), *Qualitative research in information systems: a reader*(pp. 3-12). London: Sage..

Nandi, B. (2002). Role of Telecommunications in Developing Countries in the 21st century. *14th Biennial Conference Seoul: International Telecommunications Society (ITS).*

National Informatics Centres (2005). *Good Governance through ICT.* NIC, New Deli, 2005 <http:://home.nic.in> access on 14/07/07

National Knowledge Commission Report (2007). People's Access to Knowledge can Transform India. *Digital learning, III*(2), February 2007, (pp 22-24).

Ndou, V.D. (2004). E-government for developing countries: opportunities and challenges. *The Electronic Journal on Information Systems in Developing Countries, 18*(1), 1-24.

Newhagen, C., & Levy (1995). Nightly@nbc.com: Audience scope and perception of interactivity in viewer mail in the Internet. *Journal of Communication, 45*(3), 164-175

Nielsen, J., & Levy, J. (1994). Measuring usability: preference vs. performance. *Commun. ACM, 37*(4), 66-75.

Norris, D., & Moon, M. (2005). Advancing e-government at the grassroots: Tortoise or hare? *Public Administration Review, 65*(1), 64-75.

Norris, P (2000). Digital Divide. Available at http://Ksghome.Harvard.Edu/~Pnorris/Acrobat/Digitalch1.Pdf. Accessed On 13/10/2006

O'Toole, K. & Burdess, N. (2002, October). Governance in Rural Communities: The case of Victoria. Presented at the Jubilee conference of the Australasian Political Studies Association Australian National University, Canberra. Accessed in February, 2006 from http://www. auspsa.anu.edu.au/ proceedings/2002/ otoole+burdess.pdf) .

OECD (2001) *Information and Communication Technologies and Rural Development.* http://www.oecd.org.

OECD (2005). *The contribution of ICTs to Achieving the Millennium Development Goals (MDGs).* Forthcoming. Good Practice Paper on ICTs for Economic Growth and Poverty Reduction. http://www.oecd.org/dataoecd/15/38/34662239.pdf, accessed 23 May 2007.

OECD. (2001). *The e-Government Project.* Retrieved July 7, 2005, from http://webdomino1.oecd.org/COMNET/PUM/egovproweb.nsf/viewHtml/index/$FILE/e_gov_project.htm.

OECD. (2003). *The e-government imperative: Main findings.* Retrieved from http://www.oecd.org/dataoecd/60/60/2502539.pdf.

Ojala, M. (2002). Forrester Research Hosts Portals Summit. *Information Today, 19*(10), 1-2.

Oman Telecommunication Company (2003). *Internet Services* [Internet] < http://www.omantel.net.om/services/business/internet> [Accessed March 12th 2008]

Opdahl, A.L. & Berio, G. (2007). A Roadmap for UEML. In G. Doumeingts, J. Müller, Morel, G., & B Vallespir (Eds.), *Enterprise Interoperability: New Challenges and Approaches*, Springer Verlag, London, UK, (pp. 169-178).

Osbourne, D., & Gaebler, E. (1992). *Reinventing Government: How the entrepreneurial spirit is transforming the Public Sector.* Tampa, FL.

PACE (2005). *ICT in Multi-purpose community learning centres/Gonokendras.* Bangladesh Rural Advancement Committee (BRAC), Dhaka, Bangladesh.

Pande, A.S. (2003, December). An Emergent Complex Systems Perspective on E-Governance. International Conference on E-Governance (ICEG2003). New Delhi: IIT Delhi.Rahnema, M., & Bawtree, V. (Ed.), (1997). *The Post Development Reader.* University Press Limited, Dhaka.

Parasuraman, A., & Grewals, D. (2000). The Impact of Technology on the Quality-Value-Loyalty Chain: A Research Agenda. *Journal of the Academy of Marketing Science, 28*(1), 168–74.

Parasuraman, A., Berry, L.L., & Zeithaml, V.A. (1991). Refinement & Reassessment of the SERVQUAL Scale. *Journal of Retailing, 67*(4), 420-50.

Parasuraman, A., Zeithaml, V.A., & Berry, L.L. (1985). A conceptual model of service quality & its implications for future research. *Journal of Marketing, 49*(Fall), 41-50.

Parasuraman, A., Zeithaml, V.A., & Berry, L.L. (1988). SERVQUAL: A multiple item scale for measuring consumer perceptions of service quality. *Journal of Retailing, 64*(1), 12-40.

Parasuraman, A., Zeithaml, V.A., & Malhotra A. (2005). E-S-QUAL: A Multiple-Item Scale for Assessing Electronic Service Quality. *Journal of Service Research, 7*(3), 213-233.

Patton, M.Q. (1980). *Qualitative evaluation methods.* London: Sage publication.

Pedersen, M.K., Fountain, J., & Loukis, E. (2006). Preface to the Focus Theme Section: Electronic Markets and e-Government. *Electronic Markets, 16*(4), 263-273.

Peet, R. (1995). *Theories of Development.* NY, USA: Guildford Press.

Peikari, C., & Fogie, S. (2003). *Maximum Wireless Security.* from http://www.berr.gov.uk/files/file9972.pdf.

Peng, T. (2002). *From electronic government to online governanace: US versus Taiwan.* Macao Technology University, Macao.

Pew Internet & American Life Project (2006) Home Broadband Adoption. from http://www.pewinternet.org/pdfs/PIP_Broadband_trends2006.pdf

Pigg, K.E. (2001). Applications of Community Informatics for building Community and enhancing civic society. *Information, Communication & Society, 4*(4), 507–527

Pippa, N. (2001). *Digital Divide?: Civic Engagement, Information Poverty, and the Internet Worldwide, 1.* New York, NY: Cambridge University Press.

Prakash, G. (2005). Leapfrogging into the Knowledge Era: Use of ICT for Development. *IIMB Management Review, 17*(3), 47-56.

Proenza, F.J, Bastidas-Buch, R., & Montero, G. (2001). *Telecentres for Socio-economic and Rural Development in Latin America and the Caribbean.* FAO, ITU and IADB, Washington DC

Public Record Office. (2001). E-government policy framework for electronic records management. *Govt. of UK.* Retrieved August 8, 2007, from http://www.nationalarchives.gov.uk/documents/egov_framework.pdf

Qureshi, S. (2003). Movement in the information technology for development debate: How can it meet the challenges of global competition? *Information Technology for Development, 10*(3), 147-149.

Ranganathan, C., & Ganapathy, S. (2002). Key dimensions of business-to-consumer Web sites. *Information & Management, 39*(6), 457-465.

Rau, K. (2004). Effective Governance of IT: Design objectives, roles, and relationships. *Information Systems Management, 21*(Fall 2004), 35-42.

Raul, R., & Royal. D.C. (2002). *Themes and Issues in Telecentre Sustainability.* Institute for Development Policy and Management, Manchester, Retrieved 10 October, 2005 from, <http://www.man.ac.uk/idpm/idpm_dp.htm#devinf_wp>.

Raushina, A. (2005, March). E-governance for good Governance-The national E-governance Action Plan, *Kurukshetra, 53*(5).

Ray, I. (2005, January). Good Governance and the Dilemma of Development : What lies Beneath? *Global Socio-Economic Review ABI/INFORM* (pp. 43-59).

Recommendation (2004*). Record of the Committee of Ministers to member states on electronic governance.* Adopted by the Committee of Ministers on December 15, 2004 at the 909th meeting of the Ministers' Deputies.

Reddick, C.G. (2004). A two-stage model of e-government growth: Theories and empirical evidence for US cities. *Government Information Quarterly, 21*(1), 51-64.

Reffat, R. (2003). *Developing A Successful E-Government* (Working Paper): University Of Sydney, Australia.

Reich, B.H., & Benbasat, I. (2000). Factors that influence the social dimension of alignment between business and information technology objectives. *MIS Quarterly, 24*(1), 81-113.

Reichard, C. (1998). The impact of performance management on transparency and accountability in the public sector. In A. Hondeghem (Ed.), *Ethics and accountability in a context of governance and new public management. Amsterdam etc* (pp. 123-137). The Netherlands: IOS Press.

Reichheld, F.F., Markey Jr, R.G., & Hopton, C. (2000). E-customer loyalty–applying the traditional rules of business for online success. *European Business Journal, 12*(4), 173-9.

Reynolds, M.M., & Regio-Micro, M. (2001). The Purpose Of Transforming Government-E-Government as a Catalyst In The Information Age. *Microsoft E-Government Initiatives,* from http://www.netcaucus.org/books/egov2001/pdf/EGovIntr.pdf

Rhodes, R.A.W. (1997). *Understanding Governance: Policy Networks, Governance, Reflexivity and Accountability.* Maidenhead: Open University Press.

Riley, T.B. (2003). *Defining E-Government and E-Governance: Staying the Course.* eGov Monitor.

RIRDC (1997). *A framework for developing regional communications initiatives.* Melbourne.

Ritchie, J. & Lewis, J. (2003). *Qualitative research practice: a guide for social science students and researchers,* first edn. London: Sage Publication.

Rogers, E., & Shukla, P. (2001). The role of telecentres in development and the digital divide. *Journal of* Development *Communication, 12*(2), 26-31.

Rogers, E.M. (1995). *Diffusion of innovations.* New York.

Roman, R., & Colle, R.D. (2002). *Themes and issues in telecentre sustainability.* Development Informatics Working Paper Series Paper No. 10, IDPM, University of Manchester.

Rosenau, J.N. (1992). Governance, order and change in world politics. In J.N. Rosenau & E-O. Czempiel (Eds.), *Governance without Government: Order and Change in World Politics.* New York: Cambridge University Press.

Rusay, C. (2003). *User-centered design for large government portals.* Retrieved from http://www.digital-web.com/articles/user_centered_design_for_large_government_portals/

Sabherwal, R., & Chan, Y.E. (2001). Alignment between business and IS strategies: a study of prospectors, analyzers, and defenders. *Information Systems Research, 12*(1), 11-33.

Sachdeva, S (2002, December). *e-Governance Action Plan for India..*

Safari, H., Haki, K., Mohammadian, A., Farazmand, E., Khoshsima, G., & Moslehi, A. (2004). eGovernment Maturity Model (eGMM). *ICEIS 2004: Software Agents and Internet Computing, 14*(17).

Sahu, G.P. (2004). A Study of e-Governance Acceptance in India. *A Research Plan on* ***e-Governance*** *, IIT-Delhi, 8.*

Sanchez, O.A. (2000). *The Legacy of Human Development: a tribute to Mahbub ul Haq.* (pp. 9-16). Routledge.

Sangita, S.N., & Dash, B.C. (2006). *Electronic Governance and Service Delivery in India: Theory and Practice.* The Institute for Social and Economic Change, Bangalore.

Saunders, M., Lewis, P., & Thornhill, A. (2002). *Research methods for business students* (Third edition). Harlow: Prentice Hall.

Saxena, K. (2005). Towards excellence in e-governanace. *International Journal of Public Sector Management, 18*(6), 498-513.

Saxena, N.C. (1996). *The Saga of Participatory Forest Management in India.* Center For International Forestry Research (CIFOR), Bogor.

Schneider, M. (1976). The "quality of life" and social indicators research. *Public Administration Review, 36*(3), 297-305.

Sclove, R. (1994). Democratising technology. *The Chronicle of Higher Education, B1-2*

Seifert, J., & Petersen, E. (2002). The Promise Of All Things E? Expectations and Challenges of Emergent E- Government. *Perspectives on Global Development and Technology, 1*(2), 193-213.

Sein, M., & Ahmad, I. (2001). A Framework to Study the Impact of Information and Communication Technologies on Developing Countries: The Case of Cellular Phones in Bangladesh. In *Proceedings from the BITWORLD 2001*, Cairo, Egypt.

Sein, M., & Harindranath, G. (2004). Conceptualizing the ICT Artifact: Toward Understanding the Role of ICT in National Development. *Information Society, 20*(1), 15-24.

Selhofer, H., & Hüsing, T. (2002). The digital divide index- a measure of social inequalities in the adoption of ICT, In *Proceedings of the ST 2002 Conference*, Copenhagen, November 2002.

Sen, A. (1987). Commodities and Capabilities. Monograph of Professor Dr. P. Hennipman Lectures in Economics, 1982 delivered at the University of Amsterdam, Oxford University Press.

Sen, A. (2000). A decade of human development. *Journal of Human Development, 1*(1), 17-23.

Sen, A. (2000). *Development as freedom*, (1st. ed.). New Delhi: Oxford University Press.

Sen, R. (1992). *Social constraints for working women: notes from a rural area of Jamalpur*, 75. Mohakhali, Dhaka-1212, Bangladesh.

Shang, S., & Seddon, P. (2002). Assessing and managing the benefits of enterprise systems: the business manager's perspective. *Information Systems Journal, 20*(12), 271–299.

Share, P. (1993). Telecommunication and rural remote Development. *Rural Society, 3*(16).

Siau, K., & Long, Y. (2004). Factors impacting e-government development. *International Conference on Information Systems 2004*, 221-234.

Siddiqi, A. (2001). *The United Arab Emirates: Financial Report.* The Middle East.

Sikka, B.K., Sharma, M.L., Singh, S., & Narula, S.A. (2005). On E-Marketing of Apples in Uttaranchal Conference Proceedings of Indian Society of Agricultural Marketing, Pantnagar. In *Indian Journal of Agricultural Marketing, 19*(2), Conference Spl., May-August.

Singh, A. (2002). *Bridging the digital divide: Role of universities in getting South Africa closer to the global information society.* University of Durban Westville. Retrieved 12/02/2005 from http://citte.nu.ac.za/papers/id7.pdf

Singh, K. (1999). *Rural* development*: principles, policies and management, Katar Singh (*Second Edition), *21.* New-Delhi, India: Sage Publications.

Singh, N. (2004). *information technology and rural development in India, 34.* Paper 563, Department of Economics, University of California, Santa Cruz.

Singh, N. (2008). ICTs and Rural Development in India. October 16, 2006. Available at SSRN: http://ssrn.com/abstract=950322, Accessed in May 2008.

Singh, S. H.(2000, September 26). Ways and means of bridging the gap between developed and developing countries. high-level panel on information technology and public administration, United Nations, New York.

Smith, M.A. (2004). Portals: Toward an application framework for interoperability. *Communications of the ACM, 47*(10), 93-97.

Sociocultural Barriers to E-Government: An Analysis from a Poverty Perspective: María Inés Salamancal, FLACSO Chile, DIRSI (Regional Dialogue on the Information Society), funded by the IDRC.

Soeftestad, L.T., & Sein, M.K. (2003). ICT and Development: East is East and West is West and the Twain may yet Meet. In S. Krishna & S. Madon (Eds), *Digital Challenge: Information Technology in the Development Context*, ASHGATE, (pp. 63-83).

Sood, A.D. (2003, May-June). The Kiosk Networks: Information nodes in the rural landscape, I(1). Available online at http://www.i4donline.net/issue/may03/aditya_full.htm

Sozen, S., & Shaw, I. (2002). The international applicability of "new" public management: lessons from Turkey. *International Journal of Public Sector Management, 15*(4), 475-86.

Spence, R. (2003). *Information and Communications Technologies (ICTs) for Poverty Reduction: When, Where and How*? OECD Inter national Development Rese arch Cen ter (IDRC). http://netwo rk.idrc.ca/uploa ds/user-S/10618469203RS_ICT-Pov_18_July.pdf

Spilker, B., & Revicki, D.A. (1999). Taxonomy of Quality of Life. In B. Spilker (Ed.), *Quality of life and Pharmacoeconomics in Clinical Trials*, (pp. 25–32). Philadelphia: Lippincott-Raven.

Stake, R.E. (1995). *The art of case study research.* Thousand Oaks, CA: Sage Publications.

State Services Commission (2007). *New Zealand E-government Interoperability Framework*, www.e.govt.nz.

Stauffacher, G. (2002). E-government as and instrument of public management reform. In *2nd E-Government Conference* (pp. 22-24). Kuwait Chamber of Commerce, Kuwait.

Stoker, G. (1998). Governance as theory: Five propositions. *International Journal of Social Science, 155* 17 - 28.

Stoltzfus, K. (2004). *Motivations for implementing E-Government: An Investigation of the Global Phenomenon*, University of California, Santa.

Sundar, S.S. (2004). Theorizing interactivity's effects. *The Information Society, 20*(5), 387-391.

Szirmai, A. (2005). *The Dynamics of Socio-Economic Development: An Introduction*, (1st Ed.). Cambridge University Press.

Tatnall, A. (2005). Portals, portals everywhere. In A. Tatnall (Ed.), *Web portals: The new gateways to Internet information and services.* Hershey, PA: IGI Global Publishing.

Taylor, J.A. (1998). Governance and electronic innovation: Whither the information polity' *Information, Communication & Society, 1*(2), 144-162.

Taylor, S.J., & Bogdan, R. (1984). *Introduction to qualitative research methods: the search for meanings,* (2nd Ed). New York: Wiley.

The E-Government Divide: Mutual Effects of Digital Divide and E-Government. (2003, October 12-19). *World Congress on Engineering and Digital Divide,* Tunis.

The International Bank for Re-construction and Development/World Bank (2000). *Can Africa claim the 21st Century?, 56.*

The Peninsula Newspaper. (2008). *Bursting at the seams,* from http://www.thepeninsulaqatar.com/Display_news.asp?section=Local_News&month=January2008&file=Local_News200801296298.xml.

The World Bank Report. (1992). *Governance and Development.* Washington D.C.

The World Bank Report. (1997). *Rural* Development: *From Vision to Action – A Sector Strategy.* Washington D.C.

Themistocleous, M., & Irani, Z. (2001). Benchmarking the benefits and barriers of application integration. *Benchmarking: An International Journal, 8*(4), 317–331.

Tichenor, P.J., Olien, C.N., & Donahue, G.A. (1970). Mass media flow and differential growth in knowledge. *Public Opinion Quarterly, 34,* 159-170.

Tigran, G. (2006). *Economic and Social Commission for Western Asia (ESCWA).* United Nation Networking o f Expertise on Foreign Direct Investment in the Member States of the ESCWA. http://www.escwa.un.org /divisions /pptcd/upload /EvaluationDA2.pdf, [last accessed 03/2008]

Touzi, J., Lorré, J.P., Bénaben, F., & Pingaud, H. (2007). Interoperability through Model-based Generation: The Case of the Collaborative Information System (CIS). In G. Doumeingts, J. Müller, G. Morel, & B. Vallespir (Eds.), *Enterprise Interoperability: New Challenges and Approaches,* Springer Verlag, London, UK, (pp. 407-416).

Tsagarousianou, R. (1998). Electronic democracy and the public sphere: opportunities and challenges. In R. Tsagarousianou, D. Tambini, & C. Bryan (Eds.), *Cyberdemocracy: Technology, Cities and Civic Networks* eds.. London: Routledge.

Tyndale, P. (2002). Will e-government succeed? In *2nd European Conference on E-Government* (pp. 429-438). St CatherineÆs College, Oxford.

UN (2005). *The World Summit on the Information Society (WSIS).* Geneva, Retrieved 25 November-2005, from, <http://www.itu.int/wsis/>.

UN (2008). *United Nations e-Government Survey 2008.* Department of Economics and Social Affairs, Division for Public Administration and Development Management, United Nations, New York.

UN. (2008). *World public sector report: UN E-Government survey, From E-Government To Connected Governance.* New York.

UN/ASPA. (2002). *Benchmarking e-government: A global perspective.* Retrieved from http://www/unspan/org.egovernment/benchmarking%20Egov%202001.pdf

UNCTAD (2006). *E-Commerce and Development Report.* available at http://r0.unctad.org/ecommerce/ecommerce_en/ier06_en.htm Last accessed: 30/06/08

UNDP (2002). *Human development report 2002.* New York: Oxford University Press, Inc..

UNDP (2004). *Bridging the gender digital divide.* UNDP regional centre for Europe and the CIS and UNIFEM Central and Eastern Europe, Solvak Republic.

UNDP (2006). *http://europeandcis.undp.org/home/show/1EAEB3D3-F203-1EE9-BD0C279330992AC8* Last accessed: 30/06/08

UNDP (2006). *Human Development Report.* India.

UNDP(1999). *Human Development Report 1999.* NY: UNDP/Oxford.

UNDP. (1994). *Initiatives for Change.* http://www.mirror.undp.org/magnet/policy/chapterl.htm, accessed on May 25, 2007.

UNDP-APDIP (2004). *ICT for Development: A Sourcebook for Parliamentarians* (p. 39), New Delhi: Elsevier.

UNESCO (2005). *Evaluation of UNESCO's Community Multimedia Centres.* United Nations Educational, Scientific and Cultural Organization.

United Nations (2008), *United Nations e-Government Survey 2008.* United Nations publication. http://unpanl.un.org/intradoc/groups/public/ documents/UN/UNPAN028607.pdf [last accessed 03/2008].

United Nations (2008). *Global E-Government Readiness Report 2005 for E-Givernment to E-Inclusion.* http://unpanl.un.org/intradoc/groups/public/ documents/un/unpan021888.pdf United Nations publication. [last accessed 02/2008]

United Nations (2008). *World Public Sector Report 2003: E-Government at the Crossroads.* United Nations publication. http://unpanl.un.org/intradoc /groups/public/documents/UN/UNPAN012733.pdf [last accessed 03/2008]

United Nations Department of Economic and Social Affairs 2003, *e-Government Readiness Assessment Survey.* Retrieved: August 2, 2007, from http://www.cabinet.gov.jm/docs/pdf/eGov_Readiness_Intro.pdf

UNPAN (2007). http://www.unpan.org/Library/MajorPublications/WorldPublicSectorReport/tabid/645/Default.aspx#2007: Last accessed: 30/06/08

unpanl.un.org/intradoc/groups/public/documents/UN/UNPAN028607.pdf

van der Merwe, R., & Bekker, J. (2003). A framework and methodology for evaluating e-commerce web sites. *Internet Research: electronic Networking Applications and Policy, 13*(5), 330-341.

Van Dijk, J. (1999). *The Network Society: Social Aspects of New Media.* London: Sage

van Riel, A.C.R., Lemmink, J., Streukens, S., & Liljander, V. (2004). Boost customer loyalty with online services: the case of mobile telecoms providers. *International Journal of Internet Marketing & Advertising, 1*(1), 4–23.

Venkatesh, V., & Davis, F.D. (1996). A model of the antecedents of perceived ease of use: Development and test. *Decision Sci., 27,* 451-481.

Venkatesh, V., & Davis, F.D. (2000). Atheoretical extension of the technology acceptance model: Four longitudinal field studies. *Management Science, 46*(2), 186-205.

Venkatesh, V., Morris, M., Davis, G., & Davis, F. (2003). User Acceptance of Information Technology: Toward a Unified View. *MIS Quarterly, 27*(3), 425-478.

Ventura, J. (2003). *Non-Governmental Organizations and the Digital Divide* (p. 9). Retrieved 12/05/ 2005 from http://www.uweb.ucsb.edu/~jventura/ngo.pdf

Walker, L. (2007). IBM business transformation enabled by service-oriented architecture. *IBM Systems Journal, 46*(4), 651-667

Waller, P., Livesey, P., & Edin, K. (2001). e-Government in the Service of Democracy. *ICA Information, 74.*

Walsham, G. (1993). *Interpreting information systems in organizations.* England: J. Wiley.

Walsham, G. (1995). 'The Emergence of Interpretivism in IS Research. *Information Systems Research, 6*(4), 376-394.

Walsham, G. (2002). Interpretive case studies in IS research: Nature and method, In D.E .Avison & M.D. Myers (Eds.), *Qualitative research in information systems: a reader,* (pp. 101-113). SAGE, London.

Walsham, G., & Sahay, S. (2006). Research on information systems in developing countries: current landscape and future prospects. *Information Technology for Development, 12*(1), 7-24.

Wang, H., Song, Y., Hamilton, A., & Curwell, S. (2007). Urban information integration for advanced e-planning in Europe. *Government Information Quarterly, 24*, 736-754.

Warkentin, M., Gefen, D., Pavlou, P., & Rose, G. (2002). Encouraging citizen adoption of e-government by building trust. *Electronic Markets, 12*(3), 157-162.

Wassenaar, A. (2000). E-Governmental Value Chain Models. *DEXA, IEEE Press*, (pp. 289-293).

Webster, F. (1995). *Theories of the Information Society.* London: Routledge.

Weerakkody, V., & Currie, W. (2003). *Integrating Business Process Reengineering with Information Systems Development: Issues & Implications.* In Lecture Notes in Computer Science. Springer.

Weerakkody, V., Jones, S., & Olsen, E. (2007). *E-Government: A Comparison of Strategies in Local Authorities in the UK and Norway. International Journal of Electronic Business, Inderscience, 5*(2), 141-159.

Wei, S.X., & Kuzmanovic, M. (2000). From representation to performance:responsive public space. *CPSR Newsletter, 18*. Online. Available: http://www.cpsr.org/publications/newsletters/issues/2000/Summer2000/wei-kuzmanovic.html

Weill, P. (2004). Don't just lead Govern: How top-performing firms govern IT. *MIS Quarterly Executive, 3*(1), 1-17.

Wert, J.M.V. (2002). E-Government and Performance: A Citizen-Centered Imperative. *The Public Manager, 31.*

West, D. (2000). *Assessing e-government: The Internet, democracy, and service delivery by state and federal governments.* Retrieved from www.insidepolitics.org/egovtreport00.html

West, D. (2002). *Global e-government*, Policy Report of A. Alfred Taubman Center for Public Policy and American Institutions. Retrieved from http://www.insidepolitics.org/egovt02int.html

Wikipedia (2007). *E-Democracy.* Available at <http://en.wikipedia.org/wiki/E-democracy> accessed on 17/07/2007 at 3.23 pmBaweja, Y. (2005, August). Does E-Governance means Good governance? *Yojana, 49.*

Wilson, F., Engers, T., & Peters, R. (2007). Training eGovernment actors: Experience and future trends. *European Journal of ePractice, 1*(1), 36-47.

Wilson, M. (2000). *Understanding the International ICT and Development Discourse: Assumptions and Implications.* Paper is based on research conducted for the author's M.Phil in Development Studies thesis at Oxford, U.K.

Wimmer, M., & Traunmuller, R. (2000). *Trends in e-government: managing distributed knowledge.* Paper presented at the Proceedings from 11th International Workshop on Database and Expert Systems Applications, New York.

Wishard, W.V.D. (1994). Global trends reshaping civil society. In D.E. Eberly, (Ed.), *Building a Community of Citizens: Civil Society in the 21st Century*, Lanham, MA: The Commonwealth Foundation, (pp. 57–82).

Wisniewski, M., & Stewart, D. (2004). Performance measurementfor stakeholders: The case of Scottish local authorities. *International Journal of Public Sector Management, 17*(3), 222-233.

WMRC. (2001). Global e-government survey.Retrieved from http://www.worldmarketsanalysis.com/pdf/e-govreport.pdf

Wolfinbarger, M., & Gilly, M.C. (2003). eTailQ: Dimensionalizing, measuring and predicting etail quality. *Journal of Retailing, 79*(3), 183-198.

Wolfram, E. (2004). The New Economy: Complexity coordination and a Hybrid governance approach. *International Journal of Social Economics,31*(11/12), 1029-1049.

World Bank (1999). *World Development Report 1998/99.* World Bank http://econ.worldbank.org

World Bank (2003). *Drishtee: Connecting India Village by Village* Address: http://web.worldbank.org/WBSITE/EXTERNAL/OPPORTUNITIES/GRANTS/DEVMARKETPLACE/0,,contentMDK:20208584~menuPK:21446

9~pagePK:180691~piPK:174492~theSitePK:205098,00.html Last accessed: 18/03/05

World Bank (2003). *ICTs and MDGs: A World Bank Perspective.* www.worldbank.org, accessed 26 May 2007.

World Bank (2004a). *Dm 2003 Project Implementation Progress Report.* Address: http://siteresources.worldbank.org/DEVMARKETPLACE/Resources/DM-2003-Reports/146601.pdf Last accessed: 18/03/05:

World Bank (2004b). h*ttp://Siteresources.Worldbank.Org/Devmarketplace/Resources/205097-1090596582429/1466pcr.Pdf* Last accessed: 18/03/05

World Bank (2004c). *Drishtee Telecenter Initiative* Address: http://poverty.worldbank.org/files/14646_Drishtee-web.pdf Last accessed: 23/04/2005

World Bank Group (2004). *World Development Report 2004: Making Services Work for Poor People* (p. 7). Washington, D.C., World Bank.

World Bank. (2001). *World Development Report 2000/01: Attacking Poverty.* Oxford University Press. www.worldbank.org/poverty/wdrpoverty/.

www.apdip.net/resources/case/in16/view

www.digitalopportunity.org/article/view/113259/

www.ejisdc.org/ojs2/index.php/ejisdc/article/view/462/230

www.igidr.ac.in/~susant/PDFDOCS/Thomas2003_commoditiesmkts_wb.pdf

www.patelcenter.usf.edu/assets/doc/IPSA-Singh.doc

Yah, L.C. (1991). *Development and underdevelopment.* Longman Jurong Town.

Yang, Z., & Fang, X. (2004). Online Service Quality Dimensions & their Relationship with Satisfaction. *International Journal of Service Industry Management, 15*(3).

Yang, Z., Jun, M., & Robin, P.T. (2004). Measuring customer perceived online service quality, International Journal of Operations & Production Management, 24, (11), 1149.

Yerramsetti, S. (2005). *Role of Information Technology for Rural Development – A Case Study of Rural e-Seva Project in West Godavari District.* Mphil Dissertation at Jawaharlal Nehru University (JNU), New Delhi: 126.

Yin, R.K. (1984). *Case study research: design and methods.* CA: Sage Publications.

Yin, R.K. (1994). *Case Study Research - Design And Methods* (Second Edition). London:Sage Publications.

Yoo, B., & Donthu, N. (2001). Developing a scale to measure the perceived quality of an Internet shopping site (SITEQUAL). *Quarterly Journal of Electronic Commerce, 2*(1), 31-45.

Young, I.M. (1987). Impartiality and the civic public: Some implications of feminist critiques of moral and political theory. In S. Benhabib & D. Cornell (Eds.), *Feminism as Critique: Essays on the Politics of Gender in Late-Capitalist Societies.* Cambridge: Polity.

Young, V. (1997). *ICTs and Development: Testing a framework for Evaluation.* Canada: Canadian International Development Agency.

Zakareya, E., & Irani, Z. (2005), E-government adoption: Architecture and barriers. *Business Process Management Journal, 11*(5), 589-611.

Zeithaml, V.A. (2002). Service Excellence in Electronic Channels. *Managing Service Quality, 12*(3), 135-139.

Zhang, P., & von Dran, G. (2001). User Expectations and Rankings of Quality Factors in Different Web Site Domains. *International Journal of Electronic Commerce, 6*(2), 9-33.

Zhiyuan, F. (2002). E-Government in Digital Era: Concepts, Practice and Development. *International Journal Of The Computer, The Internet and Management, 10*(2), 1-22.

About the Contributors

G. P. Sahu received his PhD in management from Indian Institute of Technology Delhi. Currently he is an assistant professor at National Institute of Technology, Allahabad, India. His research interests are in the areas of MIS and e-government. He has published several research papers in journals. He has coordinated several international conferences. He has also edited three books in the area of e-government. Dr. Sahu has acted as a reviewer for several international journals. He is also a guest editor with *International Journal of Electronic Governance.* Dr. Sahu has been on the jury for the CSI-Nihilent E-governance National Awards, India.

Yogesh K. Dwivedi is a lecturer in the School of Business and Economics at Swansea University in the UK. He was awarded his MSc and PhD by Brunel University in the UK, receiving a *Highly Commended* award for his doctoral work by the European Foundation for Management and Development. His research focuses on the adoption and diffusion of ICT in organisations and in addition to authoring a book and numerous conference papers, has co-authored papers accepted for publication by journals such as *Communications of the ACM,* the *Information Systems Journal,* the *European Journal of Information Systems,* and the *Journal of the Operational Research Society.* He is senior editor of *DATABASE for Advances in Information Systems,* managing editor of *Journal of Electronic Commerce Research,* assistant editor *of Transforming Government: People, Process and Policy* and a member of the editorial board/review board of a number of other journals, and is a member of the Association of Information Systems, IFIP WG8.6 and the Global Institute of Flexible Systems Management, New Delhi.

Vishanth Weerakkody is a member of faculty in the Business School at Brunel University, UK. VW was previously a faculty member in the department of IS and Computing at Brunel University and he has held various IT positions in multinational organisations, including IBM UK. VW is a Member of the British Computer Society, Chartered IT professional and a Fellow of the UK Higher Education Academy. He is the current editor-in-chief of the *International Journal of Electronic Government Research.*

* * *

Anand Agrawal, working as a researcher and consultant, has worked as a faculty member at ICFAI Business School at Hyderabad, India and then as associate project director at TNS India. He has completed his PhD in the field of services marketing from ICFAI University in which he developed a measurement instrument to measure e-service quality. His research area includes marketing management, services marketing and research in general. He has more than 15 national research publications and a few international research publications in his credit. He has also written case studies and magazine articles. Currently, he is also acting as associate editor of *Research World* and reviewer of many national and international journals like *Journal of Research Practice* and *Journal of Management Education.*

Moaman Al-Busaidy is a Phd researcher at the school of Information Systems, Computing and Mathematics at Brunel University in the UK. Al-Busaidy obtained a Masters in information systems engineering from Cardiff University in the UK and a Bachelors in computer science from University of Bangalore in India. Al-Busaidy has eight years of work experience in the IT industry and his final appointment was as the IT director in the Ministry of Manpower in Oman.

Shafi H. Al-Shafi is a PhD researcher at the School of Information Systems, Computing and Mathematics, Brunel University, UK. He obtained his Master in Business Administration MBA (Information Technology) from the Faculty of Engineering and Computing, Coventry University in the UK. His research interests include e-government, impact of integration technologies, strategic management and e-commerce.

Md.Mahfuz Ashraf is a PhD candidate in CIS at the University of South Australia. His research interests include IT/IS adoption and implementation in rural-urban settings, impact study of ICT for development (ICT4D) and the digital divide.

Vijayaraghavan M Chariar acquired his Master's degree in physics from IIT Bombay (India) in 1991 and the doctoral degree in physics from IIT Delhi in 1999. He has been an activist supporter associated with various movements for sustainable development in India. He has researched and taught at NISTADS, New Delhi, BITS Pilani and IIT Kharagpur. Currently he teaches at the Centre for Rural Development and Technology, IIT Delhi. His research interests include sustainable technologies, science and technology policy, integral education and participatory development.

Subhajit Choudhury is a working in Indian Institute of Technology Guwahati. He completed his PhD in information literacy from Vikram University, Ujjain, and MPhil (LIS), MLIS, BLIS. He has 17 published papers in journals and conferences. His research areas are information literacy in developing countries, information retrieval system, e-governance in third world countries and public libraries. Paper presented in IFLA World Library conference, Argentina, 2004 as Speaker by co-author.

Lalit Das is presently professor, chief design engineer and head of IDDC (Instrument Design and Development Centre) at IIT-Delhi, India. Here he is also actively involved in the design, conduct and teaching of two years interdisciplinary MDes (Masters in Design) programme in industrial design at IIT-D. He is a BTech (IIT-K), MTech. (IIT-D) and MA. He has been actively involved in several reputed international institutions like Department of Fine Art, University of Manitoba, Canada and with national level projects like design of distant education for artisans for IGNOU and recently announced National Policy on Design. With several publications to his credit, his chief areas of interest are industrial design, product design, design education, computer aided design and design & societal development. More details are available at http://web.iitd.ac.in/~lkdas/.

Vineeta Dixit has over 18 years of experience in India and UK. She worked in the areas of technology, education and governance. In the last 8 years she transitioned from mainstream corporate life to ICT for Development (ICT4D) and public policy initiatives. In the e-governance domain, she has been a senior consultant to the Department of Information Technology, Government of India for their $4Bn National e-Governance Plan and she is currently the consultant to Department of Administrative Reforms & Public Grievances, Government of India for their e-governance related initiatives. In past she has been CEO of SWApplications India P. Ltd. (SWAppIT) - a strategic partner to universities, colleges, schools, vocational training centres, distance learning programmes and executive education initiatives. She has Masters in social policy & development from London School of Economics and a Masters in business administration from The Business School, Jammu University, India.

Siddhartha Ghosh has received the BE from NIT Agartala, Tripura (previously known as TEC). He is a MTech in computer science from University of Hyderabad, India and submitted PhD in the area of natural language processing and machine learning in the Osmania University, Hyderabad. His areas of interests are natural language processing, artificial intelligence, e-governance, Web technologies, computing in local languages, machine learning and e-learning. He has 14 national and 7 international publications in various conferences and journals. He is a life member of Computer Society of India (CSI). He is aslo an Academic Initiative member of IBM for last 4 years.

Gopakumar K is working as lecturer at MBA Programme, Bapuji Institute of Engineering & Technology, Davangere, Karnataka, India. He holds an MA in economics from Mangalore University. Previously he was working as research and teaching associate at Indian Institute of Management, Ahmedabad (IIM-A). E-mail: kolangat.gopakumar@gmail.com.

Petter Gottschalk is one of Norway's leading experts on information technology management, electronic business, Internet issues, knowledge management, business strategy, police science and organized crime. He has conducted research in the systems and technology strategy area, and he has published extensively on knowledge management technology. In recent years, he has focused on knowledge management in policing. He is professor of Information Systems and Knowledge Management in the Department of Leadership and Organization at the Norwegian School of Management. In addition, he lectures at the Norwegian Police University College on knowledge management, criminal entrepreneurship and organized crime. He has extensive experience from technology management and executive management, including positions such as managing director of the Norwegian Computing Center and managing director of ABB Datacables. He has held numerous positions in public life. One example is chairman of the Children's Ombudsman, where he was appointed by the Norwegian Government for four years to chair the work of the ombudsman. Professor Gottschalk provides regular expert advice on a broad range of technology, management and policing issues to the media and has worked extensively with the Norwegian Broadcasting Corporation (NRK), newspapers and journals. He received his MBA in Germany (Technische Universität Berlin), MSc in the USA (Dartmouth College and MIT), and DBA in the UK (Brunel University).

Jo Hanisch is a lecturer/researcher in CIS at the University of South Australia. Her research interests include global software development, virtual communities of practice; the digital divide and sports IS.

Marc Holzer, dean of the Rutgers School of Public Affairs and Administration, is a leading expert in performance measurement, public management and e-governance. He is the founder and director of the National Center for Public Performance, a research and public service organization devoted to improving performance in the public sector. He also developed the E-Governance Institute, created to explore the on-going impact of the internet and other information technologies on the productivity and performance of the public sector, and how e-government fosters new and deeper citizen involvement within the governing process.

S. Kumar is a professor in the School of Studies in Library and Information Science (Faulty of IT), Vikram University, Ujjain (Madhya Pradesh) (India). With 35 years of teaching experience to post graduate classes and 4 years to MPhil 18 years experience in guiding PhD research, 7 students awarded PhD. Has 93 published papers in journals, conferences and seminars volumes. Presented papers in 49th FID 1998 and International Congress on /digital Libraries (new Delhi) 2004. Besides 23 papers presented in other international and National Conferences and Conference in ILA. Have 2 books and more than 90 articles to the credit. Paper presented in IFLA World Library conference, Argentina, 2004 as Speaker by co-author.

Vinod Kumar is a professor of Technology and Operations Management of the Sprott School of Business (Director of School, 1995-2005), Carleton University. Dr. Kumar has published over 200 articles in refereed journals and proceedings. He has won several Best Paper Awards in prestigious conferences, Scholarly Achievement Award of Carleton University for the academic years 1985-86 and 1987-88 and Research Achievement Award for the year 1993, 2001 and 2007. He is on the editorial board of two international journals. In addition, Dr. Kumar has also served for several years on the Board of Governors and the Senate for Carleton University and on the board of the Ontario Network of e-Commerce.

Uma Kumar is a full professor of Management Science and Technology Management and director of the Research Centre for Technology Management at Carleton University. Dr. Kumar has published over 160 articles in journals and refereed proceedings. Her ten papers have won best paper awards at prestigious conferences. She has won Carleton's prestigious Research Achievement Award and twice, the Scholarly Achievement Award. Recently, she won the teaching excellence award at Carleton University. Dr. Kumar is the recipient of a number of research grants from reputed research funding agencies.

Sandeep Kaur is currently pursuing her PhD in the area of rural e-governance from the Department of Communication, PSG College of Arts and Science, Coimbatore, Tamilnadu, India. She has completed Graduation in Science and Postgraduation in Arts from colleges affiliated to Bharathiar University, Coimbatore, Tamilnadu, India. She completed her MPhil Degree programme on youth attitude towards Internet use in 2002. Her major areas of interest are e-governance, new media uses and effects, media convergence and its dimensions. She has authored research papers on various aspects of e-governance and has national and international publications in the same to her credit.

Bharat Maheshwari is an asiistant professor of Information Systems at the Odette School of Business, University of Windsor. He has co-authored more than 25 peer-reviewed articles in leading journals and academic conference proceedings. He also has extensive practical experience in managing information systems. Prior to joining the business faculty of the University of Windsor he has also been part of several ERP implementation teams.

Charru Malhotra is presently assistant professor (Systems Analysis cum Programming) at Indian Institute of Public Administration (IIPA), New Delhi, India. She is registered as a PhD research scholar (2004) at IIT-Delhi in '*e-Governance for Rural Development*'. She holds a Masters in computers applications (MCA-Honours), and a "Certificate of Excellence" as Microsoft Certified Solutions Developer (MCSD). She is a MIS/GIS consultant to UN bodies (The World Bank, Winrock International). She is accredited 'Trainer of Trainers' in "Design of Training" by the Thames Valley University, Slough, U.K. and a "Recognised User (RU)" for Government of India in the same. With more than 15 years of experience in teaching, training, software Development and research in the field of information technology (IT), her current areas of interest include e-governance, Internet technologies and its impact on societies, software engineering and design of management information systems using ORACLE.

Aroon Manoharan is currently pursuing his doctoral studies in public administration at the Rutgers School of Public Affairs and Administration. His research focuses on e-governance, performance measurement and reporting, public transit issues and comparative public administration. He is currently the associate director of the E-Governance Institute, Rutgers University-Newark.

N. Mathiyalagan is currently working as reader in the Post Graduate and Research Department of Communication, PSG College of Arts and Science, Coimbatore, Tamilnadu, India. He has been teaching Journalism and Mass Communication at Post Graduate level for the last 25 years. Besides doing independent research projects, he has been guiding research students leading to MPhil and PhD in the subject. He has completed his Postgraduation and MPhil in journalism and mass communication from Madras University. He obtained his PhD on television and children from Bharathiar University, Coimbatore in 1995. His research interests include new media studies, e-governance led issues. He has to his credit national and international publications.

Vedmani Sharan is a 2nd year full-time PhD student at the Sprott School of Business, Carleton University. His research interests span from supply chain management to electronic governement. He is also interested in the areas of technology management and information systems. He brings a lot of experience in these fields having worked in the IT sector in India for almost five years. He mingles his experience in the professional world with his experience in the academic world to explore the potential of complex business and social phenomena. He has published a book chapter and five peer-review conference proceedings till now.

Paul Swatman is professor of CIS at the University of South Australia. His research interests include the diffusion of socially pervasive ICT innovations and the impact of the digital economy on rural, regional and remote (R3) communities.

Swamy Tribhuvananda H.V. is working as asst. professor at MBA Programme, Bapuji Institute of Engineering & Technology, Davangere, Karnataka, India. He holds BSc from Kuvempu University, an MBA from Kuvempu University, and MHRM from Annamalai University. His area of interest is in information systems and human resource management. Email: tribhuvananda@yahoo.co.in

Index

E

F

G

H

I

www.ingramcontent.com/pod-product-compliance
Lightning Source LLC
LaVergne TN
LVHW062137300926
849161LV00010B/2562